The Archaeology of Elam
Formation and Transformation of an Ancient Iraniaı

From the middle of the third millennium BC until the ⸻ ⸻ Cyrus the Great, southwestern Iran was referred to in Mesopotamian sources as the land of Elam. A heterogenous collection of regions, Elam was home to a variety of groups, alternately the object of Mesopotamian aggression, and aggressors themselves; an ethnic group seemingly swallowed up by the vast Achaemenid Persian empire, yet a force strong enough to attack Babylonia in the last centuries BC. The Elamite language is attested as late as the Medieval era, and the name Elam as late as 1300 in the records of the Nestorian church. This book examines the formation and transformation of Elam's many identities through both archaeological and written evidence, and brings to life one of the most important regions of Western Asia, re-evaluates its significance, and places it in the context of the most recent archaeological and historical scholarship.

D. T. POTTS is Edwin Cuthbert Hall Professor in Middle Eastern Archaeology at the University of Sydney. He is the author of *The Arabian Gulf in Antiquity*, 2 vols. (1990), *Mesopotamian Civilization* (1997), and numerous articles in scholarly journals.

CAMBRIDGE WORLD ARCHAEOLOGY

Series editor
NORMAN YOFFEE, *University of Michigan*

Editorial board
SUSAN ALCOCK, *University of Michigan*
TOM DILLEHAY, *University of Kentucky*
CHRIS GOSDEN, *University of Oxford*
CARLA SINOPOLI, *University of Michigan*

The Cambridge World Archaeology series is addressed to students and professional archaeologists, and to academics in related disciplines. Each volume presents a survey of the archaeology of a region of the world, providing an up-to-date account of research and integrating recent findings with new concerns of interpretation. While the focus is on a specific region, broader cultural trends are discussed and the implications of regional findings for cross-cultural interpretations considered. The authors also bring anthropological and historical expertise to bear on archaeological problems, and show how both new data and changing intellectual trends in archaeology shape inferences about the past.

CAMBRIDGE WORLD ARCHAEOLOGY

THE ARCHAEOLOGY OF ELAM

FORMATION AND TRANSFORMATION OF AN ANCIENT IRANIAN STATE

D. T. POTTS

CAMBRIDGE
UNIVERSITY PRESS

PUBLISHED BY THE PRESS SYNDICATE OF THE UNIVERSITY OF CAMBRIDGE
The Pitt Building, Trumpington Street, Cambridge, United Kingdom

CAMBRIDGE UNIVERSITY PRESS
The Edinburgh Building, Cambridge, CB2 2RU, UK   http://www.cup.cam.ac.uk
40 West 20th Street, New York, NY 10011–4211, USA   http://www.cup.org
10 Stamford Road, Oakleigh, Melbourne 3166, Australia

First published 1999

Printed in the United Kingdom at the University Press, Cambridge

Typeset in Trump Mediaeval 10/13 pt. in QuarkXPress® [SE]

A catalogue record for this book is available from the British Library

Library of Congress cataloguing in publication data

Potts, Daniel T.
The archaeology of Elam: formation and transformation of an
ancient Iranian state / D. T. Potts.
p.   cm. – (Cambridge World Archaeology)
Includes bibliographical references (p.   ) and index.
ISBN 0 521 56358 5 (hardback). – ISBN 0 521 56496 4 (paperback.)
Elam – Antiquities.   2. Elam – History.   I. Title.   II. Series.
DS65.P68   1998
935 – dc21   98-41051   CIP

ISBN 0 521 563585 hardback
ISBN 0 521 564964 paperback

For Hildy, Rowena, Morgan and Hallam, with much love

CONTENTS

ILLUSTRATIONS

Figures

PLATES

TABLES

PREFACE AND ACKNOWLEDGEMENTS

Of all the major constituents of the ancient Near East, Elam has surely proven one of the more difficult to come to grips with. For most students of antiquity Elam appears aloof, somewhat exotic – a place of hard-to-pronounce names, unfamiliar sites, a poorly understood language and a somewhat barbaric population to the east of Mesopotamia. Alternately subject to Mesopotamian domination or busily subverting it as best they could, the Elamites are present in the archaeological and written record for thousands of years, reacting to foreign aggression, forging local alliances of which we have few details, cropping up in the written record of their western neighbours, saying little of themselves in their own inscriptions. Archaeologists and historians have consciously or unconsciously regarded the brutal Assyrian campaigns against the Elamites in the seventh century BC as the final chapter in their troubled history, the rise of the Achaemenid Persians as a new dawn in Iranian antiquity which heralded the start of another era. Yet the Elamites and their language crop up in post-Elamite, 'Persian' Iran. Elamites appear in the histories of Alexander the Great and his Seleucid successors. In the guise of Elymaeans they fought for independence against the later Parthian dynasty. And in the early Medieval era 'Elam' became the name of an ecclesiastical province of one of the most important branches of eastern Christianity, the Nestorian church. Anyone interested in the creation of identity and ethnicity, in the past or the present, will find in the story of Elam a palimpsest of ever changing definitions of what it meant to be Elamite, glimpses of which are revealed in a patchwork of archaeological and epigraphic evidence as difficult to comprehend as any in the ancient Near East.

Numerous distinguished historians, sociologists, social theorists and anthropologists have recently explored the invention of national and ethnic consciousness and identity (e.g. Nash 1989; Hobsbawm and Ranger 1983; Hobsbawm 1990; Fullbrook 1993; Teich and Porter 1993; Gillis 1994; Pickett 1996; Ross 1996; Bischof and Pelinka 1997), leaving us in no doubt that these are socially constructed and highly mutable. By the time the reader has reached the end of this book I would hope that not merely the artificiality of the construct 'Elam', but the notion that many Elams were constructed over time, no two of which were probably coterminous culturally, politically or geographically with each other, will have become clear. Every period – each in itself an artificial construct of modern scholars – is characterised by an Elam of the external written sources (initially Sumerian and Akkadian, later Greek, Latin, Syriac, etc.), an Elam of the indigenous archaeological and epigraphic sources, and an Elam of 20th century historiography. Why I have chosen to speak of the formation and transformation of Elam in the title of this study is precisely because of the mutability of Elam through time, an entity which was constructed and recreated continuously by ancient participants in the Elamite cultural and linguistic community, ancient observers of the Elamites, and modern students of the subject.

In 1900 the French historian Henri Berr's 'terrible craving for synthesis' led him to establish the *Revue de synthèse historique* (Keylor 1975: 133; cf. Müller 1994: xvi-xvii), just as a desire for *histoire totale* eventually spurred Lucien Febvre and Marc Bloch to found the journal *Annales d'Histoire Economique et Sociale* twenty-nine years later (Lyon 1987: 200). While presuming neither to class the present work amongst the many influential studies in *Annaliste* history which have emerged since *Annales* began appearing seventy years ago, nor wishing to join an avowedly *Annaliste* club of archaeologists (e.g. Bintliff 1991, Knapp 1992), I am nevertheless adamant in declaring that this is explicitly a work of synthesis which wholeheartedly embraces the tenets of *histoire totale*, and I am happy to be counted amongst those 'rash souls who wish to move outside the limits of what they themselves have studied and aspire to a comprehensive view' (trans. Keylor 1975: 133). Because I do not believe that one can arrive at a satisfactory understanding of Elam by chopping it into chronological bits or looking only at its art or texts, I have striven to cover all periods in Elamite history using all types of available evidence, whether architectural, ceramic, numismatic, radiometric, epigraphic, literary, environmental, religious, ethnographic, etc. In my view, we need the chronologically extended synthesis as much as the particular analytical focus sometimes referred to as microhistory (Egmond and Mason 1997). Without time depth and topical breadth we would be unable to chart the repeated restructuring of Elam through time. And because I can see no justification for terminating the story of the Elamites with the campaigns of Assyria and the emergence of the Achaemenid Persian empire, the present study ranges into the Seleucid, Parthian, Sasanian and early Islamic periods, eras which have traditionally been considered 'post-Elamite'. If some readers have difficulty in this attenuation of Elamite archaeology and history, they need not bother with the final chapters. But I hope that others will see, perhaps for the first time, that the story of Elam and the Elamites does not end with Assurbanipal or the coming of Cyrus the Great.

The quantity of data presented here may suggest that I have succumbed to a kind of naive historicism and abandoned the traditional concern of archaeologists with long-term trends and societal morphology. I trust I have not fallen prey to the former, but I freely admit that I have eschewed the latter. The amount of detail which confronts readers of this book is vital to the arguments outlined in Chapter 12, however, for while I may embrace the idea of *histoire totale* in this study, I conclude by rejecting the notion of the *longue durée*. These more theoretical views, however, are largely confined to this Preface and the conclusion of this book, and readers should approach the intervening chapters without fear of suddenly finding themselves on the ideological battleground of historical method. That is not the *raison d'être* of this book. It is still a study of Elam in its many manifestations, even if that study seems to me to raise important questions about how we interpret the past.

But apart from wishing to create an *histoire totale* of Elam, there is another important reason for writing a work of synthesis like this. If Elam today is not exactly a household word, then that is less a reflection of its role in antiquity than a by-product of two major linguistic problems. For on the one hand, the difficulties posed by the Elamite language have made Elamite texts much less amenable to translation and interpretation than those of Sumer, Assyria or Babylonia, not to mention Greece or Rome. On the other hand, the fact that perhaps two-thirds of the scholarship available on Elam is written in French and German has meant that Anglophone students and lay persons, in particular, have only had access to a very limited number of primary and secondary publications on Elam. This predicament is not unique to Elamite studies, but as I have taught the archaeology and early history of Elam off and on over the past seventeen years it has become increasingly clear to me that the subject is made inherently more difficult than, for example, North American or Australian archaeology, precisely because students 'doing' Elam will only ever get a very fractured view of the subject if they are limited to the literature available in English. I do not wish to imply, of course, that there are no good, accessible works in English on Elam already available. It is, nevertheless, true to say that those book-length, synthetic studies which already exist in English (e.g. Cameron 1936, Hinz 1972, Carter and Stolper 1984) have not nearly said the last word on the subject. None of them can be remotely considered up-to-date and each concludes with the rise of the Achaemenid empire, neglecting over a millennium of later Elamite history. In spite of the impossibility of conducting archaeological fieldwork in Iran today, journals each year continue to receive and publish numerous studies of a microhistorical type which are dedicated to Elam. But like Henri Berr, I cannot help but comment on the stubborn reluctance of many contemporary authors of *Elamitica* to stand up and demonstrate '*how* obscure, marginal, or unusual cases can be used to address crucial historical issues' (Egmond and Mason 1997: 2–3). The study of Elam may not be long for this world if cogent, readable syntheses are not available with which to teach the subject. I have attempted to write such a study here. In an effort to guide readers unfamiliar with Elam through the maze of material assembled, I have offered text boxes at the beginning of each chapter which briefly summarize the matter to be discussed; an introductory map showing the sites mentioned in each chapter; and a summary chart at the end of each chapter which highlights the main points of interest within the lowlands, highlands, Mesopotamia and the entity 'Elam' in each period, and adds relevant dates for chronological orientation.

This book was written at the University of Sydney, where I have taught Elam to Australian undergraduates. For the most part, my bibliographical resources have been those of Fisher Library. While this is undoubtedly the best library for a study of this sort in Australia, it cannot compare with major libraries in Europe or the United States. Though I might sometimes agree with Aby Warburg's motto that 'God is in the detail' (Egmond and Mason 1997: 2), I have had to learn to do without and not to regret it. Nevertheless, I have not been completely averse to e-mailing and faxing colleagues with long distance requests for bibliographical aid. For their gracious help with such matters, and for sending me offprints of useful literature, I would like to express my warmest thanks to A.B. Bosworth (Perth), P. Briant (Toulouse), J.A. Brinkman (Chicago),

A. Caubet (Paris), J. Córdoba (Madrid), R.K. Englund (Los Angeles), E. Haerinck (Gent), H. Hunger (Vienna), M. Jursa (Vienna), P. Kalensky (Paris), A. Kuhrt (London), P. Magee (Sydney), P. Michalowski (Ann Arbor), P.R.S. Moorey (Oxford), H.J. Nissen (Berlin), H. Sancisi-Weerdenburg (Groningen), R. Schmitt (Saarbrücken), M.W. Stolper (Chicago), J. Teixidor (Paris), and J. Westenholz (Jerusalem). In the end, there remain publications I would have liked to consult but which remained inaccessible. In this I take comfort from Henri Berr's observation on scholars 'who cannot think of science except in terms of detailed research, and who, since detail is infinite, push forward this research of theirs only to see the goal recede before them' (trans. Keylor 1975: 133). Perhaps it is just as well that I cannot consult everything I might wish to on the subject of Elam.

The maps illustrating site distributions which accompany each of the substantive chapters were prepared by Ms Michele Ziolkowski, a PhD candidate in Near Eastern archaeology at the University of Sydney, and I would like to express my sincerest thanks to her for the long hours of digitizing contour lines which went into their creation. If sites have been misplaced, the fault is my own. Likewise, I would like to express my sincere thanks to Mr Alex Stephens, a PhD candidate in Classics at the University of Sydney, whom I employed to prepare accurate English translations of Greek texts from Susa (Table 10.1).

To write a book is one thing, to publish it quite another. I would like to thank Professor Norman Yoffee (Ann Arbor) and the other members of the board of the Cambridge World Archaeology series for accepting this book for publication when it was only a rough outline with a bit of bibliography, and for persevering with it when it appeared to be something other than what they originally expected from me. I am sincerely grateful to the readers of an earlier draft, Professor M.W. Stolper (Chicago), Professor E. Carter (Los Angeles), Professor N. Yoffee (Ann Arbor) and Mr K. Abdi (Ann Arbor) for their many detailed comments and suggestions for improving the text. I have appreciated all of their remarks and have made many changes accordingly. Further, I wish to express my sincere thanks to Jessica Kuper of Cambridge University Press for her patience and goodwill. My family knows by the dedication of this book that I have appreciated their support more than words can say. I hope they have not regretted the fact that Elam entered their lives somewhat more than they might have wished.

Finally, I would like to say a word about Iran, as opposed to Elam. To begin with, I must thank two of my professors at Harvard whose influence may be expressed only indirectly in the pages of this book, but who in very different ways sowed the seeds of a lifelong interest in Iran in me as a student. C.C. Lamberg-Karlovsky introduced me to both Iran and Iranian archaeology. Two memorable seasons of excavation at Tepe Yahya in 1973 and 1975 kindled an abiding interest in Iranian archaeology. Richard N. Frye introduced me to the pre-Islamic religions of Iran and first fostered my awareness of the incredibly rich historical, linguistic and spiritual heritage of Iran. The Iranian Revolution meant the interruption of my active involvement with the subject, but in 1995 and 1996 I was able to return to Iran with my wife and a group from the Near Eastern Archaeology Foundation of the University of Sydney. Those visits gave me the opportunity to visit Susa, Choga Zanbil, Haft Tepe, Kul-e Farah and numerous other sites of Elamite history for the first time. Parvaneh Sattari and the staff of Pasargad Tour in Teheran made both trips enormously successful and reminded me why I have spent so much of my adult life thinking about Iran's past.

Acknowledgements for photographic reproduction

It is with great pleasure that I acknowledge the kind permission of Annie Caubet, Conservateur général in charge of the Department of Oriental Antiquities at the Louvre Museum to reproduce the twenty-five plates marked © Musée du Louvre, Antiquités Orientales. The remainder of the photographs published here were taken by the author during visits to Iran in 1995 and 1996.

ABBREVIATIONS

A	Siglum of texts in the Louvre Museum
$A^{1-3}S$	Artaxerxes I–III, Susa inscriptions
AAASH	*Acta Antiqua Academiae Scientiarum Hungaricae*
AAM	Archives administratives de Mari
ABL	Harper, R.F., *Assyrian and Babylonian Letters Belonging to the Kouyunjik Collection of the British Museum*, London and Chicago: University of Chicago, 1892–1914
AfO	*Archiv für Orientforschung*
AH	*Achaemenid History*
AcIr	*Acta Iranica*
AIO	De Meyer, L. and Haerinck, E., eds. (1989), *Archaeologia Iranica et Orientalia: Miscellanea in honorem Louis Vanden Berghe*, Louvain: Peeters
AION	*Annali dell'Istituto Universitario Orientale di Napoli*
AJA	*American Journal of Archaeology*
AMI	*Archäologische Mitteilungen aus Iran*
Amorites	Buccellati, G. (1966), *The Amorites of the Ur III Period*, Naples: Ricerche 1
AO	*Der Alte Orient*
AoF	*Altorientalische Forschungen*
AOAT	*Alter Orient und Altes Testament*
AOS	American Oriental Series
ARM	Archives royales de Mari
ArOr	*Archiv Orientální*
AS	*Assyriological Studies*
Bab. 8	De Genouillac, H. (1924), 'Choix de textes économiques de la collection Pupil', *Babyloniaca* 8 (1924), 37ff.
BAI	*Bulletin of the Asia Institute*
BAH	*Institut Français d'Archéologie de Beyrouth, Bibliothèque Archéologique et Historique*
BaM	*Baghdader Mitteilungen*
BAR	*British Archaeological Reports*
BBVO	*Berliner Beiträge zum Vorderen Orient*
BiMes	*Bibliotheca Mesopotamica*
BIN	Babylonian Inscriptions in the Collection of J. B. Nies, Yale University

BiOr	*Bibliotheca Orientalis*
BM	British Museum
BSOAS	*Bulletin of the School of Oriental and African Studies*
C	Cyrus
CAH	*Cambridge Ancient History*
CANE	Sasson, J.M., ed. (1995), *Civilizations of the ancient Near East*, vols. I-IV, New York: Charles Scribner's Sons
CC	Sigrist, M. and Gomi, T. (1991), *The Comprehensive Catalogue of Published Ur III Tablets*, Bethesda: CDL Press
CDR	Gasche, H., Tanret, M., Janssen, C. and Degraeve, A., eds. (1994), *Cinquante-deux reflexions sur le Proche-Orient ancien offertes en hommages à Léon de Meyer*, Gent: Peeters
CHI	*Cambridge History of Iran*
CNIP	*Carsten Niebuhr Institute Publications*
CNRS	*Centre Nationale de la Recherche Scientifique*
Collectanea	Gasche, H. and Hrouda, B., eds. (1996), *Collectanea Orientalia: Histoire, arts de l'espace et industrie de la terra, études offertes en hommage à Agnès Spycket*, Neuchâtel/Paris: Civilisations du Proche-Orient Serie 1, Archéologie et environnement 3
CRAIBL	*Comptes-rendus de l'Académie des inscriptions et belles-lettres*
CSCO	*Corpus Scriptorum Christianorum Orientalium*
CST	Fish, T. (1932), *Catalogue of Sumerian Tablets in the John Rylands Library*, Manchester
CT	Cuneiform texts from Babylonian tablets . . . in the British Museum
CTNMC	Jacobsen, T. (1939), *Cuneiform texts in the National Museum, Copenhagen, chiefly of economical contents*, Copenhagen: C.T. Thomson
DB	Darius, Behistun inscription
DAFI	*Délégation archéologique Française en Iran*
DN	Darius, Naqsh-i Rustam inscriptions
DP	Darius, Persepolis inscriptions
DP	Allotte de la Füye, F.-M. (1908–20), *Documents présargoniques*, Paris: E. Leroux
DS	Darius, Susa inscriptions
DV	Drevnosti Vostocnyja, Moscow.
EKI	König, F.W. (1965), *Die elamischen Königsinschriften*, Graz: *AfO* Beiheft 16
EnIr	*Encyclopædia Iranica*
EW	*East and West*
FAOS	*Freiburger Altorientalische Studien*
FGH	Jacoby, F. (1923–), *Die Fragmente der griechischen Historiker*, Berlin: Weidmann
FHE	De Meyer, L., Gasche, H. and Vallat, F., eds. (1986), *Fragmenta*

	Historiae Elamicae: Mélanges offerts à M.J. Steve, Paris: Editions Recherche sur les Civilisations
HdO	Handbuch der Orientalistik
HSAO	Heidelberger Studien zum Alten Orient
HSS	Harvard Semitic Studies
H.T.	Haft Tepe text
IrAnt	*Iranica Antiqua*
IRS	Malbran-Labat, F. (1995), *Les inscriptions royales de Suse: Briques de l'époque paléo-élamite à l'Empire néo-élamite*, Paris: Editions de la Réunion des musées nationaux
IRSA	Sollberger, E. and Kupper, J.-R. (1971), *Inscriptions royales sumériennes et akkadiennes*, Paris: Littératures du Proche-Orient 3
ITT	(1920–21) *Inventaire des tablettes de Tello conservées au Musée impérial ottoman*, Paris: E. Leroux
JA	*Journal Asiatique*
JAOS	*Journal of the Ameican Oriental Society*
JEOL	*Jaarbericht Ex Oriente Lux*
JRGS	*Journal of the Royal Geographical Society*
KP	*Der Kleine Pauly*
KZ	Kaʻba-i Zardosht inscription of Shapur I at Naqsh-i Rustam
M	unpublished Mari text
MAD	Materials for the Assyrian Dictionary
MCS	Manchester Cuneiform Studies
MDP	*Mémoires de la Délégation en Perse, Mémoires de la Mission Archéologique de Susiane, Mémoires de la Mission archéologique de Perse, Mémoires de la Délégation Archéologique en Iran* (for specific text refs. acc. to vol. number see in general under Scheil 1900–39 below)
MHEOP I	De Meyer, L. and Gasche, H., eds. (1991), *Mésopotamie et Elam*, Ghent: Mesopotamian History and Environment Occasional Publications 1.
MJP	Vallat, F., ed. (1990) *Mélanges Jean Perrot*, Paris: Editions Recherche sur les Civilisations
MSKH	Brinkman, J.A. (1976), *Materials and Studies for Kassite History I: A Catalogue of Cuneiform Sources Pertaining to Specific Monarchs of the Kassite Dynasty*, Chicago: The Oriental Institute
MSVO	*Materialien zu den frühen Schriftzeugnissen des Vorderen Orients*
MVN	Materiali per il vocabolario neo-sumerico
NABU	Nouvelles Assyriologiques Brèves et Utilitaires
NH	Pliny's *Natural History*
Nik.	Nikolskij, M.V. (1908), *Dokumenty chozjajstvennoj otcetnosti drevnejsej epochi Chaldei iz sobranija N.P. Lichaceva*, St Petersburg
OECT	*Oxford Editions of Cuneiform Texts*
Or	*Orientalia*

OrAnt	*Oriens Antiquus*
OSP 1	Westenholz, A. (1975), *Old Sumerian and Old Akkadian Texts in Philadelphia Chiefly from Nippur*, Malibu: *BiMes* 1
PBS	Publications of the Babylonian Section, University of Pennsylvania.
P	Persepolis (used for seals)
PDT	Çig, M., Kizilyay, H. and Salonen, A. (1954/56), *Die Puzriš-Dagan-Texte der Istanbuler Archäologischen Museen*, Teil I: Nrr. 1–725, Helsinki; and Yildiz, F. and Gomi, T. (1988), *Die Puzriš-Dagan-Texte der Istanbuler Archäologischen Museen*, Teil II, Wiesbaden
PF	Persepolis fortification text
RA	*Revue d'Assyriologie et d'archéologie Orientale*
RA 8	Delaporte, L., 'Tablettes de Dréhem', *RA* 8 (1911), 183–98
RCS	Harper, P.O., Aruz, J. and Tallon, F., eds. (1992), *The Royal City of Susa: Ancient Near Eastern Treasures in the Louvre*, New York: Metropolitan Museum of Art
RCU	Royal Cemetery of Ur
RE	*Pauly's Real-Encyclopädie der klassischen Altertumswissenschaften*
RGTC	Répertoire Géographique des Textes Cunéiformes
RlA	*Reallexikon der Assyriologie*
RN	*Revue Numismatique*
RTC	Thureau-Dangin, F. (1903), *Recueil de tablettes chaldéennes*, Paris: E. Leroux
SAAB	*State Archives of Assyria Bulletin*
SAOC	Studies in Ancient Oriental Civilization
SEG	Supplementum Epigraphicum Graecum
SEL	*Studi Epigrafici e Linguistici sul Vicino Oriente*
SH	Tell Shemshara text
STH	Hussey, M.I. (1912), *Sumerian Tablets of the Harvard Semitic Museum*, Cambridge: HSS 3
StIr	*Studia Iranica*
STTI	Donbaz, V. and Foster, B.R. (1982), *Sargonic Texts from Telloh in the Istanbul Archaeological Museum*, Philadelphia: Occasional Publications of the Babylonian Fund 5
Susa	Anonymous, (no date), *Susa, site et musée*, Teheran: Ministry of Culture and Arts
TAVO	Tübinger Atlas des Vorderen Orients
TAD	Langdon, S.H. (1911), *Tablets from the Archives of Drehem*, Paris: Geuthner
TEN	Sigrist, M. (1983), *Textes économiques néo-sumériens de l'Université de Syracuse*, Paris: Éditions Recherche sur les Civilisations
TMO	*Travaux de la Maison de l'Orient (Lyons)*
TrD	Genouillac, H. de, (1911), *La trouvaille de Dréhem*, Paris: Geuthner
TRU	Legrain, L. (1912), *Le temps des rois d'Ur, recherches sur la société*

	antique, d'après des textes nouveaux, Paris: Bibliothèque de l'École des Hautes Études 199
TS	Tablette (de) Suse
TuM 5	Pohl, A. (1935), *Vorsargonische und sargonische Wirtschaftstexte*, Leipzig: Texte und Materialien der Frau Professor Hilprecht Collection 5
UET	Ur Excavation Texts
VAB	Vorderasiatische Bibliothek
VDI	*Vestnik Drevnej Istorii*
VR	Ville Royale (of Susa)
XP	Xerxes, Persepolis inscriptions
XS	Xerxes, Susa inscriptions
YOS 4	Keiser, C.E. (1919), *Selected Temple Documents of the Ur Dynasty*, New Haven: Yale Oriental Series 4
ZA	*Zeitschrift für Assyriologie*

Note: Articles in *NABU* are cited by their article, not their page number, e.g. *NABU* (1997), 6 = note number 6 in *NABU* (1997), not page 6.

NOTE ON TRANSLITERATION AND DATING SYSTEMS

As this book is aimed primarily at archaeologists and students of archaeology, rather than Assyriologists, I thought it simplest to forego the use of diacritical marks in the transliteration of Sumerian, Akkadian, Elamite, Aramaic, Syriac, Persian and Arabic words (principally personal names and placenames). I have not sought to impose a single, uniform system of transliteration but have used those forms most current in the archaeological and Assyriological literature today. Where I have cited Elamite and Akkadian terms, these are italicized. Sumerian words and phrases are given in bold.

As for the stipulation of dates, radiocarbon dates when cited are always given in their calibrated form. Absolute dates when cited for individual Mesopotamian rulers conform to the so-called 'Middle chronology' and follow Brinkman 1977.

ELAM: WHAT, WHEN, WHERE?

In order to discuss the origins and development of Elam we must first establish where the name comes from and what it signified. This chapter examines the etymology of the name and introduces the reader to the changing nature of its application. It also takes up the fundamental chronological issue which must be tackled before launching into an examination of the material and historical evidence covered here. When do we first find Elam mentioned? How late did Elam exist? Finally, where was Elam? Seeming contradictions between epigraphic, literary and archaeological evidence are investigated which bear on the problem of how ancient observers and modern scholars have located Elam in their treatments of the subject. Finally, the chapter closes with some observations on how and why the meanings of broad geographical and ethnic designations often change in the course of time. For us it is important to realize that the area identified as Elam in one period may not have been the same as that referred to by the same name in another period. These are some of the ambiguities which must be understood before the subject of Elam can be intelligently discussed.

What is Elam?

Elam (Fig. 1.1) is an artificial construct, a name coined by Mesopotamian scribes, gazing across the alluvium towards the Iranian plateau, who imposed it from without on the disparate regions of highland southwest Iran and its peoples. In Sumerian sources dating to the middle of the third millennium BC (see Chapter 4) the name Elam was written with the sumerogram NIM meaning simply 'high', often accompanied by the determinative KI denoting 'land, country'. The Akkadian form used was normally KUR *elammatum* or 'land of Elam' (Quintana 1996a: 50).

The etymology of Elam has been much discussed. Damerow and Englund suggest that Elam 'may be an Akkadianized rendering of both Sumerian and Elamite terms influenced by *elûm*, "to be high"' (Damerow and Englund 1989: 1, n. 1). It was not until the reign of Siwe-palar-hupak, in the 18th century BC, that a name for the land described by Sumerian and Akkadian scribes as Elam appears in the Elamite language as [hal]*Hatamti*, *hal Hatamti* or *Hatamti-* (Vallat 1996f: 89; see also 1993a: 90–3). The late Walther Hinz suggested that this term was composed of *hal* 'land' + *tamt* 'gracious lord' (1971b: 644) and it has even been suggested recently that this might be an Elamite contraction of the Akkadian expression *ala'itum matum*, meaning 'high land' (Quintana 1996a: 50), but it seems more likely that Akkadian *Elamtu* derives from Elamite *Ha(l)tamti* (Vallat 1996f: 89). Be that as it may, the fact remains that the

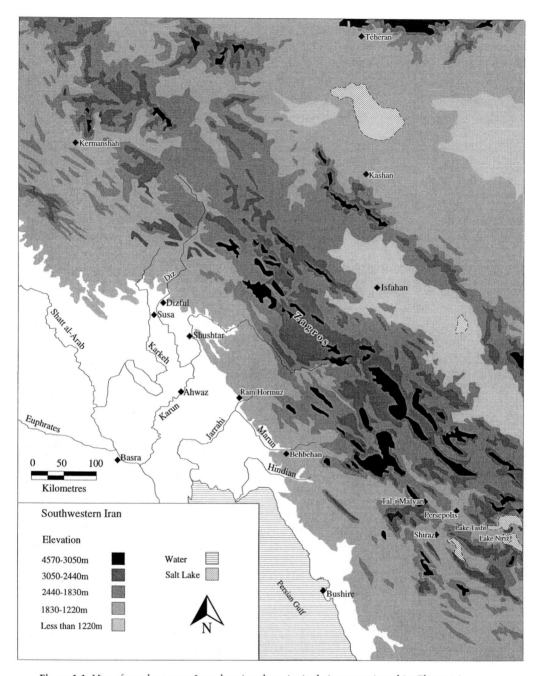

Figure 1.1 Map of southwestern Iran showing the principal sites mentioned in Chapter 1.

apparently first, indigenous name for Elam did not appear until the early second millennium BC and it is doubtful whether the region's inhabitants looked on western Iran as a single, unified country or nation. In the third millennium, when our story properly begins, the peoples of highland Iran, a disparate collection of ethnically and linguistically diverse groups, *never* identified themselves using the rubrics Elam or Elamites. That was a name given to the uplands east of Mesopotamia by Sumerian scribes who were simply referring to it, in a logical way, as 'highland'. As R. Zadok has stressed, by the late third millennium BC the Sumerian designation ELAM(.MA^{ki}) was applied to 'any highlander from the Iranian Plateau and its piedmont' (Zadok 1987: 3). Significantly, however, the sumerogram NIM was *never* used by Elamite scribes when they wrote in Elamite, and the few cases where it is alleged to have been present have all been rejected by M.-J. Steve, who has termed them 'illusory' (Steve 1992: 158–9).

Yet most people, if they have ever heard the name Elam, know of it not from the cuneiform sources of the third or second millennium BC but from scattered references in the Bible. Elam appears in the Old Testament Table of Nations (Gen. 10.22; see also Simons 1959: 27–8; Nöldeke 1874: 187–9), and an Elamite king whose name has come down to us as *Kedor-Laomer* is mentioned in a later chapter of Genesis (14.1), as well. Elam figures prominently in the forty-ninth chapter of the Book of Jeremiah (Jeremiah 49.35–39; see also Thompson 1980: 728–9; Holladay 1989: 387–9). Daniel of lion's den fame dreamt that he was 'at Shushan in the palace which is in the province of Elam' (Daniel 8.2), also the scene of the principal events described in the Book of Esther (Esther 1.1). And Jews from Elam, present in Jerusalem at Pentecost, are mentioned in the New Testament (Acts 2.9).

The late appearance of an 'indigenous' name for Elam in Elamite sources and the possibility that Elam might even be a loanword from another language may seem bizarre, but throughout history people and regions have been identified by names other than those which they and their inhabitants themselves used, and comparable examples of what could be termed 'imposed ethnicity' abound in the more recent past. The Inuit of Canada and Greenland, whose name means simply 'the people' in their own language, have been known for centuries by the term 'Eskimo', a European corruption of a Native American term meaning 'eaters of raw flesh' (*Oxford English Dictionary*). Similarly the Huron were so named by French colonists. The French term *huron* means a 'rustic rural resident' (Roosens 1989: 99) and even though the Huron were part of a larger group calling themselves 'Wendat', the name Huron was eventually adopted by the Wendat and continues to be used to this day. Moreover, it is instructive to note that neither the demise of the Huron language nor the eradication of most Huron traditional customs have diminished the intensity of current feelings of Huron ethnic identity (Roosens 1989: 96).

One thing is, in any case, certain. The available written sources which pre-date the 18th century BC give absolutely no indication that the diverse groups inhabiting the Iranian Zagros and plateau regions *ever* identified themselves by a common term as all embracing as Elam. Dozens of names of regions and population groups (see Chapter 5) attested in the late third millennium sources (principally in the Ur III period,

2100–2000 BC) give us a good impression of the heterogeneity of the native peoples of western Iran, all of whom were simply subsumed under the Sumerian rubric NIM and the Akkadian term KUR *elammatum*. Nor did the peoples of these diverse regions all speak a common language which, for lack of an indigenous term, we may call Elamite. Judging by personal names in cuneiform sources, the linguistic make-up of southwestern Iran was heterogeneous and the language we call Elamite was but one of a number of languages spoken in the highlands to the east of Mesopotamia. Yet it is not the preponderance of Sumerian, Akkadian and Amorite personal names in texts from Susa, a product of long periods of political and cultural dependency and the widespread use of Akkadian, which justifies our speaking of linguistic heterogeneity in southwestern Iran. Rather, it is the plethora of indigenous, non-Elamite languages attested to mainly by the extant corpus of Iranian (geographically, not linguistically) personal names in Mesopotamian cuneiform sources. Individuals are known from Anshan, Shimashki, Zabshali, Marhashi, Sapum, Harshi, Shig(i)rish, Zitanu, Itnigi, and Kimash with names which cannot be etymologized as Elamite (Zadok 1991: 226–30).

When did Elam exist?

As we shall see in Chapter 4, there is no certainty that the sign NIM was used by Mesopotamian scribes to refer to Elam until the middle of the third millennium BC. Some of the earlier occurrences of the sign might have had the meaning Elam, but there is no way of demonstrating this conclusively. On the other hand, the lack of a Mesopotamian term for the peoples of the eastern highlands in no way implies that the area was uninhabited, but until we find the word NIM/Elam we cannot prove any link between the archaeological assemblages of the region and the later Elamites. For this reason, if we adopt a 'minimalist' position, as is done here, we cannot in all honesty speak of Elam before *c.* 2600–2500 BC.

How late did Elam exist? This is less clear-cut than might seem to be the case from a perusal of some of the standard texts on the subject. The Assyrian conquest of Susa in the 7th century BC is seen by most scholars as the great watershed which marks the end of Elamite history (e.g. Schroeder 1925; König 1938), and the rise of the Persian empire is often taken as the beginning of a new era. Thus, G.G. Cameron's 1936 *History of Early Iran* explicitly sought to present 'in a comprehensive fashion the history of the Iranian plateau *before* Cyrus attained mastery' (Cameron 1936: vii). Although he believed that 'Elam still had an important role to play' in the Achaemenid empire, W. Hinz also used the fall of Susa to the Assyrians and the rise of the Medes and Persians as the cut-off point in his synthesis of Elamite history and archaeology (Hinz 1972: 160), as did E. Carter and M.W. Stolper, who offer just three pages on Elam during the Achaemenid, Seleucid and Parthian periods in their synthesis of Elamite political history and archaeology (Carter and Stolper 1984: 57–9).

The approach taken here is quite different. Elam's absorption into the Achaemenid empire and its legacy in the Achaemenid period in no way mark the phase at which one can legitimately conclude an assessment of Elam's history and archaeology.

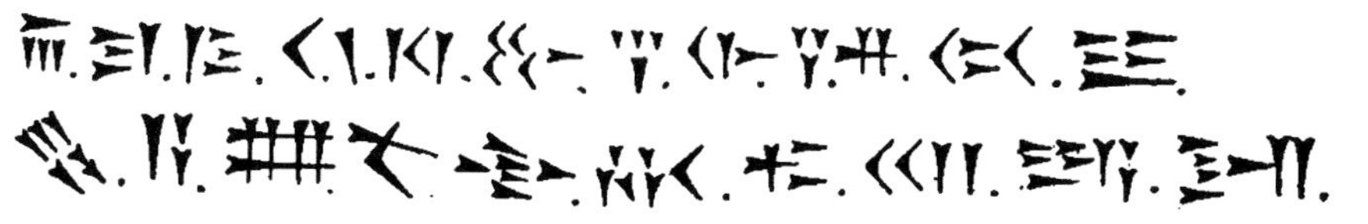

Figure 1.2 Samuel Flower's copy of an Achaemenid Elamite inscription (after Rogers 1900/I: 75).

Elam's boundaries and political status may have changed considerably from what they were during the third millennium BC, but it is clear from a reading of, for example, the late Babylonian texts which discuss the numerous incursions of Elamite troops, some of whom were commanded by officers with Elamite names (Chapter 10), that the region of Elymais and its people the Elymaeans, mentioned in Greek and Latin sources, certainly represented latter-day incarnations of Elam and the Elamites. Similarly, during the early Islamic era we continue to find the name Elam used to denote an ecclesiastical province in what is today the Khuzistan province of south-western Iran (Chapter 11).

Elam was no less an entity with a particular linguistic and cultural character in the post-Assyrian period than it had been in more remote antiquity. At no point in Elam's history were its boundaries fixed, and Elam's absorption by the Persian empire no more signalled its demise than had its suppression by the Old Akkadian or Ur III empires in the late third millennium BC. These and other episodes of political diminution certainly meant that Elam figured less prominently in written sources, but the consistent reappearance of Elam following periods of political reversal show that the essential independence – linguistically as well as culturally – of Elam and the Elamites is a phenomenon of incredible longevity. Elam and the Elamites periodically underwent a process of transformation until the disappearance of the name from Nestorian ecclesiastical sources well after the Islamic conquest. After that, it was the work of nineteenth- and twentieth-century scholars to rediscover and recreate the many Elams of the more distant past.

Where was Elam?

In 1667 an East India Company agent named Samuel Flower made the first copies of cuneiform signs (Fig. 1.2) at the Persian Achaemenid city of Persepolis and at nearby Naqsh-i Rustam. Later, it was realized that some of these belonged to the Elamite version of a trilingual inscription in Old Persian, the Babylonian dialect of Akkadian and Elamite (Rogers 1900: 74–83; Pallis 1954: 24). Even if the signs were not yet recognized as Elamite, their copies could be said to represent the first tangible evidence of Elam to have been found outside the pages of the Bible. It took more than century, however, before Carsten Niebuhr recognised in 1778 that the Persepolitan inscriptions were written in three different languages. Following this realization it became conventional to refer to the Elamite column as the 'second type' of Achaemenid inscription, and to designate the language represented by it as Elamite, Susian or Scythian (Reiner

Plate 1.1 Aerial view of Susa (from an original in the Susa Museum).

1969: 54). Although the nineteenth century witnessed the documentation of numerous trilingual Achaemenid inscriptions (Pallis 1954: 52–3), as well as many attempts at their decipherment, the Elamite versions of these texts were not satisfactorily deciphered until 1890 when F.H. Weissbach published his PhD dissertation on them (later appearing in revised form as Weissbach 1911).

The fact that the first Elamite texts found were discovered in the highlands of Fars province ought to have pointed the way towards the recognition of the highland nature of Elam, but here an accident of archaeological discovery came into play. In 1813 John Malcolm Kinneir published an extensive description of the site of Shush (Pl. 1.1) in lowland Khuzistan, arguing against older authorities that this was the site of Biblical Shushan, rather than Shushtar, another town in Khuzistan with a name similar to Shushan (Kinneir 1813: 99ff.). Opinion on this point remained divided for many years (see Forbiger 1844: 585 for a bibliography of the dispute into the mid-1840s). A.H. Layard favoured the identification of Shush with both the Susa of the Greek and Roman authors and with Shushan of the Bible, whereas H.C. Rawlinson, while accepting the identity of Shush and classical Susa, held that a site called Shushan, north of Shushtar, was the site of Daniel's dream (Layard 1842: 104; 1846: 61). When W.K. Loftus excavated the first bricks and clay cones with Elamite inscriptions at Shush in 1852, however, including amongst other things remnants of a trilingual inscription of

Plate 1.2 Château Susa, the fortified excavation house begun on the Acropole by Jacques de Morgan in 1898.

Artaxerxes II (404–359 BC) – identified by some with King Ahasuerus of the Book of Esther (other scholars believe Biblical Ahasuerus to have been Xerxes, e.g. Heltzer 1994) – mentioning the palace of Darius which had burned in the lifetime of Artaxerxes I as well as the new palace built by Artaxerxes II, there was no longer any doubt about the identity of modern Shush and Biblical Shushan (Curtis 1993: 22, 31–2), and indeed this was the basis for the resumption of investigations at the site by the French expeditions (Dieulafoy 1888; 1893; see also Harper, Aruz and Tallon 1992: 20–4) of the late 19th century (Pl. 1.2).

By extension, therefore, there could be no doubt that the name Elam referred to Khuzistan, for did not Daniel dream that he was 'at Shushan in the palace which is in the province of Elam' (Daniel 8.2)? Of course, the controversy over the identification of Shushan and by extension the 'solution' of the problem of Elam's location happened long before cuneiform scholars had realized that the sumerogram NIM implied a highland rather than a lowland setting for Elam. Yet confirmation of the lowland identification of Elam seemed to be provided by extra-Biblical sources, such as the eighth century Armenian translation of Cl. Ptolemy's *Geography* by Moses of Khorene, where we read, 'A land of Asia is that of the Elymaeans, that is Khuzastan, which the Greeks call *Šošanik*, after the city *Šošan*' (Marquart 1901: 137).

A very different notion, emphasizing the distinction between Elam and Susiana, i.e. the district of Susa, can be found, however, in other sources. After describing Susis (Susiana) and an adjacent part of Babylonia, the Greek geographer Strabo wrote, 'Above both, on the north and towards the east, lie the countries of the Elymaei and the Paraetaceni, who are predatory peoples and rely on the ruggedness of their mountains' (*Geog.* xv.3.12). Thus, it is clear that Elymais (the land of the Elymaei, as the Elamites were called in the last centuries BC), and Susiana were viewed by Strabo as two different geographical regions (see also Hoffmann 1880: 133). Moreover, although later Jewish writers, such as Sa'adya Gaon (*c.* AD 985) and Benjamin of Tudela (AD 1169) followed the Book of Daniel in equating Khuzistan with Elam, the Talmud scrupulously distinguished lowland Be Huzae, or Khuzistan, from Elam (Neubauer 1868: 325, 380; Obermeyer 1929: 205).

In the early 1970s inscribed bricks were discovered at the archaeological site of Tal-i Malyan near Shiraz in the highlands of Fars province which proved that it was the ancient city of Anshan (Reiner 1973a). This led, several years later, to a complete revision of thinking on the location of Elam, spearheaded by the French scholar F. Vallat, who argued that the centre of Elam lay at Anshan and in the highlands around it, and not at Susa in lowland Khuzistan (1980a). The periodic political incorporation of the lowlands, and the importance of the city of Susa, had given the impression to the authors of Daniel and Esther that Elam was centred around the site and coterminous with Khuzistan. The preponderance of inscriptions written in Elamite at Anshan, and the overwhelming domination of texts written in Akkadian at Susa, with largely Semitic personal names, suggested to Vallat that Elam was centred in the highlands, not in lowland Susiana. One could even suggest that ancient observers had applied the *pars pro toto* principle (Eilers 1982: 10) when it came to the use of Elam in the Bible, whereby a name which had originally designated only an area around Anshan in Fars came to be used for a geographically much more extensive state which held sway over areas well outside the original Elamite homeland. In order to distinguish between these two Elams, one might even be tempted to use terms like *Elam Minor* (for the original Elamite homeland in Fars) and *Elam Major* (for the wider state, which sometimes approached the status of an empire, created by the Elamites).

In fact, this would be wrong, and it is equally misleading to suggest that Elam meant the highlands of Fars with its capital city Anshan. For as outlined above, Elam is not an Iranian term and has no relationship to the conception which the peoples of highland Iran had of themselves. They were Anshanites, Marhashians, Shimashkians, Zabshalians, Sherihumians, Awanites, etc. That Anshan played a leading role in the political affairs of the various highland groups inhabiting southwestern Iran is clear. But to argue that Anshan is coterminous with Elam is to misunderstand the artificiality and indeed the alienness of Elam as a construct imposed from without on the peoples of the southwestern highlands of the Zagros mountain range, the coast of Fars *and* the alluvial plain drained by the Karun-Karkheh river system. For although cuneiform sources often distinguish Susians, i.e. the inhabitants of Susa, from Anshanites, this in no way contradicts the notion that, from the Mesopotamian perspective, the easterners – lowlanders and highlanders alike – were *all* Elamites in the direction of Susa and beyond.

Conclusion

All too often we take for granted the identity and ethnicity of the archaeological and historical cultures which we study, without considering whether discrepancies exist between our definitions and the self-definitions of the peoples being studied. In the case of Elam, it is now clear that we are dealing with a notion imposed by Mesopotamian scribes, not one which had any basis in indigenous notions of ethnic and linguistic self-definition. Diverse groups in southwestern Iran were subsumed under this foreign label, but at a certain point the label was adopted for it clearly served a purpose in a different context of self-definition. Elam is both a name and a concept. How these changed through time will be explored in the chapters which follow.

In a recent study of Austrian identity, Franz Mathis notes, 'When the term "Austria" in the form of *Ostarrichi* was used in a document in 996, it referred to a certain area in today's Lower Austria, which the people used to call *Ostarrichi*, a land in the east. At that time this land was ruled by the house of Babenberg. Later on, the name was gradually applied to all the lands that the Babenbergs acquired on both sides of the Danube before the end of their rule in 1246. It was not, however, applied to Styria, which had been added in 1192 . . . it was not extended over the lands that the Habsburgs acquired during the following centuries: these retained their former names such as Carinthia, Tyrol and – much later – Salzburg' (Mathis 1997: 20–1). Mathis goes on to analyze the eventual substitution of the name Austria (Österreich) for that of Habsburg, the very late adoption of that name for areas to the west and south of the original *Ostarrichi* domains, and the feelings of identity, or lack of identity, with the geographical entity so named on the part of the people who lived there. Much of this analysis of Austria and Austrian identity strikes a chord in anyone who has grappled with the problem of defining Elam in its various forms through time and will hopefully do the same in readers new to the subject as they work their way through this book.

2

ENVIRONMENT, CLIMATE AND RESOURCES

The approximate geographical boundaries of Elam are set out in this chapter, and the topographic and environmental zones within those boundaries are described. The reader is introduced to the climate, rainfall and hydrology of the relevant portions of Fars, Khuzistan and Luristan in south-western Iran. Evidence for differences between the climate of the past and that of the present is examined and in that context the possibility of anthropogenic changes to the Elamite landscape is raised. Finally, the animal, mineral and vegetable resources of the region are surveyed, showing just what earlier inhabitants of southwestern Iran had at their disposal.

Introduction

It is important in any regional archaeological or historical study to have an appreciation of what the climate, environment, land-use potential and natural resources of the region under study (Fig. 2.1) were like by the start of the period in which one is interested. Although the geographical limits of Elam changed through time, we shall consider the Elamite area at its greatest extent to have extended from Kermanshah province in the northwest to the eastern border of Fars in the southeast. For the sake of convenience we shall take as the region's northern boundary the 'Royal' or 'Great Khorassan' Road leading from Baghdad in the west to Kermanshah, Kangavar and Hamadan (and eventually Qazvin and Teheran) in the east. The western edge of the interior desert basin – the true Iranian 'plateau', as distinct from the mountains of the Zagros chain – may be taken to form the northeastern boundary of our area, while to the southeast a lack of archaeological exploration makes it difficult to define the border, but later historical evidence suggests that a true cultural boundary existed separating Kerman in the east from Fars in the west. This theoretical eastern boundary of Elam was probably located further west than Bandar Abbas, for a genuine cultural border seems to exist between Darab and Sirjan, separating Fars from Kerman (on the changing boundary between Fars and Kerman, see Aubin 1977: 285–6). Along the coast of Fars we know of a second millennium Elamite cultural presence near modern Bushire (Vallat 1984a) but whether the lower coast of what is today Laristan and Tangistan was culturally within the Elamite orbit at any time we do not know (see Pohanka 1986 for an introduction to the archaeology of the region). Politically the entire area just described encompasses most of the former *ostans* (provinces) of Kermanshah, Ahwaz and Shiraz (see Fisher 1968: Fig. 2). Here we shall briefly examine

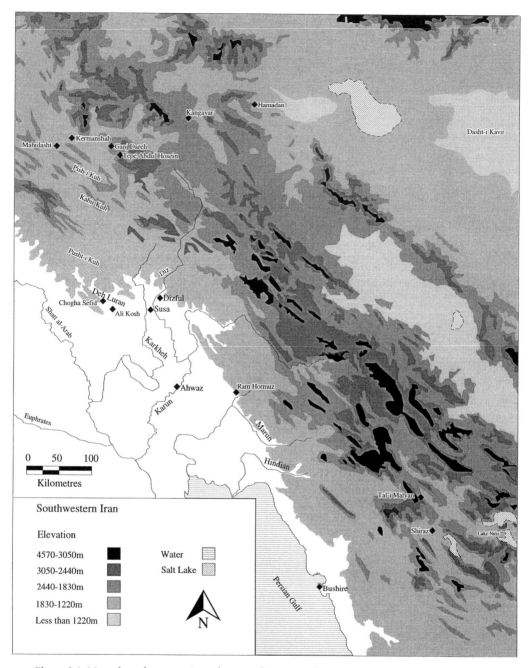

Figure 2.1 Map of southwestern Iran showing the principal sites mentioned in Chapter 2.

the main features of topography and climate which were of importance for the human populations inhabiting these regions in antiquity.

Highland Elam: the central Zagros zone

Iran has often been likened to 'a bowl, with a higher outer rim surrounding an irregular and lower, but not low-lying, interior' (Fisher 1968: 5). Very little of the country is real lowland and all of it which is lies on the peripheries of the high-rimmed 'bowl', fronting the Caspian Sea to the north, the Persian Gulf to the south, and the Mesopotamian plain to the southwest. Otherwise, the average elevation of most of the interior of the country is over 1000 metres above mean sea-level (m.a.s.l.), a feature which distinguishes Iran markedly from its neighbours, for the mountainous highlands of the Zagros region of western Iran include some of the highest peaks in Western Asia.

With the exception of Khuzistan and the coastal plain of Fars, most of the area just described falls within the central and southern Zagros mountain system, a series of deeply folded, roughly parallel mountain chains (Pl. 2.1) oriented northwest to southeast of variable length but similar alignment (Fisher 1968: 17). At its widest point, southwest of Qum, the Zagros mountains are roughly 350 km wide, while at their narrowest point, southwest of Isfahan, they are still some 200 km wide (Brookes 1982: 192). The higher Zagros ranges are separated from the lowland plain of Khuzistan by an intervening strip of foothills roughly 60 km wide. On the northeast side of the Kabir Kuh range lies the Pish-i Kuh which runs to the south of Kermanshah. The lower-lying area to the southwest of the Kabir Kuh, known as the Pusht-i Kuh, forms the backdrop to the Deh Luran plain of northwestern Khuzistan. In seeking to express the marked contrast made by the Zagros with the Mesopotamian plain, Western visitors and observers have given a number of evocative names to the Zagros mountains. Diodorus Siculus referred to a pass leading into the western Zagros as the 'ladder' in an attempt to convey the 'abruptness and the succession of terraces which lead step-like from the plain to the highlands', while the mid-nineteenth century British medical officer W.F. Ainsworth christened them the 'Persian Apennines', and during World War I the more prosaic Intelligence Department of the Admiralty Naval Staff called them simply the 'Persian Front' (Intelligence Department 1918: 29).

With annual winter rainfall often on the order of 350–500 mm (Table 1; see also van Zeist 1967: 302; Ganji 1968; 1978) and many mountain ranges reaching 3000 m or more in elevation, this is an area which, in the words of W.B. Fisher, 'exhibits much variety in scenery and opportunities for human utilization . . . Adequate, sometimes abundant, rainfall and a considerable swing of temperature – from bitterly cold winters, especially on the higher parts, to marked summer heat – result in a distinct zonation of vegetation. Though massive expanses of bare rock or gorge greatly reduce the effective soil cover, there still remains an appreciable extent of woodland, which gives way to an alpine pasture on the higher levels. Patches of alluvium also occur, and these support regular cropping' (Fisher 1968: 20). These areas, generally too small to appear on any

Plate 2.1 The Zagros between Shahr-e Kord and Izeh.

Table 2.1. *Elevation, rainfall and temperature data from southwestern Iran*

City	m.a.s.l.	Temp/Rainfall	Jan	Feb	Mar	Apr	May	Jun	Jul	Aug	Sep	Oct	Nov	Dec	Total
Abadan	3	Max. temp.	18.8	21.4	25.5	32.4	37.9	43.3	44.5	45.1	42.4	36.4	26.5	19.1	
		Min. temp.	7.2	8.7	11.9	17.5	22.2	26.2	27.7	26.8	23.0	17.8	12.5	8.3	
		Rainfall	19.9	14.5	18.5	14.6	3.7	0.0	0.0	0.0	0.0	0.6	25.9	40.6	146.3
Ahwaz	20	Max. temp.	17.7	20.7	25.3	32.3	38.9	44.5	46.1	45.9	42.1	36.0	26.0	19.2	
		Min. temp.	7.8	8.2	12.2	17.1	22.0	24.9	26.9	25.6	21.3	17.3	12.8	8.6	
		Rainfall	33.5	25.2	16.9	17.3	3.5	0.0	0.0	0.0	0.1	1.8	26.7	33.5	158.5
Bushire	4	Max. temp.	18.9	20.4	24.4	30.8	34.7	37.1	38.9	39.7	37.4	33.3	26.8	20.5	
		Min. temp.	9.7	10.4	13.7	18.1	22.3	24.9	27.6	27.3	24.1	19.2	14.9	11.5	
		Rainfall	61.4	22.4	19.4	8.6	5.0	0.0	0.0	0.0	0.0	0.8	48.4	93.3	259.3
Dizful	143	Max. temp.	19.0	20.5	24.1	31.2	37.7	43.9	46.2	45.6	42.7	36.6	26.8	19.6	
		Min. temp.	8.7	9.3	12.0	17.6	23.4	26.9	30.3	30.2	26.5	20.7	14.7	10.0	
		Rainfall	65.0	45.9	48.6	30.3	4.0	0.0	1.0	0.0	0.0	5.0	80.0	75.6	355.4
Hamadan	1775	Max. temp.	4.8	6.4	10.5	16.8	22.2	28.4	32.2	33.1	28.5	20.9	11.1	5.6	
		Min. temp.	-4.9	-3.7	0.1	5.4	8.2	12.0	15.1	14.5	10.9	6.1	-0.8	-3.5	
		Rainfall	36.0	52.8	72.9	78.9	32.7	5.6	1.3	0.5	0.7	11.8	51.8	40.2	385.2
Khorramabad	1171	Max. temp.	11.7	13.3	16.7	22.4	29.3	36.3	39.9	39.8	36.0	29.1	18.7	13.0	
		Min. temp.	0.1	0.9	4.3	8.7	11.9	15.5	19.7	19.0	14.1	9.5	5.5	1.7	
		Rainfall	66.5	73.2	88.1	82.8	28.4	0.9	0.5	0.4	0.4	10.4	76.7	75.6	504.0
Kermanshah	1322	Max. temp.	8.4	10.3	13.8	19.8	25.9	33.0	37.2	36.5	32.5	25.6	15.6	9.7	
		Min. temp.	-3.5	-3.1	0.4	0.5	7.6	10.9	16.0	15.0	10.0	5.4	1.3	-1.9	
		Rainfall	37.8	46.3	67.8	68.0	30.0	2.9	0.0	0.1	1.3	13.3	55.3	50.9	372.7
Shiraz	1490	Max. temp.	12.4	14.6	18.5	24.1	29.8	34.9	36.9	36.0	33.5	27.6	19.8	13.5	
		Min. temp.	0.6	1.8	5.1	8.3	13.2	16.9	20.1	18.7	15.3	9.4	4.4	1.6	
		Rainfall	76.9	47.3	63.4	24.4	12.7	0.0	1.2	0.0	0.0	—	65.3	93.4	384.6

soil maps of Iran, are important for cultivation, pasturage and grazing in the highland zone (Dewan and Famouri 1968: 258).

As one moves in a southeasterly direction from Kermanshah to Fars, elevations drop generally, precipitation is lower, and the rivers become more and more seasonal. Fars is part of the Iranian plateau and is consequently less wooded and poorer in pasturage than Luristan, and agriculture less productive without irrigation. Settlement in isolated oases becomes sparser as one moves eastward, and the coastal plain itself is barren with few natural harbours, the main exceptions being at Bushire and Bandar Abbas. Among the most important rivers in the region are the Kur and its affluent the Pulvar which drain into the Daryacheh-i Niriz, a large inland playa. Arable land is interspersed with salines, marshes, piedmont hills and mountains, some of which, like the Kuh-i Pinar in the north (4276 m), the Kuh-i Bul in the east (3965 m), and the Kuh-i Kharman in the east (3201 m), tower over the adjacent plains. Elevations in the highland plains are often much lower and Shiraz, the region's principal modern city, lies at 1530 m.a.s.l.

Lowland Elam: Khuzistan: physical environment, climate and hydrology

Khuzistan in southwestern Iran constitutes what was, in many periods of Elamite history, the most important lowland component of Elam. Physically and climatically Khuzistan may be divided broadly into three main zones (following Alizadeh 1992; Carter and Stolper 1984).

The *Arid Zone* of *c.* 20,000 km^2 receives under 200 mm of rainfall annually and is situated to the south of Ahwaz. This area is separated from the central and northern parts of Khuzistan by a low range of hills which runs in a southeasterly direction from the Jabal Hamrin to Ahwaz and across towards Behbehan. Agriculturally this area is unimportant as it consists of a combination of saline marshes, and arid desert steppe.

The *Semi-Arid Zone* of *c.* 15,000 km^2 receives roughly 200–300 mm of rainfall per year. This zone extends from Ahwaz as far north as the Agha Jari hills, *c.* 10–15 km south of Susa and Dizful. The approximate northern limit of this area is formed by a series of hills which runs from the Diz in a southeasterly direction towards Ram Hormuz.

Finally, the *Dry Zone* of *c.* 25,000 km^2 receives between 300 and 900 mm of rainfall annually and extends from the upper limit of the Semi-Arid Zone as far north as Deh Luran and the foothills of the Zagros mountains. In summer, temperatures may be as high as 58.9° C, while temperatures in winter have been known to fall below freezing (Johnson 1973: 19–20). Moreover, the average rainfall figures given above mask the great swings in precipitation which characterize the region. Thus, in recent years parts of central and southern Khuzistan have received as little as 85 mm and as much as 580 mm (Adams 1962: 110).

Geologically speaking, Khuzistan is an extension of the Mesopotamian alluvial plain fed by five rivers – the Karkheh, Diz, Karun, Marun and Zuhreh or Hindian – which rise in the Zagros mountains, draining between them an area of *c.* 100,000 km^2 (Kirkby 1977: 251). Moving from west to east, the Karkheh is the most westerly, originating high in the Zagros to the west of Kermanshah from a combination of smaller streams which include the Kara Su, Malayer, Gamasab and Kashkan (Sykes 1915/I: 43; Rahimi-Laridjani 1988: 232). The Diz rises near Burujird, south of Hamadan, while the Karun enters Khuzistan from the east, following a course which takes it from a point south-west of Isfahan northwest in the direction of Dizful before bending and heading south towards the Shatt al-Arab. The Diz is the least saline of all Khuzistan's rivers and its summer flow is substantial enough to permit even summer irrigation (Alizadeh 1992: 17). The Marun rises some 51 km northeast of Behbehan near the southeastern corner of Khuzistan, tending northwest before turning southwest, joining the Jarrahi and draining into the tidal floodplain and lagoons of southern Khuzistan. Finally, the Zuhre or Hindian river runs in a west-northwesterly direction from a point south of Kazerun, passing below Behbehan before turning south and running, through the town of Hindijan, into the Persian Gulf at Chatleh.

In contrast to the Tigris and Euphrates, the waters of which are derived almost entirely from the melting snows of the Taurus mountains, the rivers of Khuzistan are fed by mountain aquifers which are recharged annually by the *c.* 400–800 mm of rain-fall experienced in the Zagros (Kirkby 1977: 251). Just as Mesopotamia is an alluvial plain composed of the silt deposited each year by the Tigris and Euphrates, so too is Khuzistan the creation of the five rivers which drain it (Brice 1966: 242). Of these, the Karun, some 828 km long, is the most important, bringing with it an estimated 29,700,000 m^3 of silt per year (Cressey 1958: 449).

In 1915, Lt.-Col. (later Sir) Percy Sykes published a vivid description of the Karun (Pl. 2.2) which gives a good impression of the river which Alexander the Great's admiral, Nearchus, called the *Pasitigris* or 'Lesser Tigris':

In the heart of the Bakhtiari country there is a culminating mass of ranges. From this, on one side, springs the Zenda Rud, which runs east to Isfahan, while on the southern slope the Karun takes its rise. From its source the Karun dashes down at an incredible speed, falling 9000 feet [3000 m] before it reaches Shuster. On its way it passes through some of the grandest scenery in the world. The rugged mountain gorges are frequently inaccessible and the river appears like a riband thousands of feet below. At one point the gorge is so narrow that it can be jumped by an ordinarily active man. The river flows in every direction by turn, and often parallel to its original course. Indeed the windings between its source and Shuster measure two hundred and fifty miles [c. 402.25 km], although as the crow flies the distance is less than one-third of this total. (Sykes1915/I: 43–4)

Because of the great amount of water in the Tigris and Euphrates which is siphoned off for irrigation and subsequently lost to evaporation, the Karun actually accounts for no less than 22 out of the 27 km^3 of water discharged into the Persian Gulf annually through the Shatt al-Arab by the combined Euphrates, Tigris and Karun system (Cressey 1958: 455).

Much has been written on the changes undergone by the main watercourses of Khuzistan at different points in time, both by natural forces and by human manipulation through the construction of canals, dams and weirs (e.g. Kirkby 1977: 276ff.; Neely 1974; Christensen 1993), and enough is known about the river regimes of the main streams draining Khuzistan to be certain that present day drainage patterns are *not* the

Plate 2.2 The upper Karun, east of Izeh, in early autumn.

same as those of antiquity. It would not, therefore, be correct to project uncritically either modern climatic or geomorphological conditions onto the Khuzistan of the past. The botanist H. Pabot reconstructed the vegetation of the region between sea-level and 300 m elevation as having a scatter of tamarisk, pistachio and jujube trees, with substantial amounts of herbaceous plants suitable for wild browsers and grazers (Johnson 1973: 22). Here rainfall generally comprises 200–300 mm per annum (van Zeist 1967: 302). As Johnson has noted with respect to the northern part of Khuzistan around the site of Susa, 'destruction of forest trees by fire and overcutting; destruction of other woody plants by fuel collection; long term plowing of forest and pasture soils; depletion of organic material; overgrazing; trampling and compression of soils by herd animals, all resulting in streaming and final soil erosion' have altered the natural landscape over the millennia (Johnson 1973: 21).

Nevertheless, certain natural advantages of Khuzistan should be noted which distinguish it from its better known western neighbour, the Mesopotamian plain. To begin with, the generally higher rainfall enjoyed by much of the region gave the area an advantage agriculturally over Mesopotamia. Although artificial irrigation was widely employed and indeed, as in Assyria, greatly increased the yields achievable by dry-farming, the area's water regime was in many ways superior to that of the lower Euphrates and Tigris region. Moreover, the gravel fans of northern and central Khuzistan offer much better drainage than the silty soils of southern Mesopotamia (Adams 1962).

On more than one occasion in its history, Khuzistan has been controlled by a political force based to the west in Mesopotamia proper. Conversely, forces based in Khuzistan and/or in the adjacent Iranian highlands have raided and sometimes held southern Mesopotamia for years at a time. Why these two areas should have followed essentially distinct if interconnected paths of development is not immediately visible on most maps which suggest the continuous nature of the alluvial plain, but it must be stressed that, in all probability, features such as the Hawiza marshes, into which the Karkheh river now drains, formed real barriers between the eastern and the western portions of the alluvium. This is not to say that contact did not take place through and across those barriers, but given this obstacle and given the fact that sheep and goat herding has long been an important component in the economy of western Iran, it is not surprising to find that seasonal movements of herding groups into the mountains to the north and east during the summer and onto the plains during the winter fostered close and, as we shall see, symbiotic contact between Khuzistan and its piedmont and mountain periphery to a great degree, whereas contacts across the divide with southern Mesopotamia were more often than not politically motivated, whether Elamites attacking Babylonians or vice-versa, or Elamites aiding Babylonians against a common enemy, such as Assyria. Travellers and anthropologists working in southwestern Iran have long been aware of the close ties which have traditionally bound the Iranian highlands with the Khuzistan plain. As one example, we may cite Lt. Col. H.A. Sawyer, writing in 1894, who coined the term 'Upper Elam' for the highlands and 'Lower Elam' for the Khuzistan plain:

For want of a known general appellation, the country to the northwest of the Kuh-i-Rang has been called in this report by the name of Upper Elam. Of the ancient Elam, nothing need be said except that it lay in the plains at the foot of these hills only a few days' distant. In summer the plains were, as they are nowadays, insufferably hot, whilst this mountainous country is cool, wooded, with peaks covered with snow. It is not extravagant to suppose, therefore, that in those times, even as now, this higher level country was periodically peopled by the same inhabitants as those who had their permanent homes in the Lower Elam of the plains. (Sawyer 1894: 494)

We must, nonetheless, be wary of inferring conditions in remote antiquity from patterns of the relatively recent past, for since the sixteenth century, for example, Arabic has been spoken and Arabs of the Banu Ka'b have resided in Khuzistan, creating a situation wherein the Shatt al-Arab (the current Iran-Iraq border) was by no means a linguistic boundary separating Arabic from Persian. Furthermore, the Hawiza (Hoveyzeh) marshes themselves, alluded to above as a possible barrier between the eastern and western alluvium, may not have presented much of a barrier prior to the breaching of the dyke at Kut Nahr Hashim on the Karkheh in the 1830s (Ingham 1994: 97).

Indigenous systems of environmental classification

Western, scientific descriptions of the Iranian environment present a picture which is strikingly different from that of natural or traditional Iranian geography. From an Iranian point of view, the area treated in this book cross-cuts four major environmental zones. These are the *garmsir*, literally 'warm land', in the south, where the date-palm, sorghum and sugarcane are grown today; a strangely unnamed region of settlement where a great variety of fruits and vegetables are grown along with cotton, rice, tobacco and sesame; the *sardsir*, or 'cold land', those highland valleys up to 2900 m.a.s.l. characterized by the cultivation of cereals (except for rice and sorghum), potatoes and fruit; and finally the *sarhadd*, the 'land at the upper boundary', which is traditionally dedicated to grazing rather than cultivation (Bobek 1968: 284; Rahimi-Laridjani 1988: 62). Quite apart from the problematic state of our understanding of the palaeoclimate of Iran, using a classification such as this to help inform our understanding of agricultural potential in antiquity is problematic if for no other reason than the fact that many of the cultivars listed above were unknown in the region in more remote antiquity. We know from both Medieval and pre-modern sources that southwestern Iran has always been agriculturally productive (Christensen 1993: 117–19; 151, 155, 165) but before adopting the traditional Iranian terminology for climatic/geographical units, we must consider the difficult problem of whether or not the climate has changed appreciably since antiquity.

Climate then and now

Most authors of studies of a particular culture area feel obliged to provide their readers with some basic data on rainfall and temperature in the area under study, just as has been done here, but when it comes to addressing the knotty problem of whether or not conditions have changed appreciably since prehistoric times, one almost invariably falls back on commonplace demurrals about the lack of adequate research and the extent to which results from one area cannot be extrapolated to another. In short, the reader is often left wondering whether an understanding of the current climatic regime is at all relevant to the study of the past, or else goes away with the conviction that as nothing really can be said about palaeoclimate, all one can do is to hope that conditions have not changed so much over the millennia that the data on modern climate is rendered utterly worthless. Needless to say, this is a far from satisfactory situation.

Climatic conditions in the past which differ from those of the present can be detected in a variety of ways which include (but are not limited to) geomorphological and palynological analysis (e.g. Meder 1979). In Khuzistan, geomorphological evidence which has been gathered by M.J. Kirkby suggests that the Karkheh's peak flows have been declining since c. 1500 BC when they stood at an estimated 1100 m³ of water per second (cumecs) to their current level of only 460 cumecs (Kirkby 1977: 279). But this was not necessarily due to a gradually warming climate, and could reflect amongst other things the institution of a reservoir system siphoning off peak flow water for later use in time of low summer flows, or the adoption of better land management practices resulting in improved water retention of irrigation water in the surrounding fields (Kirkby 1977: 279). What probably does reflect changing climate is the pattern of aggradation and erosion in the rivers of Khuzistan. As Kirkby explained, 'in semi-arid areas, aggradation is associated with wetter periods, and down-cutting with drier periods. In a slightly drier period, plant cover is sparser, so that rain compacts and seals the unprotected soil surface. The effect is to reduce infiltration into the soil, and increase surface runoff, which carries with it a greatly increased sediment load. To accommodate these changes, more channels are formed and existing ones incised . . . Thus the initial effect of the drier conditions was to increase the rate of headwater erosion as hillside vegetation became sparser. To begin with, this erosion led to an increase of sediment downstream, causing aggradation all over the plains. Over the last ten thousand years, however, the continued drier climate (overall) has allowed the area of erosion to spread downstream into the Khuzistan plains, which are now more or less stable, although "wetter" conditions since the 4000 BC climatic optimum might have assisted this stabilization' (Kirkby 1977: 283–4).

Although Brookes contended that Kirkby's climatic reconstruction 'runs counter to what would be expected as a result of the climatic and cultural changes so far reconstructed for the central and southern Zagros', it in fact conforms in the main to the pollen profile at Lake Zeribar in northwestern Iran analyzed by van Zeist, who suggests that 'between ca. 10,000 and ca. 6,000 BP, a savanna with *Pistacia* [pistachio] and *Quercus* [oak] was present', i.e. warm conditions prevailed, and that 'after about 6,000 BP, the savanna thickened to an oak forest, suggesting an increase in humidity to modern levels . . . which may have been caused either by a rise in precipitation or a fall in temperature, or by a combination of both' (van Zeist 1967: 301, 310). As Bottema explains in discussing the Lake Zeribar evidence, 'the decrease of values for *Artemisia* and the parallel increase of Chenopodiaceae point to a change in conditions. Precipitation must have been the limiting factor for tree growth, while increasing temperatures did more harm than good to such vegetation. Whereas the present lower limit of forest theoretically stands at sea-level in all the other sites [examined by Bottema, i.e. Xinias and Ioannina in Greece; Lakes Vico and Garda in Italy; Trsteniki in Slovenia; the Ghab valley in Syria], oak forest in the Zagros Mountains only grows above 800 m. The conditions at the beginning of the post-Glacial were so bad that the expansion of such oak forest reached an optimum only at about 5500 BP' (Bottema 1978: 27). Post-Pleistocene warming has also been deduced from a study of the strandlines around the Neyriz playa east of Shiraz (Brookes 1982: 213) and from the calichification of gravels in the Mahidasht plain west of Kermanshah (Brookes 1989: 35).

Brookes has suggested that during the early to mid-Holocene (c. 7,000–4,000 BP) temperatures stood only 1–2° C above those of the present day. Nevertheless, he estimated that this slight difference was significant enough to completely eradicate the Iranian glaciers, thus removing one of the perennial sources of water supply available in the mountains. Brookes suggests that, 'Neolithic farming communities may have had to rely upon streamflow from winter rainfall, without spring and summer augmentation by glacier melt water. Perhaps this spurred development of irrigation techniques' (Brookes 1982: 199).

Finally, whereas the Lake Zeribar diagram shows no indication of appreciable climate change after 5,500 BP, a core drilled further south at Lake Mirabad, southwest of Khorramabad, shows signs of two 'short climatic oscillations' when the lake dried out completely, perhaps the result of drier summers which may have also thinned out the oak forest (van Zeist 1967: 310–11).

Ancient literary sources also give us some climatic data for the period from the arrival of Alexander the Great in Iran to roughly the time of Christ. In his *Geography*, the Greek geographer Strabo (64/3 BC – c. AD 25) describes Fars, or Persis as he calls it, as well as Khuzistan, ancient Susis. 'Persis is of a threefold character, both in its nature and in the temperature of its air', he wrote (*Geog.* 15.3.1). The coast of Fars was 'burning hot, sandy, and stinted of fruits except dates . . . the portion above the seaboard produces everything, is level, and is excellent for the rearing of cattle, and also abounds with rivers and lakes; the third portion, that on the north, is wintry and mountainous'. The ancient authorities on whom Strabo drew (e.g. Aristobulus, Onesicritus and Nearchus) were greatly impressed by the extreme heat of Khuzistan, about which Strabo wrote, 'although Susis is fertile, it has a hot and scorching atmosphere, and particularly in the neighbourhood of the city . . . when the sun is hottest, at noon, the lizards and the snakes could not cross the streets in the city quickly enough to prevent their being burnt to death in the middle of the streets . . . this is the case nowhere in Persis, although Persis lies more to the south . . . cold water for baths is put out in the sun and immediately heated . . . and . . . although they are in want of long beams, they need large houses on account of the suffocating heat . . . It is said that the cause of the heat is the fact that lofty mountains lie above the country on the north and that these mountains intercept all the northern winds. Accordingly, these winds, blowing aloft from the tops of the mountains and high above the plains, do not touch the plains, although they blow on the more southerly parts of Susis' (*Geog.* 15.3.10).

If we turn to the subsequent era, one of the results of Brookes' careful study of the Mahidasht plain has been to show that up to 10 m of alluvium has been deposited since a date 'no older than AD 220 and possibly as young as post-AD 1000' (Brookes 1989: 31). Devastating floods are known to have occurred in the area in 1832, and test excavations at Jameh Shuran, for example, have shown that strata datable archaeologically to *c.* 1000 BC are today located 1 m below the flood plain. The net result of these observations has been to show that many sites, particularly smaller ones, lie completely buried beneath the alluvial plain. Moreover, it completely skews our perception of the visible size of sites in this region, a factor which has obvious implications for site-size and hence putative population estimates in antiquity. The 'absence' of Chalcolithic sites within two kilometres of the Ab-i-Marik, a stream which runs through the Mahidasht, is clearly therefore an artifact of the buildup of 3–6 m of alluvium in this area, just as the over-representation of Middle Islamic period or younger sites in the same zone is a misrepresentation of real site distributions. The fact that sites earlier than this date do not appear at elevations below the 1360 m contour line (Brookes 1989: 38) reflects the areal extent of alluviation on the Mahidasht and should serve as a warning to archaeologists and historians not to interpret site distributions without some understanding of local geomorphology.

Early human impacts on the environment

In addition to having a basic understanding of climatic conditions in the past which impinged on human activities in southwestern Iran, it is also interesting to consider what the human impact on the environment has been through time.

Under the rubric 'human impacts', one often thinks of deforestation and soil degradation and in that connection of the reduction of protective vegetation cover caused by the over-grazing of domesticated goats, causing 'a high rate of denudation' (Brookes 1982: 193). To be sure, however much we may be influenced by the Green politics of the late 20th century and a visionary anthropology in which native groups live in perfect ecological harmony with their environment, it is just as possible for human-induced environmental degradation to have occurred in antiquity as it is today. In the case of historic southern Mesopotamia, with its massive irrigation system, this is precisely what has been argued by scholars who believe that wilful 'violation of fallow' led to 'engineered disaster in Mesopotamian civilization' (Gibson 1974: 7–19), or that over-intensification led to salinity problems which ultimately reduced yields (e.g. Jacobsen 1982; but see also Powell 1985).

In the Zagros, we have relatively few detailed studies which can shed light on this problem, but certainly the palaeobotanical evidence from Tal-i Malyan in Fars suggests that a slow but progressive pattern of deforestation characterizes the sequence from the late fourth through the second millennium BC. A gradual decline in the quantity of charcoal from juniper and poplar – trees which lived in the immediate vicinity of the site on the Kur River basin floor – coupled with a steady increase in oak charcoal – a species found in the higher elevations further away from the site – suggest that whether through land clearance for agriculture, in the interests of obtaining fuel to be used for domestic (cooking, heating) or industrial (firing ceramic kilns and metallurgical ovens) purposes, or a combination of such factors, the tree cover around the site grew ever sparser as time went on (Miller 1985; 1990a: 74). A similar trend has been observed in the case of Tepe Abdul Hosein in Luristan, where, as G. Willcox has noted, 'that the area around Tepe Abdul Hosein today is completely denuded of trees indicates that the area was progressively over-exploited and subsequently deforested', even though the quantities of *Pistacia* sp. and *Amygdalus* charcoal found at the site indicate 'that there was no lack of fuel occurring naturally during the mid-seventh millennium BC' (Willcox 1990: 226). Another example from Fars of later date is provided by Strabo, who says that when Alexander the Great went to Pasargadae, near Shiraz, he visited the tomb of Cyrus the Great, which was 'concealed within the dense growth of trees' (*Geog.* 15.3.7). Today, Cyrus' tomb is located in an open, undulating plain covered with savanna-like grass.

In discussing the area around Tepe Ali Kosh in Khuzistan, K. Flannery has observed that the practice of farming introduced cultivars (wheat and barley) which competed with the wild legumes and grasses (wild alfalfa, spiny milk vetch, a fenugreek-like plant, oat grass, Bermuda grass and Canary grass) formerly gathered in the area during the pre-agricultural era. As both the wild and the cultivated plants competed for the same alluvial soils, the wild plants changed from being sought after by the human communities in the region to being considered weeds. In the competition, these plants lost out. Thus, not only was the native plant cover greatly modified, but the replacement of previously economically important wild plants by cultivars meant that a reversion to plant gathering was effectively ruled out as a subsistence strategy (Flannery 1969: 87–8).

The changing percentages of wood charcoal at Tal-i Malyan are mirrored by the ever increasing amounts of weed seeds as one moves through the sequence, a sign, N. Miller suggests, that animal dungcakes were used increasingly as a wood substitute for fuel, by then an increasingly scarce commodity (Miller 1984; Miller and Smart 1984). Still, there is no indication of the sort of organized deforestation which Eratosthenes observed on Cyprus, where, according to Strabo, 'trees were cut down to smelt the copper and silver', and when even timbering for boat-building proved 'insufficient to check the growth of timber in the forest, permission was given, to such as were able and inclined, to cut down the trees and to hold the land thus cleared as their own property, free from all payments' (Strabo, *Geog.* 14.6.5, quoted in Brice 1978: 142). Rather, when it comes to 'living on the land' in an intelligent manner, Brookes' work on the Mahidasht plain is instructive, for he found that 'human settlements would unarguably have been as finely adjusted in their distribution with respect to soil and water resources as they clearly are today' (Brookes 1989: 35). A glance at Table 2.2 clearly shows this to have been the case, for the figures relating to the siting of settlements on alluvial lowland, alluvial fan and upland locations are strikingly similar.

Table 2.2. *Relative distribution of ancient and modern village sites in environmental zones within the Mahidasht survey area*

Village Sites	Alluvial lowland %	Alluvial fans %	Upland (pediment, colluvial hills and rock outcrops) %
modern	43.7	34.7	18
ancient (n = 515)	44.5	37.5	10.4

Natural resources

If we disregard the great interior desert basins of Iran, the Dasht-i Lut and Dasht-i Kavir, and parts of Baluchistan and Seistan, the rest of the country is rich in natural resources, many of which were exploited in antiquity. For the sake of this discussion, we may classify these resources under the rubrics 'animal', 'mineral' and 'vegetable'.

As the faunal assemblages from sites of all periods in our region attest, the range of vertebrate and invertebrate fauna exploited for human consumption was certainly large. Tables 2.3–5 summarize the species (mammals, reptiles, birds) present in Luristan (Table 2.3), Fars (Table 2.4) and Khuzistan (Table 2.5) from the Palaeolithic through the Chalcolithic (later fauna will be discussed in the following chapters of this book). These tables take no account of percentages and are intended only to show 'what was on the menu' in the territory which later became the Elamite zone. Clearly the range was wide and the subsistence possibilities enormous. But it should be noted that the diversity of species hunted should not be misinterpreted, for certain species were much more intensively utilized than others. For example, in spite of the seemingly wide range of species diversity during the Upper Palaeolithic, the wild ungulates hunted in the Zagros contributed 99 per cent of the total meat yield, while it is clear that in later prehistory, whether by calculating numbers of individuals of a particular species present in the faunal assemblage of a particular site, or by extension calculating the meat yield from those individuals, the broad range of animals available is deceptive in that hunted birds and mammals contributed relatively little to the diet. Nevertheless, one should not forget that animals are important not merely for the meat they yield but also for those secondary products which they are able to supply.

At the Neolithic site of Tepe Abdul Hosein in Luristan, for example, red deer (*Cervus elaphus*) antler was used to fashion tools which had tips polished (Pullar 1990: 190) by some kind of repetitive activity, such as reaming. Hare or fox bones were used to make points at Tepe Abdul Hosein, and similar objects are known from Ali Kosh (Hole, Flannery and Neely 1969: 215) and Chogha Sefid (Hole 1977: 219–25), while animal bones of undetermined species were employed as needles, spatulae, burnishers and pendants (Pullar 1990: 189–90). Modified sheep and goat scapulae were used used at Tepe Abdul Hosein and Ganj Dareh as tools for removing cereal grains (barley in the case of Ganj Dareh) from the stalk (Stordeur and Anderson-Gerfaud 1985; see the illustrations

Table 2.3. *Fauna representation in archaeological contexts (Palaeolithic through Chalcolithic) in Luristan*

Fauna		Distribution in Luristan															
		Mid. Pal.			Upper Pal.		Epipal.			Acer. Neol.		Ceramic Neol.				Chalcolithic	
Latin name	common name	War	Hou	Kho	War	Kho	War	Kho	PaS	GjD	Asi	Gur	Sar	Sia	Deh	Seh	God
Mammal (wild)																	
Insectivora																	
Hemiechinus cf. *auritus*	long-eared hedgehog															+	
Erinaceus europaeus	European hedgehog											+					
Lagomorpha																	
Ochotona cf. *rufescens*	rufescent pika	+															
Lepus cf. *capensis*	cape hare			+													
Lepus sp.	hare											+				+	
Rodentia																	
Microtus sp.	vole	+															
Mus musculus	house mouse															+	
Apodemus sylvaticus	field/wood mouse															+	
Rattus rattus	house rat															+	
Ellobius cf. *fuscocapillus*		+															
Meriones sp.	jird	+															
Mesocricetus cf. *auratus*	gold hamster	+															
Tatera cf. *indica*	Indian gerbil	+															
Cricetulus sp.	gray hamster																+
Carnivora																	
Canis lupus	wolf	+									?		+			+	
Canis aureus	jackal										?		+				

Table 2.3 (cont.)

Fauna		Distribution in Luristan															
		Mid. Pal.			Upper Pal.		Epipal.			Acer. Neol.		Ceramic Neol.				Chalcolithic	
Latin name	common name	War	Hou	Kho	War	Kho	War	Kho	PaS	GiD	Asi	Gur	Sar	Sia	Deh	Seh	God
Vulpes vulpes	red fox										+	+	+		+	+	
Hyaena sp.	hyena	+															
Felis silvestris	wild cat										+	+	+				
Felis pardus	leopard										+	+	+				
Felis sp.?	cat	+															
Lynx sp.	lynx										+	+	+				
Ursus arctos	brown bear											+					
Meles meles	badger										+	+				+	
Mustela nivalis	weasel											+				+	
Mustela sp.	weasel																
Vormela or *Martes* sp.	polecat or marten										+	+				+	
Castor fiber	beaver										+						
Perissodactyla																	
Equus ferus	wild horse	+			+		+										
Equus hemionus	onager, half-ass	+		+	+	+											
Equus caballus	horse							+	+		+						+
Equus cf. *hemionus*			+														
Equus sp.	equid unspecified	+		+	+	+	+	+		+	+	+	+	+	+	+	
Artiodactyla																	
Sus scrofa	wild boar	+		+	+	+	+	+	+	+	+	+	+	+	+	?	
Bos primigenius	aurochs	+		+	+	+	+		+	+	+	+	+	+	+		
Bos sp.																	
Gazella subgutturosa	goitred gazelle							+		+	+	+	+		+		
Gazella sp.	gazelle unspecified	?						+		+	+	+	+	+	+		
Capra aegagrus	wild goat	+	?	+	+	+	+	+	+	+	+	+	+	+	+	+	

Taxon	Common name
Ovis orientalis	Western Asiatic mouflon, red sheep
Cervus elaphus	red deer
Dama mesopotamica	Mes. fallow deer
Capreolus capreolus	roe deer
Mammal (domestic)	
Carnivora	
Canis familiaris	dog
Artiodactyla	
Sus scrofa	pig
Ovis aries	sheep
Capra hircus	goat
Reptile (wild)	
Testudo sp.	tortoise
Bird (wild)	
Egretta alba	common egret
Ciconia sp.	stork
Anas acuta	pintail
Anas crecca	teal
Aythya ferina	pochard
Tadorna cf. *ferruginea*	ruddy shelduck
Anser cf. *anser*	gray lag goose
Anser cf. *fabalis*	bean goose
Anser erythropus	lesser white-fronted goose
Gyps fulvus	griffon vulture
Aquila chrysaetos	golden eagle
Buteo lagopus	rough-legged buzzard
Circus cf. *macrourus*	pallid harrier
Alectoris graeca	rock partridge
Crex crex	Corncrake

Table 2.3 (cont.)

Fauna		Distribution in Luristan															
		Mid. Pal.			Upper Pal.		Epipal.			Acer. Neol.		Ceramic Neol.				Chalcolithic	
Latin name	common name	War	Hou	Kho	War	Kho	War	Kho	PaS	GjD	Asi	Gur	Sar	Sia	Deh	Seh	God
Fulica atra	coot											+					
Grus grus	European crane														+		
Otis tarda	great bustard														+	+	+
Bubo bubo	eagle owl											+					
Merops apiaster	European bee-eater														+		
Pyrrhocorax pyrrhocorax	red-billed chough														+		

Notes:
Information extracted from Uerpmann 1987; Young and Levine 1974; Bökönyi 1977; Bewley 1984; Hesse 1979 and 1982; Flannery 1983; Gilbert 1991; Abbreviations: War = Warwasi; Hou = Houmian; Kho = Khorramabad caves; PaS = Pa Sangar; GjD = Ganj Dareh; Asi = Asiab; Gur = Tepe Guran; Sar = Sarab; Sia = Siahbid; Deh = Dehsavar; Seh = Seh Gabi; God = Godin Tepe

Table 2.4. *Fauna represented in archaeological contexts (Palaeolithic through Chalcolithic) in Fars*

Fauna		Distribution in Fars				
Latin name	common name	Mid. Pal. Esh	Upper Pal. Esh	Epipal. Esh	Ceramic Neol. Tal-i Mushki	Chalcolithic Tal-i Gap
Mammal (wild)						
Perissodactyla						
Equus hemionus	onager, half-ass	+	+	+	?	
Artiodactyla						
Bos primigenius	aurochs	+	+	+		
Gazella sp.	Gazelle unspecified	+	+	+		?
Capra aegagrus	wild goat					?
Ovis orientalis	Western Asiatic mouflon, red sheep	+	+	+		+
Cervus elaphus	red deer	?	?	?		+
Dama mesopotamica	Mes. fallow deer					+
Capreolus capreolus	roe deer					+
Mammal (domestic)						
Artiodactyla						
Bos taurus	cattle					+

Notes:
Information extracted from Uerpmann 1987; Payne 1991; Zeder 1991; Abbreviations: Esh = Eshkaft-e Gavi.

Table 2.5. *Fauna represented in archaeological contexts (Palaeolithic through early third millennium BC)*

		Distribution in Khuzistan												
		Aceramic Neol.		Ceramic Neol.			Chalcolithic							
Fauna														
Latin name	common name	BusM	Ali K	MohJ	Sef	Sur	CMT	Sabz	Khaz	Meh	Bay	Far	P-Far
Mammal (wild)													
Insectivora													
Hemiechinus cf. *auritus*	long-eared hedgehog		+	+				+					
Rodentia													
Meriones crassus	Karun desert gerbil	+											
Nesokia indica	bandicoot rat		+	+									
Tatera cf. *indica*	Indian gerbil	+	+	+			+		+	+	+	+	
Carnivora													
Canis lupus	wolf		+	+									
Canis spp.	canid unspecified											+	+
Vulpes vulpes	red fox	+	+	+					+	+	+	+	+
Hyaena hyaena	hyena		+										
Felis cf. *Libyca*	wild cat		+	+									
Mustela nivalis	weasel		?										
Martes foina	beech marten		+					+					
Perissodactyla													
Equus hemionus	onager, half-ass	+	+	+			+		+	+	+		
Equus sp.	equid unspecified											+	+
Artiodactyla													
Bos primigenius	aurochs	+	+	+									
Sus scrofa	wild boar	+	+	+			+		+	+	+	+	+
Gazella subgutturosa	goitred gazelle	+	+	+			+	+	+	+	+		
Mammal (domestic)													
Carnivora													
Canis familiaris	dog							+	+	+	+		

Taxon	Common name	BusM	Ali K	Moh J	CMT	Sef	Sur	Khaz	Meh	Bay	Far	P-Far
Artiodactyla												
Sus scrofa	pig							+		+	+	+
Ovis aries	sheep	+	+	+	+	+	+	+	+	+	+	+
Capra hircus	goat	+	+	+	+	+	+	+	+	+	+	+
Bos taurus	cattle	+	+	+	+	+	+	+		+	+	+
Reptile (wild)												
Clemmys caspica	freshwater turtle	+		+	+	+		+		+	+	+
Bird (wild)												
Ciconia ciconia	white stork		+									
Anas platyrhynchos	mallard										+	
Aythya sp.	diving duck										+	
Anser anser	gray lag goose	+										
Anser albifrons	white-fronted goose	+										
Aquila sp.	eagle									+		
Grus grus	European crane		+									
Ardea cinerea	heron										+	+
Accipitridae	hawk or kite											+
Francolinus francolinus	black partridge	+									+	
Ammoperdix griseogularis	seesee partridge									+		
Corvus corone	hooded crow		+									
Phalacrocorax carbo	cormorant											+

Notes:

Information extracted from Hole, Flannery and Neely 1969; Uerpmann 1987; Redding 1981; Abbreviations relate to the phases of occupation identified at Tepe Ali Kosh, Tepe Sabz, Chogha Sefid and Tepe Farukhabad. BusM = Bus Mordeh, *c.* 7500–6700 BC; Ali K = Ali Kosh, *c.* 6700–6300 BC; Moh J = Mohammad Jaffar, *c.* 6300–6000 BC; Sef = Sefid, *c.* 6000–5700 BC; Sur = Surkh, *c.* 5700–5400 BC; CMT = Choga Mami Transitional, *c.* 5400–5200 BC; Saloz, *c.* 5200–5000 BC; Khaz = Khazineh, *c.* 5000–4800 BC; Meh = Mehmeh, *c.* 4800–4600 BC; Bay = Bayat, *c.* 4600–4400 BC; Far = Farukhabad, *c.* 4400–4200 BC; P-Far = Post-Farukhabad, *c.* 4200–1300 BC. After Hole 1987; Table 2.

in Pullar 1990: Fig. 72a–c). Sheep and goat long bones, particularly distal tibiae, were used as gouges at Tepe Abdul Hosein (Pullar 1990: Fig. 73), and we should also assume that the leather obtained from the larger ungulates was used for clothing, bags, buckets, etc., even if these have failed to survive in the archaeological record.

The mineral resources of highland Iran were as highly esteemed in antiquity as they were in the Medieval and early modern era and indeed continue to be to this day. In 1837, the Qara Dagh region northeast of Tabriz was described to Lord Palmerston as 'one enormous mass of the most valuable minerals, whole mountains being almost apparently composed of ores – perhaps the richest in the world – of iron, tin, and copper' (quoted in Intelligence Department 1918: 68). Hyperbole such as this notwithstanding, Iran boasts a long list of mineral resources (see Fraser 1826: 354–63), not all of which were exploited in antiquity, of course (Table 2.6). Moreover, if one examines the late antique Chinese and Medieval sources on the mineral products of Iran, it is clear that some of the things said to come from 'Persia' were not indigenous to that region, but merely passed through it before arriving at their final destinations. The list included here is far more extensive geographically than the former regions of Elam would have been, but it is intended merely to convey the wealth of mineral diversity present in Iran. Metals, semi-precious stones, pigments, and medicinal mineral compounds were all available over a wide area extending from Azerbaijan in the northwest to Khorassan in the northeast and the Makran coast in the southeast.

Finally, the vegetable resources available in the later Elamite region included a range of cultivars and their wild progenitors (Table 2.7); plants, the gums, resins and oils of which were used for medicinal and religious purposes (Table 2.8); dozens of species of trees providing wood for a wide range of uses (Table 2.9); and wild grasses and legumes, such as fenugreek and plantain, the seeds of which were employed in later history for both culinary and medicinal purposes.

Conclusion

Because we can demonstrate no unequivocal connection betewen the prehistoric assemblages of Fars, Khuzistan and Luristan, on the one hand, and the later material culture of the Elamites, on the other, it is not necessarily relevant to review the entire scope of pre-Elamite archaeology in what was later to become Elam. Nevertheless, even allowing for climatic fluctuations and changing human impacts on the environment, the land, flora and fauna of those regions in the pre-Elamite era would not have been very different from those of later periods when we know that the peoples identified as Elamite lived there. For this reason, it is useful to have an idea of the resource potential of southwestern Iran, since the resources eventually available to the Elamites were, in some cases, common to a wide range of peoples in the ancient Near East, and in other cases – rarer if not unique – to the region of Elam.

Table 2.6. *Distribution of minerals in Iran according to Chinese, Medieval and early modern records*

Mineral	Uses	Distribution	Select References
alabaster	vessels	Yazd	Beale 1973
*amber		'eastern Iran'	*Nan shi, Wei shu, Sui shu*
antimony		'Persia'	Yaqut
		Demawend (Kerman)	Intelligence Dept. 1918
		Anarak	
azurite	pigment	Anarak, Kashan	Porter and Vesel 1993
bezoar	medicinal	'Persia'	Milburn 1813
bitumen	vessels, seals, statuary, beads, etc.	Khuzistan, Luristan	Connan and Deschesne 1996
borax		near Lake Urmia	Intelligence Dept. 1918
		southwest of Isfahan	
		'Kerman'	
carnelian	beads	Helmand River basin (Seistan)	Beale 1973
chlorite	vessels, statuary, small objects	around Tepe Yahya	Beale 1973
chromite		near Takht-i Sulaiman	Intelligence Dept. 1918
cobalt	pigment	near Kashan	*Javaher-name-ye soltani*
copper	tools	northeast of Tabriz	Intelligence Dept. 1918
		near Isfahan	
		Anarak	
		Gaudi-i-Ahmer (Kerman)	
		'Kerman'	
coral	medicinal, talismanic	'Persia'	Beale 1973
diamond	drill points	'Persia'	*Chou shu, Sui shu*
			Ta T'an leu tien
erythrite	pigment?	Anarak, Meskani, Talmesi	Kashani
gold	jewellery	Hamadan	Intelligence Dept. 1918
		Kawand near Zinjan	
		Damghan (Khorassan)	
		near Assarabad	
		near Meshed (Khorassan)	
		southwest of Yazd	

Table 2.6 (cont.)

Mineral	Uses	Distribution	Select References
'green salt' (copper oxide)	medicinal, eye diseases	'Persia'	*Sui shu*
iron	metallurgical	'Persia' Bafq, east of Yazd	*Chou shu* Intelligence Dept. 1918
iron oxide	pigment	'Persian Gulf islands'	Milburn 1813
lazulite	jewellery, figurines	between Yazd and Isfahan 'northwestern Iran'	Beale 1973
lead		Demawend (Kerman) west of Teheran Anarak, northeast of Isfahan Semnan, east of Teheran northeast of Bafq (Kerman)	Yaqut Intelligence Dept. 1918
litharge	medicinal	Demawend (Kerman)	Yaqut
marble	vessels, architectural elements	northeast and southeast of Yazd 35 km west of Tepe Yahya (Kerman)	Beale 1973
mercury		Takht-i Sulaiman (Azerbaijan)	Intelligence Dept. 1918
obsidian	cutting tools, jewellery, vessels	55 km east of Bam	Beale 1973
orpiment		Takht-i Sulaiman (Azerbaijan) 'Kurdistan'	Intelligence Dept. 1918
pearls	beads	Persian Gulf	*Jowhar-name-ye nezami*
realgar		Takht-i Sulaiman (Azerbaijan) 'Kurdistan'	Intelligence Dept. 1918
sal ammoniac	medicinal	Dimindan (Kerman)	Yaqut after Ibn al-Faqih Abu Mansur Milburn 1813
salt (rock)		'Persia' Hormuz island Qishm island Kamarij, between Bushire and Shiraz	Intelligence Dept. 1918

sulphur		'Persia'	Milburn 1813
		Demawand	Intelligence Dept. 1918
turquoise	decorative	'Persia'	*Pei shi, Chou shu, Sui shu, Wei shu*
		Nishapur (Khorassan)	*Cho ken lu, Jowhar-name-ye nezami*
		Kerman	Pliny *NH* XXXVII 33
		between Kerman and Yazd	Beale 1973
		near Tal-i Iblis (Kerman)	
		Setrushteh	Ibn Haukal
vitriol		Demawend (Kerman)	Yaqut
zinc	metallurgical (ingredient in brass)	Dunbawand (Kerman)	Ibn al-Faqih
			Jawbari
			Milburn 1813
		northeast of Tabriz	Intelligence Dept. 1918

Notes: Information derived from Milburn 1813; Laufer 1919; Beale 1973; Porter and Vesel 1993.

Table 2.7. *Cultivars in early Khuzistan*

Taxon	Common name	Luristan	Khuzistan											
		AbH	BusM	AliK	MohJ	Sef	Sur	CMT	Sabz	Khaz	Meh	Bay	Far	P-Far
Hordeum distichon	2-row hulled barley	+												
Hordeum vulgare	6-row hulled barley		+	+	+				+	+	+	+	+	+
H. vulgare var. *nudum*	6-row naked barley		+	+					+	+	+	+		
Triticum dicoccum	emmer wheat	+	+	+	+				+	+	+	+	+	
Triticum monococcum	einkorn wheat		+	+					+	+	+			
Triticum aestivum	bread wheat													
Lens culinare	lentils	+		+	+				+	+	+	+		
Avena sp.	wild oats	+	+	+	+				+	+	+	+		

Notes:
Information derived from Helbaek 1969 and Hubbard 1990. Abbreviations as for Table 2.5.

Table 2.8. *Aromatics (resins, gums and volatile oils) native to various parts of Iran*

Substance	Origin	Products and uses	Distribution
asafoetida	*Ferula narthex, F. alliacea, F. foetida, F. persica, F. scorodosma*	aromatic used in medicine as a stimulant and antispasmodic; burnt as incense in religious rites; also used as condiment; leaves cooked and eaten as a vegetable	Laristan, Makran
bdellium	*Commiphora mukul*	aromatic burned in religious rites; part of Roman and Indian pharmacopeia with wide variety of uses	Makran, Media?, Bactria
galbanum	*Ferula galbaniflua, F. rubricaulis or erubescens; Dorema anchezi*	aromatic used medicinally	northern Iran, Hamadan, Demawend; between Teheran and Qazvin
labdanum	*Cistus ladiniferus, C. creticus*	resin used in perfumery and medicine, for colds	'Persia'
olibanum	*Emblica officinalis, Pongamia glabra*	aromatic used in medicine and as ingredient in	'Persia'
opoponax	*Opoponax chironium*	incense gum resin used in medicine, medicinal wine, perfumery and soap	'Persia'
sarcocolla	*Penaea mucronata, Astragalus sp.?*	resin used as blood coagulant	'Persia', Bushire
scammony	*Convolvulus scammonia*	gum resin used as a purgative	'Persia'

Notes:
Data drawn from Laufer 1919; Milburn 1813; Potts, Parpola, and Tidmarsh 1996.

Table 2.9. *Hans Wulff's 'list of useful timber . . . compiled in conversations with woodworking craftsmen and peasants' and archaeologically attested tree species from excavated sites in western Iran*

Latin name	Common name	Area of exploitation	Archaeological presence	Uses
Acacia spp.	acacia	Fars, Laristan		timber, bark used for tanning
Acer insigne, A.laetum, A. monspesassulanum, A. campestre, A. platanoides, A. opulifolium, Acer spp.	maple	Caspian provinces, Khorassan, Kurdistan	Tal-i Malyan B, K	furniture small articles timber
Albizzia julibrissin	silk tree	—		
Alnus subcordata, A. glutinosa, A. barbata	alder	Caspian provinces, Teheran, Isfahan, Shiraz Fars		produces red dye
Amygdalus communis, A. amara	bitter almond	—		
Amygdalus dulcis	sweet almond	Gilan		
Amygdalus fragilis, A. orientalis	almond			
Amygdalus scoparia Amygdalus spp. *Amygdalus/Prunus* indet.	mountain almond	—		
Buxus sempervirens	box	Caspian provinces, Gilan, Shiraz, Isfahan	Tal-i Malyan B, K Tepe Abdul Hosein AN	furniture
Caesalpina bonducella	nicker tree	—		
Caesalpina sapan	sapan wood	—		
Capparis spp.				
Carpinus betulus	common beech/ European hornbeam	Caspian provinces	Tal-i Malyan K	
Carpinus orientalis	oriental beech/hornbeam	Caspian provinces		
Castanea vesca	chestnut	—		
Cedrus spp.	cedar	—		
Celtis caucasia	nettle tree	—		
Celtis spp.			Ganj Dareh AN	small articles

Scientific name	Common name	Region	Site	Use
Cercis siliquastrum	Judas tree	Luristan, Caspian provinces		inlay work
Citrus limonum, C. medica,	lemon	—		
Citrus spp.	orange	Shiraz		
Cordia myxa, C. crenata	Sebestens tree	Bandar Abbas region		
Cornus mascula	dogwood?	Isfahan, Kargez mountains		tool handles
Cornus sanguinea	cornel tree	—		
Corylus avelana	hazelwood	—		
Cotoneaster nummularia	manna tree?	—		
Crataegus spp.			Tepe Abdul Hosein AN	
Cupressus sempervirens, C. horizontalis, C. fastigata	cypress	Caspian provinces, Fars, Elburz, Baluchistan, Luristan		timber
Dalbergia sissoo	Sissoo tree	Baluchistan		various, incl. boat-building
Dalbergia spp.	palisander, rosewood			
Daphne spp.			Tal-i Malyan B	
Diospyros ebenum	ebony	—		
Diospyrus spp.	persimmon	—		
Eleagnus angustifolia	sorb/oleaster	Caspian provinces		
Erica arborea	briar or tree-heath	—		agricultural tools
Fagus silvatica, F. orientalis	beech	Caspian provinces, Gilan, Elburz		beams, bowls arrows, spears
Ficus carica	fig	Fars, Khorassan		
Ficus altissima	Indian fig	Bandar Abbas		
Fraxinus excelsior, F. oxyphylla, Fraxinus spp.	ash	Shiraz, Caspian provinces		
Haemotoxylon campechianum	logwood	—	Tal-i Malyan K	various
Juglans regia	walnut	—		furniture
Juniperus spp.			Tal-i Malyan B, K	timber
Laurus nobilis	laurel	—		
Mangifera indica	mango	Baluchistan		
Melia azadirachta	margosa	—		
Mespilus spp.	medlar	Kerman		pipe stems, mouthpieces

Table 2.9 (cont.)

Latin name	Common name	Area of exploitation	Archaeological presence	Uses
Morus alba	mulberry	—		musical instruments
Morus nigra	black mulberry	—		musical instruments
Olea europea	olive	—		
Parrotia persica	ironwood	Caspian provinces		timber
Persica loevis	smooth almond			
Phoenix dactylifera	date-palm	—		
Pinus eldarica	pine	Caspian provinces		beams
Pistacia acuminata, P. Khinjuk	Persian turpentine tree	—	Tepe Abdul Hosein AN	
Pistacia vera, P. mutica	pistachio	Caspian provinces, Zagros mountains		
Pistacia terebinthus	white turpentine	—		
Pistacia spp.	pistachio		Tal-i Malyan B, K	
Planera cordata	alder?	Shiraz		
Platanus orientalis	plane tree	—		
Platanus spp.			Tal-i Malyan K	timber
Populus alba	white poplar/aspen	Fars, Isfahan, Caspian provinces		
Populus dilatata	green pool poplar			
Populus euphratica	poplar	Khorassan		fuel
Populus nigra, P. pyramidalis	black poplar	—	Tal-i Malyan B, K Tepe Farrukhabad JN	timber
Populus spp.				
Prosopis spicigera	mesquite	along the Persian Gulf		fuel, beams, opium pipe stems
Prosopis spp.				
Prunus cerasus, Cerasus orientalis	cherry	—	Tal-i Malyan K	
Prunus cerasifera	myrobalan tree	Kohrud mountains		spade handles

Species	Common name	Distribution	Sites	Uses
Prunus persica	apricot	—		weavers' shuttles
Prunus spp.		—	Ganj Dareh AN Tepe Farukhabad TE	
Pterocarpus santalinus	red sandalwood	—		
Pterocarya caucasia, P. fraxinifolia	Caucasian wing nut/walnut	Gilan, Gorgan, Mazanderan		
Punica granatum	pomegranate	—		
Pyrus communis	pear	—		
Pyrus malus	apple	—		
Quercus castaneifolia, Q. iberica, Q. atropatena	oak	Caspian provinces, southwest of Shiraz		fuel
Quercus valonia		—		timber
Quercus spp.	Kurdistan oak		Tepe Farukhabad JN, ED Tal-i Malyan B, K Ganj Dareh AN	
Rhamnus spp.				
Rhus coriaria	sumac	—		leaves used for tanning
Sambucus ebulus, S. niger	elder	Caspian provinces		
Salix micaus, S. fragilis, S. zygostemon, S. acmophylla	willow	—		
Salix babylonica	weeping willow			
Salix aegyptiaca	musk willow	Caspian provinces, Gorgan		
Salix spp./*Populus* spp.			Ganj Dareh AN Tepe Abdul Hosein AN	
Sambucus ebulus	elder	—		
Santalum album	sandalwood	—		
Tamarindus indica	tamarind	—		
Tamarix gallica	gall tamarisk, common tamarisk	—		timber
Tamarix pentandra	manna tamarisk	—		
Tamarix spp.			Tepe Abdul Hosein AN Tepe Farukhabad F-E	
Taxus baccata	yew	Caspian provinces, Gilan		bows, furniture

Table 2.9 (cont.)

Latin name	Common name	Area of exploitation	Archaeological presence	Uses
Tectonia grandis	teak	—		
Terminalia catappa	tropical almond	—		
Tilia rubra	lime	Teheran, Gilan, Gorgan, Caspian provinces		
Ulmus campestris, U. densa	cultivated elm	Caspian provinces, Azerbaijan		
Ulmus pedunculata	Caucasian elm	Gilan		
Ulmus spp.	beech	Caspian provinces, Turkoman steppe	Tal-i Malyan B, K	
Vitex spp.		—	Tal-i Malyan K	inlay work
Vitis vinifera	grapevine	Turkoman steppe,	Tal-i Malyan K	load-carrying shoulder bars
Zelkova crenata	elm	Caspian provinces, Gilan, Bandar Abbas		
Ziziphus vulgaris, Z. nummularia, Z. spina Christi	jujube/red Hyrcanian willow	Bandar Abbas, Fars, Kerman		beams small articles, load-carrying shoulder bars

Notes:
After Wulff 1966; Miller 1981; Willcox 1990; 1992. Key: AN = aceramic Neolithic, eighth/seventh millennium BC; B = Banesh period, *c.* 3400–2800 BC; K = Kaftari period, 2200–1600 BC (both terms specific to the Tal-i Malyan sequence); F-E = Farukh to Elamite, *c.* 4500–2000 BC; JN = Jamdat Nasr, *c.* 3100–2900 BC; ED = Early Dynastic, *c.* 2900–2350 BC; TE = Transitional Elamite, *c.* 1600–1300 BC (latter four terms specific to Tepe Farukhabad).

3

THE IMMEDIATE PRECURSORS OF ELAM

Should one, in a work devoted to an ancient state such as Elam, review the entire record of human settlement prior to the earliest unambiguous appearance of that state in the historical record? The answer to a question such as this depends in large part on whether one believes there was or was not a connection between the earliest Palaeolithic or Neolithic inhabitants of the region and the later Elamites. In general, the position adopted here is that while, for example, the late Pleistocene hunter-gatherers of the Zagros may have been related, either biologically or culturally, to the later Elamites, we have at present no way of determining that this was the case. As this is a book devoted to Elam and not to Iranian prehistory, therefore, most of the archaeological cultures which preceded the Elamites in southwestern Iran will not be discussed. Having said this, how far back in time should we look if our aim is to understand the genesis (or ethnogenesis) of Elam?

The approach taken in this book has been to look at two of the core areas of later Elamite activity – central Fars and Khuzistan, particularly the sites of Tal-i Bakun, Tal-i Malyan and Susa – beginning in the later fifth millennium BC. The justification for this is not a firm belief that the peoples of these areas can be justifiably considered ancestors of the Elamites. Rather, it is because questions which arise in the study of Elam when it first emerges in the historical record of the third millennium BC need to be addressed in the context of arguments made concerning, for instance, the original peopling of the site of Susa, or the derivation of the earliest writing system used in the region and its relationship to later written Elamite (so-called Linear Elamite). And because of the existence of a considerable body of literature devoted to the 'Proto-Elamites', even if it is argued below that this is a misnomer, it is necessary to look at certain aspects of the late fourth millennium in Fars and Khuzistan. Since the broad conclusion is that we are not justified in assuming a link between Proto-Elamite and later Elamite culture, it is unnecessary to review everything we know about the late fourth millennium at Susa, for example. Rather, only those categories of material culture are examined which bear directly on the question of whether or not the inhabitants of Susa and Fars c. 3000 BC can already be considered Elamites.

Introduction

In discussing the early peoples of central Asia, the Russian anthropologist A. Bernshtam commented, 'In reference to the first millennium BC, we can talk about ethnic names of the ancestors of the present peoples. Yet, we can not say anything positive about their ethnic affiliation. The Sarmatians-Alans of the first centuries AD do not yet represent the Turkmens, the ancient Yenisey Kirgiz of the 3rd century BC are not yet the Tien-shan Kirgiz, and the Bactrians of the end of the first millennium BC

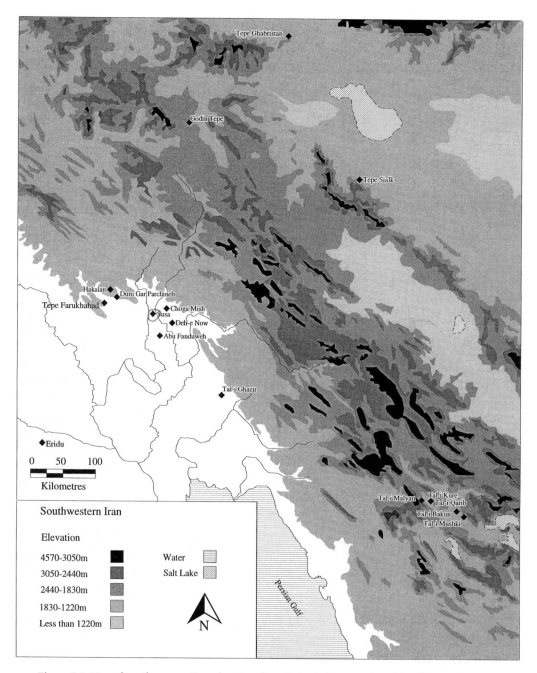

Figure 3.1 Map of southwestern Iran showing the principal sites mentioned in Chapter 3.

are not yet the Tadzhiks' (Bernshtam 1962: 119). The late Walther Hinz was less cautious in suggesting that the Elamites were 'Proto-Lurs', i.e. the ancestors of the inhabitants of modern day Luristan in western Iran (Hinz 1971b: 644). The problem of ethnogenesis – the creation of ethnicity – is one which must be faced in the study of Elam as well. Do the palaeolithic sites of Fars province represent the ancestors of the later Elamites? If not, then what about the early Neolithic sites in the region? Can we confidently claim that the Elamites are actually present in the prehistoric archaeological record of southwestern Iran? If not, when did Elam (Fig. 3.1) first appear?

These questions raise both a specific set of concerns revolving around the subject of this book, as well as the broader problem of how one recognizes an ethnic and/or a linguistic group in the preliterate archaeological record. Fredrik Barth defined an ethnic group as one which was (1) 'largely biologically self-perpetuating'; (2) shared 'fundamental cultural values'; (3) made up a 'field of communication and interaction'; and (4) had 'a membership which identifies itself, and is identified by others, as constituting a category distinguishable from other categories of the same order' (Barth 1969: 10–11). From this set of criteria it can be readily seen that ethnicity is constructed, and it need not take very long for this to happen. Indeed, anthropologists have shown how ethnicity can be created 'almost from historical scratch' (Roosens 1989: 10). Cultural symbols, territorial designations and linguistic identity can all be appropriated *ab novo* in the interests of signalling ethnic identity to the members of one's group and to the outside world. While the symbolic and linguistic vocabulary used often comes out of an already extant context or a prior, historical set of circumstances, the particular 'spin' put on these features and the combinations and modifications introduced can lead to new forms which proclaim the arrival of a group on the political, economic, religious and social scene. Ethnicity becomes particularly important in situations of competition and aggression, and it will be argued below that this is precisely what characterizes the emergence of an Elamite identity. That, however, is a feature of the third millennium BC, and there can be no grounds for suggesting that any of the prehistoric assemblages known in southwestern Iran before that time represent the vestiges of the same ethnic groups known to have inhabited the region in later periods. This conclusion, moreover, is further strengthened when we consider the archaeological sequences of Khuzistan and Fars prior to the mid-third millennium BC. We shall not review the entirety of those sequences, however, but shall instead commence around 4000 BC by looking at Susa and several sites in Fars, such as Tal-i Bakun and Tal-i Malyan, as a necessary introduction to what has often been termed 'Proto-Elamite' culture in Iran. Although, as discussed below, this is a misnomer, the term is so well-entrenched in the archaeological and historical literature of Western Asia that it must be dealt with before moving on to the first truly Elamite remains in the region.

The origins of Susa: the Susa I period

In describing the genesis of the great urban centre of Uruk in southern Mesopotamia, H.J. Nissen stressed that it was originally composed of two discrete areas, identified in the cuneiform sources as *Kullaba* and *Eanna*, which were only joined into a single entity towards the end of the fourth millennium BC, and finally circumvallated several centuries later in Early Dynastic I (*c.* 2900 BC) times (Nissen 1972). Susa presents us with a somewhat analogous situation, at least in its earliest phase of occupation. Although G. Dollfus has suggested that Susa may have been a '"city" of little hamlets', and not a continuously occupied, 15–18 ha² area as has often been assumed (Dollfus *apud* Pollock 1989: 289), this is not quite accurate. The only evidence of occupation in Susa's earliest period, which we shall call Susa I times, occurs in two discrete areas which the early French excavators referred to as the 'Acropole', or acropolis (site of the French chateau built in the late nineteenth century), and the 'Apadana' mound, so-called because of the palace constructed there in the Achaemenid period by Darius the Great (see Chapter 9). Apart from these two areas, the rest of Susa (e.g. the so-called 'Ville Royale', the 'Donjon' and the 'Ville des Artisans') was apparently unoccupied in the site's earliest phase of settlement (Steve and Gasche 1990: 25, n. 47). Soundings conducted at various points on the Apadana mound suggest that it covered an area of *c.* 6.3 ha, while trenches on the Acropole reached Susa I levels wherever they were put down, suggesting that its original extent was on the order of 7 ha (Steve and Gasche 1990: 26). The Apadana was, moreover, encircled by a packed mud (*pisé*) wall no less than *c.* 6 m wide at its base. It cannot be said whether the entirety of both the Apadana and the Acropole were in turn contained within an outer wall, but Steve and Gasche would not rule out the possibility.

The date of Susa's foundation is unclear but the earliest C14 determination from the Susa I levels on the Acropole falls between 4395 and 3955 cal. BC while the latest date from the period can be placed between 3680 and 3490 cal. BC (Voigt and Dyson 1992: Table 2; see also Weiss 1977). The wide span of time represented by these dates may be due to contamination, but on the other hand a ceramically contemporary complex at the village site of Tepe Jaffarabad (Dollfus 1978) spans the period from 4140–3865 to 3890–3655 cal. BC and is thus generally consistent with the Susa dates.

It has been suggested that the original stock of the Susian population came from many of the surrounding villages which were abandoned as a prelude to Susa's foundation (Pollock 1989: 283), and that the burning of at least a portion (see also Kantor and Delougaz 1996) of the site of Choga Mish may have had something to do with the foundation of Susa (Hole 1983: 321), possibly, as Hole has suggested, 'a deliberate attempt to reestablish some kind of a center and vacate the area of the previous one' (*apud* Pollock 1989: 292). Whatever the *raison d'être* behind Susa's foundation, and it may have been very mundane indeed, the site's subsequent development was soon distinguished by a number of architectural developments which would seem to exceed the scope of activities normally associated with village life (Dollfus 1985: 18–19).

If we begin with the Apadana first, although only partially excavated, the Susa I Building ('Bâtiment de Suse I') exposed in part of trench 25 (Chantier 25) was constructed of packed mud (*pisé*) faced with rose-coloured plaster. The walls of the building, which were only preserved to a height of 1.15 m, were nevertheless 2.10 m thick. The thickness of the walls (compare this with the .4–.6 m thick walls at the 'rural hamlet' of Tepe Djafarrabad, Wright and Johnson 1985: 25) and the unusual interior lay-out of the rooms have led Steve and Gasche to interpret the Susa I Building as some-thing more than a 'simple private habitation'. On the other hand, the fact that a grave of the following Susa II period was dug into the building suggests that neither it nor the immediate environs were part of a religious precinct. Rather, Steve and Gasche are more inclined to view this as the residence of a 'chief' of the settlement of Susa, a seat of civil authority, in contrast to what they interpret as a seat of religious power on the Acropole (Steve and Gasche 1990: 22). Whatever its function, it is clear that the Susa I building was not founded when Susa itself was established, for it stood on *c.* 2.5 m of earlier archaeological strata of the Susa I period. However, Steve and Gasche are inclined to date the foundation of the Susa I Building to the same time as the construc-tion of the second of the two major features founded on the Acropole (Steve and Gasche 1990: 26).

Early in the Susa I period (Susa IA = Acropole 27), a low mudbrick platform, referred to by the early French excavators of Susa as the *massif funéraire*, was constructed on the Acropole (Fig. 3.2). This platform, the function of which has been repeatedly dis-cussed over the years, is said by its excavators to have stood 3–4 m above the surround-ing ground level and to have been roughly 8–12 m in diameter at its base, appearing thus as a truncated cone (Hole 1990: 2). More recent excavations suggest that the *massif* was rectangular, measuring *c.* 7×14 m, with a preserved height of 1.7 m, all built of unbaked mudbrick (Hole 1990: 4). Whatever its shape, this feature appears to have served as a focal point for the burial of at least some of Susa's inhabitants in this period. As the excavations of most of the area took place early in this century, the information available is contradictory and the excavation methods employed leave much to be desired, but it has been alleged that some 2,000 individuals were buried in graves both beneath and dug into the platform, and that these burials included both primary and secondary interments as well as fractional burials in brick cists (see Pollock 1989: 286; Hole 1989: 164–6). Some scholars see this as a supra-local cemetery for the dead of a cluster of settlements around Susa (Vértesalji 1989). Alternatively, it has been inter-preted as 'a mass grave resulting from a catastrophic loss of life' rather than a cemetery used over time (Hole 1990: 1). The areal extent of the Susa I graves has been estimated at anywhere from 120 to 750 m². The graves are most famous for their tall, finely made ceramic beakers decorated in geometric and naturalistic patterns (Fig. 3.3) in black paint on a white ground (Hole 1983; 1984).

Hole interprets the *massif funéraire* as the foundation of a religious structure, 'perhaps even for priestly residences' (Hole 1990: 5). It was followed in time (Susa IB = Acropole 26–25) (perhaps one or two generations, according to Hole 1990: 7) by the con-struction of another platform, known as the *haute terrasse*, a stepped construction some 10.08 m high which was erected on top of over a metre of 'residential midden' (Hole 1990: 6), clearly signalling that the construction of the platform was not coinci-dent with the foundation of the settlement, but followed it by an indeterminable period of time. The upper surface of this second platform is reckoned to have measured *c.* 70×65 m, and to have stood on a somewhat larger socle, 2 m high (Canal 1978: 173),

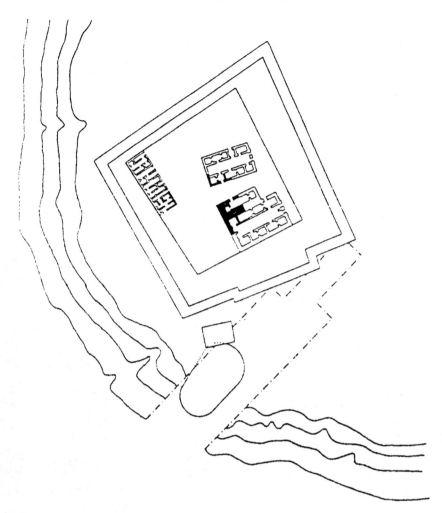

Figure 3.2 The Acropole in Susa I times (after Harper, Aruz and Tallon 1992: Fig. 23).

the south side of which was 80 m long. The exterior of the 'first stage' of the platform, i.e. that portion above the socle, was decorated with inlaid ceramic cones in groups of four or five (Canal 1978: 173), 'plaque mosaics and clay models of goat horns' (Pollock 1989: 285). According to Hole, this, too, may have served as the support for the residence of a priest or some other 'highly decorated monumental buildings' (Hole 1990: 7).

Each of these structures will remain enigmatic because of less than adequate excavation and recording, but there can be no denying that the size and height of the *haute terrasse* is considerable. S. Pollock compares it with the chateau, measuring 65 × 125 × 8–9 m, built by the early French excavators at Susa (Pollock 1989: 284), and P. Amiet has noted that it was much larger than the contemporary temple platform at the Ubaid site of Eridu in southern Mesopotamia (Amiet 1988b: 7). The imitation goat horns in clay recall the striking image of a stepped monumental building with three

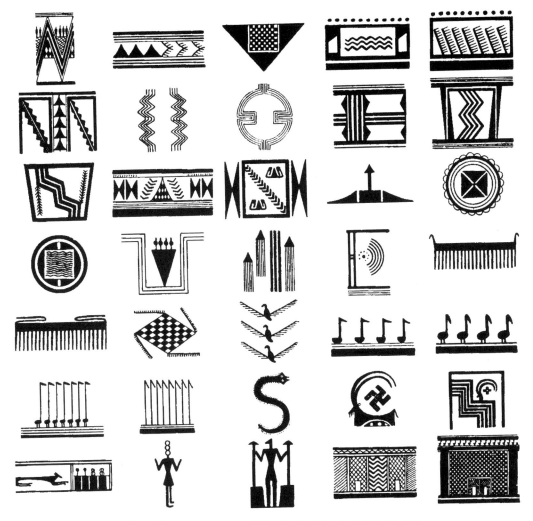

Figure 3.3 Principal motifs on Susa I pottery (after Vanden Berghe 1959: Fig. 20).

sets of protruding horns (Pl. 3.2) on a cylinder seal impression from Susa dated to late period II (Amiet 1987b: Fig. 1; see also Potts 1990a). It is, moreover, noteworthy that both the Susa I Building on the Apadana and the *haute terrasse* were destroyed by fire. However, the subsequent fate of these two areas differed. On analogy with the situation observed at Tell ed-Der in Mesopotamia, a formation of greenish soil on top of the *haute terrasse* (Acropole sounding 2) bespeaks a period of abandonment and exposure to the open air lasting well into the middle of the fourth millennium when material of Late Uruk (Susa II) type appeared above it. The Susa I Building, on the other hand, seems to have been quickly filled in with domestic debris of the Middle Uruk period, suggesting that there was no hiatus of occupation on the Apadana (Steve and Gasche 1990: 27).

With roughly forty small settlements around it on the Susiana plain, Susa in the Susa

I period was at least four times larger than any of its neighbours (Wright and Johnson 1985: 25; see also Hole 1985) and clearly, by virtue of its stepped platform, in possession of a monumental structure which, regardless of its exact function, must have been unusual in the context of Khuzistan in the late fifth and early fourth millennium BC. Whether, therefore, we wish to describe it using terms such as 'ceremonial centre', or to characterize its level of social organization as a 'chiefdom', as some scholars have chosen to do, is another matter. Certainly a number of stamp seals recovered at Susa in layers of this period show a figure whom P. Amiet has described as the 'proto-royal' (Amiet 1986c: 44; 1988c: 33; 1992a: 77) ancestor of the 'priest-king' (roi-prêtre) of the Susa II period (Amiet 1988b: 8). Amiet has linked the glyptic tradition of Susa at this time with that of the highlands of Luristan (Amiet 1979a: 196), but as the Luristan seals on which this conclusion is based were all acquired on the art market (by the Louvre Amiet 1979c: Figs. 1–14) one must be very cautious in this regard. The few which have come from controlled excavations in Luristan such as Dum Gar Parchineh and Hakalan are in general much simpler and covered with geometric decoration (Vanden Berghe 1987: Fig. 12) and do not display the human iconography of the Susa exemplars which Amiet finds so suggestive of political authority. On the other hand, in the course of over a century, the Susa excavations have yielded no fewer than 261 stamp seals and sealings dating to the Susa I period (Amiet 1986e: 17), and the variety of sealing types would certainly suggest that the seals were being employed by persons in positions of administrative authority (see also Amiet 1988b: 8) to control the flow of goods in and out of one or more offices or centres of redistribution. Certainly some of the Susa I sealings came off doors which had been locked and sealed (Amiet 1994e: 56; 1994f: 88–9; for the principal of sealing doors see Fiandra 1982).

The Late Bakun period in Fars

In Fars province, settlement contemporary with Susa I is best known from the excavations of levels III and IV at Tal-i Bakun A (for the chronology, I follow Voigt and Dyson 1992: 139) which represent the last phase of the Bakun (4500–3900 BC) and the beginning of the Lapui phase (3900–3400 BC) (these dates follow Sumner 1988b: 315).

Although the architecture of levels III and IV at Tal-i Bakun A consisted largely of multi-roomed dwellings (Fig. 3.4) and nothing was found which can compare to either the *haute terrasse* or the *massif funéraire* of Susa I, it is nonetheless important to note that, in at least two respects, the communities of highland Iran at this time were just as sophisticated as their lowland counterparts. In line with the indications of copper metallurgy at Susa in period I, sites on the Plateau – such as Tepe Ghabristan, where a smelting or refining workshop has been excavated c. 60 km south of Qazvin; Tepe Sialk, where moulds for the open casting of adzes and conical-headed pins in period III_4 were found; and Tal-i Mushki in Fars, where a single faience bead was recovered – already point to growing sophistication in metallurgy by the fifth millennium BC and, indeed, it is generally thought that the stimulus for Susa's metallurgical development derived in large measure from contacts with the highlands (Moorey 1982: 85).

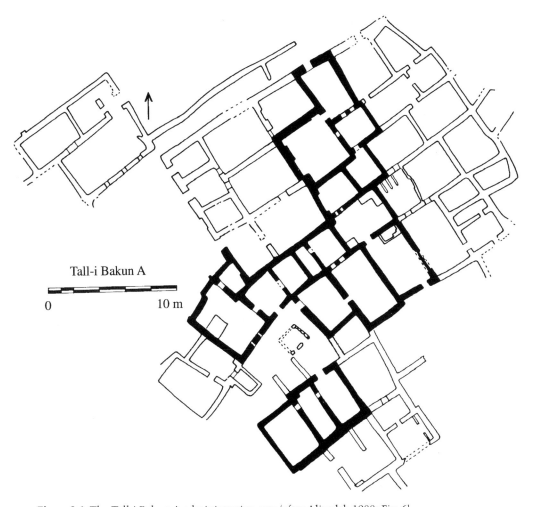

Figure 3.4 The Tall-i Bakun A administrative area (after Alizadeh 1988: Fig. 6).

Turning to the comparative evidence of seal use (Fig. 3.5), five different buildings (II-IV, VII and XIII) at Tal-i Bakun A have yielded no less than 140 seal impressions deriving from sacks or bales, doors and tags, prompting one scholar to describe this area as an 'administrative quarter' (Alizadeh 1988: Fig. 20). Nothing suggests that the operations undertaken at Tal-i Bakun A were any less sophisticated than those which must have existed in period I at Susa (Alizadeh 1994). The associated pottery (Fig. 3.6), although not of the same technical calibre as some of the Susa I wares, displays the use of a correspondingly varied and complicated range of decorative devices.

The Lapui period in Fars (named after a village near Tal-i Bakun A) was a time of small village-based settlement in the Kur River Basin, with over 100 settlements averaging 1.1 ha in size, none of which exceeds 4 ha. Apart from a very limited number of parallels between the locally produced red 'Lapui' pottery and red ware sherds from levels

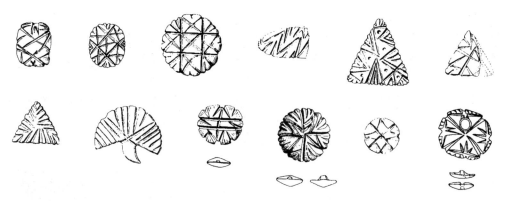

Figure 3.5 Stamp seals from Tall-i Bakun A (after Langsdorff and McCown 1942: Pl. 82.1–12).

24 and 25 in the Acropole 1 sounding (Sumner 1988a: 28, n. 1), the ceramic traditions of Fars and Susiana, unlike those of Mesopotamia and Susiana at the same time, were unrelated. By the end of the Lapui phase, Sumner estimates that poorly managed riverine irrigation was leading to increased soil salinity and decreasing agricultural yields, precipitating a drop in settled population levels (Sumner 1986a: 207). Sumner assumes cultural continuity between the Bakun and Lapui phases, noting that Lapui plain wares were introduced gradually into the painted Bakun pottery repertoire; a substantial number of sites contain both pottery assemblages, and Lapui settlement levels generally occur on sites previously occupied during the Bakun phase (Sumner 1988a: 29).

The Susa II period

A completely different orientation in the architecture, a change in brick size, and a change in the ceramic repertoire (Fig. 3.7) are the bases for distinguishing the second period in the Acropole I sounding (levels 22–17). On the Apadana, levels have been exposed which contained ceramics corresponding to levels 22–18 on the Acropole (Steve and Gasche 1990: 27). Outside of Susa itself, Wright and Johnson, working largely from survey data supplemented by excavated samples from Tepe Farukhabad, Tal-i Ghazir, Uruk, Nippur and of course Susa have used the terms Early, Middle and Late Uruk to identify the sub-periods dating to between c. 3800 and 3100 BC (Johnson 1973: 54–8; Wright and Johnson 1985: 26–9). Although by no means all scholars accept a tripartite division of the Uruk period (based largely on the Inanna Temple sequence at Nippur), and H.J. Nissen continues to stress that the sequence in the Eanna precinct deep sounding at Uruk can really only be divided into an Early (levels XII-IX) and a Late period (VIII-IV) (Nissen 1993), the important point to recognize is that ceramically, most of the material found on sites in Susiana dating to this period is a) patently different from that of the Susa I period, and b) just as obviously similar to what one finds further west in Mesopotamia proper. Thus, while we may prefer here to speak of the Susa II period because it is a culturally indigenous term which is not borrowed from another area, the fact is that when Wright and Johnson use the terms Early, Middle and

Figure 3.6 Principal motifs on Tall-i Bakun pottery (after Vanden Berghe 1959: Fig. 86).

Late Uruk, these are not merely a chronological signal for those familiar with the cultural sequence of southern Mesopotamia, but a clear statement to the effect that the ceramic types found on the Susa II-period sites surveyed in Khuzistan correspond 'remarkably well to the reported stratified sequences' mentioned above, even though 'this is not to imply that Uruk ceramic assemblages are the same everywhere' (Johnson 1973: 59). But as Wright and Johnson observe, 'During Late Uruk times . . . standard Late Uruk craft goods replaced goods in a local tradition' (Wright and Johnson 1985: 28).

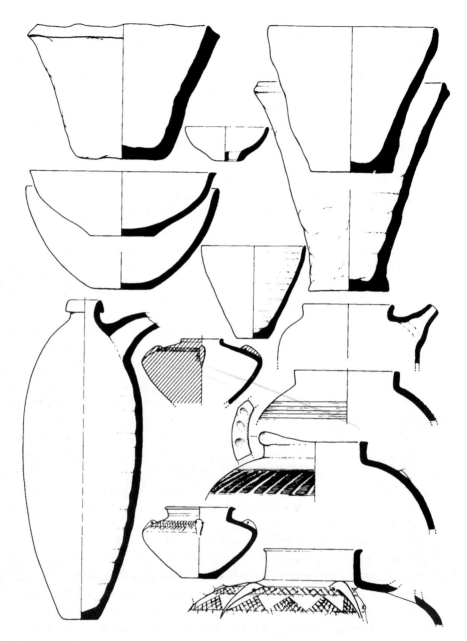

Figure 3.7 Selection of Susa II (Acropole I, level 17) pottery types (after LeBrun 1978: Fig. 34).

Wright and Johnson have documented a number of quantifiable trends in the Susa II/Uruk period, including a significant increase in the sheer number of sites on the plain and metric evidence for centralized ceramic production and distribution which are suggestive of major social transformation in the region at this time. While Susa's size, if one can believe the areal estimates based on limited soundings, may have declined in the initial Susa II period to *c.* 5 ha, the overall number of settlements in Susiana increased, and at least three other sites, including Abu Fanduweh and Deh-e Now, were comparable to Susa in size. By the middle of the period, Susa is thought to have expanded to 25 ha and to have developed a 'lower town' or residential area off the Acropole and Apadana, a pattern observable at Choga Mish and Abu Fanduweh, as well. The presence of door and jar sealings at the rural hamlet of Tepe Sharafabad suggests that small settlements were linked up with a central administration at one of the larger sites, and the size differentiation of sites in Khuzistan at this time is interpreted as a reflection of a hierarchy of settlements which may have participated in a network of local, inter-regional exchange and yet come into conflict with each other as well. This 'Susiana polity', Wright and Johnson suggest, 'distingegrated at the end of the Late Uruk Period', i.e. at the end of Susa II (Wright and Johnson 1985: 28–9). However the dynamics of culture change on the Susiana plain during the Susa II period have been characterized in the writings of Wright and Johnson over the past twenty-odd years (and that characterization has changed with virtually every published paper), the fact is that the question of 'the actual political and economic relations between Susiana and Mesopotamia proper' (Wright and Johnson 1985: 29) is an issue which has generally been sidestepped. The same emphasis on endogenous change in the history of fourth millennium Susiana is, however, absent in the works of several other scholars of note. To be more precise, the evolution of social complexity in Khuzistan cannot be treated as though the very obvious ceramic links with Mesopotamia were not in evidence (Fig. 3.8). On the contrary, the very appropriateness of terms like Early, Middle and Late Uruk in describing the ceramics of Susiana during the Susa II period begs the question of what was going on between Mesopotamia and Khuzistan, and compels us to view the problem not in terms of Khuzistan alone, but in terms of the significance of the very clear Mesopotamian character of the ceramic industry at this time.

For P. Amiet, the situation of broad cultural homogeneity in southern Mesopotamia and Khuzistan throughout much of the fourth millennium stands in marked contrast to the preceding (Susa I) and succeeding periods (Susa III). Amiet has long believed that the essential character of southwestern Iran's population in antiquity was its ethnic duality – that portion inhabiting the lowlands being essentially of 'Mesopotamian' type, and that portion inhabiting the highlands being of 'Elamite' type (Amiet 1979a; 1979b), and that Khuzistan was, throughout history, dominated in a cyclical fashion, first by one element, and then by the other. According to his reasoning, in the Susa I period Susiana was dominated by the non-Mesopotamian, highland elements with their painted pottery so different from contemporary Ubaid products in lower Mesopotamia. Susa II, on the other hand, marks a period which saw 'the insertion of Susiana into the proto-Sumerian cultural world' through the seizure of power by the

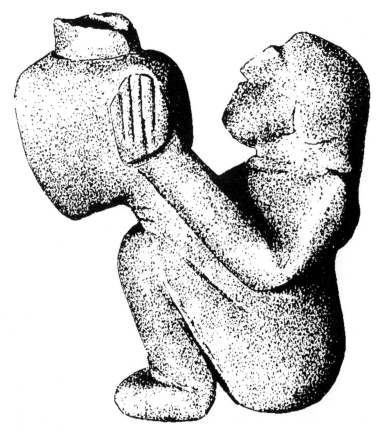

Figure 3.8 Limestone sculpture from the 'dépot archaique' excavated on the Acropole at Susa in 1909, attributed to the Susa II period (after Spycket 1981: Fig. 11).

ethnically Mesopotamian and numerically larger component of the population, at the expense of elements of the populace descended from various groups inhabiting the highlands of Iran (Amiet 1992a: 80) such that Susiana became 'a kind of second Sumerian country, though not a vassal to a then unthinkable Sumerian empire' (Amiet 1979a: 198).

A very different view is taken by G. Algaze, who suggests that Susiana was actually colonized in the Uruk period by 'settlers from the alluvium', i.e. southern Mesopotamia, in a phenomenon of 'wholescale regional colonization' (Algaze 1993: 15–17). What reasons could have prompted such a move? Algaze cites five points in defense of his hypothesis. Briefly stated, these are as follows (Algaze 1993: 16–17):

1 'it explains the overwhelmingly Sumerian character of elite activites and material culture in Susiana by the later half of the fourth millennium.'
2 'it accounts for the apparently longer evolution of the Uruk tradition in Iraq as opposed to Khuzestan.'
3 it 'explains the archaeological break in the Susiana sequence preceding *and* following the Uruk period.'

4 it 'explains the settlement pattern of the Susiana plain in the still little understood Early Uruk period, when settlements concentrate around Susa and Abu Fanduweh on the western portion of the plain – the one closest to the alluvium.'

5 it 'explains the full spectrum of Uruk sites and concomitant functions across the plain as well as the homogeneity of Uruk material culture throughout the region.'

What no authorities contest is the striking similarity of the ceramics of Susiana and southern Mesopotamia in the Susa II or Uruk period, and although Amiet is mistakenly counted by Algaze amongst the upholders of his thesis (in fact Amiet vigorously rejects Algaze's thesis, see Amiet 1994b: 92, as does M.-J. Steve in Steve 1991: 2), Amiet would not deny that Susa II ceramics are patently Mesopotamian in shape and decoration in a way which the ceramics of the Susa I and III periods are not. However, Amiet objects to Algaze's reconstruction because of a deeply held view that the basic population of Khuzistan was *always* mixed and that, when one sees the Mesopotamian element come to the fore in the Susa II period, one is looking at an element which was in that sense indigenous, not introduced via a colonial process.

P. Steinkeller, while agreeing with some aspects of Algaze's thesis, has criticized it for several essential, structural reasons. Questioning the underlying assumption that Uruk colonies were set up for purposes of controlling and extracting resources lacking in the Mesopotamian alluvium, Steinkeller contends that the procurement of resources was never the object of Mesopotamian political and military expansion, and that resources were satisfactorily obtained from many areas abroad during periods which were not characterized by expansive military policies. Indeed, the costs of far-flung expeditions, he contends, 'always vastly exceeded any gains . . . made from obtaining direct access to resource areas'(contra e.g. Butterlin 1995: 24, who, although wary of anachronistic models of colonisation, believes the Uruk expansion should be viewed in terms of the expansion of the European 'world economy' of the fifteenth through eighteenth centuries AD). Moreover, Steinkeller insists, contra Algaze, that expansion did not follow a spurt of growth or emerge as a consequence of such growth, but rather that it preceded and 'was a prerequisite for the creation of a centralized socio-economic system' (Steinkeller 1993: 109). Finally, while some scholars believe the spread of Uruk material culture was a reflection of expansion for political domination (e.g. Lamberg-Karlovsky 1996b: 92–3; see also 1996a: 92 where he is less certain), Steinkeller argues that it is simply unthinkable to suppose that Mesopotamia in the fourth millennium BC possessed the ideology, organization and resources required to launch a program of colonization on the scale envisaged by Algaze, extending from Anatolia in the north to Iran in the east.

It is nevertheless the case that Steinkeller upholds the thesis of an Uruk period penetration and colonization of Susiana in particular, although for a reason which has been completely overlooked by most other commentators on the issue. According to Steinkeller, 'Here our chief datum is the name of Inshushinak, the patron god of Susa, which, because of its undeniable Sumerian pedigree, appears to offer iron-clad proof of the Sumerian intrusion into Susiana at some very early point in time' (Steinkeller 1993:

111). The question is, of course, how early? As we shall see in Chapter 4, the god Inshushinak is attested in a god-list from Abu Salabikh by the middle of the third millennium, when he appears as *ᵈnin-šušinak*, i.e. 'lord of Susa' (Hinz 1957–71: 546; 1976–80: 117; Steinkeller 1984: 140, n. 18; Alberti 1985: 8; Mander 1986: 47), but this need not imply that the influence responsible for the Sumerian nature of Susa's chief deity occurred as early as the fourth millennium. Nevertheless, it is a novel hypothesis which warrants consideration.

Whether or not it represents a phenomenon of colonialism and incipient imperial expansion as argued by Algaze, the Uruk expansion has been conventionally dated to the Late Uruk period, i.e. to the end of the Susa II period (Algaze 1993: 56). Recent excavations at Tell Brak in northern Syria, however, have shown signs of Uruk material culture perhaps as early as the Middle Uruk period (Oates and Oates 1994: 168); Middle Uruk material appears to be present further west at Tell Sheikh Hassan on the Middle Euphrates (Oates 1993: 414); and as we have seen, Uruk types appear in Susiana in the Early Uruk or early Susa II period. It is, however, difficult to see why the ceramic shapes and decoration of the Susa II period should so closely parallel those of the Mesopotamian alluvium if they were the creation of an already present Mesopotamian element in the population (Amiet's view), and to accept the notion that by gaining the upper hand, as it were, this element threw over centuries of ceramic tradition in favour of imitating Mesopotamian types. Certainly this point speaks more for an actual introduction of potters and people from outside Susiana at the beginning of the Uruk period, rather than the simple ascendancy of a previously repressed element in the already existing population stock. On the other hand, a second consideration to which insufficient attention has been paid in this regard is the appearance of writing and the economic system thereby implied, and here the evidence does not suggest that Susiana was annexed by a Mesopotamian power. Uruk-type ceramics may reflect colonists entering the region (although one must be careful about not equating pots and people), but the differing approaches to writing found in Khuzistan and southern Mesopotamia do not suggest the subjugation of Susiana by a foreign power.

In contrasting Susa and Uruk, H.J. Nissen has stressed that the major settlements of southern Mesopotamia and Susiana are simply not comparable in size and scale of economic activities. For even if Susa did reach a late prehistoric maximum of *c.* 25 ha in the Middle Uruk (middle Susa II) period (Wright and Johnson 1985: 27), and the settlement expanded into the area known as the Ville Royale during the Late Uruk period (late Susa II) (Steve and Gasche 1990: 27), the fact remains that Uruk, at this period, expanded from 70 to 100 ha (possibly up to 250 ha judging by sherd spread, Nissen, pers. comm.), perhaps due to a shift southward of settlers from the Nippur-Adab region (Falconer and Savage 1995: 46), and was thus vastly larger than any site in Susiana (Nissen 1985a: 39). At Uruk alone, some 44,000 m² of Late Uruk and Jamdat Nasr period architecture has been exposed, far more than at any site in Khuzistan (Nissen 1993: 127). It was in this context that the bureaucratic need arose for the proto-cuneiform writing system which, already in its earliest stage of development, reveals the existence of a rigid social, professional and by implication economic hierarchy best exemplified in the lexical list of titles and professions, a long enumeration of terms which provides us with unique insight into the division of labour and hierarchical organization of Uruk-period society in southern Mesopotamia in the late fourth millennium (Nissen, Damerow and Englund 1990: 156).

What we see in Susiana at this time is not a contemporary florescence in which the local inhabitants contributed equally to the Uruk bureaucratic phenomenon. On the contrary, writing is an invention which, so far as we can tell, was unique to the site of Uruk (Powell 1981: 422) and from there spread outwards. Research has shown that no fewer than thirteen different numerical systems were employed during the Late Uruk and Jamdat Nasr periods (*c.* 3400–2900 BC) in the so-called 'Archaic' texts from Uruk to record numbers of different types of commodities (Damerow and Englund 1985). Thus, different systems were employed to record time, cereal commodities, live animals, dead animals, beer, etc. These are so involved that it is simply beyond the realm of reasoning to suppose that, where one or more of the Uruk systems is attested outside of southern Mesopotamia, e.g. at Susa, they could have been invented independently. The following list summarizes the different numerical systems found in the Archaic texts from Uruk (after Potts 1997: 237–8):

Archaic numerical notation system	*Uses*
Sexagesimal system S (1–10–60–600–3,600–36,000) [numbers alternate by a factor of 10, 6, 10, etc.]	slaves, animals (sheep, goat, cattle), wool (?), fish, fishing equipment, fish products, stone objects, wooden objects, containers (e.g. of beer, milk products)
Sexagesimal system S' (1–10–60) [numbers alternate by a factor of 10, 6]	dead animals, particular types of beer
Bi-sexagesimal system B (1/2–1–2–10–60–120–1200–7200) [numbers alternate by a factor of 2, 10, 6 etc.]	cereal/bread, fish, and milk product rations
Bi-sexagesimal system B* (1–10–60–120–1200) [numbers alternate by a factor of 10, 6, 2, etc.]	rations of uncertain type, possibly fish
GAN_2 system G (*IKU-EŠE$_3$-BUR$_3$*) [numbers alternate by a factor of 10?, 6, 3, etc.]	field and area measurement
EN system E [numbers alternate by a factor of ?, 4, 2, 2, 10]	uncertain; weight?
U_4 system U (1 day – 10 days – 30 days/ 1 month – 12 months/ 1 year or 10 months)	calendrics (day, month, year)

Archaic numerical notation system [numbers alternate by a factor of 10, 3, 12/10]	*Uses*
ŠE system Š [small units multiplied by 2, 3, 4, 5, 6, or 10, alternating by a factor of 5, 6, 10, 3, 10]	cereal, esp. barley, by volume
ŠE system Š' [units increasing by factors of 2, 5, 6]	cereal, esp. malt (for use in beer production), by volume
ŠE system Š'' [units increasing by factors of 5, 6, 10, 3, 10, 6?]	cereal, esp. types of emmer (?)
ŠE system Š* [small units multiplied by 2, 3, or 4, alternating by a factor of 5, 6, 10, 3]	cereal, esp. barley groats
DUG$_b$ system Db [units multiplied by a factor of 10]	milk product, probably ghee, by volume
DUG$_c$ system Dc [units multiplied by a factor of 5, 2]	types of beer, by volume

At Susa, cylinder seal-impressed tablets with numerical notations (Pl. 3.1, Fig. 3.9) occur in the very first building phase of level 18 of the Acropole 1 sounding (LeBrun 1985, 1990: 61; see also LeBrun and Vallat 1978: 31) and continue, in slightly more rectangular form, to be found in level 17 (Vallat 1986a: 337). Tablets of similar type are known from Uruk IVa and level 15 in the Inanna Temple sounding at Nippur in southern Mesopotamia; Khafajah in the Diyala River valley of northeastern Iraq; Habuba Kabira, Mari, Jabal Aruda and Tell Brak in Syria; Godin Tepe V in Luristan; Choga Mish in Khuzistan; and Tal-i Ghazir in the Ram Hormuz valley between Khuzistan and Fars (Friberg 1979: Fig. 1; see also Schmandt-Besserat 1981: 323). By far the largest number of such tablets comes from Susa, where 90 have been found. An early numerical tablet believed to have been found at Uruk by W.K. Loftus in 1850 (Reade 1992a; see also Englund 1994: 17, n. 26) is particularly similar to the numerical texts from Susa (as well as Tell Brak and Jabal Aruda). Englund suggests that the numerical tablets from Godin Tepe are more like those known in northern Mesopotamia (Nineveh, Khafajah) and Syria (Jabal Aruda, Tell Brak, Mari), whereas those from Susiana (Susa, Choga Mish) are most like examples from Uruk (Englund n.d.: n. 98).

From the suite of thirteen notational systems in use at Uruk, only three have been documented in the earliest period II texts at Susa. These include the sexagesimal S system, the bi-sexagesimal B system and the Š systems of capacity notation. As Friberg has noted, these systems 'were practically identical in protoliterate Uruk and Susa' (Friberg 1994: 485). The archaic Mesopotamian systems employ a restricted repertoire of 60 numerical signs (Nissen, Damerow and Englund 1990: Abb. 8a), the values of

Plate 3.1 A sealed Susa II tablet with numerical signs only (Sb 4839). © Musée du Louvre, Antiquités Orientales

which vary according to what system is employed in a given context, and hence what types of things are being counted. The fact that we are obviously dealing with only a small sub-set of the Mesopotamian suite of numerical systems leaves little room for doubting the Mesopotamian, indeed Urukean origin of the counting systems employed in the Susa II texts (for the situation in the following Susa III period, see below). It suggests, moreover, that many more different types of things needed to be counted at Uruk than at Susa.

At the same time, however, it must also be stressed that tablets with proto-cuneiform signs in addition to simple numerical tablets also occur in Uruk IV contexts. Although intuitively one might assume, as has often been done, that tablets with more complex proto-cuneiform ideograms followed chronologically and developmentally those with only numerical signs, this is by no means certain. At Uruk, for example, both types of tablet occur together (Nissen 1986: 326) and although stratigraphic arguments have been made to suggest that the numerical tablets should be dated to Uruk V, thus preceding true writing in Uruk IV times, these are problematic at best (Englund 1994: 16). Scholars who favour such a scenario may be tempted to adduce the evidence from Susa in support of such a developmental sequence, pointing to the fact that the vast bulk of the Archaic texts at Uruk were found in secondary trash deposits (e.g.

Susa Acropole I.77.2091.1

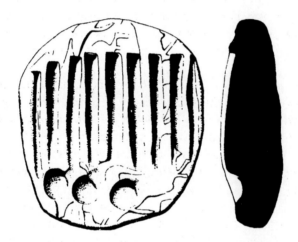

Susa Acropole I.77.2089.1

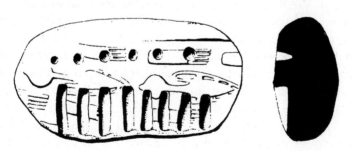

Figure 3.9 Seal-impressed Susa II (Acropole I, level 18) tablets with numerical notations (after LeBrun and Vallat 1978: Fig. 4).

Table 3.1. *Distribution and characteristics of bullae and tablets in levels 18–16, Acropole Sounding 1, Susa*

Susa Acropole 1 period and level		Document type	Shape	Contents and surface treatment
II	18	1. bullae	spherical ovoid	tokens + cylinder seal impression(s)
		2. tablets	rounded oblong	numerical signs + cylinder seal impressions
II	17	tablets	cushion-shaped	numerical signs + cylinder seal impressions
II	17x	tablets	cushion-shaped	numerical signs + one pictogram + cylinder seal impressions
III	16	tablets	rectangular	numerical signs + optional cylinder seal impressions + pictograms

LeBrun and Vallat 1978: 30; Vallat 1986a: 336). The Susa evidence is summarized in Table 3.1 and while, as noted above, it might make intuitive sense to see the development of writing proceed in this fashion, there is no telling whether the sequence at Susa, where the technology of writing was received and not invented, mirrors that of Uruk.

Moreover, the earliest true proto-cuneiform texts at Uruk include not only economic texts with signs as well as numbers, but copies of lexical texts (Fig. 3.10), including those dealing with titles and professions, vessels, metals, grain and cities (Englund and Nissen 1993: Abb. 2). The fact that these texts show a more fully elaborated type of writing using proto-cuneiform signs, conspicuous by their absence in Susiana, suggests that the language represented by the Uruk texts – as yet undetermined but possibly ancestral to Sumerian (Nissen 1985b: 354–5) – was that of Uruk and those other sites in southern Iraq and Syria with similar texts (e.g. Jamdat Nasr, where copies of the same lexical lists, such as 'vessels' and 'geography', have been found, see Englund and Nissen 1993: 66; Englund and Grégoire 1991), but *not* Susiana (see also Harper, Aruz and Tallon 1992: 53). Furthermore, although, as noted above, three out of thirteen archaic Mesopotamian numerical systems were adopted in Susiana, the physical arrangement of numerical signs on the Susa texts is completely different from that which we see developing on the proto-cuneiform economic texts at Uruk (see also Green 1981: Fig. 1). Finally, the physical shape of the Susa texts differs markedly from the earliest texts of Uruk IV times at the type-site Uruk (Fig. 3.10). These points must be a strong argument against the notion that a political force based at Uruk moved into Susiana during the Late Uruk period, and when we do find Susa and Susiana taken over by a Mesopotamian power, as was the case during the Old Akkadian period in the later third millennium (see Chapter 5), scribes were clearly brought in from outside, and written documents appear at Susa much as they did in the Mesopotamian homeland. Moreover, even if a situation of limited economic control over Susa by a small Mesopotamian elite and a few scribes could have effected the introduction of the numerical systems

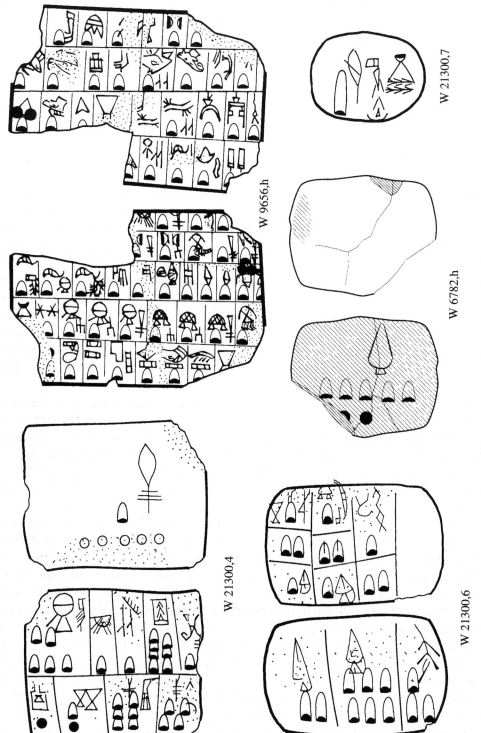

Figure 3.10 Late Uruk economic and lexical texts from Uruk (after Englund and Nissen 1993; Englund 1994).

W 9656,h

W 21300,7

W 6782,h

W 21300,4

W 21300,6

described above, the fact that many of the tablets themselves of Uruk IV and Susa II type are demonstrably different in physical proportions and graphic style makes it highly unlikely that true political and economic power at Susa was usurped by a Mesopotamian authority (see Schmandt-Besserat 1986: 115–16) in period II. If this had been the case and large numbers of Mesopotamian administrators had been involved, one would have expected to find the appearance at Susa of true proto-cuneiform texts with signs as well as numerical notations, economic as well as lexical texts, and more than just three of the proto-cuneiform numerical systems. Quite clearly, however, this is not the case.

It is increasingly likely that the written expression of these systems on clay tablets was preceded by a more three dimensional vehicle, evidence of which we also find in level 18 of the Acropole 1 sounding (Fig. 3.11), in the form of tokens enclosed within spherical envelopes or bullae (Amiet 1987c). Although long known from the early excavations at Uruk, where 25 complete or broken examples have been found, Susa, which has yielded 40 complete bullae, 15 broken ones, and fragments of 57 more, and Choga Mish, where a minimum of 28 have been recorded, it is only very recently that J. Friberg has made significant progress in deciphering the numerical systems represented by the formally diverse tokens and the signs used to mark the envelopes' exterior surfaces with which they correspond (Friberg 1994: 492–5). Friberg's work leaves us in no doubt that 'the accounts were expressed in terms of several systems of number tokens, easily identifiable as forerunners of the protoliterate systems of notations for capacity numbers and sexagesimal, bisexagesimal, or decimal counting numbers' (Friberg 1994: 495).

In sum, I shall take a different position to that of either Amiet or Algaze on the interpretation of the Susa II period. It can be suggested that the increase in the number of sites on the Susiana plain during the Susa II period and the unmistakable similarity of the ceramics found there and in southern Mesopotamia bespeak an infiltration of southern Mesopotamians, probably agriculturalists and their families, potters and other craftsmen who moved into the available agricultural land in Khuzistan and founded new settlements. They were, in a true sense, colonists. But the fact that only a small sub-set of accounting procedures, namely three of the thirteen numerical systems attested at Uruk, were introduced to Susa, and then on tablets which differed demonstrably from their proto-cuneiform counterparts, suggests that no Mesopotamian administration can have taken over power at Susa at this time. If this had happened, then we should expect to see economic account texts of the sort found in Uruk IV contexts at Uruk itself, tablets similar in shape to their Uruk counterparts, accounting procedures following the same patterns of dividing the surface of the text into distinct areas for different types of information, etc. The introduction to Susa of just a few of the numerical systems found at Uruk could have been effected by a scribe or two brought in by a local ruler whose site – a fraction of the size of Uruk – and accounting requirements were very different from those in place at Uruk. It could be argued that the Susiana region may still have been annexed by Uruk, but a local Susian put in charge, yet I would still suggest that, had this been the case, one would probably

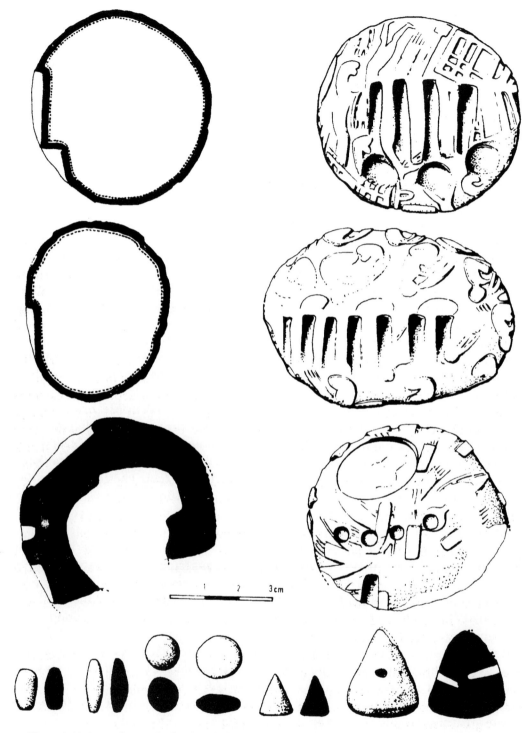

Figure 3.11 Susa II (Acropole, level 18) bullae containing tokens (after LeBrun and Vallat 1978: Fig. 3).

expect Urukean scribes and texts written *à la mode d'Uruk*. What we find instead are texts which are organized physically in a very different manner from contemporary Uruk economic texts, and only a small number of the Uruk numerical systems in use, while a large portion of the apparatus of economic control and scribal tradition found at Uruk was lacking at Susa. For these reasons, I believe we must distinguish an infiltration of Urukean or southern Mesopotamian people trying to farm the alluvium of Susiana, from a political takeover of the district as has often been implied by those who assume the more extreme colonization position. Whether or not these were refugees fleeing growing political oppression at Uruk, as suggested by Johnson, this can hardly be decided on the basis of the available evidence (Johnson 1988–9).

The potential existence of an individual or institution strong enough to have wielded sufficient political power in the fourth millennium to have effected a take-over of Susiana has sometimes been discussed in light of a series of cylinder seal impressions from Uruk, Susa and Choga Mish which, in the opinion of some scholars, depict a 'priest-king' who, it has been suggested, could represent a) 'the paramount ruler of Uruk who controls Susa'; b) 'a local surrogate of the paramount at Uruk'; or c) 'an independent ruler of Susa who is represented as identical to the ruler of a competing polity', i.e. Uruk (Harper, Aruz and Tallon 1992: 52; see also Amiet 1985b). Fig. 3.12 brings together some of the more important seal impressions from Susa, Choga Mish and Uruk on which this figure appears.

Some of the clearest representations of this figure come from Uruk and show that he probably wore a cap over his long hair (not a diadem as has been assumed on the basis of less well-preserved representations), which was pulled into a knot at the back of his head, and that he was bearded. The figure wore a skirt and was naked from the waist up. At Uruk, he appears in front of a number of captives who are apparently being beaten or driven forward by guards armed with short whips. The 'priest-king' stands before them with a spear, point down in the earth. Another representation from Uruk, which shows the figure in marshes accompanied by a pair of dogs and two wild boar (?), has our figure grasping a staff, but this too may be a spear, the point of which is lost. The same figure also appears holding a bow on a seal impression from Uruk (W 7883 + 7884, Fig. 3.12). At Susa, the figure is shown wielding a composite bow in two instances (on Sb 2125 and AO 29389, both illustrated in Fig. 3.12), aiming an arrow at opponents, some of whom he has shot, and some of whom are consequently shown falling off the roof of a two-tiered building. Finally, an impression from Choga Mish shows the figure, mace in hand, seated on a bovid, apparently in a flat-bottomed boat or barge. Larger than all of the other figures accompanying him, he grasps a rope emanating tail-like from the back of a seated figure on the vessel.

Who is this man and what is he doing at Susa and Choga Mish? For Amiet, the presence of images such as this at Choga Mish merely confirms the diffusion, far from Uruk, of those political and religious institutions which seem to immediately precede the appearance of the state in Sumer (Amiet 1986c: 64). In the case of Sb 2125 (Fig. 3.12), Amiet goes so far as to suggest that, were it not for the fact that the seal used to make the impressions in question was patently present at Susa, one would be inclined to view

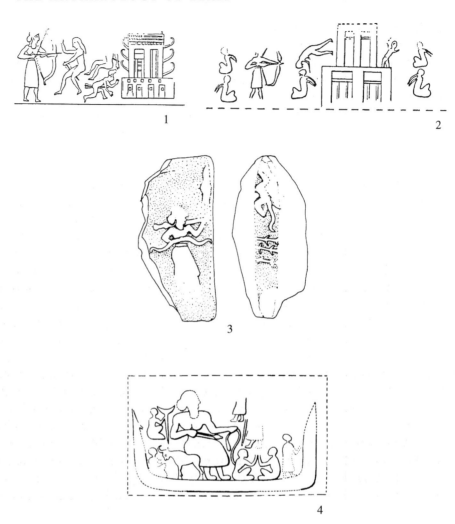

Figure 3.12 Susa II and Late Uruk seal impressions showing the 'priest-king' from Susa, Uruk and Choga Mish. 1. Susa (Sb 2125); 2. Susa (AO 29389); 3. Uruk (W 7883 + 7884); 4. Choga Mish (after Amiet 1986c: Fig. 22.1); 5. Uruk (W 6760 *et al.*).

the impressions on which this scene occurs as imports, i.e. sealings off of something sent from Uruk, since the similarities of the bearded figure on them are so striking to images known from Uruk. On the other hand, as Amiet believes the Susa I images of the 'proto-royal' figures on stamp seals to be ancestral to those of the 'priest-king', it is Susiana which is given chronological priority in the invention of the bearded male as a symbol of sacral kingship (Amiet 1986c: 60). Whatever the iconographic similarities and parentage of this figure, however, it seems unlikely to me that the virtually identical appearance of him in both the Susiana and Mesopotamian regions is merely a reflection of a shared institution of kingship, sacral or not.

Whether these representations depict a single individual, whether paramount ruler of Uruk or Susa, or a picture of a generic, 'model ruler', like the multitude of anonymous depictions of generic deities on later seals, we shall probably never know. That there was once an important individual who looked like this is made more probable, in my opinion, by the existence of several pieces of anthropomorphic statuary depicting him, but like portraits on coins which continue to be struck long after the death of the original person represented, there is no way of knowing whether the seal impressions at our disposal come from the lifetime of our hypothetical 'big man', or are merely later renditions which encapsulated the characteristics of high authority. For this reason, moreover, it is idle to speculate too much on the architectural facades depicted in the two sealings from Susa, neither of which necessarily relates to a real building at the site. It is, nevertheless, interesting to note that the building shown on Sb 2125 (Fig. 3.12), with three pairs of horns projecting from the upper story (Pl. 3.2), is adorned with horns in a fashion which continued much later in history and signified both the holiness of the building and the divine power immanent in the horns (themselves a divine symbol from the third millennium onwards) which could be transferred to secular buildings as well (see Potts 1990a; Amiet 1987b). Thus, whether or not the niched architectural facades relate to a real or ideal building, the presence of horns certainly relates to a decorative tradition well-attested at Susa during the course of several millenia.

Fars during the Early Banesh phase

The Lapui phase in Fars was followed by the Banesh phase. Although the Banesh phase has been subdivided differently by those scholars who have worked on it (see also Alden 1982a, Sumner 1986a, Zeder 1991 for different periodizations), I shall follow Sumner's division into an Early, Middle and Late sub-phase (Sumner 1986a: 199, n. 2). The Early phase is considered comparable both chronologically and culturally to Susa II: 18–17. The Kur River Basin experienced a dramatic drop in population between the Lapui and Early Banesh phases, for the latter is characterized by only 26 small sites, or roughly 26 per cent of the settlement found during the Lapui phase (Sumner 1986a: 200). In contrast, as discussed above, the number of sites occupied on the Susiana plain *increased* during Susa II times. It has been suggested that grit-tempered Early Banesh pottery was produced at one small centre, Tal-i Kureh, and distributed from another, Tal-i Qarib

Plate 3.2 A Susa II seal impression showing a horned building (Sb 2125). © Musée du Louvre, Antiquités Orientales

(Alden 1982b), but little can be said about the subsistence economy in the region at this time as Early Banesh levels were not excavated at either site, each of which is known only from surface finds (Alden 1982b: 90).

Alden considers the ceramics of the Early Banesh phase to be a new introduction from outside the region, and suggests an influx of population from Susiana, which he posits may have been reacting to Sumerian (sic) expansion (Alden 1982a: 620, 622), a view with which Sumner does not agree (Sumner 1986a: 199). For Sumner, 'similar evolutionary processes, operating in Susiana and the Zagros Highlands, simultaneously produced the first stages of Proto-Elamite civilization' (Sumner 1986a: 200), and he has described Early Banesh as 'the precursor of Proto-Elamite civilization' (Sumner 1986a: 199). In view of all that has been said above regarding the adoption of Late Uruk proto-cuneiform accounting methods at Susa, this is untenable. As the work of Friberg, Damerow and Englund reviewed above has now shown, everything points to the direct influence of Mesopotamian accounting procedures on Susa in late Susa II times, whereas the absence of Uruk IV-type tablets in the Kur River Basin clearly indicates that, from an evolutionary perspective, a crucial step in the growth of organized administration, present in Khuzistan, was completely lacking in Fars. The two areas did not evolve along similar lines.

Susa III

The interpretation of the following period of Susa's history has been as fraught with personal bias and ambiguity as the preceding one. To begin with, however, let us summarize a few stratigraphic observations made by previous scholars who have studied this material. Amiet has characterized Susa at this time as 'diminished' (Amiet 1992a: 81), certainly a reflection of the fact that occupation at the beginning of period III (levels 16–14b) is attested only on the Acropole (Fig. 3.13). Just as significant as the diminution of Susa's size, however, are the signs of a rupture in the cultural sequence on the Acropole. Although a handful of ceramic types occur in both levels 17 and 16 (Dittmann 1986: 171–2), it is difficult to ascertain whether these are in context in level 16, for the overwhelming impression of the level 16 ceramics upon the excavator, A. LeBrun, was one of a complete disjunction marked by the appearance of different fabrics and shapes (LeBrun 1978: 189–90). Moreover, as R.H. Dyson, Jr. has pointed out, the Acropole 1 section shows that the walls of level 17B were covered by 'sloping strata of secondary trash termed 17A', and the entire deposit was 'terminated by levelling activity during the construction of the structures of level 16 which have a different orientation from those of 17B' (Dyson 1987: 648). Finally, the *haute terrasse* seems to have been definitively abandoned at the end of level 17 times, as well (Canal 1978: 173). As Dyson remarked, 'There is, therefore, a discontinuity in the stratigraphy of unknown duration which must be taken into consideration' (Dyson 1987: 648).

In the late 19th century, J. de Morgan's excavators at Susa recovered two tablets which V. Scheil published briefly in 1900 (Scheil 1900). Five years later, Scheil presented a larger group of similar texts which he called 'Proto-Elamite' (Scheil 1905; see also Cruveilhier 1921: 143ff.), many of which had been sealed using cylinder seals (Pl. 3.3) differing demonstrably in both iconography and style from their Susa II/Late Uruk predecessors (Amiet 1972a; 1986c: 93ff.), and that name has been retained to the present day. Although the early Susa excavations were such that none of these tablets (Pls. 3.4–5) can be said to have been recovered from a good stratigraphic context, texts of precisely the same type were later found in levels 16 to 14b of the Acropole 1 sounding by A. LeBrun (and to a limited extent in the Ville Royale sounding by E. Carter), confirming that they date to the Susa III period. Because the linguistic relationship of these texts to later Elamite ones, and the cultural relationship of Susa to the highlands in this period are subjects which remain to be investigated, it is perhaps unwise to go on

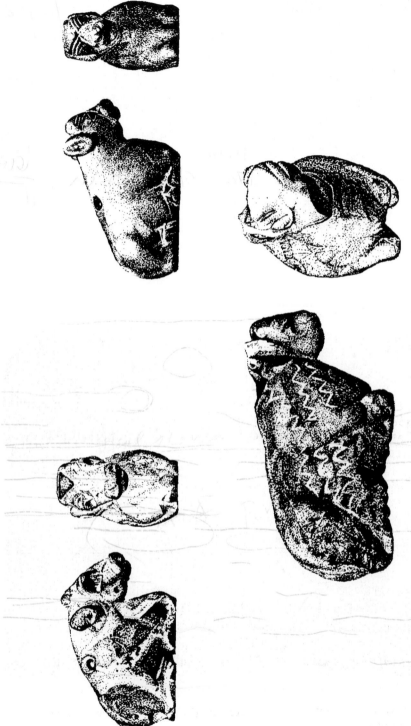

Figure 3.13 Stone figures of recumbent bovines, attributed to Susa III times (after Behm-Blancke 1979: Taf. 23.123–5).

Plate 3.3 A modern impression of a bitumen compound, Susa III cylinder seal (Sb 1484, 3.2 cm high). © Musée du Louvre, Antiquités Orientales

Plate 3.4 Obverse of Sb 2801, a Susa III account text (26.7×21 cm). © Musée du Louvre, Antiquités Orientales

Plate 3.5 Reverse of Sb 2801, with a cylinder seal impression (4.2 cm high). © Musée du Louvre, Antiquités Orientales

calling these texts 'Proto-Elamite', since this term implies a definite link with later Elamite texts before such a link has been demonstrated, either linguistically or graphically. For this reason, the tablets of so-called 'Proto-Elamite type' shall be referred to here simply as 'Susa III texts'.

All told, roughly 1550 Susa III texts have been discovered at Susa (Damerow and Englund 1989: 2; comparable texts found elsewhere in Iran will be discussed below). In order to properly assess these texts and to better evaluate the conflicting positions described above with regard to the nature of the Susa III period, we must consider their relationship to the earlier pictographic tablets of Late Uruk or Susa II date, as well as their relationship to later Elamite texts. Let us examine each of these problems in turn.

The distinctiveness of the Proto-Elamite tablets vis-à-vis their counterparts of Jamdat Nasr/Uruk III date from sites in southern Mesopotamia has long been apparent. This is due largely to the fact that 'most of the proto-elamite ideograms . . . are of a substantially more abstracted form than proto-cuneiform ideograms' (Damerow and Englund 1989: 22). As Damerow and Englund have noted, 'That there was little clear evidence for the borrowing of ideograms from the Mesopotamian into Persian writing systems or vice versa was already obvious to the first editors of the archaic texts', and as for the graphic parallelisms which do exist, these are of the type which have been observed in widely separated cultures on more than one occasion and therefore should not be accorded much, if any, significance (Damerow and Englund 1989: 6 and 7, n. 23).

Because of our inability to read and understand the texts in question, the graphic divergence between the two writing systems has tended to overshadow any other bases for comparison. Now, however, thanks to the groundbreaking work of J. Friberg, R.K. Englund and P. Damerow, a large number of structural similarities between the Susa III and Uruk III texts has become apparent (Table 3.2). As early as 1978, Friberg suggested that the similarities observed clearly support 'the tentative conclusion that the proto-Elamite ŠE-system is a slightly improved copy of a somewhat older proto-Sumerian ŠE-system. This result fits in well with the observation that the proto-Sumerian ŠE-system is used not only in several Jemdet-Nasr texts but also in some texts from the older Uruk IV stratum' (Friberg 1978: 42). More recent work by Damerow and Englund, however, has clarified the situation enormously, and it now seems certain that, with the exception of the decimal and bisexagesimal B# systems, the rest of the numerical systems in use at Susa during the Susa III period (Fig. 3.14) were either identical to or else derived from the systems found in the proto-cuneiform texts from Uruk. Moreover, as we have already seen, the ŠE-system was already in use at Susa during the Susa II period, suggesting that some of the numerical techniques of the Susa III period were derived from systems already in use at the site in the preceding two or three centuries. This does not exclude the possibility, however, that other numerical systems were first introduced at Susa during Susa III times. The originators of the Susa III writing system were thus fully competent in a wide range of Mesopotamian numerical systems, but the divergence of their sign list from that found on the Mesopotamian texts is sufficiently strong to suggest that it must be considered a separate system. The question is, whose system? The answer has great bearing on the problem of how we interpret the Susa III remains.

When Scheil baptized the texts from Susa 'Proto-Elamite', he consciously chose the term in order to underscore the linkage which he believed to exist between the newly found texts, datable to *c.* 3100–2900 BC, and the much later 'Old Elamite' inscriptions of late third and early second millennium BC date (see Chapters 4–5). This was a purely intuitive assumption. Susa, later an important city in the Elamite world, was incorrectly perceived to be the very epicentre of Elam itself. Based on this assumption, Scheil and many after him have reasoned that the Susa III texts (and their language) ought somehow to be ancestral to later Old Elamite ones. Moreover, the fact that neither Old Elamite nor 'Proto-Elamite' could be read in 1905 proved no hindrance to the assumption that Old Elamite must have been derived from Proto-Elamite. It was an assumption of an evolutionary sort, an unsystematic if not altogether untoward presumption of a genetic relationship between the languages represented by the two different writing systems.

And yet how dangerous is such an assumption. No one would ever argue that the prehistoric vestiges of the Susa I settlement were in any sense ancestral to the palace built there by the Achaemenid Persian king Darius or that the latter was ancestral to the chateau constructed by the late 19th century French excavators. Why, then, should we assume that the Susa III texts have anything to do with the later Elamite language or

Table 3.2. *Comparison of the formal and structural characteristics of Mesopotamian proto-cuneiform (Jamdat Nasr/Uruk III period) and Susa III texts*

Text Characteristic Similar/Dissimilar	Proto-Cuneiform	Susa III texts	
1. general shape	convex obverse; length:width ratio c. 3:2	as in proto-cuneiform	similar
2. use of sides	both sides used; numerical entries on obverse, summation on reverse	as in proto-cuneiform	similar
3. 'text wrapping'	when data intended for obverse overflowed onto reverse, scribe began at right edge and worked towards the left, leaving left side available for totals, summary information on tablet contents, and date	when data intended for obverse overflowed onto reverse, scribe began in upper left corner	dissimilar
4. storage procedure	stacking on shelves or in baskets with left side easily accessible for quick inspection	unknown, but pattern of reverse inscription implies different conventions for accessing tablets	dissimilar
5. semantic structure	a. subscripts qualify transactions recorded in the text	headings function like subscripts	similar
	b. cases are individual units of information	entries correspond to cases	similar
	c. graphical arrangement of cases and sub-cases reflects a syntactical hierarchy	graphical arrangement of entries is not reflected in syntactical structure of entry sequence	dissimilar
6. numerical system	a. numerals written by combination of vertical and oblique impressions of a round stylus	as in proto-cuneiform	similar
	b. numerical value of a sign varies according to the specfic context of its appearance	as in proto-cuneiform	similar
	c. sexagesimal system Š used for counting vessels, wood and stone objects, tools, humans, animals	as in proto-cuneiform	similar
	e. bisexagesimal system B used for counting rations in barley, fish, cheese?	as in proto-cuneiform	similar
	f. bisexagesimal system B# used for totalling amounts of grain recorded in the derived ŠE# system	unknown	dissimilar

g. no decimal system	decimal system used for counting animals and humans	dissimilar
h. sexagesimal ŠE systems , Š# and Š″ used for counting measures of grain	ŠE systems shows some sign variation compared to the proto-cuneiform	dissimilar
i. GAN$_2$ system used for surface mensuration less abstract than in Susa III texts	as in proto-cuneiform	similar
7. ideograms	more abstract than proto-cuneiform	dissimilar

Notes:
All information from Damerow and Englund 1989.

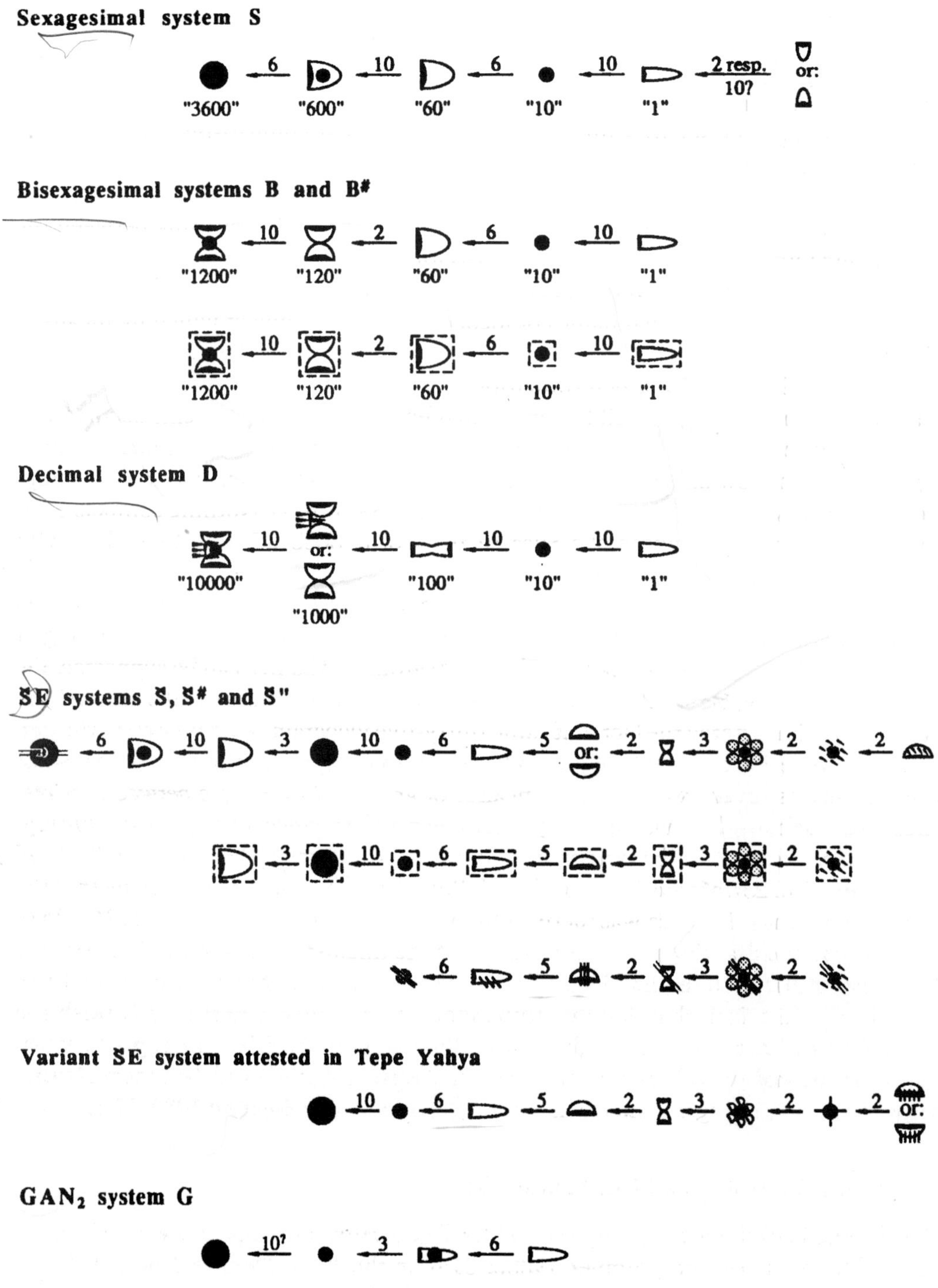

Sexagesimal system S

Bisexagesimal systems B and B#

Decimal system D

ŠE systems Š, Š# and Š"

Variant ŠE system attested in Tepe Yahya

GAN₂ system G

Figure 3.14 Numerical sign systems used on Susa III-type tablets (after Damerow and Englund 1989: Fig. 29).

people? In fact, nothing suggests that either the writing system or language of the Old Elamite texts was lineally descended from those of Susa III. Unlike the ideograms on the proto-cuneiform texts of Mesopotamia, the understanding of which has been based on graphic comparison with later forms of cuneiform writing, the Susa III texts have not been brought closer to a full decipherment through comparison with later Old Elamite texts, and indeed, 'syllabic sign readings adduced from these studies have . . . led to no successful decipherings of the archaic script' (Damerow and Englund 1989: 4). Perhaps the foremost objection to accepting the notion of a link between the Susa III and Old Elamite texts can be stated as follows: 'Given the span of *ca.* 700 years unaccounted for between proto- and Old Elamite, and given the high probability of the use in proto-elamite personal names of logographic signs, some of which by means of phonetic transfer will likely have developed into syllabic signs by the Old Akkadian period [*c.* 2350–2150 BC], a determination of any genetic relationship between Old Elamite and the language possibly represented by the proto-elamite texts seems to us at present impossible' (Damerow and Englund 1989: 5, n. 14). In sum, one can only agree with Damerow and Englund when they note that 'the evidence for this assumption seems very meager' (Damerow and Englund 1989: 1, n. 2). Nothing compels us to see any relationship between the Susa III texts of *c.* 3000 BC and the earliest Old Elamite inscriptions of *c.* 2300 BC.

Nor would it seem that comparable claims for a genetic link between the so-called Linear Elamite writing system, an innovation which began and ended with a king of Awan called Puzur-Inshushinak (see Chapter 4) around 2100 BC, can be supported. On more than one occasion, scholars searching for a link between Linear Elamite and the Susa III texts have noted the fact that some thirty-five ideograms are common to the two systems (Steve 1991: 3; 1992: 4), but Damerow and Englund, citing I.J. Gelb's stern warning against overstating the significance of graphic parallelisms between scripts, stress that such parallels may be completely meaningless 'since many pictographic representations are likely to be similar even in disparate cultures' (Damerow and Englund 1989: 6 and 7, n. 23). Moreover, even if one follows Steve and Vallat in believing that the syllabary of Linear Elamite was 'derived from proto-Elamite signs' (Vallat 1986a: 347), the fact remains that this proves nothing about the linguistic relationship between the *languages* of the Susa III and Linear Elamite texts, any more than the use of the Latin alphabet to write Turkish tells us anything about the linguistic affinities of Turkish and Latin. In sum, Damerow and Englund have dismissed the 'fruitless attempts to establish semantic and even phonetic links between the proto-elamite and the Linear Elamite script' as having no significance whatsoever (Damerow and Englund 1989: 22, n. 66).

Fars during the Middle and Late Banesh phase

The Middle Banesh phase in Fars is considered generally contemporary with 'the early part' of Susa III: 16–14a (Sumner 1988b: 315) or the Proto-Elamite 1 period (levels 16–15b) in Dyson's terminology (Dyson 1987: 650). At this time, the major settlement in the region was undoubtedly Tal-i Malyan (Fig. 3.15). Tal-i Malyan is located roughly

Figure 3.15 Contour plan of Tal-i Malyan (after Sumner 1988b: Fig. 1).

50 km north-northwest of Shiraz in a valley drained by the Kur River at an elevation of *c.* 1611 m (Sumner 1988b: 307). Although briefly sounded around 1961 by the Archaeological Department of Fars Province, Tal-i Malyan was systematically investigated in the course of five seasons between 1971 and 1978 by an expedition from the University of Pennsylvania under the direction of W. Sumner. The origins of the site may date back as far as 4800–5500 BC, for 'a few sherds' of prehistoric pottery known as 'Jarri ware' have been found on the surface, as have small numbers of Shamsabad (4800–4500 BC), Bakun (4500–3900 BC) and Lapui (3900–3400 BC) sherds (Sumner 1988b: 315). Although no actual building levels of architecture or unmixed stratigraphic contexts pre-dating the Middle Banesh phase were recovered in excavation, this may be mere chance, particularly as most of the Banesh and later exposures at the site were shallow and extensive, often limited to architectural complexes almost immediately beneath the surface, rather than deep soundings.

Be that as it may, during the Middle Banesh phase, Tal-i Malyan appears to have comprised no less than 45 ha. of settled area (Sumner 1986a: 202). Occupation is well-represented in areas ABC and TUV by an 'elaborate building (ABC 3), a large warehouse (ABC 2), and buildings with evidence of both craft production and domestic activities (ABC 4, TUV 2 and 3)' (Sumner 1986a: 206). These remains led Sumner to characterize Middle Banesh Tal-i Malyan as 'a small city inhabited by administrative officials and part-time craftsmen, many of whom were also farmers or herdsman' (Sumner 1986a: 206). Unworked and semi-worked natural resources, finished products, and production detritus attest to copper metallurgical activity, shell-working, bead manufacture and flint-knapping at the site (Nicholas 1990). It is also presumed that an industry in lime production and lime plaster manufacture must have existed at Tal-i Malyan, for the ABC 3 building and other structures were faced with lime plaster, some of which was painted in geometric patterns (Nickerson 1977; Blackman 1982; Sumner 1986a: 205; Wasilewska 1991: 145–6). Food production resulted in a yield of almost 40,000 animal bones from areas ABC (8,313) and TUV (31,480) combined (Zeder 1991: 134), the overwhelming majority of which were sheep/goat. Cylinder seals and sealings in the so-called 'piedmont Jamdat Nasr' and 'Proto-Elamite' styles were also present in both the ABC and TUV areas (Rova 1994; Pittman 1994; see also von der Osten-Sakken 1996).

Evidence of a Late Banesh phase at Tal-i Malyan, contemporary with Susa III: 14a-b (Dyson 1987: 650), is attested in the form of a mudbrick city wall, investigated in Operation By8, enclosing an area of c. 200 ha (Sumner 1985: 153). The wall, which has a length of c. 5 km, consisted of an outer construction built on a stone foundation, and at least two parallel inner walls, the innermost of which was supported by 'solid brick packing' no less than 5 m thick (Sumner 1986a: 206). That this represents a major construction is indisputable. But it clearly post-dates the major phase of contact with period III Susa. Sumner interprets it as having had 'an actual defensive function, probably against dissident sections of local pastoralists, rather than hostile forces from outside Fars' (Sumner 1986a: 209). Sumner's further ideas on the mix between nomads and sedentary villagers, or on the possibility that political authority was vested in local tribal leaders comparable to 19th and 20th century AD tribal 'khans', are highly speculative and impossible to verify.

The Susa III writing system on the Iranian Plateau

The major Middle Banesh buildings yielded a total of thirty-two texts of the Susa III type. Apart from these and the texts from Susa, tablets of comparable type have also been found at four other sites in Iran: one at Tal-i Ghazir in eastern Khuzistan, one at Tepe Sialk on the plateau, twenty-seven at Tepe Yahya in Kerman province, and one at Shahr-i Sokhta in Seistan (Lamberg-Karlovsky 1978; Damerow and Englund 1989: 2). As 'the published and unpublished tablets from Malyan . . . are in exact uniformity with texts from Susa' (Damerow and Englund 1989: 22; see also Stolper 1985), we can be certain we are dealing with precisely the same types of texts. Similarly, the texts from sites like Tepe Yahya, when carefully analyzed, have revealed numerous similarities with their western counterparts. Thus, 'all entries and column ordering of the Yahya texts . . . follow the same linear sequence noted for the Susa texts' (Damerow and Englund 1989: 13), and 'not only the structure, but also the relative complexity of the Tepe Yahya texts . . . are in full accord with the complexity and structure of the proto-elamite texts from Susa' (Damerow and Englund 1989: 15). Thus we have clear evidence for strong structural uniformity across Iran in the technical apparatus of bookkeeping procedures, and with the exception of some 'smallish attacks on graphic conventions' (Damerow and Englund 1989: 30) observed in the writing of the smallest numbers used in the ŠE-systems at Tepe Yahya, complete graphic uniformity as well.

J. Alden has called the Proto-Elamite/Susa III writing system a 'highland script' (Alden 1982a: 624), implying that it was first invented on the Iranian Plateau, perhaps at Tal-i Malyan, whence it spread westwards to Khuzistan and eastwards to Seistan and Kerman during Middle Banesh or Susa III times. In this context, it is interesting to recall the stratigraphic and ceramic evidence of a disjuncture at Susa between periods II and III noted above. As Dyson put it, 'either the discontinuity was extremely brief, or the hiatus represents a significant passage of time. If the former is the case, it would mean that the replacement of the assemblage of level 17 by that of 16 was abrupt, with no time for local development; the origin of the 16 assemblage would consequently have to be sought elsewhere. In the second situation, sufficient time would need to be involved to allow for a shift in ceramics and glyptic, and for the Proto-Elamite sign system to appear. This change would have occurred either at Susa, in the neighboring highlands, or in both places concurrently' (Dyson 1987: 649). Dyson himself opted for the second possibility, without, however, specifying where the changes occurred and how they came to manifest themselves at Susa. In Amiet's view, Susa and Susiana were 'annexed' by the highland polity centred on the site of Tal-i Malyan, ancient Anshan. A drop in the size of Susa's settled population is inferred from the reduced size of the occupied area at the site, as is an adoption of a nomadic way of life by the site's former inhabitants (Amiet 1992a: 81). Similarly, according to Alden, Susa in period III was 'no longer a major political, military, or economic force' but a 'port-of-trade, a weak but independent location where highland resources were exchanged for the products of Sumerian society' (Alden 1982a: 624). Steve has suggested that, although the steps leading up to this alteration in affairs are unclear, the fact remains that it appears as if the 'indigenous' population had finally succeeded in recapturing that control which, according to Amiet, was lost to the Mesopotamian elements in Susiana society during the Susa II period. Thereby both 'plain and plateau became confused, and one finds oneself for the first time in the presence of an Elamite country' (my translation after Steve 1991: 3). T.C. Young, Jr. is even more explicit. In his opinion, 'the prehistory for Susa 16 lies in the Marv Dasht plain. If your task is to find the origin of Susa 16, historically you can't find it in Susa 17, I think you . . . find . . . [it] in your Early Banesh' Malyan (Young 1986: 226).

Thus we have a number of scholars holding the view that Susa was in decline in period III, when it was annexed by people from Tal-i Malyan, forcing out the Mesopotamian element which had been dominant in the Susa II period and simultaneously introducing the writing system of the Susa III texts. Unfortunately for the proponents of this view, everything that has just been said about the Susa III texts emphatically contradicts it. On the one hand, it has been shown convincingly by Friberg, Damerow and Englund that, with few exceptions, the numerical systems used in the Susa III type texts were either identical to those of the Uruk IV and III tradition, or else derived from the systems in use in Mesopotamia. On the other hand, the evidence of the numerical texts found in Susa II contexts proves definitely that some of the numerical systems used in the Susa III period were already introduced at Susa during the preceding Susa II era and were most likely the forerunners of the Susa III systems. Moreover, given the fact that 'no all-numerical tablets comparable to those from Susa Acropole 18 and 17 were found in excavations at Malyan' (Stolper 1985: 5), it would seem indefensible to claim that Malyan was the site at which the writing system of the Susa III-type texts originated. In conclusion, it is the fact that the Susa III texts represent a *derived* system, a method of writing which, for all its graphic peculiarites, was founded on the account-technical procedures of the proto-cuneiform system of Susa II/Uruk IV times, which privileges Susa in the search for the homeland of the originators of the Susa III writing system.

Furthermore, recent interpretations of the Susa III texts have a direct bearing on the notion that Susa was in decline and was at best a minor outpost of a highland power *c.* 3000 BC. As Damerow and Englund have argued, 'the texts from Susa record very large numbers of animals as well as notations of grain measures as large as the largest such notations from proto-cuneiform texts', including references to 17,100 units of grain (MDP 26: 48), 23,600 animals (MDP 31:31), and 1502 small cattle (MDP 17: 275), and they go on to stress that 'tablets from Malyan/Anshan are indicative of economic activities greater than those of Tepe Yahya, yet by no means in the order of the larger Susa accounts' (Damerow and Englund 1989: 63, n. 171). Alden's suggestion that the major centre of the Susa III-period was Tal-i Malyan rather than Susa is thus not substantiated by the epigraphic evidence, any more than the notion of Susa's decline is. The likelihood that Tal-i Malyan was capable of projecting its power from central Fars into Khuzistan at the end of the fourth millennium BC, thereby reducing Susa to a 'minor outpost', thus seems remote. All of the evidence points to the opposite conclusion. Susa was the centre at which the Susa III writing system developed, and it was the centre of greatest economic activity in literate Iran (i.e. among those sites with Susa III-type texts) at the time. Finally, as Alden himself has admitted, Susa III:16 'ceramics are like (but not identical to) Late Middle Banesh pottery' (Alden 1982a: 624). In view of this evidence, the notion of Tal-i Malyan literally annexing Susa must be rejected out of hand.

Conclusion

According to my own definition of Elamite, the material discussed in this chapter has all been pre-Elamite and thus strictly speaking outside the scope of the present work. It has been necessary to treat it, however, given the fact that the term 'Proto-Elamite' is so much a part of Elamite and Iranian archaeology. Having clarified some of the misconceptions prevalent in the literature, we turn now to a consideration of developments in the early third millennium and the appearance of the first 'true' Elamites in the historical and archaeological record.

Date	Lowlands	Highlands	Mesopotamia	'Elam'
c. 4300 BC	foundation of Susa, Susa I period	Tall-I Bakun A, levels III–IV late Bakun	Ubaid period, incipient complexity	does it exist?
c. 3800–3100 BC	Susa II period; arrival of Mesopotamian settlers, limited use of proto-cuneiform, no full-scale colonization	Tall-I Bakun A, Lapui phase Tal-i Malyan, early Banesh phase	Uruk period, origins of writing and accountancy	strong Mesopotamian contacts with Susiana
3100–2900 BC	Susa III period; use of so-called 'Proto-Elamite' writing system	Tal-i Malyan, later Banesh phase; texts of Susa III type appear at various highland sites; city wall constructed at Malyan late in the Banesh phase	Jamdat Nasr period; ambiguous refs. to Elam (use of NIM and NIM.KI in Archaic texts)	distinctive writing not necessarily related to later Old Elamite; exact relationship between highlands and lowlands unclear; Susa the main centre in 'Elam'

4

ELAM AND AWAN

Although Elam may be mentioned as early as 3000 BC in the so-called Archaic texts from Uruk in southern Mesopotamia, it is not attested unambiguously in the historical record until the middle of the third millennium BC when it appears, in the Sumerian King List, as an adversary of the Sumerian city-state of Kish. A second Iranian region, known as Awan, also makes its appearance in a similar context at this time. Thereafter, both Awan and Elam are mentioned in a variety of Mesopotamian sources dating to the mid- and late third millennium. After reviewing the literary evidence, we examine those contemporary archaeological remains from Khuzistan and the central western Zagros which have the greatest likelihood of representing the material equivalent of third millennium Elam and Awan. The use of the terms 'Trans-Elam' and 'Trans-Elamite' to describe a much more easterly portion of the Iranian Plateau and its material culture is also examined.

During the period from *c.* 2350 to 2150 BC we continue to see Elam largely through Mesopotamian eyes. This was the time of the Old Akkadian dynasty in southern Mesopotamia which was founded by Sargon of Agade and ruled from an as yet unidentified capital in central Iraq. Elam figures in Old Akkadian royal inscriptions and literary works, though some of these are only known from much later copies. Repeated acts of aggression against Elam and Susiana are recorded, and the subjugation of Susa by the Akkadians is confirmed by a number of sources. It is interesting to examine the material culture of a site like Susa in light of its political history at this time. Slightly later, around 2100 BC, we are able to chart the rise and progress of an indigenous leader, Puzur-Inshushinak, the first Elamite (or Awanite) since the time of the Sumerian King List to attack Mesopotamia itself. The question of whether Puzur-Inshushinak's short-lived consolidation of power in this period should be seen as a response to Mesopotamian aggression – in other words as a case of 'secondary state formation' – is considered, as is the significance of the so-called 'Linear Elamite' inscriptions associated with Puzur-Inshushinak.

Introduction

In the middle of the third millennium BC two eastern regions, Elam and Awan, appear in Mesopotamian cuneiform sources (Fig. 4.1). In this chapter we shall first examine the earlier written sources from *c.* 3000 to 2400 BC and then turn to the material culture of southwestern Iran in order to see whether Elam and the Elamites, as constructed by Mesopotamian scribes, can be identified in the archaeological record. In the period from *c.* 2350 to 2200 BC we see a continued pattern of Mesopotamian aggression towards Susa in particular, but by 2100 BC we have evidence of a territorially expansive king of Awan named Puzur-Inshushinak whose rise and fall may be said to conclude this early period of Elamite history.

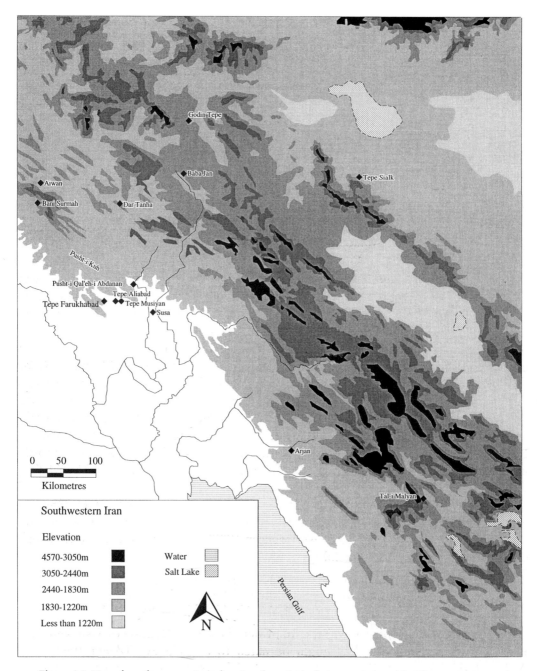

Figure 4.1 Map of southwestern Iran showing the principal sites mentioned in Chapter 4.

Earliest cuneiform sources

As noted in Chapter 1, Sumerian scribes used the Sumerogram NIM to denote Elam. When do we find this first clearly used in the cuneiform tradition? It has long been known that proto-cuneiform texts of Uruk III type from the sites of Uruk and Jamdat Nasr contain the term NIM.KI. At Jamdat Nasr, the term $NIM_{b2}KI_a$ is appended to personal names in a list of female slaves (OECT 7, 88 = MSVO 1: 217; see Selz 1991: 31), while at Uruk the sign NIM_{b2} without the geographical determinative KI occurs in an archaic lexical list of titles of officials (Englund and Nissen 1993: 269). Unfortunately, we cannot be certain that the sign as used at this early date already refers to Elam (Zadok 1994: 37; pers. comm. R.K. Englund). Leaving these references aside we next find a forerunner of the sign NIM used to identify individuals in an economic account or list of names on one of the so-called Archaic Texts from Ur of Early Dynastic I date (*c.* 2900–2700 BC). Regrettably, no actual names occur which can be analyzed linguistically as Elamite and, as in the case of the proto-cuneiform texts from Uruk and Jamdat Nasr, it may be unwise to assume the same reading of the NIM sign here as in later texts (Zadok 1994: 37). Similarly, although the Early Dynastic II (*c.* 2700–2600 BC) texts from Fara in southern Mesopotamia qualify certain individuals with the sign NIM, none of these has a linguistically Elamite name. The roughly contemporary lexical list of divine names from Abu Salabikh, also in southern Mesopotamia, mentions a god called *^{d}lugal*-NIM (Alberti 1985: 8; Mander 1986: 25). If NIM as used here stands for Elam, then the god's name can be understood as 'king of Elam'. Unlike the earlier attestations of NIM, circumstantial evidence suggests that this is a reference to Elam, for the deity named immediately before *^{d}lugal*-NIM is *^{d}lugal-aratta*, a deity apparently associated with another eastern land, whether mythic or real, by the name of Aratta. Eight lines after *^{d}lugal*-NIM we find a deity called *^{d}nin-šušinak*; this is almost certainly Inshushinak (Malbran-Labat 1995: 190), later the chief god of Susa (Hinz 1976–80; Selz 1991: 31).

   In the late Early Dynastic II or succeeding Early Dynastic III period (*c.* 2600–2350 BC) the situation becomes clearer still, for it is then that we find several lines of converging evidence. The *Sumerian King List* (Jacobsen 1939) records three encounters which are relevant, listed here in chronological order:

> Col. ii 35–7: Enmebaragesi of Kish attacked Elam
> Col. iv 5–6: Ur was attacked and its kingship carried to Awan
> Col. iv 17–19: Awan was attacked and its kingship carried to Kish

Enmebaragesi (or Mebarasi) was the first ruler of the First Dynasty of Kish, and D.O. Edzard has suggested that he should be dated to *c.* 2675 BC (Edzard 1967a: 54). Although the *Sumerian King List* gives him the fabulously long reign of 900 years, we know nevertheless that he was an historical figure, not a mythic one, for two fragments of alabaster vessels found at Khafajah in the Diyala region of eastern Iraq, one of which calls him **lugal [k]iš**, 'king of Kish', bear his name (Steible 1982/II: 213). The reference to Enmebaragesi's attack on Elam is the first unequivocal mention of Elam in the cuneiform record, but what precise district he attacked is unclear. Given that Kish is located in northern Babylonia, and that Enmebaragesi's inscriptions have been found at Khafajah (ancient Tutub), up the Diyala from modern Baghdad, one might think that his campaign(s) led him down what was later to be known to Herodotus as the 'Royal Road', through the Jabal Hamrin district and into the northwestern portion of Khuzistan, via Der and Kismar, towards Susa. That such a route was in use during the Early Dynastic period has recently been shown by D.R. Frayne, for the so-called 'List of Geographical Names' found at Abu Salabikh and Ebla contains the names of toponyms which define such a trajectory (Frayne 1992: 58–9). The same list, moreover, mentions three toponyms known to have lain in the western marches of Elam, including one known as URUxA/*ar-ù/a-ra-wa*, called in some sources *sag-kul-NIM*^{ki}, 'the bolt of Elam' (Frayne 1992: 71). In an Ur III text this town is associated with bitumen and a location somewhere near Deh Luran in northern Khuzistan has been postulated. One further piece of evidence linking Kish with Elam in Early Dynastic III times has come down to us in the form of an Ur III copy of an Early Dynastic votive inscription of Enna'il, son of A'anzu, who calls himself *elam* GIN₂.ŠE₃, '(he) who conquered Elam' (Steible 1982/II: 218; Selz 1991: 32).

The references to Awan are just as important, for Awan was almost certainly the indigenous name of one of the sub-regions east of Mesopotamia subsumed more broadly under the rubric 'Elam' by Sumerian scribes. According to the *Sumerian King List* the First Dynasty of Ur, founded around 2500 BC by Mesanepada, was undone by a dynasty from Awan which reigned for 356 years (see Stolper 1989: 112). Unfortunately, the names of the first two rulers of Awan who reigned over parts of southern Mesopotamia following this event are lost, and of the third, only the fragmentary 'Ku-ul-[...]' is preserved (Gelb and Kienast 1990: 317). As none of the names in the much later Susa kinglist of Old Babylonian date (*c.* 1800–1600 BC), which records the names of twelve kings of Awan, begins with Ku-ul- (see Scheil 1931, Glassner 1996), Gelb and Kienast have even suggested the list recounts the members of a 'second' Dynasty of Awan, as opposed to the 'first' dynasty which conquered Ur. Nevertheless, from a linguistic point of view two of the names on the Susa list, Lu-uh-ish-shan and Hi-she-ip ra-te-ip, eighth and ninth rulers of Awan respectively in the list are particularly important. Lu-uh-ish-shan is an Elamite name (Zadok 1991: 226). In all probability Hi-she-ip ra-te-ip is the same as Hi-shi-ip-ra-shi-ni, identified as 'king of Elam' and father of Lu-uh-ish-shan in two Old Babylonian copies of Old Akkadian texts from the reign of Sargon of Agade (Sargon C 7 and 13; Gelb and Kienast 1990: 180, 188), i.e. *c.* 2334–2279 BC. Not surprisingly, therefore, Hi-shi-ip-ra-shi-ni is also an Elamite name (Zadok 1991: 226). Whether the names became reversed in the Susa kinglist, or whether these are simply homonyms unrelated to the father and son contemporary with Sargon of Agade, we cannot say.

As for the location of Awan, the fact that at least some of the names of the rulers of Awan were Elamite has led Vallat to suggest a location somewhere on the Iranian Plateau north of Susiana, rather than in the Khuzistan lowlands where he suggests Akkadian names would be expected (Vallat 1993a: 26). Specific geographical informa-

Table 4.1. *Summary of the conflict between Eannatum and regions to the east*

Eannatum text	Action
22 2: 4–8	the 'mountain/mountain land' Elam, Arawa, Umma and Ur were all smitten with weapons
1 Rev. 6 10–12; 2 Obv. 3 12–16	Elam, 'the high mountain', was smitten with weapons; mounds of corpses were piled up; Arawa, whose **ensí** had raised its standard, was smitten with weapons; mounds of corpses were piled up; Umma was smitten with weapons; twenty mounds of corpses were piled up
11 5: 3–8	Uruk was smitten with weapons; Uru'aza was destroyed; Mishime was destroyed
1 Rv. 6: 10–10: 22	Elam and Subartu, the mountain land rich in (?) wood . . . was smitten with weapons; Susa was smitten with weapons; Arawa, whose **ensí** had raised its standard, was smitten with weapons; A-DU$_3$-a was destroyed . . . Ur was smitten with weapons
3 3: 11/4 3: 10	Uruk, Ur and Ki'utu were smitten with weapons; Uru'aza was destroyed, its governor killed; Mishime was destroyed; A-DU$_3$-a was destroyed
2 3: 12–16	Elam, 'the high mountain', was smitten with weapons; mounds of corpses were piled up; Arawa, whose **ensí** had raised its standard, was smitten with weapons; mounds of corpses were piled up; Umma was smitten with weapons; twenty mounds of corpses were piled up
2 4: 6ff	Uruk, Ur and Ki'utu were smitten with weapons; Uru'aza was destroyed, its governor killed; Mishime was destroyed; A-DU$_3$-a was destroyed
2 6: 15–7: 2	Elam, Subartu Arawa, Kish, Akshak, and Mari were smitten with weapons

tion is contained in three Old Babylonian copies of inscriptions of the Old Akkadian king Rimush (Rimush C 6, 8 and 10) describing his capture of Sidga'u, general of Barahshum (see Table 4.6) (Rimush C 6 also mentions Sar-GA-PI, governor of Zahara) 'between Awan and Susa, by the river Qablitum' (Gelb and Kienast 1990: 207ff.; see also Westenholz 1970: 27). Scheil supposed that a phrase of this sort implied that Awan and Susa were located close to each other (Scheil 1931: 1), and even if this is a logical deduction we have no way of estimating the distance between the Qablitum river, Awan and Susa.

Apart from Kish and Ur, Lagash also had a considerable amount of contact with Elam during the Early Dynastic III period. Eannatum (*c.* 2460 BC), one of the most powerful rulers of the First Dynasty of Lagash, left us a number of inscriptions in which he speaks of his conquests over Elam (Table 4.1), presented in their presumed chronological order (following Selz 1991: 33ff.). Selz has suggested that Eannatum undertook at least two eastern campaigns, an initial one in which Arawa was destroyed, perhaps in an effort to open up a land route to Susiana; and a second one in which the southern cities closer to the head of the Persian Gulf (Steinkeller 1982a: 242), such as Mishime (= p Bashime) and Uru'aza (and probably also A-DU$_3$-a) were attacked (Selz 1991: 36).

Perhaps as a result of these campaigns we find that, during the reigns of Lugalanda and Urukagina, two later rulers of Lagash, considerable traffic is recorded between Elam and Lagash (Table 4.2), and at least sixteen individuals with linguistically Elamite names appear in the late pre-Sargonic texts from the latter site (Zadok 1994: 38).

Several other additional Early Dynastic texts concerning Lagash should also be briefly mentioned. One text, which names two smiths attested during the reign of Urukagina, says that Lu'ena, the administrator of the E-Nin-MAR.KI temple at Gu'abba (the harbour of Lagash), defeated a force of 600 Elamites trying to transport 'booty' from Lagash to Elam (Selz 1991: 36–7). The text DP 164 mentions another administrator of the E-Nin-MAR.KI, A'agrigzi, who received various ingredients for beer-making while he was in Mishime (Selz 1991: 41), one of the cities/regions conquered by Eannatum. Uru'aza, another city conquered by Eannatum, provided a band of gardeners for work in the gardens of Urukagina (DP 339, dated Urukagina L 4), while provisions for a ship owner from Uru'aza are treated in a group of four texts (Nik 140–142; BIN 8 367) dating to the years Lugalanda 2 and 6 (Selz 1991: 42).

In conclusion, the *Sumerian King List* and the pre-Sargonic texts from Lagash reveal the following pattern: first, a brief period of rule in southern Mesopotamia by a 'dynasty' based in Awan; second, a fairly vigorous series of conquests during the reign of Eannatum when campaigns were recorded against Elam, Mishime, Arawa, and Uru'az; and third, a period during the reigns of Lugalanda and Urukagina when some of those districts, whether subservient politically or simply no longer bellicose, had commercial relations with Lagash via its port Gu'abba. Let us see how the archaeological record of southwestern Iran in this period relates to the skeletal political history just outlined.

Elam and Awan in the Early Dynastic era

The developments of the Susa III and Banesh periods at Susa and Tal-i Malyan discussed in Chapter 3 seem to have come to a conclusion in the first half of the third millennium. The absolute chronology of the Susa III period, which overlaps with both the Jamdat Nasr and Early Dynastic I periods in southern Mesopotamia, suggests that a major break in the sequence occurred around 2900 or 2800 BC when, with the exception of a few locally manufactured bitumen and bitumen-compound objects (Connan and Deschesne 1996: 148), Early Dynastic Mesopotamian styles became dominant in glyptic and statuary forms (Amiet 1992a: 82). The abandonment of the Susa III-related, period IVC enclave at Tepe Yahya, and the desertion of Tal-i Malyan at the end of the Banesh period, which Sumner would date to c. 2600 BC, were almost certainly not brought about by Mesopotamian aggression, but to match up Mesopotamian historical chronology with the archaeological and radiocarbon chronology of the Iranian Plateau is a hazardous exercise at best. P. Amiet has gone so far as to state that it is not really until the appearance of Sargon of Agade that the situation at Susa becomes clear again. Most authorities, however, agree that the graves at Susa excavated in the early part of this century, which contain painted pottery (formerly known as Susa D), show links not with Mesopotamia but with the graves believed to be those of nomads or semi-

Table 4.2. *Elam and Elamites in pre-Sargonic texts from Lagash*

Text	Date	Contents
STH 1, 15; STH 1, 16; Nik 9	Urukagina **ensí** 1/5, 1/6 (?) and 1/8	list of barley rations distributed, *inter alia*, to Abba (or the eldest?) from Elam
RTC 21	'Fifth year' (of Urukagina?)	account of commodities, including spices, mentioning a container (ceramic?) of the 'mountain-country type' as the trading expedition commission for the boats from Elam
RTC 20	Ukg. **lugal**?	list of commodities, mainly spices, purchased, mentioning a commission for the trading expedition of the Elamites
Nik 85	Lugalanda 1	barley being traded for wool from Elam
Nik 292	Lugalanda 4	delivery of silver from Elam for the purchase of trade goods
Nik 214	Lugalanda 4	reports purchase of livestock in Elam
DP 486	Lugalanda 7	mentions wooden objects, including waggon parts, ladders, vessels, brought from Elam
DP 230	Lugalanda (?)	list of cereal rations given to, *inter alia*, five women from Elam, probably either slaves or prisoners-of-war, with the otherwise unattested names of DU-*íl-íl*, *ha-ba-ra*-DU.NE, KA.A and *usùr*-DU$_{10}$.DU$_{10}$; reference to two Elamite women with typically Sumerian names, PAP.PAP-*am-da-rí* and ^{d}*nin-gír-su-ur-mu*, working for a brewer named Ilibeli at Lagash
DP 134	undated	list of emmer and barley disbursements for the festival of Baba, mentioning the 'wife of Nigduba, the Elamite' who received barley, wheat, dates and cheese
Nik 11	undated	list of names of five Elamites, including HA.NE, MI.DU and *ra-bí*
Nik 310	undated	list of commodities (grain, flour, lard and salve) being sent to Elam; mention of Siku, governor of Arawa (?)
DP 370, 371	undated	reports the harvest of 'Susian flax' in the territory of Lagash
Nik 313	undated	return of a **lú-sa$_6$-ga** from Elam to Gu'abba, Lagash's main harbour
DP 423	'First year' (of whom?)	mentions wooden objects brought by boat from Elam

Note:
Data drawn from Selz 1991.

nomads in the Pusht-i Kuh of Luristan and the Deh Luran plain of northern Khuzistan (Carter 1987, Haerinck 1986), and the question is, do some of the archaeological complexes of Luristan of early to mid-third millennium date represent the archaeological manifestation of the historical entity known as Awan? Does the shadowy figure of historic Awan lie behind the 'effervescence' of the western Zagros around 2650 BC as suggested by M.-J. Steve (Steve 1991: 3)? Let us examine these possibilities now in greater detail.

The Central Western Zagros

Because the archaeology of this region will be referred to in discussing areas further south, it is best to begin by examining developments in the Kangavar valley and the Pusht-i Kuh region.

If we begin with the Kangavar and nearby valleys, a major change in the ceramic repertoire of the region c. 2600 BC signals the start of what has been called Godin Tepe period III. For the moment, we are interested only in the earliest phase, period III:6, which is considered contemporary with Early Dynastic II and III in the Mesopotamian sequence (Levine and Young 1987: 42, 50). Apart from the plain wares present, the most striking ceramic feature of this period is the appearance of black-on-buff and occasionally cream-slipped carinated pots and jars which employ combinations of geometric motifs (chevrons, horizontal bands, spirals) and vegetal motifs. Related pottery has been found as far west as the Islamabad plain, to the west of the Mahidasht valley, and may even extend into the Hamrin basin of northeastern Iraq (K. Abdi, pers. comm.). Architecturally, the period III architecture at Godin Tepe is characterized by portions of several multi-roomed, obviously domestic, mudbrick dwellings.

Levine and Young have noted three points worth considering in any attempt to view the third millennium archaeological assemblages of Luristan as a reflection of the historical entity known as Awan. These may be enumerated as follows. First, the material which characterizes period III:6 at Godin Tepe is found 'in most of the southern and eastern valleys of Luristan along the main routes linking these regions with the lowlands of Khuzistan'; second, 'close connections with the monochrome painted pottery of Susa Dc-d/Susa IVA are clear'; and finally, 'sherds of a certain Godin III:6 type have also been found at al-Hiba [ancient Lagash] associated with tablets and sealings of Enannatum, Eannatum, and Lumatur' (Levine and Young 1987: 50). In an effort to imbue this material with historicity, R.C. Henrickson has suggested that the Godin III assemblage of Luristan represents the material correlate of ancient Shimashki, a region about which we shall have more to say in the following chapter. Yet at the time of which we are speaking, Shimashki was not a force, indeed still less a name. Awan was the region responsible for the overthrow of the house of Kish, and it is with Awan that I propose identifying the assemblage just described. Awan's position as part of Elam, from a Mesopotamian perspective, and the references to Elamites at Lagash in late pre-Sargonic times reviewed earlier, provide the context in which Godin III:6 pottery could easily have reached a lowland city like Lagash. Equally, Awan's role at this date must have brought it into constant contact with Susa, which would again explain why we find clear ceramic parallels between Godin III:6 and that site.

Moving south into the Pusht-i Kuh we have a series of cemeteries excavated by the late L. Vanden Berghe. For convenience, all of the third millennium assemblages from the Pusht-i Kuh have been summarized in Table 4.3. Of greatest interest are those assemblages which Haerinck has assigned to Pusht-i Kuh Phase III. The material from this period has been divided into three groups or zones, corresponding to a northwestern (1), southeastern (2) and central (3) zone (Haerinck 1986: 68). As Table 4.3 shows, many of the ceramic and metal weapon types known in the Pusht-i Kuh can be paralleled at sites in the Kangavar valley (Godin Tepe), the Diyala region (Khafajah, Tell Asmar, Tell Agrab), the Hamrin basin (Tell Razuk), northern Khuzistan (Tepe Farukhabad, Tepe Aliabad, Tepe Musiyan) and Susiana (Susa). The same applies to the cylinder seals found in the necropolis at Bani Surmah (Tourovets 1996). The demonstration of such links is consistent with the inclusion of this region in that of ancient Awan.

Developments in Northern Khuzistan

Tepe Musiyan (Table 4.4), the largest site on the Deh Luran plain in northern Khuzistan of early to mid-third millennium date, is poorly known. Limited French soundings there in 1902–3 by Gautier and Lampre revealed some very rich graves containing painted pottery (Pézard and Pottier 1926: 17), but we know little else about the site in this period. At Tepe Farukhabad, a much smaller site, levels of fill and mudbrick architecture dating to the Early Dynastic II period (following Carter 1987: Table 1) were revealed by H.T. Wright in Excavations A (levels 1–5) and B (19–20) (Wright 1981: 72–5). As Wright has noted, however, 'massive river erosion and intrusive pits limit our knowledge of the Early Dynastic occupation' at Farukhabad (Wright 1981: 192). Nevertheless, the polychrome pottery from Farukhabad shows numerous parallels to material from Tell Razuk in the Hamrin basin (Carter 1987: 75).

At Tepe Aliabad a series of vaulted mudbrick cist tombs were excavated by Gautier and Lampre. These yielded both painted and plain ceramics comparable to finds from Kheit Qasim I and Tell Ahmad al-Hattu in the Hamrin basin, and the Early Dynastic I assemblages from the Diyala region (Delougaz 1952: 139). They also show clear links to the material from Farukhabad, Susa and Pusht-i Qal'eh-i Abdanan in Pusht-i Kuh Zone 2 (see Table 4.3) (Carter 1987: 80).

In spite of the limited size of the Early Dynastic exposures at Farukhabad, and the poor quality of the excavated assemblages from Tepe Aliabad, the ceramic parallels just cited leave no doubt that contacts occurred between the Diyala, Hamrin, Pusht-i Kuh and Deh Luran plain at this time.

Susa in the pre-Akkadian third millennium B.C.

Following period II, the Apadana at Susa was either abandoned during the entirety of period III, or else remains of that time were completely obliterated by later activities,

Table 4.3. Overview of the archaeological assemblages of the Pusht-i Kuh

Pusht-i Kuh Phase	Major cemeteries	Finds with external parallels	Comparanda	Suggested date
I	Kalleh Nisar A1, Mir Khair	polychrome (red, black) pottery	Kheit Qasim (Hamrin), Khafajah (Diyala), Jamdat Nasr, Ur, Tepe Farukhabad, Susa	Jamdat Nasr-ED I
II	Kalleh Nisar C, Bani Surmah A and B, War Kabud Mihr 1	polychrome (red, black) pottery	'scarlet ware' from sites in the Diyala (Tell Asmar, Tell Agrab, Khafajah) and Hamrin (Tell Razuk)	ED I
III – Zone 1	Kalleh Nisar A1 16, C3 loc. VII, Bani Surmah A13, B6, 11–12, War Kabud Mihr 2	polychrome (red, black) pottery	Tell Razuk (Hamrin)	ED II–IIIa
III – Zone 2	Pusht-i Qal'eh-i Abdanan, Qabr Nahi, Takht-i Khan, Tawarsa	'fruitstands' finger-impressed jars monochrome pottery polychrome pottery convex ring base	Diyala sites (Tell Asmar, Tell Agrab, Khafajah) Susa Godin III:6 Godin III:6 Susa Tell Razuk Khafajah	ED II
III – Zone 3	Dar Tanha 1	shaft-hole axes monochrome pottery	Susa Tepe Musiyan Tepe Aliabad Kish Godin Tepe III:6 Susa	ED II ED II/III

Table 4.4. *Principal sites of the Deh Luran plain in northern Khuzistan during the early third millennium BC*

Site	Survey ID	Type	Approximate size	Periods of use
Tepe Musiyan	DL 20	settlement	13.5 ha	ED I-III
Tepe Baula	DL 24	settlement	5 ha.	?
Tepe Farukhabad	DL 32	settlement	3.5 ha.	Jamdat Nasr – Early Dynastic
Tepe Sabz East	DL 18	settlement	4 ha.	ED II
Tenel Ramon	DL 24	settlement	traces only	?
Tepe Guran	DL 34	settlement	traces only	?
unnamed	DL 104–74x	settlement	?	Jamdat Nasr-ED I
unnamed	DL 43	settlement	?	Jamdat Nasr-ED I
Tepe Khazineh	DL 28	cemetery	?	Jamdat Nasr-ED II
Tepe Aliabad	DL 71	cemetery	?	Jamdat Nasr-ED II

Notes:
Data drawn from Carter 1987:74.

such as the excavation of a large ditch during the Islamic era. The only remains of the subsequent period, IVA, are those of an unspecified number of graves and pottery kilns beneath the floors of the Achaemenid palace of Darius (Steve and Gasche 1990: 28).

The situation elsewhere on the site is only slightly better. It is believed that a temple once stood on the Acropole, but all that remains of it are 'a few stone plaques [Fig. 4.2] and statues, possibly local copies of Sumerian types' attributed to levels 4 and 3 (Carter 1985: 43; 1980: Table 1), from which an interesting mother-of-pearl inlay (Pl. 4.1) may have come (see Dolce 1978: S2). More material was recovered in the Donjon at the southern end of the site. A cache of cylinder sealings of Early Dynastic I-III types, showing clear Mesopotamian parallels, represents the principal evidence of sealing practices at the site in period IVA, to which we should add a cylinder seal-impressed storage jar fragment (Fig. 4.3) which had been sealed with the type of seal attested at sites in Syria including Hama and Ebla (Amiet 1985a: 9–10). Hundreds of tombs were excavated in the Donjon and Ville Royale by R. de Mecquenem, but of these only four can be reconstructed with any degree of certainty. These consisted of single inhumations accompanied by a range of ceramic (Pl. 4.2) and metal vessels, as well as a selection of other objects including copper/bronze arrowheads, belt buckles, and daggers or knives in leather sheaths. Of particular interest is the presence of at least one burial in the Donjon which included a four-wheeled chariot. This, as well as other tombs containing copper/bronze 'wands', comparable to examples found in Luristan, may have been those of high status individuals (Carter 1985: 45). The existence of such tombs in the mid-third millennium immediately invites comparisons with chariot burials at Ur and Kish, but there is not enough little detail available to enable such comparison. Most importantly, 'ceramic and metal objects find their closest parallels in Luristan . . . Trade with the west is evidenced by the appearance at al-Hiba in area C

Figure 4.2 Limestone wall plaque from Susa (after Boese 1971: Taf. XXIV.2).

and Ur of a few examples of early Susa IV type ceramics' (Carter 1985: 45), where an Early Dynastic III date is most likely (Carter 1987: 80). As noted above, Susa IVA ceramics show parallels with material from Pusht-i Qal'eh-i Abdanan in Pusht-i Kuh Zone 2, as well as with Tepe Musiyan, Tepe Aliabad and Tepe Farukhabad (Carter 1987: 78, 80). Interestingly, although the ceramics and metal weaponry reflect ties to the north, an important link with the Oman peninsula (ancient Magan) is indicated by the composition of a hoard of metal objects found in a large painted vessel, the so-called 'Vase à la cachette', which suggests that the copper used for their manufacture came from the Oman ophiolite (Berthoud et al. 1980: Fig. 3; see also Amiet 1986c: 126).

Undoubtedly the best stratified early to mid-third millennium material from Susa comes from levels 12–9A in the Ville Royal I excavations conducted by E. Carter.

Plate 4.1 Shell inlay of an equid excavated by de Morgan, sometimes thought to represent Przwalski's horse, from Susa (Sb 5631, 5.7×3.6 cm), dating to the second half of the third millennium. © Musée du Louvre, Antiquités Orientales

Although the architectural remains were limited to fragments of a few mudbrick walls corresponding to portions of several rooms, the ceramics recovered show clear links to the Godin Tepe III, Baba Jan IV and Dar Tanha assemblages, thus confirming once more the existence of indisputable links to Luristan in the mid-third millennium. The same applies to the material from graves 555 and 569, both of which were dug down from period IVA levels into older strata. These contained *inter alia* objects such as a shaft-hole axe comparable to those from Dar Tanha 1 and Bani Surmah (see Table 4.3; Vanden Berghe 1968: 58).

Awan in Luristan?

In discussing the various locations put forward in the past for the region of Awan, F. Vallat came to the conclusion that the name could have applied to a vast area encompassing the modern provinces of Luristan, Kermanshah, Kurdistan and Hamadan, extending as far east as Tepe Sialk near Kashan and north to an unspecified point (Vallat 1993a: CXXV). Certainly the ceramic and metallurgical evidence adduced above confirms the existence of a relatively coherent material culture complex in Luristan and the Pusht-i Kuh in the mid-third millennium, but beyond that one runs, archaeologically speaking, into different cultural provinces. I prefer a minimalist definition of Awan for the moment which focuses on those highland areas referred to here as partak-

Figure 4.3 Impression of a mid-third millennium Syrian cylinder seal on a sherd from Susa (after Amiet 1985a: Fig. 1 = Amiet 1972a: no. 1023).

ing of the culture of Godin III:6 and the Pusht-i Kuh assemblages datable to the mid-third millennium (ED II-III in Mesopotamian terms). Furthermore, it must be remembered that the period IVA material from Susa shows little if any connection to that of period III (see Amiet 1992a: 82) or to the Banesh assemblage of Fars. If one is looking for the source of at least some of it, then the parallels cited above point in the direction of Luristan and that, combined with the historical evidence of the emergence of Awan in this period, is highly suggestive.

Trans-Elam and Trans-Elamite material culture

One further aspect of Elamite identity on the Iranian Plateau in the mid-third millennium remains to be considered. In 1986, P. Amiet introduced the term 'Trans-Elamite' into the vocabulary of Iranian archaeology (Amiet 1986c: 138; see also 1986b; 1987a; 1988a; 1994a). Amiet focused on the so-called *série ancienne* or 'Intercultural Style' carved soft-stone vessels (de Miroschedji 1973; Lamberg-Karlovsky 1988) of the late Early Dynastic and Old Akkadian periods (Pl. 4.3; Fig. 4.4) as the most visible testimony of the earlier phase of this culture (cylinder seals and metal types were also included), the centre of which he saw in Kerman province at sites such as Tepe Yahya and Shahdad (see Amiet 1974a) where (at least in the first case) material of this type was actually manufactured. According to several scholars, these settlements, 'beyond the pale' of direct Elamite control in the post-Proto-Elamite era, might have formed part of either ancient Marhashi (Steinkeller 1982a) or Shimashki (Vallat 1980a; 1985b; 1993a), but in view of the uncertainty of these attributions, Amiet created a vaguer term, yet one which nonetheless acknowledged a certain tie to a heritage dating back to the Susa III or Proto-Elamite period (e.g. Amiet 1986b: 12). The term Trans-Elamite was also extended to incorporate a still later manifestation of artistic originality in the region, as expressed by the painted pottery of Bampur in Baluchistan, and Trans-Elam was formally acknowledged to encompass Kerman province and the western portions (at least) of Baluchistan.

Plate 4.2 Large polychrome ceramic vessel (Sb 2840) from a third millennium grave excavated by de Mecquenem at Susa. © Musée du Louvre, Antiquités Orientales

Plate 4.3 Carved soft-stone compartmented vessel (Sb 2829) from Susa belonging to the *série ancienne* or 'Intercultural Style' (18.3 cm long). © Musée du Louvre, Antiquités Orientales

This construct is certainly correct in focusing on a community of culture in south-eastern Iran, even though the links between Tepe Yahya and Shahdad, and between Tepe Yahya and Bampur are just that and nothing more, sets of parallels and far from an identity of material culture. But there is little justification for terming this 'Trans-Elam'. In fact, it is difficult to see how the material expressions of the mid- and late third millennium can have anything to do with an alleged 'Proto-Elamite heritage', for 500 years at least separate the Trans-Elamite from the Proto-Elamite. Whether or not it is appropriate to refer to the region of Kerman and western Baluchistan as Marhashi or Shimashki, it is clearly different ceramically, glyptically and metallurgically from Susiana, Fars and Luristan and should not be confused with Elam *per se*.

Sargon of Agade

Earlier we reviewed the evidence of hostilities against portions of western Iran (Elam, Awan, URUxA or Arawa, Mishime, Uru'aza and probably A-DU$_3$-a) by Enmebaragesi, Enna'il and Eannatum in the mid-third millennium BC. Although economic texts from Lagash may reflect the submission of some of those areas, their provision of labourers, and generally increased traffic between southwestern Iran and southern Mesopotamia

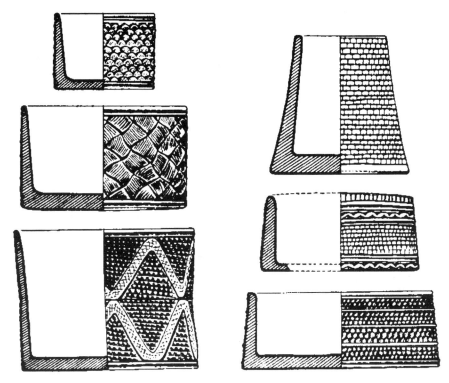

Figure 4.4 *Série ancienne* or 'Intercultural Style' soft-stone from Susa (after de Miroschedji 1973: Fig. 5).

c. 2600–2400 BC, nothing suggests that sustained political influence was ever exercised by a Mesopotamian city over one of its eastern neighbours at this date. In the mid-24th century, however, this situation changed dramatically, and for the first time in their history the regions of southwestern Iran came within the direct political orbit of a Mesopotamian power.   SARGON

The history of what has often been called the 'first world empire' is generally well known, and the qualitative and quantitative differences between the short-lived hegemony of successive city-states during the Early Dynastic period and the new political, bureaucratic and religious structures created by Sargon of Agade have been examined in detail in recent years (Westenholz 1979; Glassner 1986; Liverani 1993). After subduing both the north and the south of Mesopotamia and setting himself on the path towards the creation of an empire, Sargon turned his attention to the east. In Mesopotamia, 'each king named a particular year of his reign after an important event which had taken place in the course of the preceding year' (Sigrist 1988: 1), and no fewer than three of Sargon's four extant year names commemorate his eastern conquests (Gelb and Kienast 1990: 49–50):

> Sargon 2a: 'in the year after Sargon destroyed URUxA'
> Sargon 2b: 'in the year after URUxA was destroyed'
> Sargon 3: 'in the year after Sargon destroyed Elam'

Table 4.5. *Eastern regions named in the Old Babylonian copies of Sargon of Agade's royal inscriptions*

Old Babylonian copies of Sargon's royal inscriptions	Eastern regions mentioned
C1: 87–94, C4: 94–9	Elam stands 'in the service of Sargon, king of the land'
C7: 1–7; C7 caption b; C13: 2–7	'Sargon, king of the totality, slayer of Elam and Barahshum'
C7 caption c	'booty from URUxA' *Marhaš!*
C7 caption d; C13 caption f	'Sanamshimut, governor (**ensí**) of Elam'
C7 caption e; C13 caption g	'Luhishan, son of Hishibrashini, king (**lugal**) of Elam'
C7 caption f	'booty of Shali'amu'
C7 caption g	'booty of Kardede'
C7 caption h	'Ulul, GÌR.NÍTA of Barahshum' ✓
C7 caption i	'Dagu, brother of the king (**lugal**) of Barahshum'
C7 caption k	'booty of Heni'
C7 caption l	'booty of Bunban'
C7 caption m	'Zina, governor (**ensí**) of Huzi- . . .'
C7 caption n	'Hidarida- . . ., governor (**ensí**) of Gunilaha'
C7 caption o	'booty of Sapum'
C7 caption p	'booty of Awan'
C7 caption q; C13 caption e	'Sidga'u, GÌR.NÍTA of Barahshum'
C7 caption r; C13 caption h	'Kumdupum, judge (DI.KUD) of Barahshum'
C7 caption s	'booty of Susa'
C13 caption d	'. . . governor (**ensí**) of Shirihum'
C13 caption j	'Hishibrashini, king (**lugal**) of Elam'
C13 caption k	'Elamites . . .'

Notes:
Data drawn from Gelb and Kienast 1990.

The Old Babylonian copies of Old Akkadian royal inscriptions include fifteen attributable to the reign of Sargon. In recounting the major victories of the Akkadian monarch, these texts provide us with a series of statements relating to Sargon's eastern conquests (Table 4.5) and include a number of important personal names as well as toponyms. As noted above, both Hishibrashini and Luhishan, designated as king (LUGAL) and son (DUMU) of the king of Elam, respectively, bore Elamite names, and the same applies to Sanam-shimut (Zadok transliterates $Sa\text{-}pir_{6}\text{-}ši\text{-}mu\text{-}ut$, see Zadok 1991: 225), which contains the name of the Elamite deity Simut or Shimut, comparable to Nergal or Mars (Zadok 1984b: 40). Zina is considered 'atypical' while Hidarida- appears not to be Elamite (Zadok 1991: 226) and Kumdupum 'cannot be compared with any names' (Zadok 1993: 223). To sum up, the copies of Sargon's inscriptions give us the names of thirteen eastern cities or regions against which he campaigned (Pl. 4.4): Elam, Barahshum, URUxA, Sali'amu, Kardede, Heni, Bunban, Huzi-x, Gunilaha, Sapum, Awan, Susa and Shirihum. It is impossible to specify the precise location of each of these places, but apart from Elam, URUxA, Awan and Susa, which have been discussed already, the remainder can be classified as follows.

The location of Barahshum, or Marhashi as the name was sometimes written, is ~~dis-puted~~ *known*. While Steinkeller has suggested placing it in eastern Fars and Kerman province (Steinkeller 1982a; 1989), F. Vallat has argued that it was further east, in the area of modern Iranian Baluchistan (southeasternmost Iran, southwestern Pakistan) (Vallat 1985b: 52; 1991: 14; 1993: CXIII-CXVIII). However, Sidga'u (*Si-it-ga-ù*), described as GÌR.NÍTA of Barahshum, has a Hurrian name (Zadok 1993: 223), and this would seem *NO* to imply a more northerly (or northwesterly) location for Barahshum, closer to northern Iraq and northwestern Iran. Huzi-x is probably 'in Elam', according to Zadok (Zadok 1991: 225). Gunilaha is thought to lie 'somewhere in the Iranian Plateau' (Zadok 1991: 226). Sapum is listed as one of the regions of Shimashki (Zadok 1991: 226). As Stolper has observed, those parts of 'Shimashkian territory exposed to contact with Mesopotamian states [in the Ur III period, see Chapter 5] lay among the valley systems to the north of Khuzistan and/or Fars. More precise location, and determination of the greater extent of lands which Mesopotamian or Susian scribes considered Shimaskian, is not available' (Stolper 1982: 46). In contrast, Vallat has proposed a location for Shimashki in the northern part of Kerman province far to the east, more precisely in the area of the site of Shahdad (Vallat 1985b: 51; see also 1991: 21; 1993a: CXIII-CXVIII). For Zadok, 'Shimashki extended from Fars to the Caspian Sea' (Zadok 1991: 227). Finally, Shirihum or Sherihum is thought to have been the coastal region of Fars (Steinkeller 1982a: 256).

As uncertain as the historical geography of Iran in the third millennium may be, the provisional locations just enumerated bespeak wide-ranging conquests on the part of Sargon. However, it is also important to remember that some of these conquests may have been by proxy. In other words, some of the regions named may have been allied with groups further west, e.g. Susa or Awan, which supplied troops to defend against Sargon's incursion and ended up contributing booty to the Akkadian war chest. Their inclusion in the dedicatory inscriptions (Table 4.5) does not necessarily mean that *✳* Sargon physically visited each of them with his army.

Rimush　*older son* Maništušu

After a long and vigorous reign of thirty-seven years, Sargon was succeeded by his ~~younger~~ son, Rimush. Judging by his own, original inscriptions as well as the Old Babylonian copies of others now lost, Rimush retraced some of his father's steps in western Iran (Table 4.6). Once again Elam and Barahshum appear as the chief adversaries, with the addition of Zahara, while Gupin and Meluhha also figure in one of the variants. Although Steinkeller (1982a: 257) sees no reason to believe that the hostilities were ever carried as far east as Barahshum itself, Rimush C 6 would seem to suggest that Rimush encountered the combined forces of Zahara, Elam and Barahshum in Barahshum itself. As for Zahara, this toponym appears only in Rimush's inscriptions and its location is unknown (could it have anything to do with *Azara*, presumably in eastern Khuzistan, mentioned in the Parthian period and discussed in Chapter 10?). Vallat suggests Baluchistan (Vallat 1993a: 305) but stresses that it was politically independent of, if allied with, Elam. We have already discussed the geographical implica-

see
have
diorite

Javelin

Plate 4.4 Diorite stele fragment (Sb 3, 46×35 cm) from Susa, dated to the reign of Sargon of Agade, showing prisoners with hands bound behind their back being marched by a soldier. © Musée du Louvre, Antiquités Orientales

Table 4.6. *Eastern regions named in original and Old Babylonian copies of Rimush's royal inscriptions*

Rimush Inscription	Eastern regions mentioned
1 – repeated on fourteen booty of stone vessels or vessel fragments	'after he had conquered Elam and Barahshum, from the booty of Elam' he dedicated the vessel to Enlil
2 – repeated on eight stone vessels or vessel fragments and one macehead	text as on no. 1, vessels dedicated to Sin
3 – on one stone vessel	'after he had conquered Elam and Barahshum' he dedicated the vessel
5, C7 – repeated on one macehead and three stone vessels or vessel fragments	'conqueror of Elam and Barahshum'
C6: 3–72	'defeated Abalgamash, king of Barahshum, in battle; Zahara and Elam arrayed themselves for battle in the midst of Barahshum, but Rimush was victorious; 16,212 men were killed and another 4,216 taken prisoner; Emahsini, king of Elam, was captured . . . from Elam was captured, Sidga'u the general from Barahshum was captured, and Shar-GA-PI from Zahara was captured between Awan and Susa by the river Qablitum; mounds of corpses were heaped up in the city and he conquered the cities of Elam and razed their walls and he tore the roots of Barahshum out of the land of Elam, for Rimush, king of the totality, rules now Elam'
C6 Colophon 1: 138–51	'after conquering Elam and Barahshum he removed 30 minas of gold, 3600 minas of copper and 360 male and female slaves and dedicated them to Enlil'
C8: 3–34	'defeated Abalgamash, king of Barahshum, in battle and captured Sidga'u its general between Awan and Susa by the river Qablitum; he piled up mounds of corpses in the city and tore the roots of Barahshum out of the land of Elam for Rimush, king of the totality, rules now Elam'
C10: 10–11	mentions Gupin and Meluhha after Zahara and Elam, otherwise as C 6
C10 Colophon: 41–5	diorite, *dushû*-stone and (other) stones which I have received, pieces from the booty of Barahshum

[handwritten: Hurrian Marhaśi]

tions of the reference to the river Qablitum between Awan and Susa, suggesting that the Saimarreh, a northern tributary of the Karun, may be meant and a location in the Pusht-i Kuh thereby implied. As for the *dramatis personae*, Sidga'u, the general from Barahshum, was already active in the reign of Sargon (Table 4.5). It is important to stress that both his name and that of the king of Barahshum mentioned here, Abalgamash (*A-pá-al-ga-maš*), are Hurrian (Zadok 1993: 223), and as noted above, this may have implications for the location of Barahshum to the north rather than to the east of Susiana.

Death and captivity were inflicted by Rimush on the forces of Zahara, Elam and most probably Barahshum. We can never be certain that the numbers cited are accurate, and they are certainly large by comparison with the figures given for the combined forces of Ur and Lagash. According to Rimush, these two southern Sumerian cities suffered 8040 deaths, while 5460 men were taken captive and another 5985 were put to work as corvée labourers (Westenholz 1979: 121, n. 18). Whether the eastern forces were arrayed as part of the general rebellion on the part of Ur, Umma, Uruk, Kazallu and Lagash which Rimush faced upon his accession, we do not know, but although the likelihood certainly exists, Foster suggests that the Iranian campaigns followed the suppression of the Sumerian revolt and were not triggered by the general rebellion (Foster 1985: 27–8).

Manishtusu

[handwritten: NO, to Anśan]

Sargon's elder son was the first Old Akkadian ruler to penetrate to the heart of Fars province. In the only inscription relevant to the east (Manishtusu C 1), an Old Babylonian copy of one of his original texts, we learn that he conquered Anshan and Sherihum before crossing the Lower Sea (Persian Gulf) and continuing on his way. To have reached Anshan, modern Tal-i Malyan, and not to have mentioned Susa suggests *[handwritten margin: Ur Susa a colony]* that Susiana and the western portions of Fars offered no resistance to the king on his way east. If, as Steinkeller suggests, Sherihum should be located along the coast of Fars, then we might envisage a route of march approximating that which links modern Shiraz with Bushire on the Gulf.

During Manishtusu's reign we know that he had a governor (**ensí**) named Ilshu-rabi installed in the Iranian coastal region of Pashime, as well as a governor of Elam named Eshpum (Table 4.7).

Naram-Sin

The situation in the east during the reign of Manishtusu's son Naram-Sin is more complicated. In Naram-Sin's inscription B 7:8–13 he is called 'conqueror of Armanum, Ebla and Elam', while the Old Babylonian copy C 3:7–10 mentions Elam and Barahshum in an unclear context. In spite of the considerable amount of literature devoted to the so-called 'great revolt' which attended Naram-Sin's coming to power (Tinney 1995), the precise chronology of his wide-ranging campaigns is by no means clear. We know that he fought from Anatolia and Cilicia in the north to Oman in the south, and that he

[handwritten: NO end, 9 battles megław]

Table 4.7. *Akkadian regents in Elam during the Old Akkadian period*

Regents in Elam during the Old Akkadian period	Title	Approximate date
Eshpum	governor (**ensí**) of Elam	Manishtusu
Ilshu-rabi	governor (**ensí**) of Bashime	Manishtusu
Epirmupi	vassal? (GÌR.NÍTA) of the land of Elam governor (**ensí**) of Susa	early Naram-Sin
Ili'ishmani	vassal? (GÌR.NÍTA) of the land of Elam	late Naram-Sin, early Sharkalisharri

Notes:
Data derived from Gelb and Kienast 1990: 318–19; see also Lambert 1979:17.

engaged the Lullubum in the northwestern Zagros as well (see Glassner 1986: 20), but exactly how the campaigns against Elam and Barahshum fit into this we cannot say. It is probable, however, that changes in Naram-Sin's titulature – starting with his use of the title 'king of Agade', his adoption of the unprecedented epithet 'king of the four quarters', his deification, and finally his use of the term 'smiter of Armanum and Ebla' – can help us to chart his *cursus honorum* (see Frayne 1991: 381–2; see also Kutscher 1989: 17–19). That being the case, the conquest of Elam and Barahshum must have occurred late in his reign, for the event is named in a text (B 7) in which Naram-Sin's name is already written with the divine determinative and in which he has adopted the title 'king of the four quarters' (Gelb and Kienast 1990: 110). If Kutscher was correct in suggesting that Naram-Sin's apotheosis occurred soon after crushing the great revolt (see also Frayne 1991: 392, n. 71), then we can conclude that Elam and Barahshum, which were not attacked until afterwards, played no part in that rebellion.

Naram-Sin is the only Akkadian king whose own inscriptions attest to his having been a royal builder in the east. Two brick fragments found at Susa bear the legend 'Naram-Sin, mighty king, king of Ur, king of the four quarters . . .' and may relate to his construction at the site of a temple such as those which he is known to have built or re-built at Nippur (Enlil), Girsu (Enlil), Adab (Enlil and Inanna) and Lagash (Sin) (Malbran-Labat 1995: 21 and n. 38). Unfortunately, the state of the inscription is such that it is impossible to tell whether Naram-Sin's name was preceded by the **dingir** sign, the divine determinative, and hence it is impossible to suggest whether the building at Susa was erected early or late in his career, i.e. before or after his apotheosis.

A fragment of a human torso with arms folded across the chest found at Susa (Moortgat 1969: Pls. 150–1) bears a dedication from Suash-takal which tells us that he dedicated his statue to the god ᵈNIN.KIŠ.UNU for the life of Naram-Sin, the mighty, his (i.e. the god's) friend, king of the four quarters (Gelb and Kienast 1990: 107, Naram-Sin B 2). The text calls Suash-takal 'scribe' and 'major-domo' (**šabra-é**), and indeed we know from other sources that Suash-takal was a 'powerful official', involved in the re-building of the temple of Enlil at Nippur and influential enough to have had a town named after him near Gasur (Westenholz 1987: 55). The text gives no indication as to whether or not the statue stood originally in a temple at Susa, certainly a possibility given Suash-takal's mobility and high rank, or whether it was brought there subse-quently as booty, just as the more famous 'victory stela' of Naram-Sin, several statues of Manishtusu and the code of Hammurabi were in the 12th century BC by Shutruk-Nahhunte I.

Finally, an alabaster sherd inscribed with the name and title of Naram-Sin ('Naram-Sin, king of the four quarters'), and which bears traces of the sign BUR, meaning 'vessel', was found at Susa at the beginning of the century (Scheil 1902; see also Potts 1986: 279; T.F. Potts 1989: 152; Braun-Holzinger 1991: 161; Koch 1997: 109). This is thought to be one of a number of inscribed alabaster vessels seized as booty by Naram-Sin during his campaign against Magan (Oman peninsula) – the full inscriptions on which read BUR NAM.RA.AK MÁ.GÁN.KI, 'vessel from the booty of Magan' (Potts 1986: 278) – but how it ended up at Susa remains a mystery. Most probably it was not the alabaster vessel itself which was considered precious but its contents. In later antiq-uity alabaster jars were renowned as the 'best means of keeping unguents fresh' (Pliny, *Nat. Hist.* 36.12.60–1).

he put them in all places he controlled. (probably abroad).

Sharkalisharri

With the reign of Sharkalisharri, Agade was no longer the aggressor but the recipient of attacks from all sides (Glassner 1986: 40). Victories in battle over Elam and Zahara are recorded in two variants of one of Sharkalisharri's year formulae (Gelb and Kienast 1990: 54). Interestingly, one of these says that the battle took place 'opposite Akshak', a city located along the Tigris above Baghdad, possibly modern Tell Sinker (Frayne 1991: 395, n. 93; 1992: 47). Thus, the rebellion against Akkadian rule was carried into the heart of central Mesopotamia. At the same time, however, either Sharkalisharri or his son travelled from Nippur to the east in order to marry a princess of Marhashi. Three texts from Nippur concern 1. the onions which were given to a delegation of Marhashians 2. onions given to the prince 'when he went to Marhashi'; and 3. onions given for the prince's wedding, which is thought to have taken place in Marhashi (Westenholz 1987: nos. 129, 133 and 154).

lower Frayne 1993

Who was he? Sm!

Dudu *?.*

NO

Sharkalisharri was the last descendant of Sargon's to occupy the Akkadian throne. The period after his reign is notoriously poor in documentation, but of those names listed in the *Sumerian King List* which follow Sharkalisharri's, the fourth of the remaining 'kings of Agade', Dudu, may have campaigned against Elam. This, however, depends on the restoration of the name E[lam] in one of his year formulae and is highly uncer-tain (Glassner 1986: 42; this is not listed, for example, in Gelb and Kienast 1990).

who was he?

[handwritten: why did they do it? cnt'd? Trade]

Akkadian politics and Susiana

The incessant determination to dominate southwestern Iran, minimally from Susa and Awan in the west to Anshan in the east – for the moment we must leave aside the other regions of uncertain location – not only resulted in the spread of Mesopotamian material culture over parts of the dominated areas, but it actually incorporated some of those areas, particularly Susiana, within the immediate Akkadian political universe. Whereas the inscriptions of Sargon and Rimush mention the names of two kings (**lugal**) of Elam, viz. Hishibrashini and Emahsini, respectively (Tables 4.5–6), we find three **ensí**'s and a GÌR.NÍTA installed, in one case specifically at Susa, from the reign of Manishtusu to the beginning of Sharkalisharri's reign (following the chronology proposed by Lambert 1979: 17). The interpretation of these titles is, however, far from straightforward. Let us first consider the title **ensí**.

Hallo has shown that in the pre-Sargonic and early Sargonic periods the title **ensí** was used by independent rulers of city-states (e.g. Eannatum I and II and Entemena of Lagash) who could not perhaps claim the more substantial title **lugal**, meaning king. On the other hand, the formerly independent **ensí**'s defeated by Sargon were replaced by Akkadian **ensí**'s who functioned more properly as city governors (or even mayors) for the king (Hallo 1957: 45), and by the late Akkadian period 'ensí was the title of the ruler or governor of many of the cities of Sumer and Akkad. It did not matter whether the city was formally dependent at any given time, or whether it had succeeded in cutting even the last ties with the often ephemeral sovereigns at Akkad, Gutium, Uruk or Ur . . . But where, as at Uruk, the city had not – at least since the earliest times – been under an ensí, there the Sargonic and Ur III rulers likewise forebore to install one, relying instead in this case on en's and GÌR.NÍTA's, both members of the royal family' (Hallo 1957: 45–6). *[handwritten: general]*

What did the title GÌR.NÍTA signify? In the Sargonic era, 'as a political title, i.e., compounded with a geographical name, GÌR.NÍTA was applied at this time only to vassals of foreign kings or of the Sargonic kings themselves' (Hallo 1957: 100). Thus, in Sargon's inscriptions, Ulul and Sidga'u were both GÌR.NÍTA of the king of Barahshum, i.e. vassals of that king. Similarly, Epirmupi and Ili'ishmani (Fig. 4.5) are both qualified as GÌR.NÍTA, which would suggest that they were dependents of the Akkadian king, rather than independent rulers of Elam. In the case of an individual like Epirmupi, who is attested both as GÌR.NÍTA and as **ensí**, Hallo suggests that he may have risen 'from a courtier's rank to that of governor of Susa and Elam, still as such subordinate to the kings of Awan, Akkad, or some other higher power' (Hallo 1957: 102). Glassner (Glassner 1986: 11) and Koch (Koch 1996: 146), on the other hand, interpret GÌR.NÍTA as a title denoting a military governor. *[handwritten: yes]*

The status of Ili'ishmani does not preclude the existence of an **ensí** with ultimate responsibility over Susa (or Elam) and indeed some of the Old Akkadian texts from Susa which, judging by the personal names they contain (Legrain 1913: 127–30), originated in either Umma or Zabalam, indicate that during the reign of Sharkalisharri Susa and Susiana were considered part of the province of Girsu-Umma and were under the

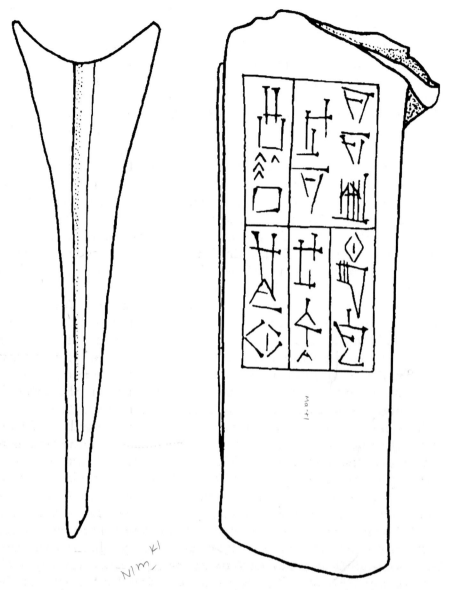

Figure 4.5 Bronze axe from Susa with an inscription reading, 'Ili'ishmani, scribe, GÌR.NÍTA of the land of Elam' (after M. Lambert 1979: Fig. 1).

control of its **ensi** Mesag (Lambert 1979: 19–20). But Ili'ishmani, whose name is purely Akkadian, and the slightly more than 80 Old Akkadian texts from Susa which probably belonged 'to Sumerian (Ummaite?) families residing at Susa' and included 'official records of the imperial administration there' (Foster 1982: 7) would seem to reflect the activities of high Akkadian functionaries and their subordinates at a city which was well and truly integrated into the empire at this time (Lambert 1979: 22).

Into this picture, however, we must now interweave yet another document, written in Old Elamite, namely the so-called 'treaty' of Naram-Sin with an unnamed ruler or high-ranking official whom G.G. Cameron supposed to have been Hita (Cameron 1936: 34), eleventh king of Awan in the Old Babylonian list of kings of Awan and Shimashki alluded to above (Hinz 1967: 66). Whether or not the king in question was Hita – neither Awan nor Susa is in fact mentioned in the text – the fact remains that the text is unlikely to concern one of the princes installed by the Akkadian government at Susa. The text is an important document which begins with the invocation of a long list of deities, some twenty-six of whom are 'Elamite' in the broadest sense of the term, i.e. Iranian and not Mesopotamian, such as Pinikir, Humban, Inshushinak, Shimut or Hutran, two of which (Ninurta and Ninkarrak) are Sumero-Akkadian, and three of which (Ishara, Ilaba and Mazziat) are specifically Old Akkadian (Lambert 1991: 54). The crux of the treaty (§3) contains the unnamed king's promise not to countenance opposition to Agade, and the lines 'Naram-Sin's enemy is also my enemy, Naram-Sin's friend is also my friend'. Gifts having been received from the Akkadian monarch, the Iranian party to the treaty promised to defend the treaty and not to tolerate anything anti-Akkadian in his realm (§7).

Following on from the discussion above of the chronology of Naram-Sin's campaigns as revealed by his changing titulature, it could be suggested that the treaty was concluded early in Naram-Sin's career, for his name is written without the **dingir**-determinative signifying his deification (Hinz 1967: 96). Lambert believes that the treaty signified the unnamed ruler's acceptance of Naram-Sin's rule over Susiana and his simultaneous desire to maintain his relative autonomy in the highlands even if it meant swearing allegiance to the Akkadian king (Lambert 1979: 29).

The installation of Akkadian officials, bureaucrats and undoubtedly their families certainly brought about an influx of Mesopotamians onto the Susiana plain unparalleled since the Susa II period. It also effected the introduction of Old Akkadian methods of accountancy (see Foster 1982) and consequently Akkadian became the language of bureaucracy at Susa. This in turn contributed to the 'Akkadianization' of the native population, with the result that patterns of name-giving undoubtedly changed, and Akkadian names became common, even among ethnically non-Akkadian Susians. This is not to say that Elamite names are absent in the Old Akkadian texts from Susa, but it does explain why they are in the minority (Table 4.8) and why, in Mesopotamia itself (Zadok 1994: 39–40) 'all the Susians mentioned in Sargonic texts bore Semitic names' (Zadok 1991: 225). There are, however, other people not specifically designated as Susians who appear in Mesopotamian sources and who have linguistically Elamite names (Table 4.9).

Susa during the Old Akkadian period

What are the physical manifestations of Akkadian sovereignty at Susa? To what extent does the material culture of the site reflect the historical trends outlined above? While nothing suggests that the Apadana was unoccupied during the Old Akkadian period

Table 4.8. *Elamite names attested at Susa during the Old Akkadian period*

Elamite names attested at Susa in the Old Akkadian period	Text reference
E-ni-ish-sha-an	*MDP* 28: 524, 9
E-pi-ir-ì-lum	*MDP* 2: A, 3 7
E-pir$_x$-mu-pi	*MDP* 43: 1547, 1
Hal-te-en$_6$-hu-ut-ta-ash	*AfO* 19 (1959/60): 10, vi 32
Ha-si-ri-ir-za-na	*MDP* 14: 75, 9'
Ha-si-ha-li-ish	*MDP* 14: 75, 7'
Hi-si-ip-ra-si-ni	Gelb and Kienast 1990: 317
In-da-su/sú	*AfO* 19 (1959/60): 10, vi 32
Kur-da-shu	*MDP* 43: 1579, 1
Mi-ish-da-ti	*MDP* 14: 79
Muk-dù-dù	*MDP* 14: 1, ii, 3
Na-ru-ti	*MDP* 14: 74, 8
Nu-ti-ish	*MDP* 14: 72 rev. ii, 6'
Ra-bí-pi-li-ir	*MDP* 14: 82, 4
Sa-pi-ru-ri	*MDP* 24: 384, 4
Si-da-ak-su-kir	*MDP* 14: 27, i 2
Si-im-pi-ru-uk	*MDP* 24: 384, 25
Si-ir-ú-lul-uk	*MDP* 24: 384, 27
Su-kir-a-bí	*MDP* 14: 6, rev. ii 14'
Ú-lu-tu-ni	*MDP* 28: 424, 3.4

Notes:
Data derived from Zadok 1984b.

(Table 4.10), the soundings made by R. de Mecquenem through the floor of the Achaemenid palace there revealed relatively little material, apart from pottery and some bronze objects recovered in graves (Steve and Gasche 1990: 28). The situation was better on the Acropole, where levels 1 and 2 have been dated by the excavators to the Late Old Akkadian period and included the foundations of a building with small, vaulted rooms interpreted as a possible granary (Steve and Gasche 1971: 77; see also Amiet 1986c: 143), while in Ville Royale I a small area of domestic remains, including an oven complex and fireplace associated with an ashy surface, as well as a grave (grave 527) were exposed in levels 8 and 7 (Carter 1980: Fig. 20) and attributed to the Old Akkadian and post-Akkadian periods, respectively (Carter and Stolper 1984: Fig. 15). In continuation of the numerical system used to denominate Susa I, II and III, the late Early Dynastic and Old Akkadian periods at Susa are termed Susa IVA (c. 2600–2400 BC) and IVB (c. 2400–2100 BC), respectively (Carter 1985: 43–5). It is estimated that the site covered approximately 46 ha. by the end of the Akkadian period (Carter and Stolper 1984: 135).

Ceramically speaking, Susa was converted to both Mesopotamian forms and modes

Table 4.9. *Elamite names attested in southern Mesopotamia during the Old Akkadian period*

Location	Name	Situation	Text reference
Adab	unnamed	Elamite prisoners receiving rations	Yang 1989: A 672, 4
Eshnunna	Ku-ru-za		MAD 1, 85: TA 1931, 9
Gasur	Pu-ul-ma	listed in a ration or wage list	HSS 10: 185, iv 15
	Si-a-ni	named amongst people delivering lard	HSS 10: 169, 9; 199, 2
	Ti-ru-sha-ki	received grain ration	HSS 10: 129, 13; 156,7; 197, 10
	Za-na	named in ration list of agricultural labourers	HSS 10: 188, ii, 18; iv, 21
Girsu	A-bi	listed in a contract	MVN 6: 500
	Am-ba/ma-ar	listed in a contract	MVN 6: 500
	Ba-ak-za-na	named in list of personnel	MVN 6: 381 rev. 7
	Ba-ar	listed in a contract	MVN 6: 500
	Ba-ar-si-ni	named in list of personnel	MVN 6: 381 rev. 7
	Da-an	listed in a contract	MVN 6: 500
	Da-an-ú-ri	mentioned in connection with a delivery of baskets	STTI 37: L. 1277, 2
	Gi-NIM		ITT 5839
	Gu-ri	listed in a contract	MVN 6: 500
	Ha-al-ka	mentioned in list of garments and recipients thereof	MVN 6: 377, rev. 15
	Ha-ap-hi-iš	mentioned in list of quantities of metals and recipients thereof	MVN 6: 100, 2
	Ha-ne	mentioned in Mesag archive	Bridges 1981: 32
	Hu-ba	receved rations	DPA 45
	Hu-ba	listed in a contract	MVN 6: 500
	Hu-hu-me	listed in a contract	MVN 6: 500
	Hu-um-ba	a shepherd	MVN 6: 351 rev. 15
	Hu-un	listed in a contract	MVN 6: 500
	Hu-un-zu-lu	listed in a contract	MVN 6: 500
	In-tar-ra	list of personal names	ITT 3107
	Ka-ka	listed in a contract	MVN 6: 500
	Ma-ad-ga	(or the region of the same name minus the geograpical determinative?)	RTC 253, 8 rev. 5
	Mu-mu-shi	list of personal names	ITT 3107
	Na-pi$_5$-ir	listed in a contract	MVN 6: 500

Table 4.9 (cont.)

Location	Name	Situation	Text reference
	Pu-ul-ma	listed amongst Susians	MVN 6: 90, 5 rev. 9
	Si-im-ta[n]	listed in a contract	MVN 6: 500
	Ú-e-li	listed in a contract	MVN 6: 500
	Ur-ᵈshushinak	mentioned in list of offerings	ITT 2855
	Uru-az^ki	geographical name used as personal name	ITT 1195 rev. 3
	U.URUxA-mes	scribe named after geographical placename	Nik. 2, 14, ii, 14
	Za-na	listed in a contract	MVN 6: 500
	Zu-zu-i-lum	mentioned in account of beer	ITT 4518
	unnamed	ensí of Susa	ITT 4560
	unnamed	ensí's of Susa and Elam holding land at Girsu	RTC 143
	unnamed	Susians	ITT 4700
	unnamed	Elamites	ITT 2905
	unnamed	Kimashians	RTC 248, 7; 251, 3'; 252, 5
	unnamed	Elamite women receiving rations	MVN 6: 105.335.492
	unnamed	Elamite with a slave who had a Sumerian name	ITT 5798
	unnamed	Elamite priest occurs in list of metal objects and military equipment	STTI 7: L. 1125, 6
	unnamed	purchasing trip to Elam	STTI 63: L. 1469
	unnamed	Anshanite	RTC 247 rev. 17
	unnamed	Susian mentioned in ration text	CT 50:148
	unnamed	people from Bashime	Nik. 2, 35, ii, 12
	unnamed	people from Uru'az	RTC 113, 3'
Nippur	Elam-mu	uncertain	OSP 1: 129, v, 2 f
	unnamed	mentioned in beer account	OSP 1: 57, i, 7
	unnamed	craftsmen	OSP 1: 57, i, 2.4.6; ii, 4.5
	unnamed	received beer and clothing	TuM 5: 38, i, 6; 108+, iv, 7
Umma	unnamed	beer text	CT 50: 56, 21
	unnamed		MCS 9; 241 rev. 11; 242 rev. 7
	unnamed	Elamite who functioned as a scribe	BV 5: 61, 3

Notes:
(data drawn from Zadok 1994: 39).

Table 4.10. *Susa and Tepe Farukhabad during the late third millennium BC*

	Susa			Tepe Farukhabad	
Apadana	Acropole	Ville Royale	Proposed date	Site	Proposed date
Chantier 24: graves,			late Early Dynastic /Old Akkadian		
pottery kilns	levels 2–1 (Steve/Gasche)	A 8-7, grave 527 (Carter)	late Akkadian Period IV? late Akkadian		
Achaemenid palace: graves beneath; tomb 329 (locus 32)	pits 8, 10, 22, 25, 27, 28 (Steve/Gasche)	A XV (de Mecquenem) B VII–VI (Ghirshman/ Gasche) A 6B-3, graves 513, 507 (Carter)	Ur III Elamite ancien II (2100–1900 BC) Period V? Shimashki (2200–1900 BC) Ur III	Exc. B, layers 18–15	Shimashki (2200–1900 BC)

of decoration with common Akkadian types replacing local ones in period IVB (Carter and Stolper 1984: 134). Moreover, the same trend can be seen in most of the metalwork recovered from the graves excavated by R. de Mecquenem and incorrectly dated to the 'XXVth' century (Tallon 1987: 61; see also Amiet 1986c: 143). Typologically, this material includes a variety of tools, weapons, toilet articles and vessels. Reliable information on the provenience of most of the metal finds from the early excavations at Susa (i.e. pre-1968), which are now in the Louvre, is, however, lacking, and typological comparison with material from other sites (Table 4.11) rarely suffices to distinguish between a late Early Dynastic, Old Akkadian or Ur III date. On the other hand, there are a few exceptional pieces with inscriptions, such as the blade of a broken socketed axe (Fig. 4.5) bearing the legend 'Ili'ishmani/scribe [DUB.SAR]/GÌR.NÍTA of the land of Elam' (Frayne 1993: 308; Tallon 1987/II: 139, no. 20) which can be securely assigned to the Old Akkadian period.

For the most part, the roughly 170 cylinder seals from Susa which are attributable to the Old Akkadian and Post-Akkadian periods also display Akkadian iconography and style. Thus, like Mesopotamian seals from the time of Sargon, the earliest of these continue to reflect the norms of the late Early Dynastic tradition, while the bulk can be compared with mature Akkadian, and some with post-Akkadian seals of Mesopotamian provenience. Some seals are, without any doubt, imports from Mesopotamia. This applies, for example, to the seal of Lugalidda, known to have been a high-ranking functionary at Adab, while the seal used by Libur-beli, a functionary of Epirmupi, who was in charge of Susa early in Naram-Sin's reign, was most probably also a Mesopotamian product (Amiet 1972a: 190). Known from its impression on a tablet found at Susa, the Libur-beli seal shows a classic Old Akkadian scene of two nude heroes confronting in one instance a water buffalo and in the other a lion. Importantly, however, Amiet has suggested that the large number of second-rate cylinder seals, often of an archaizing rather than genuinely ancient style, suggests the presence of seal-cutting workshops at Susa itself (Amiet 1972a: 189). One particular group of seals from Susa is made of frit or faience and shows horned monsters and animals. Although this was attributed to the 'Guti' (mountain-dwellers in the northern Zagros, see below) by Henri Frankfort (Frankfort 1955: 33; see also Amiet 1972a: 192; Porada 1965: 41–2), such an ethnic attribution is pure speculation.

Nearly sixty predominantly female clay figurines from Susa have been attributed to the Old Akkadian period, and while some of these, like other categories of material culture discussed above, reflect Mesopotamian styles, the majority do not, indicating rather that in this domain an indigenous tradition persisted in spite of foreign political domination (Spycket 1992: 25). Interestingly, one of the Susa figurines is decorated with paint in the style of the painted figurines known from contemporary Tal-i Malyan. The significance of these figurines is unclear. The promotion of fertility, a function as toys, substitutions for sacrifice, role-play in rituals, dedications to deities, representations of worshippers and other roles can all have applied to particular types of figurines in antiquity (Black and Green 1992: 81, 144).

Gaining an understanding of Susa and the Susians under Akkadian occupation is a

Table 4.11. *Diagnostic metal artifact types at Susa during the late third millennium* BC

Object	Type	Susa contexts	Comparanda	Date range
shaft-hole axe	A1	tombs A112, 125 Donjon	U.12484, PG 1422, RCU unpubl., PG 1395, RCU Takht-i Khan (Luristan) 'Luristan' (Ashmolean) victory stela from Tello Gudea stela in Berlin Ur-Namma stela from Ur	Ur III early Old Akkadian late Early Dynastic III Old Akkadian? Old Akkadian, post-Sargon early Ur III early Ur III
	A3a	unstratified	'Luristan' (Ashmolean, Louvre) War Kabud Mihr (Luristan) Takht-i Khan (Luristan) Tepe Giyan (Luristan) Tepe Khazineh (Khuzistan)	? Early Dynastic II? c. 2500 BC? late Early Dynastic III Giyan IVB / late third millennium late Early Dynastic, Old Akkadian?
tubular cudgel	A1	tomb A125, Donjon	U.9137, PG 580, RCU 'Luristan' (Ashmolean, Louvre) Tello	Early Dynastic IIIA ? ?
	A2	Donjon tomb 555, V.R. I	Shahdad (Kerman) 'Nihevand' 'Luristan'	? ? ?
tanged point	A3a	unstratified	RCU type 6	Early Dynastic IIIA
square-sectioned point	A4a	unstratified, V.R. I	RCU type 1/1b Assur, Ishtar temple Tell Billa Kara Hasan (Syria) Tell Mumbaqa (Syria) 'Luristan' Tepe Aliabad (Khuzistan)	Early Dynastic III Old Akkadian (Manistusu), Ur III ? late third millennium late third millennium Ur III ?
socketed point	B1a	Donjon	Mari	late Early Dynastic, early Old Akkadian
blade axe	B3, C3	unstratified	Tell al-'Ubaid sites in Palestine, N. Mesopotamia,	Early Dynastic IIIb Early Dynastic III various

Table 4.11 (cont.)

Object	Type	Susa contexts	Comparanda	Date range
burins/graver	B4, C4, F3	unstratified	Anatolia, Syria, Indus Valley	
			Cemetery A, Kish	Early Dynastic III – Old Akkadian
			RCU	Early Dynastic III – Old Akkadian
			Troy II, IV	
			Kültepe Ib	
			Byblos	nineteenth cent. BC
adze	C1	Donjon	RCU	Early Dynastic III
			Cemetery A, Kish	Early Dynastic III – Old Akkadian
			Tello	Early Dynastic III
			Tepe Gawra VI	Akkadian/Post-Akkadian
			Assur	Old Akkadian – Ur III
			Sardant (Luristan)	Old Akkadian – Ur III
sickle	A2	unstratified	Mari	Naram-Sin
pan	A5a	tomb A196, Donjon	Chanhu-Daro (Pakistan)	
			Mohenjo-Daro (Pakistan), lower and upper levels	
			Altyn-depe (Turkmenistan)	
			'Bactria' (Louvre)	
	A5b	unstratified	RCU	Early Dynastic – Old Akkadian
			Cemetery A, Kish	
			Tello	
			Tepe Gawra VI	Akkadian/Post-Akkadian
cylindrical vase	B2b	Donjon tombs	RCU	Early Dynastic III – Old Akkadian
	G1a/a′	Donjon tombs	RCU	Early Dynastic III – Old Akkadian
			Tell al-'Ubaid tomb 76	
			Cemetery A, Kish	
			Shahdad	?
square-headed pin	A2b/b′	unstratified	Geoy Tepe D	early second millennium
			Sardamt. Gululal-i Galbi	late Early Dynastic – Old Akkadian

cylindrical-headed pin	G	Acropole, unstratified	Tell al-'Ubaid	Early Dynastic III – Old Akkadian
			Tello	?
			Tell al-Wilayah	late third millennium
			Cemetery A, Kish	
			RCU	Early Dynastic III – Ur III
			Darwand (Luristan)	Old Akkadian
			Kalleh Nisar (Luristan)	Early Dynastic III – Old Akkadian
			Bani Surmah (Luristan)	Early Dynastic III
			Deh Luran (Khuzistan)	?

Note: Data drawn from Tallon 1987. Types (A1, B4, etc.) are as defined by Tallon. RCU = Royal Cemetery of Ur, P6 = Private Grave (at Ur). U-numbers (e.g. U.12484) are Ur excavation registration numbers.

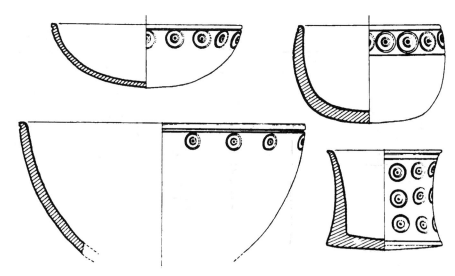

Figure 4.6 *Série récente* soft-stone from Susa (after de Miroschedji 1973: Fig. 8).

difficult task. The existence of some thirty-two small farmsteads or hamlets, ranging in size from c. .2–.7 ha, around Susa itself (Carter 1985: 45) and all unexcavated gives us only a hint of the city's agricultural hinterland in the Akkadian period. Similarly, the overwhelmingly Akkadian style of the ceramics, metals, and cylinder seals from Susa, and the cuneiform sources documenting the site's troubled relationship with the Akkadian empire, can all too easily lead one to overlook the non-Akkadian dimensions of Susa's existence. In fact, there is a varied corpus of material from Susa, most of it unstratified but generally attributable to the Old Akkadian and/or Ur III periods, which reflects relations with the Indus Valley, Oman peninsula, and Persian Gulf region generally. No fewer than 71 of the 170 cylinder seals of Old Akkadian type from Susa are made of shell (Amiet 1972a: 192–207), and both incised shell bangles and perforated discs of Mature Harappan type, all made of *Turbinella pyrum*, have been found at Susa as well (Gensheimer 1984: 71). Amiet has also drawn attention to the presence of a cylinder seal and a stamp seal with Harappan characters from Susa, as well as a single Harappan weight, and a number of etched carnelian beads, all of which derive from the Indus Valley (Amiet 1986c: 143–4) and most probably date to somewhere within the final three or four centuries of the third millennium BC. Similarly, a large number of *série récente* soft-stone bowls with double-dotted circle decoration (Fig. 4.6) found at Susa (de Miroschedji 1973) can unhesitatingly be attributed to the Oman peninsula, while a number of flasks (Fig. 4.7) are, based on their shape and decoration, just as clearly Bactrian (Amiet 1980a). Objects such as these reached Susa through mechanisms which we are at a loss to reconstruct. Nevertheless, their very presence in Khuzistan is an indication that, whatever else the Akkadian and Ur III administrations did at the site, they did not stop the flow of goods and, presumably, ideas from points south, east and north into an area which had long been connected with a wide array of distant lands.

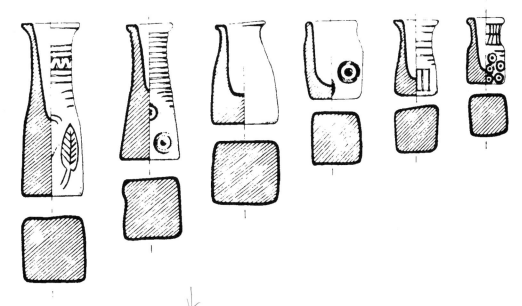

Figure 4.7 Soft-stone flasks of Bactrian type from Susa (after de Miroschedji 1973: Fig. 11).

The Fall of Agade

In the *Sumerian King List* the Old Akkadian kings are followed by twenty-one kings of Gutium, six of whom are attested in other sources (year formulae, royal inscriptions, building inscriptions of officials at Uruk and Umma) as well (Gelb and Kienast 1990: 293–4). The King List grants these twenty-one rulers a span of only 91 years. A synchronism between the last Gutian king, Tirigan, and Utuhegal of Uruk (2117–2111 BC) would thereby set the beginnings of the dynasty under Imtaa in the reign of Sharkalisharri, a date which is entirely plausible given that the third Gutian king, Sarlagab, is mentioned (as having been captured) in a year formula of Sharkalisharri's (Gelb and Kienast 1990: 54).

Although Glassner has expressed considerable scepticism about the alleged role played by the Guti in bringing about the downfall of the house of Agade (Glassner 1986: 48–50), as Frayne has observed, the fact that 'a list of 21 kings of their dynasty was included in the king list was undoubtedly a recognition by Nippur of the reality of their control, for at least part of the post Akkad period, over the city' (Frayne 1991; 404, n. 141). Furthermore, Gutians are certainly attested in cuneiform sources, e.g. at Adab, Umma and probably in the vicinity of Lagash, during the Old Akkadian period (Zadok 1994: 49). Generally identified with a portion of the northern Zagros mountains in western Iran ('some or all of the highlands northeast of the lower Tigris', Hallo 1971: 708), Gutium was probably a near, northern neighbour of areas considered to comprise Elam, for one Gutian royal name, Si-ù-um, is homonymous with a district attested in the Ur III period as part of 'greater Elam' (Zadok 1991: 226 and 1994: 49). Zadok has suggested that Gutium was located in the same region as the later region of Mannai, an area which today comprises part of Iranian Azerbaijan near Lake Urmia (Zadok 1993: 237; see also 1986a: 245).

Puzur-Inshushinak and his times

The relationship between Gutium and the regions designated properly 'Elamite' is difficult if not impossible to determine, just as the political situation at Susa following the reign of Sharkalisharri is largely unknown to us. An Old Babylonian copy of an inscription of the founder of the Third Dynasty of Ur, Ur-Namma, found at Isin, names Puzur-Inshushinak, the last king of Awan named in the Susa kinglist, as one of his adversaries (Wilcke 1987: 108). Thus, we can confidently date Puzur-Inshushinak to *c.* 2100 BC.

Puzur-Inshushinak is known to us from no fewer than twelve inscriptions (Table 4.12). His ethnicity has recently been queried by Glassner, who asks whether he was a Susian of royal blood, as his name would suggest (Inshushinak was the main deity of Susa; see Lambert 1979: 24), who made his career by rising in the ranks of the Old Akkadian political administration (presumably of Susa), or an Elamite king who was able to seize control of Susa (Glassner 1988: 51). In fact, there are at least two further possibilities. Both the Susian kinglist (André-Salvini 1992: 261) and an inscribed stone staircase fragment (André and Salvini 1989: 65) call Puzur-Inshushinak 'king of Awan', which, as argued above, may be the area of the Pusht-i Kuh and not necessarily coterminous with a portion of Elam. On the other hand, the Isin inscription (Wilcke 1987: 108–11), while it calls Puzur-Inshushinak king of Elam, suggests that the cities 'enslaved by Anshan' at the time of Ur-Namma (Steinkeller 1987: 19, n. 1) were the very ones said in the Isin text to have been conquered by Puzur-Inshushinak. Could the king then have hailed from Anshan, or are we simply witnessing a relaxed attitude to different designations like Elam, Awan and Anshan, on the part of the scribes who wrote the texts in question?

Puzur-Inshushinak's titulature varies considerably throughout his texts. Unfortunately, these cannot be ordered chronologically with any degree of certitude. In those texts with the titles still preserved, Puzur-Inshushinak appears alternately as

>governor (**ensí**) of Susa (texts 10 and 12)
>governor (**ensí**) of Susa, GÌR.NÍTA of the land of Elam, and son of Shimpi'ishhuk (texts 2, 4, 5, 6, 9 and with altered positions 3)
>the mighty (**dannum**), king (**lugal**) of Awan, and son of Shimpi'ishhuk (texts 7 and 8)

It is tempting to see the proposed sequence of titles as a reflection of a progression from governor of Susa, to ruler (however one wishes to translate GÌR.NÍTA, see the discussion above) of Elam, and finally to king of Awan (André and Salvini 1989: 69–70; see also André-Salvini 1992: 262). Gelb and Kienast have questioned whether the latter title and indeed the Susa list of Awanite kings in fact reflect any sort of political reality (Gelb and Kienast 1990: 318), and one may share their scepticism on many grounds, but

Table 4.12. *Inscriptions of Puzur-Inshushinak*

Puzur-Inshushinak text	Summary
1	P, governor (**ensí**) of Susa, GÌR.NÍ[TA] of the land of Elam, son of Simpi'ishhuk, captured the enemies of Kimash and Hurtum, destroyed Hupsana and crushed under his feet in one day 81 towns and regions; when the king of Shimashki came to him, he (the king) grabbed his (Puzur-Inshushinak's) feet; Inshushinak heard his prayers and . . .
2	after opening the canal to/from Sidari, he erected a statue in front of the gate of the temple of Inshushinak and decorated the gate with a copper-covered cedar bar/bolt; a sheep at dawn and a sheep in the evening were chosen daily for sacrifice and singers sang day and night at the temple gate; he dedicated pure oil for the care of the gate, four silver objects, the 'desired' emblem of gold and silver, a dagger, and an axe with four 'leaves'; whoever seeks to remove these votive objects should have his roots torn out and his seeds removed by Inshushinak, Shamash, Enlil, Enki, Ishtar, Sin, Ninhursag, Narunte and the totality of the gods
3	Akkadian text: dedication of a foundation text/object for Inshushinak by P.; Linear Elamite text: dedication of a 'wooden stake' for the temple of Inshushinak
4	dedication of a statue to the deity AL.UR.KA
5	dedication of a statue to the deity Belatterraban
6	commemoration of a staircase for Inshushinak erected by P., the mighty, king of Awan, son of Shimpi'shhuk
7	as no. 6
8	commemoration of the building of the temple of the deity SU.GU by P.
9	Akkadian text: dedication of a statue to the goddess Narunte by P.; Elamite text: victory effected by Narunte, whose help is sought by P.
10	door-socket naming P., governor (**ensí**) of Elam
11	Akkadian text: curse on a statue fragment calling on the gods to tear out the roots and take the seeds of anyone (i.e. who removes the statue); Elamite text: names P. as dedicant of the statue
12	bas-relief of a lion with a curse upon anyone who removes the inscription

the fact that Puzur-Inshushinak's father is not listed among the kings of Awan can hardly be one of them. This may simply reflect the fact that Puzur-Inshushinak was not of Awanite blood, or of royal Awanite blood, or of the main line of kings, assuming that the names indeed reflect a single dynasty. On the other hand, Puzur-Inshushinak may have been a Susian, as his name suggests, and not a highlander at all, and he may have simply taken on the title 'king of Awan', much like his Mesopotamian counterparts used the ancient title 'king of Kish', to legitimate his claim to sovereignty.

Alternatively, the Awan kinglist may indeed be fictitious, nothing more than a summation of the names of various Elamite kings who had preceded Puzur-Inshushinak (Gelb and Kienast 1990: 318). Unfortunately, at the moment it is impossible to know where the truth lies. The fact that a number of the inscribed objects attributable to Puzur-Inshushinak were inscribed in Elamite as well as Akkadian suggests that, if he didn't come from the highlands, then Puzur-Inshushinak was at pains to integrate both the highland and lowland regions to which he laid claim.

As to the realm which he could rightfully claim, Puzur-Inshushinak claims in one of his texts (Table 4.12.1) to have conquered eighty-one regions or towns, apparently in the Iranian, i.e. non-Mesopotamian, sphere (Gelb and Kienast 1990: 312–24). Unfortunately these are, for the most part, unattested in any other sources, although Huhnur, which occurs roughly halfway through the list, is mentioned in a large number of sources and is thought by some scholars to have been situated near modern Arjan, roughly midway between Susa and Anshan (Duchene 1986; see also Vallat 1993a: CXXXI). In his own inscriptions Puzur-Inshushinak never refers to any hostilities against the cities of Mesopotamia, but the Ur-Namma Isin text lists Awal, Kismar and Mashkan-sharrim, as well as the lands (**ma-da**) of Eshnunna, Tutub, Zimudar and Agade among the areas governed by Puzur-Inshushinak (Wilcke 1987: 110). This statement shows that Puzur-Inshushinak was particularly active in the Jabal Hamrin–Diyala–central Tigris district. Epigraphic discoveries at Tell as-Suleimeh in the Jabal Hamrin basin have identified that site as ancient Awal (Steinkeller 1981: 164); Mashkan-sharrim was situated along the Tigris, near the boundary between northern Babylonia and southernmost Assyria (Steinkeller 1982b: 289); and Kismar was located in its immediate vicinity (Steinkeller 1981: 165). Eshnunna is the site of Tell Asmar in the Diyala valley; Tutub is the nearby site of Khafajah; Zimudar is thought to have lain 'on or near the Diyala river' (Frayne 1992: 56); and the land of Agade perhaps refers to the area between the Tigris and Euphrates approximately between the latitude of Fallujah-Baghdad and Seleucia-Sippar (Wilcke 1987: 110).

The acquisition of these territories is significant, but their enumeration clearly differs from what we find in the prologue of the so-called 'Ur-Namma Code' from Sippar where we read: 'at that time, Akshak(!), Mar(a)da, X, Kazallu, and their settlements, (and) Usarum, (and) whatsoever had been enslaved by Anshan, through the strength of Nanna, my lord, I established their freedom' (Steinkeller 1987: 19, n. 1). Both Steinkeller and Glassner believe that Ur-Namma's attempt to wrest control of northern Babylonia from the Anshanites is reflected in the Isin account of his conflict with Puzur-Inshushinak (Steineller 1987: 20, n. 1; see also 1988b: 52, n. 20; Glassner 1988: 51). However, whereas Akshak has been located on the middle Tigris, Kazallu is thought to have lain along the Euphrates northwest of Babylon, while Mar(a)da is located much further south, roughly halfway between Isin and Babylon (Frayne 1992: Maps 2 and 4). If the enslavement of these latter cities by Anshan was yet a further projection of power by Puzur-Inshushinak from the Diyala–east Tigridian region into the heart of Babylonia, then it certainly bespeaks considerable effort and success on his part and may well have justified taking so grand a title as 'king of Awan', presumably after he had already become ruler (GÌR.NÍTA) of Elam and well after his original accession to the **ensí**-ship of Susa.

Be that as it may, the Ur-Namma Isin text makes it clear that Puzur-Inshushinak's pretensions to the hegemony of Mesopotamia were brought up short by his defeat at the hands of Ur-Namma. Moreover, the campaign against Puzur-Inshushinak may be echoed in yet another inscription roughly contemporary with Ur-Namma, Statue B vi 64–69 of Gudea, ruler of Lagash, who says that 'he smote the city of Anshan in/of Elam' (Steinkeller 1988b: 52). Until recently it was generally thought that Gudea flourished some decades prior to Ur-Namma's rise to power (e.g. Edzard 1967b: 122), but Steinkeller has now shown that the reigns of Ur-Namma and Gudea overlapped (Steinkeller 1988b). In view of this fact, and in view of the apparently enormous extent of Puzur-Inshushinak's realm at the time of Ur-Namma's rise to power, it seems more likely that the ruler of Lagash was acting in concert with Ur-Namma when he fought against Anshan, rather than launching his own raid deep into the heart of southwestern Iran. It may even be that two texts from Lagash (RTC 249 and MVN 10: 92) 'which record barley-allotments to the same group of foreigners', some of whom are called 'sons of Shimbishu', allude to captive members or dependents of Puzur-Inshushinak's family, for Shimbishu is thought to be the same as Shimpi'ishhuk, the name of Puzur-Inshushinak's father (Steinkeller 1988b: 53, n. 21). Certainly Gudea boasted (Cylinder A XV 6ff.) that, in connection with the construction of the Eninnu, the major temple to Ningirsu at Girsu, 'Elamites came to him from Elam, Susians came to him from Susa' (see also the discussion in Neumann 1992: 273–4).

A further point of interest in relation to the extent of Puzur-Inshushinak's 'empire' has been raised by Amiet. A seal impression found at Susa early in this century which shows two standing females, possibly wearing horned-crowns and therefore divine, has been compared by Amiet with a fragmentary cylinder seal from Tepe Yahya and a seal from the Tod treasure in Egypt. Amiet suggests that all three seals are examples of late 'Trans-Elamite' art (Amiet 1994a: 1–4). While the affinities between the seals are clear enough, the recognition of a cultural phenomenon which can be called Trans-Elamite is more problematic, as discussed above, and any relationship to the short-lived 'empire' of Puzur-Inshushinak is pure speculation.

Puzur-Inshushinak and Linear Elamite

In Chapter 3 we discussed the almost certainly fallacious link sometimes alleged to have existed between the Susa III or 'Proto-Elamite' writing system and so-called Linear Elamite. To date, twenty-one examples of Linear Elamite have been recovered (André and Salvini 1989: 58). Although the vast majority of these fragmentary, often lapidary inscriptions (Fig. 4.8) comes from Susa, examples are known from Shahdad, on the fringes of the Dasht-i Lut in northeastern Kerman province, and from the vicinity of Persepolis (see Hinz 1969; 1971a; Vallat 1986a: 342; Calmeyer 1989). The linguistic

Figure 4.8 Linear Elamite lapidary inscription (A) from Susa (after de Mecquenem 1949: Fig. 3).

details of the attempts at decipherment by F. Bork in 1905, C. Frank in 1912, W. Hinz in 1969, P. Meriggi in 1971 and F. Vallat in 1986 need not concern us. Suffice it to say that, as indicated in Table 4.12, the presence of short Linear Elamite texts on objects with Akkadian inscriptions has led to the not unreasonable hypothesis that the former may be truncated translations of the latter, and this has been the basis for most attempts at decipherment. However, as Vallat has stressed, 'of the 103 signs recorded, more than 40 are hapax legomena, i.e. the signs are attested only once, or they are always attested in the same context', making decipherment especially difficult (Vallat 1986a: 343). As all of the Linear Elamite inscriptions from Susa relate to Puzur-Inshushinak, it is probably safe to assume the same date for the examples from Shahdad and Fars. In view of the now certain synchronism between Ur-Namma and Puzur-Inshushinak, the time gap between the Susa III and Linear Elamite writing systems, once thought to be on the order of 700 years (when Puzur-Inshushinak was considered a contemporary of Naram-Sin's) is actually more like 900 years. Thus, the notion of continuity between them is impossible to sustain. Whether or not the Linear Elamite system was actually invented by a scribe serving under Puzur-Inshushinak, or whether it had any antecedents in the highlands, the paucity of texts and their absence follow-ing Puzur-Inshushinak's reign suggests that at Susa, which had been heavily Akkadianized in the preceding two centuries, the cuneiform writing system and Akkadian language were found to be much more practicable than the nascent Linear Elamite one which seems to have died out with the demise of the Awanite king's realm.

The secondary state of Awan under Puzur-Inshushinak?

It has been suggested that a later response to Ur III hegemony in western Iran (see Chapter 5) was the creation of a 'secondary state' centred on Shimashki, but if the logic of that argument is accepted, and if we adopt the perspective of those texts in which Puzur-Inshushinak is regarded as 'mighty king of Awan', then one might be tempted to draw a similar conclusion with respect to the Awan of Puzur-Inshushinak and describe it as a secondary state as well. Unlike 'primary' states, which are thought to 'have been formed, by means of internal or regional development, without the stimulus of other pre-existing state forms', secondary or 'derived' states 'result from a "response" imposed by the presence of a neighbouring state, a power centre that eventually modifies the equilibrium established over a wide area' (Balandier 1972: 154).

Whether or not one chooses to term Awan a secondary state – and I am not persuaded that this alone advances the cause of its analysis very far – the coalescence of Awan as an entity in opposition to Early Dynastic Mesopotamia (itself far less monolithic than the term might imply to the casual reader) and later the Old Akkadian empire is likely to have involved some reaction to foreign aggression. As Roosens has observed, 'the intensity with which a group profiles itself as an ethnic group, and with which individuals stress their ethnicity, generally increases when there is intense spatial-geographical and social contact between groups. The most isolated "traditional" group of people is probably the least ethnically self-defined' (Roosens 1989: 13).

This is not to say that there were no trends towards greater social differentiation, stratification or organizational complexity already present in the region which became identified as Awan before we see Awan in the guise in which it appears in the *Sumerian King List* or the Ur-Namma inscription from Isin. But of any such trends we are ignorant, and recourse to the archaeological assemblages of the Pusht-i Kuh, adduced as a likely location for Awan, can provide little evidence of complexity or otherwise. The image we have of Puzur-Inshushinak from the Isin account of his conquests is one of an expansive leader in the tradition of Sargon himself, and this may prompt some readers to accept the possibility that Puzur-Inshushinak's Awan was indeed a secondary state. But if Puzur-Inshushinak had any role models, these may have been very different from the Akkadian kings and purely local, such as the king of Awan who attacked Ur and carried off its kingship according to the *Sumerian King List*. An ambitious leader like Puzur-Inshushinak scarcely needs 'explaining' through recourse to a simplistic model of secondary state development. His abilities and ambitions may have been quite unique and his awareness of Old Akkadian or Early Dynastic precedents quite deficient. Yet his annexation of Susa and his conquests in Mesopotamia bespeak a ruler of considerable talent who was able to organize support and a military contingent capable of seizing territory in both the periphery and core area of his western neighbour. To dismiss his social formation, whether state or not, as ephemeral would be unjust, for the Old Akkadian state went through periods at least as traumatic and fraught with disintegration as Awan seems to have done once Puzur-Inshushinak had been dealt with by Ur-Namma.

Date	Lowlands	Highlands	Mesopotamia	'Elam'
2900–2350 BC	predominance of Early Dynastic Mesopotamian styles (seals, statuary) at Susa; graves there have clear ceramic links to Luristan and northern Khuzistan	Godin Tepe III and cemeteries in Pusht-i Kuh show ceramic links with Diyala, Hamrin, northern Khuzistan, Susa, Lagash; identification of Pusht-i Kuh with Awan? abandonment of Tal-i Malyan c. 2600 BC	Early Dynastic (ED) period; Sumerian King List refers to attacks on Elam, attacks by Awan in ED II or early ED III; Eannatum of Lagash Claims conquest of Elam in late ED III times	Elam and Awan appear as adversaries of Kish and Lagash; Awan a highland entity in Luristan which spread its influence to Susiana; did Mesopotamian scribes use 'Awan' and 'Elam' interchangeably? Is greater independence in 'Elam' compatible with ED influence at Susa? Was the rise of Awan a reaction to an ED Mesopotamian presence at Susa?
c. 2330 BC	conquest of Susa by Sargon of Agade	aggression by Sargon against Awan, Barahshum, Elam, parts of Shimashki and Sherihum	consolidation of Akkadian empire	a mosaic of regions allied against Akkad; leaders have linguistically Elamite names as well as non-Elamite ones in Mesopotamian sources; 'king' of Elam mentioned
c. 2275 BC	campaigns against Susa by Rimush; introduction of Akkadian bureaucratic officials, accounting procedures; use of Mesopotamian pottery	campaigns against Barahshum, Zahara and Gupin	general rebellion in Mesopotamia, crushing of revolt by Rimush	Elam and Barahshum appear as chief adversaries of Akkad; 'king' of Elam mentioned

	shapes, metal types, cylinder seals; contacts with Indus and Oman			
c. 2260 BC	Akkadian governors in Elam and Pashime	Manishtusu campaigns against Anshan and Sherihum	Akkadian expansion in Assyria	Akkadian governors, rebellions in highlands signal attempted consolidation of power around Anshan?
c. 2250 BC	Akkadian governor at Susa; construction of a temple at Susa by Naram-Sin	campaigns against Elam and Barahshum	general rebellion against Naram-Sin, apotheosis of Akkadian king	continuing rebellion in highlands against Akkadian rule, ongoing Akkadian presence at Susa, treaty between Naram-Sin and unnamed ruler in Old Elam
c. 2200 BC	Akkadian governor at Susa, administrative texts	forces from Elam and Zahara take fight against Akkad to northern Babylonia; inter-dynastic marriage with princess of Marhashi	rebellions against Sharkalisharri	consolidation of forces to the point where Elam and Zahara were capable of attacking Babylonia
c. 2100 BC	status of Susa following fall of Akkadian state unclear; Puzur-Inshushinak called 'governor' of Susa; use of Linear Elamite writing system	Puzur-Inshushinak, king of Awan, campaigning in east Tigris region; use of Linear Elamite writing system	following fall of Akkad, period of rule by Gutian kings from northwestern Iran (?); attacks by Puzur-Inshushinak; eventual liberation by Ur-Namma, Founder of third Dynasty of Ur	use of Awan, Elam and Anshan with reference to Puzur-Inshushinak may reflect political realities, or may be Mesopotamian scribal usage without particular meaning

THE DYNASTY OF SHIMASHKI

Puzur-Inshushinak's reign was followed by a period of renewed Mesopotamian control over Susa, this time by a dynasty established by Ur-Namma at Ur in southern Mesopotamia around 2100 BC which lasted for almost a century (the so-called Third Dynasty of Ur or Ur III empire). Apart from controlling Susa the Ur III state entered into relations with other Iranian regions such as Anshan and her neighbours on the Iranian Plateau through a pattern of dynastic inter-marriage with local elites.

But as texts from the mid- to late Ur III period show, a new power centred on the region of Shimashki was on the rise in western Iran, no doubt partly as a reaction against Ur's political imperialism. It is important therefore to investigate the role played by Elam in general and Shimashki in particular in the eventual downfall of the Third Dynasty of Ur around 2000 BC, particularly the contribution made by Kindattu, the sixth king mentioned in a list of the kings of Awan and Shimashki found at Susa. Shimashkian influence in the wake of Ur's collapse, while difficult to gauge accurately, clearly extended beyond the confines of Susiana. The difficulty of defining the boundaries of Shimashkian influence makes it awkward to point to specific archaeological assemblages from Fars and Khuzistan which can be associated with Shimashki, but it is important to keep the political history of the period in mind when assessing the material culture of the late third and early second millennium BC. It is also important to bear in mind what the relative contributions of the Iranian highlands and lowlands may have been in the often shadowy political processes which we seek to follow at this time.

Susa, Anshan and the Third Dynasty of Ur

As we have seen, Puzur-Inshushinak's westward expansion was checked by Ur-Namma, founder of the Third Dynasty of Ur. Yet his defeat signalled not merely a loss of those areas near the Diyala and Tigris which he had formerly held. It also marked Susa's loss of independence, opened the way for Mesopotamian attacks deep into Iranian territory and ushered in an era which would witness the vassaldom of Anshan (Fig. 5.1).

Apart from the reconquest of northern Babylonia and the Trans-Tigridian area discussed above, it is difficult to ascertain just how much was achieved in the Iranian sphere by Ur-Namma himself. None of his year names (Sigrist and Gomi 1991: 319–20) mention Susa, Elam or any other points east, and it is not until the reign of Ur-Namma's son and successor, Shulgi, that we find clear evidence of Ur's control over Susa. The documentation reflecting Shulgi's involvement with Susa is limited but nonetheless informative. A macehead, dedicated by a maritime trader (**garaš-a-ab-ba**)

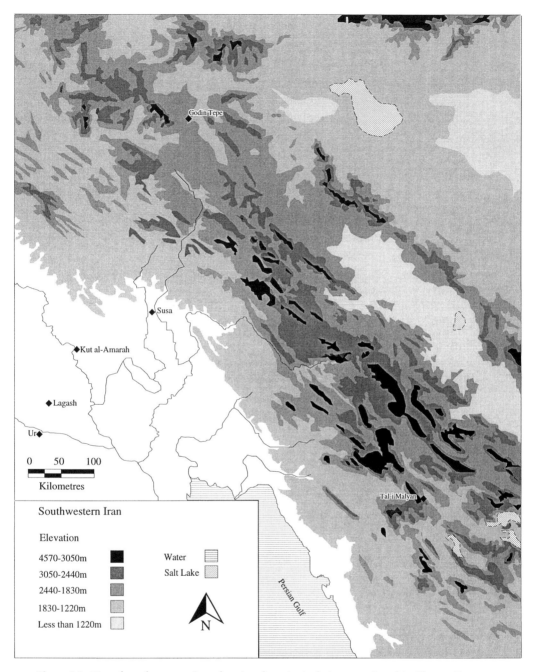

Figure 5.1 Map of southwestern Iran showing the principal sites mentioned in Chapter 5.

'to (the goddess) Ninuruamugub, his lady, for the life of Shulgi, the mighty male, the king of Ur' (Lambert 1979: 30), and four bricks commemorating Shulgi's restoration of the temple of Inshushinak at Susa (Malbran-Labat 1995: 22) all bear the king's name without the divine determinative. This implies that they should be dated prior to Shulgi's apotheosis which occurred in the 23rd year of his reign (Sigrist 1992: 8). Activities after this year are, however, indicated by a foundation figurine (Pl. 5.1) from the temple of Ninhursag at Susa (Tallon 1987/I: 63, II: 130–1, 341–3; see also Carter 1990: 95), a carnelian bead with a dedication to Ningal (Pl. 5.2), and a bronze hammer with two birds heads, perhaps given to a high functionary serving under Shulgi (de Mecquenem 1953: 82; Amiet 1986c: 146; Brentjes 1991: 5), bearing an inscription which reads 'Shulgi, the mighty male, king of Ur, king of Sumer and Akkad' (Lambert 1979: 29). On both of these objects Shulgi's name is preceded by the divine determinative **dingir**.

Shulgi is credited with a thorough overhaul or 'modernization' of the realm inherited from his father. This included initiatives in the military (reorganization of the army), bureaucratic (reform of the writing system, reform of weights and measures, creation of a powerful and centralized bureaucracy), judicial (promulgation of a law code, that known as the Ur-Namma code), calendric (unification of calendars throughout the empire), taxation (unification of the tax system throughout the empire), communication (creation or reform of a system of rapid flow of information throughout the empire) and land tenure (reform of land tenure principles relating to the palace and temples) spheres (Sigrist 1992: 9; Steinkeller 1987: 20–1). In one of the royal hymns of Shulgi, we even read 'I actually know the tongue of Elam like the tongue of Sumer' (Castellino 1972: 257, C: 122), a sure sign that he took his relations with the east seriously.

Of particular interest for us is the fact that to the east of the Mesopotamian core area of the empire (roughly between the Diyala and Ur), as defined by Steinkeller (Steinkeller 1987: Fig. 1), lay a series of 'unincorporated territories' in which large numbers of soldiers were settled in 1. small settlements commanded by junior captains; 2. medium-sized settlements under the command of senior captains; and 3. large settlements run by generals or governors. Susa, Sabum and Urua were each controlled by a governor. An individual named to such a high-ranking post might serve in either a civil (governorship) or military (generalship) capacity, and in the case of Zariqum, we know that he served in turn as governor (**ensí**) of Susa, captain (**nu-banda**) of Assur, governor (**ensí**) of Assur, and again governor (**ensí**) of Susa, where he spent the final eight years (Amar-Sin 4/XII-Shu-Sin 4/II/2) of a twenty-two year career spanning the period from Shulgi 40 to Shu-Sin 4 (Hallo 1956: 221; see also Kutscher 1979: 81). In the twelfth month of the year Shulgi 40, Zariqum and Shamshi-illat were given leather shoes at Puzrish-Dagan (modern Drehem) for their journey from Nippur to Susa (Kutscher 1979: 81; Sigrist 1992: 397), and in the year Amar-Sin 9, a payment in silver was made to Zariqum at Ur (Sigrist 1992: 384, Tab. 1458).

All of the military personnel in the periphery of the Ur III state were required to pay 'tax of the province' (**gú/gún** or **gún ma-da**) (Sigrist 1992: 100; Steinkeller 1987). Of the roughly 90 settlements from which this tax was collected, several are of particular

Plate 5.1 Bronze foundation figurine from Susa (Sb 2881) with a nine-line inscription reading, 'the god "Lord of Susa" [Inshushinak], his king, Shulgi, the mighty male, king of Ur, king of Sumer and Akkad, the . . . , his beloved temple, built' (trans. after Thureau-Dangin 1907: 193). © Musée du Louvre, Antiquités Orientales

Plate 5.2 Carnelian bead from Susa (Sb 6627) engraved with a Sumerian dedication reading, 'Ningal, his mother, Shulgi, god of his land, king of Ur, king of the four world quarters, for his life dedicated (this)' (trans. after Thureau-Dangin 1907: 195). © Musée du Louvre, Antiquités Orientales

interest: Sabum, Susa, Shu'irhum, and Urua (Steinkeller 1987: 36–7, n. 56). As discussed in Chapter 4, Urua figured alongside Awan in the pre-Sargonic and Sargonic periods as an eastern adversary, as did Sabum and Shu'irhum. Susa's tax payment of 1869 animals in the 46th year of Shulgi's reign (CST 124) is the first such tax recorded, followed two years later by payments from Adamdun (near Kut al-Amara? see Frayne 1992: 125, n. 327) and Sabum (another payment from Sabum is attested in Amar-Sin 4; see Sigrist 1992: 368), while on another occasion in the reign of Shu-Sin, Urua delivered one mina (*c.* 500 g) of silver (Michalowski 1978: 35; Sigrist 1992: 100). In other cases, livestock was transferred to Susa, as for instance when Abbashaga, the official in charge of all deliveries and transferals of livestock at Puzrish-Dagan during the reign of Amar-Sin, transferred 3586 sheep to Beli-arik, governor (**ensí**) of Susa (DV 5: 479; see Sigrist 1992: 65, n. 82), or when Abbashaga received 150 sheep from Beli-Arik (Sigrist and Butz 1986: 30). Given the distance involved, however, and the likelihood that travel for upwards of ten days overland could seriously diminish a herd moving between Susa and Puzrish-Dagan, it is thought likely that these were 'technical transfers' of credits and debits in the ledgers of Puzrish-Dagan, rather than physical transfers of livestock (Sigrist 1992: 65).

Susa and the other nearby cities in this peripheral zone did not, however, participate in the **bala** institution, whereby taxes were paid by the core cities and livestock were drawn from a central fund administered at Puzrish-Dagan (Steinkeller 1987: 29), and the fact that Zariqum is recorded (PDT 1: 557; Hallo 1960: 98) as having paid **bala** is interpreted by Hallo as 'an apparent exception to this rule, for it was a kind of personal obligation due when, in or about Amar-Sin 4/XII, he was transferred from Assur to Susa' (Hallo 1960: 92). On the other hand, the military colonists of Sabum are known to have sent voluntarily no fewer than 600 sheep as a votive offering to Ninhursag of Al-sharrukin via the livestock depot of Puzrish-Dagan on one occasion (Sigrist 1992: 134).

Beyond this taxable area, however, lay still more distant lands (Table 5.1), such as Marhashi, Anshan, Huhnur, Kimash, Hu'urti and Shimashki, comprised of a number of constituent parts, the most important of which was Zabshali. These regions were not considered part of the Ur III periphery, and their status varied through time. The rulers of these areas were apparently indiscriminately referred to as kings (**lugal**), e.g. the 'king of Marhashi', or governor (**ensí**), e.g. the 'governor of Zabshali', 'governor of Anshan' or 'governor of Marhashi' (Tables 5.2–3). One might be tempted to suggest, therefore, that Marhashi was more independent of Ur's influence than Anshan because of the fact that at least one of its rulers was designated king, whereas Anshan's ruler was called governor, but this is pure speculation, and Michalowski notes that the term **ensí** 'was used in Ur III documents to refer to appointed governors as well as to independent foreign rulers' (Michalowski 1978: 38–9). At times these areas were drawn into the political and presumably economic orbit of Ur by means of arranged marriages between the daughters of the kings of Ur and local rulers. At other times, however, these areas became the target of Ur's naked military aggression, yielding sizable amounts of booty including objects made of semi-precious stones, such as carnelian and lapis lazuli necklaces, as well as metals, including gold, silver, copper and bronze

Table 5.1. *Groups and countries constituting 'Elam' during the Ur III period*

'Nuclear' Elamite territory	Elamite areas the relative locations of which are unknown
1. Anshan	10. Itnigi/Anigi
2. Pashime (Parparrahupa)	11. Barbarranamba
3. Huhnur	12. Danhili (Gili)
4. Adamdun	13. Girkinam
5. Susa	14. Gisha
6. Iabrat	15. Gizili
7. Shimashki with 6 core	16. Hupum
dependencies	17. Hutum
a. Zabshali	18. NE-duhu(l)ni
b. Sig(i)rish	19. Siri
c. Iapulmat	20. Sitinrupum
d. Alumiddatum	21. Sium
e. Garta/Karda	22. Ulum/Ullium
f. Shatilu	23. Urri
	24. Zurbati
and another 11 semi-	25. Daba
dependencies	26. Garnene
g. Azahar	27. Iab/pib/pum
h. Pulma	28. Shazibi/Shaziga
i. Nushushmar	29. Husan
j. [x]-[x]-li	
k. Arahir	
l. [Lu?]-lu-bi-im	
m. Sisirtum	
n. Nishgamelum	
o. [x]-[x-x-a]m	
p. Ti-ir-mi-um	
q. Zitanu	
8. Zaul	
9. Iapru	

Notes:
Data drawn from Zadok 1991.

(Edzard 1959–60: 7; Pettinato 1982). Shulgi's campaigns against Kimash (years 46 and 48) and Shimashki (year 47) may explain why a number of Shimashkians (**lú Šimaški**) are recorded as having sworn an oath of allegiance in the first year of Shu-Sin's reign, and why some Kimashians (**lú Kimaš^ki**) did the same in the temple of Ninurta at Nippur in the same year (Sigrist 1992: 194–5).

Interdynastic marriage, as we have already seen, is first attested in this region during the reign of Sharkalisharri, whose son married a princess of Marhashi. Three of the five kings of Ur – Shulgi, Shu-Sin, and Ibbi-Sin – married their daughters to princes of Marhashi, Anshan, Pashime, and Zabshali (Table 5.2). Although the marriage of Shu-Sin's daughter to the ruler of Anshan is not commemorated in a year formula, an economic text, probably from Lagash or Girsu, records the commodities given out for the journey of the Ur princess to Anshan. She took with her 10 l of butter fat (**ì-nun**), 10 l of hard cheese (**ga**-ŠAR), 64 l of sesame oil (**ì-giš**), 120 l of apples (**hašhur-duru₅**) 180 kg of onions (**sum-sikil**) and 210 kg of garlic (**sum-gaz**) (Sigrist and Butz 1986: 28). One would think that the marriage of Shulgi's daughter to the governor of Anshan was especially significant, for the event served not just for the year name of the king's thirtieth year, but the following year was designated, in some sources, the 'year after the year the king's daughter was married to the governor of Anshan' (Sigrist and Gomi 1991: 323). And yet, judging by the dates of these marriages and the dates of the Ur III campaigns against some of the very same areas, the success of this strategy of interdynastic marriage is questionable (see Hallo 1976: 31; Pettinato 1982: 53). Moreover, the destruction of Anshan in year 34 was still invoked as the event by which the subsequent two years (35 and 36) were named (i.e. year after the year Anshan was destroyed and year after the second year, Anshan was destroyed), just as the subsequent destruction of Kimash in year 47 was still recalled in year 48 of Shulgi and year 1 of Amar-Sin, and the destruction of Zabshali in Shu-Sin's seventh year was remembered in year 8 (Sigrist and Gomi 1991: 323, 325, 327).

Nor were these 'conquests' simply propagandistic boasting which never occurred in reality. As proof that such conquests most certainly did occur, we have not only references to booty, such as that accumulated in the year Shulgi 48 as a result of the campaign against Kimash, Harshi and Susa (Sigrist 1992: 108), but also ration texts, such as one written in the fifth month of the year Amar-Sin 6, which records 17 **gur** of coarse flour (*c.* 2.57 tons) and 15 **gur** of bran-bread (*c.* 2.27 tons) which were allotted by the governor (**ensí**) of Umma for the prisoners 'from the land of Susa and from the land of Elam'. It is impossible to be certain how many prisoners might have been involved, but if the standard daily ration used for women of 2 l. is adopted, assuming that prisoners would receive less than their working male counterparts, then the quantity specified would have sufficed to feed 320 men (Sigrist and Butz 1986: 31).

Communications between the peripheral regions, the still more distant vassal states, and the centre at Ur were maintained by an efficient system of roads with rest houses resembling later Medieval *caravanserais*, in part established by Shulgi (Sigrist 1986: 51). These were used regularly by couriers (**sukkal** or **kaš₄**) and high officials (e.g. **ensís**) alike. Allotments made to travellers were laconically registered in the thousands of so-called 'messenger texts' of Ur III date (see Table 5.3). Those texts concerning messengers travelling between Elam and Lagash, a major transit point on the route from Susa to the capital Ur, have been treated in detail by a number of scholars over the years (e.g. Jean 1922; Jones and Snyder 1961: 297–300; Grégoire 1970: 202–14; Sigrist 1986). They show us Urkum, **ensí** of Susa, returning to Susa via Lagash; Aburanum, **ensí** of Sabum, passing through Lagash on his way to Nippur; and Dada, son-in-law of the king (possibly Amar-Sin), heading to Susa (Sigrist 1986: 55, none of these texts is dated).

Ambassadors from the Iranian east came frequently to the cities of the empire, and

Table 5.2. *Synopsis of relations between the Third Dynasty of Ur and Elam*

Monarch	Date	Event	Reference
Shulgi	Shulgi 18	year, 'Liwwir-mittashu, the king's daughter, was elevated to the ladyship (i.e. given in marriage) of Marhashi'	CC: 321
	Shulgi 30	year, 'the king's daughter was married to the governor (**ensí**) of Anshan'	CC: 323
	Shulgi 34	year, 'Anshan was destroyed'	CC: 323
	Shulgi 46	year, 'Shulgi, the mighty man, king of Ur, king of the four quarters, destroyed Kimash, Hu'urti and their lands in a single day'; ambassadors from Marhashi at Puzrish-Dagan	CC: 325
	Shulgi 47	booty of LÚ.SU, i.e. Shimashki, registered at Puzrish-Dagan (Drehem)	
	Shulgi 48	Shulgi's daughter, Taram-Shulgi, mentioned as wife of Shudda-bani, king of Pashime; year, 'Harshi, Kimash and u'urti and their lands were destroyed in a single day'; Kutu of Shigrish received as ambassador at Puzrish-Dagan	
Amar-Sin	AS 1	Rashi, ambassador of Zidanum in Elam, arrives at Puzrish-Dagan, remaining until AS 4; ambassadors from Shimashki also present	
	AS 3	return of the messenger Barashum from Marhashi	TRU 318
	AS 4	ambassadors from Kimash and Marhashi present at Puzrish-Dagan; messengers from Libanugshabash, **ensí** of Marhashi, present, along with messengers from Kimash	
	AS 7	year, 'the king Amar-Sin destroyed Bitum-rabium, Jabru, their neighbouring territories and Huhnur	CC: 326
Shu-Sin	SS 2	unnamed daughter of Shu-Sin travelled to Anshan, presumably for marriage	Tab. 2751
	SS 7	year, 'Shu-sin, the king of Ur, king of the four quarters, destroyed the land of Zabshali'; dedicated a statue of himself for Enlil, made of gold taken as booty in the lands of the Su people; the lands of Zabshali, Shigrish, Iabulmat, Alumiddatum, Karta, Shatilu, Bulma, Nushushmar . . . Shulgi captured	CC: 327; Edzard 1959–60
Ibbi-Sin	IS 1	Banana of Marhashi went to Uruk	Tab. 1535
	IS 5	year, 'Tukin-hatta-migrisha, the king's daughter, was married to the governor (**ensí**) of Zabshali'	CC: 328
	IS 9	year, 'Ibbi-Sin, the king of Ur, went with massive power to Huhnur, the bolt to the land of Anshan, and . . .'	CC: 328
	IS 14	year, 'Ibbi-Sin, the king of Ur, overwhelmed Susa, Adamdun and Awan like a storm, subdued them in a single day and captured the lords of their people'	CC: 329

Table 5.2 (*cont.*)

Monarch	Date	Event	Reference
	IS 22/IE 16	year, 'Ishbi-Erra the king smote the armies of the Su people and of Elam'	BIN 9: 77 etc.
	IS 23	year, 'the "stupid monkey" in the foreign land struck against Ibbi-Sin, the king of Ur'	CC: 329
	IS 24	Ur attacked by the Elamites and Shimashkians, Ibbi-Sin taken to Anshan as a prisoner	

are particularly well represented in the Puzrish-Dagan archives, where they appear receiving disbursements (Table 5.3) in the form of food and drink, equipment for their journeys such as sandals, and gifts such as rings (e.g. for the ambassadors of Kimash in the year Amar-Sin 5 according to TrD 83; Sigrist 1992: 378). Some of the ambassadors remained so long at Puzrish-Dagan that one would be justified in thinking of them as hostages rather than emissaries (Sigrist 1992: 363). Large numbers of people with linguistically Elamite names are attested at Girsu, Umma and Puzrish-Dagan, and in smaller numbers at Nippur and Ur in the Ur III period, and in all at least 340 people have been identified (Zadok 1990: 39; 1994: 40–5), making Elamites the largest group of non-Semitic speaking foreigners in late third millennium Mesopotamia (Zadok 1993: 231).

M. Lambert has cast the history of Susa and Elam during the Ur III period in terms of two major periods, from Shulgi to Amar-Sin 4, and from Amar-Sin 5 to the end of Ibbi-Sin's reign (Lambert 1979: 29–39). It is beyond the scope of this study to situate every major event connected with the east in the context of the totality of Ur III politico-military history, nor is it necessarily certain that to do so would be a profitable exercise. The events summarized in Table 5.2, like the comings and goings and receipts and disbursements registered at Puzrish-Dagan (Table 5.3), project an illusion of historical progression susceptible to sequential description, but the documentary record is so fragmentary and the events leading up to the major eastern campaigns attested in the year formulae so obscure, that we are unable to write an Ur III political history in the form of a continuous narrative. The fact is that embassies came and went and inter-dynastic marriages were arranged in times which also witnessed brutal attacks on highland regions. We are far from understanding the interplay of domestic and foreign political and economic pressures which gave rise to the sequence before us. Even Shulgi, whose reign might give the impression of being one of the more consolidated vis-à-vis foreign powers, was forced to lead his armies against the recalcitrant east.

Political disintegration and the rise of Shimashki

From the year Shulgi 47 until the fall of Ur, the Shimashkians played a major part in the uprisings or acts of disobedience which must in part have been responsible for pro-

Table 5.3. *Expenditures for travellers to and from Elam at Puzrish-Dagan (Drehem) during the Ur III period*

Officials at Drehem	Years of service	Involvement with the east	Source
Endingirmu	Shulgi 40 – AS 9	expenditures for the messenger of Arbimazbi, governor of Marhashi and the messenger of the son of the governor of Marhashi	MVN 1: 124 (Sigrist 1992: 322)
Enlilla	Shulgi 41 – SS 2	received deliveries for the king from colonists of Kimash received bala contributions from the governors of Babylon, Push and Urum for the great banquet held the day Kimash was destroyed	TRU 144 (Sigrist 1992: 251) YOS 4: 74 (Sigrist 1992: 256)
Urkununna	Shulgi 42 – IS 2	expenditures for Badatma of Shimashki	MVN 11: 184 (Sigrist 1992: 272)
Lu-dingirra	Shulgi 46– AS 3	expenditures for Shushalla and Shurushkin, ambassadors of Marhashi	RA 8: tab. 1, MVN 13: 529 (Sigrist 1992: 326)
Igi-Enlilshe	SS 1–2	expenditures for the man of Kimash and Niabru	TEN 480 (Sigrist 1992: 323)
Abbashaga	AS 1–9	receipt of deliveries from Beli-arik of Susa, mentioned together with his son Idnin-Sin	BIN 3: 537 (Sigrist 1992: 278)
		transfer of livestock (3586 sheep, 14 he-goats) to Beli-arik of Susa (AS 6)	DV 5: 475; TAD 16
Intaea	AS 3–9	receipt of deliveries from the elders of Garnene in Elam	MVN 8: 195 (Sigrist 1992: 297)
Ahu-Wer	AS 6 – SS 7	expenditure for Babdusha of Shimashki	Bab. 8: tab. 30 (Sigrist 1992: 317)
		expenditure for Banana of Marhashi	CST 436 (Sigrist 1992: 317)
		expenditure for Dashal-Ibri of Shimashki	AOS 32 rev. 11 (Sigrist 1992: 317)
		expenditure for Libanashgubi, messenger of Libanugshabash, ensi of Marhashi	RA 8: tab. 11, MVN 13:539, 635; TRU 344 (Sigrist 1992: 317)
		expenditure for Shilatini of Anshan	Bab. 8: tab. 30 (Sigrist 1992: 317)
Shu-mama	AS 7–8	expenditure for messengers from Anshan, Iabrad and Digidihum	BIN 3: 477 (Sigrist 1992: 331)
Dugga	AS 8 – IS 1	expenditure for the people of Kimash and Zidahri on the occasion of their swearing an oath of allegiance in the temple of Ninurta	JCS 14: tab. 14 (Sigrist 1992: 304)
Dudu	SS 5–6	expenditure for the messengers of Marhashi and Kimash	CTNMC 7
Aba-Enlilgim	SS 6 – IS 2	expenditure for Niusha, son of Mega of Kimash	*Amorites*: tab. 21 1.9

Notes:
Key: SS = Shu-Sin; AS = Amar-Sin; IS = Ibbi-Sin

voking the campaigns of the Ur III kings listed in Table 5.2. Precious geographical information on the region known as Shimashki appears in a pair of texts copied from the bases of statues or stelae dedicated by Shu-Sin, king of Ur (Kutscher 1989: 90–1). According to one of these texts, 'the lands of Shimashki' were comprised of six districts called Zabshali, Sh/Sigrish, Nibulmat/Iapulmat, Alumiddatum, Garta/Karda and Shatilu. A number of other lands are mentioned as well, including Azahar (see also Zahara in Chapter 4 and Azara in Chapter 10), Bulma, and Nususmar, at which point the tablet breaks off where at least ten more lines would have followed. These and other toponyms are preserved in a second text, which presents a variant of the first inscription. According to this text, Shu-Sin defeated 'LÚ.SU^{ki}, of [Steinkeller 1990: 10 translates 'which comprises'] the lands of Zabshali, from the border of Anshan to the Upper Sea, their rise, like locusts, Nibulmat, [X], Shigrish, Alumiddatim, Garta, Azahar, Bulma, Nushushmar, Nishgamelum, Sisirtum, Arahir, Shatilu, Tirmium and [X]' (Kutscher 1989: 90; see also Zadok 1991: 227), and this surely refers to the campaign in year 7 of Shu-Sin's reign.

Some years ago Steinkeller suggested (1988a; 1990) to the satisfaction of most scholars (e.g. Frayne 1991: 406; Zadok 1991: 228; but cf. Vallat 1991: 12, n. 13; 1993a: CXXVIII-CXXIV) that LÚ.SU^{ki} was a rebus writing of Shimashki adopted by Ur III scribes. This has recently been confirmed by the publication of a text from Emar in Syria which is a syllabic Sumerian version of an Old Babylonian letter from Sin-iddinam to the sun god in which the name Shimashki appears in place of the term LÚ.SU^{ki} used in the original (Civil 1996: 41). Of all the lands of Shimashki, Zabshali seems to have been the most important, judging by the fact that Shu-Sin commemorated his Iranian conquests by naming the seventh year of his reign the year in which he 'destroyed the land of Zabshali' (Steinkeller 1988a: 199; Sigrist and Gomi 1991: 327).

Whereas the term 'Upper Sea' was conventionally used to denote the Mediterranean by Mesopotamian scribes, the Shu-Sin account of the conquest of Zabshali uses 'Upper Sea' to refer to a body of water beyond Anshan. In this context, therefore, 'Upper Sea' almost certainly denotes the Caspian Sea (see Frayne 1991: 406; Zadok 1991: 228). In discussing the location of Sapum (Chapter 4), the broad outlines of the debate surrounding Shimashki's location were sketched out. If the Upper Sea in Shu-Sin's inscription does indeed refer to the Caspian, then the position of Shimashki, located between Anshan, modern Fars province, and the Caspian (see Steinkeller 1990: 13), extended much further to the north than most scholars have thought. One further point which is surely relevant (though problematic) in determining the location of Shimashki is its linguistic makeup. Some fifty-nine individuals identifiable as Shimashkians are known in the cuneiform literature. Leaving aside those with broken, atypical and unparalleled names, roughly one dozen can be classified as Elamite or Elamite-related, while at least one Zabshalian named In-da-su also had an Elamite name (Zadok 1991: 228). This might suggest that the lands of Shimashki were not too far removed from Fars, the centre of Elamite language use. On the other hand, apart from the evidence of excavated texts in Susiana and at Tal-i Malyan, we know virtually nothing about the geographical extent of spoken Elamite in the late third and early second millennium BC. How far north and west it ranged is largely a matter of guesswork.

As we saw in the last chapter, an Old Babylonian copy of one of Sargon's royal inscriptions (Table 4.5) mentions 'booty of Sapum', a veiled reference to Shimashki in the early Old Akkadian period (even if Shimashki itself is not named in pre-Sargonic or Sargonic texts; see Selz 1989: 94), while a king of Shimashki bowed down before Puzur-Inshushinak (lit. 'grabbed his feet') as a result of the latter's conquests of his other Iranian neighbours (see Table 4.12). Booty from Shimashki was received at Puzrish-Dagan in the year Shulgi 47; messengers with Elamite names from Shimashki and Sapum are attested at Lagash (ITT 2 893, i, 6; iii, 25; Zadok 1994: 41). We have mentioned already Shu-Sin's destruction of Shimashkian lands in the seventh year of his reign (Table 5.2). Yet even as the monarchs of the Third Dynasty were attempting to solidify their alliances with the elites of Marhashi, Anshan, Pashime, and Zabshali through dynastic inter-marriage (see Steve 1991: 4), Shimashki was emerging as the leader of a hostile and far more potent anti-Ur coalition.

Stolper has suggested that Shu-Sin's campaign against the lands of Shimashki was the primary catalyst for the formation of a secondary state. He writes, 'Conflict stiffened local opposition and created communities of interest among Ur's adversaries. Loose political affiliations perhaps antedated the campaign. Shu-Sin's war stimulated or accelerated political or military liaisons among the several regions' (Stolper 1982: 51). As we have seen in the case of Awan, Shimashki may or may not have been the first secondary state to coalesce in southwestern Iran in response to Mesopotamian aggression. But the fact remains that an Elamite-Shimashkian coalition, whatever the mechanics of its formation, was a formidable combination which was to change the political dynamics of southwest Asia in a significant way, for it achieved nothing less than the destruction of the once mighty Ur III state.

The distintegration of the Ur III empire had already begun in the early years of Ibbi-Sin's reign (see Gomi 1984) when, as Jacobsen stressed long ago, the year formulae of the Ur monarch were ignored. By so doing, Ibbi-Sin's rule was no longer acknowledged, beginning in the second year of his reign at Eshnunna; by the third year of his reign at Susa; by the fifth year of his reign at Lagash; by the sixth year of his reign at Umma; and by the seventh year of his reign at Nippur (Jacobsen 1970: 174; see also Edzard 1967b: 158). In other words, the very core of Ur's dominions was in open rebellion shortly after Ibbi-Sin's accession. Added to this, Ishbi-Erra of Isin reported in a letter (PBS XIII 9) to Ibbi-Sin that 'hostile Martus had entered the plains', threatening the western flank of the empire.

To this equation we must now add the forces of Elam and Shimashki. In a hymn to Ishbi-Erra (2017–1985 BC), founder of the First Dynasty of Isin, we learn that it was he who put to flight 'Kindattu, the man of Elam' (**lú-elam**[ki]), and that it was Kindattu who had dealt the death blow to the Ur III empire (van Dijk 1978: 197; on Kindattu, see Quintana 1998). Nevertheless, the relationship between Ibbi-Sin, Ishbi-Erra and Kindattu is far from transparent and speculation on it has been great. Falkenstein once suggested that, although Ishbi-Erra was Ibbi-Sin's military commander at Isin, the former was in fact trying to subvert the ruler of Ur and succeeded in setting himself up as ruler of Isin by the year Ibbi-Sin 10 or 11. In Falkenstein's view, Ishbi-Erra's treachery forced Ibbi-Sin into an unlikely alliance with the Elamites, resulting in his eventual flight to Anshan where he went, not as a captive, but as a refugee (Falkenstein 1950: 62ff.). Thorkild Jacobsen and others, however, rejected this scenario and saw nothing but 'constant enmity with Elam, often flaring into open war' in the ill-fated career of Ibbi-Sin (Jacobsen 1970: 182). Indeed, his year formulae would hardly support the notion of a pact with Elam. Apart from the fact that his daughter Tukin-hatti-migrisha 'was married to the governor of Zabshali' in the fifth year of his reign, Ibbi-Sin's attacks on Huhnur and Anshan in year 9, and on Susa, Adamdun and Awan in year 14 (Table 5.2) would hardly lead one to envisage an alliance with Elam during the subsequent and final ten years of his reign.

Tantalizingly fragmentary, the hymn to Ishbi-Erra mentioned above relates that one 'Zinnum, he who had escaped' into the burnt earth of the steppe, was forced to eat *zubud*-fish from the Euphrates, Tigris, the Mirsig and the Kish canal, but, haunted by spectres, died of thirst. Upon learning of this, Kindattu retreated to Anshan and disappeared forever (van Dijk 1978: 198–9). An important letter from Puzurnumushda, governor of Kazallu, to Ibbi-Sin, identifies Zinnum as **ensí** of Kish, and van Dijk believed the letter implied that Zinnum was an ally of Ibbi-Sin's. The Ishbi-Erra hymn, on the other hand, which describes Zinnum's demise at the hands of Ishbi-Erra, might suggest that at some point Zinnum shifted his allegiance from Ibbi-Sin to Kindattu (van Dijk 1978: 200). Otherwise, how is one to explain Kindattu's flight upon hearing the news of Zinnum's death? Curiously, B. André-Salvini has recently suggested that Kindattu was actually in league with Ishbi-Erra against Ibbi-Sin (André-Salvini 1992: 262). If such were the case, then Ishbi-Erra's eventual triumph and Kindattu's flight can only mean that Ishbi-Erra turned on Kindattu once Ibbi-Sin had been dealt with. This, however, seems to be pure speculation.

The bare skeleton of events which ensued during the final three years of Ibbi-Sin's reign is provided by a combination of his own and Ishbi-Erra's year formulae. In the sixteenth year of his reign, equivalent to year 22 of Ibbi-Sin (following the synchronism Ishbi-Erra 18 = Ibbi-Sin 24; Sigrist 1988: 4), 'Ishbi-Erra the king smote the armies of the Su people and of Elam' (Sigrist 1988: 16). In the following year (Ibbi-Sin 23), 'the stupid monkey in the foreign land struck against Ibbi-Sin, the king of Ur', and although the fragmentary year formula for the following year tells us that 'Ibbi-Sin, the king of Ur . . . struck' (Sigrist and Gomi 1991: 329), the *Lamentation over the Destruction of Sumer and Ur*, a Sumerian composition which vividly commemorated the fall of Ur at the hands of Shimashki and Elam, confirms the fate decreed for Ibbi-Sin, namely 'that Ibbi-Sin be taken to the land of Elam in fetters/That from the mountain Zabu, which is on the edge of the sealand, to the borders of Anshan/Like a bird that has flown its nest, he not return to his city'. This, too, is confirmed by another Isin dynasty text published many years ago by Jacobsen (Jacobsen 1953: 182). Finally, the expulsion of Kindattu, the Su-people and the Elamites is commemorated in the year formula for the twenty-sixth year of Ishbi-Erra's reign which was the year 'Ishbi-Erra the king brought

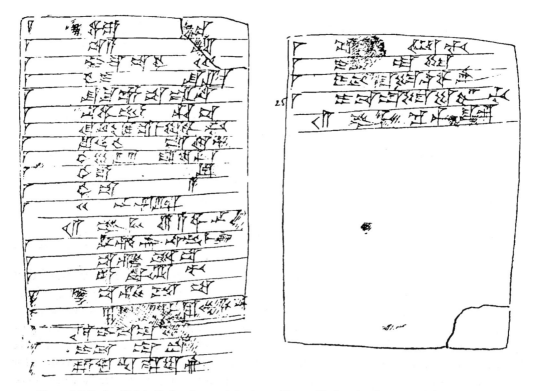

Figure 5.2 Father V. Scheil's handcopy of the Awan/Shimashki kinglist from Susa (after Scheil 1931: 2).

down by his mighty weapon the Elamite who was dwelling in the midst of Ur' (Sigrist 1988: 20).

The same tablet from Susa (Fig. 5.2) which enumerates the twelve kings of Awan also lists the names of twelve kings of Shimashki, as follows: 'Girnamme, Tazitta, Ebarti, Tazitta, Lu[?]-[x-x-x]-lu-uh-ha-an, Kindattu, Idaddu, Tan-Ruhurater, Ebarti, Idaddu, Idaddu-napir, Idaddu-temti, twelve Shimashkian kings' (André-Salvini 1992: 261). There is no reason to doubt that the Kindattu who appears as the sixth king of Shimashki is anyone other than the Kindattu of the Ishbi-Erra hymn. On the other hand, as Stolper has argued, Ur III and Isin-Larsa period texts suggest that, far from representing a diachronic sequence of successive Shimashkian leaders, the first portion of the Shimashki 'king list' represents a collection of names of contemporary leaders (Table 5.5) who were all alive in the period c. 2044–2032 BC (Stolper 1982: 50). Filiation is nowhere indicated in this list, and identifying lineal descent is a problem in the Shimashkian documentation. Recently, Vallat has suggested that the Shimashki kinglist must be read in an even more radical fashion, namely as two parallel lists of contemporary rulers, the contents of which have been listed one after the other (Vallat 1996e: 298). Thus, he suggests that some of the rulers on the list (e.g. Ebarti/Ebarat II) ruled in Susiana while others (e.g. Tan-Ruhurater) held sway on the Plateau, and that the last Shimashkians (from Ebarat II onwards) were vassals of the early Susian *sukkalmahs* who gradually overtook them completely (Vallat 1996e: 315–16).

Table 5.4. *Shimashkian kings attested in texts and cylinder seal legends*

Louvre #	MDP 53	Texts mentioning royalty
Sb 7391 = TS B 10	1675	Tan-Ruhurater / **ensí** of Susa / X[broken proper name] / son of I-da-d[u?]
Sb 7390	1676	Mekubi / the great queen [**nin-gula**] / Aabanda . . . / Aza, son of Id . . . / scribe, his servant
Sb 2033+2294+2299+6972	1677	Idadu / **ensí** of Susa / beloved hero / of Inshushinak / son of Tan-Ruhurater / to Kuk-Simut the scribe / to his beloved servant / has given [this seal]
Sb 6682	1678	Idadu / **ensí** of Susa/Kuk-Inshushinak / messenger / [is] his servant
Teheran Museum tablet 2514	1679	Imazu / son of Kindadu / **lugal** of Anshan

Although we have no precise information on the point, it is sometimes assumed that the abandonment of Ibbi-Sin's year formulae at Susa signalled the beginning of the annexation of the site and surrounding hinterland by the Shimashkians. Subsequent campaigns by Ibbi-Sin show, however, that the loss of Susiana was not taken lying down. The marriage of his daughter to the ruler of Zabshali in his fifth year may have been an attempt to retain or strengthen an alliance, but if so, it must have failed, for why else would he have campaigned against Huhnur in year 9 and against Susa, Adamdun and Awan in year 14? It seems more likely, then, that the expulsion of the remnants of Ibbi-Sin's forces from Susiana was effected by Kindattu, who followed this up by delivering the ultimate *coup de grace* to the Third Dynasty of Ur. Indeed Amiet has suggested that it was only then, halfway through the fictive Shimashki kinglist, that the 'Shimashki epoch' truly began (Amiet 1992a: 85).

In the Sumerian composition the *Lamentation over the Destruction of Sumer and Ur* we read that Shimashki and Elam 'dwelt' in Ur, and her shepherd, Ibbi-Sin, was 'taken to the land of Elam in fetters' (Michalowski 1989: 39). Another composition belonging to the same genre, known as the Eridu lament, tells us that the Su-people and Elamites, 'the destroyers', looked at 'the holy kettle, which no one may look at' (Green 1978: 137). Their attack is compared to a 'roaring storm', distorting the 'essence' of the city, tossing the ziggurat 'into a heap of debris'. Nor were Eridu and Ur alone, for Kesh, Uruk and Nippur were also destroyed.

In the post-Kindattu period of Shimashki, a text (BIN IX 382) dating to the nineteenth year of Ishbi-Erra's reign, i.e. some seven years prior to his expulsion of the Elamites from Ur, refers to messengers from *Ki-in-da-du* and *I-da-[x]*. As Stolper has stressed, it is tempting to see these two individuals as Kindattu and Idaddu (Stolper 1982: 48; see also Vallat 1996a), the sixth and seventh kings according to the Shimashki king list. Whether these two were father and son, however, cannot be determined. A son of Kindattu who was never acknowledged by the kinglist tradition as a king of Shimashki may be mentioned in a cylinder seal inscription (Table 5.4), known only from an impressed tablet from Susa, which reads '*I-ma-zu* / DUMU *Ki-in-da-du* / LUGAL *An-ša-*

an-na[ki], or 'Imazu, son of Kindadu, king of Anshan'. Later kings known from the Shimashkian kinglist, including Idaddu I, Tan-Ruhurater, Ebarti II and Idaddu II (Table 5.5) are also attested in seal legends (Fig. 5.3) and in a Middle Elamite text; some of these do give us positive proof of filiation (there is disagreement over whether MDP 43: 1678 and 2325 should be attributed to Idaddu II; U. Seidl attributes these to Idaddu I, see Seidl 1990). Thus one seal inscription, if restored, makes it highly probable that Tan-Ruhurater, eighth king of Shimashki, was the son of Idaddu I, the seventh king of the list. Tan-Ruhrater himself had a son whom he called Idaddu (II), and this son, who is called 'ensí of Susa, beloved of Inshushinak, son of Tan-Ruhurater' on a cylinder seal given by him to Kuk-Simut, his chancellor (Vallat 1996e: 302), may have been serving in this capacity before becoming the tenth Shimashkian king following the accession of his elder brother (?) Ebarti, ninth king of Shimashki (Stolper 1982: 55).

As far as the absolute chronology of the Shimashkian kings goes, we have seen that the earliest kings can be linked quite confidently with points in the reign of Shu-Sin and Amar-Sin: two of the kings in the middle of the list, Kindattu and Idaddu I, can be fixed to the middle of Ishbi-Erra's reign; Tan-Ruhurater was a contemporary and son-in-law of Bilalama of Eshnunna, himself a contemporary of Shu-ilishu of Isin (1984–1975 BC); and finally the eleventh king on the list, Idaddu-napir, can be tied to the reign of Sumuabum of Babylon (1894–1881 BC) based on the fact that a cylinder seal used to seal a tablet from Susa dated in the reign of Sumuabum (MDP 10: no. 2) was also used on another Susa text (MDP 10: no. 21) mentioning Idaddu-napir (Vallat 1988a: 174, n. 13; 1989a: 34).

As can be readily seen, the texts mentioning the kings named in the Shimashki kinglist contain a variety of titles including

- king (**lugal**) of Anshan (Imazu)
- governor (**ensí**) of Susa (Idaddu I, Tan-Ruhurater, Idaddu II)
- GÌR.NÍTA of Elam (Idaddu I)
- king (**lugal**) of Shimashki and Elam (Idaddu I)
- king (**lugal**) of Anshan and Susa (Ebarti II)
- king (**lugal**) (Ebarti II)

How are we to interpret this multiplicity of high offices? What functions did their office-bearers actually perform? Most scholars view the occurrence of these titles as confirmation of the fact that the territory of Shimashki, to which Susiana had now been added, 'was not easily suited to centralized control' but rather to 'a political structure with a high order of regional autonomy: rulers of unequal age and rank, tied to each other by marriage and descent' in charge of 'individual regional centers' (Stolper 1982: 53–4). Following L. de Meyer, Vallat has suggested that, in the slightly later *sukkalmah* period (Chapter 6), the title 'king of Susa' in effect denoted something like 'mayor of Susa' (Vallat 1996a), implying that a title such as 'king of Anshan' may have carried with it similar connotations. Likewise, 'ensí of Susa' or 'GÌR.NÍTA of Elam' may have been similarly restricted in scope, while 'king of Shimashki and Elam' and 'king of Anshan and Susa' may be two temporal variants of an essentially identical title of paramount rank.

Table 5.5. *Shimashkian kings attested during the Ur III and early Isin periods, with those named in the Shimashki kinglist*

Shimashki kinglist	Source	Text
1. Girnamme	CTNMC 7: 8∞	Ki-ir-na-me (dated Shu-Sin 6)
2. Tazitta	Bab. 8: Pl. 7.30/3 BIN 3: 477/	Da-a-zi-te, 'man of Anshan' (dated Amar-Sin 8) Da-a-zi (dated Shu-Sin 2)
3. Ebarti I	CTNMC 7: 8	Ià-ab-ra-at, 'man of Su' (dated Shu-Sin 6)
4. Tazitta	—	—
5. Lu-[(x)-r]a-ak-lu-uh-ha-an	MDP 24: 385/9 EKI §48: 2, 48a: 3 EKI §39: II	Hu-ut-ra-an-te-im-ti H[ut-rant]epti Hutran-tepti mentioned as builder of the Inshushinak temple
6. Ki-in-da-at-tu	BIN 9: 382 EKI §48: 2 MDP 43: 1679	Ki-in-da-du, 'man of Elam' (dated Ishbi-Erra 19) Itaddu, 'sister's son' of H[ut-rant]epti Imazu / son of Kindadu / king of Anshan
7. Idaddu I	BIN 9: 382 IRSA IVO1a MDP 14: 26/4	I-da-[du] Inda[ttu]-Inshushi[nak], **ensí** of Susa, GÌR.NÍTA of Elam, son of Pepi I-da-du, 'king of Shimashki and Elam'
8. Tan-Ruhurater	MDP 43: 1675 MDP 43: 1674 IRSA IVO2a MDP 43: 1676	Tan-Ruhurater / **ensí** of Susa /[broken proper name] / son of I-da-d[u?] Nur-Sin / scribe / son of Puzur-Ishtar / servant of Tan-Ruhurater Tan-Ruhurater, **ensí** of Susa, mentioned as husband of Mekubi, daughter of Bilalama, governor of Eshnunna Mekubi / the great lady [nin-gula] / Aabanda . . ./ Aza, son of Id . . ./ scribe, his servant
9. Ebarti II	IRSA IVO6a MDP 23: 291–305 MDP 43: 1685 MDP 43: 1686 MDP 43: 1680	Ebarat, king of Anshan and Susa and Shilhaha *sukkalmah* and priest of Anshan and of Susa, Adda-hushu regent and scribe of the people of Susa E/Ia-ba-ra-at king Ebarat the king / Kuk-ᵈKalla / son of Kuk-sharum / servant of Shilhaha Buzua / servant of Ebarat . . .-Inshushinak / scribe / [son of . . .]-ᵈKalla (?) / servant of Ebarat
10. Idaddu II	MDP 43: 1677	Idadu / **ensí** of Susa / beloved hero / of Inshushinak / son of Tan-Ruhurater / to Kuk-Simut the scribe / to his beloved servant / has given [this seal]

Table 5.5 (*cont.*)

Shimashki kinglist	Source	Text
	IRSA IVO3a-c	Indattu, **ensí** of Susa, son of Tan-Ruhurater
	MDP 43: 1678*	Idadu / **ensí** of Susa / Kuk-Inshushinak / messenger /[is] his servant
	MDP 43: 2325*	Shurimku the doctor / [son of] Puzur-Ishtar / (servant of) Idadu
11. Idaddu-napir	MDP 10: 35, 21.4	I-da-du-na-pi-ir
12. Idaddu-temti		

Notes:

∞ numbers here generally refer to specific texts or seals and not to pages.

* Seidl 1990 attributes this seal to Idaddu I, not Idaddu II

Figure 5.3 Drawing of the seal of Kuk-Simut given by Idaddu II (after Lambert 1971: Fig. 1).

Mention has already been made of the fact that Tan-Ruhurater, eighth king of Shimashki, was married to the daughter of the governor of Eshnunna, an important city in the Trans-Tigridian Diyala Valley (to the northeast of Babylonia proper). This, along with two other events, would seem to signal a rapprochement between Shimashki and the kings of Isin following Kindattu's reversal at the hands of Ishbi-Erra. Ishbi-Erra's successor at Isin, Shu-ilishu (1984–1975 BC), is said to have restored the cult statue of Nanna to Ur from Anshan (Sollberger and Kupper 1971: 172). One does not know whether this came about as the result of a hostile raid or a peaceful arrangement. Given the history of Mesopotamian-Shimashkian relations one would hardly be inclined to envisage the former were it not for the fact that two diplomatic marriages occurred about this time. The year formula for the first year of the reign of Iddin-Dagan (1974–1954 BC), Shu-ilishu's son and successor on the throne of Isin, reads 'Year Iddin-Dagan (was) king and (his) daughter Matum-niatum was taken in marriage by the king of Anshan' (Sigrist 1988: 24). Vallat has recently suggested that this marriage may have taken place with Kindattu's son Imazu, called in a seal inscription 'king of Anshan' but never acknowledged by the Shimashkian kinglist as paramount ruler of Shimashki (Vallat 1996a). These snippets of information go some way towards supporting the notion that, in the middle of the Shimashki period, Isin and the kings of Shimashki indeed put the history of Ur's downfall behind them and attempted to re-establish friendly relations based in part on the time-honoured practice of diplomatic marriage. Unfortunately for Shimashki, Isin was soon to be rivalled in southern Mesopotamia by another power based at Larsa under the vigorous leadership of Gungunum. The consequences of this change will be explored in the following chapter.

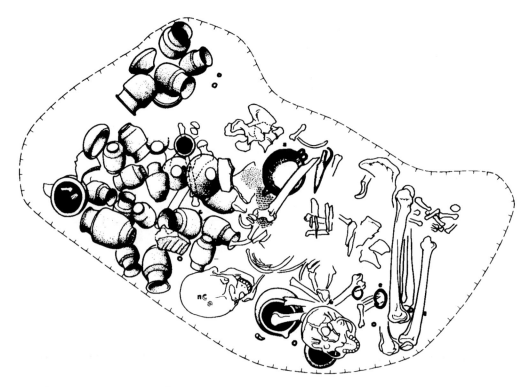

Figure 5.4 Grave 507 in Ville Royale A at Susa, containing the remains of two or three separate interments. The corpses had been wrapped in bitumen-coated reed mats, and a wide variety of
grave goods were interred, including ceramic and metal vessels, weaponry, jewellery and,
judging by the animal bones recovered, food offerings (after Carter 1980: Fig. 44).

Some archaeological correlations

Up to this point most of the discussion of Shimashki has centred on its history, and
little has been said about its material culture. Shu-Sin brought back 'the image of a he-
goat . . . as the gún of Anshan during a campaign against the lú-SU.A [Shimashkians]
and Zabshali' while Ibbi-Sin returned from a campaign with 'an image of a speckled
Meluhhan dog which came as gún from the land of Marhashi' (Michalowski 1978: 43),
but these can hardly be seen as typical examples of the material culture of the time. In
any case they are known only from attestations in votive inscriptions, not from the
objects themselves which have long since disappeared. During the plundering of Ur
described in the *Lamentation over the Destruction of Sumer and Ur*, 'the great tribute
that they had collected was hauled off to the mountains' (Michalowski 1989: 63, l. 419).

Although Carter refers to the period between *c.* 2200/2100 and 1900 BC at Susa (Figs.
5.4–5) as the 'Shimashki phase' (Table 4.10), it is archaeologically impossible to discern
a clear break between the late Akkadian and Ur III periods when Susa was under
Mesopotamian control, and that point in Ibbi-Sin's reign when, presumably, Susa was
lost to Shimashkian forces under Kindattu or one of his predecessors. In one area of the
site, however, a very fine distinction can be drawn. R. Ghirshman excavated a series of

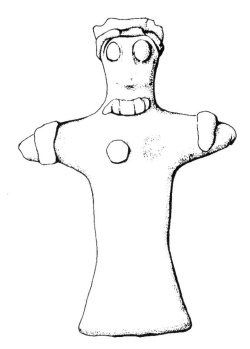

Figure 5.5 A terracotta figurine from Ville Royale A, level 4, at Susa (after Carter 1980: Fig. 53.1).

fragmentary buildings in Ville Royale Chantier B, and it is possible to precisely date the so-called Archive Building ('Bâtiment aux Archives') in level VII where two distinct floors, some 40–55 cm apart, were isolated in rooms (loci) 29 and 32 (de Meyer 1986). In fact, the term Archive Building is somewhat misleading, for the structure appears to have been the private house of a scribe named Igibuni (Fig. 5.6). The distance between the two floors in his house, while seemingly substantial, belies the fact that the texts from the lower and upper floors date to a very narrow span of time (Table 5.6) which coincides with the late Ur III, immediately pre-Shimashkian era.

A distinctive glyptic style (Fig. 5.7), once referred to by Amiet as 'popular Elamite' and now identified as 'Anshanite', can be linked in one case by inscriptional evidence to Ebarti or Ebarat II (W.G. Lambert 1979; 1992; Amiet 1992b; 1994c). Iconographically, the group is extremely coherent and shows, *inter alia*, females wearing 'crinoline' gowns which strongly resemble those shown on figurines and small portable statuary of allegedly Bactrian origin (Amiet 1986c: Figs. 203–4). The term 'Anshanite' is used because of the fact that original seals of this type have been found in early second millennium contexts at Tal-i Malyan, the site of ancient Anshan.

Surprisingly, the historical phases at Susa dealt with in Chapters 4 and 5 – Old Akkadian, Ur III and Shimashki-period – are not replicated at Anshan itself. Abandoned at the end of the Banesh period *c.* 2600 BC, Tal-i Malyan was re-settled *c.* 2200 BC and the entire time span down to 1600 BC is characterized by a fairly uniform material culture (Fig. 5.8) referred to as 'Kaftari' (Sumner 1989). Within this six hundred year long phase, W. Sumner has identified three 'stages': early Kaftari (2200–1900 BC),

Table 5.6. *Distribution of dated tablets belonging to the archive of the scribe Igibuni in Ville Royale B, level 7*

Floor	Dated tablets	Date	Calendar year (middle chronology)
Upper	TS.B. 120, 121, 126	Ibbi-Sin 1	2028/2027 BC
	TS.B. 131, 139	Shu-Sin 8	2031/2030 BC
	TS.B. 138	Shu-Sin 7	2032/2031 BC
	TS.B. 108, 133	Shu-Sin 5	2034/2033 BC
Lower	TS.B. 147	Ibbi-Sin 1	2028/2027 BC
	TS.B. 151	Shu-Sin 8	2031/2030 BC
	TS.B. 145	Shu-Sin 7	2032/2031 BC
	TS.B. 148	Shu-Sin 4	2035/2034 BC

Notes:
After de Mayer 1986: 76.

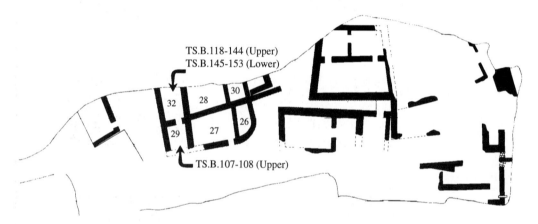

Figure 5.6 The house of Igibuni at Susa (after de Meyer 1986: Fig. 1).

Middle Kaftari (1900–1800 BC) and Late Kaftari (1800–1600 BC). Beginning with a substantial 39 ha of occupied area in the Early Kaftari stage, Tal-i Malyan rose in size to a massive 130 ha of settled area during the Middle Kaftari period, when it was more than ten times the size of all but one other site (Kaleh at 15 ha) in the Kur River basin. By the Late Kaftari stage, the site's size is estimated to have fallen to 98 ha (Table 5.7).

The degree of ceramic and settlement discontinuity between the Banesh and Kaftari periods suggests a real hiatus in sedentary occupation in the region during the mid-third millennium (Sumner 1989: 136). Apart from a coarse, quartz-tempered grey ware used for cooking vessels which runs through the Banesh, Kaftari and subsequent Qaleh periods, and rare sherds of grey burnished ware, possibly imported from Mesopotamia in Carter's opinion, the dominant wares of the Kaftari assemblage are a red-slipped ware which is most commonly used for open bowls, and a smooth, buff ware, often with

Figure 5.7 Cylinder and stamp seals of 'Anshanite' type: 1. the seal of Ebarat in the Gulbenkian Museum, Durham; 2, 3, 6, 8. seals in the Rosen collection; 4. sealing of Ilituram, servant of Pala-ishshan; 5, 7. unprovenanced seals; 9. seal from Tal-i Malyan (after Porada 1990: Pls. II-III).

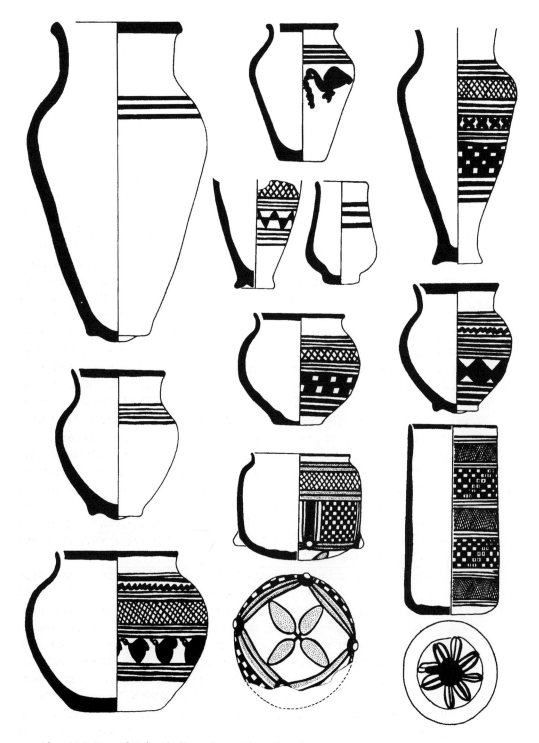

Figure 5.8 Painted Kaftari buffware from Tal-i Malyan (after Sumner 1974: Fig. 6).

Table 5.7. *Kaftari site distribution in comparison to the growth of Malyan*

Kaftari	Number of sites occupied	Hectares of settlement	Size of Malyan
Early	35	83	39
Middle	74	278	130
Late	43	210	98

simply painted bands and meanders around the shoulder, occasionally showing the use of vegetal and geometric motifs as well as birds (Sumner 1992: 287). The non-ceramic assemblage, consisting of flaked and ground stone tools, stone vessels, metal (copper/bronze) objects and casting debris, seals and sealings, figurines, and jewellery (Nickerson 1991), hardly projects an image of a cosmopolitan centre linked by marriage to the greatest power in Western Asia, and if they accurately portray daily life in Anshan, then the Ur III princesses who went there to live must have felt like their nineteenth century Russian counterparts when banished to the country. On the other hand, it is entirely possible that more elite residences and palatial constructions of late third millennium date exist at Tal-i Malyan which have yet to be investigated archaeologically.

Several interesting points can be made about the economy of Kaftari-period Malyan. Cultivars included wheat, barley, lentil and grape, while wild pistachio and almond were collected as well. Although barley was ten times as common as wheat in excavated domestic contexts, 'a mineralized Kaftari latrine deposit yielded twice as much wheat as barley', suggesting that 'wheat was more important as human food, and barley was grown primarily as fodder'. The fact that the seeds of weeds commonly associated with irrigated fields, including *Chenopodium*, *Avena*, *Lolium*, *Fumaria* and *Hyoscyamus*, were found in Kaftari contexts suggests that some irrigation agriculture was being practised at this time, drawing water from the Kur River and nearby springs (Sumner 1988b: 317), perhaps alongside dry-farming (Miller 1990b: 80–1). In addition to the expected complement of sheep, goat and cattle, horse made its first appearance at Malyan in the Kaftari period as did, in all likelihood, a hybrid cross between *Equus caballus* and *asinus* (Zeder 1986: 406).

In spite of the strong glyptic links between Kaftari-period Tal-i Malyan and Susa alluded to above, Sumner believes that Anshan's 'role as a political unit' is one of 'unclear status in the Shimashkian state' (Sumner 1988b: 317). Some years ago an argument was made for locating the core of that state in the highlands of central western Iran, specifically in those intermontane valleys where one finds pottery of Godin Tepe III: 6 (2600–2300 BC), 5 (2300–2100 BC), 4 (2100–1900 BC) and 2 type (1900–1600 BC) (Godin III: 3 is described as an 'ephemeral phase' of 'little archaeological or historical significance'; Henrickson 1984: 101, n. 5). The dearth of Godin III: 4–2 material at Susa, however, must be seen as a strong counter-argument to the claim that the Mahidasht, Kangavar, Malayer, Hulailan and other intermontane valleys of central western Iran were the main source of the relatively brief cultural florescence in the lowlands known as the dynasty of Shimashki, just as the absence of clear ties between these areas and the Kur River basin argues against the hypothesis as well.

Conclusion

The Iranologist Walther Hinz once described late third millennium Elam as 'a federal state', and wrote, 'In an attempt to unite the very diverse areas of the federation, the kings, being sovereign, strove to bind the minor princelings to themselves by ties of blood relationship. The result was a body politic constructed on lines that were unusual, complicated, and indeed unparalleled elsewhere. The ruling houses most adept at this task all seem to have sprung from the high land and not from Susiana, although Susa itself early attained the status of capital' (Hinz 1972: 69). As we have seen, the various groups/peoples mentioned in Mesopotamian cuneiform sources as having come under attack by the Old Akkadian and Ur III kings were spread in a wide arc extending from the central Zagros to the frontiers of Kerman province and possibly even Baluchistan. Speaking only of the northern portion of this arc, Steinkeller has described the six Shimashkian lands defeated by Shu-Sin as a 'confederation' (Steinkeller 1988a: 199), while Stolper has called them 'an extensive interregional union' (Stolper 1982: 49). The Shu-Sin texts which describe the defeat of the Shimashkian lands make it clear that each one had its own ruler, styled 'great ensí' (**ensí-gal-gal**) or 'king' (**lugal**) in the case of those who ruled a land, and simply **ensí** for those whose domain was a city or town (Kutscher 1989: 99). Kutscher has suggested that Ziringu, named as the paramount ruler of Zabshali in one of the Shu-Sin texts, ruled a Shimashkian 'empire' which he envisaged as 'a confederacy of lands whose leading force was the land of Zabshali under Ziringu' (Kutscher 1989: 100).

To what extent was Elam, as Hinz suggested, an 'unparalleled' socio-political formation in the context of ancient Western Asiatic history? In the Greek world federations are attested as early as the late 6th century BC (Larsen and Rhodes 1996). Nevertheless, in ancient Western Asia federations were rare. The dispersed, trucial nature of the coalitions which faced the Mesopotamian armies of the late third and early second millennium BC, coming together to wage war against a common enemy, is very different from a 'unitary state . . . in which there is a central monopoly of power, exercised by a specialised administrative staff within defined territorial limits' (Southall 1956: 260). In this respect Elam resembles much more what political anthropologists define as a 'segmentary state', a structure with 'extended zones of authority' which is characterized by competition between the centre and its peripheries, a pyramidal power structure with segments enjoying comparable powers, and peripheral segments which shift their allegiance and may belong to more than one power pyramid at any one time. Thus, segmentary states have been called both 'flexible and fluctuating' (Southall 1956: 248–9). As Georges Balandier has stressed, segmentary states are characterized by a high degree of 'ethnic and cultural heterogeneity', so that the system 'appears more centralized at the ritual level than at the level of political action' (Balandier 1972: 142, 155).

As we have seen there is good evidence to suggest ethnic and linguistic diversity at the same time as we find some level of Elamite influence throughout the arc extending from Kermanshah to eastern Fars. Power, judging by Shu-Sin's inscriptions, was decentralized, concentrated in numerous small pyramids which might, at any particular time, fall under one or another of the major protagonists in the region, whether Zabshali, Shimashki itself, Elam, Anshan or Marhashi. Southall has further noted that 'under certain conditions, the interaction of diverse ethnic groups of contrasted social structure may predispose them to coalesce into a composite social structure of dominance and subjection out of which state forms develop. This process cannot adequately be described as conquest' (Southall 1956: 245). While conquest is usually cited as the prime mover in the creation of so-called secondary states, the incorporation of groups within a segmentary state may also come about as a result of the development of trade relationships, the development of client or tributary relations between a dominant centre and an area which it has not actually conquered, and the voluntary submission of one group to another, seeking the benefits of protection, or identification with a charismatic leader. Viewed in this light, it would be simplistic to suggest that, throughout its history, Elam and its neighbours were only bound together through outright conquest. Both temporary and longer-lasting alliances seem to have been forged between the constituent members of the greater Elamite segmentary federation which benefitted all parties and drew them together in opposition to a common enemy. In this regard the conflict between Elam and Ur in the last century of the third millennium emerges as a clash between two very different political forms: the hyper-centralized, unitary state *par excellence* of Ur, and the 'tribalized', segmentary state of Elam.

When Ibbi-Sin went to Anshan (if he in fact lived to see the city), he would have been instantly aware of just how different those two political systems were. Anshan must have seemed like a country town compared to Susa, and Ur must have seemed like Manhattan in comparison to his final home. Yet how difficult it is to be comfortable with such generalizations. One of the great difficulties lies in the fact that we are obviously dealing with sites excavated in such diametrically different fashions that the results are virtually incompatible. We have small exposures and fine-grained recovery of utilitarian debris (pottery, stone, metal, animal bones, plant remains, etc.) from Anshan, while at Susa we have inadequately excavated and recorded swathes through an enormous site, an abiding impression of that site's size and importance in just about all periods, and fragments of an historical record which brings the Third Dynasty of Ur into direct contact with its late third millennium Susian or Elamite counterparts. We certainly sense the 'common man' in the material record of Tal-i Malyan, but this is quite clearly not the material counterpart of princesses journeying there from Ur and Ibbi-Sin in exile. The drama of the princesses' marriages and the captivity of Ur's last king find no echo in the Kaftari levels of ancient Anshan and, apart from emphasizing the site's sheer size in comparison with other prehistoric settlements in the region, the excavators of Tal-i Malyan are hard pressed to demonstrate even the provincial importance of the city at that time. Historical links between Anshan, Shimashki and Susa find little corroboration in the material record, and this fact alone should warn us that the archaeology of Iran in the early historic period should never be treated in isolation from the available written record. Both types of evidence are necessary, for neither is sufficient on its own to give us a picture of conditions in the late third millennium BC.

Date	Lowlands	Highlands	Mesopotamia	'Elam'
2094–2047 BC	Susa under Ur's control by reign of Shulgi; involvement of Shulgi with temples to Inshushinak and Ninhursag; taxes paid to Ur by Susa;	polities in Anshan, Zabshali, Marhashi identified in Mesopotamian sources as having governors and/or kings; inter-dynastic marriage with Ur princesses; Ur campaigns against highlands; re-settlement of Malyan, appearance of distinctive 'popular Elamite' glyptic	consolidation/expansion of Ur III state under Shulgi	references late in period to Shimashkians; mosaic of lands of Shimashki attested in cuneiform sources; Shimashkians bear Elamite and non-Elamite names; lack of ceramic ties between Luristan, Susiana and Fars
2046–2038 BC	raids by Amar-Sin; Susa under Ur's administration	dispatch of couriers, ambassadors between Ur and highlands		
2037–2029 BC	appearance of popular Elamite glyptic; Susa under Ur's administration	Shu-Sin active in campaigning; absence of ceramic links to Susa or Fars	construction of the 'Martu wall' in north-ern Babylonia against foreign incursions	first kings of Shimashki mentioned; Shu-Sin's aggression a possible catalyst for coalescence of 'Shimashkian' state
2028–2004 BC	raids by Ibbi-Sin; liberation of Susa; Susa comes under control of Shimashkian kings	raids by Ibbi-Sin, as well as inter-dynastic marriage	disintegration of Ur III empire; fall of Ur, foundation of First Dynasty of Isin by Ishbi-Erra	Elamite-Shimashkian coalition under Kindattu crushes Ur; alternate use of Anshan, Elam, Susa, Shimashki in titulature reflects

			constituents of new political order
2004–1940 BC	Susa part of Shimashkian 'kingdom'	polities in alliance with Isin through inter-dynastic marriage	First Dynasty of Isin

6

THE GRAND REGENTS OF ELAM AND SUSA

From the era of Shimashki we move to the period of the *sukkalmahs*, a title of some antiquity in Mesopotamia which has been interpreted variously in its Iranian context. The mechanics of the transformation of the line of Shimashkian kings into the line of Susian *sukkalmahs* is obscure but one thing is certain: under the *sukkalmahs*, particularly those of the late nineteenth and early eighteenth centuries BC, the prestige and influence of Elam throughout Western Asia was unprecedented. The break-up of the Ur III empire witnessed the rise of independent, rival dynasties in the southern Mesopotamian cities of Isin and Larsa. Isin's power was greatest during the first three quarters of the twentieth century BC, and this was a period in which the Elamites suffered a series of political and military setbacks. But, beginning in the late twentieth century BC, the power of Isin waned as that of Larsa waxed, and the Elamites came to have substantial influence in the kingdom of Larsa. Ultimately we see Elam emerge as the major powerbroker in a web of relations which bound Assyria, Babylonia and other neighbouring regions, such as Eshnunna (in the modern Diyala River basin) and Mari (on the Middle Euphrates in Syria), often in uneasy alliances which eventually broke down. Elam provided the much sought after tin which Mari dispensed to the kingdoms of western Syria and Palestine. Elamite involvement with regions to the south and east, such as Dilmun (Bahrain) and Magan (Oman) in the Persian Gulf, and the resource-rich region of Bactria (northern Afghanistan/southern Uzbekistan), is also documented during this period. While the archaeological evidence of this era is abundant at Susa and in some of the plains of northern and eastern Khuzistan, it is slim in Fars, although several important rock reliefs exist. Ultimately, Hammurabi of Babylon put an end to this phase of growth and influence which saw Elam change from a regional to a world (still in the limited Western Asiatic sense) power.

Introduction

The plurality of royal titles which characterized the later Shimashki period at Susa continued, in altered form, throughout the first half of the second millennium BC, that time known to historians and archaeologists as the *sukkalmah* period. *Sukkalmah* is a title which first appears in the pre-Sargonic texts from Girsu, where the title seems, from its use in an inscription of Urukagina, to denote something like 'prime minister' or 'grand vizier', an office clearly subservient to the **ensí** or paramount ruler in the territory of Lagash (Hallo 1957: 113). The *sukkalmah* is well-attested in Mesopotamia during the Ur III period, and it seems to have remained linked to the city-state of Lagash. This may help explain why the title should have been used for the paramount leader in post-Shimashki Susa and Elam, for the control of the eastern front of Ur during the Ur III period, and thus Susa and Susiana (Fig. 6.1), seems to have fallen to the lot of

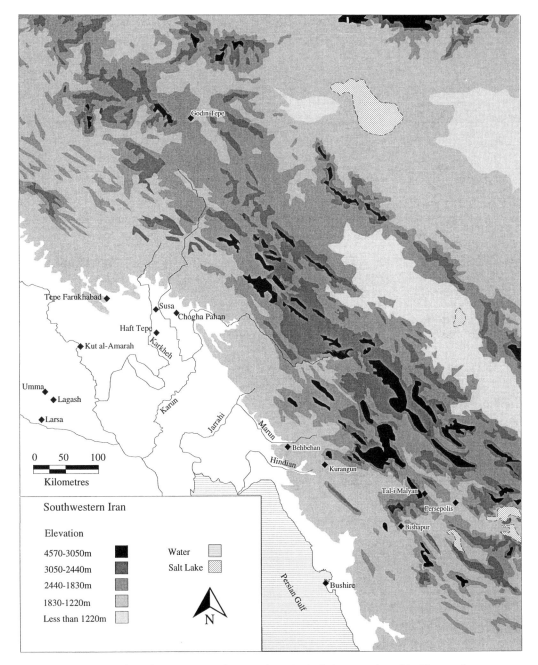

Figure 6.1 Map of southwestern Iran showing the principal sites mentioned in Chapter 6.

the *sukkalmah* at Lagash (Hallo 1957: 118; see also Vallat 1990a: 121). At Susa, Kuk-Kirmash was the first to call himself *sukkalmah*, but his predecessor Shilhaha was the first ruler to be called *sukkalmah* (Vallat 1990a: 121), and he is generally considered the founding ancestor of the long line of *sukkalmahs* who reigned in the early second millennium BC. On the other hand, Shilhaha is identified in one text as the 'chosen son of Ebarat', and it is generally believed that this refers to the same ruler as Ebarti II, ninth king in the Shimashki kinglist discussed in Chapter 5 (Stolper 1982: 55).

Ebarat's own position in all of this, and the historical mechanics of the transition from the rule of Shimashki, the kinglist of which claims Ebarti II as one of its own, to that of the *sukkalmahs*, the later sources for which identify Ebarat as 'king of Anshan and Susa', must remain unclear so long as the absolute chronology of the early *sukkalmahs* is sketchy, but as noted above Vallat has recently suggested that the Susian *sukkalmahs* gradually overtook their highland Shimashkian 'vassals', finally achieving a position of predominance in the political arena of southwestern Iran (Vallat 1996e: 315–16). As already described, Ishbi-Erra's expulsion of Kindattu from Ur was followed by a period of rapprochement between Isin, Eshnunna and Shimashki, marked once more by several diplomatic marriages involving the daughters of Bilalama of Eshnunna and Iddin-Dagan of Isin. However, the maintenance of cordial east-west relations was soon interrupted by the appearance of a more aggressive ruler on the throne of Larsa. Gungunum (1932–1906 BC), the fifth monarch to have ruled over Larsa since the demise of the Ur III state, attacked and destroyed Bashime in his third year and Anshan in his fifth year (Sigrist 1990: 7; Vallat 1996e: 313), and may have been in control of Susa in his sixteenth year, depending on how one interprets a text from Susa (MDP 10: 21/4) dated to this year of his reign (Stolper 1982: 56). The disbursement of sesame oil at Larsa in year twelve of Sumuel's reign (i.e. 1882 BC) to an anonymous 'king of Anshan', however, suggests cordial relations with a highland ruler, not continuous subjugation of this distant region by Larsa. It is tempting to interpret the demise of the Shimashki line as a result of Gungunum's hostilities, and the rise of the *sukkalmahs* as a resurgence following the region's recovery from Larsa' aggression, but this must remain speculative (Carter and Stolper 1984: 27). An alternative reconstruction of early *sukkalmah* history would situate Gungunum's attack *c.* 1927 BC just prior to the appearance of Atta-hushu (Vallat 1989a; see also Pétrequin 1990), whom Vallat regards as a usurper of the throne and not a biological descendant of Shilhaha (Vallat 1990a: 124; 1996e: 310).

Although there is still some uncertainty over the precise sequence of rulers in the post-Shimashki period (Vallat 1996e), the variety in their titulature, consisting of no fewer than seventeen different titles including all variants (Vallat 1990a: 120), has long been recognized. Over half a century ago the late G.G. Cameron suggested that political power was vested in a triumvirate consisting of the *sukkalmah* in the position of paramount authority, followed by the *sukkal* ('minister') of Elam (and Shimashki), and finally by the *sukkal* of Susa in third position (Cameron 1936: 71; see also Grillot and Glassner 1991: 85). Upon the death of the reigning *sukkalmah*, the *sukkal* of Elam and Shimashki acceded to his position, the *sukkal* of Susa moved up a rank to replace him, and a new family member was chosen to be *sukkal* of Susa. In fact, as the provisional list of office-bearers and their titles shows (Table 6.1), the notion that simple triumvirates always operated in the period *c.* 1900–1600 BC – as few as fourteen and as many as twenty-four have been suggested (Carter and Stolper 1984: 77, n. 178) – does not seem to be borne out by the evidence.

Obviously there are titles additional to the three main ones just discussed which are associated with the *sukkalmahs* and their relatives. *Ippir* of Susa may mean something like 'magistrate of Susa', while **adda lugal** of Anshan and Susa may be an acknowledgement of the ancestral primacy of Shilhaha as founder of the *sukkalmah* line since the title means literally 'father king' (Vallat 1989b). The combined title '*sukkal* of Elam, Shimashki and Susa' may reflect real sovereignty over a more extended region than either the *sukkal* of Elam or the *sukkal* of Susa enjoyed. How prince of Elam should be differentiated from *sukkal* of Elam is unclear, just as the difference between the king of Susa and *sukkal* of Susa is uncertain. The fact that a single individual, such as Kuk-Kirmash could be simultaneously called not only *sukkalmah* but also *sukkal* of Elam, Shimashki and Susa, or that Tan-Uli was called *sukkalmah* and *sukkal* of Elam and Shimashki, clearly suggests that a tripartite division of power did not always obtain (Vallat 1990a: 120).

Vallat has argued persuasively that Atta-hushu's peculiar titulature demands a special explanation, for he and Tetep-mada are the only 'rulers' not associated in economic or legal texts with another *sukkal* or *sukkalmah*, as well as the only ones to bear the title 'shepherd of the people of Susa'. Furthermore, Atta-hushu is unique in using the titles 'shepherd of Inshushinak', '*sukkal* and *ippir*' and 'he who holds the . . . of Susa' (Vallat 1996e: 309–10). One might well ask whether Atta-hushu ever enjoyed the status of supreme ruler if he never took the title *sukkalmah*? In fact, noting that Atta-hushu is the only leader of the *sukkalmah* period whose texts are dated according to a Babylonian era (in one case to year 16 of Gungunum, in another to year 1 of Sumu-abum), Vallat has suggested that this lends weight to the idea that he came to power with the help of Gungunum and was not a rightful inheritor of the position *sukkalmah* (Vallat 1996e: 311). This might also explain why he never used this title, for his status may have been that of a client of Larsa's rather than an independent *sukkalmah*.

Equally problematic, and much debated over the years, has been the significance of the term *ruhushak*, literally 'sister's son' (see most recently Glassner 1994 and the critique by Vallat 1997a). Koschaker long ago signalled several possible interpretations of the phrase, including that of the biological issue of a true marriage between siblings; the biological issue of an exogamous marriage between a male and a female not of the same social group as a result of which the *ruhushak* was recognized, however, as having the juridical rights of a sister of her husband; the issue of biological parents who were not siblings but who belonged to a society in which descent through a particular female line needed to be indicated; and a legitimate descendant of a distant ancestor acknowledged as the founder of a dynasty (Koschaker 1933: 54–5). The latter interpretation is certainly the only one possible in some cases where the individual so named is separated in time by more than a century from the female identified as his father's sister, but

Table 6.1. *Tentative sequence of the sukkalmahs and their relationships to other high-ranking officials*

Sukkalmah	Other officers	Stated filiation	Titles	Reference
Ebarat II			king (**lugal**) of Anshan and Susa	MDP 28: 7, #4, 7
Shilhaha		chosen son of Ebarat	king (**lugal**)	MDP 28: #455
			sukkalmah, **adda-lugal** of Anshan and Susa	MDP 28: 7, #4
Pala-ishshan	Lankuku			?
	Kuku-sanit			MDP 28: #399
Kuk-Kirmash		'sister's son of' Shilhaha,	*sukkal* of Elam, Shimashki and Susa	VAB 1: 182, #5
		son of Lankuku	*sukkalmah*	VAB 1: 182, #5
	Tem-sanit			EKI 48 §2; 48a+b §3
	Kuk-Nahundi			MDP 24: #351
				MDP 24: #352
Kuk-Nashur I[1]		son of Shilhaha	*sukkalmah*	MDP 28: #8, 430
	Atta-hushu	'sister's son of' Shilhaha	*sukkal* and *ippir* of Susa	EKI 48 §2; 48b §3
				MDP 28: 7, #4
			shepherd of the people of Susa	MDP 28: 8–9, #5–6,
				MDP 2: 79 and Pl. 15.5
			shepherd of Inshushinak	MDP 6: 26, Pl. 5.3
			he who holds the . . . of Susa	Dossin 1962: 157
Shiruk-tuh[2]	Tetep-mada	'sister's son of' Shilhaha		?
	Simut-wartash I	'sister's son of' Shilhaha		EKI 48 §2; 48a+b §3
		son (?) of Shiruk-tuh		?
Siwe-palar-huppak[3]		'sister's son of' Shiruktuh	*sukkal* of Susa	MDP 28: #396, 397
			prince of Elam	EKI 3
	Kudu-zulush I[4]	'sister's son of' Shiruktuh	*sukkal* of Susa	MDP 28: #397
			sukkalmah	MDP 23: #179
Kutir-Nahhunte I		son (?) of Kudu-zulush		?
	Atta-merra-halki			MDP 24: #379
	Tata			MDP 24: #391
	Lila-irtash		*sukkal*	VAB 1: 184, #9
				MDP 28: #398
Temti-Agun			*sukkal* of Susa	MDP 28: #398
Kutir-Shilhaha		'sister's son of' Shiruktuh	*sukkal*	MDP 23: #212

Ruler	Relationship	Title	References
Kuk-Nashur II[5]	'sister's son of' Temti-Agun,	sukkalmah	MDP 22: #10, 133
		sukkal of Susa	MDP 23: #283
Temti-raptash		sukkal of Elam	MDP 22: #160
			MDP 23: #169, 183, 212–14, 216–20, 240, 315
			MDP 22: #8, 10, 101, 116–17, 133
Simut-wartash II			MDP 24: #341, 345, 393
			MDP 23: #221?, 222, 246
			MDP 25: 91, Fig. 15
			MDP 28: #420
Kudu-zulush II		king of Susa	MDP 22: #160
Sirtuh	'sister's son of' Kuk-Nashur	king of Susa	MDP 23: #284
Kuk-Nashur III	'sister's son of' Shilhaha	sukkal of Elam	MDP 23: #282
		sukkal of Elam, Shimashki and Susa	MDP 23: #282; VAB 1: 184, #7; VS 7: #67
		sukkalmah	MDP 23: #282; VAB 1: 184, #7; VS 7: #67
Tan-Uli	'sister's son of' Shilhaha	sukkal	MDP 23: #177–8, 186, 196, 206
			MDP 24: #335–6
		sukkalmah	MDP 22: #7, 9; MDP 23: #173;
			MDP 24: #338, 353, 370
Temti-halki	'sister's son of' Shilhaha	sukkal of Elam, Shimashki and Susa	VAB 1: 184, #7
		sukkalmah	VAB 1: 184, #7
Kuk-Nashur IV	'sister's son of' Tan-Uli	sukkalmah	EKI 48 §2, 48b §3
			EKI 48 §2, 48b §3

Notes:
[1] The arrangement of rulers by the name of Kuk-Nashur follows that proposed in Quintana 1996. Synchronisms with Mesopotamian rulers are noted in notes 2–5.
[2] Shamshi-Adad I of Assyria (1813–1781 BC).
[3] Hammurabi of Babylon (1792–1750 BC).
[4] Hammurabi of Babylon (1792–1750 BC).
[5] Ammisaduqa of Babylon (?) year 1 (1645 BC).

this explanation is just as obviously unsuited to other situations. In such cases, according to F.W. König, we may be dealing not with the issue of an incestuous brother-sister marriage, but with the adopted younger brother of a ruler (König 1957–71: 227) or perhaps, more plausibly, with the adopted son of a ruler's sister in cases in which a ruler either had no biological issue of his own or in which his own son had predeceased him. Doubtless because of the many unknowns involved in such speculations, Cameron interpreted *ruhushak* simply as 'descendant' (Cameron 1936: 61). M. Lambert, on the other hand, followed by Vallat, preferred to understand the term to mean 'son of the sister-wife of X', an incestuous, biological reality perhaps in the time of Shilhaha which became, from the time of Atta-hushu onward, an element of the royal titulary signifying legitimacy rather than genealogical affiliation (Lambert 1971: 217; Vallat 1989a, 1994, 1995a: 1028–9; 1996e: 300–1). For the Soviet scholar, Y.B. Yusifov, on the other hand, the term *ruhushak* 'originally meant a son born to one related, or not, married couple', and he further suggested that it was a survival 'of the dominating role of descent on the female side, namely, on [the] sister's line which gave the descendant the right of succession to the throne' (Yusifov 1974: 328). It must be stressed, however, that any notion of 'residual matriarchy' (Vallat 1994: 8) in the earlier periods of Elamite or Shimashkian history is pure speculation.

The early second millennium levels at Susa have yielded a large number of legal and administrative documents, all written in Akkadian, and naming by and large individuals with Akkadian personal names. This is in stark contrast to the names of the *sukkalmahs* themselves which are strictly Elamite. W.G. Lambert has suggested that one explanation for this imbalance may lie in the fact that, just prior to and following the fall of Ur, 'the area received a sudden insurge of Akkadian speakers', probably from the southern districts of Umma and Lagash (Lambert 1991: 57), which would account for the fact that 'most names from OB [Old Babylonian] Susa are Semitic' (Zadok 1991: 225).

Finally, a small group of seven texts, written in Akkadian, may be described as 'funerary documents' (Steve and Gasche 1996). These documents, dating most probably to the very end of the *sukkalmah* period, were found in 1914 in an area to the east of the Achaemenid palace of Darius, possibly in association with a number of tombs excavated there by de Mecquenem. Judging by the longest example the texts, which are unparalleled in Mesopotamia, concern the taking of the deceased by the hand and accompanying him to the final judgement.

Assyria, Babylonia and the sukkalmahs

Gungunum was far from the only aggressive ruler to have attempted to extend his influence eastwards. Siniddinam (1849–1843 BC), well-known for his building activities in the Ebabbar shrine at Larsa, conquered the town of Ibrat on the Tigris, possibly to be located near modern Kut el-Amara (Zadok 1987: 6). If Ibrat was under the control of the *sukkalmah* of Susa and/or his *sukkal*, its loss might help explain the forging of an alliance a few years later between Zambija of Isin (1836–1834 BC) and Elam, a coalition the defeat of which was commemorated in the year formula for Sîn-iqisham of Larsa's (1840–1836 BC) fifth year, 'year Uruk, Kazallu, the army of the land of Elam and Zambija the king of Isin were defeated' (Sigrist 1990: 29). A text from Uruk found in the palace of Sinkashid, a contemporary of Warad-Sin of Larsa (1834–1823 BC), which records the disbursement of nearly 1.5 *minas* of gold (*c.* 750 g) for the manufacture of vessels destined for the *sukkalmah* of Elam (Durand 1992), may well reflect the short-lived alliance between Uruk and Elam. Just a few years later, however, perhaps in 1835 BC, Kutur-mapuk, son of Simti-Shilhak and father of Manzi-wartash, in turn conquered Larsa. Kudur-mapuk, his father and his daughter all have seemingly Elamite names, but he is called 'father' or 'sheikh' of Yamutbal or Emutbal (Zadok 1987: 6), a region located just east of the Tigris (Edzard 1957: 105; Stol 1976: 63–72; see also Frayne 1992: 93 and Map 13), as well as 'father of the Amorite land (or mountain)' (Hallo 1980: 194). As these are generally held to be 'Amorite' designations, it has often been suggested that, in spite of their names, the family of Kutur-mapuk were Amorites who had settled at some point in the Trans-Tigridian area and there came under Elamite influence (e.g. Lambert 1991: 55), perhaps even serving the Elamites militarily (Edzard 1957: 168). In this connection it is interesting to note that, in some of the letters from Susa dating to the *sukkalmah* period, Ishtaran, the city-god of Der, chief city of Yamutbal, is mentioned (Lackenbacher 1994: 54).

It is not clear whether Kutur-mapuk's conquest of Larsa was an independent act on the part of the sheikh of Yamutbal or whether he was acting as an Elamite proxy (Edzard 1957: 168). Either way, it transformed Larsa's political history, and for the next seventy years a combined kingdom of Larsa and Yamutbal was ruled over by his two sons, Warad-Sin (1834–1823 BC) and Rim-Sin I (1822–1763 BC). Not surprisingly, therefore, most of the individuals with linguistically Elamite names who are mentioned outside of Susa itself are to be found in the Old Babylonian texts from Larsa (Zadok 1987: 6). Rim-Sin's Elamite or quasi-Elamite origins seem to be reflected in a 'Hymn to An' (UET VI 102), in which those origins 'in the mountains where the divine powers are dispensed for the principality' are juxtaposed against the legitimacy of his calling as 'shepherd of Sumer and Akkad' (Steible 1975: 7). For many years it was thought that the dating formula for Rim-Sin's eighth year should be read 'year Rim-Sin the king had built the temple of Enki in Ur and the temple of Ninlil of Elam in the temple(-complex) of Ninmara' (Edzard 1957: 177, n. 970; see also Carter and Stolper 1984: 28), but more recently a new reading of the divine name in question has resulted in **ᵈnin.é.NIM.ma** instead of **ᵈnin.líl-elam.ma**, such that Ninlil of Elam has vanished and been replaced by a 'temple of Ninenimma' (Stol 1976:19; Sigrist 1990: 41).

One of Rim-Sin's most important contemporaries on the political stage of Western Asia was certainly Shamshi-Adad (1813–1781 BC), the expansive ruler from Syria who, after growing up as an exiled prince in Babylonia, marched northward, conquered Ekallatum and Assur, and created the first Assyrian empire (Læssøe 1963: 41–2; Villard 1995). Shamshi-Adad's eventually successful attempts to expand that empire east of the Tigris late in his reign, beginning in his twenty-fifth year (1789 BC), certainly threatened the inhabitants of the Zagros (Gutians, Turukkeans) as well as Elam itself, and a letter from Tell Shemshara (SH 827), which dates to Shamshi-Adad's twenty-eighth year (1785 BC) or one to two years subsequent to it (Eidem 1992: 16), informs us that 'Shuruhtuh, the king of Elam', i.e. the *sukkalmah* Shiruk-tuh, had raised an army of 12,000 troops as a contribution towards a joint force with Assyria, Eshnunna and perhaps the Turukkeans (a Zagros people), the purpose of which was the destruction of the Guti (Eidem 1985: 90; 1992: 18; Wu 1994: 186–7). A fragmentary alabaster stele commemorating a long series of conquests in Elamite by naming a toponym and adding the phrase 'I took' is probably to be attributed to Shiruk-tuh (Farber 1975: 78). If one of the personal names there is restored as Indassu (Wu 1994: 186), then the likelihood that the text indeed recounts Shiruk-tuh's conquests is made even greater, for the Tell Shemshara letter mentioned above specifically says that Shiruk-tuh's 'intention is towards Indassu', king of the Guti (Eidem 1985: 90; 1992: 18, 49). Interestingly, Indasu was also the name of an **ensí** of Zabshali in the Ur III period (Kutscher 1989: 91)

A tantalizing glimpse of the status of the *sukkalmahs* at about this time is afforded by a letter (A 7537) which was probably sent by Rimsin-Enlilkurgalani, an official in the service of Rim-Sin, or Sin-muballit, Rim-Sin's brother and viceroy of the northern portion of his kingdom (thus Wu 1994: 169; Rowton 1967: 269 and Charpin and Durand 1991: 62 believe the letter's author to have been Rim-Sin himself), to their Larsan ambassadors at the court of the king of Eshnunna. Although badly damaged, the letter instructs the envoys to tell the king of Eshnunna that 'our lord', i.e. Rim-Sin, 'sent (envoys) to the great king of Elam'. The letter is undated but was written when Dadusha (?-1780 BC; Sasson 1995: 904) was king of Eshnunna. Whether this was before or after Dadusha's invasion of the Middle Euphrates district of Suhu *c.* 1783–1782 BC (Villard 1995: 881), we do not know. At any rate, Eshnunna was obviously strong at the time, but it is the 'great king of Elam' who would seem to be the most important monarch of the period, and this is one of the first hints of the power of the *sukkalmahs* in the late Isin-Larsa period (Charpin and Durand 1991: 62).

Although initially successful in his eastward expansion, Shamshi-Adad was to die in 1781 BC and it has been suggested that the power vacuum thereby created was instrumental in allowing the expanding power of the *sukkalmah* to reverse the trend of Assyrian expansion and, in league with Babylon and Mari, conquer the powerful kingdom of Eshnunna (Charpin and Durand 1991: 64) at the end of Zimri-Lim's eighth year on the throne (a conquest which may have also caused the destruction of Tell Harmal, ancient Shaduppum, at modern Baghdad; Charpin 1987: 117; for the date see Durand 1994: 18) and possibly even allow the *sukkalmah* to make Eshnunna his temporary home (van Dijk 1970: 65). But however that may be, it was the *sukkalmah* who was in the predominant position vis-à-vis his subordinate allies. The Mari royal archives contain examples of letters and extracts of letters sent by the *sukkalmah* to Hammurabi of Babylon (1792–1750 BC) telling him to leave the towns of Eshnunna alone or run the risk of invasion by the Elamite ruler, and enjoining him to sustain no correspondence with his counterpart at Mari, Zimri-Lim (1776–1761 BC) (Durand 1994: 16). A similarly haughty tone was used in correspondence with Zimri-Lim and his ambassadors; with Atamrum, king of Allahad, who was made to journey all the way to

Anshan to receive a pardon; and with Ishme-Dagan, grandson of Shamshi-Adad and a refugee at Babylon (Charpin and Durand 1991: 63). Even the prince of Qatna in Syria proposed surrendering his principality to the Elamite king if the latter would take up the fight on his behalf against the kingdom of Aleppo. That cities in Syria should defer to the *sukkalmah* is remarkable to say the least, and a sure sign of the Elamite's high standing. Moreover, the Elamite king's status is confirmed by the fact that the Syrian and Babylonian rulers, each of whom addressed the other as 'brother', considered themselves 'sons' of the *sukkalmah* (Charpin and Durand 1991: 64). The reasons for this great deference – apart from the conquest of Eshnunna and the disappearance of a powerful rival with the death of Shamshi-Adad – might lie in the historical memory of the part played by Shimashki in the downfall of Ur; in the vast resources of the Iranian Plateau, human as well as natural, which helped prop up the *sukkalmah's* legitimacy; and in the eventual intrusion of Elam into the lucrative commercial network of Anatolia and northern Mesopotamia (Charpin and Durand 1991: 64–5). Or was the latter in fact the objective of that Elamite expansion in the year Zimri-Lim 9 which brought soldiers from Elam and Eshnunna to Shubat-Enlil, Shamshi-Adad's capital (Charpin 1986), along with a governor?

Whatever the material and psychological modalities of the esteem in which the *sukkalmah* was held by his western colleagues, it is obvious from the Mari texts that gift exchange between Elam and Mari went hand in hand with the exchange of envoys, and that one of the material benefits accruing to Mari for a period of about two-and-a-half years from the beginning of Zimri-Lim 7 to the middle of year 9 was the opportunity of acquiring tin (Table 6.2). As the texts show clearly, a number of leading merchants or commercial agents were entrusted with mounting trading expeditions to Susa, but the king was personally involved in some cases as well (Durand 1986: 122–5; see also 1990). Zimri-Lim is known to have had at his disposal some 970 *minas* (1 *mina* = c. 500 g) during a voyage which he undertook early in his eighth year and to have distributed as gifts no less than 821 *minas* (410.5 kgs) to the kings of Aleppo, Hazor, Ugarit and Ursum (Joannès 1991: 68). It is probable, particularly given the archaeological evidence for links between Susa and Bactria at this time (see below), that Afghanistan was the source of Elam's tin (Potts 1997: 269). This suggestion finds corroboration, moreover, in the fact that lapis lazuli, most probably from the Badakhshan region of Afghanistan and much sought after by Zimri-Lim, was acquired from Elam at this time as well (Guichard 1996).

The brief period of cordial relations just described was one result of a rapprochement between Mari and Elam following their joint conquest with Babylon of the kingdom of Eshnunna, prior to which time Eshnunna and Assur had stood between Mari and the acquisition of Elamite tin at a good price (Joannès 1991: 68, 70). This situation, however, was soon to change. Although we do not have all of the details, it seems clear that the *sukkalmah* had no intention of sharing the advantages gained by the conquest of Eshnunna with his colleagues at Mari and Babylon, and when Hammurabi occupied Mankisum and Upi, two towns along the frontier of the kingdoms of Eshnunna and Babylon, he was threatened by Siwe-palar-huppak of Elam (see Grillot and Glassner

Table 6.2. *Relations between Mari and Elam according to texts from Mari*

Action	Date	Agent	Reference
wine sent to Siwe-palar-huppak of Anshan and Kudu-zulush of Susa	7-i-ZL 7	—	AAM 2
silver and gold vessels sent to same	8/9-ii-ZL 7	Yatar-Addu	ARM XXV 3, 5, 6
96 minas 25 shekels of tin and 2 minas of gold brought to Mari by Iddiyatum, chief of the Mari merchants	3-vi-ZL 7	Haya-Addu Belânum	ARM XXV 301
more gifts sent to Elam	27-vi?-ZL 7	Ishhi-Dagan Haya-Addu	ARM XXIV 162
receipt of Elamite silver at Mari	25-viii-ZL 7	Lishtamar	ARM XXV 201
dispatch of Ishhi-Dagan with 1 mina of gold to buy tin in Elam	11-ix-ZL 7	Ishhi-Dagan	ARM XXI 218
arrival of garments from Elam	2-i-ZL 8	—	AAM 2
dispatch of precious vessels to Siwe-palar-huppak and Zibir-Anshan	11-i-ZL 8	—	ARM XXIV 1
dispatch of wine to Elam	i/iii-ZL 8	Ishhi-Dagan	ARM XXIII 355
dispatch of Ishhi-Dagan with 1 mina of gold to buy tin in Elam	7-vi-ZL 8	Iddiyatum	AAM 2
announcement of arrival of envoys from Elam	ii-vi-ZL 8	Yatar-Addu, Inneri	ARM VI 19
Elamite envoys in transit to Qatna pass Mari	vi?-ZL 8	Inneri, Kukkumanzu	ARM VI 19
dispatch of precious vessels to Siwe-palar-huppak	2-viii-ZL 8	—	ARM XXV 2
arrival of silver from Elam	25-viii-ZL 8	Yatar-Addu	ARM XXI 201
arrival of 107 minas 45 shekels of tin	30-viii-ZL 8	Isshi-Dagan, Yatar-Addu	ARM XXV 368
arrival of 107 minas 40 shekels of tin	?	Isshi-Dagan, Yatar-Addu	AAM 2
dispatch of 138 minas 40 shekels of tin to Carchemish, Ursum and Aleppo	15-ix-ZL 8	—	ARM XXIII 524
dispatch of 14 talents of tin by boat to the West	8-xii-ZL 8	Yantin-Addu	ARM XXV 450
dispatch of a gift to Kudu-zulush on his capture of Eshnunna	late ZL 8	—	M. 8806
dispatch of precious vessels to Elam	iv-ZL 9	—	ARM XXIII 542
gift of precious vessels to Elamites at Aleppo	iv-ZL 9	Inneri, Kuksiyari Shamash-ili	ARM XXI 251

Notes:
Zimri-Lim reigned from 1776–1761 BC according to the middle chronology. Data from Joannès 1991.

1990), who claimed them for himself, ordered their liberation forthwith, and threatened to invade Hammurabi's kingdom if this were not done (Charpin and Durand 1991: 63). Simultaneously the *sukkalmah* demanded that the king of Mari terminate his relations with Hammurabi (Charpin 1990: 109). This was apparently going too far, and it would appear that the *sukkalmah*'s dictatorial manner prompted the formation of an anti-Elamite axis consisting of Mari, Babylon and the kingdom of Aleppo (Charpin and Durand 1991: 65).

Thanks to a letter describing the oath of alliance between Zimri-Lim and Hammurabi we have a rare window on the actual ceremony at which a formal agreement between Babylon and Mari was sealed, while the text of Hammurabi's oath of allegiance, prepared by a scribe at Mari, shows the king of Babylon committing himself in no uncertain terms: 'From now on, as long as I live, I shall indeed be the enemy of Siwepalarhuppak. I shall not let my servants or my messengers mingle with his servants, and I shall not dispatch them to him. I shall not make peace with Siwepalarhuppak without the approval of Zimri-Lim . . . If I plan to make peace with Siwepalarhuppak, I shall certainly consult with Zimri-Lim' (Sasson 1995: 909; see also Charpin 1990: 110). Considering the fact that Zimri-Lim had concluded a treaty with Ibal-pi-El II, king of Eshnunna, in the fourth year of his reign, yet by his eighth year had joined the coalition with Babylon and Elam against Eshnunna, which resulted in the probable massacre of Ibal-pi-El and his entire family (Durand 1994: 18; witness the year name for Zimri-Lim 8: 'year when Zimri-Lim sent allied troops to Elam'), the king of Mari may have had a jaundiced view of alliances such as these. If not, he certainly ought to have. In the thirtieth year of his reign (1764/3 BC), Hammurabi defeated the army of Elam which had recruited from the extremity of Marhashi, Subartu, Gutium, Eshnunna and Malgium (van Dijk 1970: 65); the following year (1763/2 BC) he again campaigned against Eshnunna, Subartu and Gutium, and crushed Larsa as well; and the next year (1762/1 BC) Hammurabi's troops marched into Mari, defeated Zimri-Lim and destroyed his kingdom (Sasson 1995: 911).

Thereafter historical sources on the *sukkalmahs* become very sparse. Neither a reference to cereals, perhaps intended to be sold in Elam, in the twenty-sixth year of the reign of Ammiditana of Babylon (i.e. 1658 BC) nor an allusion to Kuk-Nashur of Elam in a source from the first year of Ammisaduqa of Babylon's reign can be adduced as evidence that Elam had become tributary to the Babylonian king (Zadok 1987: 11).

Khuzistan in the time of the sukkalmahs

Architectural remains from the period of the *sukkalmah*s have been exposed both on the Ville Royale and on the Apadana at Susa. In the course of some twenty-one seasons of excavation on the Ville Royale, R. Ghirshman revealed no fewer than fifteen major stratigraphic levels in a deposit *c.* 15 m deep. Levels XV to XII in Chantier A show a changing plan of domestic and public architecture and can be assigned to the *sukkalmah* period. As Carter has observed, 'a "chapel" from A XV, the large households of A XIV (Fig. 6.2), the industrial area of A XIII with its kilns, and the house of the temple

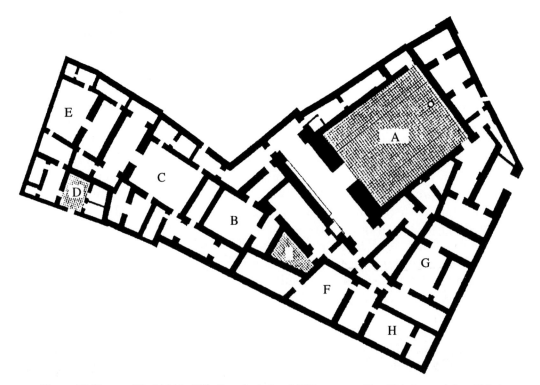

Figure 6.2 House of Ra-bi-bi in Ville Royale A, level XIV, excavated by Ghirshman (after Ghirshman 1965: Fig. 3). The letters identify the individual courtyards within the house.

prostitutes in A XII (Fig. 6.3) give some idea of the variety of functions within the city during the early second millennium' (Carter 1985: 47; see also Trümpelmann 1981). As Steve has shown (Steve 1994: 25–7), tablets recovered in the large house on the east side of the Ville Royale excavation ('Complexe Est') in A XII and A XI can be linked to the reigns of half a dozen of the latest *sukkalmahs*, as well as to Kidinu, 'king of Susa and Anshan' and founder of the first post-*sukkalmah* dynasty (Table 6.3; see also Chapter 7). As Steve has stressed, this is a sure sign that the first 'kings of Susa and Anshan' followed on directly from the last of the *sukkalmahs*. On the Apadana, excavations in what had been a huge pit dug in the Islamic era (Chantier 24) revealed a complex of rooms with many associated, intramural graves built up against a large packed mud (*pisé*) wall of Susa I date. The third phase ('troisième état') of this complex could be associated ceramically with levels A XV and B VI-V in Ghirshman's Ville Royale excavations, *c*. 1970–1750 BC (Steve and Gasche 1990: 16, 18, 23).

Building inscriptions in the form of dedications inscribed on bricks are a source of precise information on the building activities of various *sukkals* and *sukkalmahs* at Susa during the early second millennium BC. Five rulers from this period were active at the site (Table 6.4), where work was done on a ramp, a temple for Ishmekarab, and a temple for Inshushinak known as the 'Ekikuanna'. The goddess Ishmekarab was

Table 6.3. *References to* sukkalmahs *in texts from ville Royale A, levels XI and XII*

Ville Royale A level	Text	Royal references
XI	7	Temti-halki, Kuk-Nashur (IV?)
	11	Tan-Uli, Kuk-Nashur (IV?)
	12, 19, 20	Kuk-Nashur (III?), Kudu-zulush II
XII	91	Kuk-Nashur (III? IV?)
	13	Kidinu

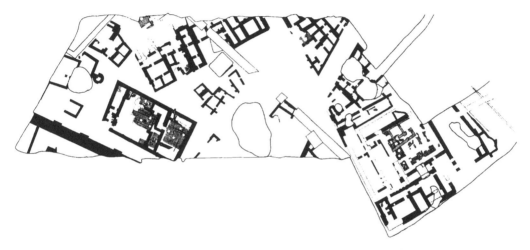

Figure 6.3 Ville Royale A, level XII (after Steve 1994: Fig. 2).

thought to escort the dead on their way to final judgement by Inshushinak, chief deity of Susa (Malbran-Labat 1995: 194). The building activities of the *sukkalmahs* outside of Susa are also attested by inscribed bricks (or fragments thereof) at several sites. Material attributable to Temti-Agun is known from the site of Choga Pahan East in Khuzistan (Stolper and Wright 1990), while the name of Siwe-palar-huppak is attested on a brick inscription from Tal-i Malyan which tells us that 'Siwe-palar-huppak, *sukkal* of Elam, [built] a temple' (Stolper 1982: 60). A fragment of an alabaster socle belonging to Simut-wartash is also known from Liyan, near Bushire (see below) (Malbran-Labat 1995: 19, 217, n. 23).

There are a number of distinctive categories of material culture dating to the *sukkal-mah* period which deserve some attention. Generally speaking, the ceramics at Susa continue to follow the traditional, largely Mesopotamian forms of the preceding Shimashki phase (Carter and Stolper 1984: 148). Large vats set in the ground beneath the plastered, baked brick floor of a building in Ville Royale A XII, contained in one case

Table 6.4. *Brick inscriptions showing the building activities of various* sukkalmahs *at Susa*

Ruler	Text	Reference
Kuk-Kirmash	For Inshushinak, his lord, Kuk-Kirmash, *sukkalmah*, *sukkal* of Elam, of Shimashki and of Susa, sister's son of Shilhaha, did not re-do the ancient temple but restored the Ekikuanna (with) a new wall of baked bricks; he built (it) for his life	IRS 18
Atta-hushu	Atta-hushu, the shepherd of the people of Susa, beloved servant of Inshushinak, sister's son of Shilhaha, built a ramp	IRS 10
"	Atta-hushu, the shepherd of Inshushinak, sister's son of Shilhaha, restored the ancient sanctuary; he did it for his life	IRS 11
"	Atta-hushu, the shepherd of Inshushinak, sister's son of Shilhaha, made a stele of justice, he had it erected in the marketplace. He who does not know the just price, May the Sun (Utu? Shamash? Nahhunte?) inform him.	IRS 12
"	Atta-hushu, the shepherd of the people of Susa, sister's son of Shilhaha, his beloved dwelling which he de[sired? . . .]	IRS 13
Temti-Agun	Temti-Agun, *sukkal* of Susa, sister's son of Shiruktuh, has built a temple of baked bricks for Ishmekarab, for the life of Kutir-Nahhunte, for the life of Lila-irtash, for his own life, for the life of Temti-hisha-hanesh, for the life of his venerated?/gracious? mother Welkisha	IRS 14
Temti-halki	Temti-halki, *sukkalmah*, *sukkal* of Elam, of Shimashki and of Susa, sister's son of Shilhaha, beloved brother of Kurigugu, for his life, he has built the temple of baked bricks for Inshushinak	IRS 15
"	For Inshushinak, the great king, Temti-halki, *sukkalmah* of Elam (and) of Shimashki, sister's son of Shilhaha, his beloved brother of Kur[igugu . . .]	IRS 16
Kuk-Nashur	For Inshushinak, his lord, Kuk-Nashur, *sukkalmah*, *sukkal* of Elam, of Shimashki and of Susa, sister's son of Shilhaha, has built for his life the High-temple of baked bricks of the Acropole of Inshushinak	IRS 17

Notes:
IRS = Malbran-Labat 1995

a set of five beakers. This has been interpreted as an ancient beer keg and drinking mugs by one scholar (Trümpelmann 1981: 39ff.). Fine grey pottery with incised and punctate decoration, including geometric shapes and concentric circles filled with a white substance (Fig. 6.4), forms a coherent group found over a large area extending from Nuzi in the northeast, to Tell Asmar (ancient Eshnunna) and Tell Hasan in the Diyala region, Godin Tepe and Chogha Gavaneh in central western Iran, Tello in southern Mesopotamia, Susa in Khuzistan, and Tal-i Malyan in Fars (Carter 1990: 96). The style of much of this material is so similar that the existence of a single production centre has been suggested (Delougaz 1952: 120). Given the extensive interaction between the

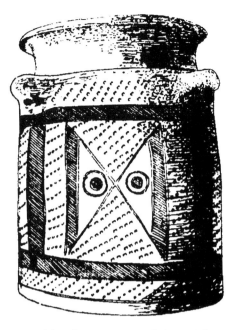

Figure 6.4 Punctate and incised greyware vessels from Susa (after de Mecquenem 1943: Fig. 46).

sukkalmahs, Eshnunna, Larsa and Babylon, the distribution of this pottery is scarcely surprising.

Vessels made of a unique bitumen compound containing ground-up calcite and quartz grains are also characteristic of Susa in the early second millennium. Naturally available at many spots around Susa and in Khuzistan generally (Connan and Deschesne 1996: 228–337; see also Marschner, Duffy and Wright 1978), bitumen compound was used as early as the Susa I period, but its most extensive exploitation seems to have occurred during the early second millennium when a wide range of artistically fashioned tripod vessels, bowls and cups, some with animal protomes (Pl. 6.1, Fig. 6.5), were fashioned from this material (Harper, Aruz and Tallon 1992: 99–105; Connan and Deschesne 1996: 238–62). It is now clear that the bitumen compound was formed into bars or blocks and fired at 250° C. In this way it acquired the hardness of a stone and could be carved as such (Connan and Deschesne 1996: 117). One of the finest examples of a bitumen compound vessel, showing a recumbent ram, was discovered in the Ishtar-Kititum temple at Tell Ischali in the Diyala (Porada 1965: 52, Fig. 33; see also Calmeyer 1995a: 445, Abb. 1) and is surely a sign of the frequent contact which took place between the kingdom of Eshnunna and Susa during the *sukkalmah* period. A fragmentary caprid head, broken at the neck, is known from Uruk (Lindemeyer and Martin 1993: Taf. 11.139A), while a nearly complete vessel was discovered at Choga Mish as well (Kantor 1977). Bitumen compound was also used extensively to fashion cylinder and stamp seals at Susa during this period (Connan and Deschesne 1996: 289ff.).

In the realm of terracotta we find an enormous number of both male and female fig-

Plate 6.1 Bitumen compound bowl (Sb 2740) with carved animal decoration from Susa (22 cm long). © Musée du Louvre, Antiquités Orientales

urines at Susa during the *sukkalmah* period. Male figurines were most numerous at this time and include a diverse range of types including bearded figures with horned crowns, most likely representing deities; musicians holding e.g. *oud* or mandolin-like string instruments and 'crooked pipes', presumably a wind instrument; men holding monkeys; and men, perhaps priests, grasping kids or lambs to their chest. Turning to the female figurines, these normally show the complete human figure nude with the arms folded across the chest, hands clasped beneath the breasts. The majority of these figurines were mould-made, as the recovery of actual moulds attests (Spycket 1992). Nude females lying on terracotta bed models are also known, as they are from contemporary contexts in Mesopotamia, such as Isin and Tello (Trümpelmann 1981: 42–3). Females wearing the fleecy garment known in Mesopotamian iconography as the *kaunakes* are also depicted. These are interpreted as representations of deities because of their horned crowns (Spycket 1992: 123–4). Finally, Susa has yielded several examples of apparently handmade terracotta plaques with incised 'drawings', apparently 'artists' trial pieces or studies for sculptural production' (Winter 1996: 398).

Turning now to the metal work of the period (Tallon 1987: 341ff.), much of it derives from the poorly published and as yet largely unevaluated terracotta 'sarcophagus'

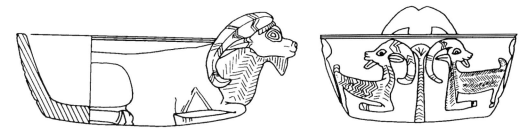

Figure 6.5 Sb 2740 = Pl. 6.1 (after Connan and Duschesne 1996: 242).

graves excavated by R. de Mecquenem. Weapons were represented by a typologically broad range of socketed axeheads, spear and lanceheads, arrowheads, and daggers. Agricultural or horticultural tools included adzes, sickles and hoes, while metal vessels included open bowls, cauldrons, deep 'buckets', vases, and an embossed bowl. Alongside silver and gold bracelets, earrings, and beads, sometimes used in conjunction with semi-precious stones such as agates in bracelets and necklaces, copper or bronze jewellery was also found. Small copper figurines (*c.* 10–20 cm high) of horned deities, one of which was originally gold-plated and another of which is shown seated in a chariot (Fig. 6.6) are also attested at this time. One of the more important metal types found at Susa in the early second millennium is a socketed axe with a flaring blade (Pl. 6.2) which has come to be known as the 'Atta-hushu type' axe because of the fact that one of the known examples bears the following engraved inscription: 'Atta-hushu, sister's son of Shilhaha, he who holds the reins (?) of the people of Susa, Ibni-Adad his servant, has given him this bronze axe' (Sollberger and Kupper 1971: 261). Ibni-Adad was a well-known scribe whose son Rim-Adad and grandson Adad-rabi also served Atta-hushu (Vallat 1989a: 34, 1996e: 304; see also Grillot and Glassner 1993). At least one terracotta figurine from Susa, although headless, shows the male figure clearly grasping an axe with an 'Atta-hushu-type' axehead in his left hand (Spycket 1992: Pl. 92.775). Moreover, similar axes are attested on *sukkalmah*-period seals and seal-impressions from Susa. The incidence of tin use in bronze, particularly favoured for weaponry, increased in the early second millennium (Tallon 1987: 351), hardly surprising given what was said above about Elam's access to tin during this period.

The glyptic of Susa during the early second millennium was as heterogeneous as its metalwork. Nearly one hundred cylinder seals from Susa can be considered 'Old Babylonian' in style, strongly reflecting Mesopotamian styles and iconography, while somewhat more than that number differ enough from the glyptic of the Isin-Larsa and Old Babylonian periods to be classified as 'popular Elamite' (Amiet 1972a: 226–64). Seals attributable to this latter group are also known from Tal-i Malyan, Persepolis and the art market (Seidl 1990; Porada 1990). At least two cylinder seals from Susa, one of which has been heavily worn, can be considered 'Cappadocian', i.e. deriving from Anatolia and showing clear similarities to material from level 1b at Kültepe (ancient Kanesh), while several seal-impressions and at least one seal are just as clearly Syrian

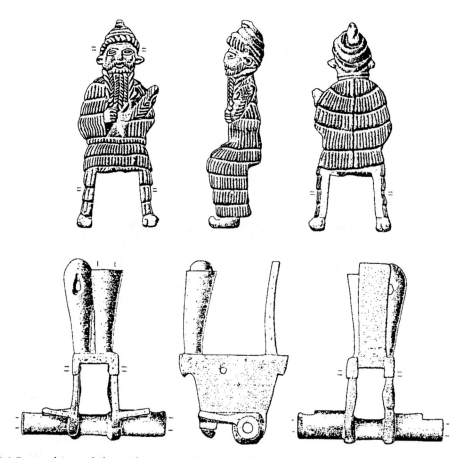

Figure 6.6 Bronze deity and chariot from Susa (after Tallon, Hurtel and Drilhon 1989: Pl. II).

in origin. The historical ties between Mari and the *sukkalmahs*, and the activities of the latter in northern Syria discussed above undoubtedly provide the explanation for the appearance of such material at Susa (Amiet 1985a: 11; see also 1972a: 212).

Susa is thought to have covered an area of *c.* 85 ha by the *sukkalmah* period, when roughly twenty new villages were founded as well (Carter and Stolper 1984: 150). Settlement, though sparser, is also attested at this time in some of the adjacent valley systems to the east, including Ram Hormuz and Izeh (Bayani 1979: 99–103), while *sukkalmah*-period levels are found at Tepe Farukhabad in the Deh Luran plain to the north as well (Wright 1981, Carter 1981).

Dilmun, Magan, Bactria and Elam

From the time of the *sukkalmahs* comes a growing body of evidence, both epigraphic and archaeological, reflecting ties between Susa, Elam and Anshan, the regions bordering the Persian Gulf and Bactria (northern Afghanistan/southern Uzbekistan).

Plate 6.2 Atta-hushu-type bronze axe (Sb 10236) from Susa. © Musée du Louvre, Antiquités Orientales

I/Enzag/k, the chief deity of Dilmun – a name denominating Bahrain and the adjacent mainland of what is today eastern Saudi Arabia (Potts 1990b) – was either venerated at Susa by a temple and a paved walkway of early second millennium date dedicated to Ea, Inshushinak and Enzag (Vallat 1983a: 93), or else Inshushinak had, as one of his epithets, the name of the Dilmunite deity (Vallat 1997d). Be that as it may, contact with Dilmun is in any case evinced by four 'classic' Dilmun stamp seals made of softstone which have been found at Susa, six imitation Dilmun stamp seals made of bitumen compound which are probably local copies of actual Dilmun-style seals (Connan and Deschesne 1996: 291–2, nos. 299–304), two cylinder seals reminiscent both in iconography and execution of Dilmun stamp seals, a clay sealing with the impression of a Dilmun seal, and a tablet (Pl. 6.3, Fig. 6.7) bearing the impression of a Dilmun seal (Amiet 1986f: 265–8). These last two finds are particularly interesting, for while the sealing may have come off of a commodity sealed in Dilmun and shipped to Susa, the tablet is a contract resembling others from Susa, which concerns three brothers (Elamatum, A'abba, and Milki-El son of Tem-Enzag) who loaned 10 *minas* of copper to one Ekiba, about to depart on a business trip, against a guarantee by one Milku-danum (Lambert 1976: 71). An answer to the question of why the tablet, probably written at Susa, was sealed using a Dilmun seal, is suggested by the Milki-El's father's name, Tem-Enzag, which contains in slightly variant form the name of the chief deity of Dilmun,

Plate 6.3 Economic text (Sb 11221 + 12404, 4.7×6.3 cm) from Susa with an impression made by a Dilmun stamp seal. © Musée du Louvre, Antiquités Orientales

I/Enzag/k. Nor is this the only written source for such a link with Dilmun, for another account text found in 1965–66 in 'Chantier A' and probably belonging to a small archive dating to the reign of the *sukkalmah* Kutir-Nahhunte I, records the delivery of 17.5 *minas* of silver 'brought by the Dilmunite' (de Meyer 1966: 117). If the fragmentary Akkadian inscription found in 1913 at Bushire, on the Persian Gulf, by M. Pézard which names Simut-wartash is indeed attributable to the *sukkal* of this name, son of Shiruk-tuh (Vallat 1984a: 258; Carter and Stolper 1984: 31), then this might suggest that the control of the *sukkalmahs* was well entrenched along the Gulf coast and that the links with Dilmun may have proceeded via Fars just as easily as up the Gulf and along the Karkheh river.

Soft-stone vessels from the Oman peninsula (ancient Magan) were certainly finding their way to southwestern Iran in the second millennium BC. Although the number of extant examples is small, a characteristic lid with dotted circle decoration is known from the foundation deposit of the Inshushinak temple on the Acropole at Susa (de Miroschedji 1973: Pl. 7e; Häser 1988: Abb. 42.531), while a similar lid and a large fragment of a hole-mouth vessel were discovered by M. Pézard during his excavations at Bushire (ancient Liyan) in 1913 (Häser 1988: 100). As with the alabaster 'booty of Magan' discussed in Chapter 4, it is most likely that the contents of these soft-stone

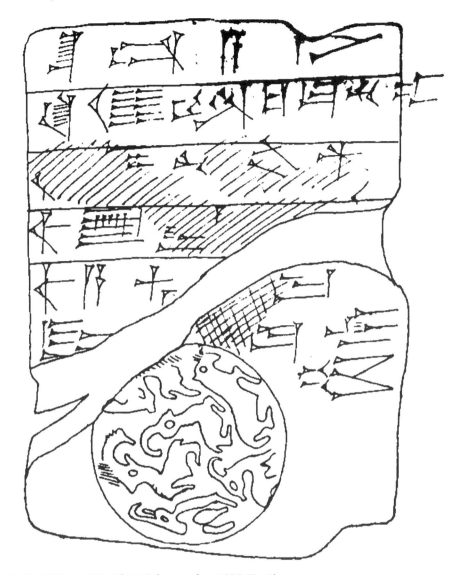

Figure 6.7 Sb 11221 + 12404 = Pl. 6.1 (after Lambert 1976: Fig. 1).

vessels were the desired commodity, rather than the vessels themselves. Whether copper from Magan reached Susa at this time, as it had done in the late Early Dynastic era (see Chapter 4), we do not know.

Bactria was the source of a distinctive group of square-based, soft-stone flasks found at Susa (Amiet 1980a), as well as a small number of pieces of imported stone statuary, an inlaid eagle pendant, a stone column, and a compartmented bronze stamp seal (Amiet 1986c: Figs. 97, 106, 108). These Bactrian objects are likely to have travelled to Susa as a by-product of the much more important trade in tin discussed above.

Sites in Fars

In Chapter 5 it was noted that the Kaftari period at Tal-i Malyan overlapped with the late Akkadian, Ur III, Isin-Larsa and Old Babylonian periods, or the Shimashki and *sukkalmah* periods at Susa. For this reason it is unnecessary to again review the situation there. Two rock reliefs datable to this period have been located in Fars, and these show strong iconographic links to some of the popular Elamite glyptic mentioned above.

The best preserved of the two reliefs is at Kurangun (Seidl 1986; Vanden Berghe 1986a with earlier lit.), roughly halfway between Bishapur and Behbehan in western Fars (Fig. 6.8). The left and right-hand panels are of much later, Neo-Elamite date (eighth/seventh centuries BC). The central panel shows a male deity with horned crown seated on a coiled serpent throne. Behind him sits a female deity, likewise crowned, wearing the *kaunakes* garment. Each holds a pair of serpents in his/her left hand. In his right hand the male deity holds a 'flowing vase' out of which streams of water flow towards the first of three worshippers who flank the divine pair on either side. The identification of the deities in question has never been clearly ascertained, but it has been suggested that they may represent the god Inshushinak and the goddess Napirisha, the 'divine Anshanite couple' par excellence (Vanden Berghe 1986a: 159 with further refs.; cf. Carter 1989: 147 for a contrary view).

As for the date of the relief, it should be noted that the representation of a deity seated on a serpent throne found in the central panel is attested on a number of impressions of seals assigned to the 'popular Elamite' group (Amiet 1980c: 48–9; see also de Miroschedji 1981a; Trokay 1991), including some made by seals belonging to specific *sukkalmahs* or other royalty. These include the seals of 'Sirahupitir, the scribe, son of Inzuzu, servant of Atta-hushu' used on two tablets from Susa (Amiet 1972a: 296, no. 2327); Tetep-mada, 'shepherd of Susa, sister's son of Shilhaha' (Amiet 1972a: 260, no. 2016); Kuk-Nashur II, '*sukkal* of Susa, sister's son of Temti-agun' (Amiet 1972a: 260, no. 2015; see also Steve 1994: 26; Vallat 1997c); and Tan-Uli (Pls. 6.4–5), '*sukkalmah, sukkal* of Elam and Shimashki, sister's son of Shilhaha' (Amiet 1972a: 297, no. 2330; Harper, Aruz and Tallon 1992: 117; Vallat 1989c). The serpent throne appears on several more pieces from Susa, none of which can be attributed to a specific personnage (e.g. Amiet 1972a: 260, no. 2017; 1994c: Fig. 5), as well as on a seal impression from Haft Tepe in Khuzistan (de Miroschedji 1981a: 15; Harper, Aruz and Tallon 1992: 117). The glyptic evidence supports a date in the *sukkalmah* period for the Kurangun relief (e.g. Amiet 1992b: 259; see also Vanden Berghe 1983: 114; 1986a: 162, n. 23; Seidl 1986; Carter 1989: 145).

A badly preserved remnant of a second relief, located at Naqsh-i Rustam, near Persepolis, also shows two seated deities, one of whom sits on a serpent throne (Fig. 6.9). Unfortunately, a much later Sasanian relief has destroyed most of the earlier Elamite relief (Porada 1965: 67; Vanden Berghe 1983: 29).

Conclusion

The prestige and influence of the *sukkalmah* during the early second millennium undoubtedly represent the apogee of Elamite political influence in Western Asia. Never

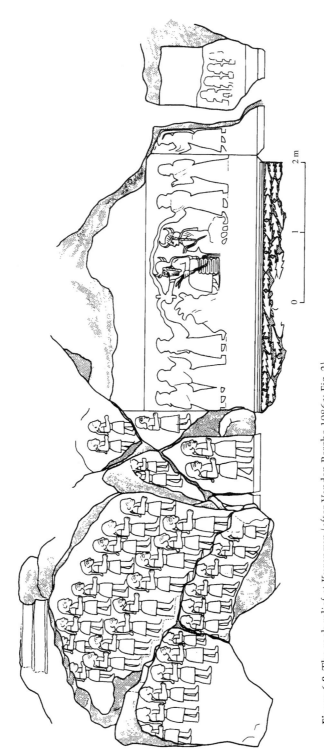

Figure 6.8 The rock relief at Kurangun (after Vanden Berghe 1986a: Fig. 2).

Plate 6.4 Tablet fragment (Sb 8748, 6.9×5.8 cm) from Susa impressed with the seal of Tan-Uli. ©
Musée du Louvre, Antiquités Orientales

Plate 6.5 Sealed, upper edge of Sb 8748. © Musée du Louvre, Antiquités Orientales

Figure 6.9 Elamite rock relief at Naqsh-i Rustam (after Seidl 1986: Abb. 2b).

before had Elamite political power been projected so far to the west, and it is unlikely that it had ever been projected equally far to the east. At no later period did any Elamite monarch enjoy a role comparable to that played by the *sukkalmah* in the balance of power between Babylonia, Assyria and Mari. As in the preceding Shimashki-period, it is difficult to find physical manifestations in the archaeological record of Susa, Tal-i Malyan or Tepe Farukhabad which corroborate the enormous influence of Elam at this time. Yet this very fact may be an indication that we are looking in the wrong places for the sources of Elamite power and prestige. These lay, perhaps, not with the settled communities of Susa or Anshan, the former a thoroughly Mesopotamianized city, the latter a fairly provincial centre in the highlands, more a Dodge City than an El Dorado. Perhaps the 'wealth of nations' in this case grew from the manpower on which the *sukkalmah* could draw. Without entering into the debate concerning the evidence required in order to recognize 'nomads' in the archaeological record, perhaps we must look to the mountain-dwellers of Elam for the levees raised by the *sukkalmah* when he marched against the Guti. Perhaps these were little different from the fierce tribes who refused to submit to Alexander the Great fifteen hundred years later (see Chapter 9). Perhaps it was human as much as natural resources which bought the influence of the *sukkalmah* in the courts of Hammurabi, Shamshi-Adad and Zimri-Lim. Admittedly, this is a difficult assertion to prove, for as yet our archaeology is the archaeology of Susa and Anshan, our texts limited largely to the perspective of the cuneiform-using West.

During the early second millennium BC tin was probably the most important exotic commodity in circulation in Western Asia. Assur traded it to the cities of Anatolia, as the Old Assyrian caravan texts make clear, and the king of Mari, as we have seen, distributed it to his clients further west (Kuhrt 1995: 94, 101 with extensive bibliography). The tantalizing references to tin from Elam in the Mari letters suggests that the power of the *sukkalmah*, while not exclusively based on the ownership of this scarce resource, may have rested to a not inconsiderable extent on an ability to control the flow of tin to the West.

Date	Lowlands	Highlands	Mesopotamia	'Elam'
1932–1906 BC	Susa subjugated by Gungunum of Larsa?	Anshan and Pashime sacked by Gungunum	eclipse of Isin and rise of Larsa under Gungunum	end of Shimashkian 'independence'?
1900–1600 BC	Susa part of a polity governed by a ruler with the title *sukkalmah*; continued use of Akkadian; maritime links to Dilmun and Magan (Bahrain and Oman); major occupation levels at Susa, building activities of *sukkalmahs* attested at Susa, Choga Pahan East, Liyan; strong Mesopotamian influence in glyptic at Susa; occupation at other sites such as Tepe Farukhabad	Anshan and Shimashki part of the *sukkalmah*'s kingdom; later Kaftari period occupation at Malyan, building activity by Siwe-palar-huppak; rock reliefs at Kurangun and Naqsh-i Rustam	rival kingdoms of Isin, Larsa, Babylon, Assyria, Mari, etc.; recognition of authority of Elamite *sukkalmah*; Elamite conquest of Larsa; Elamite-Amorite connections in east Tigris region; eventual defeat of Elam by Hammurabi c. 1764/3 BC	Susa, Anshan, Shimashki, together constitute most powerful 'Elamite' entity in history; Elam provides tin for Mari, implying strong links further east

7

THE KINGDOM OF SUSA AND ANSHAN

The period of the *sukkalmahs* was followed by the Middle Elamite period. While details of the transition between these two eras are lacking, the onset of the Middle Elamite period is usually put at *c.* 1500 BC, its end *c.* 1100 BC. Three phases have been distinguished, each marked by a different dynasty named after its founder or most significant early leader (thus the Kidinuids, Igihalkids, and Shutrukids). This is the period when the title 'king of Susa and Anshan', as it is expressed in Akkadian texts, or 'king of Anshan and Susa', according to the usage of the Elamite sources, is attested.

 The first phase of this period (Middle Elamite I, *c.* 1500–1400 BC) is notable not only for the wealth of evidence from Susa but for the foundation of a new and important site at Haft Tepe by a king named Tepti-ahar. The second phase (Middle Elamite II, *c.* 1400–1200 BC) is characterized by inter-marriage with the royal family of the contemporary Kassite dynasty in Babylonia. This was also the time when one of the Middle Elamite II period's most important rulers, Untash-Napirisha, founded yet another important new site at Choga Zanbil, ancient Al Untash-Napirisha, complete with a stepped temple tower or *ziggurat*, where the deities of the highlands were worshipped alongside those of the lowlands. Susa, too, provides abundant evidence of occupation at this time. The third phase (Middle Elamite III, *c.* 1200–1100 BC) saw the overthrow of the Kassites by one of the most important figures in Elamite history, Shutruk-Nahhunte. It was he, following his conquest of southern Mesopotamia, who brought to Susa such significant monuments as the law code of Hammurabi, the victory stele of the Old Akkadian king Naram-Sin, and many other pieces of Mesopotamian statuary, booty taken during his victorious campaign in 1158 BC. Shutruk-Nahhunte's son and successor, Kutir-Nahhunte, meted out even more punishment to his western neighbours, removing the all-important cult statue of Marduk from his temple at Babylon. Likewise Kutir-Nahhunte's successor, Shilhak-Inshushinak, campaigned widely, particularly in eastern and northeastern Mesopotamia.

 Important archaeological finds from this latest phase of the Middle Elamite era have been recovered at Tal-i Malyan in Fars, and rock reliefs in the Bakhtiyari mountains add yet another dimension to our understanding of political fragmentation and religious practice in this period. A number of significant sites, as yet unexcavated, are also known in Fars and Khuzistan where bricks inscribed in Elamite, often mentioning shrines to particular deities, have been found.

 If the Mesopotamian literary tradition is to be believed, the Middle Elamite period was brought to a close by Nebuchadnezzar I (1125–1104 BC), the fourth king of the southern Babylonian Dynasty of the Sealand (a term which refers to the southern marshes of Iraq) who is said to have revenged Kutir-Nahhunte's removal of the statue of Marduk by conquering Elam. Thus we reach the end of an important era in Elamite history, one in which the unity of highland Anshan and lowland Susa was expressed in the titulature of its kings, and revealed in a wealth of archaeological remains from sites like Tal-i Malyan, Kul-e Farah, Choga Zanbil, Haft Tepe and Susa. It is a period from which much information on Elamite religion has come down to us, and one in which Elam again figured prominently in political affairs which transcended the boundaries of modern Iran.

Introduction

Due to the scarcity of synchronisms between the later *sukkalmahs* and Babylonian historical chronology, as well as a dearth of radiocarbon dates, it has long proven difficult to fix the end of the *sukkalmah* period and the beginning of what is generally referred to as the Middle Elamite era (Fig. 7.1). For the most part it has been a matter of making educated guesses, yet even so estimates have run the gamut from *c.* 1600/1500 to 1300/1200 BC. Some years ago Stolper argued that, given the existence of at least five rulers following Kuk-Nashur II, the contemporary of Ammisaduqa of Babylon (1646–1626 BC), 'The *sukkalmah* dynasty therefore certainly lasted through the seventeenth, probably well into the sixteenth, and possibly as late as the early fifteenth century BC' (Carter and Stolper 1984: 32). A decade later M.-J. Steve reviewed the evidence in the context of his analysis of the epigraphic evidence from Ville Royale A XII, as discussed in the previous chapter, stressing the following points (Steve 1994: 28):

1. given the synchronism between Ammisaduqa and Kuk-Nashur II (Vallat 1993b), the mid-point of the latter's reign might be reasonably placed around 1620 BC
2. following Kuk-Nashur one must account for at least four rulers, Kudu-zulush II, Tan-Uli, Temti-halki and Kuk-Nashur III, before the advent of Kidinu and a new dynasty (Middle Elamite I)
3. one might therefore allot the time span from 1620 to 1500 BC for the last of the *sukkalmahs*

As noted in Chapter 6, Ville Royale A XII contained tablets impressed with the seal of Kuk-Nashur III (or IV?), the iconography of which is extremely reminiscent of that found on the seal of another late *sukkalmah*, Tan-Uli. Moreover, the same level produced a text sealed with the cylinder of Kidinu, first 'king of Susa and Anshan' and founder of a new, post-*sukkalmah* dynasty. Thus, whatever his absolute dates may be, it is clear that, barring severe stratigraphic perturbation in A XII, no time gap of any sort existed between the last *sukkalmah* and the first Middle Elamite ruler. Nevertheless, the differing titulature clearly suggests that a major dynastic change had occurred and with it a departure, if not a rupture, had taken place in Elamite history.

To what extent that change did or did not have something to do with events in the wider world is, however, unclear. Some scholars have pointed to the rise of the kingdom of Mitanni under Shaushtatar in the period *c.* 1500–1450 BC, and to his conquest of Assyria and Babylonia (Steve, Gasche and de Meyer 1980: 91), but just how this may have impacted on the late *sukkalmahs* is difficult to assess. A tempting if obscure historical correlation is suggested by the Babylonian *Chronicle of Early Kings* which reports that Ea-gamil, eleventh and last king of the First Dynasty of the Sealand, went to Elam (Brinkman 1968: 150) after which Ulam-Burash (Ulam-Buriash), brother of the Kassite king Kashtiliashu, 'conquered the Sealand and became its overlord' (Brinkman 1976: 318). The term 'Sealand' denoted appropriately enough that region of southernmost Mesopotamia largely comprised of the swampy region south of Ur (Brinkman 1993a). Zadok assumes that Ea-gamil in fact fled in the wake of a Kassite conquest (Zadok 1987: 13), whereas the *Chronicle* makes it clear that the conquest only followed

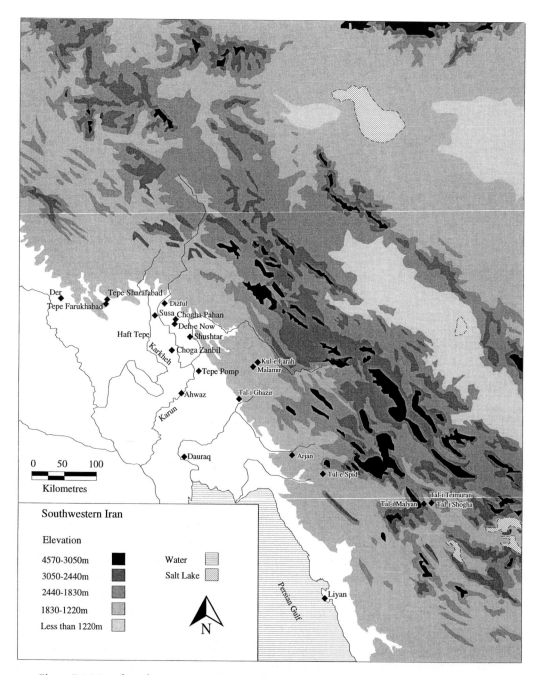

Figure 7.1 Map of southwestern Iran showing the principal sites mentioned in Chapter 7.

Ea-gamil's departure. In either case, it is interesting, as Zadok notes, that the fourth and
fifth kings of the First Dynasty of the Sealand – Ishkibal and Shushshi – had names
which 'are perhaps explicable in Elamite terms' (Zadok 1987: 25, n. 51). While the
notion of a link between the Sealand dynasty and one or more noble Elamite families
is intriguing, it is still too early to speculate on how such a link, and Ea-gamil's trans-
ferral to Elam, may have affected the last of the *sukkalmahs*. Certainly a chronological correlation, while plausible, is far from certain.

Based on the broad lines of dynastic succession, the Middle Elamite period may be
divided into three phases: Middle Elamite I (*c.* 1500–1400 BC), whose rulers are sometimes called the 'Kidinuids' after the first ruler of the group, Kidinu; Middle Elamite II
(*c.* 1400–1200 BC), generally referred to as the period of the 'Igihalkids' after Igi-halki,
founder of a dynastic line of ten rulers; and Middle Elamite III (*c.* 1200–1100 BC), the
time of the 'Shutrukids', named after one of the most powerful of the dynasty's early
rulers, Shutruk-Nahhunte I (Vallat 1994: 13–14).

Middle Elamite I (*c.* 1500–1400 BC)

The first real dynasty assigned to the middle Elamite period began with Igi-halki, *c.*
1400 BC (Middle Elamite II), but before him we must place five rulers, none of whom
can with certainty be considered to have been related. All but one of these rulers used
the title 'king of Susa and Anzan', the latter a variant of Anshan. Obviously this title
recalls that of the Shimashkian/*sukkalmah* Ebarat who styled himself 'king of Anshan
and Susa'. It is unclear whether the transposition of the two toponyms in the title is
significant. E. Quintana has suggested that kings styled 'king of Susa and Anshan' ruled
only in Susa, while those styled 'king of Anshan and Susa', ruled only at Anshan
(Quintana 1996c), but Vallat has shown that this was not the case, pointing out that the
title 'king of Susa and Anshan' is only attested in Akkadian texts, while 'king of Anshan
and Susa' is confined exclusively to Elamite texts, as if the authors of these inscriptions
were appealing to and perhaps even flattering the Akkadian and Elamite speakers of
their realm, respectively, reversing the order of the linguistically different areas depending on the intended audience (Vallat 1997b). Be that as it may, Anshan was certainly of
less importance during this period than Susa and other sites in Khuzistan. The order of
the five 'Kidinuids' is as uncertain as their filiation, but we shall briefly introduce them,
beginning with their namesake, in the order recently suggested by F. Vallat (Vallat 1994:
13; for an alternative arrangement, see Steve, Gasche and de Meyer 1980: 78).

Kidinu is known only from the tablet (TS.XII.13) mentioned above which bore the
impression of his cylinder seal, identifying him as 'Kidinu, king of Susa and Anzan, son
of Adad-sharru-rabu (^dIM.SAR.GAL), servant of his god, Kirwashir' (Amiet 1980c: 139,
no. 11). To date, Kidinu's seal inscription appears to be the earliest attestation of the
use of the logogram EŠŠANA for the Akkadian word *šarru*, i.e. king (Steve, Gasche and
de Meyer 1980: 93).

Tan-Ruhurater II obviously shared his name with the eighth ruler of Shimashki (see
Chapter 5). He, too, is known only from a cylinder seal in a private collection, the

legend of which closely resembles that of Kidinu in calling him 'king of Susa and Anzan' (Steve, Gasche and de Meyer 1980: 83, 95, Pl. IV.2).

An individual named Shalla is mentioned without title in a group of approximately twelve texts originally alleged to have come from Malamir in the Bakhtiari mountains to the east of Susiana but more likely, on prosopographic grounds, to derive from Haft Tepe itself (Stolper 1987–90: 280; Glassner 1991: 117, however, is not convinced), and is otherwise known only from a single legal text found at Susa where a wish for his prosperity is expressed (Glassner 1991: 117). Despite the absence of a royal title, most scholars agree in recognizing Shalla as a likely 'king of Susa' because of the fact that his name is invoked in a formulaic oath used in legal texts along with that of Inshushinak, in precisely the same way as the 'king of Susa' Tepti-ahar's is (Steve, Gasche and de Meyer 1980: 96). It has been suggested that Shalla may have been 'an immediate predecessor of Tepti-ahar' (Stolper 1987–90: 280; see also Steve, Gasche and de Meyer 1980: 96).

Tepti-ahar and Inshushinak-shar-ilani (Akkadian; or Inshushinak-sunkir-nappipir in Elamite) have both been known from inscribed bricks found at Susa since the beginning of this century. In a sale text from Susa (MDP 23: 248, no. 18), the oath 'may Inshushinak live for ever, may Tepti-ahar prosper' is found (Reiner 1973b: 94). Tepti-ahar is also mentioned on approximately fifty-five tablets from the site of Haft Tepe, 10 km east-southeast of Susa, where the impressions of his cylinder seal call him 'king of Susa and Anzan, servant of Kirwashir and Inshushinak' (Glassner 1991: 111), and on a stele found there which identifies him simply as 'king' (Reiner 1973b: 89, l.27). Finally, Tepti-ahar is mentioned on a single 'Malamir' text (Scheil 1902: 191, no. 15; 1930: 76; see also Glassner 1991: 117; Stolper 1987–90: 280), where once again the parties to a sale 'took an oath by Tepti-ahar and Inshushinak' (Reiner 1973b: 94).

As for Inshushinak-shar-ilani, he has also been known since the beginning of the century from some two dozen inscribed bricks found at Susa which report that, having entered the temple of Inshushinak and seen that the construction of his *sukkalmah* predecessor, Tepti-halki, was collapsing, 'he removed that which was (made) of dried bricks and built beside it (i.e. replaced it) in baked bricks' (Malbran-Labat 1995: 56). Unlike Tepti-ahar, Inshushinak-shar-ilani is called simply 'king of Susa', the same title by which he is identified in three seal impressions from Haft Tepe made with a cylinder seal belonging to one Adad-erish, who identifies himself as 'servant of Inshushinak-shar-ilani, king of Susa' (Herrero and Glassner 1990: 6–7; Glassner 1991: 111; Amiet 1996: 140).

Two points are particularly important about Tepti-ahar and his reign, the first chronological, the second culture-historical. To begin with the chronological issue, one of the administrative texts from Haft Tepe is dated 'year when the king expelled Kadashman-dKUR.GAL', and in publishing this it was suggested by P. Herrero that dKUR.GAL should be read 'Enlil', thereby implying that the individual in question was the Kassite king Kadashman-Enlil I who reigned from 1374 or earlier to 1360 BC (Herrero 1976: 102, no. 6/11–12). Obviously, if this interpretation is taken as correct, then an important synchronism is afforded for anchoring at least part of the Middle Elamite I period, and many scholars have embraced this possibility (e.g. Carter and Stolper 1984: 34; Amiet 1985a: 11; Gassan 1986: 189; Zadok 1987: 13; Negahban 1991:108; Spycket 1992: 231, n. 429; Malbran-Labat 1995: 53). However, over twenty years ago J.A. Brinkman cast doubt on the validity of reading ^{d}KUR.GAL as Enlil, noting that it most often seemed to refer to the deity Amurru in Kassite period texts (Brinkman 1976: 144–5) and this has led many to reject an alleged synchronism with Kadashman-Enlil I (e.g. Steve, Gasche and de Meyer 1980: 97, n. 57; Seidl 1990: 130; Amiet 1996: 135; Glassner 1991: 119 remains undecided) which, in any case, seems far too late by roughly a century. The absence of a royal title for Kadashman-^{d}KUR.GAL is also suspicious, and suggests that this may not have been the Kassite king Kadashman-Enlil I.

The culture-historical point of greatest significance in relation to Tepti-ahar is his apparent foundation (thus Negahban 1994: 31), or re-foundation of the settlement and religious/mortuary complex at Haft Tepe, and the relationship of this act to the ongoing existence of Susa and Tal-i Malyan. As indicated above, there is nothing to suggest a hiatus of even the shortest duration between the last *sukkalmahs* and the reign of Kidinu, and certainly the Ville Royale continued to be occupied into the Middle Elamite II period. It is important to stress, however, that the texts from Ville Royale A XI as well as the inscribed bricks of Inshushinak-shar-ilani and Tepti-ahar from Susa show very clear graphic similarities with the 'Malamir' texts and the tablets from Haft Tepe, where, as noted above, Tepti-ahar figures prominently (Steve, Gasche and de Meyer 1980: 98–9). Moreover, the few human figurines found at Haft Tepe (Negahban 1991: Pls. 25–26; see also Van den Boorn, Houtkamp and Verhart 1989: Pl. III.5) are said to be 'identical' to those from Ville Royale A XII and XI at Susa (Spycket 1992: 231). Thus, in assessing the political and social situation at Susa in the Middle Elamite I period, it is clear that the site was certainly occupied, and that it figured in the titulature of Tepti-ahar. On the other hand, a major effort seems to have been expended at Haft Tepe (see below).

At the same time, it would appear that there was no substantial settlement in the Kur River basin following the end of the Kaftari period (*c.* 1600 BC) until the Middle Elamite II phase, although W.M. Sumner suggests that the early 'Qaleh' period from *c.* 1600–1350 BC may be attested 'in the upper levels at GHI, ABC, TT-F, and possibly XX', areas largely located in the northwestern portion of the site (Sumner 1988b: 316). Both ceramic parallels to Susa and a series of radiocarbon dates suggest, however, that the first major, post-Kaftari construction at Tal-i Malyan did not occur until the second half of the fourteenth century BC. All of this implies that the use of the title 'king of Susa and Anzan' in the Middle Elamite I (and II, see below) phase was ceremonial and anachronistic, much as the title 'king of Kish' was used by various Old Babylonian rulers or 'king of Ur' was used by the kings of Isin and Larsa (Hallo 1957: 17, 26). These titles might imply control over Ur or Kish, and the same may have been true of Susa and Anshan, but the cities in question need not have been capital cities any longer. Certainly it would seem that Tepti-ahar's residence may well have been Kabnak, where he was buried, rather than Susa.

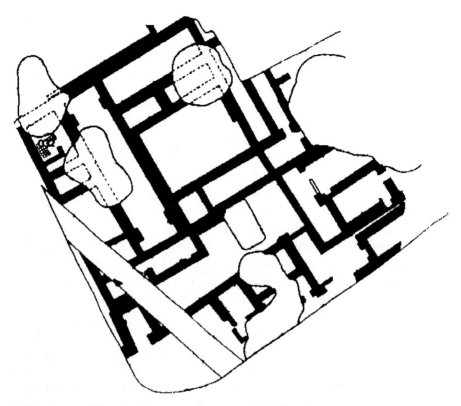

Figure 7.2 Building T in Ville Royale A, level XI (after Steve 1994: Fig. 1).

Middle Elamite I settlement at Susa and minor sites in Khuzistan

As noted above, there is evidence of occupation at Susa in various areas. In Ville Royale A XI, a large area of domestic houses (Steve, Gasche and de Meyer 1980: Fig. 8) was excavated as well as a large, almost square building ('Building T', Fig. 7.2) which may have been founded late in the preceding period represented by A XII (Spycket 1992: 157). Along with quantitites of pottery, roughly fifty fragments of nude female figurines were found in Building T. In each case, the female has an elaborate coiffure and stands erect with the hands cupping each breast (e.g. Spycket 1992: no. 953). Terracotta figurines depicting clothed females with their hands clasped beneath their breasts, as well as figurines showing clothed females suckling an infant at the left breast, were also found in A XI (Spycket 1992: 182, 187). Male figurines of musicians playing a hand-held string instrument (so-called 'lutenists') and terracotta model beds depicting naked couples (male and female) on the upper surface, were also found in A XI (Spycket 1992: 196, 209).

A small sounding adjacent to R. Ghirshman's Ville Royale excavation was opened up in 1975 by P. de Miroschedji. Levels 12 and 13 in this area, known as Ville Royale II, contained only very little in the way of mudbrick architecture and pottery (de

Miroschedji 1978: Fig. 50; 1981b: 36) but are probably contemporary with Middle Elamite I (Steve, Gasche and de Meyer 1980: 76–7, Fig. 13). Very little glyptic evidence from secure contexts can be assigned to A XI (as opposed to graves or pits dug into it) but there is at least one faience cylinder seal (Amiet 1980c: 142, no. 17) showing a typical linear, geometric design which has close parallels in the large corpus of Middle Elamite material from Choga Zanbil.

According to a series of eighteen fragmentary bricks describing in some detail a rite to be carried out by four female guardians of the temple, Tepti-ahar, who calls himself 'king of Susa', built a baked brick structure at Susa called the É.DÙ.A which he dedicated to Inshushinak (Malbran-Labat 1995: 57). The text, although somewhat cryptic, is nevertheless of interest and reads as follows: '(1) Tepti-ahar, king of Susa [made?] a statue of himself and of his servant girls to whom he is gracious, and interceding female figures (2) who would intercede for him and for his servant girls to whom he is gracious; he built a house of baked bricks (3) and gave it to his lord Inshushinak. May Inshushinak show him favor as long as he lives! (4) When night falls, four women of the guardians of the house . . . they must not act in concert (5) to peel off the gold; their garments should be fastened with strings; they should come in and (6) sleep at the feet of the *lamassu-* [protective genius] and the *karibu*-figures; they should . . .' (Reiner 1973b: 95). Because of the similarity of this text to that of a stele recovered at Haft Tepe (discussed below) E. Reiner has suggested that they may both refer to the same building, which she describes, paraphrasing the original building inscription as 'constructed of baked bricks, under Tepti-ahar, and . . . dedicated to Inshushinak; it housed the statue of Tepti-ahar and the statues of his "servant girls", as well as statues of protective deities (*lamassati*) whose role was to invoke blessings upon the king and the "servant girls". As the stele specifies funerary offerings to be made [see below], the "servant girls" may refer to dead female members of Tepti-ahar's family' (Reiner 1973b: 96). Reiner's belief that the building mentioned in the text of the inscribed bricks from Susa is in fact the structure which E.O. Negahban identified as Tepti-ahar's tomb at Haft Tepe is discussed below.

At Tepe Farukhabad in the Deh Luran plain occupation continued from the preceding *sukkalmah* period, and at least some of the pottery recovered there finds parallels in the Ville Royale A XIII-XI and Haft Tepe assemblages (Carter 1981: 214). A small sounding by R. Schacht at Tepe Sharafabad (Schacht 1975) produced both ceramics and female figurines comparable in style to that known from A XI at Susa (Spycket 1992: 182), while some of the material recovered from the test excavations at Izeh (Sajjadi and Wright 1979: 107) and in survey on the Izeh plain (Bayani 1979) should be considered contemporary as well.

It is not really possible to assess overall settlement trends in Khuzistan at the level of the periodization adopted here, since most of the ceramic indicators cannot be distinguished as Middle Elamite I, II or III, and this fact, no doubt in the absence of epigraphic evidence, has given rise to some of the conflicting periodizations expressed in the literature for the late second millennium assemblages of Susa. Nevertheless, it is certainly true in broad terms that Susa's pre-eminence seems to have been on the wane

Plate 7.1 A view of Haft Tepe showing areas excavated by E.O. Negahban.

as a number of other sites in Susiana (e.g. KS-3, 7, 96, 120, 172 and 233) appear to have grown in size; new settlements were founded in the northwest at Tepe Goughan and Tepe Patak, and sites such as Tepe Bormi and Tal-i Ghazir in the Ram Hormuz region southeast of Susa, and KS 2X near Ahwaz assumed greater importance vis-à-vis the old centre of Susa. No 'new' site, however, rivalled Haft Tepe in significance, although excavations at any one of the sites just mentioned could radically alter this image.

Haft Tepe

Haft Tepe is the name given to a cluster of mounds (Pl. 7.1) spread over an area of at least 30 ha (Carter and Stolper 1984: 158) which is located *c.* 10 km east-southeast of Susa. First described in 1908 by J. de Morgan, then engaged at Susa, the site was excavated by E.O. Negahban between 1965 and 1978 during the course of fourteen seasons (Negahban 1991: xxvii-xxix). Excavations (Fig. 7.3) focused on the 'tomb-temple complex of Tepti-ahar', so called because of the discovery of a stele fragment in the central courtyard of the complex which names him (see below), and two 'terrace complexes' (I and II) to the southeast of the tomb-temple area.

Before describing the so-called 'tomb-temple complex', it is important to say a word about terminology. What is the basis for this designation? In his final report on the

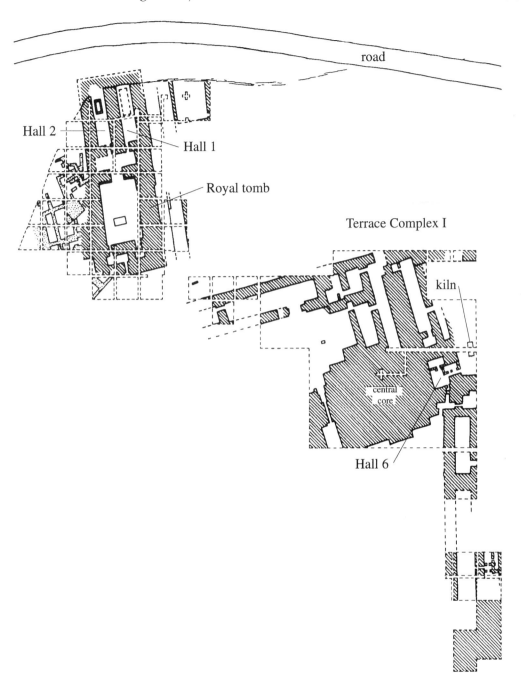

Figure 7.3 Plan of the excavated areas at Haft Tepe (after Negahban 1991: Plan 2).

Saparru = Subir

Saparru wagon

Table 7.1. *Summary of Haft Tepe stele 1*

Lines	Simplified description of contents
1–19	obligation of the six guards of the house – Kuk-Allatu, Kuk-eshru, Iribamma, Agunannu, Attameten and Irib-Adad – to sacrifice specified amounts of flour, beer and sheep per month or year as *terru shetru* offerings, and at the festivals of Abu and Tashritu
20–27	summary of the above plus additional amounts to be sacrificed before the chariot of Inshushinak and the *saparru*-wagon of Tepti-ahar
28–31	summary of offerings plus sheep for the festivals of Abu, Kirawashir, Tashritu and the chariot
31–38	summary of funerary offerings to be made by the six guards
39–46	further duties of the guards, admonition against negligence
47–55	duties of the women of the guards

excavations of Haft Tepe, Negahban has given no justification for the use of the term 'tomb-temple'. The designation, in slightly altered form, has been taken over by Carter, who refers to it as a 'funerary temple' (Carter and Stolper 1984: 158). In fact, the inscription on the Haft Tepe stele, written in Middle Babylonian dialect (not Elamite), does not use one of the Akkadian terms for temple commonly used on inscribed bricks at Susa, such as *kizzum*, *kukunnam* or *siyan/ziyanam*, but rather the much vaguer and certainly more neutral designation, É.DÙ.A, meaning 'house, construction' (Malbran-Labat 1995: 185) in referring to the '6 guards of the "house"' (e.g. Reiner 1973b: 88, l. 15; 90, l. 39). In her discussion of the Haft Tepe stele, moreover, Reiner at no point suggested that the text came from a temple context, but always spoke of it as deriving from a royal tomb. Her suggestion (Reiner 1973b: 95) that the inscribed bricks of Tepti-ahar from Susa mentioning his construction of an É.DÙ.A might in fact have originated at Haft Tepe by way of local workmen who could have picked them up there and given them to the French at Susa seems no longer tenable now that we have Malbran-Labat's full publication of no fewer than eighteen fragments of the Tepti-ahar bricks from Susa. Moreover, the text of the Haft Tepe stele (Table 7.1) is clearly a record of food offerings in the form of beer, sheep and flour to be delivered throughout the year for the deceased (see the discussion of similar Mesopotamian ceremonies in Potts 1997: 221ff.) along with provisions for the six guards of the 'house'. This would seem to exclude the possibility of identifying the complex simultaneously as both a tomb and a temple, and as Reiner has observed, 'the purpose of the "house" (always referred to as É.DÙ.A, as customary in the orthography of Akkadian texts from Elam) could be ascertained from the mention of funerary offerings alone (lines 31, 34), even if its function as a tomb had not been established from the archaeological evidence' (Reiner 1973b: 94). For these reasons the 'tomb-temple complex' will simply be referred to here as the 'royal tomb'.

Built entirely of brick, some of it baked, the Haft Tepe royal tomb resembles an elongated H with a narrow entrance through a southern wall leading into a small room, and a further doorway leading northwards into a large courtyard (15×24.5 m) paved with baked brick in the centre of which a ruined brick altar or platform (3×5 m) stood. Negahban suggests that the stele discussed above, two fragments of which were found in the courtyard, may once have stood on this platform (Negahban 1991: 13). A doorway at the northern end of the courtyard opened onto another room, described as the 'long portico' (5.5×17 m) from the northeastern side of which access was gained to 'Hall no. 1', a large chamber (6×9.2 m) paved with baked bricks. The interior walls of the hall had been plastered and decorated with 'incised geometric designs including squares, rectangles, circles, and triangles' (Negahban 1991: 14). At the north end of this hall stood a baked brick chamber (5.8×12.9 m ext. dimensions, 10×3.25 m int. dimensions) with a vaulted roof some 3.75 m high which Negahban describes as the tomb of Tepti-ahar. It is said to have contained 'possibly 21 skeletons', seven of which were found at the north end of the chamber; 'at least two' of which were near the south end, and twelve of which lay 'carelessly dumped inside the southern entrance' into the tomb from the hall (Negahban 1991: 15). A second 'hall' which was probably once identical in dimensions to Hall 1 was located just west of it, separated by a 4.8 m thick wall. This, too, contained a vaulted burial, known as the 'mass burial tomb', roughly half the size (2.65×5.20 m ext. dimensions; 1.85×4.80 int. dimensions) of the so-called tomb of Tepti-ahar, and with the articulated remains of twenty-three individuals. The entrance to this chamber had been blocked up with rubble, and the vaulted roof had been destroyed. Given the fact that sacrifices to be made before Tepti-ahar's chariot are mentioned in the Haft Tepe stele inscription, Reiner suggested 'that the sacrifices were instituted during or immediately after the reign of Tepti-ahar' (Reiner 1973b: 94). This makes it conceivable, though far from certain, that the tomb complex was that of the king himself, although the notion that the two skeletons found 'together with an elongated pottery vessel in the southern section' of Hall 1 indeed represented 'the remains of the king and his favorite girl servant' as Negahban has suggested (Negahban 1991: 15, 21), is sheer speculation. Jar burials and simple pit graves were also found outside the walled royal tomb area, particularly to the west of the structure where they were obscured by the walls of a series of mudbrick houses built during the Sasanian period.

Terrace Complex I is a large mound to the southeast of the royal tomb area which is comprised of a massive, nearly square (40×44 m, *c.* 14 m high) brick terrace and a network of adjacent rooms running off it. To the south, a second, 'much higher' structure was also detected in an area of limited horizontal excavation. The rooms, corridors and courtyards of these two complexes yielded a diverse collection of material, and included a craft workshop area in Hall 6 in which sculpted human heads of clay, ivory figures (witness the recovery of 'a nearly complete elephant skeleton in Trench M XXXIII/XXXIV'), mosaic fragments, and decorative bitumen roundels were recovered (Negahban 1994); a ceramic kiln in the 'eastern courtyard'; bronze weaponry (Negahban 1991: 46); some three hundred seal impressions; and an unspecified proportion of the 'nearly four thousand complete and partial clay tablets' (Negahban 1994: 31) recovered at the site. In spite of this wealth of material, little serious attention has been paid as yet to the actual function of the terrace complexes.

Figure 7.4 The bronze plaque from Haft Tepe (after Negahban 1991: Ill. 48).

While their excavator, by the very neutrality of his designation, appears to eschew any attempt at identifying its function, others have suggested that Terrace Complex I represents either a series of temples or the royal palace (e.g. Glassner 1991: 115, n. 48). As a common, domestic function of workshops intermingled with private houses would seem to be excluded by the massiveness of the high terraces, can we determine whether a religious or palatial explanation best fits the evidence? It is unfortunate that virtually nothing is known about the mound called Haft Tepe B, opposite the rail-road station to the east of the main site, where 'a massive construction' was partly revealed in 1976 and where an unspecified number of tablets was recovered (Negahban 1991: 11, 103). Nevertheless, as an educated guess it may be suggested that the terrace area is not a palace – there are no demonstrable living quarters in the area – but a temple precinct where, on analogy with the great temples of southern Mesopotamia, a wide range of craft activities were concentrated, including pottery, statuary, and other craft production destined to manufacture goods for the gods, the priesthood, and the large number of dependents attached to the temple. The temple almost certainly incorporated a scribal school (see the school texts among the Haft Tepe tablets) and a corps of scribes (see the economic text and letters found as well) alongside a band of specialized priests, some of whom performed acts of extispicy (see the extispicy and omen texts recovered; extispicy may be defined as 'the inspection of the entrails of the sacrificial animal' for the purposes of divination, Jeyes 1980: 13). A decorated bronze plaque (10×7.5 cm, Fig. 7.4) found 'on the ground in front of the entrance door' of Hall H2, showing 'a deity, possibly the god Nergal . . . standing on the back of a lion with a nude female kneeling in front of him and a praying figure

behind him' (Negahban 1990) might support the attribution of a religious function for the complex.

The texts from what we may therefore call the Haft Tepe temple complex are diverse (Table 7.2), and both their content and date formulae raise some interesting questions about the life of the site and the interpretation of its remains. References to the 'house', called the É.DÙ.A, in both the stele fragments from the courtyard south of the royal tomb and in an undated letter, make it reasonable to suggest that the structure so designated was indeed the tomb. Whether or not the 'great house' (É.DÙ.A GAL) referred to in two year formulae of an unnamed king refers to the same building we cannot tell. These formulae commemorate the initiation of the construction of the É.DÙ.A and the erection of another wall surrounding it. Alternatively, if the É.DÙ.A refers specifically to one of the tomb chambers, the term É.DÙ.A GAL might plausibly refer to the larger complex in its entirety. On the other hand, could the É.KUR referred to in one of the year formulae, if indeed the reading is correct, signify the great brick massif of Terrace Complex I? The most famous temple of this name – the '"Mountain house", whence Enlil, surnamed the "Great Mountain" (^{d}kur-gal), rules his human subjects' (Wiggermann 1996: 209) – was certainly the temple of Enlil at Nippur (Westenholz 1987: 21–29). Was the decision to build the mudbrick massif and associated temple complex an attempt to recreate something of the grandeur of the great religious centre at Nippur which, even in the Kassite period, was still an impressive monument, or perhaps the Kassite ziggurat at Dur Kurigalzu (E. Carter, pers. comm.)? Several of the year formulae used at Haft Tepe refer to messengers travelling to and from Babylonia, and even if this suggests that contact between the areas was rare enough to warrant special mention (M.W. Stolper, pers. comm.), it might suggest that some knowledge of the Nippur sanctuary reached Haft Tepe.

According to Haft Tepe stele 1, the 'six guards of the house', i.e. of the É.DÙ.A, 'should sacrifice before the chariot of the god to Inshushinak', and they were required to both 'provision' and to celebrate a festival in honor of 'the chariot of the god' (Reiner 1973b: 89). These references are interesting in light of the discovery at Susa of a 15.7 cm. high fragmentary copper figurine of a deity seated in a chariot, even if this piece (Fig. 6.6), which lacks a provenience, has been dated stylistically to the *sukkalmah* period (Tallon, Hurtel and Drilhon 1989: 123–4). It is unclear, however, whether the same sort of small, portable chariot is being referred to in the letter H.T. 2, where the adjective GAL, 'great', is applied to the term used for chariot (GIŠ.GIGIR), or whether the chariot fittings discussed in a number of the other economic texts from Haft Tepe (Table 7.2) were for models or life-size chariots (for life-size bronze 'tyres' and other fixtures from mid-third and early second millennium BC contexts at Susa, see Tallon 1987/I: 297–307; 1987/II: 336–7; Littauer and Crouwel 1989: 111 and Pl. I; see also Littauer and Crouwel 1979 with earlier lit.).

We shall close this section with some thoughts on the ancient name of Haft Tepe and Tepti-ahar's relationship to it. The seal impressions of Athibu call him 'great governor of Kabnak' and this has been taken as evidence in support of the hypothesis that Haft Tepe = ancient Kabnak, the same city as *Kabinak* mentioned in the Neo-Assyrian king

Table 7.2. *Summaries of selected texts from the Haft Tepe temple complex*

Type	Text	Reference	Summary	Year formula
religious	Stele 1	Reiner 1973b	enumeration of flour, beer and sheep 'given' by six guards of the É.DÙ.A who are to perform sacrifices during various festivals; instructions relating to funerary offerings to be made which involve the *ippu* and priestess of Susa; injunctions regarding maintenance to be carried out by the guards and sweeping to be performed by eight women	undated
"	Stele 2	Herrero/Glassner 1990: 3	enumeration of flour, sheep and beer offerings; reference to the É.DÙ.A	
epistolary	H.T. 2	Herrero 1976: Fig. 21	Awilu to Sin-rimeni the porter, the scribe(s?), and the guards of the É.DÙ.A, requesting that a great chariot with gold fittings be brought to him by Temtu-hahpu	undated
economic	H.T. 28	Herrero 1976: Fig. 16	account of silver paid for bracelets	'year when the king . . . Pir'i-Amurru messenger of Babylonia'
"	H.T. 38	Herrero 1976: Fig. 19a	account of silver and gold	'year when the king expelled Kadashman-^{d}KUR.GAL'
"	H.T. 1	Herrero 1976: Fig. 22	account of flour which Pir'i-Amurru will deliver to the attendants and give to the king	'year when the king began construction of the É.DÙ.A GAL (and?) the É.KUR
"	H.T. 12	Herrero 1976: Fig. 23a	account of linen disbursement	'year when the king surrounded the É.DÙ.A GAL with a wall of clay (i.e. unbaked brick?)'
"	H.T. 39	Herrero/Glassner 1990: 8	account of silver for the decoration or manufacture of various chariot parts	—
"	H.T. 106	Herrero/Glassner 1990: 9	account of silver for the decoration or manufacture of a wheel, running board, yoke, reins, and pole for chariots	—

	H.T. no.	Reference	Description	Year name / notes
"	H.T. 246	Herrero/Glassner 1990: 10	account of gold for the manufacture of various parts of great chariots	—
"	H.T. 9	Herrero/Glassner 1990: 13	account of vessels made of gold and lapis lazuli	—
"	H.T. 40	Herrero/Glassner 1990: 16	account of gold used for the manufacture of bracelets	'year when the king ordered Habil-banutu to build an *arattu*'; seal impression of Tepti-ahar'
"	H.T. 435	Herrero/Glassner 1990: 23	account of vessels, bracelets, divine figurines, and other figurines of gold	—
"	H.T. 61	Herrero/Glassner 1990: 38	account of silver	'year when Pir'i-Adad took up his place beside the king'
"	H.T. 27	Herrero/Glassner 1990: 40	receipt of bronze	'year when the king ordered the construction of the stairway of . . .' undated; seal impression of Tepti-ahar'
"	H.T. 101	Herrero/Glassner 1990: 44	account of armour plates, belts, and other elements of armour in silver	'year when the king placed the cone (?) of Ina-bubla'
"	—	Beckman 1991	account of oxen	—
"	H.T. 605	Herrero/Glassner 1991: 42	list of females each receiving a gift (?) weighed out in talents and minas	—
unknown	H.T. 443	Herrero 1976: Fig. 17a	?	'year when [. . . u]sh-tu came from Babylonia'
"	H.T. 317	Herrero 1976: Fig. 17b	?	'year when Ili-barna came from Babylonia'
"	H.T. 129	Herrero 1976: Fig. 18a	?	'year when Ili-barna came from Babylonia'
"	H.T. 114	Herrero 1976: Fig. 18b	?	'year when Atta-. . . went to Babylonia'

Table 7.3. *References to Tepti-ahar and other high-ranking officials in the Haft Tepe texts*

Name	Text	Reference	Legend
Tepti-ahar	H.T. 445, H.T. 40, H.T. 101, H.T. 20, H.T. 450, 590 H.T. 60, 16	Herrero 1976: Fig. 20a Herrero/Glassner 1990: 16 Herrero/Glassner 1990: 44 Herrero/Glassner 1991: 40 Herrero/Glassner 1991: 48 Herrero/Glassner 1991: 52	Tepti-a[har], king of Susa and Anzan, [serva]nt of Kirwashir (and) of Inshushinak, may they in the good grace of their heart recognize him for as long as he lives
Athibu	H.T. 38 H.T. 14	Herrero 1976: Fig. 19b Herrero/Glassner 1991: 51	Athibu, great governor of Kabnak, administrator and confidant of Tepti-ahar, king of Susa (and) [serva]nt of the god IM
Adad-erish	H.T. 567, H.T. 3	Herrero/Glassner 1990: 6	Adad-erish, chief of the stable-hands, servant of Inshushinak-shar-ilani, king of Susa, servant of Adad (his god?)

Assurbanipal's account of his conquest of Susa and other cities in its environs (thus Herrero 1976: 113; Negahban 1991: 109; Malbran-Labat 1995: 53). It has also been suggested by some scholars that Tepti-ahar, notwithstanding his title 'king of Susa and Anzan', both lived and died at Haft Tepe (thus Glassner 1991: 115). That he may have been buried at Haft Tepe is plausible, and in spite of the damaged state of the Haft Tepe stele inscriptions, it does seem as though the prescriptions concerning funerary offerings were *for* Tepti-ahar, not merely ordered *by* him. But as for living at Haft Tepe, this is more difficult to determine. Regardless of the absence of imposing remains from this period at Susa, the fact remains that the site was surely inhabited concurrently, that it was still an urban centre, and that the king had a governor at Kabnak, Athibu, 'administrator and confidant of Tepti-ahar' (Table 7.3). Does the use of Tepti-ahar's seal at Haft Tepe, as demonstrated by numerous sealed tablets, necessarily mean that Tepti-ahar himself lived there? Haft Tepe is only 10 km from Susa, and the seals of both Athibu, Tepti-ahar's man in Kabnak, and Adad-erish, Inshushinak-shar-ilani's stable chief, refer to their respective bosses as 'king of Susa'. One could interpret this literally, and suggest that, whether or not the royal tomb was at Kabnak, the residence remained at Susa. In this regard, it is interesting to recall that many a Mesopotamian monarch was buried outside of the city where he reigned (Potts 1997: 233–4). Thus Yahdun-Lim of Mari was buried at Terqa, and the Ur III emperor Shu-Sin, although he ruled at the capital Ur, was buried at Uruk (Charpin 1992: 106). Similarly, one wonders whether Tepti-ahar, although reigning at Susa, might not have been buried at Kabnak because of a particular familial association with the place?

On the other hand, a further possibility suggests itself as well. Several scholars have recently questioned whether, at this stage in its history, Elam was indeed 'a monarchy controlling at a minimum both Susa and the nearby city at Haft Tepe . . . with at least titular claim to Anshan' (thus Carter and Stolper 1984: 34). Rather, they point to references in several of the Haft Tepe texts (H.T. 29, 30 and 72) to a 'king of Huhnuri' (Herrero and Glassner 1990: 14; Glassner 1991: 118), another city to the east of Haft Tepe and Susa, possibly near modern Arjan (Duchene 1986). Although the internal chronology of the Haft Tepe texts is largely unknown (except, e.g., in the case of texts dated by the year formulae referring to the beginning of work on the É.DÙ.A GAL and the subsequent surrounding of that building with an outer wall), and the relationship of, e.g., Tepti-ahar to Inshushinak-shar-ilani a complete mystery, the existence of at least one other king at Huhnur, roughly halfway between Susa and Anshan, may be an indication of a politically fragmented landscape at this time (thus Malbran-Labat 1995: 53). In spite of his title 'king of Susa and Anzan', if Tepti-ahar had lost control of Susa, not to mention Anshan, in such a competitive situation he may well have been forced to create a new base from which to press his claim to legitimate authority. If this indeed happened, then Kabnak may have been the new foundation where Tepti-ahar lived, in a kind of internal exile, as well as died.

Middle Elamite II (c. 1400–1200 B.C.)

In our present state of knowledge we have no idea how the situation at Kabnak, Susa or Anshan may have evolved from the period just discussed to one in which a new dynasty appeared claiming Igi-halki as its founder. However, it is important to underscore the fact that Steve, Gasche and de Meyer (1980: 67) have shown that a hiatus in occupation occurred in the Ville Royale A area between levels XI (Middle Elamite I) and X-IX. Based on the presence of numerous inscribed bricks attributable to various rulers of the Shutrukid dynasty (Steve, Gasche and de Meyer 1980: 56–7) and on ceramics comparable to the latest phase of occupation at Choga Zanbil (Pons 1994: 48 and n. 48), levels X-IX can be dated to the Middle Elamite III period (1200/1100–1000 BC). Susa was certainly occupied in the interval, however, for a large pit on the Acropole excavated in 1966–67 yielded twenty inscribed brick fragments (Table 7.4) dating to a series of monarchs beginning with Untash-Napirisha (mid-Igihalkid/Middle Elamite II) and ending with Shilhak-Inshushinak (mid-Shutrukid/Middle Elamite III) (Steve, Gasche and de Meyer 1980: 85). Shilhak-Inshushinak is important for various reasons, not least because he left a building inscription enumerating the rulers who preceded him in restoring the temple of Inshushinak at Susa (König 1965: 110, §48.2). There he names the earliest rulers of the Igihalkid dynasty (Table 7.5) as follows:

> Pahir-ishshan, son of Igi-halki
> Attar-kittah, son of Igi-halki
> Untash-Napirisha, son of Humban-numena
> Unpahash-Napirisha, son of Pahir-ishshan, and
> Kidin-Hutran, son of Pahir-ishshan

Parts of this genealogy have been confirmed by other, contemporary sources, including a stele fragment attributed to Kidin-Hutran (Steve and Vallat 1989: 224–5), although it omits to identify Humban-numena as a son of Attar-kittah, a fact known to us by his

Table 7.4. *Stratigraphic distribution of texts mentioning rulers from the Middle Elamite II and III periods at Susa*

King	Area of site	Location of text	Steve, Gasche and de Meyer 1980:
Untash-Napirisha	Acropole	locus 313 (pit)	85
"	Acropole	locus 292 (pit)	85
Shutruk-Nahhunte	Acropole	locus 292 (pit)	85
"	VR A IX	locus 103	120
Kutir-Nahhunte	Acropole	locus 313 (pit)	85
"	Acropole	locus 292 (pit)	85
	VR A IX	locus 104	120
	VR A IX	locus 35?	120
Shilhak-Inshushinak	Acropole	locus 313 (pit)	85
"	Acropole	locus 292 (pit)	85
	VR A IX	locus 104	120
Hutelutush-Inshushinak	VR A IX	floor, unspecified	120

inscribed bricks from Susa (Malbran-Labat 1995: 59). A second, even more remarkable document (Table 7.6) is a Neo-Babylonian copy of a literary text from Babylon, now in the Vorderasiatisches Museum in Berlin, which takes the form of a letter and belongs to a group of texts concerned with the period in question. The text, which is addressed to the Kassite court by an Elamite king, confirms that Untash-Napirisha (Hundasha-napirisha) was the son of Humban-numena (Humban-immeni) (see also the brick fragment from Chogha Pahan East, Cameron A, in Stolper and Wright 1990: 156); that a second Kidin-Hutran (i.e. II; Kidin-hudurudish) was Untash-Napirisha's son; and that a Napirisha-Untash (Napirisha-hundash) was Kidin-Hutran II's son (van Dijk 1986: 163; see also Steve and Vallat 1987: 226; Vallat 1994: 14). The incompleteness of these sources is important to remember, but this is to be expected given the fact that Shilhak-Inshushinak's inscription refers only to kings who had carried out work on the temple of Inshushinak, while the 'letter' to the Kassite court refers only to kings who had married Kassite princesses.

Igi-halki himself is known from an inscription (Table 7.7), several copies of which were found at Deh-e Now (KS-120), *c.* 20 km to the east of Haft Tepe. The invocation of deities who have granted the writer of a royal inscription his kingship has a long history in the ancient Near East and usually implies that the writer was not descended immediately from his predecessor on the throne (see Quintana 1996c: 106). In other words, divine intervention is invoked to legitimize a *coup d'état*. In the case of Igi-halki this seems particularly clear, for he mentions no royal ancestors, but instead ascribes his rule over Susa and Anzan to the goddess Manzat-Ishtar. The simplest explanation for the presence of his inscriptions at Deh-e Now would be that this, and not Susa, was his birthplace and/or power base. Although we do not know for certain that Deh-e Now

Table 7.5. *Tentative family-tree of the Igihalkids*

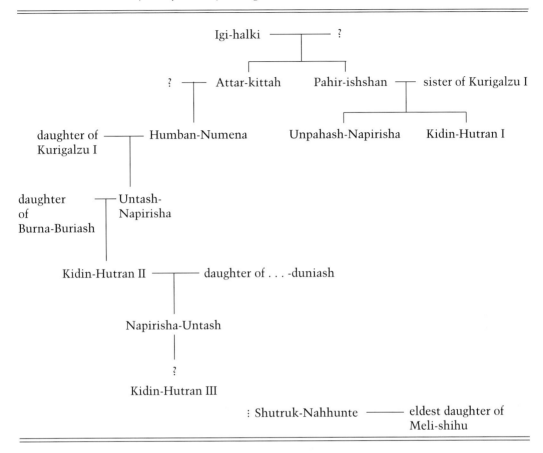

had been settled continuously since its foundation in the Early Uruk period (Johnson 1973: 77, 81), the site covered 9.5 ha by the Middle Elamite period and could well have been the source from which a dynasty arose to rival that of Tepti-ahar or Inshushinak-shar-ilani. Finally, Igi-halki is mentioned as Attar-kittah's father on two inscribed maceheads from Choga Zanbil (Steve 1967: 112).

If we follow the genealogy established by Shilhak-Inshushinak's building inscription, then Igi-halki was succeeded by his son Pahir-ishshan. This king has left us no original inscriptions, but we know from Shilhak-Inshushinak that he carried out work on the temple of Inshushinak at Susa, while a text of Shutruk-Nahhunte I's tells us that Pahir-ishshan did something, the sense of which is obscure, in a place called Aahitek (König 1965: 81, §28A/19; Carter and Stolper 1984: 36). Furthermore, the Berlin 'letter' alluded to above informs us that Pahir-ishshan (called Pihiranu-[d]U, van Dijk 1986:161, l. 9; see also Vallat 1987b: 89) married a sister of 'the powerful king Kurigalzu' (van Dijk 1986: 163). Because of other synchronisms between later Middle Elamite and Kassite kings, this can only refer to the Kassite king Kurigalzu I who reigned sometime before 1375

Table 7.6. *Shutruk-Nahhunte's letter to the Kassites*

Author	Text	Provenience	Content
Shutruk-Nahhunte (1190–1155 BC)	Van Dijk 1986	Babylon	ll. 1–8: too fragmentary for translation Pihiranu-ᵈU married . . . | the sister?] of the mighty Humban-immeni [married] his daughter; this one bore (him) Hundasha-naprisha. Hunda[sha-naprisha] married the daughter of Burnaburiash; this one bore (him) Kidin-[hud]uru[di]sh. Kidin-[hudurudish] married the daughter of [. . .]-ᵈduniash; this one bore (him) Nap[risha-h]und[ash?]. I, the [daughter's]-son married the eldest daughter of Meli-shihu . . . . . which the (PN) . . . will not fling away; [their] descen[dants?] will take possession of Babylonia; I will rise up, I have approached my land . . . Regarding that which was written to me: 'They given princesses of Babylonia, since the land was. . ., to all countries: in truth, a son of such a daughter, whom one has put on the throne of Babylonia, does not exist! The PN . . . who [. . .had go]ne, whom you [to Babylon's misfortune] chose and put [on the throne] of Babylonia: He has occupied Babylonia, and to this day his reign is [no]t acknowledged like that of the [daugh]ter's son, no, how . . .! Adad-shuma-usur, son of Dunna-Sah, from the region by the bank of the Euphrates, whom you chose and put on the throne of Babylonia; h[ow has h]e frustrated the daughter's son! Nabu-apal-iddina, the son of a Hittite (fem.), an abomination for Babylon, a Hittite (masc.), whom you chose to the detriment (?) of Babylon and put on the throne of Babylonia; you have experienced his sins, his failure, his crime and his . . . Why I, who am a king, son of a king, seed of a king, scion of a king, who am king (?) for the lands, the land of Babylonia and for the land of El[am], descendant of the eldest daughter of mighty King Kurigalzu, (why) do I not sit on the throne of the land of Babylonia? I sent you a sincere proposal, you however have granted me no reply: you may climb up to heaven, [but I'll pull you down] by your hem, you may go down to hell, [but I'll pull you up] by your hair! I shall destroy your cities, dem[olish] your fortresses, stop up your (irrigation) ditches, cut down your orchards, [pull out] the rings (of the sluices) at the mouths of your (irrigation) canals, . . : [. . . and I shall . . .]

Table 7.7. Selection of important Middle Elamite II inscriptions from Susa, Bushire and Deh-e Now

Author	Text	Provenience	Content
Igi-halki (1400–1380 BC)[1]	Steve 1987: 11–13	Deh-e Now	Igi-halki, Manzat-Ishtar having granted him the kingship of Susa and Anzan, after having restored the ancient *kukunnum*[2] of baked brick for Manzat he made an offering to her. May Manzat, having accorded him a long life grant him to achieve a happy reign
Humban-numena (1350–1340 BC)	Vallat 1984a: 258	Bushire	[I am Humban-numena, son of Attar-kittah . . .] king of Susa [and Anshan . . .], [. . .] Inshushinak [gave me the kingship of Susa and of Anshan . . .], [. . . for my life, for the li]fe of Mishi[mruh, for the life of Rishapanla . . .], [. . . I constructed] the *kukunnum* [. . .] [. . . at X . . . I ga]ve it. My Napirisha, Ki[ririsha . . .] [. . . grant [a happy reign]].
	IRS: 59	Susa	O great god, Kiririsha and the (divine) protectors of the earth, (gods) of Liyan, I, Humban-numena, son of Attar-kittah, I (am) the enlarger of the kingdom, the master (of the) Elamite (land), the holder of the Elamite throne, the king of Anzan and Susa; on account of the continuity by (my) mother, (the) great god chose me and loved me: prosperity established (?), the crown restored (?), Inshushinak gave me kingship. For my life, for the life of Mishimruh and the life of Rishap-La, for this, the temple having been completely destroyed (?), on its site I built a *kukunnum* and gave it to the great god, to Kiririsha and to the (divine) protectors of the earth. May (the) great god, Kiririsha and the (divine) protectors of the earth grant me a long life, may they grant me a continuously prosperous kingship.
Untash-Napirisha (1340–1300 BC)	IRS: 66	Susa	I, Untash-Napirisha, son of Humban-numena, king of Anzan and of Susa, I built the temple of Pinigir in baked bricks; I placed in it (a) Pinigir of gold; may the work which I created, as an offering, be agreeable to Pinigir-of-*siyan-kuk*!
	IRS: 71	Susa	I, Untash-Napirisha, son of Humban-numena, king of Anzan and of Susa, desirous (that) my life (be) continually one of prosperity, that the extinction of my lineage not be granted (when it shall be) judged (?), with this intention I built a temple of baked bricks, a high-temple of glazed bricks; I gave it to Inshushinak-of-*siyan-kuk*. I raised a ziggurat. May the work which I created, as an offering, be agreeable to Inshushinak!

Table 7.7 (cont.)

Author	Text	Provenience	Content
	IRS: 77	Susa	I, Untash-Napirisha, I built a high-temple in bricks of gold and silver, obsidian and alabaster and I gave it to the great god and to Inshushinak-of-*siyan-kuk*. Whosoever tears it down, destroys its brickwork, removes and takes to another country its gold, its silver, its obsidian, its alabaster and its brickwork, may the wrath of the great god, of Inshushinak and of Kiririsha-of-*siyan-kuk* be on him and may his descendants not prosper under the sun!
Napir-Asu	EKI §16[3]	Susa	I, Napir-Asu, wife of Untash-Napirisha. He who would seize my statue, who would smash it, who would destroy its inscription, who would erase my name, may he be smitten by the curse of Napirisha, of Kiririsha, and of Inshushinak, that his name shall become extinct, that his offspring be barren, that the forces of Beltiya, the great goddess, shall sweepdown on him. This is Napir-Asu's offering . . .

Notes:
[1] All dates are of course approximate. They follow Steve and Vallat 1989: 234 unless otherwise stated.
[2] For the *kukunnum*, a type of temple, see Malbran-Labat 1995: 187.
[3] Trans. after Harper, Aruz and Tallon 1992: 83.

BC (Brinkman 1977: 338). As the Berlin letter shows, generations of Igihalkid kings and Kassite princesses married each other.

Igi-halki's other son, Attar-kittah, carried on the operation begun by his brother mentioned in Shutruk-Nahhunte's letter, this time however in relation to the temple of Inshushinak at Susa (König 1965: 81, §28A/20). Recently, E. Quintana has suggested that the two brothers or their descendants may have divided the rule over Susa and Anshan between themselves, Attar-kittah ruling over Susa and Susiana, and Pahir-ishshan ruling over Anshan (Quintana 1996c: 106). The major justification for this view is the fact that, whereas Attar-kitah's son Humban-numena calls himself 'king of Susa and Anzan' (Malbran-Labat 1995: 59), Pahir-ishshan's son Kidin-Hutran inverted the title and called himself 'king of Anshan and Susa' (thus Steve and Vallat 1989: 224). Since Humban-numena is known to have styled himself both 'king of Susa and Anshan' and 'king of Anshan and Susa' in different contexts (Table 7.6), according to whether the text was written in Akkadian (Susa and Anshan) or Elamite (Anshan and Susa), Vallat has rejected the proposal of divided rule (Vallat 1997b), as discussed above.

Be that as it may, it is not inconceivable that rivalry erupted between the cousins descended from the two sons of Igi-halki, Pahir-ishshan and Attar-kittah. Again, if we follow the order of rule given in Shilhak-Inshushinak's building inscription, and insert Humban-numena in front of his son Untash-Napirisha (even if the former did not carry out restoration work on the Inshushinak temple, but assuming that he reigned before his son), then we find that Humban-numena and his son Untash-Napirisha ruled before Pahir-ishshan's two sons, Unpahash-Napirisha and Kidin-Hutran I. This would be explicable if Pahir-ishshan, who ruled before Attar-kittah, had died before his own eldest son could succeed him (i.e. if Unpahash-Napirisha had only been a young boy at the time), and Attar-kittah had instead become king. The shift in descent from Pahir-ishshan's line to that of Attar-kittah, however, may have caused friction, and if the order in Shilhak-Inshushinak's text is taken as a true, sequential account of Elamite rule in this period, then it can only mean that after passing down the line from Attar-kittah to his son Humban-numena and his grandson Untash-Napirisha, the kingship over Susa and Anzan shifted back to the collateral line emanating from Pahir-ishshan, to his two sons Unpahash-Napirisha and Kidin-Hutran I. For no apparent reason, Vallat has assumed that the kingship reverted to Pahir-ishshan's sons, Unpahash-Napirisha and Kidin-Hutran I, after the death of Attar-Kittah. He has suggested, furthermore, that each of these sons died without issue, at which point kingship reverted back to Attar-kittah's son, Humban-numena (Vallat 1994: 14, chart). There seems no evidence to support this series of assumptions, however. Moreover, it stands in conflict with the evidence of Shilhak-Inshushinak's enumeration of Elamite kings who contributed to the maintenance or re-building of the temple of Inshushinak at Susa, as we have already seen.

Humban-numena I clearly states in his brick inscriptions from Susa that he was chosen by the 'great god' by reason of his descent from his mother, and although the text is difficult to understand, he seems to claim that Inshushinak granted him kingship once he had re-established prosperity and restored the crown (Table 7.6). Claims such as these are unlikely to have been made if his accession to the throne of his father had been a smooth one. Moreover, continuity with his predecessor is scarcely to be inferred from Humban-numena's allegation that he built a high-temple or *kukunnum* on the site of a temple which had been completely destroyed. How we are to interpret his construction of a temple for Kiririsha-of-Liyan at Liyan, near modern Bushire on the Persian Gulf (Vallat 1984a; Walker 1981: 130, no. 192) is unclear, but it surely indicates a close relationship with that site (contra Malbran-Labat 1995: 82; Vallat 1997b notes that none of the bricks referring to this work were found at Susa, all came from Bushire).

Malbran-Labat has suggested that the survival of Humban-numena's line may likewise have been in question, and that royal inscriptions which cite the names of family members (e.g. Mishim-ruh, presumably his wife, and Rishap-La, another female, perhaps a daughter) may reflect the uncertainties surrounding either the foundation or the prolongation of a royal line (Malbran-Labat 1995: 204). The survival of his line, however, may have owed something to his marriage to the daughter of 'the mighty king Kurigalzu', i.e. Kurgalzu I, possibly the Mishim-ruh of his inscriptions, as revealed in the Berlin letter referred to above. The letter goes on to tell us that the Kassite princess gave birth to Untash-Napirisha, who himself married the daughter of Burna-Buriash (II), the nineteenth king to sit on the Kassite throne (1359–1333 BC).

Apart from the inter-dynastic nature of his marriage, we are far from having even a rudimentary understanding of Untash-Napirisha's foreign relations. A fragment of a statue of the god Immeriya taken to Susa as war booty by Untash-Napirisha bears an inscription, but the vital name there is broken. Originally read as [Kashtil]iash (Scheil 1908: 85), i.e. Kashtiliashu, the twenty-eighth ruler of the Kassite dynasty (1232–1225 BC), it was later suggested that it might be [Tupl]iash, the name of a city or region in the east-Tigridian area north of Der (Carter and Stolper 1984: 38; for the location see Reade 1978: 138 and Fig. 2), but Brinkman has noted 'that there is little evidence in favor of the new restoration' (Brinkman 1976: 189; see also Steve, Gasche and de Meyer 1980: 102). Thus, while we can be certain that Untash-Napirisha campaigned somewhere in the Mesopotamian arena, we still do not know where.

Domestically, however, Untash-Napirisha left us ample evidence of his activities. An inscribed brick discovered in a sondage at Tepe Bormi in the Ram Hormuz valley between Khuzistan and Fars alludes to his building activities there, as do bricks found at Tepe Deylam (KS 47), Tepe Gotvand (Steve, Gasche and de Meyer 1980: 81–2) and Chogha Pahan East (KS 102; see Stolper and Wright 1990). At Susa he left no fewer than eleven different building inscriptions (with even more variants) incised on bricks (Table 7.8). According to these, he had statues carved and temples or other types of religious buildings erected for Belala, Belet-ali, Ea?-sunkir, IM, Inshushinak, Ishnikarab, Kiririsha (Grillot 1986), Nabu, Nahhunte, Napirisha (the 'great god'), the Napratep gods ('the protectors'; Vallat 1987a), Nazit, NUN-EŠŠANA, Pinigir, Shala, Shimut, Sin and Upurkubak (Pl. 7.2). No program of public/religious building on this scale had previously taken place at Susa. Unfortunately, much of the architecture which must have resulted from this burst of activity has been lost to us through subsequent construc-

Table 7.8. *Deities for whom Untash-Napirisha built or reconstructed various religious buildings*

Deity	Structure	Location	Meaning	Reference
Belala	siyan . . . upat hussip	Susa	temple of glazed brick (Steve), painted brick (Vallat)	IRS 30; EKI §10a–c
			temple of glazed brick (Steve), painted brick (Vallat)	
Ea?-sunkir	siyan	Susa	temple	IRS 24
Hishmitik and Ruhurater	siyan hunin	Choga Zanbil	unknown type of temple (s.v. Belala)	EKI §6h = MDP 41: no. 20
	siyan . . . upat hussip	Choga Zanbil		EKI §7IIb, 11C = MDP 41: nos. 19, 39
	hadien hapshir sukartah	Choga Zanbil	unknown type of structure	EKI §11C = MDP 41: no. 39
Humban	siyan . . . upat hussip	Choga Zanbil	(s.v. Belala)	EKI §12D = MDP 41: no. 39
IM and Shala	siyan silin	Susa	temple of?	IRS 24
	siyan . . . upat hussip	Susa	(s.v. Belala)	IRS 25
	siyan silin	Choga Zanbil	temple of?	EKI §6g = MDP 41: no. 14
	siyan . . . upat hussip	Choga Zanbil	(s.v. Belala)	EKI §7IIc = MDP 41: no. 13
Inanna	siyan	Choga Zanbil	temple	EKI §10A = MDP 41: no. 45
Inshushinak	siyan ubqumimma	Susa	temple of artificial sandstone bricks (Hinz-Koch) or glazed bricks? (Malbran-Labat)	IRS 24
	kukunnum	Susa	high temple	IRS 31
	kukunnum ubqumimma	Susa	high temple of artificial sandstone bricks (Hinz-Koch) or glazed bricks?	IRS 28
	siyan . . . upat hussip	Susa	(s.v. Belala)	IRS 28
	zagratume	Susa	ziggurat	IRS 28
	nur kiprat	Susa	(temple of) 'moonlight'	IRS 29
	siyan ubqumimma	Choga Zanbil	temple of artificial sandstone bricks (Hinz-Koch) or glazed bricks? (Malbran-Labat)	EKI §5e = MDP 41: no. 33
	siyan likrin	Choga Zanbil	unknown typeof temple	EKI §6i = MDP 41: no. 34
	siyan . . . upat hussip	Choga Zanbil	(s.v. Belala)	EKI §12a–c = MDP 41: no. 1, EKI §12A = MDP 41: no. 5

Table 7.8 (cont.)

Deity	Structure	Location	Meaning	Reference
	kukunnum ubqumimma	Choga Zanbil	high temple of artificial sandstone bricks?	EKI §12a-c = MDP 41: no. 1
	zagratume	Choga Zanbil	ziggurat	EKI §13a
	x-x-x mushia	Choga Zanbil	bull? and griffin of glazed clay	MDP 41: nos. 53–5
	tush pitteka	Choga Zanbil	enclosed courtyard? (Steve)	MDP 41: no. 22
	kukunnum	KS 937 along the old Dizful-Shustar route?	high temple	MDP 53: No. 7
Ishnikarab	*siyan . . . upat hussip*	Susa	(s.v. Belala)	IRS 24
	siyan . . . upat hussip	Choga Zanbil	temple	EKI §6e = MDP 41: no. 8
	ligi mushitta	Choga Zanbil	blue-glazed terracotta knob	MDP 41: no. 57
Kilah shupir	*siyan limin*	Choga Zanbil	'fire' temple	EKI §9Va
	siyan . . . upat hussip	Choga Zanbil	(s.v. Belala)	EKI §9Vb = MDP 41: no. 51
Kiririsha	*kishtum.ma*	Choga Zanbil	temple 'in the grove'	EKI §9IVc = MDP 41: 25
	siyan . . . upat hussip	Choga Zanbil	(s.v. Belala)	EKI §12B = MDP 41: no. 7
Kirm/washir	*siyan*	Choga Zanbil	temple	MDP 41: no. 30
Manzat	*siyan . . . upat hussip*	Choga Zanbil	(s.v. Belala)	EKI §12G = MDP 41: 48
Nabium	*siyan . . . upat hussip*	Choga Zanbil	(s.v. Belala)	MDP 41: no. 42
Nabu	*siyan*	Choga Zanbil	temple	EKI §71a
	siyan . . . upat hussip	Choga Zanbil	(s.v. Belala)	EKI §12E = MDP 41: no. 41
	siyan . . . upat hussip	Susa	(s.v. Belala)	IRS 25
Nahhunte	*siyan . . . upat hussip*	Choga Zanbil	(s.v. Belala)	EKI §10a
	siyan . . . upat hussip	Susa	(s.v. Belala)	IRS 30
Napirisha	*ain kuten*	Choga Zanbil	'house of justice' (Steve, Malbran-Labat)	EKI §8 = MDP 41: no. 38
	siyan	Choga Zanbil	temple	MDP 41: no. 28
	siyan talin	Choga Zanbil	temple of? (something related to writing?)	EKI §11D = MDP 41: no. 9
	ain kuten	Susa	'house of justice'	IRS 26
	siyan	Susa	temple	IRS 27

Napirisha and Belet-ali	siyan . . . upat hussip	Susa	(s.v. Belala)	IRS 25
Napirisha and Inshushinak	siyan mielki ilani	Choga Zanbil	temple of?	EKI §9II
	siyan	Choga Zanbil	temple	EKI §9IIIa-c = MDP 41: nos. 2–4
	nur kiprat	Choga Zanbil	(temple of) 'moonlight'	MDP 41: no. 21
	abullu kinunni	Choga Zanbil	'gate of the oven'	EKI §11A, a-b; MDP 41: nos. 36–7
	shunshu irpi kushih	Choga Zanbil	unknown type of structure	EKI §11B = MDP 41: no. 6
	kukunnum	Choga Zanbil	high temple	EKI §13A-B = MDP 41: nos. 31–2
	siyan mielki ilani	Choga Zanbil	temple of the 'king of the gods'? (Steve)	MDP 41: no. 35
	ulhi	Choga Zanbil	type of temple	MDP 41: nos. 2, 4A-B
	siyan mielki ilani	Susa	temple of the 'king of the gods'? (Steve)	IRS 27
	kukunnum	Susa	high temple	IRS 32
Napratep gods	siyan	Choga Zanbil	temple	EKI §6d = MDP 41: no. 17
	sir halte	Choga Zanbil	columned doorway? (Steve)	EKI §6k = MDP 41: no. 18
	siyan . . . upat hussip	Choga Zanbil	(s.v. Belala)	EKI §7IId
	siyan . . . upat hussip	Susa	(s.v. Belala)	IRS 25
Nazit	siyan	Susa	temple	IRS 27
NIN.É.GAL	siyan . . . upat hussip	Choga Zanbil	(s.v. Belala)	EKI §12F = MDP 41: no. 47
NUN-LUGAL	siyan	Susa	temple	IRS 27
Nushku	murti	Choga Zanbil	podium? (Malbran-Labat)	EKI §7III = MDP 41: no. 24
	siyan . . . upat hussip	Choga Zanbil	(s.v. Belala)	EKI §12C = MDP 41: no. 43
	ipillati	Choga Zanbil	courtyard? (Steve)	MDP 41: nos. 23 and 44
Pinigir	siyan . . . upat hussip	Susa	(s.v. Belala)	IRS 22, 25
	ashtam	Susa	building where statues/figurines signifying the goddess's fecundity role in procreation were gathered; cf. link with sacred marriage rites or divine prostitution	IRS 24
	siyan . . . upat hussip	Choga Zanbil	(s.v. Belala)	EKI §6a, 7Ib = MDP 41: nos. 10–11
	ashtam	Choga Zanbil	(s.v. Belala)	EKI §5d = MDP 41: no. 12

Table 7.8 (cont.)

Deity	Structure	Location	Meaning	Reference
Shimut and Belet-ali	*siyan kinin*	Choga Zanbil		EKI §6f = MDP 41: no. 16
	siyan	Choga Zanbil	temple	EKI §7IIa = MDP 41: no. 15
	siyan . . . upat hussip	Susa	(s.v. Belala)	IRS 25
Shushmusi or Damusi and Belilit	*siyan*	Choga Zanbil	temple	EKI §10B = MDP 41: no. 50
Siiashum	*siyan*	Choga Zanbil	temple	EKI §8A
Sin	*siyan . . . upat hussip*	Susa	(s.v. Belala)	IRS 30
Sunkir risharra ('Great god')	*pukshi takkippi*	Choga Zanbil	'house of life, place of destinies' (Steve)	MDP 41: no. 46
	siyan	Choga Zanbil	temple	MDP 41: no. 26
Upurkubak	*siyan*	Susa	temple	IRS 23
	siyan	Choga Gotvand	temple	MDP 53: no. 5
	zagratume	eastern Susiana	ziggurat	MDP 53: no. 6

Plate 7.2 Bronze relief fragment (Sb 133, 1.05 m long) from Pit 15, excavated in the Inshushinak temple at Susa in 1898/99 by de Morgan. Seven warrior deities, each *c.* 36 cm tall (note the horned crowns) are depicted and the inscription (EKI 69) mentions the Elamite gods Nahhunte, Lagamar, Pinikir and Kirririsha. The king who may have commissioned this has yet to be determined. © Musée du Louvre, Antiquités Orientales

tion and disturbance, so that the inscribed bricks which record this or that building project are often all we have to go on. The absence of the buildings themselves in most cases makes it difficult to fully comprehend the variety of terms used to denote the different types of structures erected by Untash-Napirisha. The main shrine to Inshushinak was one of the rare examples of a Middle Elamite religious building still extant at Susa when excavations began, but this was largely excavated in the late nineteenth century when recording left much to be desired, and 'while excavators give elaborate descriptions of some of the architectural details (crenellated roofs and polychrome inlaid terracotta wall knobs)' and 'mention glazed inscribed relief brickwork on the main doorways on the southeastern side of the temple of which we have examples' (Harper, Aruz and Tallon 1992: 123), the finds thus described no longer survive.

Two hoards of material from the Inshushinak temple area are important as they provide us with a glimpse of the variety of Middle Elamite material culture. Deposit I, as I shall call it, was found on New Year's Day, 1904, in a three-sided brick cist which measured 1.5×1.2 m (Tallon, Hurtel and Drilhon 1989: 121). Along with unpierced beads, unengraved cylinder seals and scrap metal, several dozen male and female metal figurines were found. These included examples made from nearly pure copper with trace impurities (e.g. zinc, lead, arsenic, iron, silver, etc.) as well as some low tin content bronzes with up to 5.9 per cent tin (Tallon, Hurtel and Drilhon 1989: Fig. 1). On 22 February 1904 a second hoard, Deposit II, was found to the south of the temple itself, clustered on a green-glazed, brick platform c. 96×64 cm. It was originally believed to be a foundation deposit by the excavator R. de Mecquenem, but he later changed his mind and suggested it represented the 'remnants of a funerary deposit from a vaulted tomb that had been looted' (Harper, Aruz and Tallon 1992: 145). This included a pair of nearly identical, 6 cm. tall statuettes of male worshippers made of gold and silver; a series of faience figurines depicting male worshippers; a lapis lazuli dove inlaid with gold; limestone animal figures mounted on bitumen compound sledges; a schist whetstone with an elaborate gold lion's head finial at one end showing fine granulation and repoussé work; and an agate bead inscribed in Akkadian with the legend, 'To Ishtaran [city god of Der, see Chapter 6], Kurigalzu has dedicated [this]' (Harper, Aruz and Tallon 1992: 153).

Perhaps the most outstanding find from this period yet discovered at Susa is the 1.29 m high cast bronze statue of Untash-Napirisha's wife, Napir-Asu (Pl. 7.3), which was recovered from the upper levels of a room in the temple to Ninhursag founded on the east-central portion of the Acropole by Shulgi. The late E. Porada called it 'rightly the most famous work of Elamite art' (Porada 1971: 30). If this was the Elamite king's principal wife then she must have been the daughter of the Kassite king Burna-Buriash II mentioned in the Berlin letter. Could this account for the fact that her statue, which depicts her in a gesture of perpetual prayer, was erected in the temple of a Mesopotamian deity rather than in the great temple of Inshushinak? Discovered in 1903, the statue shows the queen wearing a long dress with short sleeves. The upper part of the dress is covered with dotted circles which might represent eyelet-like decoration, while the skirt, which appears to be wrapped around the figure, has panels of geometric decoration running around the waist and down the front, as well as wavy lines suggesting a border of fringe at the bottom. The eyelet pattern covers large portions of the body of the skirt as well, although one area has been inscribed in Elamite (Table 7.6) with a curse on anyone who would do damage to the statue or its inscription, invoking the Elamite deities Napirisha, Kiririsha and Inshushinak. Napir-Asu wears a four-banded bracelet on her right wrist, and at her right shoulder a clasp is shown attached to her dress.

Although fragmentary, Napir-Asu's statue still weighs 1750 kg and represents but one of a number of fragments of large, cast bronzework from Middle Elamite Susa. The construction of Napir-Asu's statue is intriguing. A solid core of 11 per cent tin-bronze supports an outer shell of copper cast in the lost-wax process with 1 per cent tin and various other impurities including lead, silver, nickel, bismuth and cobalt. Although most of the decorative work on Napir-Asu's dress was originally cast, the inscription, eyelets, and portions of the geometric borders were chased after casting. It is not certain whether the statue was originally covered with gold or silver plate which has since been lost, but the possibility exists, for grooves were found on the arm and on either side of

Plate 7.3 Bronze statue of Napirasu (Sb 2731, 1.29 m tall) from Susa. © Musée du Louvre, Antiquités Orientales

Plate 7.4 White limestone statue fragment (Sb 67) from Susa, possibly representing the god Napirisha, patron deity of Untash-Napirisha (see also Amiet 1973a: 18, Spycket 1981: 307). © Musée du Louvre, Antiquités Orientales

the skirt which, in other situations, have been known to help secure sheets of precious metal to base metal statuary (Harper, Aruz and Tallon 1992: 134–5).

Susa has also yielded fragments of one or more statues of Untash-Napirisha (Vallat 1988a) along with fragments of an inscribed (Vallat 1981) stele showing, in four registers, the king before a seated god wearing a horned crown (I); Napir-Asu, Untash-Napirisha, and the priestess U-tik (Untash-Napirisha's mother?) (II); two goddess with horned crowns holding the streams emanating from a number of flowing vases (III); and two standing mountain goats with bearded, human faces grasping the leaves of a tree (IV) (Harper, Aruz and Tallon 1992: 128–9). Meandering serpents with dragons' heads frame the scenes. Both the stele and the statues of, or commissioned by, Untash-Napirisha (Pls. 7.4–5, Fig. 7.5) are thought to have been brought to Susa by the later Middle Elamite III ruler Shutruk-Nahhunte, who says in one of his inscriptions, 'I (am) Shutruk-Nahhunte, son of Hallutush-Inshushinak [the beloved servant] of [the god Inshushinak]. I removed the statues which Untash-Napirisha had placed in the *siyan-kuk* when Inshushinak, my god, demanded it of me, and at Susa dedicated them to Inshushinak, my god' (König 1965: 75–6, §21; see also Grillot and Vallat 1978: 82, n. 3; Vallat 1981: 32). The *siyan-kuk* where Untash-Napirisha originally displayed these

Plate 7.5 Detail of the inscribed forearm of Sb 67. © Musée du Louvre, Antiquités Orientales

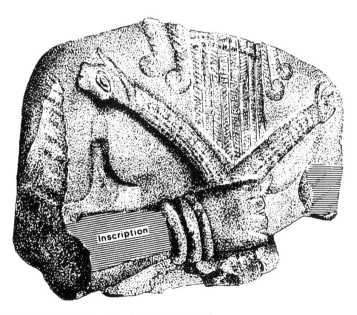

Figure 7.5 Sb 67 = Pl. 7.4 (after Spycket 1981: Fig. 75).

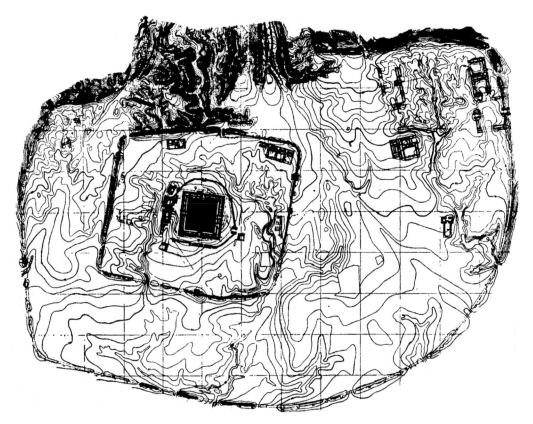

Figure 7.6 Plan of Choga Zanbil (after Ghirshman 1966: Plan I).

works was at Al Untash-Napirisha, modern Choga Zanbil, an entirely new city founded by the king approximately 40 km southeast of Susa.

Choga Zanbil

In the mid-1890's, a geologist prospecting for oil brought an incised brick from the surface of a site overlooking the Diz river to the French working at Susa, and in this way Choga Zanbil was first made known to archaeologists (Ghirshman 1966: 1). Although R. de Mecquenem undertook limited soundings at the site in 1936 and 1939, it was R. Ghirshman who, in the course of nine seasons of excavation (1951–1962), succeeded in uncovering a vast area of Choga Zanbil (Fig. 7.6), complete with ziggurat, temples, a palace, and a perimeter wall exceeding 4 km in extent which enclosed an area of roughly 100 ha. Subsequent exploration in the environs have revealed the site of a temple to Manzat and NIN.DAR.A *c.* 3 km away, built by Shutruk-Nahhunte (Mousavi 1990; Vallat 1990c), while study of aerial photographs of Choga Zanbil have located what has been described as a 'ceremonial way' leading to the east gate of the outer city wall (Tourovets 1997).

With the exception of two stone maceheads bearing the name of 'Attar-kittah, son of . . . king of Susa and Anshan' (Steve 1967: 112), all of the epigraphic evidence from Choga Zanbil – somewhere between 5000 and 6500 inscribed bricks plus assorted other texts – underscores the fact that the city was a new foundation, the work of Untash-Napirisha. However piously he may have acted at Susa, and as we saw above the inscribed bricks found there attest to his fostering of the cults of no fewer than eighteen different deities, Untash-Napirisha exceeded every one of his predecessors in the zeal and energy expended on the Elamite, Susian and Mesopotamian deities worshipped at Choga Zanbil. Looking again at the building inscriptions (Table 7.8) we find that twenty-five deities – Belet-ali, Belilit, Hishmitik, Humban, IM, Inanna, Inshushinak, Ishnikarab, Kilah shupir, Kiririsha, Kirwashir, Manzat, Nabium, Nabu, Nahhunte, Napirisha, the Napratep gods, NIN.É.GAL, Nushku, Pinigir, Ruhurater, Shala, Shimut, Shushmusi, and Sunkir risharra – were honoured in one or more shrines at Choga Zanbil.

These were all clustered within an inner, walled area, which Ghirshman referred to by the Greek term *temenos*. The perimeter wall of this precinct was 1625 m long, the individual sides of which measured 470 m (NE wall), 325 m (NW wall), 450 m (SW wall) and 380 m (SE wall), respectively. The temples of Pinigir, IM and Shala, Shimut and Belet-ali, and the Napratep gods were located, one after the other, to the right of the royal entrance in the southeastern wall of the *temenos*. The first three of these adjacent temples had identical plans with a series of rooms on the southern and western sides, presumably for the priests and temple functionaries, and a pavement leading diagonally from the entrance across the interior courtyard to a two-roomed shrine with decorative buttresses on the exterior and a pair of altars (only one in the case of Pinigir) in the interior. Although Mallowan compared the lay-outs of these three identical shrines to the Enki temple at Ur built by Rim-Sin, suggesting that his descent from Kudur-Mapuk and the alleged Elamite connection of the family may have been responsible for their similarity (Mallowan 1970: 270), the differences between the temples in question seem as great as any similarities.

To the northeast of the complex just described was the temple of Hishmitik and Ruhurater, while the temples of Ishnikarab, Nabu, Kiririsha, and Napirisha were situated just northwest of the ziggurat located in the approximate centre of the enclosure. The ziggurat was encircled by yet another wall, adjacent to which were further chapels, and built into this wall were shrines to Inshushinak (A and B). Within the *temenos* were distinct roadways leading from the northeast gate and the northwest gate (the so-called 'Susa gate') towards the ziggurat, but the rest of the interior seems not to have been built upon.

The ziggurat itself (Pl. 7.6, Fig. 7.7) was built of millions of bricks, three types of which were noted in excavation: sun-dried, baked, and sun-dried with fragments of baked brick used as temper (Ghirshman 1966: 12). The structure was principally built of sun-dried bricks topped off with a 2 m thick 'skin' of baked brick to prevent erosion. Inscribed bricks (Pl. 7.7) proclaiming Untash-Napirisha's dedication of the ziggurat to Inshushinak occurred after every tenth row of uninscribed bricks. Throughout the zig-

Plate 7.6 A view of the approach to the stairway of the ziggurat of Choga Zanbil.

gurat, layers of mud mortar were used between the rows of brick, and in one area tree trunks coated with bitumen were used as dowels to help secure the mantle of baked brick to the core of sun-dried brick (Ghirshman 1966: 13).

The ziggurat consisted of four levels, estimated by Ghirshman to have been origi- nally 12 m high (Ghirshman 1966: 59; see also Roche 1986), one on top of the next. These shrank in size from bottom to top, the lowest measuring 99.40 m on a side, resting on a slightly larger socle 105.20 m on a side (I; approximately equal to 200 Elamite cubits of 52.5 cm. each, see Trümpelmann 1976: 325); the second measuring 67 m on a side, resting on a socle 71.2 m on a side (II); the third measuring 51 m on a side, the socle of which had been eroded (III); and the fourth measuring 35.2 m on a side, the socle of which was likewise no longer extant (Ghirshman 1966: 36). As in the case of Babylonian ziggurats, the uppermost stage supported a shrine, in this case the *kukunnum* of Napirisha and Inshushinak. Faced with bricks glazed blue and green, with touches of gold and silver as well, and decorated with blue and green glazed square plaques with a raised pommel in the centre and palmette decoration (Nunn 1988: 161) – most inscribed with the name of Untash-Napirisha (Steve 1967: 103) – this high temple was surely an impressive sight.

One of the most extraordinary aspects of the Choga Zanbil ziggurat is the preserva- tion of the gateways, galleries, and staircases which gave access ultimately to the

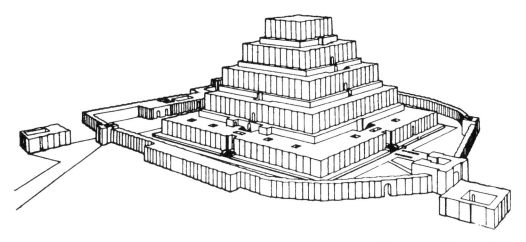

Figure 7.7 Axonometric reconstruction of the ziggurat at Choga Zanbil (after *Susa*, n.d.: Fig. 11).

kukunnum. In contrast to the ziggurats of southern Mesopotamia, where access to the uppermost shrine was external, i.e. via staircases external to the individual levels themselves (Mallowan 1970: 267), the ziggurat at Choga Zanbil was entered through a monumental stairway and scaled internally. Equally fascinating is the building's history which was only really revealed when Ghirshman and his colleagues daringly excavated an exploratory tunnel through the ziggurat. This exposed a method of construction completely unattested in Mesopotamia, a point stressed by Mallowan in his comparison of Mesopotamian ziggurats with that of Choga Zanbil (Mallowan 1970: 266–7). Briefly stated, in its earliest configuration, the square space occupied by the ziggurat was in fact a sunken courtyard (believed by Gropp 1989: 243 ff. to have been a 'pool' filled with water for ritual purposes, comparable to the so-called 'Great Bath' at Mohenjo-Daro in Pakistan, a far from convincing hypothesis) entered through one of three monumental gateways on the northeast, southeast and southwest sides of the square, and surrounded by the L-shaped temples of Inshushinak (A and B). Within the centre of this space a solid brick tower was constructed, the upper surface of which would appear to have been the fourth level of the ziggurat. This in turn was surrounded by a second skin of brick, the surface of which represented the third level of the ziggurat, and a third skin of brick, the surface of which marks the second level of the ziggurat. The 'first' level of the ziggurat was nothing more than the ceiling of the Inshushinak temples and the walls which were eventually added on to them so as to complete the northern sides of the square (Ghirshman 1966: 38–45). This must surely be one of the most ambitious brick constructions ever attempted in the ancient Near East.

The ziggurat at Choga Zanbil yielded a wide variety of important finds. During the excavation of the northeastern entranceway the remains of a blue-glazed bull (1.35 m tall, 1.105 m long) were recovered (Ghirshman 1966: Pl. LXIX, top). The bull's back bore a sixteen-line inscription in the glaze identifying the object as 'a bull in glazed terra-

Plate 7.7 Inscribed brick in the ziggurat of Choga Zanbil.

cotta, such as the ancients never made' which Untash-Napirisha set up as a guardian of the precinct of Inshushinak (Steve 1967: 95). Similarly, excavations in the northwest entrance to the ziggurat yielded fragments of a blue-glazed griffon (Ghirshman 1966: Pl. LXIX, bottom) badly broken but presumably of approximately the same size as its bovine counterpart, with a badly preserved inscription (Steve 1967: 97). A surprising number of stone tools, including flint scrapers, knives, burins and projectile points were found around the ziggurat, confirming that stone tools were well and truly still in use in the Late Bronze Age in Khuzistan (e.g. Ghirshman 1966: Pl. LXVI, LXX-LXII). Large numbers of small animal figurines (including birds, turtles, rams, boars, bulls), beads, and maceheads were found in the series of 'chapels' along the southwest side of the ziggurat, presumably having been donated as votive offerings by worshippers. Finally, 127 of the 160 cylinder seals discovered by Ghirshman at Choga Zanbil came from these chapels (Porada 1970: 3), including both pseudo-Kassite and Elamite ('élamite élaborée') seals, the majority of which were made of faience or frit (see now Matthews 1992: 15ff.).

The various temples in close proximity to the ziggurat also yielded finds, some of which may have been used in temple ritual, some of which may have been *ex voto* offerings. Thus, the tall ceramic beakers (Ghirshman 1966: Pl. LXXXII) from the temple of Napirisha (the 'great god') could have been employed by priests for domestic use or for pouring libations, while a fragmentary frit statuette of a female with arms crossed across her stomach (Ghirshman 1966: Pl. LXXXII, G.T.Z. 273) probably represents a worshipper in an attitude of prayer which was dedicated by the worshipper herself. A pair of bronze shaft-hole axes, one of which has a boar (?) reclining on the shaft and the blade emanating from a lion's mouth, as well as a bronze celt (small blade-axe), all of which were found in the temple of Kiririsha, were engraved with the name of Untash-Napirisha (Steve 1967: 102; Ghirshman 1966: Pl. LXXXIII, LXXXV). Small bronze animal figurines, rings, pendants, stone maceheads bearing the name of Untash-Napirisha, and a selection of short swords and dagger blades were also recovered from the temple (Ghirshman 1966: Pl. LXXXIV-XCIII). The temple of Ishnikarab, on the other hand, yielded a number of examples of the ceramic dish-on-stand (Ghirshman 1966: Pl. XCVI), which, on analogy with modern day incense burners, may have been used for a similar purpose, while excavations in the temple of Pinigir brought to light a number of frit vessels in the form of a female head (Ghirshman 1968: Pl. LXX). Finds such as these, along with alabaster vessels (Ghirshman 1968: Pl. LI-LIII, XCIII-XCIV), closely paralleled at Middle Assyrian Assur (von Bissing 1940: Figs. 12–14; Haller 1954: Pl. 31), show that representative examples of international art styles in wide circulation during the Late Bronze age were well known at the court and in the temples of Al Untash-Napirisha.

In the eastern corner of the site, well away from the *temenos* area, Ghirshman excavated four major buildings in what he called the 'royal quarter' of the city. This area of buildings lay approximately 300–600 m away from the *temenos* wall. Although the intervening area has in recent times been subject to intense erosion during the winter rains, Ghirshman imagined that it had never really been built up with domestic houses, but that 'pilgrims', journeying to the great complex of deities within the centre of the city, had camped there in the wide open spaces (Ghirshman 1968: 47). This remains, however, pure speculation, and there is no concrete evidence that Choga Zanbil was in fact ever a place of pilgrimage.

A monumental 'royal' gateway complex slightly south of the northeastern corner of the site gave access to this part of Al Untash-Napirisha. Here inscribed bricks identified a 4.9 m wide entrance through the outer city wall as the 'great gate'. This opened onto a large courtyard measuring almost 64 m square (actually 64×62.3 m) with rooms, perhaps for guards, built into the surrounding walls. Finally, directly opposite the 'great gate', on the opposite side of the courtyard, was the 4 m wide 'king's gate' (Ghirshman 1968: 87–9).

Immediately to the east of the gate/courtyard complex was a large building (90.1× 42.9 m) consisting of a gallery of rooms built around two nearly identical, internal courtyards measuring 29.3 m on a side and 29.5×29.3 m, respectively. This structure, composed of two symmetrical sets of rooms each surrounding a courtyard, was termed Palace III by Ghirshman, who felt that the general dearth of finds, consisting only of some jar lids and a few sherds (Ghirshman 1968: 83), apart from a buried hoard of twelve alabaster vessels (Ghirshman 1968: Pl. XCIII-XCIV), suggested that the building may have been systematically looted, perhaps by the Assyrians under Assurbanipal in the late 7th century BC. More recent analysis of the latest ceramics from Choga Zanbil, however, suggests that its destruction probably occurred much earlier (Pons 1994: 43), when Nebuchadnezzar I (1125–1104 BC) brought the Middle Elamite III Shutrukid dynasty to an end.

To the northeast of the gateway and Palace III lay the ephemeral remains of what Ghirshman took to be another palace (IV), and beyond this was yet another building, called Palace II, which was comprised of three courtyards, each surrounded by a gallery of rooms, the whole arranged in an L-shape. The perfect symmetry of this building is shown by the fact that it was made up of three square units, 58 m long, so that at its widest point the building measured 116 m. The internal courtyards here measured c. 38.4×37.8 m. As in the case of Palace III, finds were rare. Although the term 'palace' is retained here for purposes of reference, the palatial function of these structures is far from proven.

Approximately 70 m to the west of Palace II lay a building with a completely different plan, the so-called *palais hypogée* (Fig. 7.8). Covering an area c. 70×56 m, it consisted of a large, internal courtyard (22.9×29.75 m) on the south side of the building, flanked by sets of rooms of varying dimensions to the northwest and northeast, and a pair of long, narrow rooms along the southwestern and southeastern sides. As interesting as this building may have been above ground, it proved to be far more interesting below ground, where Ghirshman discovered no fewer than five monumental, subterranean, vaulted tombs, all built of brick. Access to each of these was via a staircase of seventeen steps (sixteen in the case of Tomb V), but the tombs themselves differed from each other in plan. Thus, the stairway might be placed at one end of a long, narrow chamber, as in Tomb I, which measured 3.65×12.6 m internally, whereas in Tomb IV the entrance and staircase were in the middle of the long side of a 4.1×15 m chamber, and in the case of Tombs II, III and V, the tomb consisted of two long chambers of roughly similar dimensions (II: 6.25 and 6.85 m; III: 6.15 and 6.6 m; V: 9 m) connected by a narrow passageway. These were monumental constructions, the height of the vaulted roof above the chambers in general reaching c. 4 m and, as suggested by the steeply inclined staircases, the floors of the tomb chambers themselves lying up to 5.25 m below the floor of the palace above.

The use of these tombs was indicated in a variety of ways. In Tomb II two small concentrations of carbonized bone and ash, one in each chamber, were recovered. These proved to be the remains of three individuals in the first chamber, and five in the second, all of whom had been cremated together with a variety of grave goods including weapons (swords and arrowheads) and items of personal jewelry (e.g. beads, buttons, a silver torque) (Ghirshman 1968: 63–5). On the other hand, a completely different form of burial seemed to be indicated by the evidence from Tomb IV, where the fully articulated skeleton of a female, age c. 40–50 years, was found in flexed position, lying on its left side, on top of a solid brick platform measuring 2×2.25×.8 m. The skeleton was lying crosswise near one end of the platform (rather than lengthwise as on a proper bed), accompanied by the cremated remains of two other individuals and their personal belongings (weaponry, jewelry), also resting atop the platform. Similar remains may

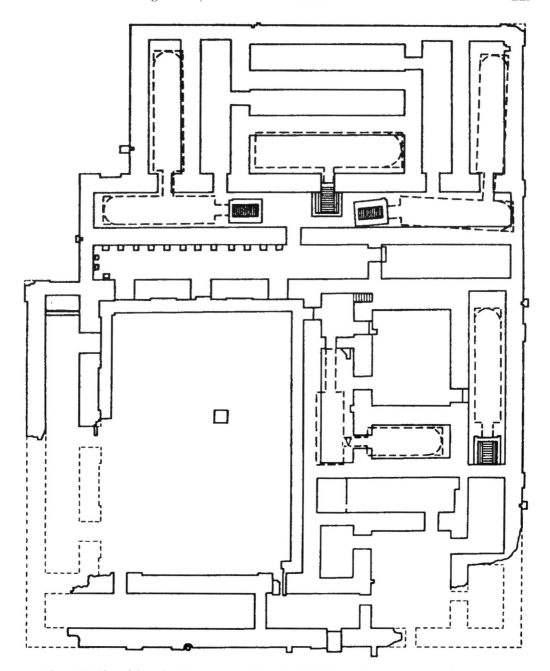

Figure 7.8 Plan of the palace hypogeum at Choga Zanbil (after Mallowan 1970: Fig. 6).

once have existed in Tomb V, but the evidence of pillaging here – again ascribed by Ghirshman to the violent destruction wrought by Assurbanipal in the 7th century BC, but perhaps more likely to be the result of Nebuchadnezzar I's conquest – obliterated most of the evidence (Ghirshman 1968: 73).

While reminiscent of the slightly earlier, vaulted tombs at Haft Tepe, the tombs just described are far more elaborate architecturally, and the evidence they provide of cremation is enormously important for our understanding of the varieties of Middle Elamite mortuary practice. Ghirshman was at pains to stress that, in the course of roughly 70 years of excavations by the French at Susa, not a single instance of cremation had been uncovered (Ghirshman 1968: 73). Assuming that all of the tombs found in the 'palais hypogée' were, in some sense, royal, he suggested that the uncremated female may have belonged to a princess of foreign origin for whom cremation would not have been an appropriate mode of burial, and he recalled that diplomatic marriages, particularly those involving Egyptian, Mitanni, Kassite and Hittite royalty, were common at the time (see also Pintore 1978). Knowing as we now do that Untash-Napirisha was himself married to the daughter of Burna-Buriash II (Table 7.5), and that inter-marriage was common between the princes of Susa and Anshan and the princesses of Kassite Babylonia, it is tempting indeed to suggest that the uncremated female from Tomb IV at Choga Zanbil was, as Ghirshman suggested, of foreign blood, most likely Kassite (Vallat 1988a: 175). Diplomatic and commercial contacts with areas as far away as Assur in northern Mesopotamia, Tell Zubeidi in the Hamrin basin or Marlik near the Caspian Sea are also attested to in this period by the diffusion of Elamite cylinder seals (Amiet 1986d; 1989; 1990a).

In conclusion, Choga Zanbil is in many ways a remarkable site. With respect to urban development and religious reform the achievements of Untash-Napirisha are unparalleled, even if it is far from certain that Choga Zanbil was 'an ambitious attempt to replace Susa as the political and religious center of the Elamite kingdom . . . a kind of federal sanctuary where the gods of the highlands and the lowlands were worshiped on an equal footing' (Harper, Aruz and Tallon 1992: 121). Nothing, however, suggests that Untash-Napirisha was followed in these areas by his immediate offspring.

After Untash-Napirisha

The genealogy of Untash-Napirisha's successors is, in part, revealed by the Berlin letter (Table 7.5) which tells us that his Kassite wife bore him a son called Kidin-hudurudish or Kidin-Hutran (II) in Elamite. The latter himself married yet another Kassite princess, daughter of . . . -^{d}duniash, who gave birth to Napirisha-Untash. As noted above, the Shilhak-Inshushinak building inscription listing those kings who contributed to the maintenance of the Inshushinak temple at Susa suggests that following the reign of Untash-Napirisha, whether directly or indirectly, he was succeeded by his second cousins, i.e. Pahir-ishshan's sons, Unpahash-Napirisha and Kidin-Hutran I. If this was indeed the case, then both men must have been fairly advanced in years, but it is not an impossibility. Vallat has suggested that these two may have died without issue

(Vallat 1994: 5), and if this were so then it would explain why succession reverted to Untash-Napirisha's son Kidin-Hutran II, who was in turn succeeded by his son, Napirisha-Untash. However, although not named in the letter, presumably because he did not take a Kassite bride, a third Kidin-Hutran has been postulated by some scholars for the simple reason that an Elamite king by this name was active in the last quarter of the 13th century and cannot, therefore, be synonymous with Kidin-Hutran II (Steve and Vallat 1989: 228; Steve 1991: 6). According to the Babylonian Chronicle P, this Kidin-Hutran (III) attacked the east Tigris region, destroying Der and its main temple Edimgalkalamma, before moving into Babylonia where he captured Nippur, deported some of its inhabitants and overthrew Enlil-nadin-shumi, twenty-ninth ruler of the Kassite dynasty, in 1224 BC. In reality, the Kassite king was himself only a puppet of the Assyrian state, for Tukulti-Ninurta I had conquered Babylonia by attacking and defeating Kashtiliashu I approximately a year earlier (Weidner 1959: 4; see also Brinkman 1968: 86; 1976: 125). A few years later, according to Chronicle P (Brinkman 1968: 87; 1976: 87), Kidin-Hutran attacked the third Assyrian appointee to the Kassite throne, Adad-shuma-iddina (1222–1217 BC), striking at both Marad and Isin.

The reason for these attacks is nowhere stated explicitly, but one may suppose that, as the legitimate Kassite royal house had long been linked by marriage with that of the kings of Susa and Anshan, Tukulti-Ninurta I's overthrow of Kashtiliashu IV provided ample excuse for the Elamites to take up arms against the Assyrian client. The lack of any Assyrian response to attacks against one of its clients may seem strange, but the fact that Tukulti-Ninurta was assasinated shortly thereafter (c. 1207 BC) might indicate that the king had more than enough troubles to deal with on the homefront. Unfortunately, we have no sources relating to the end of Kidin-Hutran's aggressive reign, but we know that after Tukulti-Ninurta's death, the son of Kashtiliashu IV, Adad-shuma-usur, regained the throne, restoring the legitimate rule of the Kassite royal house and even gaining supremacy over its arch-rival Assyria (Brinkman 1968: 87).

The complete absence of inscriptions at Choga Zanbil attributable to Untash-Napirisha's successors – Kidin-Hutran II, Napirisha-Untash and Kidin-Hutran III – strongly suggests that, upon Untash-Napirisha's death, all major construction at the site ceased as did, one might deduce, the patronage of the sanctuaries of Al Untash-Napirisha. As noted above, some occupation of the site after the time of Untash-Napirisha may be inferred on ceramic grounds (Pons 1994), but this does not alter the fact that his successors seem to have abandoned the site for official purposes (Steve, Gasche and de Meyer 1980: 103). Any ongoing, non-royal occupation is almost certain to have ended if, as the Babylonian literary tradition asserts, Nebuchadnezzar I terminated the Shutrukid dynasty in the eleventh century.

Middle Elamite III (*c.* 1200–1100 B.C.)

We have no clear idea of how the Igihalkid dynasty came to an end, but it is thought that Kidin-Hutran died early in the reign of his Kassite counterpart Adad-shuma-usur (Steve, Gasche and de Meyer 1980: 103). What followed is unclear. The next historical

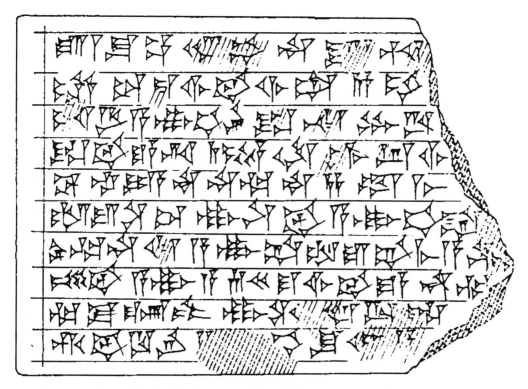

Figure 7.9 The inscribed brick Deh-e Now 1, face B (after Steve 1968: 301).

figure to call himself 'king of Anshan and Susa' is Shutruk-Nahhunte, son of Hallutush-Inshushinak. Of the latter, we know nothing apart from his name as given by his son on more than 450 inscribed bricks from Susa (Malbran-Labat 1995: 79–83) and on several bricks from Deh-e Now (KS 120) and Choga Pahan West (KS 3A) (Steve 1987: 20–6).

Shilhak-Inshushinak's enumeration of the re-builders of the Inshushinak temple at Susa names Shutruk-Nahhunte amongst them (König 1965: §48.2), and indeed 439 of his own inscribed bricks tell us that he built a *hiyan*, usually interpreted as a columned hall, for Inshushinak which became the 'family chapel' of the Shutrukids (Malbran-Labat 1995: 79, 100 and n. 133). In addition, four brick fragments tell us of the restoration of the temple to Kiririsha-of-Liyan originally built by Humban-numena (Malbran-Labat 1995: 82). At Deh-e Now (KS 120), on the other hand, Shutruk-Nahhunte restored the temple of Manzat which Igi-halki had likewise rebuilt several centuries earlier. A pair of inscribed brick fragments from the site (Fig. 7.9) also mention the originally Sumerian goddess ᵈNIN.DAR.A (Steve 1968: 300–3; 1987: 20, 27). Shutruk-Nahhunte's building activities are also attested by fragments of glazed terracotta plaques with raised pommels which name him (Steve 1987: 29). These are similar to those used by Untash-Napirisha to decorate the high temple at Choga Zanbil. Whether this indicates a particular connection with the family of Igi-halki and/or with the site is impossible to ascertain but certainly plausible. As two of the inscribed brick fragments from Deh-e Now seem to call ^dNIN.DAR.A (and Manzat?) 'god of Elam land of Hubshen' (Steve 1987: 27; see also 1968: 303) it has been suggested that this may have been the ancient name of the site (e.g. Hinz 1972: 121), but the fact that specific reference is made to the land and not to the city/town of Hubshen makes this doubtful.

Apart from these various building projects, Shutruk-Nahhunte's presence at Susa is best attested by the booty which he brought back from Mesopotamia, but before describing this, it is best to set the historical scene. As the Berlin 'letter' discussed above (Table 7.5) makes clear, its author was married to the daughter of the thirty-third Kassite king, Meli-Shihu or Meli-shipak (1186–1172 BC). He bitterly resented the fact that, in spite of his descent from a Kassite royal mother, he 'did not sit on the throne of the land of Babylonia'. As his letter reveals, he was incensed at not receiving a civil reply to his 'sincere proposal', presumably that he ascend the Babylonian throne. He threatened to 'destroy your cities, demolish your fortresses, stop up your (irrigation) ditches, cut down your orchards' and '[pull out] the rings (of the sluices) at the mouths of your (irrigation) canals'. While the name of the author of the Berlin letter is no longer preserved, it seems likely that it must have been none other than Shutruk-Nahhunte (Steve and Vallat 1989: 228; Steve 1991: 7) rather than his son, Kutir-Nahhunte as assumed by van Dijk (van Dijk 1986: 166; followed by Foster 1993: 284, n. 1, and Lambert 1994: 67). There are two main reasons for preferring Shutruk-Nahhunte. First, we know that Shutruk-Nahhunte invaded Babylonia and overthrew the thirty-fifth Kassite king, Zababa-shuma-iddina, in 1158 BC (Brinkman 1968: 88). Second, he seems shortly thereafter to have ceded the throne of Babylonia to his son, Kutir-Nahhunte, which would make it less likely that the latter would have written in such a manner.

Shutruk-Nahhunte brought a vast amount of booty back from his Mesopotamian campaign. This included numerous *kudurrus*, or boundary stones recording royal Kassite land grants (Seidl 1968); stone tablets; stelae, such as the famous victory stele of Naram-Sin, most probably the Law Code of Hammurabi, and a Kassite monument (Fig. 7.10) to which Shutruk-Nahhunte had his own image added (Amiet 1976: Fig. 12; 1992c: Fig. 2); and statues, including life-size representations of the Old Akkadian king Manishtusu (Table 7.9). Many of these, or fragments of them, bear one or another version of a standard inscription in which Shutruk-Nahhunte identifies himself as 'son of Hallutush-Inshushinak, beloved servant of Inshushinak, king of Anshan and Susa, enlarger of my realm, protector of Elam, prince of Elam'. This is then followed by a reference to Inshushinak, at whose behest Shutruk-Nahhunte undertook a specific action, e.g. 'I destroyed Karaindash [i.e. Babylonia]', 'I destroyed Sippar', or 'I destroyed Eshnunna'. Thereafter the Elamite king identifies what it was he seized as booty, e.g. 'the stele of Naram-Sin', 'the statue of Manishtusu' or 'the stele of Meli-Shihu' (all refs. are to König 1965: §22–24a). Additionally, there are numerous other Babylonian pieces, mainly *kudurrus*, from Susa, without a specific label attached telling us who seized it (Table 7.9; Seidl 1968). These may have been acquired by later kings, such as Kutir-Nahhunte, and it has even been suggested that some may have been brought back much

Figure 7.10 Babylonian stele re-cut by Shutruk-Nahhunte I, showing the Elamite king, left, before a Babylonian deity (after Calmeyer 1995b: Fig. 16).

Table 7.9. *Mesopotamian booty seized by Shutruk-Nahhunte and other Elamite kings which was recovered at Susa*

Object	'Author'	Date	Seized by	Reference
stele	Sargon	2334–2279 BC	unknown	Jéquier 1905: 9–41 = RCS 105
"	"		unknown	Nassouhi 1924: 65–74 = RCS 106
statue	Manishtusu	2269–2255 BC	Shutruk-Nahhunte	EKI §24a = RCS 107
statue	Naram-Sin	2254–2218 BC	Shutruk-Nahhunte	EKI §22 = RCS 109
stele	unknown	Ur III?	unknown	de Morgan 1900: Pl. 3 = RCS 110
statue	unknown	Ur III/Isin-Larsa?	Shutruk-Nahhunte	Pézard and Pottier 1926: 191–192 = RCS 111
statue	unknown	Isin-Larsa/Old Bab.	Shutruk-Nahhunte	Scheil 1905: 12–13 = RCS 112
statue head	unknown	Old Babylonian	unknown	Frankfort 1954: 59 = RCS 113
stele (law code)	Hammurabi	Old Babylonian	unknown	de Morgan 1905: 28–29
limestone statue	Kurigalzu I or II	pre-1375 BC; 1332–1308 BC	unknown	Scheil 1939: 11–12 = MSKH Q.2.2
agate scaraboid	"	"	unknown	Scheil 1905: 30 = MSKH Q.2.105
stone tablet	Nazi-Maruttash	1307–1282 BC	unknown	Scheil 1900: 86–92 = MSKH U.2.19
sceptre pommel	Shagarakti-Shuriash	1245–1233 BC	unknown	Scheil 1933: 32 = MSKH V.2.1
kudurru	Kashtiliashu IV	1232–1225 BC	unknown	Scheil 1900: 93–94 = MSKH O.2.5
stone tablet	post-Kashtiliashu?		unknown	Scheil 1900: 95–96 = MSKH O.2.6
kudurru	Adad-shuma-usur	1216–1187 BC	unknown	Scheil 1900: 97–98 = MSKH C.22.6
"	"		unknown	Scheil 1905: 42–43 = MSKH R.2.6
"	Meli-Shihu	1186–1172 BC	unknown	Scheil 1900: 99–111 = MSKH S.2.6 = RCS 115
"	"		unknown	Scheil 1900: 112 = MSKH S.2.7
"	"	"	unknown	Scheil 1908: 87–94 = MSKH S.2.8
"	"	"	unknown	Lampre 1900: 180 = MSKH S.2.9
stele	"	"	Shutruk-Nahhunte	Scheil 1902: 163–165 = MSKH S.5.1
kudurru	Marduk-apla-iddina I	1171–1159 BC	unknown	Scheil 1905: 39–41 = MSKH R.2.5
stele	uncertain	twelfth century BC?	unknown	de Morgan 1905: Pl. 99 = RCS 117

earlier, e.g. by Kindattu (Harper, Aruz and Tallon 1992: 171). Finally, an inscribed agate bead, said to come from Iran and bearing a dedication by the Kassite king Shagarakti-Shuriash to the goddess Namma, may also have been acquired as booty (Gassan 1986), although the stated provenience is by no means reliable.

Shutruk-Nahhunte was also active in removing stelae from other cities in Iran and re-erecting them at Susa. Thus, the inscription on one stele fragment (König 1965: §20) talks about a stele made in Anshan which Shutruk-Nahhunte, at Inshushinak's behest, took and brought back to Susa. 'The king, who set it up, I do not know', he writes. In the same text he speaks of monuments taken from Choga Zanbil and the city of Tikni which he set up at Susa for Inshushinak and the goddess Balippiti. At least one more stele was moved from Choga Zanbil to Susa (König 1965: §21), while a third stele from . . . amkiru was taken to Susa as well (König 1965: §28A). These actions would certainly suggest that, while Choga Zanbil may not have been completely uninhabited after Untash-Napirisha's death, the shrines there were perhaps neglected and, out of piety, Shutruk-Nahhunte felt it incumbent upon himself to remove certain holy monuments to a safer locale where they could be cared for. Ritual paraphernalia, including a sacred basin which Siwe-palar-huppak, Pala-ishshan, Pahir-ishshan and Attar-kittah had each moved to a different city in their lifetimes, was also re-consecrated by Shutruk-Nahhunte at Susa (König 1965: §28A).

Several of Shutruk-Nahhunte's inscriptions, although fragmentary, record military exploits. One refers to his camp while on campaign and to action near the Ulai, the modern Karkheh river, in Khuzistan (König 1965: §28B; for the Ulai, see Steve, Gasche and de Meyer 1980: 104, n. 71). Another refers to 700, 600 and 400 cities/towns, presumably in different districts and presumably conquered (König 1965: §28CIa). The longest lists tribute exacted from various defeated cities in Mesopotamia, citing an illegible amount of gold, 54 talents (i.e. 1620 kg) and an illegible number of *minas* of silver, from the Kassite capital Dur-Kurigalzu; an uncertain number of talents and 90 *minas* (*c.* 45 kg) of something (gold or silver?) from Sippar; a number of talents and 23 *minas* (*c.* 11.5 kg) of something from Akkad; illegible amounts from Upi and Dur-. . .; and finally commodities such as copper bricks (ingots?), clothing, trees (or timber?) and swords (König 1965: §28CI). This last text is undoubtedly an actual record of the tribute received as a result of his campaign of 1158 BC.

Two texts, known principally from Neo-Assyrian copies belonging to the library of Assurbanipal and described as 'highly poetic accounts of the deliverance of Babylonia from the Elamites' (Brinkman 1968: 13), provide important, if biased information on the subsequent course of Kassite-Elamite relations. One of these, generally attributed to Nebuchadnezzar I, fourth king of the Second Dynasty of the Sealand (1125–1104 BC) and eventual 'liberator' of Babylonia, tells us that after driving away (?) Zababa-shuma-iddina, Shutruk-Nahhunte 'be[stowed royal authority] upon his eldest son, Kudur-Nahhunte' (Foster 1993/I: 294). This does not suggest anything like total abdication on the part of the father, merely the appointment of his eldest son as a kind of military governor of Babylonia following its conquest. In spite of Shutruk-Nahhunte's apparently ruthless campaign in Mesopotamia, yet another Kassite king, Enlil-nadin-ahi, was able to garner enough support to rule for three more years during which time land grants were issued and economic texts dated in his name (Brinkman 1976: 122).

How Kutir-Nahhunte and his father may have acted in this period is unclear. The same text states, '[The Babylonians? elevated] Enlil-nadin-ahi, my predecessor, [K.?] set to hostility, vowing destruction (?)', and this seems to be the background to the so-called 'Kedor-Laomer' texts (so-called because of a tenuous and improbable argument that Kedor-Laomer, king of Elam, mentioned in Genesis 14, was in reality Kutir-Nahhunte [see Lambert 1994: 67]), three texts dating to the Achaemenid period which treat the Elamite-Kassite conflict (Foster 1993/I: 282–9). One of these texts takes the form of a letter from Kutir-Nahhunte to the Babylonians. There the Elamite king speaks of the punishment meted out to Babylon by Marduk and of the god's decree that the 'property of the Babylonians' should become Elam's (Foster 1993/I: 284). Ultimately Kutir-Nahhunte attacked Babylonia. As another of the Kedor-Laomer texts says, he 'over[ran] all the people of Akkad like the deluge, He turned all the sublime [hol]y places into [ruin heaps] . . . He carried off the [possessions] of Sumer and Akkad [to Elam], He took Enlil-nadin-ahi [to Elam]' (Foster 1993/I: 294). The third Kedor-Laomer text treats the Elamite sack of Nippur in the following terms: 'To all of his warriors he sped the blasphemy on, "Plunder Ekur [Enlil's temple at Nippur], take its possessions! Obliterate its design (regulations? see Lambert 1994: 69), cut off its rites"'. The Elamites attacked another temple, the E-sharra, 'carried off its cult objects'; Kutir-Nahhunte 'called up the barbarian horde, [it level]led the land of Enlil', then 'headed north towards Borsippa . . . torched its sanctuary . . . [plun]dered all the temples . . . took their possessions and carried them off to Elam' (Foster 1993/I: 285–7). Most notoriously of all, however, as the later composition attributed to Nebuchadnezzar I tells us, Kutir-Nahhunte committed that crime which 'exceeded those of his forefathers, whose monstrous sin was the greatest of them all' (Foster 1993/I: 294) by removing the statue of Marduk from his temple (Esagila) in Babylon, taking it with him to Susa (Brinkman 1968: 89).

Scarcely more than fifty inscribed bricks and fragments of Kutir-Nahhunte's have been found at Susa. These commemorate various projects including the replacement of some sun-dried brick with baked brick on an 'exterior chapel' of Inshushinak's, and the restoration of the great gate of Lagamal, the deity who, together with Ishnikarab, accompanied the dead to the divine judge Inshushinak (Malbran-Labat 1995: 83–7; see also König 1965: §29–30; Steve 1987: 30). Outside of Susa, Kutir-Nahhunte was active at Deh-e Now, where two fragmentary bricks mention the deity Manzat (Steve 1987: 31), presumably in connection with her temple, already attested in the inscriptions of Igi-halki and Shutruk-Nahhunte from the site. The restoration of the temple of Kiririsha-of-Liyan, which had been built originally by Humban-numena (see above), is also attested in a text from Bushire (König 1965: §31). This last inscription provides a further piece of information in telling us that the restoration of the temple was done for the life of not only Kutir-Nahhunte but for a female, Nahhunte-Utu, and 'her descendants'. Most scholars have assumed that this was Kutir-Nahhunte's wife (e.g. Carter and Stolper 1984: 41). Malbran-Labat has suggested, on the other hand, that this was not

Table 7.10. *Shilhak–Inshushinak's building works at Susa*

Projects undertaken at Susa	Reference
restoration of the temple of Inshushinak built/restored by Kindattu, Ebarti, Shilhaha, Tan-Ruhuratir, Idadu, Atta-hushu, Shiruk-tuh, Siwe-palar-huppak, Humban-numena, Hutran-tepti, Kuk-Nashur, Tepti-halki, and Kuk-Kirwash	IRS §38, 49
restoration of the temple of Inshushinak, construction of a doorway in glazed brick with gold fixtures	IRS §43
restoration of the gate of Inshushinak	IRS §50
restoration of the 'exterior chapel' of Inshushinak	IRS §40
completion of a moulded brick façade on the 'exterior chapel' of Inshushinak begun by Kutir-Nahhunte	IRS §41
refoundation and (re-?)construction of the throne/seat? of Tab-migirshu (?) in mudbrick	IRS §44
restoration of the temple of Kiririsha-of-Liyan	IRS §39
decoration of the temple of Kiririsha-of-Liyan with glazed brick	IRS §42
reconstruction of the 'temple of the grove' built by unknown predecessors	IRS §45

Kutir-Nahhunte's wife but his sister, and that this reveals a particularity of Elamite dynastic succession in the absence of a male heir, namely succession via the sister of the king (Malbran-Labat 1995: 87). Against this argument one must point out that, upon his death, Kutir-Nahhunte was succeeded not by a nephew but by his brother.

As he tells us in a brick inscription, Shilhak-Inshushinak (*c.* 1150–1120 BC), who calls himself 'son of Shutruk-Nahhunte' in the many inscriptions for which he is known, succeeded his brother Kutir-Nahhunte when the latter died (Malbran-Labat 1995: 94). In one text he calls himself the 'chosen brother of Kutir-Nahhunte' (König 1965: §54), and in fact, one of Kutir-Nahhunte's building projects involving the construction of a façade of moulded brick was completed by Shilhak-Inshushinak (Table 7.10). The vast majority of Shilhak-Inshushinak's texts come from Susa, where he undertook a great variety of building works as recounted on his inscribed bricks, stelae and door sockets. Elsewhere, inscribed bricks from Bandar Bushire confirm that he restored Humban-Numena's temple to Kiririsha there (König 1965: §57–59; see also Grillot and Vallat 1984); brick fragments from Choga Pahan West relate to the restoration of the 'temple of the grove', seemingly the same building referred to at Susa (?) (Stolper 1978: 89–91; Steve 1987: 32); and a stamped brick found at Tul-e Sepid near Fahlian in Fars province invoking the beneficence of Kilahshupir (König 1965: §41A) has been taken as a sign that Shilhak-Inshushinak built a temple to this deity there (e.g. Lambert 1972: 61). However, Shilhak-Inshushinak's activities were far more wide ranging, for two of his stelae from Susa also mention the restoration of temples to various deities, including Huban-elu, Inshushinak, Lagamar, Manzat and Shimut, and one of them specifies that he carried out this work in twenty different cities (e.g. Attata-ekal-likrub, Attata-mitik, Bit Hulmi, Bit Turni . . . , Ekallate, Hantallak, Marrut,

Plate 7.8 The *sit shamsi* (Sb 2743, 60×40 cm) from Susa. © Musée du Louvre, Antiquités Orientales

Peptar-siyan-sit, Perraperra, Pinigir, Shuhshipa and Tettum, as well as some, the names of which are broken) (König 1965: §47–48).

Two discoveries made at Susa cast further light on religious practice there during the reign of Shilhak-Inshushinak. The first of these is a cast bronze model (Pl. 7.8) with a short inscription in which Shilhak-Inshushinak, after identifying himself and giving us his titles, writes, 'I have made a bronze sunrise (*sit shamshi*)' (König 1965: §56). Discovered in the area of the Ninhursag temple on the Acropole, the *sit shamshi*, as it has come to be known, is a unique representation of ritual in action. The model consists of a flat, 60×40 cm. base which supports a pair of nude male figures, each of whom crouches. One holds a spouted vessel while the hands of the other's are extended flat, palms up. The figures are surrounded by various items, some of which were cast in one piece with the men and platform, while others were attached with rivets. Two stepped structures, vaguely reminiscent of the ziggurat at Choga Zanbil, flank the figures. Two rectangular basins, a large pithos, three trees, a stele-like object, an L-shaped platform, and two rows of four semi-spheres fill out the scene. The interpretation of the *sit shamshi* is far from clear. It has been described as a model of 'a cult activity taking place at the break of day in which two persons, presumably priests, engage in ritual cleansing at the very spot where the day's sacrifices and libations will be carried out' (Harper, Aruz and Tallon 1992: 140). Alternatively, F. Malbran-Labat suggests that it may represent a funerary ceremony for kings interred nearby which was celebrated at dawn on a sacred esplanade by two priests who performed a rite of ablution (Malbran-Labat 1995: 214). Whatever the precise meaning of the scene depicted, it is certainly one of the most evocative finds ever made at Susa.

The second major find of religious significance dating to the reign of Shilhak-Inshushinak comes from the Apadana mound where, in a badly disturbed context (Harper, Aruz and Tallon 1992: 141–4, 281–2), portions of a moulded brick façade were discovered which depict two figures, a standing bull-man grasping a date-palm (Fig. 7.11) and a frontal female (?) with arms raised and hands cupped in front of the chest. The inscribed bricks which run across the centre of both the bull-man and the palm tree record that Shilhak-Inshushinak made a 'statue of brick' (*salmu erientum-ia*) for the 'exterior chapel' (*kumpum kiduya*) of Inshushinak. The text in question was used only on this façade, which is thought to represent a sacred garden, blessed and guarded by the beneficent figures of the bull-man and the partially destroyed frontal figure (Malbran-Labat 1995: 95). In Kassite Babylonia, the bull-man was viewed as a protective demon (Black and Green 1992: 49; Wiggermann 1992) and the use of moulded, baked brick to create architectural façades at sites such as Uruk as early as the fifteenth century (temple of Inanna built by Karaindash) is likely to have exerted an influence on the Elamite architects who designed Shilhak-Inshushinak's brickwork.

The degree of piety evinced by Shilhak-Inshushinak would seem to have surpassed that of any of his predecessors, including Untash-Napirisha. For while he may not have founded a new religious centre, Shilhak-Inshushinak certainly took extreme care to propitiate a wide variety of gods and goddesses at every turn. Nowhere is this better illustrated than in the long inscription engraved on a roughly 1×2 m limestone stele from Susa (König 1965: §54). The text begins with a long invocation to many different deities, 'gods of the heavens, gods of Elam, gods of Susa', beseeching their blessings for his life, the life of his wife, Nahhunte-Utu, and the lives of their nine living children (Hutelutush-Inshushinak, Ishnikarabat, Urutuk-Elhalahu, Shilhina-hamru-Lagamar, Kutir-Huban, Utu-ehihhi-Pinigir, Temti-turkatash, Lil-airtash and Bar-Uli) and any more to come. Much of the text concerns offerings made to Inshushinak and requests that the consanguinity of the royal couple be sanctioned by the gods of Elam, Anshan, and Susa, along with the princes of Elam, the nobles of Susa, and the priesthood (König 1965: 124).

But after dwelling further on offerings made, Shilhak-Inshushinak then moves into an enumeration of political and administrative steps undertaken in a wide variety of places. Unfortunately, many of the toponyms mentioned are illegible, and the sense of the text is often interrupted, but it seems clear that the king, by carrying out sacrificial offerings, was praying for Inshushinak to sanction some fundamental administrative initiatives which included the creation of a large number of provinces (one paragraph mentions twenty-two) and the installation of administrators following his successful conquest of the areas in question. While König's attempted translation (König 1965: §54.30) of Shilhak-Inshushinak's text is problematic (M.W. Stolper, pers. comm.), Brinkman has nevertheless noted that 'many towns and cities lying within the normal sphere of influence of Assyria or Babylonia' (Brinkman 1968: 89) were subjugated (see Carter and Stolper 1984: 41) at a time co-eval with the early years of a new dynasty in

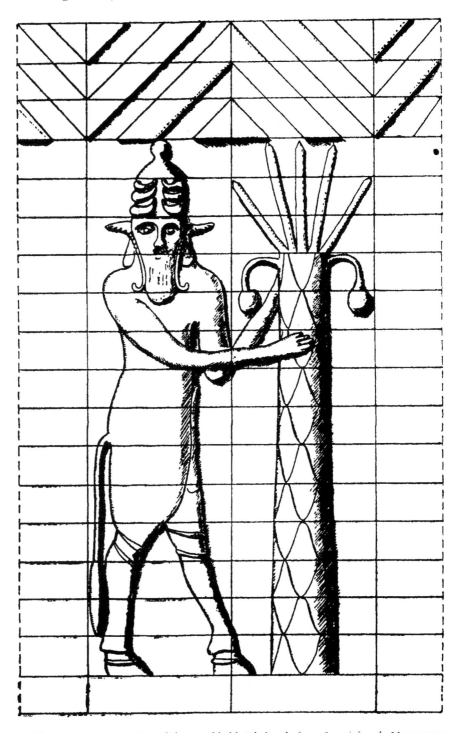

Figure 7.11 De Mecquenem's restoration of the moulded brick façade from Susa (after de Mecquenem 1947: Fig. 8).

southern Mesopotamia, the Second Dynasty of Isin, and 'the declining years of the aged Ashur-Dan I' in Assyria. Allusions to these campaigns are also contained in the inscriptions on three door sockets from Dizful, Shushtar and Tepe Pomp (Steve, Gasche and de Meyer 1980: 80–2). The power vacuum created by the collapse of the Kassite dynasty was obviously exploited by Shilhak-Inshushinak in a great way.

Judging by some of the names which are legible – some Akkadian, some Kassite, and others Elamite – a number of the conquered cities seem to have lain in the Zagros east of the Tigris, at least some of them in the region later known as Namri (perhaps west of Kermanshah, see Reade 1978: 139), while some were further north towards the Lower Zab (König 1965: 126). Although most of the names mentioned early in the text cannot be identified, a number beginning with Ashuhash can, and these continue in a northwesterly direction towards the area of Nuzi (Table 7.11). This suggests that Shilhak-Inshushinak probably invaded from Susa, following a portion of what was later to become the Achaemenid royal road through Kismar, Der and on to the Diyala. This route, recently called the 'Elam-Kismar-Der-Diyala Road', appears in various guises, most notably as part of the 'List of Geographical Names' known from Abu Salabikh and Ebla during the mid-third millennium (Frayne 1992: 58–60). The third millennium sources also record a route to the north of this which led from the Diyala (or Der) through Awal and eventually on to Gasur (Nuzi) and Assur. This route seems clearly to have been used by Shilhak-Inshushinak, as a comparison of a number of toponyms suggests. Thus, moving from south to north, we can recognize a whole cluster of names mentioned in the Nuzi texts (Fincke 1993; G.G.W. Müller 1994), including Ashuhish (=Ashuhash), Matka (=Matka), Shehala (=Sha Hala), Kipri (=Kiprat), Arraphe (= Arrapha), Nuzi (=Nuza), Hapate (=Hanbate) and Shinishhe (=Sha Nishe).

According to Cameron, who first noted a large number of correspondences between toponyms mentioned in Shilhak-Inshushinak's list and those of the Assyrian kings such as Shamshi-Adad V, the Elamite king headed east from the Nuzi area, and this raises the question of the Elamite relationship with the peoples of the Zagros. One of Shilhak-Inshushinak's stelai (König 1965: §46) reports that 'The Balahute have plundered cult vessels and . . . of Inshushinak, but I brought them back. O Inshushinak, my god, therefore I ask you, . . . my camps and . . . my . . . and Susa . . . Anshan . . . Ulan'. Unfortunately, we do not know who the Balahute were and where they lived, although Cameron has suggested that they were somewhere in the central Zagros (Cameron 1936: 16). The statement by no means suggests that the Balahute actually plundered one of Inshushinak's temples at Susa, however, for as Shilhak-Inshushinak's references to his restoration works make clear, there were temples to the supreme deity of Susa in many places.

Another fragmentary text of Shilhak-Inshushinak's records the plundering of cattle at Hussi, a city located near Upi/Opis in northern Babylonia, and it also mentions the Tigris, the Euphrates and Nippur, suggesting that the conquests extended both west and south of the northeastern frontier belt just described. In view of conquests such as these, one must query the status of the early kings of the Second Dynasty of Isin who 'ruled' at this time. Some scholars have gone so far as to suggest that they were in fact

Table 7.11. *Shilhak–Inshushinak's western campaign as related in Šil S 27: EKI §54*

EKI §54	Content	Reading	Location	Reference
	15–20 names	illegible		
	c. 15 names	[. . .]-e-a		
		[ ]-un-nu		
ii 37		Sha Shilitu		Vallat 1993a: 312
		rest illegible		
	c. 21 names	[. . .]-ri		
ii 44		Shenkuru		
ii 45		Bit-Nappahie		
		Kur . . .		
ii 46		Sha Imire		
		Ha . . .		
ii 48		. . . kitekku		
		Bit-Nakiru		
		. . pilantu		
		rest illegible		
ii 59	number illegible	Sha Barbari		
		Sha Alta . . .		
ii 60		Sha . . . nankari		
		rest illegible		
ii 71	c. 16 names	Sillam	Tell Suleimah in Hamrin?	Frayne 1992: 56
ii 72		Tunni		
		Arti . . .		
ii 73		Bit - . . . arrika		
ii 74		Sha Puh . . .		
		Matku- . . .		
		. . . pisi		
ii 75		Sha Si		
ii 76		Bit-dSin-iriba		
ii 77		Bit-Kadashman	e. of the Tigris	Brinkman 1968: 258, n. 1641
		rest illegible		
ii 81		**Ashuhash**	Ashuhish? of Nuzi texts, on southern edge of Arappha region, around modern Kirkuk; OB Ashuh between Awal and Gasur/Nuzi	Fincke 1993: 58
				Frayne 1992: 54

Table 7.11 (cont.)

EKI §54	Content	Reading	Location	Reference
ii 82		Bit-Lassi		
ii 82		Bit-dSin-shemi		
		Bit-Etellie		
		... shaya		
ii 83		**Matka**	Madga? modern Kifri north of Jabal Hamrin; Matka of Nuzi texts	Vallat 1993a: 179, Frayne 1992: 57 Fincke 1993: 176
ii 83		**Sha Hala**	Shehala? near Nuzi	Zaccagnini 1979: 156, Fincke 1993: 256
ii 84		Appisinipeti		
ii 84		Sha dArad-ekalli	Ekalli near Nuzi?	Fincke 1993: 71
ii 84		**Kiprat**	Kipri near Nuzi?	Fincke 1993: 146; a fortified city with a city gate!
ii 95	8 names	**Arrapha**	Arrapha, modern Kirkuk	Fincke 1993: 38
ii 95		**Nuza**	Nuzi (Yorgan Tepe)	Fincke 1993 208
ii 96		**Hanbate**	Hapate? near Nuzi	Fincke 1993: 92
		Titu...?		
ii 97		**Sha Nishe**	Shinishe	Fincke 1993: 256
		rest illegible		
iii 8	c. 20	Tunnati		
iii 9		Sha Hanta		
iii 10		Bit-Rierabbi		
		rest illegible		
iii 14	18 names	Bit-Bahe		
iii 15		Sha Kush . . .		
		Sha Purnamashhum		
		Ma . . .		
iii 16		Bit-Ishtar		
		Huratu		
iii 17		Ishirtu sha dAdad		
		Sha Anpima		
		Hurat-dSharie-GUD?		
iii 18		Bit-Riduti-rabû		
		Bit-Riduti-sehru		

Table 7.11 (*cont.*)

EKI §54	Content	Reading	Location	Reference
		Bit-Nashumaliya		
		...lue		
iii 51		Bit-Tasak-sharri		
iii 52		Uzzi...		
		...ik		
iii 53		Bit-Barbari		
iii 54		...ia		
		URU?-kaplu		
iii 65	18 names	Bit-Kilalla		
		Zaka...		
iii 66		Bit-Nangari		
		Bit-...		
		...silti		
iii 67		Tansillam		
		...tukar...		
		...kanbateya		
		Bit-Shi...		
iii 69		Bit-Kunzubati		
		Ata...pna...		
iii 70		Puhutu		
		Nakapu		
		Zalla...		
iii 71		Ki...su		
		Bit-Rapiqum	Rapiqu on the Middle Euphrates	Brinkman 1968: 127, n. 748
iii 81	c. 20 names	Kitan		
iii 82		Narsillam		
		Bit...hatu		
		Bit...napsira		
iii 85		Bit-Ummashap		
iii 86		Harap		
iii 88		Bit-Amurri?		
iii 89		Bit-Kilak...		

Elamite vassals. While not implausible, there is no evidence that such was the case (Brinkman 1968: 89, n. 467).

In those texts where Shilhak-Inshushinak names his children, Hutelutush-Inshushinak appears as his eldest son and it was he who succeeded Shilhak-Inshushinak *c.* 1120 BC. His mother was none other than Nahhunte-Utu, sister and wife of Kutir-Nahhunte and Shilhak-Inshushinak (Vallat 1985a: 46). Hutelutush-Inshushinak used the unparalleled title 'king of Elam and Susiana' (Vallat 1985a: 45; see also Steve 1987: 41; Malbran-Labat 1995: 117) and claimed descent from the *suk-kalmah* Shilhaha (e.g. Vallat 1978: 98). At Susa he rebuilt the temple of Inshushinak 'of the grove' (Vallat 1985a: 45) as well as the *kukunnum* of Inshushinak, the deity's principal shrine on the Acropole (Malbran-Labat 1995: 119–22). He renovated the temple of Upurkupak in the land of Salulikki, perhaps to be identified with the region known in the Middle Ages as Surraq or Dauraq in eastern Khuzistan (Steve 1987: 43–5). He also rebuilt the temple of Ishnikarab 'of the grove' at a place called Kipû which, because it is mentioned in a series of bricks from Susa, may have been nearby, perhaps even a district of the city (Malbran-Labat 1995: 117; Vallat 1993a: 140).

The inscription commemorating the latter deed is interesting in that Hutelutush-Inshushinak says that he did it, not for the lives of his wife and offspring, but 'for my life and the life of my brothers and sisters, for the life of my nephews, for the life of my nieces, of those of my house' (Malbran-Labat 1995: 117). This had led some scholars to suppose that the king never married and never had children of his own, but inscribed bricks from Tal-i Malyan inform us of two children – a girl named Utuk-ᵈHute-kasan and a boy named Temti-pitet – without identifying their mother (Lambert 1972: 65; Reiner 1973a: 59). Brick fragments stored at Susa, however, identify Hutelutush-Inshushinak as the 'beloved brother of Ishnikarab-huhun' and it may well be that the king's sister was the mother of his children (Vallat 1985a: 50).

Inscribed bricks from Tal-i Malyan, ancient Anshan, proclaim that Hutelutush-Inshushinak built a baked brick temple there to Napirisha, Kiririsha, Inshushinak and Shimut (Lambert 1972: 66), and it is probable that some of the texts found there relate to that project. Before considering the political history of his reign, let us examine the evidence from Middle Elamite Tal-i Malyan, particularly that which dates to the time of Hutelutush-Inshushinak.

Developments in Anshan

The Middle Elamite or 'Qaleh' occupation of Tal-i Malyan was concentrated largely in the northwestern sector of the site (Sumner 1988b: 308). It was in the area which eventually became known as EE that the inscribed bricks of Hutelutush-Inshushinak were first discovered, although subsequent soundings were unsuccessful in identifying the structure from which they derived (Carter 1994a: 16). Some 430 m west of EE lay the highest point on the site where, in a series of ten 10×10 m squares, a building (Level IV) was exposed in sector EDD (Fig. 7.12). Although excavation was not extensive enough to recover the entire ground plan, it is clear that the structure consisted of a

large number of rooms arranged around an interior, rectangular courtyard which measured 10×14 m. In plan this is generally reminiscent of the smaller courtyard and adjacent rooms in the *palais hypogée* at Choga Zanbil. The Level IV building was destroyed
by fire and although the northeast quadrant of the structure was subsequently used as
a pottery workshop with four or more kilns (Level IIIB), all dating to the Qaleh phase,
this and the later Neo-Elamite and Sasanian-era use of the site are of no great interest
here. Based on ceramic parallels with Susa and Choga Zanbil, the burned building in
EDD has been dated to the eleventh century BC (Pons 1994: 50), but an analysis of the
available C14 dates (Table 7.12) from Level IV has led the excavator to suggest a construction date of *c.* 1250–1150 BC and a destruction date of *c.* 1100–1000 BC (Carter
1996: 16). Among the 246 tablets and fragments recovered in excavation were four
which can be considered 'royal' and which provide us with absolute dating criteria. The
earliest of the three royal texts (Stolper 1984: 142, no. 100) employs a word (*tenti*) which
is otherwise only attested in the inscriptions of Shilhak-Inshushinak. A second small
fragment contains part of a curse formula used by both Shilhak-Inshushinak and
Hutelutush-Inshushinak (Stolper 1984: 143, no. 101). A third fragment includes a personal name, . . . tir-^dHuban, which, if restored to Kutir-Huban, probably refers to the
Kutir-Huban who was both the son of Shilhak-Inshushinak and brother of Hutelutush-
Inshushinak (Stolper 1984: 144, no. 102). A fourth fragment (Stolper 1984: 122, no. 88)
mentions the silver of (the) king (EŠŠANA) Hu-[. . .], possibly a reference to Hutelutush-
Inshushinak. Palaeographical considerations also point to the reign of Shilhak-
Inshushinak (*c.* 1150–1120 BC) or later (Stolper 1984: 9; Steve 1992).

In this regard, it is interesting to re-examine the calibrated C14 dates from the building. Of the three short-lived samples (reed matting) dated, one (P-2332) gives calibrated
ages between 1152 and 1130 BC, while the other two are considerably later. As is to be
expected, a sample taken from a roof beam (P-2230) is considerably older, with a calibrated age likely to fall between 1251 and 1205 BC, but this tells us the date of the
wood, possibly a century-old tree trunk, not the date of its use.

It is unlikely, however, that the EDD building is in fact the temple built by
Hutelutush-Inshushinak mentioned in the inscribed bricks from Tal-e Malyan. The
content of the texts recovered is overwhelmingly metallurgical. Gold, silver, copper or
bronze are mentioned, most frequently as raw metal and/or finished objects issued or
transferred, although metal received is probably also implied as well (Stolper 1984: 13).
The fact that roughly one quarter of all the texts were impressed with a single seal 'indicates a single point of origin or control' (Stolper 1984: 26). As Stolper noted, texts
dealing with gold and silver, and those dealing with copper and tin, were clustered in
two separate but nearby parts of the building. The fact that Anshan is virtually the only
toponym mentioned (a fragmentary name occurs in text no. 85, [. . .]-*li-na*) demonstrates that the matters dealt with at EDD were purely internal. Whether they indeed
related to the temple built by Hutelutush-Inshushinak, as suggested by Carter (Carter
1994a: 18), is difficult to say. The presence of glazed or faience tile and knob fragments
(Fig. 7.13) probably does bespeak high status. Carter believes that 'the courtyard and its
surrounding rooms were used for the formal reception, redistribution, and storage of

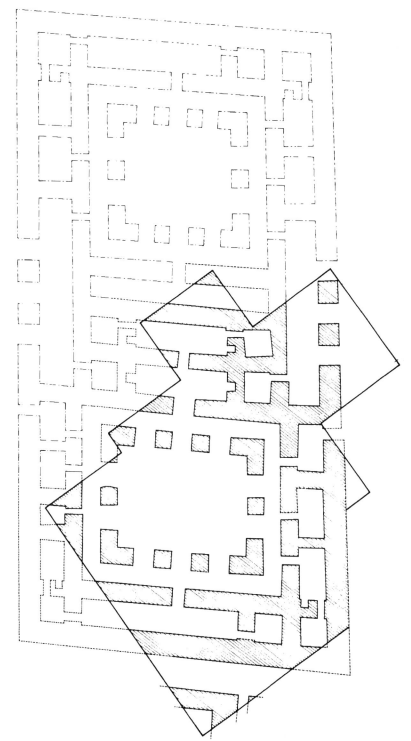

Figure 7.12 Plan of the Middle Elamite building at Tal-i Malyan (after Carter 1996: Fig. 16).

Table 7.12. Radiocarbon chronology of Middle Elamite occupation at Tal-i Malyan

Lab #	C14 age	Calibrated age	Calibrated BC 1σ range (probability method)	Relative contribution to probabilities	Calibrated BC 2σ range (probability method)	Relative contribution to probabilities
P-2060	3170±50	1424	1507–1474 1465–1399	.29 .71	1522–1313	1.00
P-2061	3060±60	1312	1399–1257 1236–1223	.93 .07	1429–1125	1.00
P-2230	2980±60	1251, 1248, 1205	1301–1275 1269–1114 1093–1081	.10 .86 .04	1385–1338 1324–1013	.07 .93
P-2331	2830±60	987, 956, 944	1110–1108 1053–899	.01 .99	1153–1148 1130–831	.00 1.00
P-2332	2950±60	1152, 1149, 1130	1256–1238 1219–1046	.08 .92	1375–1348 1317–988 956–944	.02 .97 .01
P-3261	2900±60	1045	1194–1185 1163–1142 1138–990 954–946	.03 .09 .86 .03	1259–1232 1227–916	.04 .96
P-3257	2640±60	805	894–878 850–770	.09 .91	917–757 681–546	.86 .14

Note: all samples were charcoal. My thanks to Dr. P. Magee for calibrating these dates using the CALIB 3.0 program from the University of Washington's radiocarbon laboratory. Sample type is as follows: charcoal (P-2060, 2061, 3261), roof beam (P-2230), reeds and charcoal (P-2331, 3257), matting and charcoal (P-2332).

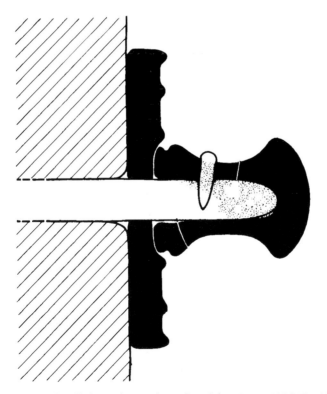

Figure 7.13 A glazed wall plaque from Tal-i Malyan (after Carter 1996: Fig. 31).

goods necessary for the functioning of the empire' (Carter 1996: 49). On the other hand, it has been suggested that the zooarchaeological finds from the excavation, which included 16 per cent cattle, 4 per cent equid (horse, *Equus caballus*) and 2 per cent camel (*Camelus bactrianus*) over and above the dominant 76 per cent sheep/goat (out of an assemblage of 685 identifiable bones, Zeder 1991: 217, Table 57), suggest that 'EDD IV may . . . have served as a kind of Elamite *entrepôt*, an area to which nomadic groups traveling through the valley came to exchange goods and animal products with Elamite administrators of Malyan' (Zeder 1991: 236). While this is an interesting notion, it finds no confirmation in the texts found at the site.

Before leaving the subject of Tal-i Malyan it is interesting to note that, alongside the Qaleh buffwares which display some continuity in painted decoration with earlier Kaftari material and show clear parallels in shape to both Susa and Choga Zanbil, a new tradition appears in the Kur River basin. Both handmade and wheel-made orange wares, known as Shogha and Teimuran, respectively, have been found at sites such as the type sites of Tal-i Shogha and Tal-i Teimuran (Overlaet 1997) and at Darvazeh Tepe (Nicol 1970; 1971; Jacobs 1980; 1994), *c.* 80 km southeast of Tal-i Malyan, in association with small amounts of Qaleh pottery. While the former are decorated with naturalistic motifs (fish, birds, animals, plants) and hatched lines, the latter tend to be decorated with horizontal lines and triangles (Carter and Stolper 1984: 174). It is tempting to see these three traditions – Qaleh on the western side of the valley, Shogha and Teimuran in the east – as expressions of different, co-existing groups in the Kur River basin separated by a 'cultural boundary' of sorts (Sumner 1988b: 318). Following up on a hypothesis of Nicol's (Nicol 1971), Sumner has recently suggested that the Shogha/Teimuran wares may represent the earliest ceramic manifestations of Persian-speakers in Fars (Sumner 1994). Needless to say, this is a highly speculative yet interesting challenge to traditional views concerning the infiltration and arrival of 'Persians' in western Iran (see Chapter 8).

Babylonian revenge and the end of the Middle Elamite era

According to a poem recounting the deeds of Nebuchadnezzar I (1125–1104 BC), fourth king of the Dynasty of the Sealand, the Babylonian king prayed to Marduk saying, 'Have mercy on me, in despair and prostrate, Have mercy on my land, which weeps and mourns . . . How long, O lord of Babylon, will you dwell in the land of the enemy?' (Foster 1993/I: 301). Ever since Kutir-Nahhunte's removal of the cult statue of Marduk from the Esagila at Babylon, the Elamites had enjoyed apparent superiority over their Babylonian neighbours, even if they had not chosen to colonize and dominate them outright. Shilhak-Inshushinak's campaigns, however, had left no doubt about the military might of the kingdom of Susa and Anshan. The poem just cited tells us that Marduk, heeding Nebuchadnezzar's prayer, commanded him to, 'Take me from Elam to Babylon. I, lord of Babylon, will surely give you Elam'. This was the beginning of the end for Hutelutush-Inshushinak.

An initial Babylonian foray into Susiana ended disastrously by the banks of the

Karkheh (Uqnu) river, where Nebuchadnezzar's army was struck by plague (Brinkman 1968: 106). As one text written in the first person tells us, 'Erra, mightiest of the gods, decimated my warriors ... a demon was killing my fine steeds. I became afraid of death, did not advance to battle, but turned back. With heavy ... I camped, stupefied, at the city Kar-Dur-Apil-Sin ... the Elamite [advanced] and I withdrew before him. I lay on a bed of misery and sighs ...' (Foster 1993/I: 295). An account by Sitti-Marduk, a chariotry commander who styled himself as 'head of the house of Bit-Karziabku', a Kassite family and tribal unit (Brinkman 1968: 253), tells us that an attack was launched from Der in July, 'With the heat glare scorching like fire, the very roadways were burning like open flames ... The finest of the great horses gave out, the legs of the strong man faltered' (Foster 1993/I: 297). The Babylonians pressed on to the Karun (Ulai) river where Nebuchadnezzar finally engaged Hutelutush-Inshushinak in battle: 'Both kings met there and made battle. Between them a conflagration burst out, the face of the sun was darkened by their dust, whirlwinds were blowing, raging was the storm'. When the dust cleared, 'Huteludish, king of Elam, retreated and disappeared. Thus king Nebuchadnezzar triumphed, seized Elam, and plundered its possessions' (Foster 1993/I: 298). According to a much later text in the form of a letter from Nebuchadnezzar to the citizens of Babylon, Hutelutush-Inshushinak 'abandoned his strongholds, and disappeared' (Foster 1993/I: 302).

For many years it was thought that this was the end of Hutelutush-Inshushinak, although the fact that we cannot date his brick inscriptions, combined with the fact that Nebuchadnezzar certainly did not occupy Elam or annex it as his Old Akkadian and Ur III forebears had, always meant that his survival somewhere could not be entirely ruled out. New impetus was given to a 'survival' hypothesis with the discovery of Hutelutush-Inshushinak's bricks at Tal-i Malyan. Indeed, it was in this sense that M. Lambert interpreted the king's building activities at Anshan, suggesting that these were effected *after* Nebuchadnezzar's campaign and that Hutelutush-Inshushinak retreated to Anshan rather than 'disappearing' as the Babylonian tradition would have it (Lambert 1972: 74; see also Vallat 1978: 104–5; Steve, Gasche and de Meyer 1980: 104–5; Steve 1991: 7; Pons 1994: 43). More recently, Vallat has suggested that Hutelutush-Inshushinak returned to Susa after Nebuchadnezzar's campaign. He bases this on the fact that his Anshan bricks mention only two children, whereas one of his brick inscriptions from Susa mentions his 'sister's sons' and 'sister's daughters' in the plural (Vallat 1996b: 88; see also König 1965: §60 = Malbran-Labat 1995: 117). This is a tenuous argument, however, not merely because Hutelutush-Inshushinak does not identify the latter group as biological children, but because it is always possible that, of a larger number of children, several had died leaving only two. In such a case, the Susa inscription would have to be dated before, not after, the Malyan bricks.

Amiet has recently suggested that two rock reliefs at Kul-e Farah (Pls. 7.9–11), near Izeh/Malamir, should be dated to the period following Nebuchadnezzar I's Elamite conquest. On either side of the Izeh-Malamir plain in the Bakhtiyari mountains, 150 km northeast of Susa, stand two areas of rock reliefs known as Kul-e Farah and Shikaft-e Salman (Vanden Berghe 1963a, with prev. bibliog; 1983: 111–13; de Waele 1972; 1976;

Plate 7.9 The south face of the rock relief Kul-e Farah III (4–4.9 m wide, 2.5–3 m tall).

1981; 1989; Stolper 1987–90). Although Sir H.C. Rawlinson was made aware of the existence of these reliefs and their associated inscriptions in 1836, it was Sir A.H. Layard who first visited them five years later. Of the six reliefs at Kul-e Farah and four at Shikaft-e Salman, only one of these, Kul-e Farah I, seems to be an original work of an apparently local ruler named Hanni, son of Tahhi (see Chapter 8), who nevertheless added inscriptions to the remainder of the reliefs at these sites which date to the reign of Shutruk-Nahhunte I and/or to the period just after Nebuchadnezzar I's conquest of the Middle Elamite state (Amiet 1992c: 81, 86; with the possible exception of Kul-e Farah V), or perhaps to the earlier Neo-Elamite period (de Waele 1989). Kul-e Farah has been interpreted as an 'extramural sanctuary' which was used 'on the occasion of certain feasts' such as the New Year celebration (de Waele 1989: 35), possibly involving 'animal sacrifices, processions with music, and symposia' (Seidl 1997: 202).

It was noted above that the final abandonment of Choga Zanbil has been attributed, on ceramic grounds, to the campaign of Nebuchadnezzar I (Pons 1994). Such was not, however, the case at Susa. According to the most recent analysis of the pottery from the latest phase of occupation at Choga Zanbil and Susa, Ville Royale A X and IX, these latter levels should be dated to the eleventh century BC, i.e. after Nebuchadnezzar I's attack on Susa (Pons 1994: 48 and n. 48). Comparable ceramic forms are attested sporadically in Ville Royale II levels 11–8 and Ville Royale B I, as well (Pons 1994: 49). In

Plate 7.10 Detail of the badly eroded figures, partially buried beneath the modern ground surface, at the base of Kul-e Farah III.

this regard it is interesting to note that some 300 years after Nebuchadnezzar I and Hutelutush-Inshushinak, the Neo-Elamite king Shutruk-Nahhunte II (716–699 BC) referred on a tablet found at Susa to three of his ancient predecessors as having been king – Hutelutush-Inshushinak, Shilhina-hamru-Lagamar and Humban-numena (König 1965: §72; see also Montagne and Grillot-Susini 1996: 33, who interpret the passage there as a reference to *statues* of the three kings in question). From the many brick inscriptions of Shilhak-Inshushinak we know that Shilhina-hamru-Lagamar was Hutelutush-Inshushinak's next younger brother (e.g. Malbran-Labat 1995: 90, 101, 108, 110, 116). Thus, although we have none of his original inscriptions, Shilhina-hamru-Lagamar presumably reigned in the early eleventh century BC, following Nebuchadnezzar's campaign and precisely at the time to which the various levels in the Ville Royale mentioned above have been dated. As for Humban-numena, this name does not appear in Shilhak-Inshushinak's inscriptions as that of one of his sons, nor is it attested as that of a child of Hutelutush-Inshushinak who, according to his inscribed bricks from Tal-i Malyan, had a girl named Utuk-[d]Hute-kasan and a boy named Temti-pitet, discussed above. It is possible, however, that this Humban-numena came from another family and indeed reigned after Shilhina-hamru-Lagamar, which would extend the Shutrukid dynasty down to the middle or even the end of the eleventh century.

Plate 7.11 Kul-e Farah II.

Conclusion

The Middle Elamite period is one of the most richly documented in the history of Elam and Anshan, and the exploits of kings such as Untash-Napirisha, Shutruk-Nahhunte, Kutir-Nahhunte and Shilhak-Inshushinak are unparalleled in earlier or later Elamite history. Although the full impact of Nebuchadnezzar's campaigns is difficult to judge, they certainly marked a watershed in Elamite history and we have little evidence whatsoever from the succeeding three centuries.

One of the trends which has been noted in studying the inscriptions of Tal-i Malyan and those of Hutelutush-Inshushinak from the end of the Middle Elamite III period is an increase in the use of syllabic signs which find their closest parallels in the contemporary Assyrian sign-list beginning with the reign of Tiglath-Pileser I (1114–1076 BC) (Steve 1992: 12). In addition, certain administrative terms were borrowed as well. These changes may well have been a by-product of Shilhak-Inshushinak's extensive activities, both military and administrative, on the fringes of Assyria a half-generation before Hutelutush-Inshushinak. Whatever the explanation, we shall see in the following chapter that Assyria, rather than Babylonia, was to loom largest in the political history of Elam during the early first millennium BC.

Date	Lowlands	Highlands	Mesopotamia	'Elam'
1600/1500 BC	end of *sukkalmah* dynasty		end of First Dynasty of Babylon, rise of kingdom of Mitanni in north, First Dynasty of the Sealand in the south	kingdom of 'Susa and Anshan' established by Kidinu
1500–1400 BC	Middle Elamite I, 'Kidinuids', based at Susa? continued settlement in Deh Luran, foundation of Haft Tepe (Kabnak?) by Tepti-ahar	limited evidence of settlement at Malyan; petty kingdom around Huhnur near Arjan?	Kassite dynasty ruling in Mesopotamia	unclear relationship between Susa, Kabnak, Huhnur; kingdom of 'Susa and Anshan' a title without geographical meaning?
1400–1200 BC	Middle Elamite II, 'Igihalkids', rupture in Susa sequence? Igi-halki linked to Deh-e Now; building activity at Liyan on Gulf coast near Bushire and at various sites in Khuzistan; building activity at Susa by Untash-Napirisha and foundation of new city, Choga Zanbil	highland deities worshipped at Choga Zanbil, but scant evidence from Anshan itself	Kassites linked to Igihalkids by marriage	continued use of title king of 'Susa and Anshan'(in Akkadian) or 'Anshan and Susa' in Elamite
1200–1100 BC	Middle Elamite III, 'Shutrukids'; building activity at Susa, Deh-e Now, Choga Pahan, war booty from Mesopotamia	rock reliefs at Kul-e Farah and Shikaft-e Salman; foundation of major building complex at Malyan (Qaleh period)	Kassite rule contested by Shutruk-Nahhunte who invaded Babylonia and overthrew Kassite king in 1158 BC;	continued use of title king of 'Susa and Anshan'

	invasion of Susiana by fourth king of Dynasty of the Sealand, Nebuchadnezzar I; end of occupation at Choga Zanbil	brought to Susa by Shutruk-Nahhunte	Babylonia again invaded by Kutir-Nahhunte; east Tigris area invaded by Shilhak-Inshushinak
1125–1104 BC	retreat to Anshan by last Shutrukid king, Hutelutush-Inshushinak? autonomous rulers near Izeh?	Nebuchadnezzar I, fourth king of the Dynasty of the Sealand	end of dynasty at hands of Nebuchadnezzar I

THE NEO-ELAMITE PERIOD

The Neo-Elamite period is dated from *c.* 1000 BC until the conquest of Babylonia in 539 BC by Cyrus the Great. For simplicity we have divided it into three phases. While the earliest phase (Neo-Elamite I, *c.* 1000–744 BC) is poorly known, the middle phase (Neo-Elamite II, 743–646 BC) is amply documented in Assyrian sources, for it was a period of intense conflict between the Assyrian kings and a series of Elamite rulers, often allied with insurrectionists in southern Babylonia. The inscriptions of Shutruk-Nahhunte II (c. 717–699 BC) from Susa reveal continuities with earlier periods in Elamite history, but much of the contemporary archaeological material from the site is badly disturbed. Similarly, it is impossible to correlate much of the military history of Assyria's aggression with Elamite archaeology for the simple reason that many of the towns in western Khuzistan which must have borne the brunt of Assyrian aggression have yet to be identified on the ground, let alone excavated. It is also likely that, under intense Assyrian pressure, Elam as it had existed in the Middle Elamite period was no longer a unified state linking the highlands of Fars and the lowlands of Khuzistan, and that individual cities, such as Hidalu or Madaktu, were no longer bound by the authority of a single Elamite king at any one time.

It is clear that, given the paucity of indigenous Elamite sources at this time, we are to some extent a prisoner of the Assyrian royal inscriptions and the Babylonian Chronicle which present us with a sequence of Elamite rulers through foreign eyes. In this regard it is important to note that the scarcity of references to Anshan at this time leaves us very much in the dark about contemporary historical events in the highlands. Rock reliefs at Kul-e Farah and Shikaft-e Salman seem to relate to petty kings in the highlands who wrote in Elamite but were not necessarily under the authority of the Elamite kings mentioned in Assyrian and Babylonian texts.

When the Assyrians under Assurbanipal finally descended upon Susa and destroyed the city, seizing the Elamite king Tepti-Huban Inshushinak, or Te-Umman as he is known in the Assyrian sources, the event was commemorated in stone in Assurbanipal's palaces at Nineveh. Importantly, if the Assyrian propaganda is to be believed, Assurbanipal's victory over the Elamites is said to have provoked a number of Iranian leaders, possibly including the grandfather of Cyrus the Great, to send tribute to Assyria. The problems surrounding this episode are discussed below, but it is important to stress that with it the Persians are introduced into our story for the first time. In the following Neo-Elamite III period (647–539 BC) we see evidence of close links between Persian and Elamite elements. This is the period to which a number of important Biblical references to Elam must be related, and it is a period from which we have a particular group of cylinder seals in which Elamite and Persian aspects are blended. Linguistically, too, this is a period in which the written Elamite which has survived shows close links to that which was later employed during the reign of Darius at the great Achaemenid city of Persepolis (see Chapter 9).

Introduction

Following the reign of Hutelutush-Inshushinak it becomes extremely difficult to track the Elamites until the late eighth century, for we have nearly three centuries with no textual evidence. Because of an eventual renaissance of the title 'king of Anshan and Susa' it has become common to refer to the earlier first millennium, pre-Achaemenid era in southwestern Iran as the Neo-Elamite period (Fig. 8.1). Proposals to further subdivide it have, however, varied and for the most part have been based on mutually incompatible data sets. For example, on stratigraphic and ceramic grounds, de Miroschedji identified two phases at Susa, Neo-Elamite I (c. 1000–725/700 BC) and II (c. 725/700–520 BC) (de Miroschedji 1981c; 1982; see also Carter and Stolper 1984: 182; Carter 1994b: 68), whereas, based on an analysis of the Elamite syllabary of the early first millennium – focusing on the total number of signs used and the varying number of logograms amongst them – Steve has divided the Neo-Elamite period into four phases: IA (c. 1000–900 BC), II (c. 750–653 BC), IIIA (c. 653–605 BC) and IIIB (605–539 BC) (Steve 1992: 21–2; one assumes the first phase is called IA rather than I because Steve wished to leave open the possibility of a IB between 900 and 750 BC when and if evidence emerges which fills this *lacuna*). Malbran-Labat, on the other hand, has to some extent combined Steve's schema with historical considerations, resulting in three phases: Neo-Elamite I (1000– c. 760 BC), II (c. 750–653 BC) and III (653–539 BC) (Malbran-Labat 1995: 129). Most recently, Vallat has proposed a slight modification of Steve's periodization as follows: I (c. 1100–770 BC), II (c. 770–646 BC), IIIA (646–c. 585 BC), and IIIB (c. 585–c. 539 BC) (Vallat 1996d: 393).

Further north in the Zagros region, where there is abundant though generally not Elamite-related occupation reflected in a variety of ceramic styles, the terms Iron Age I (c. 1450–1100 BC), II (c. 1100–800 BC) and III (c. 800–500 BC) have been used. It is scarcely surprising that the historical phases of the Neo-Elamite period do not correlate precisely with the ceramic phases of the west Iranian Iron Age. Obviously the earliest Iron Age occupation of the Zagros region correlates broadly with the bulk of the Middle Elamite period, discussed in the previous chapter; Iron II covers a period which begins prior to and lasts into the century after Neo-Elamite I; and Iron III subsumes the bulk of Neo-Elamite II and III. In general this will not cause us any difficulties, but it is important to be aware of, not only when reading archaeological literature, but in considering certain developments in Assyria and the Zagros which may have had an indirect influence on the Elamite area.

A modified version of a tripartite periodization will be used in the following discussion, based largely on historical considerations. Thus, Neo-Elamite I (c. 1000–744 BC) will refer to the period between the end of the main Middle Elamite occupation at Tal-i Malyan and the appearance of the earliest Elamite ruler of first millennium BC date in the Babylonian Chronicle, signifying the reconnection of Elam to Mesopotamian political affairs. Neo-Elamite II (743–646 BC) will refer to the century of intense interaction between Assyria and Elam, culminating in Assurbanipal's brutal sacking of Susa. The schema proposed by Steve and followed in modified form by Malbran-Labat draws

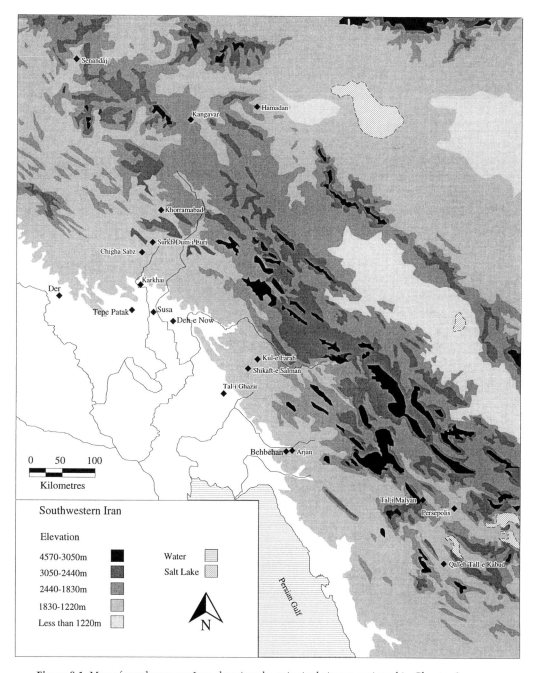

Figure 8.1 Map of southwestern Iran showing the principal sites mentioned in Chapter 8.

a line between the campaign against Te-Umman and the next phase of Assyrian hostilities which, while defensible on linguistic grounds, is hardly satisfactory from an historical point of view. Finally, Neo-Elamite III (646–539 BC) will be used to refer to the period from Assurbanipal's last Elamite campaign until the eventual consolidation of a new empire under the Achaemenids and the consequent eclipse of the ancient kingdom of Susa and Anshan.

Neo-Elamite I (*c.* 1000–744 B.C.)

Because of a dearth of sources we can say very little about this period. At Susa, scattered remains of Neo-Elamite date turned up sporadically in the early excavations on the Apadana and the Ville Royale (de Miroschedji 1978: 213; Amiet 1967a), but it was not until soundings were undertaken in Ville Royale II that levels attributable to the earliest Neo-Elamite phase were clearly revealed. These, however, consist only of fragmentary mudbrick walls and surfaces (de Miroschedji 1978; 1981b; 1981c; Carter and Stolper 1984: 182) in levels 9 and 8, attributed to the Neo-Elamite I period. The fact that these levels contained examples of tall, Middle Elamite goblets should probably not be interpreted as an indication of ceramic continuity, for the pieces in question could well be out of context (Pons 1994: 48). Rather, the overriding impression is of a ceramic assemblage, characterized by bowls and jars with convex bases, bottles and wavy-line incised vessels (Carter and Stolper 1984: 184), which is distinct from that of the preceding Middle Elamite III phase (thus de Miroschedji 1978: 227) and gives scant indication of continuity.

In Fars, on the other hand, the documentation is even scantier. The Kur River basin shows no signs of sedentary occupation between the late Middle Elamite and the Achaemenid periods (Sumner 1988b: 314). Qal'eh Tal-e Kabud, a hilltop fortress some 73 km south of Shiraz on the road to Jahrom, has been attributed to the Iron Age on the basis of surface sherds (Kleiss 1995), but it is difficult to assign a more precise date within the Neo-Elamite period. Similarly, some of the many cairn burials found throughout Fars (Boucharlat 1989) may date to the Neo-Elamite I period, but far too few have been excavated and far too little diagnostic material has been recovered to seriously entertain the possibility.

It is to this early period that the so-called 'Elamite Dynasty' in Babylonia can be assigned. In fact, the dynasty consisted of a single ruler, Mar-biti-apla-usur (984–979 BC) who, in spite of his Akkadian name, was called 'remote (?) descendant of Elam' in the Dynastic Chronicle (Brinkman 1968: 165). Apart from his existence, we have practically no other knowledge of him. The fact that four bronze arrowheads inscribed with his name and the title 'king of the world' wound up in a well-known Iranian collection of antiquities (Dossin 1962: 160), many of which came from Luristan, is no reason for either supposing that Mar-biti-apla-usur's remote affiliation with Elam was significant or that he had dealings with groups in western Iran.

From this point on we have no written sources on Elam, either internal or external, for over 150 years. The next information available consists of a reference to a contingent of Elamite troops which, in company with Kassite, Aramaean and Chaldaean units, went to help the Babylonian king Marduk-balassu-iqbi (-813 BC) liberate Dur-Papsukkal, a royal city near Der (modern Tell 'Aqar at Badra in eastern Iraq) in the east Tigridian area, which was being besieged by Shamshi-Adad V (823–811 BC) (Brinkman 1968: 209). This episode, briefly reported as it is, nonetheless serves to illustrate two important points. First, Shamshi-Adad V's immediate predecessors, Assurnasirpal II (883–859 BC) and Shalmaneser III (858–824 BC) had each conducted campaigns into the northern Zagros and east Tigridian zone, attacking regions such as Allabria, Andia, Ellipi, Mada, Manna, Namri, Parsua and Zamua (Levine 1973; 1974; Reade 1978; Dandamaev and Lukonin 1989: 45–6; Chamaza 1994). Although we have no indigenous, Iranian sources which throw light on Assyrian aggression, we are fairly well informed from the Assyrian side by their royal inscriptions. Even though the theatre of war was often far removed from Susiana, it is likely that Assyrian expansion was seen as a threat by the Elamites. The second point which arises from this observation is that, in attempting to thwart Assyria's expansionist tendencies, the Elamites were perfectly prepared to collaborate with their former arch-rivals, the Babylonians. In sending troops to help Marduk-balassu-iqbi, the Elamites were setting a precedent which they would follow for most of the Neo-Elamite period.

At least two texts from Nimrud throw some light on this otherwise poorly documented period. A text dating to 784 BC, and hence falling near the end of the reign of Adad-nirari III (810–783 BC), mentions the presence of an Elamite ambassador at the Assyrian court, and demonstrates that the Assyrian army both manufactured and used the 'Elamite' bow at this time (Dalley and Postgate 1984: 256, no. 145; Zadok 1994: 47).

Neo-Elamite II (743–646 B.C.)

According to the Babylonian Chronicle, a king named Ummanigash (Huban-nukash), son of Umbadara (Huban-tahra), came to the Elamite throne in 743 BC and continued to reign until 717 BC (Cameron 1936: 157; Brinkman 1968: 234). Thus, most of his reign overlapped with that of the Assyrian king Tiglath-Pileser III (745–727 BC). Although he targeted none of his forays against Elam *per se*, Tiglath-Pileser campaigned twice against the Aramaean tribes of southern Babylonia and on one occasion pursued them as far as the Uqnu river, the modern Karkheh, in Khuzistan (Gerardi 1987: 5). The second campaign of 737 BC took him all the way to Media (Diakonoff 1991: 15ff.) on the Iranian plateau (the ancient capital of which, Ekbatana, is modern Hamadan). A stele commemorating this campaign was found during the mid-1960s 'somewhere in western Iran, perhaps Luristan' (Levine 1972: 11).

Despite the fact that none of his Elamite texts have survived, Huban-nukash is again attested in 720 BC when he led his troops in battle against Sargon II (721–705 BC) at Der on behalf of Merodach-Baladan II of Bit-Jakin ('house' [or tribe] of Jakin) in Chaldaea (southernmost Babylonia), who had put together an alliance in an attempt to throw off the yoke of Assyrian authority following Shalmaneser V's death (Brinkman 1965; 1968: 245). As Brinkman has observed, 'Thus Babylonia and Elam were enemies in the late second millennium, but later united in opposition to Assyria in the early first millennium. With the weakening of the Babylonian monarchy, the Babylonian army also declined as an effective force; whereas Babylonian kings under the Second Isin Dynasty and occasionally in the ninth century could muster Babylonian military forces, by the late eighth century there is little trace of a Babylonian army and eventually – under Merodach-Baladan – the Elamites bore the brunt of campaigning on behalf of Babylonia' (Brinkman 1968: 317). In fact, the incident provides an interesting lesson in historiography for, as Stolper has stressed, 'Sargon's official account boasts of overwhelming triumph; Merodach-Baladan's building inscription claims credit for expulsion of the Assyrians; and the Babylonian Chronicle, the least prejudiced source, credits Huban-nukash both with the initiative and with unqualified success, adding that Merodach-baladan's forces arrived too late to participate' (Carter and Stolper 1984: 45). The battle, however, seems to have produced no clear-cut result, and while the Elamite army may have been victorious on the field of battle, the Assyrians retained their forward post at Der (Gerardi 1987: 7; Tadmor 1958: 38). As Levine has noted, this was vital for the pursuit of Assyrian policy in the Zagros, and may have been enough of a satisfaction to Sargon to justify claiming victory in the action. In Levine's opinion, Elam 'was the expansionist state, and its attempts to advance beyond Der made its victory a pyrrhic one at best. A few miles of mountain talis [sic] and a handful of villages can hardly have been Humanigash's objective, but it is all he managed to achieve' (Levine 1982: 51, n. 70).

The Babylonian Chronicle tells us that, upon his death, Huban-nukash was succeeded by Ishtar-hundu, otherwise known in Assyrian sources as Shutur-Nahundu/i or, to the Elamites, as Shutruk-Nahhunte II (*c.* 717–699 BC). With Shutruk-Nahhunte we once more have indigenous Elamite sources. Four different brick inscriptions of his are known from Susa. In one text from Susa, Shutruk-Nahhunte describes the re-installation (perhaps also reconsecration?) of the statues of Hutelutush-Inshushinak, Shilhina-hamru-Lagamar and Huban-numena before the cult image of Inshushinak in his *kukunnum* at Susa, and calls himself the son of Humban-numena (Montagne and Grillot-Susini 1996: 33). Whether or not this is the same Huban-numena whose image he mentions in the text itself is unclear, although it is certainly possible. At any rate, the text shows clearly that Shutruk-Nahhunte was not a son of his predecessor, Huban-nukash.

Another of Shutruk-Nahhunte's Susa texts speaks of his manufacture of glazed brick, alleging incorrectly that none of his predecessors had done so (Malbran-Labat 1995: 131). Shutruk-Nahhunte's bricks all come from a small, square temple, excavated between 1898 and 1901, which was once decorated in green glazed brick depicting griffons, horses, lions, winged scorpions and vegetal motifs (Amiet 1967a: 27; Nunn 1988: 157). A second project, either the construction of a new temple or the rebuilding of an old one, was dedicated to the deity Ishnikarab (Malbran-Labat 1995: 134). It has also been suggested (Vallat 1995b) that Shutruk-Nahhunte II, and not Shutruk-Nahhunte I, was responsible for the construction of one or more unnamed buildings at Deh-e Now, where three fragments of glazed wall plaques and pommels have been found, the best preserved examples of which simply say, ' . . . that which the king Shutruk-Nahhunte built' (Steve 1987: 29).

Other evidence for occupation in this period at Susa comes mainly from de Miroschedji's excavations in Ville Royale II levels 7–6 which, however, were disturbed by later graves (Carter and Stolper 1984: 182). Several forms, including the tall 'Elamite goblet', the vat, and the band-rim jar, all of which were present in Neo-Elamite I times, are no longer found, and Carter interprets these changes, along with 'disjunctions in the stratigraphy', as signs of a disruption between the Neo-Elamite I and II ceramic/stratigraphic phases (Carter 1994b: 73). Scattered occupation is also attested elsewhere on the site, and burials are known from the Ville Royale and the Apadana (Carter and Stolper 1984: 183).

Following the battle of Der in 720 BC Sargon II spent the next decade actively engaged on the borders of Egypt and in Israel, Syria, Urartu, and the upper Zagros (Tadmor 1958: 94–6; a stele of Sargon's commemorating his sixth campaign against areas in northwestern [e.g. Mannea] and central-western Iran [e.g. Media] in 716 BC was discovered at Najafehabad *c.* 15 km northeast of Kangavar in 1965; see Levine 1972: 25ff.), apparently too occupied to pay much attention to Merodach-Baladan in Babylonia. In 710 BC, however, the Assyrian monarch again turned his attention southward, alleging that Marduk, having seen the wicked deeds of the Chaldaean chieftain, had ordered Sargon 'to take the sceptre and throne of his kingship away from him [Merodach-Baladan]' (Fuchs 1994: 327). Sargon's annals, inscribed on the walls of his palace at Khorsabad, ancient Dur-Sharrukin, tell the tale of the king's twelfth year, naturally from a very biased perspective. In his recent edition of Sargon's Khorsabad texts, A. Fuchs has carefully reconstructed the entire campaign as a series of seven major episodes (Fuchs 1994: 399–405) which differ slightly (Table 8.1) from the chronological order in which the events are related in the Khorsabad Annals (see also Olmstead 1923: 251ff.; Brinkman 1964: 19ff.; 1965: 163ff.).

The ultimate goal of the campaign was the capture of Babylon, Merodach-Baladan's royal residence, but to achieve this Sargon set out on a rather elliptical course designed to neutralize the Chaldaean's eastern, Aramaean tribal allies, hinder any potential cooperation with Shutruk-Nahhunte, and isolate Merodach-Baladan's tribal seat of Dur-Jakin. This bespeaks a great deal of caution on Sargon's part, for with the Assyro-Babylonian frontier of the day running through Dur-Kurigalzu near modern Baghdad, a frontal assault on Babylon might seem the more logical approach to us. The fact that Sargon did not take this direct option would suggest that he feared a repeat of the battle of Der, for, even if the Babylonian army was itself fairly weak (see Brinkman 1965), Elamite reinforcements might always be sent quickly to the defense of Babylon. Thus, eliminating this possibility in the first place seems to have been foremost in Sargon's mind. The story of the campaign of Sargon's twelfth year is really the story of Sargon achieving this tactical goal. Having accomplished this, Sargon did not tarry long and passed up the opportunity of attacking the Elamites at Bit-Imbi in order to move quickly to his forward camp in the ruined city of Dur-Ladini, where he received a delegation of priests and citizens from Babylon and Borsippa who entreated the king to

Table 8.1. *Summary of Sargon II's Elamite campaign*

Event	Khorsabad annals reference, line
1. Sargon sent troops to Bit-Dakkuri, ostensibly to cut the route between Babylon and Merodach-Baladan's homeland of Bit-Jakin; the troops camped in the ruined city of Dur-Ladini	305
2. hearing of Sargon's planned invasion, M-B reinforced his fortresses and gathered his forces; he put the entire Gambulu tribe in the city of Dur-Athara with 600 cavalry and 4000 soldiers, raised the height of the city walls, and flooded the moat around the city	266–9
3. Sargon besieged and took Dur-Athara, deporting its 18,430 inhabitants and all their livestock; Sargon renamed the city Dur-Nabu, and received eight shaikhs of the Gambulu who lived by the Uqnu, and who brought presents to the Assyrian king; Sargon installed one of his eunuchs as governor, and created a new province out of six districts and 44 fortified cities; thereupon he dammed the Tublijas river in order to force the surrender of the Ru'ua, Hindaru, Jadburu and Puqudu sections of the Gambulu tribe who had fled to the marshy areas of the Uqnu river; the shaikhs of these tribes eventually gave up, bringing tribute and gifts; as for those who refused to surrender, their towns were razed, their gardens destroyed, and finally after sending troops into the marshes, these too gave up	271–94
Merodach-Baladan meanwhile left Babylon, heading for Jadburu, bringing with him a bed, throne, table, and wash basin of silver, as well as jewelry which he gave as a 'bribe' to Shutruk-Nahhunte in the hope of securing his help against Sargon; the Elamite king took the gifts, but would not joint Merodach-Baladan; hearing this Merodach-Baladan gathered his forces and leaving Jadburu retreated to Iqbi-Bel	305–10
4. Sargon seized control of Sam'una and Bab-Duri, two towns of the region Jadburu which Shutruk-Nahhunte had fortified, capturing their commanders and 7520 Elamite soldiers, as well as 12,062 of the local inhabitants and their livestock; a whole series of shaikhs from the district came to pay homage to Sargon	295–301
5. Sargon's army takes control of Lahiru and other cities of the region Jadburu, as well as Ahilimmu and Pillatu on the banks of the river Naditu 'in Elam', successfully driving a wedge between the Elamites and Merodach-Baladan	301
6. turning northward again towards Der, the Assyrian army advanced through through Rashi, the inhabitants of which, fearing Sargon's attack, retreated to the city of Bit-Imbi, while their ruler, Shutruk-Nahhunte, sought refuge in the mountains	302–4
7. Sargon made no attempt to besiege Bit-Imbi but, having effectively neutralized Elam and any potential Elamite-Chaldaean manoeuvers, left the area, crossing the Euphrates and heading for Dur-Ladini where he had already stationed troops	304–5

Note:
After Fuchs 1994.

enter Babylon. This he did, unopposed, for Merodach-Baladan had retreated to Iqbi-Bel in his native Bit-Jakin. Thus ended Sargon's twelfth year.

It is obvious that the Chaldaean-Elamite alliance quickly began to fracture if not entirely to break down, and Shutruk-Nahhunte must have been mindful of the fact that this alliance had brought down the full weight of the Assyrian military machine on lands and towns which were in spitting distance of Susa itself. Even if we cannot believe everything Sargon tells us, nothing suggests that any effective Elamite offensive operations took place, only defensive ones. The story of Sargon's thirteenth year shows us the Assyrian king once more making preparations for an offensive against Merodach-Baladan, who this time evacuated the inhabitants of neighbouring towns such as Ur, Kishsik and Nemed-Laguda to his tribal capital Dur-Jakin. Merodach-Baladan reinforced the city wall and dug a 100 m wide, 9 m deep moat *c.* 60 m from it which he flooded with water diverted from the Euphrates (Powell 1982). These defensive measures, according to Sargon, were of no consequence and he captured the city, putting to death most of its soldiers and seizing immense quantities of booty, but Merodach-Baladan, although injured in the hand by an arrow, 'slipped through the gate of the city like a mongoose' (Fuchs 1994: 334; Brinkman 1964: 21). Where he went we do not know, but in order to block any approach by the 'Elamite enemy', Sargon had Nabu-damiq-ilani build a fortress in the city of Sagbat (not to be confused with Bit-Sagbat, a city in Media, Fuchs 1994: 456) and, when not too busy defeating the Chaldaeans and Aramaeans, the Assyrian king 'let the inhabitants of Elam (enjoy) the bitter taste of his weapons' (Fuchs 1994: 336, Ann. 385).

A year later Shutruk-Nahhunte was once more involved in Assyrian politics. This time it was prompted by the death of Dalta, king of Ellipi, a 'half-Iranized kingdom' (Diakonoff 1991: 16) bordering both Elam and Media which is thought to have been coterminous with modern Luristan and the area south of Kermanshah (Levine 1974: 104–6; Reade 1978: 141; Chamaza 1994: 103). An enemy of Assyria's in the first or second year of Sargon's reign, Dalta had switched his allegiance, paid tribute in Sargon's eighth year, and was himself rescued by Assyrian troops from an attempted *coup d'état* the following year (Fuchs 1994: 432). Dalta apparently died without children, and a power struggle erupted between his nephews, Nibe and Ishpabara. While Nibe turned to Shutruk-Nahhunte for support, Ishpabara appealed to Sargon. According to Sargon's annals, the Elamite king sent 4500 bowmen to aid Nibe, who had taken refuge in the fortress of Marubistu. The Assyrian army sent to Ispabara's aid was, however, victorious and Sargon 'filled the entire (land of) Elam with paralyzing fear' (Fuchs 1994: 339, Anm. 422–3). Once more Shutruk-Nahhunte's attempt to check the growth of Assyrian influence seems to have been costly and ineffectual.

Following his death in 705 BC, Sargon was succeeded by his son Sennacherib (Tadmor 1958: 98). The otherwise scarcely attested Marduk-zakir-shumi seized power in Babylon (Brinkman 1965: 24; Frahm 1997: 9), but in 703 BC he was easily deposed by Merodach-Baladan. Sennacherib immediately went to work organizing a campaign to unseat his father's old rival, while Merodach-Baladan summoned the aid of the Aramaean and Chaldaean tribes of the south and, most importantly, the Elamites.

According to the account of Sennacherib's first campaign, 'Merodach-Baladan, king of Kardu[niash . . .] a rebel plotting treachery, a criminal abhorring justice, turned to Shutruk-Nahhunte, king of El[am, for help] and bestowed upon him gold, silver, (and) precious stones and asked him for support. As help for him (i.e. Merodach-Baladan), he (Shutruk-Nahhunte) sent to Sumer and Akkad Imbappa, the general, . . . Tannanu, the *tashlishu*-official, ten *rab-kisri* commanders, together with Nergal-nasir, the Sutian chieftain, fearless in battle, eighty thousand bowmen . . . (and) horses with them' (Brinkman 1965: 164–5). Like the contingent sent to help Dalta of Ellipi, the troops sent to Merodach-Baladan were overwhelmingly archers, apparently a specialty of Elamite warfare (Brinkman 1986: 203).

One wonders why Shutruk-Nahhunte chose to proffer aid, even for a price, at this point? Perhaps he had less respect for Sennacherib's military prowess than for Sargon's. Perhaps he preferred any fighting to take place on Babylonian soil, well away from his own western borderlands. In Brinkman's view, 'it would be more accurate to say that the services of the Elamite army and of various high Elamite officials were purchased rather than that mercenaries were hired' (Brinkman 1964: 25, n. 139), but this does not explain *why* Shutruk-Nahhunte agreed to the request. As on all previous occasions, Merodach-Baladan stayed well out of the main theatre of war, engaging only in a skirmish with an advance party of the Assyrian army near Kish before fleeing and leaving the Elamite forces to face the major Assyrian contingent near Kutha (Brinkman 1964: 165; 1965: 25; Levine 1982: 36). Once more Merodach-Baladan fled into the marshes, while what was left of Shutruk-Nahhunte's forces presumably retreated, leaving the way clear for Sennacherib to enter Babylon, just as his father had several years earlier.

Sennacherib chose not to immediately pursue the Chaldaean chieftain but became involved once more in the Zagros, where, interestingly, Ispabara of Ellipi, whom Sargon had set on the throne, undoubtedly out of no love for the Ellipian but as a counterpoise to Elamite ambitions in that arena, had turned against him (Levine 1982: 38; Frahm 1997: 10). It was not until 700 BC that Sennacherib moved against Merodach-Baladan. His invasion of Bit-Jakin, however, only prompted Merodach-Baladan to flee to the city of Nagite, described as being on an island but quite possibly located in 'swampy land in the region of Elam reached by crossing the Persian Gulf' (Brinkman 1964: 27), taking with him both the cult statues of his cities ('the gods of his whole land in their shrines', Luckenbill 1924: 35) and the bones of his ancestors ('the bones of his fathers, [who lived] before him, [which] he gathered from their coffins', Luckenbill 1924: 85), lest they be defiled or destroyed (Brinkman 1964: 27; Cassin 1982: 365 and n. 49).

Thereafter Merodach-Baladan is heard of no more. In concluding his description of Merodach-Baladan's flight to Nagite, Sennacherib simply says, 'and in that place he died' (Luckenbill 1924: 85–6). In the aftermath of these events, according to the Babylonian Chronicle (ii 32–4), Shutruk-Nahhunte was deposed by Hallushu, 'his brother', who thereupon became king of Elam (Grayson 1975: 77; Luckenbill 1924: 158). Whether this *coup* was prompted by the unpopularity of Shutruk-Nahhunte's support of Merodach-Baladan and the consequent suffering inflicted on the Elamites at Assyrian hands, we cannot say. It has been customary to identify Hallushu of the

Babylonian Chronicle with a king variously identified as Hallushu-Inshushinak (thus Cameron 1936: 163; Hinz 1972–1975: 61; Carter and Stolper 1984: 47), Hallutash-Inshushinak (König 1965: 168, n. 10; Steve 1987: 50–1; 1992: 22), or Hallutush-Inshushinak (Malbran-Labat 1995: 129), although Vallat considers Hallushu to have been distinct from the king of this name whom he would date to after Assurbanipal's destruction of Susa (Vallat 1995b, and see below).

Another contradiction emerges between the Chronicle, which accords Hallushu a reign of six years (iii 8), and a Neo-Babylonian legal text discovered at Nippur which is dated to Hallushu's fifteenth year (Brinkman and Kennedy 1983: 60–1; Weisberg 1984; see also Stolper 1986: 239). Attempting to resolve this problem, Weisberg has suggested that the two 'brothers' may have ruled at the same time, with Shutruk-Nahhunte the paramount 'king of Elam' and Hallushu a 'king' of some smaller portion of Khuzistan for at least nine years prior to being recognized by the Babylonian scribes who composed the Chronicle as paramount king. This same solution has been adopted by P. de Miroschedji, who suggests that, during the Neo-Elamite period, a *cursus honorum* existed in which 'kings' passed from sovereignty over Susa and Hidalu (in which order he does not specify) to that of Madaktu, a capital city about which we shall hear more in discussing events during the reign of Kutir-Nahhunte II. This sequence of rule, de Miroschedji believes, mirrors the much earlier sequence *sukkal* of Susa, *sukkal* of Elam and Shimashki, leading finally to the position of *sukkalmah* (de Miroschedji 1986: 218). This view has been challenged by Quintana, however, who suggests a bipartite apportionment of rule between the king of Elam, with royal seats at both Susa and Madaktu, and a secondary 'king of Hidalu' (Quintana 1996d). If this were the case already in the time of Shutruk-Nahhunte, then one would have to imagine that he occupied the paramount position, while Hallushu functioned as king of Hidalu.

In 694 BC Sennacherib decided 'to root out the Chaldean refugees' of Bit-Jakin who had fled with Merodach-Baladan to Elam (Levine 1982: 41). According to the Oriental Institute prism inscription (Frahm 1997: 102–3), Sennacherib crossed the sea in 'Hittite ships', conquered Nagite, Hilmu, Billatu and Hupapanu, 'provinces of Elam', deported the inhabitants of Bit-Jakin 'and the people of the king of Elam' to Assyria, and destroyed their cities before crushing Shuzubu the Babylonian (i.e. MUshezib-Marduk, see below) who had rebelled against the rule of Sennacherib's son Assur-nadin-shumi, once more with Elamite help (Luckenbill 1924: 39). The Babylonian Chronicle (ii 38–44), however, tells a rather different tale, for after recounting Sennacherib's conquests in the south, it says, 'Thereupon, Hallushu, king of Elam, came against Akkad, entered Sippar toward the end of the month of Tashritu, and slew the inhabitants. Shamash did not leave Ebabbara. Assur-nadin-shumi was captured and carried off to Elam . . . The king of Elam placed Nergal-Ushezib on the throne in Babylon and invaded (or defeated) Assyria' (see also the discussion in Mayer 1995: 367). Levine has suggested that Hallushu was prompted to launch an attack on northern Babylonia (i.e. Akkad and Sippar) by the fact that these areas were vulnerable so long as Sennacherib and his forces were tied up in the far south (Levine 1982: 43). From a letter later written to Sennacherib's eventual successor, his youngest son Esarhaddon, we also know that

Figure 8.2 Depiction of the city of Madaktu from Slab 6, lower register, Room XXXIII in Sennacherib's palace at Nineveh, bearing Assurbanipal's epigraph, KUR *ma-dak-te* 'land of Madaktu' (after de Miroschedji 1986: Fig. 2; cf. Gerardi 1987: 279).

Sennacherib's eldest son, Ashur-nadin-shumi, was captured by some of the rebellious Babylonians and turned over to Hallushu, after which he was taken away to Elam (Parpola 1972; Brinkman 1973: 92).

The fact that at least three extant texts were dated to Hallushu's reign (years one and fifteen, the date of the third text is missing; see Stolper 1986: 235) shows that, despite being omitted from Kinglist A (Brinkman 1976: 433), Hallushu's control over Babylonia was real. Were it not for the problematic reference to year fifteen of Hallushu's reign, the one text dated to his first year would sit well with the fact that, towards the end of 694 BC, Nergal-Ushezib assumed the throne of Babylon. As Levine suggests, there may be some truth in both the Assyrian and the Babylonian points of view, the former alleging that Nergal-Ushezib (not to be confused with Shuzubu the Babylonian, i.e. MUshezib-Marduk, in Sennacherib's annals) had seized power 'during an uprising in the land', and the latter asserting that he was 'placed . . . on the throne in Babylon' by the king of Elam (Levine 1982: 43; Brinkman 1995). According to the Babylonian Chronicle (ii 46 – iii 2), in the spring of 693 BC Nergal-Ushezib seized control of Nippur, evidently in a bid to widen his sphere of influence beyond Babylon, but several months later the Assyrians launched a counter-attack, seizing Uruk (which probably indicates that by then it had come under Nergal-Ushezib's control) and prompting Nergal-Ushezib to seek refuge with the Elamites. Nergal-Ushezib replied by attacking 'the Assyrians in the province of Nippur' (again presumably lost by then to the Assyrian army), but he was 'captured in open battle and carried off to Assyria' (iii 4–5). Sennacherib's own Nebi Yunus inscription is more graphic, claiming that his soldiers 'threw him [i.e. Nergal-Ushezib] fettered into a cage and brought him before me. I tied him up in the middle city-gate of Nineveh, like a pig' (Luckenbill 1924: 87–8), while in the Oriental Institute prism text, the Assyrian monarch says, 'I seized him alive with my (own) hands, I threw him into bonds and fetters of iron and brought him to Assyria' (Luckenbill 1924: 39).

Scarcely two weeks after this battle, if the Babylonian Chronicle can be believed, 'his people rebelled against Hallushu, king of Elam, imprisoned and slew him' (iii 7–8). In an unexpected manner, however, Hallushu's image lived on in Assyria. We know from several of Sennacherib's inscriptions (e.g. the Chicago Prism VI.10; see Frahm 1997: 21) that he mutilated his Elamite captives by cutting their lips (or moustaches? see George 1996). In a text from the reign of Sennacherib's grandson Assurbanipal (Frahm 1997: 21–2), the Assyrian king reports that he performed the same act of mutilation on a statue of Hallushu – one of thirty-two statues of Elamite kings brought back from Susa and other Elamite cities – which is said to have stood in Sennacherib's Southwest Palace at Nineveh, possibly at the entrance to Room XXXIII in which Assurbanipal's own Elamite campaigns were commemorated.

According to the Babylonian Chronicle, Hallushu was succeeded by 'Kudur', in whom we recognize the 'Kudur-nahundu' of Sennacherib's annals (Luckenbill 1924: 40–1), i.e. Kutir-Nahhunte II. As we have no original inscriptions of this king from Elamite territory, we have no knowledge of his antecedents and family relations. The Babylonian Chronicle does not specifically implicate Kutir-Nahhunte II in the killing of Hallushu, which it attributes to 'his people'. The reasons for this *coup* are also withheld, but one could well imagine that Elamite foreign policy, so costly and seemingly unproductive with respect to Assyria and Babylonia, was a perennial justification for overthrowing any ruler who pursued such a line. In Hallushu's case, his actions seem to have indeed set the stage for a major reply from Sennacherib. Undoubtedly the Assyrian ruler sensed the time was right for a strike against Susiana in the aftermath of Hallushu's death and the Assyrian capture of Nergal-Ushezib, particularly given the instability which these events must have caused in Elam itself. Possibly beginning within weeks of his victory over the Babylonian pretender, Sennacherib 'descended against Elam, devastated the land from Rashi to Bit-Burnakka and carried off its spoil', according to the Babylonian Chronicle (iii 10–11). In his annals Sennacherib says he marched against 'the strong cities, his treasure-houses, and the small cities of the environs, as far as the pass of (or, entrance to) Bit-Burnaki, I besieged, I captured, I carried off their spoil, I destroyed, I devastated, I burned with fire' (Luckenbill 1924: 88).

According to Sennacherib, his advance into Elam prompted Kutir-Nahhunte II to organize the evacuation of his people into 'strongholds', while he himself 'forsook Madaktu, his royal city, and turned his face toward Haidala which is in the midst of the mountains'. Sennacherib marched on to Madaktu, but foul weather halted the chase. By now it was autumn, 'severe weather (cold) set in, uninterrupted rains came on, and snow. I was afraid of the swollen mountain streams and turned back and took the road to Assyria' (Luckenbill 1924: 88). Assuming that the Assyrian campaign was launched from Der, long an important staging post for forays into the region, de Miroschedji has proposed that Bit-Bunakki should be located around Deh Luran, to the north of Susa. Assuming that it is identical with Badakê (Diodorus Siculus XIX.19), a place mentioned in connection with wars of the successors following Alexander the Great's death, Madaktu (Fig. 8.2) has been identifed with Tepe Patak, a 6 ha site between the Karkheh and Duwairij rivers close to the modern road between Andimeshk and Deh Luran (de Miroschedji 1986: 215). Not all scholars, however, accept this view and Vallat has recently concluded that its precise location remains a mystery (Vallat 1993a: 162). As for Haidala or Hidalu/i, this city is mentioned in slightly later Neo-Elamite texts from Susa, but it is most frequently attested in the Achaemenid fortification texts from Persepolis, according to which it was roughly a seven days' journey southeast of Susa (Vallat 1993a: 96). De Miroschedji has suggested that this would accord well with a location roughly halfway between Susa and Persepolis, probably in between Ram Hormuz and Behbehan (de Miroschedji 1986: 217), and this location would be corroborated by the evidence of the Persepolis fortification texts (Koch 1986: 142–3 and Abb. 1).

The fact that Sennacherib calls Madaktu Kutir-Nahhunte II's 'royal city' is important for several reasons. For a start, this may explain why no inscriptions attributable to the king have yet been found at Susa, which may not have been his royal residence at all. It may also be that, following the removal of Hallushu from power, Kutir-Nahhunte II preferred to live outside of Susa, perhaps fearful of the fates which had befallen his immediate predecessors. Whether in this case Susa still retained enough importance for its governance to have been a stage on the *cursus honorum* of the Neo-Elamite kings, as suggested by de Miroschedji, remains a moot point.

Before the year 693 BC was out, Sennacherib's old nemesis Shuzubu the Babylonian, or MUshezib-Marduk as the Babylonian Chronicle calls him, 'ascended the throne in Babylon' (iii 12), and by the spring of 692 BC 'Kudur, king of Elam, was seized during an uprising and killed. Ten months he reigned in Elam. Menanu ascended the throne in Elam' (iii 14–15). Menanu's Elamite name was the well-attested Humban-numena as we can deduce from Sennacherib's version, 'Umman-menanu' (Luckenbill 1924: 42, 47), making him Humban-nimena III (Vallat 1995b). According to Sennacherib, 'the king of Elam gathered to himself a large body of confederates – (the men) of Parsua, Anzan, Pasiru, Ellipi, the whole of Chaldaea, and all the Aramaeans. These, with the king of Babylon, drew near *en masse*, and set upon me, offering battle. (Trusting) in the might of Assur, my lord, I fought with them in the plain of Halulê' (Luckenbill 1924: 88). This offensive, which almost certainly took place in 691 BC, marks a radical departure from those of the previous century. It is not the alliance with the king of Babylon, i.e. MUshezib-Marduk, which is of any particular interest, for Elamite and Babylonian kings had been jointly facing Assyria for some time. Rather, it is the fact that the expeditionary force included Ellipi, Assyria's buffer state in the Zagros, as well as Parsua, another Zagros area the name of which means 'borderland' in Old Iranian (Diakonoff 1991: 14) and which has often been identified mistakenly with the 'Persians' (e.g. Levine 1974: 106–12; Reade 1978: 139–40; Chamaza 1994: 101). These were areas which had borne the brunt of many an Assyrian campaign, but hitherto they had not joined in the Elamite-Babylonian coalition.

Equally interesting is the reference to Anzan, all but forgotten in the earlier Neo-Assyrian sources which deal with Elam and an area for which, archaeologically speaking, little material evidence exists, as noted above. P. Briant has suggested that the omission of all mention of Anshan in the Neo-Elamite titulature following Shutruk-Nahhunte II might be an indication that Anshan had been lost by the kings of Susa to an emerging highland power, namely the Persians, who would become truly visible in the reign of Assurbanipal, and that the contribution of contingents from Anzan to Humban-numena III's forces was already an indication of the growing strength of the new polity (Briant 1984: 82). In fact, this argument is flawed since we now know that it was not Shutruk-Nahhunte II who used the title 'king of Susa and Anshan', but a later ruler by the same name who lived after the time of Assurbanipal (Vallat 1995b). On the other hand, Hallushu-Inshushinak, the only other Elamite king of the pre-Halule period attested by original inscriptions at Susa, did call himself 'enlarger of the kingdom of Anshan and Susa' (Malbran-Labat 1995: 136). Note, moreover, that in this case Anshan was cited *before* Susa. While this could be construed as denoting stronger Elamite control over the highlands, this is highly doubtful given that it was the norm for Anshan to precede Susa in Elamite versions of the royal title, while Susa preceded Anshan in Akkadian ones (M.W. Stolper, pers. comm.). Nevertheless, given the fact that Anshan is listed as one of the participants in the force which fought at Halule, Briant is probably correct in seeing this as an indicator of the emerging independence of a kingdom of Anshan, whether Persian or not, no longer linked to that of Susa/Madaktu. As for Briant's suggestion that 'Persian' participation in the coalition was paid for by Elamite recognition of Persian territorial sovereignty over Fars (Briant 1984: 82), this is an interesting hypothesis, but one which is highly speculative.

Apart from the fact that the annals tell us it was somewhere on the Tigris, the site of Halule is unknown (Brinkman 1973: 93, n. 25). Like the battle of Der in 720 BC, the battle of Halule is one for which conflicting accounts exist. The Babylonian Chronicle says that 'Menanu mustered the armies of Elam and Akkad, made an attack upon Assyria at Halule and defeated Assyria' (iii 16–18). Sennacherib's accounts of the encounter vary. In his Nebi Yunus inscription he says, 'I defeated them, cutting down with the sword 150,000 of their warriors', naming Nabu-shum-ishkun, son of Merodach-Baladan, among those whom he captured alive. As for the protagonists, 'the king of Babylon and the king of Elam, the chilling terror of my battle overcame them, they let their dung go into their chariots, they ran off alone, and fled their land' (Luckenbill 1924: 89). The Oriental Institute prism gives much more detail, for in addition to the Iranian lands which joined the coalition, it gives the precise names of the Chaldaean and Aramaean districts involved, and describes the battle graphically, including Sennacherib's slaying of Humban-undasha (Huban-Untash), the Elamite field commander whom he acknowledged as 'a trustworthy man' (Luckenbill 1924: 45).

Once again, there may be some truth in both versions of the battle. Certainly Assyria was not defeated with any finality, because Sennacherib was able to start the siege of Babylon in an effort to root out MUshezib-Marduk by the spring of 690 BC (Brinkman 1973: 93; Levine 1982: 49). Although the Babylonians remained strong enough to withstand that siege until the autumn of 689 BC, the costs were high. As a legal text in the Yale Babylonian Collection relates, 'In the time of MUshezib-Marduk, king of Babylonia, the land was gripped by siege, famine, hunger, want, and hard times. Everything was changed and reduced to nothing . . . The city gates were barred, and a person could not go out in any of the four directions. The corpses of men, with no one to bury them, filled the squares of Babylon' (Brinkman 1973: 93). In the middle of the siege came news that Humban-nimena had suffered a stroke and died. As the Babylonian Chronicle says, 'In the fourth year of MUshezib-Marduk, on the fifteenth of the month Nisan [January], Menanu, king of Elam, suffered a stroke, his jaw was locked (mouth seized) so that he could not speak . . . On the seventh of the month Adar [December], Menanu, king of Elam, died' (iii 19–25). In the interval, Babylon had fallen to Sennacherib and was thereupon razed (Brinkman 1973: 94).

According to the Babylonian Chronicle, Menanu/Humban-nimena was succeeded on the Elamite throne by Humbahaldashu (iii 27), or Humban-haltash I (for the name, see Zadok 1976a: 63). This occurred at a time when 'there was no king in Babylon', i.e. after the destruction of Babylon when, for eight years, Sennacherib was content to just let the land 'languish' (Brinkman 1973: 95). Humban-haltash I ruled from 688 to 681 BC when, according to the Chronicle, 'he was seized with fever and died from the attack' (iii 30–1). He was succeeded by his son Humban-haltash II but neither king is known from any original, Elamite inscriptions.

For reasons which are not entirely clear, as heir presumptive following the abduction (and presumably execution) of his eldest son, Ashur-nadin-shumi, Sennacherib had chosen his youngest son, Esarhaddon, bypassing three older children (see the discussion in Porter 1993: 16ff.). Not surprisingly this aroused the jealousy and opposition of Esarhaddon's elder siblings, one of whom, Arda-Mulishshi, murdered his father as a result in January of 680 BC (Parpola 1980: 174). By this time Esarhaddon was in hiding, but the murder was followed by a power struggle between the other brothers (Porter 1993: 24). An apparently sizable faction was still loyal to Esarhaddon, however, who returned to the outskirts of Nineveh, dispatched his brothers in battle, sending them fleeing to Urartu, and assumed the Assyrian throne in February/March of the same year. Perhaps it is not coincidental that Esarhaddon apparently used a Median contingent as bodyguards (Liverani 1995). He may have felt insecure in Assyria amidst the followers of his rebellious brothers.

Before the year was out, Nabu-zer-kitti-lishir, a son of Merodach-Baladan who was then governor of the Sealand, seizing on what must have been fairly unsettled conditions, besieged Ur and, pursuing a tried and true policy used often before, attempted to lure Humban-haltash II into a new *entente* by sending him lavish gifts (Weidner 1954–6). With the relief of Ur by an Assyrian army, Nabu-zer-kitti-lishir and his brother, Na'id-Marduk, fled to the Elamite king, who promptly executed the former, according to the Babylonian Chronicle (iii 39–42), while the latter fled back to Esarhaddon, begging for mercy. Esarhaddon, in a move which revealed more astuteness than any of his predecessors had shown, installed Na'id-Marduk as the new governor of the Sealand, effectively ending decades of Assyrian strife with Bit-Jakin and winning an ally in the fight to stay Elamite interference in what Assyria undoubtedly saw as its 'internal affairs' (Porter 1993: 34).

The new influence won by Assyria in the Sealand may have prompted Humban-haltash II to attempt a counter-move designed to undo that new relationship, although the evidence is by no means clear. A letter to Esarhaddon (ABL 1114), apparently written by some elders of the Sealand, reports the arrival of an Elamite envoy alleging that Na'id-Marduk was dead (one wonders where he was at the time?) and proposing that they accept his brother, Nabu-ushallim, as their leader (Porter 1993: 35, n. 75). Another letter (ABL 576) repeats this intelligence, but includes a reiteration of the loyalty of the writers and expresses the belief that they do not think their leader is dead. Finally, a third letter (ABL 1131) to Esarhaddon announces that Nabu-ushallim had invaded the Sealand with the help of Elamite warriors (Dietrich 1970: 24–5; Porter 1993: 35, n. 75). Whether this should be construed as 'official' Elamite policy and intended subversion by Humban-haltash II, or whether it simply reflects a power struggle between the two surviving sons of Merodach-Baladan, one of whom had some support from the Elamite side though not necessarily royal sanction, is difficult to say. Brinkman seems inclined to believe that Humban-haltash II 'resisted Babylonian attempts to involve him in anti-Assyrian resistance in Esarhaddon's early years' (Brinkman 1991: 44).

How then is one to explain the fact that Humban-haltash II attacked and sacked Sippar in 675 BC, as recounted in the Babylonian Chronicle (iv 9–10)? Scholars have been inclined to view the attack on Sippar either as a part of new disturbances which were linked to the deportation of the chief of the Bit-Dakkuri and the governor of Nippur in the same year, or else as a scribal error on the part of the chronicler who inserted events here which happened twenty years earlier in the time of Ashur-nadin-shumi, the cuneiform spelling of whose name (AN.SÁR-MU-MU) differed but slightly from that of Esarhaddon's (AN.SÁR-ŠEŠ-MU) (Brinkman 1990: 92; 1991: 44). As Brinkman has noted, 'this stands out as an isolated event, the only apparent disruption in a quarter-century of otherwise good relations between Assyria and Elam' (Brinkman 1991: 44). Nevertheless, these disturbances may have prompted Esarhaddon to fortify his border with Elam (Borger 1956: 53).

The Babylonian Chronicle relates that Humban-haltash II 'died in his palace without becoming ill' (iv 11–12) and was succeeded by his brother Urtak (thus contra Dietrich 1970: 37, the letter ABL 839, which speaks about a king of Elam who suffered a stroke, cannot refer to Humban-haltash II; see Brinkman 1978: 308, n. 27), whose Elamite name was probably Urtagu (Zadok 1976a: 63). This occurred in the sixth year of Esarhaddon's reign and was soon followed by a treaty between the Assyrian and Elamite kings (Borger 1956: 19) involving the return of some plundered cult statues, for in Esarhaddon's seventh year, according to the Babylonian Chronicle, 'Ishtar of Agade and the gods of Agade left Elam and entered Agade . . . ' (iv 17–18; Brinkman 1990: 88; 1991: 44). This must have taken place *c.* 674 BC (Gerardi 1987: 12–13).

Urtak is not attested in original Elamite inscriptions. He was still in power when Esarhaddon died in 669 BC and in the early years of the reign of his son and successor,

Assurbanipal, grain was sent to Elam to relieve a famine which, according to Assurbanipal (ABL 295), was so bad that 'there wasn't even a dog to eat' (restoration acc. to Malbran-Labat 1982: 250). Furthermore, Elamite refugees were allowed to settle in Assyria until such time as the harvest improved in Elam (Piepkorn 1933: 54). Assurbanipal was explicit in justifying his gesture of aid as a by-product of Urtak's treaty with his father Esarhaddon (Nassouhi 1924–5: 103). But in 664 BC Urtak attacked Babylonia (for the date see Gerardi 1987: 129), apparently at the instigation of an anti-Assyrian trio including Bel-iqisha, chief of the Gambulu tribe, Nabu-shum-eresh, governor of Nippur; and Marduk-shum-ibni, an Elamite official in Urtak's administration. After receiving news of the Elamite invasion and checking it by sending his own messenger to Babylonia, Assurbanipal says, 'In my eighth campaign, I marched against Urtak, king of Elam, who did not heed the treaty of (my) father, my sire, who did not guard the friendship' (Gerardi 1987: 122). Assurbanipal's account of the events which followed is very brief, noting only that the forces of Urtak retreated from their position near Babylon, and were defeated near the border of Elam. Later, Urtak himself died and according to Edition B of Assurbanipal's annals, 'Assur . . . , (and) Ishtar . . . , his royal dynasty they removed. The dominion of the land they gave to another; afterwards Te-Umman, image of a *gallû* demon, sat on the throne of Urtak' (Gerardi 1987: 133), whereupon the remaining members of both Urtak's family and those of his predecessor, Humban-haltash II, fled to Assyria (Gerardi 1987: 123–4; Brinkman 1991: 52). If this is the same event referred to in the Shamash-shum-ukin Chronicle, according to which 'the Elamite prince fled [to] Assyria' on the 12th of Tammuz in the fourth year of Shamash-shum-ukin's regency over Babylonia, then it can be placed around June-July 664 BC (Millard 1964: 19; Gerardi 1987: 128).

In Te-Umman we recognize Tepti-Huban-Inshushinak (a view not shared by Vallat 1995b), known from four separate brick inscriptions attested at Susa which inform us of his work on the Inshushinak and Pinigir temples there (Malbran-Labat 1995: 138–40). Whatever the rhetoric of Assurbanipal's version of divine intervention in Te-Umman's rise to power, it seems certain that he came from a family which was not that of one of the immediately previous Elamite rulers. This is confirmed, moreover, by Te-Umman's own inscriptions, according to which he was the son of a Shilhak-Inshushinak (II) and apparently unrelated to either Urtak or Humban-haltash II. But while the families of these two Elamite kings may have fled to Assyria, others stayed behind, including Ishtar-nandi, i.e. Shutruk-Nahhunte, king of Hidalu, and Umbakidinu, i.e. Humban-kidin.

A decade was to pass before Assurbanipal and Te-Umman were to meet on the battlefield, but in the interval there was no shortage of diplomatic contact between them, for as Assurbanipal says in Edition B of his annals, Te-Umman 'repeatedly sent his nobles for the extradition of those people who fled to me, who submitted to me. I did not order their extradition because of the insolent messages that he continually sent, monthly, by the hand of Umbadara and Nabu-damiq' (Gerardi 1987: 135–6; for the history, see Mayer 1995: 403ff.). In this context Assurbanipal names 'Ummanigash, Ummanappa, Tammaritu, the sons of Urtak, king of Elam, (and) Kudurru (and) Paru sons of Ummanaldash, brother of Urtak, king of Elam', along with 'sixty of the royal family, countless bowmen, free Elamites', all of whom, fearing for their lives, 'fled from the murderous intent of Te-Umman and took hold of my royal feet' (Millard 1964: 19; Streck 1916/II: 109). In 653 BC (for the date, see Gerardi 1987: 145) Te-Umman began raising an army with which to attack Assurbanipal who, in Edition B of his seventh campaign, quotes Te-Umman as saying, 'I shall not give up until I come and make war on him', attributing this bellicose behaviour to Ishtar, who 'had confounded his reason' (Gerardi 1987: 136). In response, Assurbanipal himself set off with an army from Der towards Elam. Te-Umman had apparently already started to move up the traditional road from Susa towards Der and on to Assyria and had reached Bit-Imbi but fell back at the approach of the Assyrians. In a pitched battle at Til-Tuba, on the banks of the Ulai river, he was killed along with his son Tammaritu and decapitated. As Assurbanipal says, 'I cut off the head of Te-Umman, their king, the boaster, who plotted evil. Countless of his heroes I killed' (Gerardi 1987: 138). The decapitation of Te-Umman is most likely referred to in a slightly later historical omen which drew its subject matter from Assurbanipal's Elamite campaigns as well (Starr 1985: 60, 65 l. 15).

Assurbanipal decorated Room XXXIII in the Southwest palace (i.e. Sennacherib's palace, which Assurbanipal continued to use) and later Room I in his own North palace at Nineveh (Reade 1976: 99ff.; Gerardi 1987: 139ff.) with a cycle of roughly ten compositions depicting the campaign against Te-Umman. These were arranged in two registers of five compositions each, some of which consisted of more than one episode strung together in cartoon-strip fashion. While the lower reliefs depicted the actual battle scenes, the upper reliefs illustrated the celebrations in Assyria which followed (Reade 1983: 61). These scenes (Table 8.2) were often accompanied by epigraphs (Table 8.3) which can be likened to captions accompanying the illustrations. Originally, the scenes were arranged around either side of the entrance to Room XXXIII, slabs 1–3 on one side, 4–6 on the other (Gerardi 1987: 139).

The difference between the scantily armed Elamites, whose only weapon appears to have been the bow, and the heavily armoured Assyrian cavalrymen, wearing helmets and upper body armour (see Born and Seidl 1995) and wielding both long lances and bows, is striking in these reliefs and underscores the technical superiority of the Assyrian army over its Elamite foe (see Saggs 1963, Reade 1972, Mayer 1995: 419–82; Córdoba 1997: 7–8), not least because of its use of iron weaponry (Pigott 1984: 626). Apart from personal weaponry, the only equipment employed by Elamites appears to have been their carts (Fig. 8.3), 'open back and front . . . usually drawn by mules – exceptionally by bovids or horses' which functioned 'chiefly in the role of troop transports, moving at speed and carrying four men' (Littauer and Crouwel 1979: 101). The wheels of these carts were notable for their unusual number of spokes, sometimes as many as sixteen (Littauer and Crouwel 1991: 357; Hrouda 1994: 53). In contrast to the Assyrians with their protective tunics of lamellar armour (Thordeman 1939: 277; Salonen 1965: 100–8), the Elamites wore nothing but a short-sleeved tunic, generally shorter in front than in back, a headband, and an arrow quiver on their backs, held in place by straps run over the shoulders and fastened to a baldric in front. Generally they went barefoot

Table 8.2. *Epigraphs elucidating the depictions of Assurbanipal's triumph over Te-Umman in Room XXXIII of Sennacherib's palace at Nineveh*

Slab	Register	Depiction	Epigraph[1]
1	lower	above chariot, heading left, carrying Te-Umman's head	Head of Te-Um[man king of Elam], which in the midst of bat[tle] a common soldier in my army [cut off]. To (give me) the good ne[ws], they hastily dispatched (it) to Assy[ria].
2	lower	above officer on the ground	Urtak, in-law of Te-Umman, who was wounded by an arrow, but did not die, to sever his own head, he called to an Assyrian thus: "come, cut off my head. Bring (it) before the king your lord and make a good name (for yourself)."
3	lower	midst of battle scene	Te-Umman, in desperation, said to his son, "take up the bow!"
3	lower	above Elamite being beheaded	Te-Umman, king of Elam, who in fierce battle was wounded, Tammaritu, his eldest son, took him by the hand and to save (their) lives they fled. They hid in the midst of a forest. With the encouragement of Assur and Istar I killed them. Their heads I cut off in front of each other.
4	upper	above two men being flayed	[PN$_1$] and [PN$_2$] spoke great insults against Assur, my creator, Their tongues I ripped out, their flesh I flayed.
5	lower	above figure being led by the hand by an Assyrian soldier	[Umman]igash, the fugitive, servant who submitted to me at my command, joyfully into the midst of Madaktu and Susa I caused my *sut-reshi*, whom I sent, to enter and he set him on the throne of Te-Umman, whom my hands conquered.
6	upper	above royal chariot	I, Assurbanipal, the king of the world, king of Assyria, with the encouragement of Assur and Ishtar my lords, my enemies I conquered. I attained whatever I wished. Rusa, king of Urartu, heard of the strength of Assur, my lord, and fear of my dominion overcame him; he sent his nobles to ask my health. In the midst of Arba-ili Nabu-damiq and Umbadara, nobles of Elam, with writing boards with messages of insolence I made (them) stand before them.
6	lower	in the midst of an illustration of a city	land of Madaktu

Notes:
[1] Translations are from Gerardi 1987: 274–9.

Table 8.3. *Synopsis of the content of Assurbanipal's Elamite room (XXXIII) in Sennacherib's palace at Nineveh*

Register	Slab 1	Slab 2	Slab 3	Slab 4	Slab 5	Slab 6
Upper	fragmentary, two Elamite captives grinding bones	not preserved	two files of Elamite captives being deported	procession of Assyrians moving towards flaying and decapitation of Gambulians		Assurbanipal in his chariot
Lower	Assyrian army attacking the Elamites, decapitation of Te-Umman	battle (cont.)	battle (cont.)	Ulai river with floating corpses,	as Slab 4 and Assyrian soldiers, chariots, cavalry meeting Elamite delegation, installation of Ummanigash	as Slab 4 and prostrate delegation before Assyrian officer standing in front of Madaktu

Figure 8.3 'Assyrian warriors in a cart captured from the Elamites' (after Layard 1882: 246).

(Reade 1972: 107; Strommenger 1994: Tafs. Ic-d, IIa-b). Only the members of Te-Umman's royal house wore rounded helmets with ear flaps and a single feather extending backwards (Hrouda 1994: 54, Abb. 3).

As it turned out, these did not protect their wearers, and Te-Umman's head, severed on the field of battle by an Assyrian soldier, was taken back to Nineveh along with quantities of other war booty where it was suspended by a ring from a tree in Assurbanipal's garden, as illustrated on a well-known relief in the British Museum (Reade 1976: 104; 1983: 68). Lest knowledge of the fate of Te-Umman somehow escape his allies, Assurbanipal attacked Dunanu, chief of the Gambulu, who had supported Te-Umman, on his way back to Nineveh from Susiana. After capturing Dunanu, Assurbanipal had Te-Umman's head hung around Dunanu's neck and thus was the ruler of Gambulu made to enter Nineveh, along with the Elamite prisoners-of-war. The two envoys who had delivered Te-Umman's haughty requests for the extradition of the Elamite princes were made to watch as Te-Umman's skin was paraded through the city, and while one of them merely tore at his beard, the other is said to have committed suicide (Streck 1916: 125).

The removal of Te-Umman paved the way for a major, if unrealized re-orientation of Elamite-Assyrian relations in that Assurbanipal was now in a position to turn his hostile neighbour into a client state. This he attempted to do by installing two of the refugee princes whom he had been harbouring at Susa – and for whose return Te-Umman had long been clamouring – as 'kings' in Elam. As noted above, Assurbanipal had given refuge to 'Ummanigash, Ummanappa, Tammaritu, the sons of Urtak, king of Elam' as well as to their cousins, 'Kudurru (and) Paru sons of Ummanaldash, brother of Urtak, king of Elam'. By virtue of the fact that he is mentioned first, Ummanigash was presumably the eldest of Urtak's three sons, and this would explain why he was installed as king at Madaktu, while his brother Tammaritu (not to be confused with the homonymous son of Te-Umman) was made king at Hidalu (Millard 1964: 19). Whether Ummanappa, presumably older than Tammaritu, had in the meantime died or defected, we do not know, but something must account for his having been passed over in favour of Tammaritu, seemingly the youngest son of Urtak, whom Assurbanipal calls

Ummanigash's 'third brother' (Streck 1916: 27). As noted in Table 8.3, the installation of Ummanigash, i.e. Humban-nikash III, was illustrated in the cycle of reliefs depicting the second Elamite campaign. The loyalty of the newly appointed vassal had, however, already been called into question by Assurbanipal's brother, Shamash-shum-ukin, who had written to the Assyrian king warning him that the Elamite prince might prove treacherous (Millard 1964: 19 and n. 24; see also Streck 1916: 127).

Treacherous he indeed proved to be, but not solely of his own doing. Rather, Shamash-shum-ukin, dissatisfied with what he perceived to be his second class role as regent of Babylonia while his brother occupied the throne of Assyria, plotted a rebellion against Assurbanipal and, to prepare the way, entered into alliances with other potential enemies of Assyria including Ummanigash, the Elamite whom he had himself suspected as a prince and whose help he now sought as a king (Millard 1964: 19, 24). Assurbanipal recounts the treachery of his brother who, in spite of all that had been given him – troops, horses, chariots, cities, fields, grapevines (!) and people – incited the population of Babylonia to rebel against Assyrian overlordship (Streck 1916: 29). 'Also Ummanigash, the refugee, who had seized my royal feet, whom I had placed on the throne of Elam' (Streck 1916: 31) joined league with Shamash-shum-ukin, 'Ummanigash for whom I had done many favours, made king of Elam, who was not mindful of the good relations; he did not keep the oath of the great gods; he accepted a bribe from the messengers of Shamash-shum-ukin, faithless brother my enemy' (Gerardi 1987: 158).

In 652 BC Ummanigash sent troops to join the rebellious forces of Shamash-shum-ukin, enlisting further support on their way through southern Babylonia. Included in the expedition was a son of Te-Umman's, one Undashi, i.e. Untash, who had not perished with his father at Til-Tuba, and to whom Ummanigash is said by Assurbanipal to have spoken as follows: 'Go! Exact vengeance from Assyria for your father, your sire' (Gerardi 1987: 159). The expeditionary force met an Assyrian army coming south from the Tigris crossing at Mangisi and fought a battle at Hiritu, a fortress in the Diyala region (Millard 1964: 25, n. 52; cf. Grayson 1975: 257 who locates it 'in the extreme south of Babylonia . . . near the Elamite border' or Frame 1992: 291 who places it in northern Babylonia, 'in the province of Sippar'). The Elamite-Babylonian army was defeated, and the Elamite generals, Nesu and Attametu, along with Te-Umman's son, Undashi, were all killed, whereupon Assurbanipal sent an envoy to Ummanigash, who, however, neither replied nor released the messenger (Gerardi 1987: 159).

While the envoy's subsequent fate is shrouded in mystery, that of his host is not. Ummanigash was soon dethroned and murdered in yet another *coup d'état* by one Tammaritu who, in an Assyrian text dedicated to the god Nergal, is called 'heir of Ummanigash, brother of his father' (Streck 1916: 181; Gerardi 1987: 178–9). This makes it clear that Ummanigash, Assurbanipal's ex-client king of Elam, was Tammaritu's uncle, not his brother, and hence the Tammaritu (II) who overthrew Ummanigash was not the Tammaritu (I), brother of Ummanigash, who had been installed as king of Hidalu by Assurbanipal. One wonders if the father of Tammaritu was none other than Ummanappa, the brother of Ummanigash who had been a fugitive at the court of

Assurbanipal but had not been installed in either Madaktu or Hidalu after the rout of Te-Umman's army. At any rate, Tammaritu II could not have objected to his predecessor's support of the Babylonian insurgents for he soon led troops into the field in support of Shamash-shum-ukin where, however, he was overthrown by an Elamite general named Indabibi who turned on him in the midst of the battle, sending Tammaritu, his brothers and 85 supporters fleeing to Nineveh (Streck 1916: 35; Malbran-Labat 1975: 27). This must have occurred in 650 or early 649 BC (for the date see Gerardi 1987: 176; Frame 1992: 293).

From this period dates the correspondence between Assurbanipal and his general in the Sealand, Bel-ibni, who, as his letters make clear, was charged particularly with containing the rebellious Nabu-bel-shumate, a grandson of Merodach-Baladan who had early on allied himself with Shamash-shum-ukin (Brinkman 1991: 56–7). The difficulty of dating Bel-ibni's letters has led to varied interpretations of the precise sequence of events in this period, but it is in any case clear that the Sealand was both a place of refuge for Nabu-bel-shumate and a breeding ground for endless intrigues against Assyria in which the Elamites usually took part. From Bel-ibni's correspondence with Assurbanipal we can glean many details otherwise unmentioned in the Assyrian annals. For example, we read that Indabibi killed one of Tammaritu II's brothers during the battle in which he revolted (ABL 521), and that Tammaritu and his entourage fled in the first instance to Bel-ibni who sent them on to Assurbanipal (ABL 284). We hear of a famine amongst the Elamites on the border with the Sealand; we learn that Nabu-bel-shumate was able to organize 250 men of the Gurashimmu tribe to harrass the Assyrian general's forces; but we also see that Bel-ibni mobilized 400 archers in squadrons of 100 who crossed the head of the Persian Gulf to Elam, massacred members of the tribes of Hilim and Pillatu, and seized 500–600 head of cattle before returning (ABL 1000; see also Malbran-Labat 1982: 78). Bel-ibni organized other raids on Elamite territory, passing through the marshes by boat and, on one occasion, capturing 1500 head of cattle belonging to the Elamite king and the prince of Pillatu, a border town in the region (ABL 520), using 600 archers and 50 cavalrymen.

Perhaps because he realized that Shamash-shum-ukin's position was becoming untenable and because he could perceive no advantage for Elam in continuing its support for Assurbanipal's rebellious brother, Indabibi decided to treat for peace with Assurbanipal (Cogan and Tadmor 1981: 233). He released a number of Assyrian prisoners and sent an ambassador to Nineveh with a view to concluding a treaty (Streck 1916: 131), but there were others who were not released, prompting Assurbanipal to send back a message with Indabibi's envoy enjoining him to release these or risk the destruction of Susa, Madaktu and Hidalu and experience the fate of Te-Umman (Streck 1916: 1431). For whatever reasons, the messenger never arrived, Assurbanipal marched against Elam, and hearing of the approach yet again of an Assyrian army, 'the people of Elam revolted [against] Indabibi and [killed him. Ummanaldash, son] of Attametu, [took] his throne' (Gerardi 1987: 161).

Ummanaldash, i.e. Humban-haltash III, is not known from original Elamite inscriptions, and while it has generally been assumed that his father Attametu was the Atta-hamiti-Inshushinak known from Susa (thus e.g. Malbran-Labat 1975: 28, n. 68; Gerardi 1987: 222, n. 93; against this view see Vallat 1995b) the grammar of the latter's inscriptions would suggest that this was not the case (see below).

Beginning in mid-summer 650 BC, Babylon was under siege, but by mid-summer 648 BC, after great cost of human life, the city had been taken and Shamash-shum-ukin had died in a fire (Streck 1916: 37; Millard 1964: 29). Thus relieved of one running sore, Assurbanipal was able to turn with more effect to his Elamite problem. The situation in Elam was anything but stable. In a letter (ABL 280) concerned mainly with his troops' raids into Elamite territory, Bel-ibni reported to Assurbanipal that 'Ummanigash, son of Amedirra, has fomented a revolt against Ummanaldash. From the Hudhud river to the town of Hadanu, (the people) have rallied to him. Ummanaldash has gathered his troops. Right now, they've taken up a position on the river facing each other' (Malbran-Labat 1975: 29–30; Gerardi 1987: 226, n. 141). A second letter (ABL 462) from Bel-ibni reports that 'all of the inhabitants of Elam have revolted against their king Ummanaldash', who, fearing to fall into the revolutionaries hands, took refuge in the mountains. In this atmosphere of chaos and internal revolution, Assurbanipal decided it was timely to make a further strike against Elam.

The Assyrian king marched to Bit-Imbi – described in the annals as 'the fulcrum of Elam, which bars (i.e. protects) Elam like a great wall' (Streck 1916: 43) – conquered the city (Cogan and Tadmor 1981: 234) and deported all of its surviving inhabitants, including Imbappa, the Elamite commandant (var. chief archer) and brother-in-law of Ummanaldash, king of Elam, and the 'palace wife' and sons of Te-Umman, to Assyria. Assurbanipal had with him 'Tammaritu, the king of Elam, who had fled from Indabibi, his servant, and seized my feet' (Streck 1916: 43). Hearing of the invasion Ummanaldash is said to have fled to the mountains from his residence at Madaktu, whereupon Umbahabua seized the throne, established himself at Bubilu, but soon fled as well 'and like a fish, sought the depths of distant waters'. All opposition gone, Assurbanipal says he led Tammaritu II 'into Susa and made him king' (Streck 1916: 45). His vassaldom, however, must have been shortlived, for the very next sentence in the annals reports Tammaritu's objection to the Assyrian plundering of his country, whereupon he was promptly removed from the throne and deported for a second time. In a rage, Assurbanipal proceeded to destroy twenty-nine Elamite cities on his return to Assyria, including Madaktu and Susa (Streck 1916: 47).

Although the annals present this episode as if it were solely due to Assurbanipal's intervention, the parallelisms between the cities mentioned early in the account and those listed in a letter by Bel-ibni as having been taken by his troops, suggest that both Assyrian forces, striking from the northwest and the southwest, may have been involved in the action (Gerardi 1987: 188). While the Assyrian army under Assurbanipal was obviously more concerned with routing Ummanaldash and installing Tammaritu II, Bel-ibni seems to have been mainly intent on continuing to harrass the Elamites on their western marches and, in so doing, effect the long sought capture of Nabu-bel-shumate.

In fact, Assurbanipal's fourth Elamite campaign ended in an equivocal manner.

Tammaritu II had been installed and then removed from office and no one else had been substituted in his place. Thus, in spite of the destruction of over two dozen cities and the seizure of quantities of booty, Assurbanipal's army left Elam to Ummanaldash, who was able to return from his hiding place and resume rule over Madaktu and whatever else remained loyal to him. A fifth campaign was launched against Ummanaldash, however probably within months of the aborted attempt to re-install Tammaritu II, in mid-647 BC (for the date see Gerardi 1987: 208). Assurbanipal's army once more took the road to Bit-Imbi, and once more Ummanaldash, hearing that two of his frontier towns had fallen, fled from Madaktu to Dur-Untash (Streck 1916: 49). In Chapter 7 the ceramic evidence for the chronology of Choga Zanbil, identical with Al Untash Napirisha, was presented, suggesting that the city was not occupied after Nebuchadnezzar I's conquest. Whether certain areas, unexcavated by Ghirshman, continued to be in use down to the seventh century BC, or whether Dur-Untash here refers to an altogether different city, we cannot say, but nothing in the extant archaeological evidence is suggestive of occupation into the Neo-Elamite II period at Choga Zanbil.

Crossing the Idide river, Ummanaldash prepared his forces for battle, using the river as a line of defence (Streck 1916: 49). City after city fell to Assurbanipal's forces, sending Ummanaldash once more into flight toward the mountains. At this point the Assyrian forces pressed eastward as far as the border of Hidalu, and along the coast of the upper Persian Gulf to Pashime, destroying cities and towns, smashing some cult statues and seizing others as booty, laying waste to an enormous area 60 double-hours (c. 600+ km) in extent, before turning back and heading for Susa. Here Assurbanipal entered the Elamite palaces, opened their treasuries (or what was left of them), seized hold of the booty taken by earlier Elamite kings from Sumer, Akkad and Babylonia, and took everything previously given by Shamash-shum-ukin to buy Elamite allegiance, jewellery, clothing, chariots, horses, gold and silver plate (Streck 1916: 53). All of the gods and goddesses of Elam, along with their treasures, their possessions, their ritual paraphernalia, and their priesthood, along with statues of kings made of gold, silver, bronze and limestone were seized and taken back to Assyria as booty. The graves of former kings were opened and destroyed, and the monarchs' bones were also transported to Assyria. The destruction lasted one month and twenty-five days (Streck 1916: 57).

Assurbanipal specifically says that he destroyed the ziggurat of Susa and broke off its 'horns' of shining bronze (Streck 1916: 53). This reference to the horns of the ziggurat at Susa is particularly interesting in light of a number of literary allusions to horns and religious architecture. One of Shilhak-Inshushinak's stele texts refers to the casting of horns for a place of sacrifice (König 1965: 106, §46.15), while a horned building appears on a Late Uruk-style seal impression of Susa II date, discussed in Chapter 3 (Pl. 3.2, Fig. 3.12; see also Potts 1990a). Moreover, the manufacture of horns in gold is mentioned in one of the Middle Elamite texts from Tal-i Malyan (Stolper 1984: 68–9). Finally, the so-called 'ziggurat relief' in room I of Assurbanipal's palace at Nineveh depicts a four-stage temple tower or ziggurat at Susa with projecting horns (Dombart 1929; Reade 1976: 101 and Taf. 25; but see also Unger 1938: 353, who located the structure in question at Babylon).

As Assurbanipal says, 'In a month of days I levelled the whole of Elam, I deprived its fields of the sound of human voices, the tread of cattle and sheep, the refrain of joyous harvest songs. I turned it into a pasture for wild asses, gazelles, and all manner of wild animals' (Brinkman 1991: 59). Amongst the treasures recovered from the ancient city of Susa was the statue of Nanaya of Uruk, which had been taken 1635 years earlier (Streck 1916: 59). And yet with all of the destruction and plundering involved in this campaign, Assurbanipal had once again failed to capture Ummanaldash, who returned to his ruined city of Madaktu where he received a messenger from the Assyrian king demanding the extradition of his arch-rival Nabu-bel-shumate. Hearing of this request, the Chaldaean rebel and his shield bearer killed each other, apparently preferring this to flaying and decapitation at the hands of the Assyrians, and Ummanaldash, fearing the dissatisfaction of Assurbanipal, packed the body of Nabu-bel-shumate in salt along with the head of his shield bearer and gave it to the Assyrian messenger. On its arrival at Nineveh, Assurbanipal had Nabu-bel-shumate's head cut off and hung around the neck of Pa'e, an ally of his rebel brother's, who is said to have ruled Elam simultaneously with Ummanaldash before fleeing to Assyria along with the inhabitants of a long series of Elamite towns and cities, who found themselves promptly enlisted in the Assyrian army (Streck 1916: 63). In 645 BC, following Assurbanipal's victories over the Arabs (Gerardi 1992), Pa'e, Ummanaldash and Tammaritu were humiliated before the Assyrians by being forced to draw Assurbanipal's carriage in a celebration staged at Nineveh (Frame 1992: 208).

This marked the end of Assurbanipal's violent campaigns against his Elamite and Chaldaean foes. His brother had perished, his Chaldaean enemy had been delivered to him, and he had laid waste to most of Khuzistan, stopping short at Hidalu. According to a fragmentary letter (ABL 1007+), a LÚ.SAG (a high officer) was placed in charge of the villages of Arashu and Bit-Burnakka, while another was given responsibility for Hilim and the Pillatu tribe, and a 'governor (?) of the officers' was sent to Susa (Malbran-Labat 1982: 132; Gerardi 1987: 256).

Notable by its absence in all of the foregoing accounts of Assurbanipal's campaigns has been any mention of Anshan. The silence of the historical sources is matched by a paucity of archaeological material as well. Virtually the only locus at Tal-i Malyan which can be dated to sometime within the first half of the first millennium is burial 47 in area DD43 (Fig. 8.4), the shallow pit grave of an individual buried with items of personal jewellery and three ceramic vessels (Carter 1994b: 66 and Fig. 3; 1996: 47 and Fig. 45). As Carter has emphasized, however, 'these ceramics show no relation to either Neo-Elamite I or II pottery known from Susa', and the date of the burial is based mainly on generalized parallels between a faience cylinder seal which was strung along with seven beads to form a necklace on the deceased and the Iron Age glyptic of Marlik in northern Iran.

As we have seen, Madaktu figures prominently in the Assyrian annals, less so Hidalu and, in the climax of the Assyrian-Elamite confrontation, Susa. Certainly the long lists of toponyms included by Assurbanipal make it clear that the population of Khuzistan was ample at this time, and surveys in the Ram Hormuz plain, roughly halfway

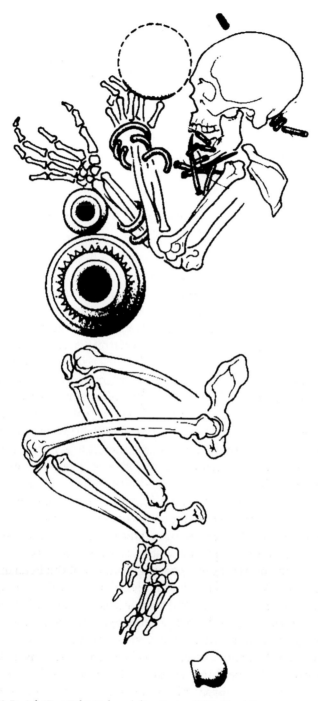

Figure 8.4 Burial 47 at Tal-i Malyan (after Carter 1996: Fig. 46).

Table 8.4. *Early Achaemenid genealogy according to Herodotus, the Behistun inscription, the Cyrus Cylinder and P. de Miroschedji*

Herodotus VII 11	Behistun §2	Cyrus Cylinder	de Miroschedji 1985
Achaemenes	Achaemenes		
Teispes (I)		Teispes (I)	Teispes (I), *c.* 635–610 BC
Cambyses (I)			
Cyrus (I)		Cyrus (I)	Cyrus (I), *c.* 610–585 BC
Teispes (II)	Teispes (II)		
Ariaramnes	Ariaramnes		
Arsames	Arsames	Cambyses (I)	Cambyses (I), *c.* 585–559 BC
Hystaspes	Hystaspes	Cyrus (II)	Cyrus (II), 559–530 BC
		Cambyses (II)	
Darius (I)	Darius (I)		
Xerxes			

between Anshan and Susa, have identified a number of sites with early first millennium occupation, the largest of which were Tepe Bormi at 18 ha and Tal-i Ghazir at 7.5 ha, where Neo-Elamite ceramics and smallfinds were discovered in recently published soundings by D. McCown (Carter 1994b: 68ff.). Settlement in central Khuzistan is sparse, however, with little continuity from the Middle Elamite period, and equally little between the Neo-Elamite I and II ceramic phases (Carter 1994b: 73).

According to the latest edition (Edition A, from *c.* 643 BC) of Assurbanipal's annals, at the conclusion of the last Elamite campaign, two Iranian leaders – Kurash king of Parsumash, and Pizlume king of Hudimiri – sent tribute to Assurbanipal upon hearing of his decisive victory over Elam (Weidner 1931–1932), and Kurash even sent his son Arukku to Nineveh 'to do obeisance' (Frame 1992: 209 and n. 86). This episode has spawned a considerable amount of controversy revolving around the identity of Kurash and the location of his kingdom. Ever since Weidner's publication of the fragment of Assurbanipal's annals mentioning Kurash, it has been conventional to identify him with Cyrus I, ancestor of the better known Cyrus II, founder of the Persian empire (e.g. Cameron 1936: 204; Eilers 1964: 181; 1974: 3; Dandamaev 1977; Briant 1984: 83; Bollweg 1988; Dandamaev and Lukonin 1989: 54; Grayson 1991: 155; Shahbazi 1993: 516; Stronach 1997: 39, hesitantly). Given the long reigns implied if one relies on the later genealogical information contained in the Cyrus Cylinder and the inscription of Darius at Behistun (Table 8.4), Weidner's view has been challenged as chronologically impossible by de Miroschedji (de Miroschedji 1985: 283–5; Briant 1996: 28). As Shahbazi has argued, however, it is perfectly possible for Cyrus I, the alleged Kurash king of Parsumash, to have reigned in the 640s BC, and his grandson Cyrus II to have been born *c.* 600 BC and to have died *c.* 530 BC (Shahbazi 1993: 516). Admittedly, as the name Kurash is attested in Neo-Babylonian sources from Babylon and in late Neo-

Elamite texts from Susa, there is no reason to assume that the name was unique to the Achaemenid royal family (Zadok 1976a: 63 and n. 12). Some scholars even think it may be Elamite (Andreas 1904: 94).

As for Parsumash, it is important not to conflate this with Parsua, as has been done so often in the past (e.g. Levine 1973: 106, n. 35; Dandamaev 1977: 41; Reade 1978: 139; de Miroschedji 1985: 277). G. Windfuhr has suggested that both Parsua and Parsumash represent the names of groups/regions ultimately derived from the east Iranian region *Parthawa* (< *Parsu/awa*) whence the later Parthians (see Chapter 10) hailed (Windfuhr 1974: 466–7; see also Diakonoff 1991: 14). Parsua of the Neo-Assyrian sources should perhaps be located east of Senandaj (Reade 1978: 139) or in the Mahidasht (Windfuhr 1974: 467), whereas Parsumash, which later changed under Persian influence to Old Persian *Parsa* (see also Greek *Persis*), must have been coterminous with some portion of Fars (Windfuhr 1974: 467; Reade 1995: 41).

One final point which should be made in regard to Assyrian aggression against Elam concerns the matter of deportation. As we have seen, the residents of Elamite cities and towns were deported on numerous occasions during the seventh century, and one may well wonder just how these aliens were absorbed into their new environments. We know from a combination of royal inscriptions and letters that the Assyrians deported Elamites to Nimrud in Assyria, Samaria in Israel (referred to in Ezra 4: 9–10; see Frame 1992: 203), and even as far as Egypt (Oded 1979: 29, 30, 61). Moreover, both Assurbanipal and Esarhaddon drafted large numbers of Elamite captives into their armies (Oded 1979: 52–3 with refs.). The discovery of four late Neo-Assyrian texts at Tell Shaikh Hamad, ancient Dur-Katlimmu, on the lower Khabur river in Syria, sheds unexpected light on this question. Two of the texts, dating to 602 BC and 600 BC (for the dates see Brinkman 1993b: 135), mention estates at a place called Magdalu 'bordering the land of the Elamites' (Postgate 1993b: 117–18). J.N. Postgate has suggested that these Elamites were 'presumably deportees from about half a century before' (Postgate 1993: 110; see also Zadok 1995a). Their presence in Syria would suggest that, after reaching Assyria, many Elamites (Zadok 1995d) may have been sent on to yet more distant locales where they pursued an agricultural, craft-related or pastoral existence.

Neo-Elamite III (647–539 BC)

In recent years a small amount of pre-Achaemenid glyptic, combined with a number of undated texts both from Susa and elsewhere, have been used as the basis of an historical reconstruction according to which Susa and Elam experienced a revival in the period following Assurbanipal's last Elamite campaign. Before examining this evidence, let us consider the few points of historical and chronological integrity which have survived from this period.

It has been suggested that in the aftermath of Assurbanipal's conquest of Susa, Susiana, if not all of Elam, became an Assyrian province until the fall of the Assyrian empire and the destruction of Nineveh in 612 BC. G.G. Cameron adduced several texts in support of this theory, including a 'schedule' from Nineveh listing agricultural lands, their location and owners, which may refer to a place called Susanu, linked hesitantly by Cameron to Susa (Cameron 1936: 211). Apart from the fact that this reading is by no means certain, all of the districts dealt with in the text in question seem to lie in northern Mesopotamia (Fales 1973: 5–6, 74). Another text adduced by Cameron was a list of officials at the court of Nineveh which names an individual whose name is broken, [. . .]gi, and describes him as *shaknu*, i.e. governor or prefect, of the Elamites (Fales and Postgate 1992: 10, no. 5). But it is not possible to use this text as an indication of a post-647 BC Assyrian administrator in Elam, for the text's date is broken, and according to its most recent editors, it could date to the reign of either Assurbanipal or Esarhaddon (Fales and Postgate 1992: xix).

Following the destruction of Susa, therefore, the next fixed point in the history of Elam occurred in 625 BC. Both Assurbanipal and the mysterious Kandalanu, whom the Assyrian king had installed as 'king of Babylon' following the death of Shamash-shum-ukin (Frame 1992: 191ff. and Appendix F for a discussion of the problems surrounding the identity of Kandalanu; see also Zawadzki 1988: 57ff.; Oates 1991: 170–1), had died in 627 BC, and during the next two years the Babylonians, led by Nabopolassar, possibly another Chaldaean from the Sealand, and possibly an Assyrian-appointed general originally commissioned by Assurbanipal (Brinkman 1984: 110, n. 551; Wiseman 1984: 5–6; Frame 1992: 211), renewed their armed struggle against Assyria. In 626 BC Nabopolassar was proclaimed 'king of Babylon', and according to the Nabopolassar Chronicle, following his defeat of an Assyrian army, and in his accession year, 'Nabopolassar returned to Susa the gods of Susa whom the Assyrians had carried off and settled in Uruk' (Grayson 1975: 88; see also Wiseman 1956: 51).

The significance of this statement is certainly open to interpretation. Wiseman suggested that the gesture 'was but a proper acknowledgement of help received from Elam, for it appears that when Nabopolassar captured Erech [Uruk] sometime before 626 BC, the Elamites had taken its temple library to their country for safe-keeping' (Wiseman 1956: 9). This view was based on Wiseman's interpretation of the colophon of an Akkadian ritual text (AO 6451) which describes bread-making at the Anu temple in Uruk. The colophon concludes, 'tablets which Nabopolassar, king of the Sealand, carried off as plunder from the city of Uruk; but now Kidinanu, a citizen of Uruk, a *mashmashu*-priest of Anu and Antu . . . looked at these tablets in the land of Elam, copied them in the reign of the kings Seleucus and Antiochus, and brought (his copies) back to the city of Uruk' (Pritchard 1969: 345). Nabopolassar's defeat of an Assyrian and Nippurean army at Uruk is mentioned in Chronicle 2 ('Chronicle concerning the early years of Nabopolassar') (Grayson 1975: 88) and probably occurred just prior to his defeat of the Assyrians (Zawadzki 1988: 30). If we combine the evidence of the ritual text's colophon with that of the Chronicle, then one would have to suggest that, having seized the temple library at Uruk, Nabopolassar took it all the way to Elam, where he deposited it, but this seems a curious turn of events and one for which there is absolutely no corroborating evidence. Moreover, Wiseman later changed his mind about the veracity of the colophon, arguing 'there is no evidence that Nabopolassar even had to attack Uruk, let alone plunder it' (Wiseman 1984: 6). Be that as it may, even if we remain unsure of how the tablets copied by the Uruk priest in the time of the Seleucids reached Elam – by which Susa is presumably meant – the fact remains that Nabopolassar's restitution of divine statues originally seized by the Assyrians has been interpreted by Elamite scholars as evidence of the existence of a new, revived government at Susa by 625 BC since it presumes the presence there of authorities competent to receive the returned goods (Amiet 1973b: 24; also de Miroschedji 1982: 62). Stolper has suggested that Nabopolassar was desirous of establishing 'a new entente with Elam' because he had not yet subdued Assyrian forces in the northern part of Babylonia and was, in time honoured fashion, seeking 'Elamite support for his insurrection' (Carter and Stolper 1984: 53).

In discussing the revolt of Der from Assyrian control which, according to the Chronicle, occurred in 623/2 BC, Wiseman spoke of 'the new status of Elam which had also regained its independence of Assyria by this time' (Wiseman 1956: 10), while Zadok has suggested that 'Elam might have been an ally of Babylonia during Nabopolassar's reign . . . when both countries had a common enemy, namely Assyria' (Zadok 1979b: 171). If, however, such an alliance ever existed, then why did the Elamites not participate in the final destruction of the Assyrian empire, alongside the Babylonians under Nabopolassar and the Medes under Cyaxares? Surely if Nabopolassar had persuaded the Elamites to aid him in any substantial way, the Elamites would not have missed the opportunity to return to Nineveh in 612 BC, not as deportees and humiliated prisoners, but as conquerors. And how would one reconcile a Babylonian-Elamite *entente* with the rising power of Media, and the hint of an Elamite-Median alliance against Babylon prophesied in Isaiah 21:2, where we read, 'A grievous vision is declared unto me; the treacherous dealer dealeth treacherously, and the spoiler spoileth. Go up, O Elam; besiege, O Media; all the sighing thereof have I made to cease'. These are difficult questions to answer, but they must be posed lest we uncritically assume that a single reference to Susa in the Chronicle denotes a new alliance on a par with those of the period before 646 BC.

Nabopolassar died in the summer of 605 BC and was succeeded by his son, Nebuchadnezzar II. According to Chroncle 5, which concerns the early years of Nebuchadnezzar II's reign, Babylonian forces clashed with those of a foreign king along the Tigris in 596 BC (Wiseman 1956: 72; Grayson 1975: 102). Wiseman originally suggested that the broken geographical name associated with the king who 'took fright and fear overcame him so he we[nt] home' could be restored as Elam, but he later vacillated, calling his suggested restoration 'possible though doubtful' (Wiseman 1984: 34; cf. 1991: 233). Indeed, the capacity of Elam to attack Babylonia at this point in its history has been called into question by Zawadzki (1988: 140), who points to the prophecy in Jeremiah 49: 34–9, which suggests that Elam lost its independence early in the reign of Zedekiah of Judah (597–586 BC) and reads as follows: '[34]The word of the Lord that came to Jeremiah the prophet against Elam in the beginning of the reign of Zedekiah king of Judah, saying, [35]Thus saith the Lord of hosts; Behold, I will break the bow of Elam, the chief of their might. [36]And upon Elam will I bring the four winds from the four quarters of heaven, and will scatter them toward all those winds; and there shall be no nation whither the outcasts of Elam shall not come. [37]For I will cause Elam to be dismayed before their enemies, and before them that seek their life: and I will bring evil upon them, even my fierce anger, saith the Lord; and I will send the sword after them, till I have consumed them: [38]And I will set my throne in Elam, and will destroy from thence the king and the princes, saith the Lord. [39]But it shall come to pass in the latter days, that I will bring again the captivity of Elam, saith the Lord'.

Even if the prophecy was written after the events 'forecast' had taken place, it is important for it implicitly contrasts Elam's loss of power and 'captivity' with a prior state of independence. Is such a state perhaps to be associated with the brief interval of time between the death of Assurbanipal and the early years of Nebuchadnezzar II? Considering the part played by the thousands of Elamite bowmen mentioned in the Assyrian annals (Fig. 8.5) during the seventh century, the reference to the 'bow of Elam' as 'the chief of their might' is particularly apposite.

Some scholars have assumed that the encounter referred to in the Chronicle preceded an all out conquest of Elam by Nebuchadnezzar II (e.g. König 1931: 23; Weidner 1939: 929; Zadok 1976a: 61), a view which was bolstered early in this century by the discovery of a number of objects (Langdon 1905–6; 1912: 44; Thureau-Dangin 1912: 24–5) bearing the name of Nebuchadnezzar II, as well as inscribed bricks (Scheil 1927: 47–8) with the king's name, at Susa (Table 8.5). Scheil was of the opinion that whereas inscribed objects, such as the stone vessels with Nebuchadnezzar's name or the stone weights with the names of Nebuchadnezzar and his successors, Amel-Marduk (562–560 BC) and Neriglissar (560–556 BC), could have reached Susa at any time, this was much less likely with bricks, which were probably made close to each building site where they were eventually used (Scheil 1927: 47; see also Dandamaev and Lukonin 1989: 59). This is certainly a reasonable assumption, although Zawadzki has pointed to the discovery of an inscribed brick of Nebuchadnezzar's at Persepolis, a site not founded until the Achaemenid period, suggesting therefore that the discovery of an inscribed brick at a site need not perforce imply the building activity there of the king named (Zawadzki 1988: 142, citing Schmidt 1953: 144, 179). Certainly the inscribed Neo-Assyrian and Neo-Babylonian eyestones (Fig. 8.6), seals and beads recovered in the Persepolis treasury (Schmidt 1957: 57ff.) must have arrived long after they had originally been manufactured.

In fact, although inconclusive, there is some evidence to suggest that Nebuchadnezzar may not have erected a building at the site. The Susa bricks all bear the very simplest formula giving the king's name and title, an epithet and his filiation – 'Nebuchadnezzar, king of Babylon, provider for Esagil and Ezida, first/chief son of Nabopolassar' (Berger 1973: 22). Bricks with this standard formula are known from Babylon, Borsippa, Eridu, Hillah, Kish, Sippar, Seleucia and Tell Nasrat Pasha near Baghdad (Berger 1973: 180, 185–6, 195–6). Far more common, however, are inscribed bricks actually naming specific buildings, examples of which are known from Babylon, Borsippa, Ur and Uruk (Berger 1973: 105–7). One might suggest, therefore, that the Susa bricks, with their 'generic' inscriptions, could have come from almost anywhere Nebuchadnezzar was active as a builder, whereas only an inscribed brick naming a specific building can be accepted as ironclad proof of such activity at Susa.

Figure 8.5 Depiction of an Elamite cutting his bow in an Assyrian relief (after Strommenger 1994: Taf. 1d).

Table 8.5. *Objects inscribed by Neo-Babylonian kings from Susa and Persepolis*

King	Object	Provenience	Text	Reference
Nebuchadnezzar II	alabaster vessel	Susa	'palace of Nebuchadnezzar, king of Babylon, who walks forth with the support of Nabu and Marduk, his lords, son of Nabopolassar, king of Babylon'	Langdon 1912: 207
	onyx eye-stone	Persepolis treasury room 41	'to (the goddess) Sarpanitum, his lady, Nebuchadnezzar, king of Babylon, for his life, presented (this)'	Schmidt 1957: 58
	eye-stone fragment	Persepolis treasury room 33	'. . . Nebuchadnezzar, king of Babylon . . .'	Schmidt 1957: 58, n. 89
	chalcedony bead	Persepolis treasury room 33	fragment of the name 'Nebuchdnezzar'	Schmidt 1957: 58
	limestone paver	Susa	'palace of Nebuchadnezzar, king of Babylon, son of Nabopolassar king of Babylon	Langdon 1905/6: 147
	3 baked bricks	Susa	'Nebuchadnezzar, king of Babylon, provider for Esagil and Ezida, first/chief son of Nabopolassar, king of Babylon'	Scheil 1927: 47–8
Amel-Marduk	2 stone vessel fragments	Susa	'1 *sutu* 6 1/2 NINDA, of the palace of Amel-Marduk'	Scheil 1904: xxiii
	alabaster vessel	Susa	'3 GAR 1/3 [*qa*] palace of Amel-Marduk, king of Babylon, son of Nebuchadnezzar, king of Babylon'	Thureau-Dangin 1912: 24
Neriglissar	stone vessel fragment	Susa	'2 *qa* 1/2 NINDA, Neriglissar king of Babylon'	Scheil 1908: 96

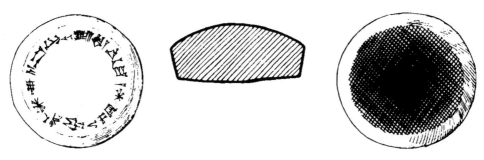

Figure 8.6 Concave onyx disc from the Persepolis treasury (hall 41), bearing the inscription, 'To (the goddess) Sarpanitum, his lady, Nebuchadnezzar, king of Babylon, for his life presented (this)' (after Schmidt 1957: Pl. 25.2).

A fragmentary basalt stele from Babylon of Nabonidus (556–539 BC), the last king of the Neo-Babylonian dynasty, mentions (col. III 43) 'the Ishtar, the lady of Elam, the princess who dwells in Susa (two lines missing)' (Pritchard 1969: 309) in connection with building works carried out by one of his predecessors, almost certainly Nebuchadnezzar (Beaulieu 1989: 20–2). The context is somewhat cryptic, and surely the text does not justify the inference made by Berger that Nebuchadnezzar had himself built a temple to Ishtar at Susa (Berger 1973: 104). As recognized long ago, it is just possible that the long 'captivity' of Ishtar at Susa mentioned by Assurbanipal (see above) when he 'liberated' her (statue) caused Ishtar of Uruk to receive the epithet 'lady of Elam' (Langdon 1912: 277, n. 1). Even an inscribed limestone paver, the inscription of which says that it came from the 'palace of Nebuchadnezzar', is thought by Berger to have been 'deported' to Susa from a Babylonian site because of its curious concave surfaces which made it a curio (Berger 1973: 25). All in all, there is no reliable evidence to speak of for Neo-Babylonian building activity at Susa.

Wiseman once suggested that during the post-Assyrian era the Medes acted as a kind of check against Elam's growth, making a Babylonian annexation of Elam unnecessary (Wiseman 1956: 36). Nevertheless, Weidner was of the view that a ration list from Babylon dating to 592/1 BC in which oil rations for no fewer than 713 Elamites are mentioned was a reflection of the presence of an Elamite military unit in the service of Nebuchadnezzar along the lines of the units of Elamites in Assurbanipal's army mentioned above (Weidner 1939: 929; see also Dandamaev and Lukonin 1989: 59). In Zadok's opinion, a Babylonian named Nabû-le', mentioned in the same text and identified as an 'officer (^{LÚ}SAG) in charge of Elamites', may have been their commander (Zadok 1976a: 62). Moreover, Dandamaev and Lukonin have pointed to the lamentation for Egypt in Ezekiel 32:24 mentioning 'Elam and all her multitude round about her [i.e. Egypt's] grave, all of them slain, fallen by the sword', suggesting that the Babylonian conquest of Elam had occurred between the time of Jeremiah's prophecy c. 597/6 BC and 584 BC to which Ezekiel may be dated (Dandamaev and Lukonin 1989: 59). Dandamaev and Lukonin have also suggested that Babylonian control over Elam was lost late in the reign of Nabonidus (556–539 BC), when it was wrested from him by Astyages, king of the Medes (Dandamaev and Lukonin 1989: 61). Zawadzki, who sees no firm evidence for Babylonia ever having controlled Elam, believes that Elam may have fallen under Median control as early as 584 BC, when Astyages succeeded his deceased father (Zawadzki 1988: 143). In such case, if one were to follow Jeremiah and Ezekiel, Elam lost its independence not to Babylonia at all but to Media. The few texts from Babylonia which date to the mid-sixth century and which concern Elamites, such as a promissory note from 541/40 BC concerning an Elamite debtor at Babylon (Zadok 1976a: 62–4), cannot help us decide whether or not Elam was independent at the time.

Any historical reconstructions based on such sparse data are, of course, highly speculative and very much at odds with those proposed by scholars such as Amiet, de Miroschedji, Steve and Vallat, who suggest that a Neo-Elamite renaissance – a state of independence rather than subjection to any rival, whether Babylonia or Media – occurred in the wake of Assurbanipal's destruction of Susa. In epigraphic terms, such a renaissance would have occurred in the phase defined by Steve as Neo-Elamite IIIA (*c.* 653–605 BC). In historical terms, IIIA represents the period from the capture and death of Te-Umman through the reign of Nabopolassar – thus overlapping the period both before and after Assurbanipal's sack of Susa – while IIIB equates to the period from the reign of Nebuchadnezzar II through the defeat of Nabonidus and the ascension of Cyrus the Great. Steve's separation of IIIA and IIIB, however, is based on the evolution of the Neo-Elamite syllabary, not on Mesopotamian historical chronology, while Vallat has modified the chronology somewhat, using the sack of Susa as the *terminus post quem* for Neo-Elamite IIIA (646–585 BC).

The only excavated object assigned by Steve to the Neo-Elamite IIIA phase is a bronze plaque from Persepolis with a largely illegible inscription (Cameron 1957; assigned to IIIB, however, by Vallat 1996c). Apart from this, the remainder of the material attributed to this phase (Steve 1992: 22) are five cylinder seals of unknown provenience (Amiet 1973b: 29; Bollweg 1988; Garrison and Root 1996: 7) illustrated in Fig. 8.7. Iconographically speaking, these five seals present us with three different styles which may be called 'Assyrianizing', 'Elamo-Persian', and 'Neo-Babylonianizing'. Fig. 8.7.1 shows a scene in Neo-Assyrian style, with a deity in his winged disc above a stylized tree. The latter is flanked by two fish-men (Akk. *kulullû*), each of which is surmounted by a genie. The legend on this seal is too damaged to permit a reading. Fig. 8.7.2 shows a very Assyrian-looking goddess wearing a feathered tiara who rests one foot on the back of a reclining lion. The Elamite legend identifies the seal as the property of 'Parsirra, son of Kurlush' (Amiet 1973b: 29). Because he believed these names to be Persian, Amiet proposed that seals be called 'Elamo-Persian' (Amiet 1994c: 63–4). In fact, Parsirra is 'apparently an Elamite gentilic form meaning "Persian"', while Kurlush, 'a name that occurs in the Persepolis Fortification texts . . . may be Iranian' (M.W. Stolper, pers. comm.). A figure holding two fish in his/her hands is shown in Fig. 8.7.3. This unusual gesture is otherwise only attested in Neo-Assyrian glyptic, although in a different fashion (Amiet 1973b: 18). The fragmentary Elamite legend reads 'I . . . na, son of Hupanna'. Finally, two seals show evidence of strong Neo-Babylonian influence. The first of these (Fig. 8.7.4) shows two rampant, horned dragons on either side of the upright, triangular-headed spade of Marduk. The legend reads

Figure 8.7 Neo-Elamite IIIA (653–605 BC) cylinder seals (after Amiet 1973b).

'Huban-kitin, son of king Shutur-Nahhunte' (Amiet 1967a: 45; 1973b: 29). The muscular animals recall Babylonian glyptic from the time of Nebuchadnezzar II and are in many respects comparable to the glazed brick dragons on the processional way and Ishtar gate of Babylon, while the ornate spade recalls that found on a seal in the Yale Babylonian Collection attributed to the late Neo-Babylonian period (Amiet 1967a: 44). The final seal of this group (Fig. 8.7.5) is similar in style to the preceding example, only this time two rampant bulls are depicted and the spade of Marduk is absent. The legend reads 'Kitepatin, son of Pinriri' (Amiet 1973b: 29; Porada 1971: 34).

Undoubtedly, the seal of 'Huban-kitin, son of king Shutur-Nahhunte' has generated the most discussion over the years. From the beginning of scholarship on this piece, Amiet and M. Lambert were clear about the distinction between Shutruk-Nahhunte II (717–699 BC), the contemporary of Merodach-Baladan II and Sargon II, and the Shutur-Nahhunte of this seal. For Lambert, the reign of Shutur-Nahhunte, otherwise unattested at Susa by epigraphic finds, should be situated in the brief interval following the destruction of Nineveh and the conquest of Susiana by Nebuchadnezzar II, after which, in his view, Susa became a Babylonian dominion (Lambert 1967: 51). In this Amiet and Lambert have been followed by Vallat (1996d: 393), who attributed to Shutur-Nahhunte the two stone horns from Susa, each over a metre in length, which are described as 'horns of alabaster' in the text engraved upon them. These were for the decoration of the temple of Pinigir (Vallat 1990b; 1995b).

In Vallat's opinion (Vallat 1996d: 393), Shutur-Nahhunte was succeeded by Hallutash-Inshushinak, a king known only from a single series of inscribed bricks which commemorate his rebuilding of the temple of Inshushinak (Malbran-Labat 1995: 136–7) and a fragmentary glazed knob which may have come from the same structure (Steve 1987: 50–1). There he calls himself 'son of Huban-tahra, enlarger of the kingdom of Anshan and Susa'. Vallat further suggests that Hallutash-Inshushinak was succeeded by Atta-hamiti-Inshushinak, with whom we can associate some limestone stele fragments found at Susa (Pl. 8.1) which identify him as 'Atta-hamiti-Inshushinak, son of Hutran-tepti, king of Anshan and Susa' and speak of his work on a project begun by a king Halkatash in the time of the Atta-hamiti-Inshushinak's father (König 1965: 173, n. 5, §86). In one of the fragments Atta-hamiti-Inshushinak says that he 'loved' or perhaps chose Susa (König 1965: 174, §87). As for his own father, Hutran-tepti, he is otherwise unattested in Assyrian records, while Halkatash, one of Atta-hamiti-Inshushinak's predecessors, was tentatively identified by König with one of the earlier Elamite kings named Humban-haltash (König 1965: 173, n. 5).

Archaeologically and epigraphically, evidence assignable to Neo-Elamite IIIB is much more abundant, both at Susa and elsewhere. Excavations at the turn of the century on the Acropole at Susa suggest that however badly damaged the area was by Assurbanipal's soldiers, the area must have been re-settled within a few decades of the Assyrian onslaught. In 1901 a cache of 298 economic texts (Scheil 1907) was discovered on the Acropole, in proximity to but slightly higher than (Amiet 1973b: 4, n.1) the small temple to Inshushinak built by Shutruk-Nahhunte II (Amiet 1967a: 27–9) discussed above. Later, an additional text belonging to the same group was also discovered, bring-

Plate 8.1 Restored stele of Atta-hamiti-Inshushinak (Sb 16, 93.5×65.6 cm) from Susa. © Musée du Louvre, Antiquités Orientales

ing the total to 299 (Scheil 1911: 89ff.). Most of these texts 'deal with textiles, leather items, and tools, weapons, utensils, and vessels of bronze, iron, silver, and gold' (Harper, Aruz and Tallon 1992: 268). A number of points about these texts deserve brief mention.

To begin with, Vallat has suggested that the Huban-kitin mentioned in one of these texts (MDP 9: no. 5) may well be the same Huban-kitin identified as the son of Shutur-Nahhunte on the cylinder seal (Fig. 8.7.4) described above (Vallat 1995b; 1996d: 389). He also suggests that the Ummanunu (for the name as an Elamite hypocoristicon [i.e. nickname], attested also at Persepolis, see Zadok 1983b: 97, 100 and n. 138) mentioned in MDP 9: no. 165 is the Ummanini (reading uncertain) named as the father of Shilhak-Inshushinak II on an inscribed bronze door socket (König 1965: §78) from Susa which was made for use in a temple dedicated to the goddess DILBAT. Further, if this is correct, then it situates not only Shilhak-Inshushinak II in time, but also his son, Tepti-Huban-Inshushnak (*not* Inshushinak), known from a series of inscribed bricks and several stele fragments found in the early excavations at Susa (König 1965: §79–85). In two of his texts, Tepti-Huban-Inshushnak refers to campaigns against the lands/peoples of Balahute and Lallar (König 1965: §79, 80). Although neither has been located conclusively, both have been located generally in the region of Luristan or the lower Zagros ranges below the region of the Lower Zab (Vallat 1993a: 33, 155 with prev. lit.).

This sort of military activity, combined with the building or rebuilding of shrines to Inshushinak, Pinigir and possibly Umu (unless a model like the Middle-Elamite *sit shamshi* is referred to in the Acropole text Scheil 1907: no. 49, l. 11, rather than a true 'ziggurat'; see Vallat 1988c) at Susa (e.g. König 1965: §80, 82–4), is certainly suggestive of an Elamite renaissance free from Babylonian interference. In addition to the references to hostile relations with Balahute and Lallar, the Acropole texts also mention many other peoples and toponyms including Unsak (Vallat 1992), Zari (MDP 9: nos. 48, 71, 178), Huhnur (Vallat 1993a: 101–2), Ayapir (modern Izeh-Malamir) (Vallat 1993a: 26–7), and Parsirra or Persia (Vallat 1993a: 209–11). Vallat has suggested that whereas some of these names, such as Persia, Huhnur, or Ayapir, are preceded by the determinative AŠ, used to designate geographical names in Elamite, others are preceded by the determinative BE, used to qualify personal names, followed by a patronym (i.e. BE-name-patronym). In line with the practice of name-giving amongst the tribes of southern Mesopotamia during the post-Kassite period, Vallat suggests that names preceded by BE might refer to nomadic tribes (Vallat 1992; on BE, see Vallat 1997e: 260). Whether or not some of these were Old Persian speakers is not clear, but certainly there is a handful of personal names which are Iranian or Iranian-related (e.g. Bama, Irmakka, Kitikka, Pirna, Unukaka and possibly Kunaramika) in the Acropole texts (Zadok 1984a: 388).

The Acropole texts are also important in that over a third of them bear cylinder seal impressions, and these have been the basis for the definition of a stylistic group by Amiet (1973b: 6ff.). Based on the inscriptions on these seals, Steve has assigned four of the Acropole seals to his Neo-Elamite IIIB phase (Steve 1992: 22). These are shown in Fig. 8.8. Fig. 8.8.1 shows a seal impression attested on over 100 tablets. It is a

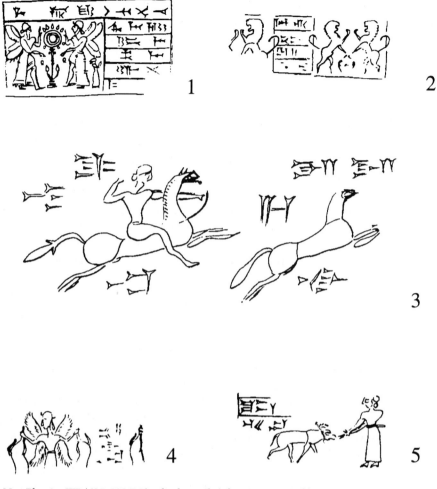

Figure 8.8 Neo-Elamite IIIB (605–539 BC) cylinder seals (after Amiet 1973b).

Babylonian scene consisting of two winged genii flanking an ornamental tree surmounted by a solar disc, with a prayer invoking Marduk and Nabu in Babylonian on
the right. A pair of rearing lions decorate a seal (Fig. 8.8.2) which once belonged to an
individual whose name began Huban-. . . , while the seal of one Kitdada (Fig. 8.8.3)
shows a mounted bowman in pursuit of an equid. The cuneiform signs of the text are
placed in an almost random manner throughout the open spaces, above and below the
figures. Amiet has pointed to the presence of generally comparable galloping riders on
two sealed jar stoppers from Nineveh (Herbordt 1992: Taf. 31.1–2), noting further that
the recent suggestion of a date for them in the reign of Assurbanipal is based on purely
circumstantial evidence (Amiet 1994c: 63). Finally, a robed figure shown feeding a
quadruped adorns yet another seal used on an Acropole text (Fig. 8.8.5).

In 1909, during soundings on the Apadana mound beneath the palace of Darius, R. de

Mecquenem recovered seven more tablets which Scheil immediately compared to those found on the Acropole (Scheil 1911: 89), but whether this area, too, was re-occupied prior to the reign of Darius I is open to question since neither stratigraphic nor architectural evidence of Neo-Elamite occupation has been published and there seems to be a gap in the Apadana sequence between the middle of the second millennium and the Achaemenid period (Steve and Gasche 1990: 28). Based on the Elamite text of the seal used on one of these texts (Scheil 1911: no. 302), Steve has assigned it to the Acropole group defined by Amiet. The scene on the seal impression (Fig. 8.8.4) shows a winged genie or deity in a master-of-animals attitude with two quadrupeds suspended upside down from his outstretched hands. An omen text discovered by de Mecquenem (Scheil 1917) has also been assigned to the Neo-Elamite IIIB phase by Vallat (1996d: 386).

After the interruption of work at Susa occasioned by World War II was over, R. Ghirshman undertook excavations just to the east of the old city in an area which the French excavators dubbed the Ville des Artisans, the largest of the mounds of which Susa is comprised (Stronach 1974: 244 and n. 53). There, excavations revealed a portion of a multi-roomed building, badly damaged by later Parthian graves and Islamic pits (Ghirshman 1954: 14). Although the number of epigraphic finds here was minimal, an Elamite tablet was discovered in a large jar in Level I, and this text, along with two others (one from Level II and one found near the surface) share a proper name (Tal-lak-ku-tur), certain phraseology, and orthographic peculiarities (Paper 1954) with the Acropole and Apadana texts mentioned above (Steve 1992: 22), as well as with 25 fragmentary Elamite letters found at Nineveh (Weissbach 1902; Walker 1980: 79). Although it was once suggested that the Nineveh texts could have originated at Malamir and not in Assyria (Vallat 1988b), this seems highly unlikely (Reade 1992b; Dalley 1993: 143). Other onomastic and grammatical similarities suggest that the inscribed bronze plaque from Persepolis mentioned above (Cameron 1957), the rock inscriptions of one Hanni, carved at Shikaft-e Salman near Malamir (Stolper 1987–90), and an Elamite letter from Argishti-henele in Armenia (Vallat 1997e: 268) are roughly contemporary. As Vallat noted in discussing the Acropole texts, the language used in these inscriptions is no longer 'classic Elamite' but not yet 'Achaemenid Elamite' (Vallat 1996d: 386). Vallat has dated all of this material to the Neo-Elamite IIIB period, i.e. 585–539 BC (Vallat 1996c).

The precise dating of these texts, however, is problematic. Thus, whereas Weissbach assumed a *terminus ante quem* prior to 612 BC (when Nineveh was destroyed by the Median-Babylonian coalition) for the texts from Nineveh (Weissbach 1902: 170–1; see also Cameron 1936: 169; Amiet 1973b: 5), de Miroschedji argued that the Nineveh letters were the products of the royal Elamite chancellery at Susa which must have been reconstituted at the latest by 625 BC (when, as noted above, Nabopolassar restored the cult statues of Elamite divinities to Susa) and continued to exist until the Persian conquest of 539 BC (de Miroschedji 1982: 62). It is somewhat circular, however, to suggest that the revival of an Elamite kingdom at Susa after Assurbanipal's campaign of 646 BC provides evidence for the continued occupation of Nineveh after the Median-Babylonian destruction of 612 BC (Dalley 1993: 143).

Finally, during the most recent excavations at Susa by the French mission, de Miroschedji excavated a brick tomb (locus 693) in Ville Royale II which, based on parallels between bronze vessels found there (de Miroschedji 1981b: Fig. 40) and those from a tomb at Arjan (see below), should probably be assigned to the Neo-Elamite IIIB phase. The same tomb also yielded two small iron pins, the heads of which were covered with bitumen compound and then wrapped in gold or electrum foil (de Miroschedji 1990: 184; Connan and Deschesne 1996: 371–2). These have close parallels amongst the material excavated by Vanden Berghe in an Iron Age III tomb at Karkhai in Luristan (Vanden Berghe 1973: 25–9).

One Elamite town which was occupied during the late Neo-Elamite period and which may almost be considered a western borough of Susiana is Avva (var. ^{URU}A-ma-a, ^{URU}A-ma-te, ^{URU}A-ú-a; Ivvah of 2 Kings 17:24), a place located on the Uqnu river (the modern Karkheh) in Khuzistan, according to Sargon II's annals. Texts written at Avva in the mid-sixth century BC are known from Nippur, and although the population was probably West Semitic, judging by the onomastic evidence, the Avvites deported to Samaria by the Assyrians are known to have worshipped the Elamite deities Tartaq (Dirtaq) and Nibhaz (Ibnahaza). At least some Avvites had hybrid Aramaean-Elamite names, such as Sham-Agunu (Zadok 1977: 120–1).

Late Elamite manifestations outside of Susiana and Anshan

The toponyms mentioned in the Acropole texts from Susa, coupled with Elamite inscriptions and inscribed objects found outside of the traditional heartlands of Susiana and Fars, all point to the persistence of an Elamite cultural *koiné* throughout much of western Iran following the Assyrian conquest of Susiana and prior to the rise of the Achaemenids. We turn now to an examination of the most important of these remains.

As noted in Chapter 7, the relief known as Kul-e Farah I dates to the Neo-Elamite period. A carved panel *c.* 1.10–1.30 m high and 1.66 m long, Kul-e Farah I is dominated by the large figure of Hanni (1.18 m tall), facing right, who wears a long, embroidered garment, with his arms bent and hands clasped in prayer over his chest (Vanden Berghe 1963a: Pl. X). Behind him are two officials, the chief minister of the army, Shutruru, above (.38 m tall; measurements taken from de Waele 1989: 29) and his vizier or cup-bearer, Shutrurura, below (.47 m tall), each of whom is identified by carved epigraphs. The former holds a bow in his left hand and carries a quiver on his belt, while the latter holds his hands in an attitude of prayer much like Hanni. The right side of the panel is made up of two separate scenes. The upper one consists of three musicians wearing long garments, processing towards the right. The two towards the 'front' of this line (i.e. to the right) each carry a harp. A triangular harp with four strings is held vertically by the first harpist, while the second carries a harp with nine strings horizontally. The two harpists are accompanied by a musician carrying a square tambourine. Below we see several 'snapshots' relating to a sacrifice. A priest appears to be throwing something (e.g. incense) on an altar, while two men lead a bovid forward towards him, one grasping the animal's horns and the other prodding him from behind. Another individual accompanying a zebu bull is shown above the priest, while to the left of him are three ram carcasses and their severed heads (de Waele 1989: 30).

The upper part of Kul-e Farah I is covered with a twenty-four line inscription (König 1965: §75; Hinz 1962), carved after the figures had been completed, while the individuals depicted are identified by short epigraphs written over their garments or just to their sides. The contents of the principal text may be summarized as follows. The text opens (§1–6) with an invocation of Elamite deities including Tepti, Tirutur of Shilhite (the deity to whom the Kul-e Farah sanctuary was principally dedicated), Napir, Shimut and Huban. This is followed by the author's introduction of himself in the first person (§7) as Hanni, son of Tahhi, enlarger of his realm (cf. the earlier Elamite titulary), who dedicated the relief to Tirutur (§8–9). The following passages (§10–15) are unclear but contain a reference to a king Shutur-Nahhunte, son of Indada (§14), who may have been Hanni's patron since he himself never refers to himself as king (Stolper 1987–90: 277). The following passages (§16–28) have generally been taken as an account of the offering ceremony depicted on the relief, but Stolper believes they may instead summarize Hanni's exploits, which included the suppression of a revolt in Shilhite (§16–17), the capture of twenty rebellious chieftains (§18), the erection of a temple at Ayapir (§18) and the dedication of booty or prisoners resulting from the suppression of the revolt (§23–4). Mention of a second revolt (§25) followed by the capture and possible dedication of more prisoners (§27–8) seem to follow. The text concludes with a request for divine protection of the text and relief (§29, 36), and a curse on those who would seek to damage them (§30–5).

As noted above, the reliefs at Shikaft-e Salman are thought by Amiet to date to the time of Shutruk-Nahhunte I in the Middle Elamite period, although Hanni superimposed inscriptions of his own on them. These vary in both their 'form and contents' from the text at Kul-e Farah I, 'but there is much overlapping detail' (Stolper 1987–90: 278). For example, Hanni mentions his intention of creating images of not only himself but his wife Huhun and his children at Tarrisha, which some scholars take to be the ancient Elamite name of Shikaft-e Salman itself. The text at Shikaft-e Salman III also stresses the role of Masti, 'mistress of Tarrisha', as opposed to Kul-e Farah I where Tirutur of Shilhite was seemingly the most important deity invoked.

Turning now to the area of Behbehan, a stone chamber tomb (Fig. 8.9) of the late Neo-Elamite period was discovered at Arjan by the banks of the Marun river in 1982 (Alizadeh 1985a). In addition to a number of metal vessels with parallels in tomb 693 at Susa (Carter 1994b: 73) and an intricate bronze stand found clustered at one end of the tomb (Stronach 1997: 41), the chamber contained a bronze bath-tub coffin containing a gold object of uncertain function (Fig. 8.10) bearing the Elamite inscription 'Kidin-Hutran, son of Kurlush' (Vallat 1984b: 1). The gold object bears an engraved scene of two rearing griffins which recalls the common motif of rearing animals on Neo-Elamite III cylinder seals. Indeed, Vallat has observed that the personal name Kurlush is also attested on one of the Neo-Elamite IIIA seals (Fig. 8.7.2) and on four of the Neo-Elamite IIIB Acropole texts (Scheil 1907: nos. 16, 50, 127, 276), suggesting that, in view of the rarity of the name Kurlush, which is otherwise known only from a pair of much later

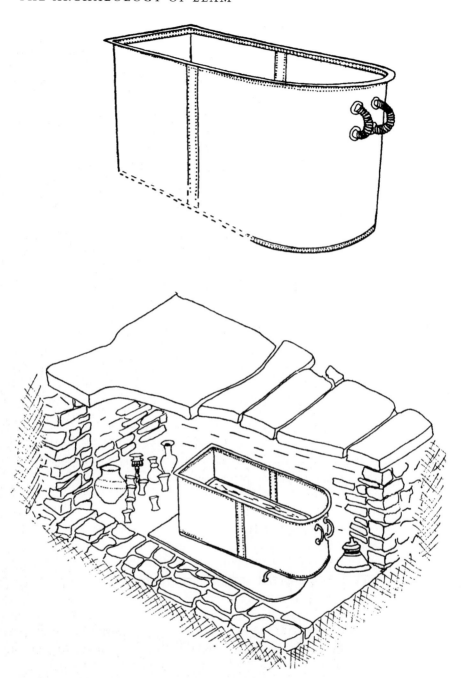

Figure 8.9 The coffin and tomb of Arjan (after Alizadeh 1985a: Fig. 2).

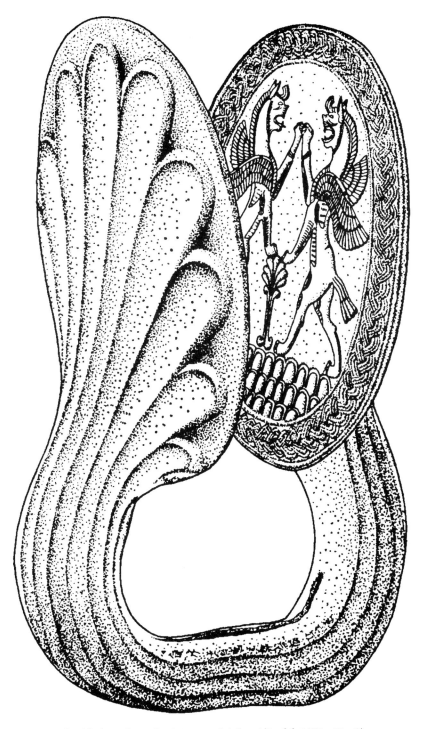

Figure 8.10 A decorated gold object from the Arjan tomb (after Alizadeh 1985a: Fig. 3).

texts found at Persepolis (Hallock 1969: 716, PF 98:3 and Fort. 6770:3; see also Mayrhofer 1973: 183), all of these references may be to one and the same individual (Vallat 1984b: 4).

If we move now to the northwest of Susa into the Zagros, excavations by E.F. Schmidt in the 1930s brought to light several more cylinder seals comparable in style to those discussed above. At Surkh Dum-i Luri, a sanctuary was uncovered and at Chigha Sabz, a Bronze Age mound was sounded in which an Iron Age hoard had been buried. Each deposit yielded a cylinder seal showing a mounted rider (Van Loon 1988; Schmidt, Van Loon and Curvers 1989: Pls. 243.153 and 259c; see also Amiet 1994c: 63), generally comparable to those found on Neo-Elamite IIIB seals.

Moving to the northeast, we have a remarkable collection of hammered silver vessels and animals allegedly excavated in the 1930s in a cave near Khorramabad (Mahboubian 1995), some of which bear Elamite inscriptions. Four individuals, including Ampirish, Unzi-kilik, Anni-Shilha, and Unsak, are called LUGAL Sa-ma-tir$_e$-ra, i.e. 'king of Samati', while several others, including Aksi-marti, Pirri, Anni-ilha (the king or another by the same name?) and Umba-dudu, appear in the Acropole texts from Susa. While some or all of these could be homonyms, the likelihood is lessened by the fact that one of the Acropole texts in which some of these names occur (Scheil 1907: no. 94) identifies the individuals in question as coming from Samati (Vallat 1996c). A reference to the goddess Dilbat also provides a link with both the Kul-e Farah I inscription and the Acropole texts from Susa. Although this material comes from an area which has traditionally been assigned to 'Media', the use of Elamite and the overwhelmingly Elamite nature of the personal names suggests that this was an area of Elamite cultural and linguistic influence.

The fate of the Elamites

Earlier in this chapter we discussed the problematic issue of the identity of Kurash, king of Parsumash, and whether or not he can be identified with Cyrus I. Part of the problem arises from the fact that a cylinder seal used on some of the Achaemenid tablets from Persepolis (Fig. 9.10) has an inscription which names its owner as 'Kurash, the Anshanite, son of Teispes', and this has always been taken to be Cyrus I. Thus, would Kurash the Anshanite and Kurash, king of Parsumash, be likely to occur as alternate names for the same individual? One point against such an assumption is the fact that the seal of Kurash shows a mounted rider very much in the style of the Neo-Elamite IIIB glyptic discussed above, which, if correctly dated, must be considerably later than the time of Assurbanipal, with whom Kurash of Parsumash was contemporary (de Miroschedji 1985: 286; Vallat 1996d: 392).

Be that as it may, the mere fact that Kurash, son of Teispes, identifies himself in Elamite as an Anshanite, just as Cyrus the Great identifies all of his ancestors in the so-called Cyrus Cylinder from Babylon as 'kings of Anshan' (Dandamaev 1976: 92), is an intriguing indication that the Achaemenid empire, however 'Persian' it may have been, in one sense evolved from the Neo-Elamite social, cultural, linguistic and perhaps even political milieu, or at least made the claim of Anshanite ancestry. Without denying the ethnic and linguistic identity of the early Persians, Amiet has nevertheless suggested that the Elamites *became* Persian by a process of acculturation, a process which he refers to as the ethnogenesis of the Persians via Elamite acculturation (Amiet 1992a: 93), while Steve suggests that centuries of symbiosis in highland Fars effected a fusion of Elamite and Persian ethnic elements (Steve 1991: 7).

The rise of the Achaemenids began in Anshan at a time when, as we have seen, numerous petty kings held sway in other parts of western Iran, including Shutur-Nahhunte and his vassal (?) Hanni around Malamir, the kings of Samati near Khorramabad, and perhaps Ummanunu in Susiana (Vallat 1996d: 393). But one should not overestimate the power of these 'kingdoms'. Certainly we read of no 'conquest' of Elam, Susa, Samati, Shilhite or Ayapir by the Persians in the same sense as we hear of the conquest of Media and the removal of gold and silver from Ecbatana to Anshan *c.* 550 BC (Grayson 1975: 106; Dandamaev 1976: 94). Perhaps this indicates that the Elamites and Persians were much more closely bound than otherwise thought and should not be treated as opponents. The onomastic evidence from Susa cited above shows that Persian speakers were present there by the mid-sixth century BC, and some were present in Babylonia (Zadok 1976a: 66–7) and Assyria (Zadok 1979a: 299) as well in this period. The presence of Persians amongst the individuals mentioned in the Acropole texts, most of which deal with craft production, should warn us against accepting Herodotus' simplistic division of Persians into nomads and agriculturalists. The symbiotic existence of Persians and Elamites, whether in Susiana or in the highlands, had acculturated the Persians to Elamite and, via the Elamites, Babylonian and Assyrian culture as much as an acculturation of Elamites was effected by their contact with the Persians (Briant 1984: 95). In this sense, the rise of the Achaemenids was more comparable to a change in political leadership via an *ethno-classe dominante* (Briant 1990: 53) in an area long accustomed to the institutions of kingship and statehood, than it was to the ascendancy of a 'new' tribal group over an 'exhausted' civilization. As de Miroschedji has rightly observed, the arrival of Cyrus the Great in Susiana, which must have occurred by 540 BC, considering that Babylon was taken in 539 BC, may have appeared to a lowland Elamite as nothing more than the restoration of the old kingdom of Anshan and Susa (de Miroschedji 1985: 305). To speak of Cyrus' arrival as a conquest (e.g. Dandamaev 1993b: 518), however, is in all likelihood wrong. The route to Babylon may have led through Susa, but Susa was already part of the Elamo-Persian world and hardly a hostile entity.

Date	Lowlands	Highlands	Mesopotamia	'Elam'
1000–744 BC	Neo-Elamite I period, sporadic occupation at Susa	little or no evidence of occupation in Fars; beginnings of Assyrian aggression in western Zagros	Bazi, 'Elamite' and mixed dynasties in Babylonia; rise of Assyria in north	Elamite troops in Babylonia, envoy in Assyria suggests some political power recognized in Mesopotamia
743–646 BC	Neo-Elamite II period, Susa functions as main cult centre and capital; numerous smaller towns and cities in Khuzistan mentioned in Assyrian annals along Elamite-Babylonian frontier; Madaktu called a 'royal city' by Assyrians as well as Susa; massive Assyrian assault on Susa razed the city in 646 BC	continued Assyrian aggression in western Iran; Anshan mentioned rarely; appearance of highland leaders with Persian names, e.g. Kurash, at end of period signals growing importance of Persians perhaps linked to decline of Elam under constant Assyrian pressure	Assyrian campaigning in and eventual control over Babylonia; guerrilla war in south waged by Chaldaeans; commemoration of campaigns against Elam on Assyrian palace reliefs	Elamites in league with Chaldaeans; succession of kings based at Susa bore brunt of Assyrian aggression; attempts by Assyrians to install Elamite puppet rulers
645–539 BC	Neo-Elamite III period, restoration of Susian gods following Babylonian expulsion of Assyrians in 626 BC; Susa under Babylonian control? Median influence at Susa? appearance of Shutur-Nahhunte, late Neo-Elamite texts containing Iranian names	growing power of Medes and Persians; appearance of Elamo-Persian glyptic; rich tomb at Arjan; reliefs at Kul-e Farah, Shikaft-e Salman, petty kingdoms in highlands? Elamite influence in Luristan; fusion of Elamite and Persian ethnic elements in highlands	expulsion of Assyrians, appearance of Neo-Babylonian dynasty	Elamite revival in sixth century, use of title 'king of Anshan and Susa', toponyms in Elamite texts from Susa suggestive of multiple centres of power

9

ELAM IN THE ACHAEMENID EMPIRE

The emergence of the Persians as a major power in western Iran must have been aided by the sustained Assyrian assault on Elam in the seventh century BC. But it is important to stress that, notwithstanding the severity of Assyrian aggression against Elam, the Elamites were neither annihilated nor reduced to a state of utter insignificance. Although it is not uncommon for historians and archaeologists to ignore the role of Elam and the Elamite population in the emergence of the better known Achaemenid Persian empire (539–331 BC), there is much to say on this matter. The very facts that Cyrus the Great established his capital in the heartland of what had been Anshan, that Elamite was the language of the earliest Achaemenid inscriptions and the language of the thousands of administrative texts found at Darius' city of Persepolis, that a number of Elamite rulers tried to rebel against Persian authority, and that Elamite deities continued to be worshipped in the Persian-controlled cities, point to the continuation of an Elamite tradition in southwestern Iran long after Cyrus came to power. Nor was Susa, an important city throughout all earlier periods of Elamite history, neglected by the Achaemenids, and it is from Susa that much of the archaeological evidence of the period comes. The survival of Neo-Elamite iconography on cylinder seals used in the Achaemenid period is another phenomenon which attests to the survival and transformation of Elamite identity in the Persian period, as does the use of military equipment specifically designated 'Elamite' or 'Susian' at this time. In the late Achaemenid period, at the time of Alexander the Great's conquest of the Persian empire, we see that the highlands of southwestern Iran were inhabited by a tribal group known as the Uxians, who may well mask the Elamites by another name.

Introduction

The so-called Dynastic Prophecy (II 17–21) made the following prediction concerning the fall of the Neo-Babylonian state: 'A king of Elam will arise, the sceptre . . . [he will take?]. He will remove him (the preceding king) from his throne and [. . .]. He will take the throne and the king whom he will have removed? <from> the throne [. . .], the king of Elam will cha[nge] his place and settle him in another land' (Beaulieu 1989: 231). The 'king of Elam' in question, Cyrus the Great (559–530 BC), called 'king of Anshan' in the Cyrus Cylinder (Lecoq 1997: 182–3) and 'king of Parsu' in Chronicle 7 (Grayson 1975: 107), fulfilled this prophecy in 539 BC with his conquest of Babylonia. In this chapter we shall consider what became of Elam (Fig. 9.1) in the wake of this momentous alteration in the balance of power in Western Asia.

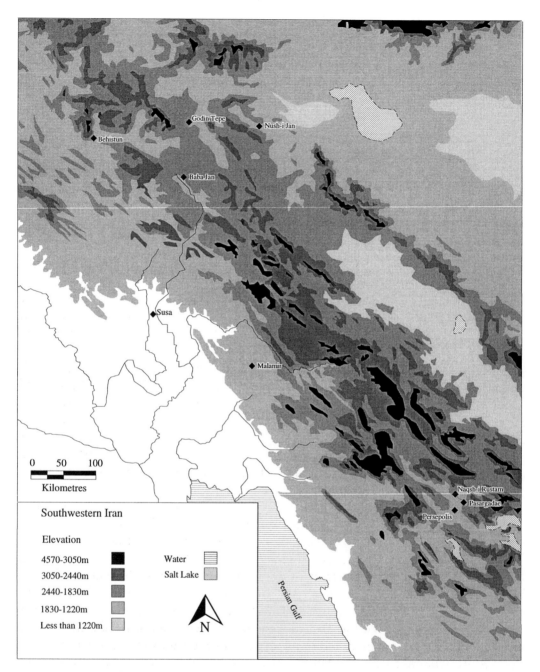

Figure 9.1 Map of southwestern Iran showing the principal sites mentioned in Chapter 9.

Elam in the early Achaemenid period

As discussed in the preceding chapter, there is much evidence, both archaeological and literary/epigraphic, to suggest that the rise of the Persian empire witnessed the fusion of Elamite and Persian elements already present in highland Fars. The very fact that Anshan was the source of the new polity no doubt meant that the differences between Persians and Elamites were fast becoming blurred during the course of the sixth century. In fact, as shown in the previous chapter, 'Elam' did not exist as a political unit at this date. Rather, sub-areas of what had formerly been the kingdom of Anshan and Susa, and perhaps some districts which had always lain outside the bounds of that polity, were peopled by Elamites (i.e. Elamite speakers) who were in no sense politically unified. This was the milieu in which Cyrus, king of Anshan/Parsu/Elam, created a new state. In southwestern Iran, Cyrus was able to exploit a power vacuum where no Elamite state of any substance had existed since the time of Assurbanipal, for it is by no means clear that a Median empire ruled by Astyages held control of Elam (contra Petit 1990: 28; see also Sancisi-Weerdenburg 1988).

After entering Babylon, one of Cyrus' first acts, according to the so-called 'Cyrus Cylinder' from Babylon, was the restoration of a number of plundered cult statues to the sanctuaries in which they had originally stood. One site to which cult statues were repatriated was Susa (Beaulieu 1989: 228; Lecoq 1997: 184). While nothing suggests that Cyrus undertook any major building works there (Briant 1996: 98; see generally Haerinck 1997: 28), the continued importance of the ancient city cannot be doubted, for it functioned as an administrative capital from the reign of Darius (Boucharlat 1997: 57) onward and may have already functioned as such under Cyrus. Indeed, Strabo says that 'the Persians and Cyrus, after mastering the Medes, saw that their native land was situated rather on the extremities of their empire, and that Susa was farther in and nearer to Babylonia and the other tribes, and therefore established the royal seat of their empire at Susa' (*Geog.* XV.3.2).

In his Persian homeland, however, Anshan lay uninhabited, an unoccupied ruin throughout the Neo-Elamite period (Sumner 1988b: 314). It is hardly surprising therefore that Cyrus founded a new 'Anshanite' capital at Pasargadae (Stronach 1978; 1997: 42ff.) on the Murghab plain (Pl. 9.1), slightly less than 40 km northeast of Tal-i Malyan. It was at Pasargadae, Strabo tells us (*Geog.* XV.3.8), that Cyrus had vanquished his Median rival Astyages, and in the Greek geographer's opinion this was Cyrus' justification for locating his new capital there. But Briant (1996: 98) points out that this was certainly not the last time the Persians fought the Medes and instead attributes the location of Cyrus' new capital to the importance of the Pasargadai, a tribal section of the Persians considered the 'most noble' by Herodotus (I.125). This argument is fragile, however, particularly if F.C. Andreas was correct in suggesting that Herodotus' use of Pasargadai as a tribal name was an error and should have simply read Parsa, i.e. the term 'Persian' used by Darius I to describe himself in his grave inscription at Naqshh-i Rustam (Andreas 1904: 96; but see also Herzfeld 1908: 28; for the text, see Kent 1953: 138, DNa). Be that as it may, it is scarcely surprising that the establishment of a new

Plate 9.1 A view over the site of Pasargadae.

royal seat was accompanied by the growth of settlement in the area, and even the Kur River basin, where little or no sedentary occupation had existed for centuries, was soon dotted with a series of new hamlets, villages, and towns (Sumner 1988b).

Because of a dearth of settlement in Fars during the Neo-Elamite period we cannot look to that era to find the antecedents of the monumental stone platform of Tall-i Takht on which Cyrus intended to construct his residential palace, or the tomb in which he was finally laid to rest after falling at the hands of the Massagetae in what is today northern Uzbekistan (Cyrus' tomb may have antecedents in some unpublished Neo-Elamite tombs near Kazerun reported on by A.A. Sarfaraz (K. Abdi, pers. comm.)). Nor does a wider search in Luristan or northwestern Iran provide us with any answers. Indeed, the lack of Neo-Elamite architecture in the region is really of little consequence for our understanding of Pasargadae because, as both Nylander and Stronach have emphasized, the masons' marks, marginally drafted and pecked limestone masonry, and dovetail clamps (Pl. 9.2), not to mention the overall design of the terrace walls, point undisputably to Lydia and Ionia as the source of both inspiration and masons (Nylander 1970; Stronach 1978: 20–3 and his discussion of Darius' later use of 'Ionians and Sardians' as stone masons at Susa). Thus, Elamite input in this new mode of imperial architecture would seem to have been singularly lacking. Whether or not the tomb of Cyrus, while modelled on Lydian funerary architecture (Stronach 1978: 42), was laid

Plate 9.2 Detail of clamp holes in stone masonry at Pasargadae.

out using the 52.5 cm long unit of measurement employed in the Middle Elamite zig-gurat of Choga Zanbil (Trümpelmann 1976: 325), it must remain a moot point.

At an entirely different level, that of imperial administration, it is important to note that all of the earliest satraps known from the reigns of Cyrus and his son Cambyses bore Old Persian names (Briant 1996: 93). As we have seen in earlier cases, the ethnic-ity of a person cannot necessarily be determined by the linguistic affiliation of his/her name, but the absence of etymologically Elamite names amongst the earliest satraps is striking and, considering the political situation at the time, may probably be taken as a reflection of the fact that trusted, ethnic Persians close to the Great King were employed in satrapal positions rather than non-Persians, e.g. Elamites. Still, one must be very careful here, for a text belonging to the Egibi archive from Babylon which dates to the reign of Cambyses (BM 30704) mentions an Elamite (*^{LÚ}E-la-mu-ú*) who bears an etymologically Iranian name (*Ni-ri-a-bi-ig-nu* or **Narya-bigna*), just as we know of Babylonians who bore Iranian names, e.g. *Ba-ga-'-pa-da* (**Baga-pata*) the son of *Nabu-zera-iqisha* (Zadok 1976a: 74).

Many scholars have noted the absence of all reference to a satrap in Elam during the early years of the Achaemenid empire, and it has been suggested that not until the reign of Darius II do we find a satrap of Elam mentioned in any of the sources (Petit 1990: Annex 2). Josephus (*Ant.* XI.33) refers to 'the governors of Media, the satraps of Persia and the toparchs of the countries from India to Ethiopia, and the generals of the one hundred and twenty-seven satrapies' in the time of Darius I (see also Tarn 1930: 134), but whether we should attach much importance to this is doubtful. Briant, however, has stressed the importance of the fact that, according to Herodotus, Darius was not necessarily the first Achaemenid king to levy taxes or tribute, but rather the first to *fix* the amount to be paid (Briant 1996: 80). As he says, viewed in this light the institution of tribute was not created from scratch by Darius. Rather, the conditions of its perception were profoundly modified (Briant 1996: 81). If this is a correct interpretation, then we must assume that, recorded or not, tribute or taxes were levied upon the ancient territories of Elam beginning already in the reign of Cyrus himself. Certainly Xenophon, in his *Cyropaedia* (VIII.6.10), attributed to Cyrus an order to his satraps to hold court in their satrapies in imitation of the royal Achaemenid court (see also Petit 1990: 147). Furthermore, the *Cyropaedia* includes the following assertion: 'And the institutions which Cyrus inaugurated as a means of securing the Kingdom permanently to himself and the Persians, as has been set forth in the foregoing narrative, these the succeeding kings have preserved unchanged even to this day' (Hirsch 1985: 88). The idealized aspects of Xenophon's work are well known, however, and even if the sentiments often betray concrete knowledge of things Persian, it is hazardous to ascribe such an order to the Achaemenid royal founder, particularly without corroboration from either Old Persian or Greek sources.

Elam in the time of Darius I

The reign of Ka^mbugiya (for the name see Eilers 1964: 211–13; 1974: 5), or Cambyses (530–522 BC) as he is better known (Prášek 1913; Duchesne-Guillemin 1979; Briant 1996: 60ff.), Cyrus' son and successor, was marked by the conquest of Egypt (525–522 BC), largely known to us through the filter of Herodotus. Cambyses' reign was brought to an abrupt end when, having learned of a rebellion led by Gaumata, Cambyses died, probably in Syria, by an accidentally self-inflicted sword wound (thus Herodotus) as he was on his way back to Susa (Dandamaev 1976: 108ff.; Briant 1996: 72).

The rise of Darius (522–486 BC), who presents himself as the restorer of the Achaemenid realm of Cyrus and the slayer of Gaumata, is recounted in the first person in the king's famous, if highly tendentious trilingual (Elamite, Akkadian [Babylonian] and Old Persian) Behistun inscription (for the text, see Kent 1953: 116–34; Von Voigtlander 1978; Schmitt 1990a, 1990b, 1991c; Malbran-Labat 1994; Zawadzki 1996b; Lecoq 1997: 87–96, 187–214; for an extensive analysis of the episode, see Wiesehöfer 1978]. Scholars have long recognized that 'the relief . . . was intended to be the centerpiece of the whole monument' and that the texts were of only secondary importance (Schmitt 1990b: 300), but it was Luschey who first realized that the Elamite texts (beginning with Dba; see Table 9.1, Pl. 9.3, Fig. 9.2), composed early in 519 BC (Schmitt 1990b: 301; see also Borger 1982), predated the Babylonian and Old Persian ones (Luschey 1990: 292). Briant has suggested that Darius may originally have intended that his relief be seen as a continuation of the royal Elamite tradition of carving rock reliefs

Table 9.1. *Development of the Behistun monument*

Stage	Relief	Major inscription	Minor inscription
I	entire relief minus Skunkha, Scythian wearing pointed cap on far right	none	Elamite: DBa
II		1st Elamite: §1–69	Elamite: DBb-j
III		Babylonian: §1–69	Babylonian: DBb-j
IV		Old Persian: §1–70 [Elamite: §70 = DB1]	Old Persian: DBb-j
V	addition of Skunkha	elimination of 1st Elamite; Copy: 2nd Elamite	Elamite and Old Persian: DBk
VI		Old Persian: §71–76 = col. V	
VII		Old Persian: DBa	

Notes:
After Schmitt 1990b: Table 8.

Plate 9.3 The Behistun relief of Darius I.

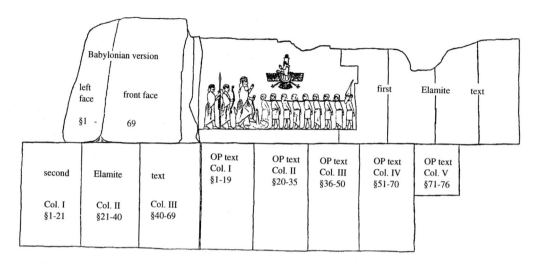

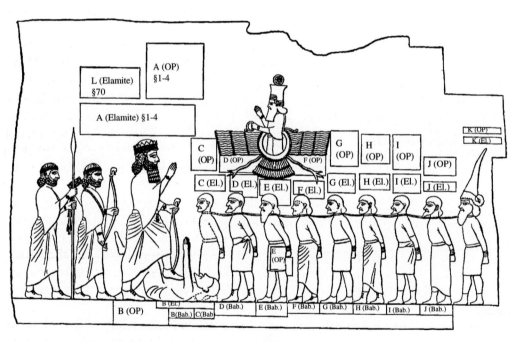

Figure 9.2 The Behistun relief (after King and Campbell Thompson 1907: Pl. VI, XIII; Borger 1982: Abb. 1–2; Schmitt 1990b: Figs. 21–22).

with associated text (Briant 1984: 93), but there is nothing surprising as such about the use of Elamite by someone whose vernacular may have been Old Persian. Walther Hinz had suggested as early as 1938 that the Old Persian cuneiform script did not originate until the reign of Darius, and indeed the studies of Luschey, Hinz and others have confirmed that the Old Persian text, like the Babylonian one before it, was squeezed into space around the main relief which had originally never been intended to hold a written accompaniment to the carved scene itself (Luschey 1968: 90ff.; Hinz 1968: 95). But most importantly, it is clear from §70 of the Old Persian text that 'this was the first time Old Persian cuneiform was used and that the script was created expressly for this purpose' (Schmitt 1990b: 302). In the words of Darius himself, 'Says Darius the king: By the will of Ahura Mazda that is my script, which I made. Also, it was in Aryan, and it was placed (?) on clay tablets and parchment. Also, I made my name (?). Also, I made the lineage. And it was inscribed and was read before me. After that I sent this script everywhere into the lands. The people learned (?) (it)' (Schmitt 1990b: 302).

The Behistun inscription records that after killing Gaumata on 29 September 522 BC and becoming king, Darius faced a series of rebellions throughout the lands formerly loyal to Cyrus. Nine rebellious 'liar kings' are depicted in the relief in the order in which they rebelled. The first region to revolt was, in fact, Elam. The names and ethnicities of the ringleaders in what were actually two separate Elamite revolts illustrate well the fusion of Elamite and Persian elements described above. The first Elamite revolt was led by one Açina (El. Hasina; for the name, see Edel and Mayrhofer 1971: 2; Mayrhofer 1973: 157, 8.487) who 'rose up in Elam', probably in mid-December 522 BC (Schmitt 1990b: 303), declared himself king and incited the Elamites to rebellion (Kent 1953: 120, DB§I.16). Zadok has suggested that Açina may be an Elamite name (Zadok 1976b: 213), although other scholars consider it Indo-European (e.g. Schmitt 1973: 290; Mayrhofer 1973: 157), pointing out that Açina's father, Upadarma, had an Iranian, not an Elamite name (Schmitt 1973: 290). The Babylonian version of Darius' Behistun inscription calls Açina an Elamite, even though it renders his name as At-ri-na in its Median form (Lecoq 1997: 193).

Darius says, 'I sent (a message) to Elam. This Açina was led to me bound [as we see him on the Behistun relief itself]; I slew him' (Kent 1953: 120, DB§I.17). Dandamaev has argued that, unfortunately for them, the Elamites did not realize that a new rebellion was simultaneously breaking out in Babylonia. Had they maintained their resistance to Darius, they might well have won back their former independence (Dandamaev 1976: 128). Instead, they turned over their leader, who was summarily executed.

Revolts by Nidintu-Bel in Babylonia and Fravartish in Media followed that of Açina, and Elam again revolted, this time under 'Martiya, son of Cincikhri – a town by name Kuganaka, in Persia – there he abode. He rose up in Elam; to the people thus he said, "I am Imanish [El. Umman-nuish, see Zadok 1984b: 12], king in Elam" ' (DB §II.22). To judge by his name alone, Martiya was a Persian (Mayrhofer 1973: 193; Schmitt 1973: 290; Lecoq 1997: 195), although there is no reason why an Elamite of this period could not have borne an Old Persian name. The name of his father remains, as ever, etymologically mysterious (Schmitt 1990a: 22). The locus of Martiya's rebellion is also some-thing of a mystery. Darius says that Martiya lived at Kuganaka in Persia, a town plenti-fully attested in the Persepolis Fortification texts (Vallat 1993a: 142). On the other hand, the text says that he revolted 'in Elam'. Because Darius' army was near, 'Thereupon the Elamites were afraid of me; they seized that Martiya who was their chief, and slew him' (DB §II.23). Thus ended a second rebellion against Darius involving Elam.

Finally, during the second or third year of Darius' reign, the Elamites again revolted against the Great King (DB §71). This time they were led by 'a man, an Elamite by the name of Atamaita', probably a shortened form of the Elamite name Atta-hamiti-Inshushinak (see Table 9.6 and Mayrhofer 1973: 131). Darius again sent an army against them, led by the Persian Gaubaruva. After engaging the Elamites in battle, Atamaita was captured, brought before Darius and killed. 'Thereafter, the people [the Elamites] became mine', Darius tells us.

As Briant has noted, it is difficult to assess the severity of the Elamite revolts against Darius, although the fact that in each case the leader was handed over to the Persian king by his Elamite brethren would not suggest that these revolutions were particu-larly popular ones (Briant 1996: 132). For their troubles, both Açina and Martiya were immortalized in the bas-relief at Behistun around which Darius' long account of his rise to power is written. Like their fellow insurgents, the Elamites are shown with a rope around their necks and their hands bound behind their back, standing like chas-tened schoolboys before the larger figure of Darius, who raises his right hand in what appears to be a sign of beneficence (Choksy 1990: 31).

It has long been recognized (e.g. Sarre and Herzfeld 1910: 189; Herzfeld 1920: 16; Porada 1965: 143; Root 1979: 198–201) that the scene at Behistun recalls that of a relief called Sar-i Pol 1 (also known as Sarpol-i Zohab) which is located near Qasr-i Shirin in Luristan (Fig. 9.3), not far from Behistun. The relief depicts the victory and investiture of Anubanini, king of the Lullubi, in the Isin-Larsa period (Hrouda 1976; Vanden Berghe 1983: Fig. 1). Like Anubanini, Darius stands on one of his captives. In place of a hover-ing Inanna/Ishtar, Ahuramazda rises above the Behistun relief in his winged sun-disk. Whereas the enemies of the Lullubi king are each shown naked and with his hands bound behind his back, the opponents of Darius face him clothed, yet bound at the hands and linked by a rope around their necks. These minor differences notwithstand-ing, there is a remarkable similarity between the reliefs, so much so that one assumes Darius and his sculptors had probably seen Sar-i Pol 1.

The first phase of Darius' career was marked by the suppression of all rebels and the conquest of new regions to the east and west. This behind him, he crowned his achieve-ments with an act of administrative and fiscal reform c. 518 BC which solidified the institution of the satrap, the 'protector of power/kingdom/kingship', already nascent under Cyrus and Cambyses (Briant 1992a: 32). Sekunda has pointed out that, 'although both Herodotus and Thucydides use the term "satrapy" they do not use "satrap"', and it is apparently in the lost but excerpted and epitomised work *Persica* by Ctesias of Cnidos, court physician to Artaxerxes II, that *satrap* first occurs in a Greek source (Sekunda 1988: 72; see also Petit 1990: 18). Nevertheless, there is no doubt that Elam was administered within the satrapal system from the time of Darius onward, when

Figure 9.3 The Sar-i Pol 1 relief (after Vanden Berghe 1983: Fig. 1).

the word 'satrap' appears as an Old Persian loanword in Elamite (Stolper, pers. comm.). As Herodotus (III.89) says, after winning his kingdom, Darius 'proceeded to establish twenty governments of the kind which the Persians call satrapies, assigning to each its governor, and fixing the tribute which was to be paid him by the several nations . . . During all the reign of Cyrus, and afterwards when Cambyses ruled, there were no fixed tributes, but the nations severally brought gifts to the king'. According to Herodotus, 'Susa, and the other parts of Kissia, paid three hundred talents. This was the eighth satrapy'. Kissia will be discussed below when we turn to the question of Elamite ethnicity in the Achaemenid period.

Administrative organization in Elam under Darius

As Perrot has stressed, by virtue of the continued use of its language, scribes, adminis-trators and soldiers, Elam and the Elamites played an important role in the reorganiza-tion of the Achaemenid empire effected by Darius the Great (Perrot 1981: 79–80). Let us examine these new administrative developments in their Elamite context.

The administrative structure of the Persian empire is best revealed by the roughly 4500 published tablets written in Elamite (out of a total of c. 30,000 excavated) from E. Herzfeld's excavations in the fortification at Persepolis, the ceremonial and adminis-trative centre founded by Darius I (Hallock 1969; 1977). These texts span the thirteenth to the twenty-eighth year of Darius' reign (509–494 BC), although most of them date to years twenty-two and twenty-three. The mere fact that these texts were written in Elamite rather than Old Persian (thereby transmitting to us important Elamite vocab-ulary from this era; see Hinz 1973: 70–104) is significant testimony of the importance of the Elamite cultural, linguistic and scribal/archival legacy in the Achaemenid era. Statistically speaking, moreover, roughly 10 per cent of the c. 2000 personal names in the Persepolis treasury and fortification texts published as of 1973 can be etymologized as Elamite (Mayrhofer 1973: 310).

Persepolis functioned as a central archive for the satrapies of Persis (Fars, ancient Anshan) and possibly Elam (although it is not impossible that another major archive existed at Susa, Stolper, pers. comm.) in which copies of transactions involving dis-bursements from state supplies were held. While the so-called 'fortification texts' are concerned exclusively with agricultural produce – movement of goods and livestock, rations, receipts, etc. – the later 'treasury texts', which date to the period 492–458 BC, are concerned solely with payments made in silver. Other types of disbursements, e.g. of textiles, clothing or weaponry, are not represented by specific groups of texts but almost certainly existed (Koch 1990: 217). Darius instituted a series of fixed tributary sums, payable in various forms of *naturalia* (e.g. livestock, barley or oil; see Koch 1989: 121) or in precious metals (Stolper, pers. comm.) for each satrapy of the empire (Briant 1992a: 33), and a variety of officials were charged with booking the receipt of that tax or tribute in the Persepolis bureaucracy (Koch 1989: 122ff.). Work projects of various sorts involved the importation of labourers and craftsmen from all over the empire and their stationing in many smaller centres where the need for such manpower arose (Uchitel 1991). Undoubtedly this had an impact on the ethnic make-up of Persis and Elam generally, for the number of workers in such teams often ran into the hundreds (e.g. 547 Egyptian workers mentioned in PF 1557; see Koch 1993: 9).

The satrapy of Elam is named more often than any other satrapy attested in the Persepolis fortification texts (Koch 1993: 8). The residence of the satrap was at Susa, and it was here (Fig. 9.4) that Darius built a palace (Fig. 9.5) as well where he often stayed. Hence, Susa figures in a large number of texts (for full references see Vallat

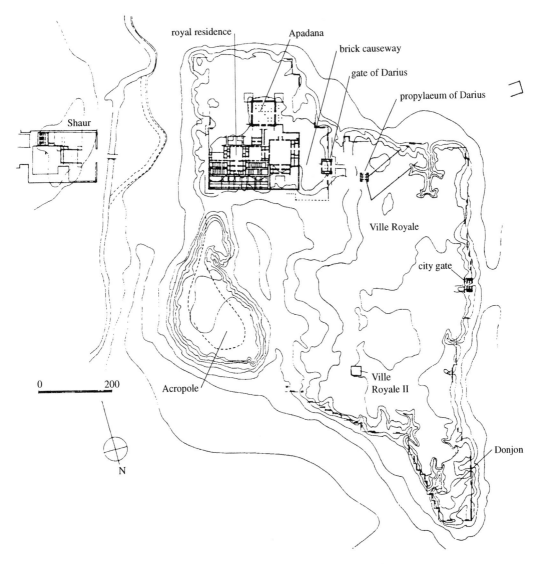

Figure 9.4 Susa during the Achaemenid period (after Perrot 1985: Fig. 1).

1993a: 265–7) which were generated by a variety of different types of transactions (Table 9.2), as does Elam in the sense of Khuzistan (Table 9.3). Naturally, the king's presence insured heavy traffic along the Persepolis-Susa highway (Koch 1986) and the frequent attestation of places in Elam in the fortification archive, most of which cannot be identified (Hinz 1973: 77–80; Sumner 1986b; Koch 1990:156–216). Susa was, moreover, the eastern terminus of the so-called 'Royal Road' which ran all the way to Sardis in Lydia and served as the main east-west route across the empire (Sumner 1986b: 17; Briant 1991; 1992b; Herrenschmidt 1993a; 1993b). This direct connection with Asia Minor, combined with the historical precedent of Cambyses' use of Greek soldiery, certainly

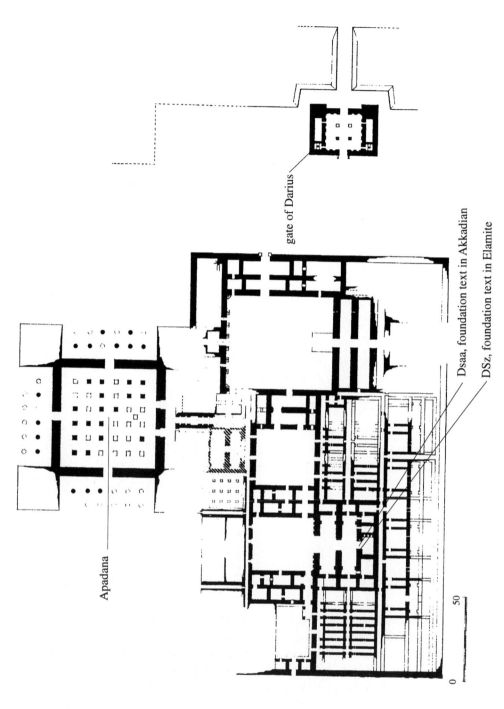

gate of Darius

Dsaa, foundation text in Akkadian

DSz, foundation text in Elamite

Apadana

50

0

Figure 9.5 The palace of Darius at Susa (after Vallat 1986b: Fig. 1).

Table 9.2. *Selection of Persepolis fortification texts of various types mentioning Susa*

Text	Hallock's type	Date	Summary
57	A. transportation of commodities	22nd yr	4 sheep (?) taken as tax from Maturban to Susa
88	B. delivery of commodities	22nd yr	46 *kurrima* [measure of volume equal to 9.7 l (Hinz and Koch 1987/I: 531]] of flour delivered at Susa
318	D. general receipts	23rd yr	65 BAR [dry measure equal to 10 QA or the equivalent of the *kurrima*] of barley loaves received at Susa
737	J. royal provisions	22nd yr	236 *marrish* [liquid measure roughly equal to the *kurrima* and BAR] of wine expended on behalf of Irdabama at Susa
1246	P. daily rations	missing	flour for woodworker, his companions and servants from Susa
1355	Q. travel rations	28th yr	flour for travellers from Persepolis to Susa
1752	S1. regular rations for animals	25th yr	flour for fowls at Susa
1781	S3. travel rations for animals	missing	grain for horses travelling to Susa
2056	miscellaneous: rations for a group	28th yr	grain for men, horses and mules travelling from Areia to Susa

Table 9.3. *Selection of Persepolis fortification texts of various types mentioning Elam*

Text	Type	Date	Summary
1497	travel ration	22nd yr	flour received by Mishshena and 50 workers; M. travelled from Persepolis to Elam
1565	"	missing	wine given to 100 workers who went to Elam (from Persepolis?)
1575	"	21st yr	barley and other cereal products received by 26 workers who went to Elam (from Persepolis?)
1577	ration text	missing	dates given to 108 workers who went to Elam (from Persepolis?)
1780	travel ration for animals	missing	wine received by Sada the horseman who fed [?] it to 11 horses; 'He went from Anshan (and) from Elam' (meaning?)
1858	letter	missing	Mirinzana to Marduka regarding the pending arrival of an official who will 'make the accounts' 'in the area of Elam'

accounted for the ongoing presence of ethnic Greeks in both military and non-military roles at sites like Susa (Seibt 1977). Furthermore, it may have provided the context for the spread of limited amounts of Attic red-figured pottery to Susa in the early fifth century which C. Clairmont believed was brought 'not by traders, but either by Persians or more likely by Greeks who lived at the Persian court working for the Persian kings' (Clairmont 1957: 90).

Darius at Susa

Achaemenid Susa comprised four quarters: the palace on the Apadana mound; a small fortress on top of the Acropole mound, surrounded by a fortification wall uncovered by de Morgan but later removed; a residential quarter in the area known as the 'Ville Royale', surrounded by a monumental brick and earthen glacis some 20 m wide at the base and 10–12 m high; and a large empty space originally dubbed the 'Place d'Armes' by the early excavators (Perrot 1981: 80). Some twenty-four inscriptions and fragments thereof from Susa (Table 9.4) are attributable to Darius (for complete translations, see Lecoq 1997: 231–47; these are referred to as DSa-ab, but the total is less than 28 because in recent years a number have been re-attributed, thus DSh is now assigned to Darius II [=D²Sa], DSr is attributed to Artaxerxes II [=A²Sd], DSx is a fragment of DSe while DSy is part of DSv) and there can be little doubt that the Great King was very active in the ancient city. Like many of his Elamite predecessors, Darius restored buildings which had fallen into disrepair, and he rebuilt the city wall as well (DSe §5), but as P. Calmeyer noted, Darius never speaks of restoring or building any temples, a clear break of tradition with his Elamite predecessors (Calmeyer 1992: 107). Nevertheless, there is clear evidence, as Perrot has stressed, that Darius' engineers largely remodelled the ancient city, re-locating much of the population to the north and east, on the far side of the channel dug to conduct water from the Shaur river.

This major alteration in the physical form of Susa is matched by a demonstrable discontinuity in the material culture of residential, non-royal occupation as well. In the area known as Ville Royale II (levels 5 and 4), de Miroschedji found evidence of a stratigraphic hiatus between the Neo-Elamite and Achaemenid levels with absolutely no trace of any continuity whatsoever between the ceramic traditions of the two eras (de Miroschedji 1987: 35). Because of the absence of epigraphic finds dating to the reigns of Cyrus and/or Cambyses, de Miroschedji suggested that Susa remained culturally an 'Elamite' city until the reign of Darius, when it was transformed into an Achaemenid centre.

If we ignore the mysterious *tachara* (not necessarily a palace, contra Harper, Aruz and Tallon 1992: 216) and several statues, it is the palace Darius had built for himself which demands most attention in considering the Great King's activities at Susa. This is scarcely surprising for, as noted above, Susa was for all intents and purposes just as important as Persepolis. The materials and workmen involved in the construction of Darius' palace at Susa are vividly described in one of his most famous inscriptions, DSf. Assyrians transported cedar from Lebanon to Babylon, whence it was taken to Susa by

Table 9.4. *Summary of Darius' inscriptions from Susa*

Siglum	Object type	Language(s)	Summary/Quotation
DSa	brick	Old Persian	'I am Darius, the great king' . . . his genealogy; 'By the favour of Ahuramazda I have done that which I have done; to every one may it seem excellent'
DSb	brick	Old Pesian	'I am Darius, the great king' . . . his genealogy
DSc	column base	trilingual: Old Persian, Elamite, Babylonian	'I am Darius, the great king' . . . his genealogy
DSd	column base	bilingual: Old Persian, Elamite	'I am Darius, the great king' . . . his genealogy; 'By the favour of Ahuramazda, I made the *tachara'*, a building or construction of unknown type
DSe	stone tablet	trilingual	praise for Ahuramazda 'who created the earth . . . who made Darius king'; I am Darius, the great king . . . his genealogy; enumeration of peoples and countries ruled over by Darius and who brought him tribute: the Mede, Elamite, Parthian, Arian, Bactrian, Sogdian, Chorasmian, Drangianan, Arachosian, Sattagydian, Makan, Gandharan, Indian, Amyrgian Scythian, Tigraxauda Scythian, Babylonian, Assyria, the Arab, Egyptian, Armenian, Cappadocian, Lydian, Greeks by the sea, Scythians across the sea, Thrace, Greek across the sea, Carians; institution of law and order by Darius, restoration of buildings and city wall of Susa; request for Ahuramazda's blessing
DSf	stone and clay tablets, glazed bricks	trilingual	praise for Ahuramazda; 'I am Darius, the great king' . . . his genealogy; acknowledgement of Ahuramazda's beneficence; description of the construction of Darius' palace at Susa by craftsmen from all over the empire and the materials used
DSg	column base	bilingual: Old Persian, Babylonian	'I am Darius, the great king' . . . his genealogy; 'I built this palace with columns'
DSi	column base	bilingual: Old Persian, Elamite	'I am Darius, the great king' . . . his genealogy; 'by the favour of Ahuramazda everything I did (was) good'

DSj	column base	trilingual	'I am Darius, the great king' . . . his genealogy; acknowledgement of Ahuramazda's beneficence; 'By the favour of Ahuramazda, to every one who shall see this palace which has been built by me, may it seem excellent'
DSk	brick	Old Persian	'I am Darius, the great king' . . . his genealogy; acknowledgement of Ahuramazda's beneficence
DSl	brick	Old Persian	'By the favour of Ahuramazda, what I thought I will do, all that was successful for me'
DSm	glazed bricks	trilingual	praise for Ahuramazda 'who created the earth . . . who made Darius king'; I am Darius, the great king . . . his genealogy; enumeration of peoples and countries ruled over by Darius and who brought him tribute, see DSe
DSn	statue fragment	trilingual	'This sculpture Darius the king commanded to make'; request for protection of both Darius and his statue from Ahuramazda
DSo	marble stele fragment	bilingual: Old Persian, Babylonian	declaration by Darius of the beauty of his building at Susa
DSp	marble plaque fragment	Old Persian	'Great Ahuramazda, the greatest of the gods, he created Darius the king; he bestowed upon him the kingdom, good, possessed of good charioteers, of good horses, of good men . . .'
DSq	marble stele fragment	Old Persian	very fragmentary, mentioning Darius
DSs	marble stele fragment	Old Persian	praise for Ahuramazda, request for his protection
DSt	marble stele fragment	Old Persian	praise for Ahuramazda, request for his protection
DSu	marble stele fragment	Elamite	'I am Darius, the great king'; fragmentary
DSv	marble stele fragment	Babylonian	'I am Darius, the great king' . . . his genealogy; fragmentary list of subject peoples
DSw	marble stele fragment	Babylonian	fragmentary acknowledgement of Ahuramazda's favour
DSz	stone stele fragments	bilingual: Old Persian, Elamite	variant of DSf
DSaa	limestone stele frag.	Babylonian	shortened variant of DSf
DSab	statue of Darius	quadrilingual: Old Persian, Elamite, Babylonian, Egyptian	praise of Ahuramazda; 'Here is the statue of stone which the king Darius ordered to be made in Egypt'; genealogy of Darius; request for Ahuramazda's protection

Carians and Ionians. Sissoo wood was imported from northwest India (Gandhara) and Kerman (Karmania) province in southeastern Iran. Gold came from Sardis in Lydia and Bactria in Central Asia, while lapis lazuli and carnelian arrived from Sogdia and turquoise from Chorasmia (on turquoise, see Vallat 1983b).

The stone used to make columns (Pl. 9.4) was quarried at an Elamite village called Abiradu (Elamite *Hapiradush*; Vallat 1993a: 78; for Achaemenid stone quarrying sites, see Huff 1994). The Elamite contribution of raw materials, in this case stone for the columns used in the palace, is echoed in two further texts. When Perrot and his team resumed work on the Apadana, two foundation tablets, one in Elamite (DSz; Vallat 1972; Lecoq 1997: 243–5) and one in Akkadian (DSaa; Vallat 1986b; Lecoq 1997: 245–6) were discovered on either side of the entrance to room 751 of the palace (Perrot 1971:49; Vallat 1971). While the Akkadian text simply lists Elam as one of the twenty-three lands which furnished materials for the decoration of the palace, the Elamite version gives the more precise information that the stone columns came from *Hapiradush*.

In addition to the raw materials just mentioned, skilled craftsmen were imported as well. As Darius says (DSf, §3k), 'The goldsmiths who wrought the gold, those were Medes and Egyptians. The men who wrought the wood, those were Sardians and Egyptians. The men who wrought the baked brick, those were Babylonians. The men who adorned the wall, those were Medes and Egyptians'. As Nylander has stressed, DSf 'was a propagandistic demonstration of the vast resources in materials and manpower of the empire and a glorification of its ruler', not 'a precise and truthful recording of the particulars of the construction process' (Nylander 1974: 317). He has noted, moreover, 'important omissions in the text, such as the Elamites who, of course, must have been employed in great numbers' (see also Stronach 1985: 438). After all, Susa was still an Elamite city and overall Persians must have been in the minority. That Persians were, however, in the majority at the court of Susa is suggested by the onomasticon of the main characters in the Book of Esther, most of whom have Old Iranian or Avestan rather than Elamite names (Zadok 1977; 1986b).

Exactly when Darius began to build his palace at Susa is a question which has troubled a number of scholars. As Briant has stressed, Herodotus' information on Darius is of little chronological value since virtually everything to do with the Achaemenid king is situated by the Greek historian at Susa (Briant 1993). It may be significant that, in his autobiographical inscription, the Egyptian ex-naval commander and sometime physician at the courts of Cambyses and Darius (James 1991: 724), Udjahorresnet, reports receiving an order to return to Egypt 'while his majesty was in Elam' (Briant 1993). Many authorities suggest that this took place in 519 BC, and Briant seems to infer from this reference that if Darius was at Susa, he must have had a palace to reside in, but this seems a slender argument on which to base the chronology of the palace. That Darius' major building works followed the suppression of the second Elamite revolt (Amiet 1988c: 124) is an unproven if most probably safe assumption. Basing himself on a careful study of the stoneworking techniques used on discarded column drums recycled as casings for bronze doorsockets, C. Nylander has suggested that Ionians and Lydians were most certainly at work on the columned hall, or Apadana, of Susa 'around

Plate 9.4 Fragment of an Achaemenid column in the palace of Darius at Susa.

520–510′ BC (Nylander 1974: 320–1). Building on arguments adduced by Perrot and his colleagues, and comparing the orthography of the DSaa and Behistun texts, Vallat has suggested that the foundation texts could not have been deposited any later than 519 or 518 BC (Vallat 1986b: 281).

In spite of the reservations expressed by H.C. Rawlinson as to the location of 'Shushan the palace . . . in the province of Elam' – the scene of both Daniel's dream (Daniel 8.2) and the main events related in the Book of Esther (see Chapter 1) – W.K. Loftus' topographic survey of the site in 1850 left him in no doubt that the main north mound of Susa, known to us as the Apadana mound, was the site of Biblical Shushan (Curtis 1993: 2). Indeed, the same conclusion had already been reached in the twelfth century by the traveller Benjamin of Tudela, who not only identified modern Khuzistan with Elam, but declared that the main archaeological site there, Shushan, was 'the site of the palace of King Ahasuerus' of the Book of Esther (Adler 1907: 51). Surface survey and excavations by Loftus in 1851 and again in 1852 confirmed the presence of column bases belonging to the Apadana (Loftus 1856: 425, 429ff.) of Darius' palace, as well as glazed bricks and fragmentary, trilingual inscriptions recording Artaxerxes II's restoration of the palace built by his great-great-grandfather Darius (= A^{2}Sa; see also Kent 1953: 154, Lecoq 1997: 272–3). Although Loftus rightly maintained, after his investigations of 1851–2 that 'Susa is not yet exhausted', Rawlinson was of the opinion that the results achieved did not warrant further excavation at the site, and British operations were therefore terminated (Curtis 1993: 15).

In 1885 M. and J. Dieulafoy resumed excavations on the Apadana (Dieulafoy 1888; Dieulafoy 1893; see also de Mecquenem 1980: 2–4; Mousavi 1996: 4ff.), recovering among other things the famous glazed brick lion, griffon, archer and Immortals friezes (Nunn 1988: 194–9), as well as the glazed brick Apadana staircase decorated with lotuses and numerous glazed and inscribed bricks (Dieulafoy 1893: 274ff.; Pézard and Pottier 1926: 205). Monumental bull-protome column capitals and column bases confirm, as do the pieces recovered earlier by Loftus and subsequent excavators, that the stone columns referred to in DSf were very real indeed, even if much of the physical fabric of both the palace and Apadana was made of brick.

Under J. de Morgan a new program of excavations was begun at Susa in 1897, concentrating principally on the Acropole. The season of 1897–8 saw G. Jéquier continue work on the Apadana mound (Pillet 1914: 97; see also de Mecquenem 1980: 8), which, among other things, resulted in the recovery of a small number of badly broken Achaemenid stone vessels, some bearing fragmentary inscriptions of Xerxes (Amiet 1990b). In 1907 a further series of glazed brick panels depicting Persian archers was discovered to the east of the Apadana mound, followed in the season of 1908–9 by column bases inscribed with the name of Xerxes (de Mecquenem 1980: 19, 21). In September of 1912 de Morgan resigned for health reasons as chief of the French mission, and the following year, under the direction of R. de Mecquenem, the young architect M. Pillet was charged with completing the excavation of the palace, recovering further glazed brick panels (Pl. 9.5, Fig. 9.6), capitals and column bases in the process (de Mecquenem 1980: 23). Before the year was out, Pillet had produced a schematic plan of the entire palace-

Plate 9.5 Glazed brick panel (Sb 3336, 36×31×8 cm) excavated at Susa in 1914 by de Mecquenem. © Musée du Louvre, Antiquités Orientales

Figure 9.6 Relief brick façade showing lions from Susa (after *Susa* n.d.: Fig. 4).

Apadana complex, and in May 1914, a few short months before the outbreak of war would see him mobilized, Pillet published a small monograph (Fig. 9.7) devoted entirely to the palace of Darius (Pillet 1914). Pillet described his 104-page study as 'a simple notice intended for French visitors to the Salon des Artistes'. With its reproductions of his handsome watercolours showing general views of the excavations, and reconstructions of the palace and Apadana, and its attempt to lead the reader through the rooms and open spaces of the complex, *Le palais de Darius Ier* is an important document which captures the pride, enthusiasm and concerns of the French endeavour at Susa in a way which the many subsequent academic studies of the palace, however accurate architecturally, fail to do.

In spite of their best intentions, the French were by no means able to complete the excavation of the palace and Apadana of Darius before the First World War, but further excavations there by de Mecquenem (1947), Ghirshman (1965) and Perrot (1971; 1981; 1985; see also Steve and Gasche 1990: 28–32; Boucharlat 1990a) largely completed the plan of the palace and resulted in the discovery of the monumental gateway leading

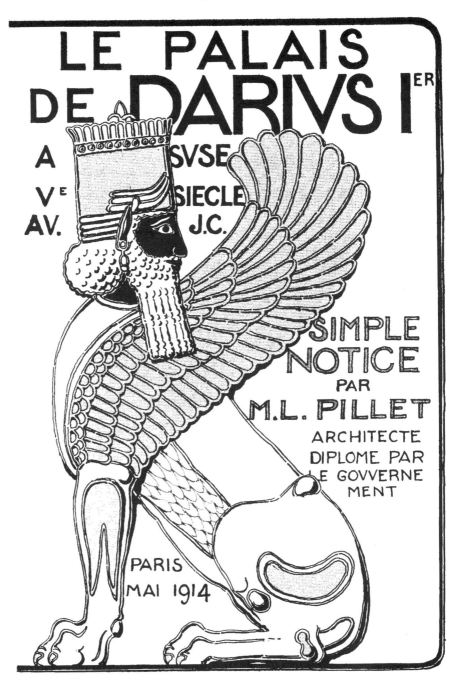

Figure 9.7 Cover of Maurice Pillet's *Palais de Darius* (after Pillet 1914).

towards it. The palace and audience hall of Darius stand on an irregularly shaped, quadrilateral platform covering no less than 13 ha, the unbuilt portions of which may have been planted with gardens (Perrot 1981: 83; for the problem of the royal garden at Susa, see also Pillet 1914: 101; Tuplin 1996: 90; see generally Stronach 1989a; 1990a;1994; Esther 1.5, 7.7–8 where a garden is mentioned in association with the palace of Ahasuerus [probably Xerxes I; see Ackroyd 1990: 10; Heltzer 1994] at Shushan; on the difficulty of determining the density of *intra muros* habitation at Achaemenid Susa, see Boucharlat 1985a: 73). A 30–60 cm thick layer of river gravel was brought in to level the Apadana, where, as noted already, much earlier remains existed (viz. Steve and Gasche 1990), and at its highest the platform stood up to 18 m high (Perrot 1981: 84). Upon the platform stood the palace itself, covering an area of *c.* 38,000 m² (246×155 m), or *c.* 5 ha, and the audience hall itself measuring 12,000 m² (109×109 m). Access to the main platform would have been via staircases faced with the glazed brick friezes of archers and animals discovered in varying states of preservation during the earlier years of excavation at Susa (Amiet 1988c: 127).

As Nylander has stressed, 'The main part of the palace stands in a Mesopotamian and Elamite tradition with a minimum use of worked stone' (Nylander 1974: 319), but this statement leaves open a wide variety of possibilities which need to be addressed. Thus, after excavating the monumental Middle Elamite structures of Choga Zanbil, Ghirshman was convinced that the plan of the palace of Darius must have been inspired by Elamite architecture and may well have been designed by Elamite architects, even if their absence in DSf, as noted above, is striking (Ghirshman 1965: 93). M. Roaf, on the other hand, suggested that Darius in fact copied the plan of Nebuchadnezzar's palace at Babylon (Roaf 1973: 80), while Amiet has pointed to the great similarity between the arrangement of rooms around courtyard XIX in the palace of Sennacherib at Nineveh and the plan of the Susa palace (Amiet 1974b: 69–70; 1994d: 1). Perrot seems to consider the parallels with Babylon and Nineveh equally compelling (Perrot 1981: 94), and it is clear, as Roaf has shown, that the particular room arrangement known as the *salle à quatre saillants* which Ghirshman found in both earlier Elamite architecture and the palace of Darius, could not have *directly* influenced Darius' architects, whereas its reappearance in Neo-Assyrian and Neo-Babylonian architecture could.

It is certain from DSf that skilled craftsmen from distant parts of the empire were brought to Susa to work on Darius' new palace, and one could perhaps overlook the omission of all reference to the architects, as opposed to builders, who conceived the palace and audience hall. Nevertheless, the effects of Assurbanipal's sack of Susa should not be underestimated, and when one reflects on that dark episode in Neo-Elamite history it is perhaps not surprising that so little of a demonstrably Elamite nature can be discerned in the new palatial complex erected by the Great King. Certainly, glazed brickwork existed in the Neo-Elamite period (see Chapter 8), but this was obviously not the parent of the work done for Darius, which was executed by Babylonian craftsmen.

No scholars, however, dispute the original, Iranianness of the columned hall, the antecedents of which can be found, albeit in more modest guise, in Iron Age Iran (e.g. at Hasanlu, Godin Tepe, Nush-i Jan, Baba Jan). These, however, are not Elamite sites. As related in a trilingual inscription engraved on four column bases for Artaxerxes II (A²Sa; Lecoq 1997: 273) who restored it, Darius' Apadana burned during the time of Artaxerxes I. Nylander has observed, however, that the square, stepped column bases used to support the Apadana columns stood on 'big squarish foundation blocks which were not made' for them, suggesting that 'they must be remains of the Darius building on the same spot and with the same ground plan' (Nylander 1974: 320). If this is correct, and we assume that the plans of the two columned halls were generally similar, then the 109 m square structure incorporated a central square measuring 58×58 m with thirty-six columns (6×6), flanked on three sides (north, west and east) by porticos with a double row of six columns, and square towers at each corner.

Apart from the palace of Darius, a number of other important features of Achaemenid Susa have also been located during the past century of excavations. These include the city gate, the gate of Darius, and the propylaeum of Darius. Located roughly midway along the eastern side face of the Ville Royale, the city gate of Susa was first located by Dieulafoy. It is a rectangular construction of brick measuring 36×18 m with walls between 3.5 and 3.9 m thick (Perrot 1981: 81). Several hundred metres to the northwest of the gateway and close to the northwest edge of the Ville Royale stands the so-called propylaeum of Darius, a 24×24 m pavillion with columned porticos to the north and south and four rooms arranged symmetrically around a square, central space partially divided by internal walls. A trilingual inscription left by Xerxes (XSa) on a column base found here attributes the construction of the building to his father Darius (Lecoq 1997: 262). It is interesting that Xerxes refers to the propylaeum as a *hadish*, literally 'seat', the same word used by Darius (DSf) when referring to his much vaster palace. This being the case, a more general term like 'building' might be warranted for *hadish*, since the propylaeum of Darius can in no way be compared to his palace.

Access from the propylaeum and the west side of the Ville Royale to the palatial complex on the Apadana mound was afforded by a 30 m long brick causeway, 17 m wide at its base and at least 10 m wide along its surface, which crossed the 10–15 m deep depression between these two parts of the site (Perrot 1981: 83). The causeway led directly to the retaining wall of the platform on which the palace stood, access to which was gained via the monumental gateway which again, thanks to an inscription of Xerxes' attributing its construction to his father (XSd; Lecoq 1997: 262), can be safely attributed to Darius. Amiet has rightly compared this to an 'Arc de Triomphe' (Amiet 1988c: 125).

The palace of Artaxerxes I and Darius II

During the season of 1931–2 R. de Mecquenem excavated a palatial structure on the southern mound of Susa known as the 'Donjon', which he incorrectly took to be a Sasanian building (de Mecquenem 1943: 70–6). Ghirshman and Amiet later realized that this was an Achaemenid palace (Fig. 9.8), suggesting that it was built by Artaxerxes

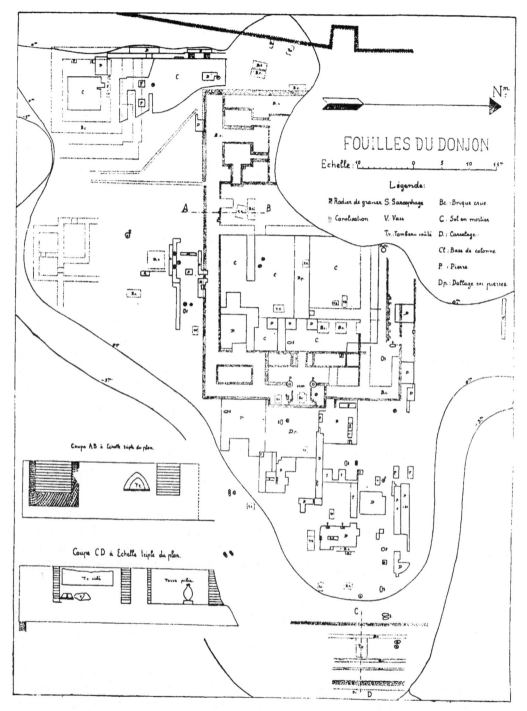

Figure 9.8 De Mecquenem's plan of the 'Sasanian' building excavated on the Donjon, more probably an Achaemenid palace (after de Mecquenem 1943: Fig. 60).

I (465–425 BC) following the destruction by fire of the palace built by his father Darius (522–486 BC) (Amiet 1972b: 167, n. 5; 1973a: 28). Although this was not fully justified, it is true that of two fragmentary inscriptions of Darius II (424–405 BC) known from Susa (D²Sb), one contains a reference to a building (*hadish*) erected by his father, Artaxerxes I, whose own inscriptions have only been found at Persepolis (Lecoq 1997: 268). It must be stressssed, however, that the attribution of fragmentary stone reliefs showing Persian guards and servants found in the Donjon region is far from certain, and Boucharlat does not believe that there are any secure grounds for dating the Donjon building prior to the Seleucid or Parthian period (Boucharlat and Shahidi 1987: 324, n. 13). Be that as it may, the Donjon building was the source of an important series of carved ivories in Achaemenid (Fig. 9.9), Egyptian and Syro-Phoenician styles (Amiet 1972b), suggesting that an Achaemenid royal building must have once stood on the site. Furthermore, Stronach has noted that 'the particular situation of the "Donjon" – a lofty protuberance jutting beyond the main outline of the site – was one well fitted for a Persian apadana' (Stronach 1985: 435).

The palace of Artaxerxes II

In 1969 bulldozing to the west of Susa on the far side of the Shaur revealed column bases which, as subsequent excavation proved, belonged to yet another columned hall, originally with eight rows of columns (64 in total), attributed to Artaxerxes II (Perrot 1971: 36ff.; Boucharlat and Labrousse 1979). Further Achaemenid stonework, including part of a staircase and a column base, have been found in the modern village of Shush less than 1 km northeast of the Shaur palace site (Boucharlat and Shahidi 1987).

Ethnicity and cultural identity in Achaemenid Elam and its environs

Mention has already been made of the apparent rupture in the ceramic tradition at Susa between the Neo-Elamite and Achaemenid levels on the site. Indeed, as de Miroschedji notes, the Achaemenid pottery from Susa is most comparable to that known from contemporary sites in Mesopotamia (e.g. Babylon, Ur, Uruk, Nippur, Tell al-Lahm and Sippar), while showing few if any parallels to Choga Mish or sites in northwestern Khuzistan, which in turn exhibit clear links to the Iron Age III tradition of the Zagros, and virtually no links to assemblages from Fars (de Miroschedji 1987: 32ff.; for Achaemenid assemblages in Fars, see Sumner 1986b: 5–6). Commenting on Susa's apparent orientation, at least in the ceramic domain, towards Babylonia, de Miroschedji noted the strong ties between the two areas at this date, and indeed the evidence of this is compelling. Members of the Egibi family from Babylon, for example, travelled frequently to and from southwestern Iran on business during the reign of Cyrus, Cambyses, Bardiya and Darius I (Zadok 1976a: 71ff.; Wunsch 1993; Abraham 1995; Zawadzki 1996a), as did members of the Murashu family from Nippur during the reign of Darius II, whose business took them to Susa for months at a time (Stolper 1992; Joannès 1988; Dandamaev 1992: 151ff. for Babylonians in Elam). A text from Dilbat,

Figure 9.9 Achaemenid ivories from the Donjon (after de Mecquenem 1947: Fig. 56).

dating to 512/11 BC, also documents a man named Urash-ana-bitishu being sent to Elam to perform an unspecified type of work for three months (Zadok 1995b). Conversely, Elamites worked in Babylonia, e.g. on lands belonging to the Ebabbar temple at Sippar (Dandamaev 1991; 1993a: 122). Movement between Babylon and Susa is also attested in the late Babylonian astronomical diaries (see generally Rochberg-Halton 1991; van der Spek 1993). Thus, one such text from the twelfth year of Artaxerxes III's reign (347 BC) includes the remark, '[of Ba]bylonia made . . . at the command of . . . and entered Babylon, and the . . . /left Babylon for Susa' (Sachs and Hunger 1988: 149, s.v. -346.rev.14). Another text, from the thirty-eighth year of Artaxerxes II's reign (367 BC) contains the cryptic remark, 'the administrator [. . .]/in Susa to the governorship [. . .]' which might imply that an Achaemenid administrator in Babylonia was elevated to satrapal status at Susa (Sachs and Hunger 1988: 131, s.v. -366.col.ii.7–8). Finally, contracts from Susa written in Akkadian and dating to the reign of an Artaxerxes show us people with Babylonian, Egyptian and Iranian names involved in marriage and real estate matters (Joannès 1990).

While examples such as these go some way towards providing a context in which to view cultural similarities between Achaemenid Babylonia and Achaemenid Elam, they do not address the more difficult issue of Elamite cultural identity *within* the more immediate Persian sphere. This is a problem which can be approached by examining a variety of sources, both literary and archaeological. We begin with the literary evidence first.

In his account of the battle of Doriscus, Herodotus (VII.62) lists a people called the *Kissians* third amongst the nations which fought in Xerxes' army, immediately after the Persians and Medes. At Thermopylae they fought alongside the Medes against the Spartans (VII.210; Diodorus XI.7.2). The distinguishing characteristics of the Kissians at Doriscus were described by Herodotus as follows: 'The Kissians were equipped in the Persian fashion, except in one respect: they wore on their heads, instead of hats, fillets' (VII.86). The earliest attestations of Kissia and Kissian, however, are to be found in *The Persians* by Aeschylus, where the opening scene is meant to be in the palace of Xerxes (sic!) at Susa. There the chorus of Persian elders speaks of the Persian force which 'flowed westward' 'from Susa, from Ecbatana, from ancient Kissian ramparts' (*Pers.* 17), and worries 'Lest Susa's ancient stones / And the high Kissian wall / Echo with frenzied groans / Of women for their dead' (*Pers.* 120).

Apart from their appearance in the description of Doriscus, the Kissians and the toponym Kissia are attested several more times in Herodotus. He speaks of 'Susa and the other Kissian lands' (III.92), clearly assigning Susa and the river Choaspes on which it lay to Kissian territory (V.49). In describing the Royal Road, he notes that after entering Kissia, 'eleven stations and 42.5 parsangs bring you to another navigable stream, the Choaspes, on the banks of which the city of Susa is built' (V.52). These references make it clear that while Susa lay in Kissia, Kissia was not coterminous with Susiana but began well north of it (see the description of the Royal Road) in the mountains of Luristan (Nöldeke 1874: 174), a point which might lend some credence to Lehmann's suggestion that Kissia was a Greek term derived ultimately from Kashshu (Lehmann

1892). For this reason it is understandable that in the tribute list of Darius, as preserved by Herodotus (III.89), 'Susa and the other parts of Kissia' comprise a single satrapy, and further it explains why Strabo says, 'the Susians are also called Kissians' (*Geog.* 15.3.3), and why the late antique geographer Stephen of Byzantium referred to 'Susa of the Kissians' (Σοῦσα Κίσιοι). As Weissbach noted, the toponym Kissia is used by Herodotus as a substitute for Elam (Weissbach 1921: 520). Certainly this would explain the absence of any reference to Susians in Xerxes' army at Doriscus. Moreover, Nöldeke long ago pointed to the parallelism between the order of the first three names in Herodotus' list of units which fought at Doriscus – Persians, Medes, Kissians – and that of two Old Persian inscriptions in which the Elamites stand in third position after the Persia and Media (Nöldeke 1874: 175). In fact, although the order varies and may be Persia-Media-Elamite (e.g. DNa §6, XPh §3) or Persia-Elam/Elamite-Media (e.g. DPe §2, DSaa), Elam or the Elamites consistently figure in the first three satrapies named, and the parallelism with Herodotus' account confirms that Kissia was synonymous with Elam. It has been suggested that Greek Kissioi was derived from *Khuja, a postulated Median form of *u-va-ja*, the Old Persian for 'Elam' (Jacobs 1994: 202 citing W. Nagel), but this is highly questionable. It has also been noted that in transcribing Greek names in Akkadian, Greek -*i*- sometimes became Akkadian -*a*- (e.g. Gr. Laodike = Akk. *Lu-da-ke*). Hence, Gr. Kissia may correspond, if it reproduces an Akkadian name or a name transmitted via Akkadian, to *Kaššu*, the Akkadian term for the Kassites (Lehmann 1892: 333). Later references to Kissia (see Chapter 10) are anachronistic (Nöldeke 1874: 177), but in sum it is clear that the distinctiveness of the Kissians generally and Susians in particular was sufficient to enable them to be easily distinguished from the Persians during the Achaemenid period.

We turn now to an examination of some of the material evidence which reflects cultural diversity and Elamite survival and acculturation in the Achaemenid world. The survival of late Neo-Elamite seals into the Achaemenid period is a phenomenon which has long been recognized, thanks to the impressions preserved on the texts from Persepolis. At least one example (PF 610) of a Neo-Elamite seal which had had its cuneiform legend effaced and was still used to seal an Achaemenid tablet is known from Persepolis (Amiet 1973b: 14), but certainly the most famous example of a seal in late Neo-Elamite style used on a Persepolis text (in fact on five different tablets, PF 692–5 and 2033) is a seal, the legend of which bears the name of Kurash the Anshanite, son of Teispes (Fig. 9.10), already discussed in Chapter 9 (see Garrison 1991; Garrison and Root 1996). This is a remarkable piece, more for its use during the reign of Darius I, than for the fact that it may mention the founder of the Achaemenid empire. But the fact that it is so early in the Achaemenid series means that we should hardly be surprised to find that the seal, while culturally Achaemenid, is iconographically Neo-Elamite. In that sense, it tells us little about the survival or perpetuation of Elamite style in the Achaemenid period. To document such a process one ought to look to material considerably later than the reign of Cyrus. In fact, as Amiet has stressed, the excavations of Susa provided very little in the way of glyptic finds from the Achaemenid period, and what has been recovered is more in the style formerly called 'Greco-Persian', hence

Figure 9.10 Composite drawing of the seal of Kurash (after Garrison and Root 1996: Fig. 2a).

reflecting iconographic and stylistic links with Greek cut gems and ring seals (Amiet 1973a: 26–7).

Persians and Elamites are often said to have shared elements of material culture. For Hinz, Elamite influence was tangible in Persian dress and weaponry (Hinz 1969: 63; see also Trümpelmann 1988: 79, 82). In the opinion of some scholars, such as the late P. Calmeyer, the similarities between the Elamites depicted in the Neo-Assyrian reliefs (see Unger 1938) and the Persians depicted on the Persepolis reliefs can only be explained if one assumes a wholesale adoption of Elamite dress, coiffure and armament by the Persians after the arrival of Persian-speaking tribes in Fars (Calmeyer 1988). What is the likelihood of such a scenario, however? One might have expected that, reduced to a second rate political status by the Assyrian onslaught of the seventh century, and unable to stage a significant recovery in the earlier sixth century due to the power of the Medes, Babylonians and increasingly the Persians, the Elamites would have been the ones doing the assimilating, not the Persians. In other words, it seems more logical to suggest that the Elamites increasingly adopted Persian customs and dress as they were gradually absorbed into the rapidly evolving Persian realm. Although it may be hazardous to use Greek literary testimony in support of such a trend, it is interesting to recall the passage from Herodotus noted above, according to which the Kissians (viz. Susians/Elamites) at Doriscus were said to have dressed like the Persians except for their headgear (VII.62). Moreover, we have a second relevant reference in a fragment of the early Greek historian Hecataeus (sixth/fifth century BC), preserved by Harpocration (second century AD), according to whom 'the Kissians wear the Persian *kypasseis* [a short tunic] as clothing' (Weissbach 1921: 520; see also Calmeyer 1988: 27, 49).

In fact, E. Strommenger has shown that the comparisons between the Persian dress shown on Achaemenid reliefs and Elamite dress as rendered on the Neo-Assyrian reliefs are far from compelling (Strommenger 1994). The belted tunic of the Elamite warriors on Neo-Assyrian reliefs, with baldric-like straps running over the shoulders and under the arms to support a quiver suspended in the centre of the back, is scarcely comparable to the long robe with multiple drapery folds shown in Achaemenid depictions of

Elamites at Persepolis. Whether such a comparison is valid, however, is another question. There is certainly no reason why Elamites or for that matter any people would wear the same dress in both battle and when approaching the Great King on a ceremonial occasion. Nor is there any reason to assume that Assyrian craftsmen would have understood the precise nature of the garment of one of the many enemies they were commissioned to represent on an Assyrian palace relief.

What remains clear, however, is the great similarity between the Persians and Elamites in the Achaemenid period palatial and tomb reliefs at Persepolis and Naqsh-i Rustam (Calmeyer 1987: 11; Bittner 1987; Hachmann 1995) where they are depicted in three capacities: 1) as bearers of gifts, depicted on the east façade of the Apadana staircase; 2) as 'throne bearers', in which role they appear supporting the throne of the Great King alongside the other subject peoples in the throne and council halls at Persepolis; and 3) as 'podium bearers' on the Achaemenid royal tomb façades where they and other subject peoples support the podium on which the Great King stands. In the latter two cases both Persians and Elamites alike are shown with a rounded and trimmed beard, wearing a stiff cap and a robe (whether this is in fact two separate garments, one for the torso and one for the legs, is of no relevance here) with pronounced pleats in the lower drapery (German 'Faltengewand'). The upper part of the garment is so cut or depicted that the arms emerge from it as though it were sleeveless. Earrings and wrist bracelets are sometimes shown. Finally, a dagger is worn at the belt (Hachmann 1995: 196–7 and Abb. 1.I). The podium- and thronebearers appear to be barefoot. In the depictions of Elamites bearing gifts, on the other hand, the headgear is different, for a headband is worn, knotted at the back, as are ankle-high boots typically shown with six rows of laces (e.g. Walser 1980: Figs. 11, 31–2).

Because of the dangers of arguing from Assyrian reliefs depicting Elamites in battle dress, it is perhaps hazardous to conclude that the differences in Elamite dress between the Neo-Assyrian and Achaemenid periods are due to Persian influence on Elamite fashion. But it seems more logical to suggest that Elamites attempting to adapt to the ways of a new ruling elite may have been more likely to assume Persian costume, than it does to suggest the Persian adoption of Elamite dress.

What does seem to have been adopted by the Persians, however, is what Hinz called the 'Elamite dagger' (Hinz 1969: 79; see also Calmeyer 1988: 32–3). Clearly depicted on the Apadana reliefs showing Elamite delegates advancing with gifts is a pointed dagger with convex, rounded pommel set in a scabbard with an asymmetrical extension (Pl. 9.6) in one direction (e.g. Walser 1980: Fig. 32) which differs clearly from the Persian short-sword or *akinakes* (Bittner 1987: 199ff.) worn at the belt (Pl. 9.7). The same type of weapon is shown being worn by Persian guards and the 'royal hero' killing a lion at Persepolis (Calmeyer 1988: 32–3). Although no actual metal examples of this dagger type are known, B. Brentjes has suggested (Brentjes 1993: 21) that an Elamite dagger is in fact depicted at the waist of an apotropaic figure on a Neo-Elamite plaque (Sb 43) from Susa (Harper, Aruz and Tallon 1992: 201, no. 142), and indeed it is shown several times at the waists of Elamite warriors in the Neo-Assyrian reliefs (Calmeyer 1988: Taf. 15, 17, 18). Bittner has suggested that the Elamite dagger was a 'cult dagger' or 'sign of

Plate 9.6 Detail of a Persian nobleman wearing an 'Elamite' dagger at Persepolis.

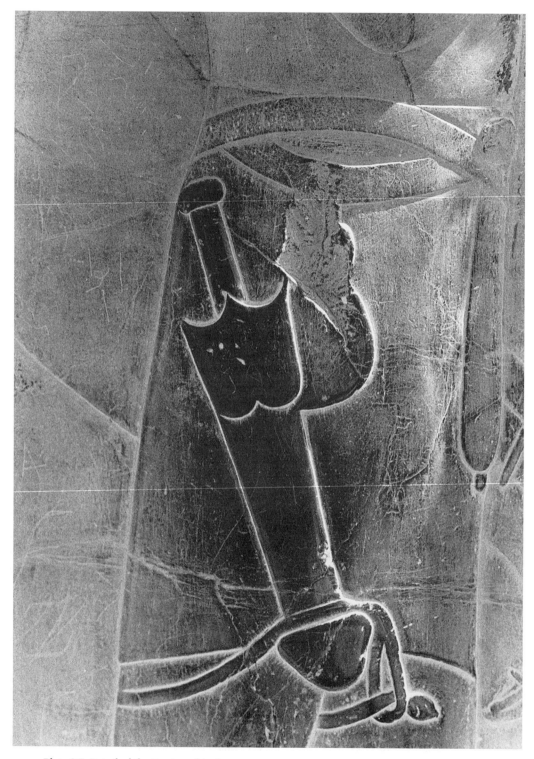

Plate 9.7 Detail of the Persian *akinakes*.

rank for bearers of high state office' (Bittner 1987: 134), as shown by the fact that it was worn by Darius himself on a statue from Susa which was made in Egyptian style (Kervran et al. 1972: Fig. 3), most probably in Egypt and of stone quarried in the Wadi Hammamat (Trichet and Vallat 1990), and is probably represented on early Achaemenid coinage of the royal archer variety (Stronach 1989b: 277, type IV). As Stronach has suggested, the 'asymmetrical extension at the top of the scabbard . . . served to hold the scabbard in place when it was thrust through the belt. It is probable, moreover, that the scalloped underside of the extension helped to prevent the scabbard from riding past the central, frontal knot on the wearer's belt' (Stronach 1989b: 277, n. 114).

Along with their daggers, the Elamite delegates on the Apadana stairway reliefs also proffer bows with duck-finials. These too have been considered typically Elamite by Hinz, who believed that the Persians had more or less adopted wholesale the archery equipment of their Elamite predecessors (Hinz 1969: 79). Bittner is less inclined to such an extreme view (Bittner 1987: 151–2) but it is striking to recall the numerous references to Elamite archers in earlier chapters, particularly during the long years of Elamite-Assyrian warfare. As the Elamites were noted for their prowess as archers, it is scarcely surprising that Elamite archery techniques and equipment, both bows and quivers (see Bittner 1987: 135ff. for 'Susian quivers') should have survived into the Achaemenid period. Indeed, Elamite bowmen were active well into the Parthian period (see Chapter 10). Thus, while there were certainly other important contributors to the evolving art of Achaemenid archery, notably the Medes and Scythians (see Herodotus I.73 for the idea that the composite bow was adopted by both the Medes and the Persians from the Scythians, who may have also transmitted it to the Greeks; see also Marsden 1969: 8, n. 4), the Elamite contribution in this field should not be underestimated. After all, as we saw in the last chapter, the Elamite bow was in use in Assyria in the early eighth century BC.

Elamite religion in the Achaemenid heartland

Over the years much has been written on the religion of the early Achaemenids. A full analysis of early Achaemenid religion is not our concern here (see Gnoli 1980: 199ff.; Boyce 1982; Boucharlat 1984: 119ff.; Schmitt 1991a; Lecoq 1997: 154ff.). Rather, we are concerned with evidence of the survival of Elamite religion in an increasingly Zoroastrian environment. M. Boyce has argued recently that 'the ruthless and appalling destruction of neighbouring Elam by the Assyrians' may have created the conditions in which Zoroastrianism 'made swift progress among the Persians' (Boyce 1988: 31). Certainly the Elamite version of Darius' Behistun inscription describes Ahuramazda as 'the god of the Iranians' (DB §62) while castigating the Elamites as 'felons' who 'do not worship Ahuramazda' (DB §72; see also Stronach 1984: 485; Lecoq 1997: 160).

Such a critical view of Elamites and their native religion is not, however, reflected in other sources. That Elamite religion was tolerated, at least during the reign of Darius, is shown clearly by an examination of the Persepolis Fortification texts where four deities of certain Elamite origin and a further four of questionable attribution are attested (Table 9.5; see also Koch 1977; 1991). Just as significant as the continued worship of these deities during the earlier Achaemenid era at Persepolis is the fact that they and their priests were being issued with commodities from state coffers for the performance of ongoing ritual offerings. Thus, contrary to whatever impression Darius may have wished to convey in his Behistun inscription, the tolerance of Elamite religion was apparently never under threat in early Achaemenid Iran. Given what we know of Cyrus' widely proclaimed tolerance of Judaism and Babylonian religion, Achaemenid toleration of Elamite beliefs is perhaps to be expected. Yet tolerance is one thing, financing offerings using state revenue another. Furthermore, it is interesting to see one and the same priest (El. *shatin*) being issued with wine or grain for sacrifices to both Iranian and Elamite deities. Thus, Turkama received wine to be used for Ahuramazda and Humban (PF 339), while Appirka received wine for Ahuramazda, Mithra and Shimut (PF 338). Undoubtedly there were many more cases like this which we can no longer recognize, for most of the texts dealing with commodities issued for sacrificial and ceremonial purposes simply describe the ultimate purpose as 'for the gods' without specifically naming them (e.g. PF 352, 353, 356–78, etc.).

Stronach has suggested that Cyrus, Cambyses and Darius were 'nominal Zoroastrians' and 'eminently pragmatic rulers' who were both aware and tolerant of Mesopotamian religious tradition, as well as mindful of the 'Elamite legacy' to which they had fallen heir (Stronach 1984: 489). In discussing burial practices during the Achaemenid period, Frye has suggested that since 'much, if not most, of the population of Fars was Elamite, it would have been impolitic to ban burials there' in an effort to enforce Zoroastrian practices relating to the treatment of the corpse (Frye 1984: 176). Further, he likens the 'horns on the parapet of the southwest walls of Persepolis' to the Elamite use of horns on shrines (Frye 1984: 175), such as those attested during the Middle and Neo-Elamite periods (see Chapters 7 and 8).

Earlier it was noted that of the roughly 2000 personal names preserved in the Persepolis Fortification texts, roughly 10 per cent can be classified as Elamite. These too are a potential source of information about Achaemenid Elamite religion, for a number of Achaemenid-period Elamite personal names were theophoric (Table 9.6). Yet we should not underestimate the degree to which Elamites must have been assimilated into an increasingly Persian cultural milieu during the interval between the last years of the Neo-Elamite period and the reign of Darius. Certainly there are names with Elamite theophoric elements, just as there are sacrifices recorded to Elamite deities. But overall, these appear as minor survivals in an increasingly Persian world.

One point of tangential interest about religion in Achaemenid Elam is raised by a dedication to Apollo by two Milesians, Aristolochos and Thrason, written in Archaic Greek (SEG 7.9) on a bronze weight (93.7 kg) found at Susa (Pézard and Pottier 1926: 107, n. 234). The weight, which is dated palaeographically to the early sixth century BC (Oppenheimer 1983: 427), was apparently seized at Miletus in 494 BC when Darius sacked the oracular shrine of Apollo at Didyma 16 km south of the city, as reported by Herodotus (VI.19). The piece must have been part of the rich booty which, according to

Table 9.5. *Elamite deities attested in the Persepolis fortification texts*

Deity	Sources (PFT)	Loci	Administration Area	Characterization
Humban	PF 339–51, 2029	—	I	chief god of the Elamite pantheon; mainly attested as recipient of wine, barley and flour offerings
		—	II	
		Hibarsh	III	
		Nishama	IV	
		Vanta		
		Brdatka	V	
		Umpura		
		Vrataka		
		Taspak	VI	
		Ibata		
		Palak		
		Zulushuna		
		Hazur		
		Zila-Humban		
Napirisha	PF 353–4, 596	—	I	the 'great god'; recipient of barley offerings
		—	II	
		Eyana	III	
		Akrna	IV	
		Mazdagush		
		Raznavatish		
		Hidali	VI	
		Zila-Humban		
		nr. Pitava		
Shimut	PF 338	—		the 'Elamite god' of the Middle Elamite era
Nabbazabba	PF 2073	Tigrash	III	otherwise unattested; worshipped together with the Babylonian god Adad
An(?)turza	PF 770	—	—	otherwise unattested; libations made for the god at six shrines (?)

Table 9.6. *Elamite personal names with theophoric elements in the Persepolis fortification texts*

Name	Reference	Etymology
*Atameta (?)/Atamaita	DB §71	from Atta-hamiti-Inshushinak, 'a considerate father is Inshushinak', 'lord of Susa'
Haldash	PF 362	shortened from Hu(m)ban-haltash (?)
Hupan'ahpi	P seal 77	from Humban, divine name
Hutrara	PF 255, 425, 1018	from Hutran (son of Napirisha and Kiririsha)
Manzana	PF 531, 591–2, 651	from Zana, 'mistress'
Shati-Dudu	PF 106, 440, 519, 556, 820, 1395, 1811, 1849–50	from Shati, divine name
Shati-Kitin	PF 88, 99, 100, 799, 845, 997, 2028; seal 81	from Shati
Shati-Ku[?]-[. . . .]	P seal 98	from Shati
Shati-Shimut	PF 434, 551–2	from Shati and Shimut, divine names
Shati-Tikash	PF 222	from Shati and Tikash, divine names
Ummanana	PF 117–18, 320, 682(?), 685, 1273–5, 1532–3, 1576	from Humban

Notes:
Follows generally Mayrhofer 1973 with corrections based on Zadok 1984b.

Herodotus, Darius brought back to Susa. As a trophy of war it is certainly a curiosity, but the likelihood that the soldiers who stole it had any idea of the import of its inscription is very slim. Certainly it does not reflect the presence of a cult of Apollo at Susa in the Achaemenid period.

Elam in the time of Darius III

Thanks in large measure to information gathered in the wake of the campaign of Alexander the Great, we have details concerning Elam in the reign of the last Achaemenid ruler, Darius III, which are wholly lacking for any of his predecessors. Arrian (III.8.5; III.11.3) names Oxathres, son of Abulites, as the general of a unit of Susians and Uxians at Gaugamela (for full refs. on Abulites and Oxathres, see Berve 1926/II: 5, 291). After the battle, when Alexander was on his way to Susa, Oxathres rode out to meet and hand over the city to him, delivering as well a letter from Philoxenos, who had gone on ahead of Alexander to secure the treasury and take possession of the city (Seibert 1985: 97). Abulites later appears as satrap of Elam on the occasion of Alexander's entry into Susa in mid-December, 331 BC, according to both Diodorus (XVII.65.5) and Quintus Curtius (V.2.8). Thus, it is clear that this is the same individual designated as Oxathres' father (Petit 1990: 212). The vast sum of 49,000 (Plutarch, *Alex.* 36.1; Diodorus XVII.66.2) or 50,000 (Arrian III.16.7; Curtius V.2.11–12) talents of silver is reported to have been seized by the Macedonians at Susa, and even if this figure is exaggerated, the purport of the statement is nonetheless clear – Susa and the satrapy of Elam were enormously wealthy.

Alexander received reinforcements at Susa and upon his departure for Persepolis left a force of 3000 men behind under the command of Archelaos and Mazaros, with Abulites remaining as satrap (Spiegel 1971: 524; Hamilton 1987: 470; Seibert 1985: 98). Heading eastwards he crossed the Pasitigris and entered the territory of the Uxians. Accounts of Alexander's campaign(s) against the Uxians are preserved in Arrian (III.17), Quintus Curtius (V.3.1–11) and Diodorus Siculus (67.1–4), and have been scrutinized by a number of ancient historians (most recently Atkinson 1994: 69–83; see also Bosworth 1980b: 321–4, 1996: 146; Briant 1982; 1996: 387–8). Arrian clearly distinguished two groups of Uxians, those of the plain and those of the hills. He writes, 'The Uxians who inhabited the plains had obeyed the Persian satrap, and now surrendered to Alexander, but the Uxian hillmen, as they were called, were not subject to Persia, and now sent a message to Alexander that they would only permit him to take the route toward Persia with his army if they received what they used to receive from the Persian king on his passage' (III.17.1).

Briant has suggested that the distinction made by Arrian between lowland and highland Uxians should be coupled with the account of Alexander's campaign against the Uxians recorded by Quintus Curtius (V.3) in which a number of further details appear (Briant 1982). Thus, according to Quintus Curtius, the Uxians were commanded by a *praefectus regionis* called Madites/Medates/Madates, who was a relative by marriage of Darius III (Berve 1926/II: 243). Madates was unwilling to submit to the Macedonian invasion and fought tenaciously from an 'insignificant and obscure fortress' which, nevertheless, was located in an area 'precipitous and encumbered by rocks and crags' (Curtius V.3.8–9). A difficult battle in rough terrain eventually ended in a Macedonian victory, with the result that 'Alexander incorporated the subdued race of the Uxii in the satrapy of the Susiani' (Curtius V.3.16). Afterwards, 'having divided his forces with Parmenion', Alexander 'with a light-armed band took the ridge of the mountains whose back runs without interruption into Persia . . . laid waste all this region, [and] on the third day he entered Persia' (Curtius V.3.16–17).

Pointing to Arrian's lowland-highland Uxians, Briant suggests that two campaigns in fact took place, the first against Madates and his lowland Uxians fighting from a fortress which overlooked the Uxian plains, followed by a second campaign against the highland Uxians (Briant 1982; 1996: 747–9). The lowland campaign in question, he argues, is that directed against Madates and recorded by Quintus Curtius and Diodorus, while that against the highlanders is the one recorded by Arrian. It is not impossible, however, that Arrian's reference to the obedience of the lowland Uxians in submitting to their Persian satrap is an allusion to those Uxians, situated in eastern Khuzistan, who fell under the jurisdiction of Abulites, while the Uxians who put up resistance seem clearly to be those led by Madates in the highlands, especially as the entire scene of the siege is described in terms reflecting the ruggedness of the terrain around the Uxian fortress. Seibert suggests that Arrian's reference implies the subordination of the lowland Uxians to the satrap of *Persis* (Seibert 1985: 102), but it seems more likely, given their location, that the Uxians in question were subject to the *Persian* satrap of Elam/Susiana, who was much closer and had readier access to the area.

Madates was possibly a *hyparch*, or governor, of a sub-region below the level of the satrapy (Jacobs 1994: 204; Petit 1990: 212; Tarn 1930: 134). Baron de Bode suggested that the site of Madates' stronghold was that of Malamir, for both Quintus Curtius and Arrian make it clear that Alexander and his forces had to penetrate 'through the defiles' to get there, and this description precisely suits Malamir, which is in a high plain surrounded by the lower ranges of the Zagros mountains (de Bode 1843: 108; see also Spiegel 1971: 627). Describing the 'territory of the Uxii', where the Choaspes river (by Susa) is said to have had its source, Strabo writes, 'a kind of mountainous country intrudes between the Susians and Persis; it is rugged and sheer, and has narrow defiles that are hard to pass, and was inhabited by brigands, who would exact payments even from the kings themselves when they passed from Susis into Persis' (*Geog.* XV.3.4; see also Curtius V.3.3). Topographically speaking, this describes well the mountainous stretch between Malamir and the heartland of Fars, and in this connection it is interesting to note that, according to Diodorus (XIX.21.2), the overland journey from Susa to Persepolis took 24 days.

Quintus Curtius notes that after subduing the Uxians, Alexander incorporated them into the satrapy of the Susiani (V.3.16). As noted above, Uxians and Susians constituted a single contingent at Gaugamela, but these Uxians may have been exclusively from the lowland region which was subject to Abulites. With their pacification by Alexander, the remainder of the Uxians were apparently brought into the same administrative structure (although in describing the wars of the successors fifteen years later, Diodorus described the Uxians as 'unconquered tribesmen', Diodorus XIX.17.3). Leriche has described as 'absurd' the notion that the Great King ever paid tribute or protection money to the mountain inhabitants of the Zagros when travelling through the region, suggesting rather that their quasi-independence was granted for the price of supplying elite troops, such as those who fought at Gaugamela (Leriche 1977: 300). Briant, on the other hand, envisages that a regular pattern of gift exchange may have operated between the nomadic Uxians of the mountains, of whom Arrian writes that 'they have neither silver nor arable land, and the majority of them are herders (*nomeis*)' (III.17.6), and the Great King (Briant 1996: 751).

Scholars have long compared the Greek ethnonym Uxii with *u-va-ja*, the Old Persian word for 'Elam' and the equivalent of Akkadian *E-lam-mat* and Elamite *Hal-tam-ti* in the Behistun inscription (see already Nöldeke 1874: 184; Hoffmann 1880: 133; Sykes 1915/I: 56; Bork 1925: 73). It was not until fairly recently, however, that O. Szemerényi was able to demonstrate the derivation of Greek Ουξιοι (perhaps an error for Ουζιοι, i.e.

Uzii, see Frye 1962: 60) from Old Persian Huziya, i.e. the inhabitants of Elam (Szemerényi 1966: 191; for the relationship between these toponyms and 'Khuzistan', the modern name of the southwest Iranian province, see already Nöldeke 1874: 185–7; Herzfeld 1968: 303–4; Eilers 1982: 27). The relevance of this for our perception of Uxian ethnicity is unclear, however. But generally speaking, it is interesting to see a distinction in the late Achaemenid period, at least in the Greek sources, between the inhabitants of Susiana (western Khuzistan) and those of Uxiana (eastern Khuzistan and the adjacent mountains). How one should interpret the derivation of Uxii from the name for 'Elamites' is a more difficult issue to resolve, particularly since we have no sources on the Uxians before the very end of the Achaemenid era, and no way of linking them with the archaeological assemblages known, e.g. from the Malamir plain or Bakhtiyari mountains. At any rate, here we have yet another ethnic group, distinguished from the Susians by the Alexander historians, but apparently unknown to Herodotus or Hecataeus whose ethnographic knowledge of the region extended only to the Kissians described above.

Late Babylonian astronomical diaries give some sparse notices concerning Susa between Alexander's conquest of Iran and his death in Babylon on 13 June 323 BC. Thus, a notice in a diary from month VIII (October/November) of his eighth year according to Babylonian reckoning, i.e. 329 BC, records, 'That month, I hea[rd that . . .]/the chief of the troops [. . .] from Susa to the land of Ha[nî . . .]' (Sachs and Hunger 1988: 191, s.v. -324.rev.26'-27'). Hanî or Hanû has been taken to be a general designation for 'the regions west of Babylonia' (Zadok 1985: 151), but as the astronomical diary in question is specifically dated to the reign of 'Alexander, the king who is from the land of Hanî', it is doubtful that the term could have had such a vague connotation. Unfortunately, the text is too fragmentary to gain a sense of what was happening beyond a transfer of troops stationed at Susa.

Conclusion

The Achaemenid period presents us with one of the most interesting cases of ethnogenesis and acculturation in Iranian history. The assimilation of Elamites and their interactions with the Persians can be studied on a variety of levels and in a plethora of domains – linguistic, religious and material. From cylinder seal styles and weaponry to deities and bureaucracy, what was once an unambiguous Elamite identity in material and mental culture becomes increasingly shadowy and elusive as we move down in time from the moment when Cyrus came to power to the last days of Darius III. We must look for and analyze these Elamite elements in an increasingly Iranian cultural milieu on a number of operational levels. When this is done, however, it becomes clear that Elamite cultural identity did not simply evaporate in the wake of the Assyrian conquest and the Persian ascent to political supremacy. The fact that Elamite identity is, if anything, even clearer in the subsequent Seleucid and Parthian periods is surely a sign that it was not completely overtaken by the forces of assimilation during the Achaemenid period.

Date	Lowlands	Highlands	Mesopotamia	'Elam'
539–530 BC	Susa comes under Persian rule	establishment of Cyrus the Great's capital at Pasargadae	Babylonia and Assyria conquered by Cyrus	Elam and Anshan still used in Babylonian works with reference to Cyrus
529–486 BC	suppression of rebellions; construction of palace at Susa by Darius; movement of businessmen and workers between Babylonia and Susa	suppression of rebellions, Darius proclaims sovereignty in words and images at Behistun; construction of Persepolis; development of Old Persian script; continued use of Elamite for administrative texts; Neo-Elamite III seals still in use	uprisings followed by reconquest in Babylonia; construction of palace at Babylon; relative continuity in Babylonian institutions	'Elamite' rebellions cited by Darius; use of Elamite language; frequency of Elamite names in Persepolis texts attests to survival of ethnically Elamite elements in society
485–465 BC	Xerxes' inscribed column bases at Susa, possibly 'Shushan the Palace' of the Book of Esther (Ahasuerus)	major building works at Persepolis	uprisings in Babylonia; reprisals by Xerxes	Elamite weaponry in use by Persians; Elamite deities still worshipped
464–424 BC	Apadana at Susa burned during reign of Artaxerxes I; construction of new palace (Donjon)?	continued building at Persepolis		
423–405 BC	building activity at Susa by Darius II			
404–359 BC	Artaxerxes II restores palace of Darius at Susa and builds			

	new one west of Susa on the Shaur river			
335–331 BC	Darius III defeated at Gauga-mela, Susa taken by Alexander the Great in 331 BC; city gar-risoned by Macedonians	Alexander subdues highlands en route to Persepolis	region conquered by Alexander, placed under Macedonian rule	Uxii represent re-mains of Elamite ethnic group in highlands

10

ELYMAIS

The survival of the Elamites as a distinct ethno-linguistic group is well-attested in the period following Alexander the Great's conquest of Western Asia. In Khuzistan we find continued occupation at major sites like Susa in the last centuries BC and first centuries AD, along with the foundation of important new sites like Masjid-i Solaiman, Tang-i Sarvak and Bard-e Nechandeh. Greek and Latin sources from the period speak of Elymais and the Elymaeans, in whom we can recognize without difficulty latter day Elamites. To a large extent the Elymaeans resisted the imposition of foreign rule by the successors of Alexander the Great, the Seleucid emperors (so named after the founder of the dynasty, Seleucus I). The geography of Elymaean territory was described by Strabo and attacks against them were made by several Seleucids, notably Antiochus III and IV.

With the demise of the Seleucid empire in the east, the major state in Iran was that of the Parthians. Originating in what is today the Khorassan province of northeastern Iran and adjacent portions of Turkmenistan, the Parthians appeared on the historical scene late in the third century BC when their first king, Arsaces I (c. 238–211 BC), began minting coins in his capital Nisa, near modern Ashgabat in Turkmenistan. By about 140 BC, the Parthian king Mithridates I had probably taken possession of Susa and was threatening Babylonia. Yet, for all its ability to contest Rome on the battlefield, the Parthian 'empire' was perhaps never more than a very loosely knit agglomeration of provinces in which local rulers exercised considerable autonomy. Certainly the fact that coins were minted by a series of Elymaean kings beginning with Kamniskires I, probably in the 140s BC, is a clear indication of the independence of the Elymaean rulers, and although the sequence and chronology of Elymaean coinage is, in many respects, unclear, the existence of an Elymaean political force is corroborated by contemporary Babylonian astronomical texts which parenthetically mention attacks on cities in Babylonia by Elamite troops.

Elymaean archaeology is best approached not at an urban center like Susa, which shows strong Greek and later Parthian influence, but at the sites of major Elymaean rock reliefs, like Hung-i Nauruzi, Tang-i Sarvak and others in the mountains north of Izeh, or at the shrines of Bard-e Nechandeh and Masjid-i Solaiman.

Introduction

The voyage of Nearchus, described in detail by Arrian and other ancient authors, ended with the arrival of the Greek admiral and his fleet at Susa (Bosworth 1987), where the long-awaited rendezvous with Alexander and his army was finally achieved (for the route along the Iranian coast, see Tomaschek 1890; Berthelot 1935). The Achaemenid empire was no more, Alexander's round of conquests had come to an end, and Macedonian domination, however nominal it may have been, was a reality across much of Western, Central and South Asia. Alexander's conferral in marriage of the daughter of his Persian mistress Barsine (Berve 1926/II: 102–4) on Nearchus (Arrian, *Anab.* VII.4.6) has sometimes been seen as symptomatic of the 'fusion' planned by the conqueror between Hellenic and Oriental societies (Badian 1975: 167). Eighty of the highest ranking Macedonians followed suit, marrying Persians of equal rank (Hamilton 1987: 467). In the classical tradition Susa thus became the scene of what was perceived by some as a major transformation in Western Asiatic history, whether or not that perception was correct. How did the descendants of the ancient Elamite and Susian populations (Fig. 10.1) fare in the wake of these momentous events?

Elymais and the Seleucid Successors

Alexander's death was followed by the wars between the generals who survived him, known as the Diadochoi. Much of the conflict between two of the protagonists of this period, Eumenes of Cardia and Antigonus the One-Eyed (see generally Wehrli 1968; Briant 1973; Will 1979: 52–3), took place in 316 BC in Susiana and Media, where Eumenes was eventually defeated (near Gabiane) and killed a year later by his own troops (von Gutschmid 1888: 17). According to Diodorus, after arriving at Susa Antigonus 'appointed Seleucus satrap of that country, gave him troops, and ordered him to lay siege to the citadel, since the treasurer, Xenophilus, refused to accept his orders' (XIX.18.1), and we know that at least some of the Alexander-type coins minted at Susa were in fact minted by Antigonus in the years 318–316 BC (Bellinger 1950–1: 45). As noted in Chapter 9, Antigonus halted at Badakê (Diodorus XIX.19.1), identified by some scholars with Elamite Madaktu and modern Tepe Patak. He is said to have received contributions to his war chest of 5000 talents of silver each from Susiana and Media (Diodorus XIX.48.8). In 301 BC, however, Antigonus lost his struggle for power with Seleucus (321–280 BC) at the battle of Ipsos, and thereby Seleucus' control over Susiana and Media was secure. From these beginnings sprang the empire of Seleucus and his successors, known as the Seleucids.

Beginning around 300 BC Seleucus began minting coins at Susa and Persepolis or Pasargadae (Newell 1938: 154–61; Jenkins 1978: 198). While very few coins from the Susa mint are extant, more are known from Fars, and it has been suggested that the mint there (whether at Persepolis or Pasargadae is uncertain) remained in operation until the end of Seleucus' reign in 280 BC. Thereafter no Seleucid emissions are known from Fars and this has been taken as one indication of the loss of Seleucid political control over Persis and the beginnings of autonomous rule there by the so-called *fratcaraka* dynasty (Will 1979: 280; see also Wiesehöfer 1994: 115–17 with lit.). The loss of Seleucid control in Persis cannot have been complete, or else it was later reversed, for during the reign of Antiochus III (223–187 BC) we know from Polybius that Alexander, brother of Molon the satrap of Media, was satrap in Persis (Newell 1938: 161). Indeed, Wiesehöfer has recently argued convincingly that Persis did not free itself from Seleucid domination until after the reign of Antiochus IV (175–164 BC) (Wiesehöfer 1994: 122ff.).

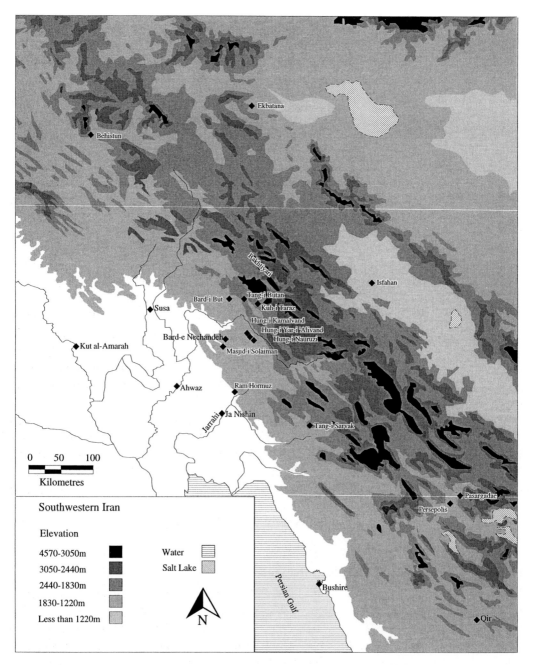

Figure 10.1 Map of southwestern Iran showing the principal sites mentioned in Chapter 10.

Seleucus and his son Antiochus I (280–261 BC) are credited with the founding or re-founding of a large, if indeterminate number of cities in Asia. Of those which can be located somewhere in southwestern Iran we can name Seleucia-by-the-Eulaios (ancient Susa, see LeRider 1965a; Fraser 1996: 33), Seleucia-by-the-Hedyphon (Hansman 1978; Fraser 1996: 32) in eastern Susiana, Antiochia-in-Persis (near modern Bushire?) (Potts 1990b/II: 16; Sherwin-White and Kuhrt 1993: 162ff.; Fraser 1996: 31, n. 68), and Laodicea-in-Persis, near the 'edge' of Persis ('extremis finibus', Pliny, *Nat. Hist.* VI. 26.115; Tscherikower 1927: 168; Wiesehöfer 1994: 61). Although Seleucus inherited twenty-one Asian satrapies, he subdivided these, creating out of them no fewer than seventy-two.

As we learn from the account of the revolt of Molon, satrap of Media, against Antiochus III sometime prior to the accession of Antiochus in 223 BC, southernmost Babylonia (the former 'Sealand') and Susiana had been joined administratively to form the 'satrapy of the Erythraean Sea' (Schmitt 1964: 34; Bengtson 1964/II: 37; LeRider 1965b: 36–7). We do not know whether this occurred as early as the reign of Antiochus II (261–246 BC), but with his death and the accession of his son Seleucus II (246–226 BC), the Ptolemaic king Ptolemy III (246–221 BC) seized the opportunity to conquer much of the Seleucid empire (Third Syrian War, 246–245 BC), including important areas of Syria and Asia Minor, although the likelihood that this included 'Babylonia, Susiana, Persis, Media and all the rest [of the Seleucid realm] as far as Bactria', as the Adulis inscription, copied in the sixth century AD by Cosmas Indicopleustes, claims, is unlikely (Will 1979: 251). This interruption of Seleucid rule brought about revolt in the Upper Satrapies which lasted many years.

As soon as he came to power, Antiochus III was forced at once to deal with the revolt of Molon, satrap of Media, and his brother Alexander, satrap of Persis. Before long Susiana, with the exception of Susa itself (Sherwin-White and Kuhrt 1993: 189), had fallen to Molon, as well as most of Mesopotamia as far west as Dura Europus on the Euphrates. After finally suppressing Molon, Antiochus in 222 BC installed one Apollodoros as *strategos* of Susiana (Polybius V.54.12). Let us briefly examine the archaeological context of Seleucid rule in southwestern Iran.

Southwestern Iran in the Seleucid period

A global understanding of settlement in the third and second centuries BC is hampered by the fact that the one major survey devoted to sites of this time period (Wenke 1976; 1981) unknowingly mistook Achaemenid ceramic forms for Seleucid-era types and mixed Seleucid and Parthian forms when attempting to chart Parthian occupation (de Miroschedji 1987: 43, n. 85; Boucharlat 1993: 41, n. 1). Thus, to speak of occupation in the 'Seleuco-Parthian' period, *c.* 325 BC to AD 25, may be an archaeological necessity because of continuity in ceramic forms and decorative styles throughout this period, and the inability to distinguish Seleucid from Parthian variants due to a paucity of research, but it does not contribute much to our understanding of land-use and settlement patterns in the region in a time which saw some profound changes at a political level.

Fortunately several ancient authors give us some precise indications of land-use patterns in the Alexandrian or early Seleucid period. Speaking of Alexander's preference for Babylon over Susa, Strabo (XV.3.9–11) noted that, 'Although Susis is fertile, it has a hot and scorching atmosphere, and particularly in the neighbourhood of the city [Susa]', but he went on to say that 'Susis abounds so exceedingly in grain that both barley and wheat regularly produce one hundredfold, and sometimes even two hundred', and further that 'the vine did not grow there until the Macedonians planted it'. While Strabo's description of the climate of Khuzistan will not surprise anyone who has visited the region, his account of the phenomenal yields achieved for wheat and barley crops strains all credulity. Without going into the enormous problems raised by the calculation of yields in ancient sources (see Potts 1997: 80–2 with lit.), suffice it to say that 100– and 200–fold yields far outstrip modern yields and returns even remotely approaching these could only have been achieved through the use of the seeding plough.

Strabo's reference to the introduction of the grape by the Macedonians is unlikely to be reliable, particularly since we know that grapes were cultivated and wine was manufactured in neighbouring southern Mesopotamia from an early date (Potts 1997: 69–70, 148–50). Moreover, there are at least two additional cultivars attested in Susiana by the late fourth century BC which seem to have escaped Strabo's notice. According to Diodorus Siculus (XIX.13.6), when Eumenes and his troops were in Susiana c. 318/7 BC 'marching through the country . . . he was completely without grain, but he distributed to his soldiers rice, sesame, and dates, since the land produced such fruits as these in plenty'. Elsewhere Strabo also confirms that rice was grown in Susis (XV.1.18), but it is difficult to know whether this information derives from the earlier period of Alexander and Eumenes or his own era, i.e. the first century BC (Potts 1991).

Although there are numerous unexcavated sites which were occupied during the Seleucid period, e.g. KS-15, KS-204 (Tepe Gallegah) and KS-316 (de Miroschedji 1987: 43), there are only two sites from which we have any appreciable quantity of excavated material: Susa and Masjid-i Solaiman.

Susa

As we have seen, Susa figures prominently in accounts of Alexander's conquests, beginning with the Macedonian's ceremonial occupation of Darius III's throne there during his first visit to the city (Bosworth 1980a: 5), and it continues to appear in accounts of the Diadochoi and Seleucid rulers, right through to the end of the reign of Demetrius II (146–140 BC). Pottery and other finds of Seleucid date have been found since the beginning of excavations at Susa in the mid-nineteenth century when Loftus unearthed the first two Greek inscriptions known from site on the Apadana mound (Curtis 1993: 11, Pl. 7b; see also Table 10.1.6). Sporadic finds (Pl. 10.1, Figs. 10.2–3) of Seleucid date were also made by Dieulafoy (Apadana, Ville Royale), de Morgan (Acropole, Apadana, Ville Royale) and de Mecquenem (Ville Royale, Donjon, Apadana, Ville des Artisans), but it was not until Ghirshman's excavations in the 1940s that the first remains of this date were found in stratigraphic context (Boucharlat 1993: 43). Excavations in level VII

Plate 10.1 Greek-style terracottas from Susa (top row, l. to r., Sb 3834, Sb 3621, Sb 3610; bottom row, l. to r., Sb 3620, Sb 3607, Sb 3910). © Musée du Louvre, Antiquités Orientales

in Ville Royale A revealed 'large, well-built houses (about 20m long) with inner court-yards, sometimes decorated, having a bathroom and containing numerous artefacts including terracotta figurines and fragments of Greek architectural decoration' (Boucharlat 1993: 44). Subsequent excavations by de Miroschedji in Ville Royale II (levels 3E/D) and Boucharlat in the Apadana East/Ville Royale (level 5e) areas yielded Hellenistic ceramics (e.g. fish-plates, bowls with inverted rim, carinated bowls, egg-shell ware; Boucharlat 1993, Haerinck 1983: 19–37; for Greek black-glazed pottery from Susa, see Clairmont 1957: 124–30; for stamped Rhodian and Thasian amphora handles from the site, see Börker 1974: 44) and coins (LeRider 1965a), but little in the way of architecture or stratigraphy (de Miroschedji 1987: 35–43). Important evidence for the re-occupation of the Achaemenid palaces of Darius and Artaxerxes II by squatters in the early Diadochoi-phase, i.e. prior to the Seleucid era proper, has also been recovered in the work initiated by Perrot on the Apadana mound (Boucharlat 1990b; 1993: 45). Industrial areas with ceramic kilns have been located in the eastern Ville Royale and in the Ville des Artisans, while shaft graves dug into the Achaemenid retaining wall are known from the eastern and southern slopes of the Ville Royale and western slope of the Ville des Artisans (Boucharlat 1993: 44).

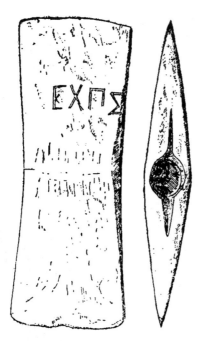

Figure 10.2 Bronze axehead with Greek inscription from de Mecquenem's Acropole Sondage I at Susa (after de Mecquenem 1934: Fig. 5).

Over thirty Greek lapidary inscriptions (Fig. 10.4) have been recovered at Susa, perhaps nine of which date to the period of the Diadochoi and the Seleucids, the rest belonging to the Parthian era (Table 10.1). These provide an important window on the political, social and juridical status of the Greek settlement there. Where a particular Greek title, office or institution is only referred to in an inscription of Parthian date it is probably safe to assume that this represents the perpetuation of a feature in the late period which already existed in the Seleucid era. One text from the late third century BC (Table 10.1.4) refers to a soldiers' association, and this strongly suggests that Susa was settled as a typical Seleucid military colony by soldiers who were either organized into an association while still on active duty, or who formed an organization soon after they were settled at the site (Cohen 1978: 76). A dedication from AD 1/2 by the guardians (*phrouroi*) of the citadel (*akra*) honours the Parthian administrator who had made improvements to the irrigation system which greatly enhanced the fertility of the guardians' land allotments (*kleroi*). Cohen has suggested that 'most likely these guardians of the citadel were descended from the original colonists or garrison soldiers who were settled in the *akra*' (Cohen 1978: 23). Land grants (*kleroi*) were typically given to new settlers, military or civilian, but here it seems clear that the guardians had a military status. These indications, however sparse, strongly suggest that Susa was originally settled with retired soldiers who were given land around the city, if not in the lifetime of Alexander then early in the Seleucid era.

On the other hand, the city may well have evolved from a military colony to a city-

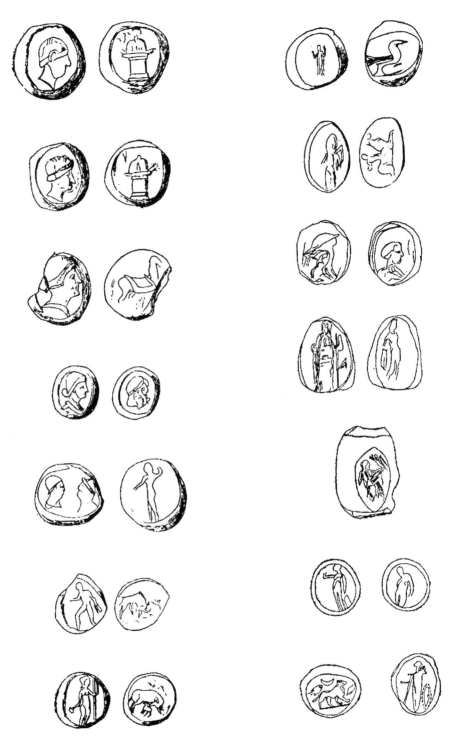

Figure 10.3 Hellenistic seal impressions from Susa (after Unvala 1934b: 242).

Figure 10.4 Greek lapidary inscriptions from Susa: 1. SEG 17.3 (after Cumont 1933: 264); 2. SEG 17.26 (after Cumont 1933: 261); 3. SEG 17.12 (after Cumont 1930: 211).

Table 10.1. *Greek inscriptions from Susa published in SEG 17 (texts 12 and 13 are treated in main text)*

SEG 17	Original	Date	Translation
1	Cumont 1932a: 238–59	AD 21	It was received during the two hundred and sixty-eighth year, as the King reckons, and as formerly (reckoned), the [three hundred and thirty-third year].
			King of kings Arsaces, to Antiochus and Phraates, being the two archons in Susa, and to the city – greetings.
			[Whereas Hestiaios, son of Asios, one of] your citizens, and one of the First and Preferred Friends, and one of the Bodyguards, having held the office of Treasurer in, [according to the former] reckoning, the three hundred and twenty-ninth year, conducted himself in this office in the best and most just manner and with all scrupulousness, having held back [no expense] on his own account towards outlay on behalf of the city; and (whereas) twice, when the city during his term of office [had need of an envoy, he went out] himself, placing at nought attention to his private interests and considering the city's interests of greater consequence, and, sparing neither resources nor trouble, he gave [himself up unreservedly] to both embassies, and, having pursued what was of benefit to his native city, he received appropriate honours, as indeed the decree [concerning him] in the three hundred and thirtieth year bears witness; and (whereas) in the three hundred and thirtieth-first year, when there was need of a good man (honest man?), [he was again proposed] for the same office for the three hundred and thirty-second year, and after a full examination – Petasos, son of Antiochus, having been chosen archon with [Aristomenes], son of Philip – he came forward and pleaded that he was barred according to established practice from holding the same office twice, unless a period of three years intervened; and (whereas) the city, [as it had formerly experienced] his good character and remembered the administration of the aforementioned office, decided to choose him to hold the office, upon which he was chosen for the three hundred and thirty-[second] year, in the archonship of Petasos, son of Antiochus, and Aristomenes, son of Philip; therefore since [they unjustly charge] Hestiaios on the above grounds, we decide that his election is valid and that he is not to be ejected from office (or 'that he is not to be prosecuted'?) on the grounds that he has held the

Table 10.1 (*cont.*)

SEG 17	Original	Date	Translation
			same office (twice) without a period of three years intervening, nor on the grounds of any other royal order whatsoever [which might be presented] concerning these matters, and that in general, setting aside any interdiction or investigation, it is necessary to discharge the [summons?] expressly mentioned, of this [investigation?] or any other (??). (Below in smaller letters:) (On the left:) This statue of Hestiaios was set up by Asios, son of Demetrius, the 'Eisagogeus', the father of Hestiaios, in the 337th year according to the former reckoning. (On the right:) Leonides, son of Artemon, citizen of Seleucia-by-the-Eulaios, inscribed the stele.
2	Cumont 1928: 81–4	177/6 BC	In the reign of Seleucus, in the year 136, in the month [*name and day*], and in Seleucia-by-the-Eulaios [*day*] of the month L[ôios], in the time of Ammonios (eponymous magistrate?); [it was decided by the assembly] following the resolution of the secretary Demetrios and [the councillors]: [whereas *name*] of Attalos [the chief-priestess of Laodice] [wife] of Seleucus [the king], and of Laodice [the elder] the mother [of Seleucus, and] of Laodice the [younger the daughter of Seleucus . . .]
3	Cumont 1933: 264–8	150–100 BC	– –	. . . . – –	– – Nicolaos, son of Ma[cedon(?), winner in the games and] wreath-wearer and one of [the First Friends and of the Body]guards [– –] and upon [becoming] gymnasiarch he [lavishly furnished] the stadium for the city; [so that thus] a fine memorial [would exist for all time of the service] rendered [to the city – –] . . . . – – || – – . – –
4	Cumont 1932b: 272–4	late third cent. BC	Leon and the commanders and soldiers under him, to Arete, daughter of Timon, who is in charge of the king's Court, and of Atheno.
5	Cumont 1931: 234–8	third cent. BC?	[– – *name*], son of Nikandros, the commander (*or poss.* governor/chief-magistrate), and in charge of processions (*or poss.* revenues).
6	Cumont 1931: 234–8	first cent. BC	Those of the middle Service-Group, to Lysimachus, son of Apollophanos, one of the Bodyguards, to him from amongst the others on account of his good service. In the year [2]14. Diophantos inscribed the stele.

No.	Reference	Date	
8	Haussoullier 1902: 159	?	– – of those amongst the F[irst and Preferred Friends – –]
9	Pézard and Pottier 1926: 107	sixth cent. BC	These statues (or votive offerings) Aristolochus and Thrason dedicated to Apollo out of booty as a tenth-part; Isikles, son of Kudimandros, cast them.
10	Cumont 1928: 80	late third cent. BC	To Ma, Apollodoros, son of Krateros.
11	Cumont 1932b: 274–7	third cent. BC	To Chaireas, son of Eumenes, I was entirely helpful, appearing in this guise, saviour of Antigona, his wife, and Cleio, his child, and by this image giving thanks in return, the sculptor himself, in Greek lyrics, celebrates me, Phoebus, the archer-renowned.
14	Cumont 1928: 89–96	first cent. AD	[Dedicated] to Ap[ollo, by Herodorus, son of Artemon, of Seleucia-by-the-Eulaios: he was victor in – –] Already . . . . and . . . . and you, god, ... [. . . . . . all]shining, Hyperion, and you hang decorated branches before the doors on houses O [. . . . .] and of [fertile] Nanaya; And [they shudder] beneath calamities . . . . for you to help [I know(?); your] impetuous strength moves the heaven in its circle, You, [over both the earth] prolific and the place [below], [shed your light, nowhere your] bound and limit exceeding, ... you separate(?) [. . . . . [. . . . . [. . . . . [. . . . . [. . . . . [. . . . . [. . . . . [. . . . .] you provide . . [. . . . .] of your store-house(?) [. . . . . a quantity] uncountable of sand [. . . . .] . . . . . . new you draw off, And from the impassable mountain you divide the floating depths, And you rain abundantly upon the pious a prosperity flowing with gold, And you stroke wild beasts in their lairs, immortal one, you soothe (them),

Table 10.1 (*cont.*)

SEG 17	Original	Date	Translation
			And instantly you (soothe?) leopards in cultivated glens, And you cover with cleverness the most-unlearned who hymn you, You do not dispense to the wise a fair-flowing (prosperous?) wealth which may be removed; Therefore, nations and cities hallow the sun (*lit.* eye *sc.* of heaven), Worshipped under many names, since you alone are the object of reverence of all; Yes, divine Mara, everywhere [– – – – –] All-seeing, highest of [the gods – – – – –]
15	Cumont 1928: 84–8	second cent. BC	In the reign of [Antiochus, in the year one hundred and *year*, in the month] Audnaios the 20th (day), in S[eleucia-by-the-Eulaios], Bacchios, [son of *name*, declaring] himself to be in [the *e.g.* horse-squadron] of Euandros, has dedicated to the goddess [Nanaya], for the preservation of Ant[iochus the king] and of Laodice the [wife of the king], his young female slave Mikra, at 30 years (of age), [and let it not be permitted to Bac]chios nor [to any other on his behalf] to ens[lave her in any way nor] by any pretence; [but if] they should do [any of these things], let the claim [and the seizure] and the enslavement [be invalid] and let [Bacchios] or the person doing any of these things pay besides [to the goddess] 3000 [drachmas of silver]. Witnesses: [*name* son of *name*] secretary of the public archive; and civilians, Artemidorus, son of Lysanios, [*name* son of *name*], Heraios son of Isidorus, [*name* son of *name*], Attalos [son of *name* . . .]
16	Cumont 1928: 88–9	?	– –	3000 drach(mas) of silver.
17	Cumont 1931: 279–85	183 BC	In the reign of Seleucus, in the year 130, in the month Daisios, in Seleucia-by-the-Eulaios, Kalliphon, son of Diodorus, declaring himself to be in the cavalry under Alexandros, dedicated to Apollo and Artemis 'Daittais', for the preservation of Seleucus the king and Laodice the queen – –
18	Cumont 1931: 285–8	209–193 BC?	[In the reign of A]ntiochus and Antiochus, [in the year] two hundred and [*number*], [in the month *name*, on the twenty-[first?] (day), [in Seleucia-by-the-Eula]ios, [*name*, son of *name*, dedicated to Lady Artemis?] Nanaya,

	Reference	Date	Text
			[for the preservation of An]tiochus [the king and Antiochus the younger the king – –]
19	Cumont 1931: 290	second cent. BC	[– – for Antiochus' (or Seleucus?) the king and] Laodice's – – Archias, son of Aristomenos and having dedicated – – according to the contr[act – –] on . . . – –
20	Cumont 1931: 291	second cent. BC	[– – in the year – – nine]ty, [in the month] Dystros the 5th (day), [in Seleucia-by-the-Eu]laios – –
21	Cumont 1931: 289–90	second/third cent. BC?	[– – Witnesses:] Antimachos [son of *name*], Drakas son of Mega[reus?. And] civilians: Diodorus, son of Diogenes, Apollonios, son of Agathocles.
22	Cumont 1932b: 278–9	142/1 BC	In the year 171, in the month – – Straton, son of Simias, dedicated to the goddess Nanaya Kan . . ., his young female slave, at 30 years (of age), for the preservation of the king and the queen, and let it not be permitted to Straton nor to any other on his behalf in any way whatsoever to lay claim to the above-mentioned slave nor to sell? (her). If he does any of these things, let it be invalid and let him pay besides to the temple of Nanaya 3000 drachmas of silver.
23	Cumont 1932b: 281–2	second cent. BC	[– – let it not] be permitted to Diom[edes? nor to any other] to lay claim [to the above-mentioned] slaves [nor] to effect [any seizure of them] nor [– –] to them anything [in any way whatsoever – –]
24	Cumont 1932b: 284–6	second cent. BC	– –	– –	– – in Seleu[cia-[by-the-Eulaios] having proclaimed it, [*name*, son of Oly]mpios [– – for the] preservation of Antiochus the king and [Laodice the q]ueen – – , having prayed, [dedicated} to the goddess Nanaya [– – S]korpion his slave.
25	Cumont 1932b: 279–81	131 BC	In the year [116, as the] king reckons, as formerly 181, in the month Xandikos, Apollonides, son of Philip, dedicated Baccheiades, his young female slave, at the age of thirty, and let it not be permitted to anyone to lay claim to the afore-mentioned slave nor to enslave her. If any of these things should happen, let it be invalid and let the person who had done it pay besides 3000 drachmas of silver.
26	Cumont 1933: 261–3	200–150 BC	[– – and let it not be permitted] to Beltibanatis nor to [her husband nor] to any other on behalf on her [to lay claim] to Sozaia, the afore-men[tioned, nor] to effect the seizure of her, [nor to enslave] her in any way or by any [pretext]; if any of these things [should happen, let the] claim and the seizure [and the slavery] be invalid and let Beltibanatis, or [the peson who

Table 10.1 (cont.)

SEG 17	Original	Date	Translation
			has done any of these things] on her behalf, [pay besides 3000 drachmas of silver].
27	Cumont 1928: 79–80	fourth cent. BC	Nikokles, son of Nikoles, of Sinope.
28	Cumont 1928: 97	?	– –	– – from them 1,	– – . . . 1,	– – . . . from them 1,		[– – (he) ex]amines 2 of ours,	[– – from] them 1.
29	Cumont 1928: 97–8	?	– – of John	– – of the service group	– – to Abinna
30	Cumont 1931: 291/2	?	[– –] Apollonios, in charge [of the first?] service group.
31	Cumont 1932b: 286	?	– – Asclepiadorus, son of Artemon, of the service-group.
32	Cumont 1930: 209	?	– – of Demetrios, Timé, daughter of Dinarios.

state (*polis*) by the end of the third or beginning of the second century BC. In describing the process whereby Bethesda was elevated from a village to a *polis* by Philip the Tetrarch (died AD 34), Josephus says that he introduced new settlers, rebuilt the town's fortifications, and changed its name (*Jewish Antiquities* 18.28). As Cohen notes, 'the adoption of a dynastic name was a right associated with the transformation of a colony into a *polis*' (Cohen 1978: 84), and based on this criterion we are probably safe in assuming that Susa, when it was renamed Seleucia-by-the-Eulaios, was also elevated in status from military colony to *polis*. The fact that we have no literary references to the new name until the reign of Antiochus III (Tarn 1938: 27; Tarn and Vickers 1996: 1458; Boucharlat 1985a: 75) is perhaps fortuitous, for the name suggests strongly that the change occurred under Seleucus I (321–280 BC) or his son Antiochus I (280–261 BC), who may have named it after his father (Tscherikower 1927: 168, 175). It was perhaps in association with the new status of the city that a gymnasium and stadium were founded at the site, archaeologically unattested but implied by a text from the early first century BC (Table 10.1.3) honouring one Nicolaos, victor in the sacred games held at Susa (Cohen 1978: 36), which mentions the gymnasiarch and stadium (Oppenheimer 1983: 427). Similarly, a letter sent to the people of Susa in AD 21 (Table 10.1.1) by the Parthian king Artabanus III (Cumont 1932a; Bengtson 1964/II: 297 with earlier bibl.) shows that the city 'still had many of the governmental accoutrements of a Greek *polis*, including the election of officials by the citizen body and a *boule* which proposed candidates and held a *dokimasia* [examination of candidates by outgoing officials]. There were also two eponymous archons [magistrates] and a treasurer' (Cohen 1978: 2). An administrative building or public archive (*chreophylakion*) is also mentioned in one text (Table 10.1.15).

The Susa inscriptions are also an important source of information on religion in the Seleucid era. Four texts (Table 10.1.14, 18, 22, 24) mention Nanaya, while a fifth, to 'the goddess' (Table 10.1.15), probably applies to her as well. Rostovtzeff emphasised the role of 'the famous temple of Nanaya . . . a large and handsome building, which certainly was not neglected either by the kings or by their local representatives. Among the stones of the temple, which were used later by the Sasanians for the construction of their palace, were found scores of Greek inscriptions of the Seleucid and Parthian periods, among them several manumissions, which shows that at this time the temple was the chief centre of the city, the place where important documents were published, statues erected, and so on' (Rostovtzeff 1941/I: 428, 436–7). Ma, the warlike Cappadocian goddess who was thought to confer victory on her followers, is named in a dedication cut into a circular limestone statue base found on the Apadana at Susa on behalf of one Apollodoros, son of Krateros (Table 10.1.10). Cumont believed that this was the same individual whom Polybius (V.54.12) says Antiochus III installed as *strategos* of Susiana around 222 BC, but the text in question refers to one Apollophanos, not Apollodoros (Table 10.1.6).

Turning finally to the subject of slavery, although recent publications on Iran during the Parthian period has tried to downplay the role of slavery in the Seleucid era there (Wolski 1983: 149; 1993: 104), there are no fewer than five Greek texts from Susa which concern slaves. The original publications of the Susa texts by B. Haussoullier and F. Cumont (Haussoullier 1902; Cumont 1928; 1930; 1931; 1932a; 1932b; 1933) led to considerable discussion of the alleged differences between Oriental and Greek law with regard to the manumission of slaves (e.g. Koschaker 1931), but L. Robert showed convincingly that much of the debate was due to questionable restorations of certain key passages in the texts. The texts in question are almost all manumissions accompanied by dedications of the freed slaves, who are both male (Table 10.1.24) and female (Table 10.1.15, 17, 22, 25), to the goddess Nanaya. In fact, manumission by consecration to the chief divinity of a city was perfectly normal in ancient Greece (Robert 1936: 144, 147) and nothing suggests that the procedures followed at Susa were anything other than standard Greek ones. Indeed, most of the manumittors at Susa, as well as the witnesses, bore Greek names (one female witness, Beltibanatis, has a Babylonian name). Whether or not these manumissions entailed service for a specified period of time in the temple of Nanaya we cannot tell, but the suggestion that several of these slaves were young girls being dedicated to Nanaya for a period of thirty years was disproven by Robert who showed that, on the contrary, the slaves were *thirty years old* at the time of their manumission. At any rate, whether their freedom was conditional or unconditional, it was quite normal that 'the god acted as a guarantor of the former slave's new status' in all such cases (Potter 1996).

The worship of Nanaya at Susa has never been properly explained. Although von Gall considers a text from Parthian Nisa in Turkmenistan dating to 190 BC to be the earliest evidence for the worship of Nanaya (von Gall 1986b: 410), the goddess is in fact attested in Mesopotamia as early as the reign of Shulgi during the Ur III period (Westenholz 1997: 82). Nevertheless the inscribed bricks from Susa which originally belonged to temples built or re-built by Elamite kings give no indication that Nanaya was worshipped there prior to the Seleucid era. On the other hand, as we saw in Chapter 8, Assurbanipal says that he repatriated a statue of Nanaya to the Eanna temple at Uruk which had been taken to Susa 1635 years earlier, and in the reign of Sennacherib an apparently different statue of Nanaya was taken by Elamite forces and subsequently restored to Assyria (Westenholz 1997: 74). These incidents, if true, provide a concrete context for the introduction of the worship of Nanaya to Susa long before the Seleucid period.

And what of the much older shrines to Inshushinak and other native deities at Susa? Did they survive the Achaemenid and Macedonian conquest? It is of course difficult to say in the absence of any epigraphic evidence, but one unexpected insight is offered by a recension of the Akkadian ritual text describing bread-making at the Anu temple in Uruk which was discussed in Chapter 8. As noted above, the colophon of this text tells us that a priest from Uruk 'looked at these tablets in the land of Elam, copied them in the reign of the kings Seleucus and Antiochus, and brought (his copies) back to the city of Uruk' (Pritchard 1969: 345). Furthermore, the colophon adds that the text was one of a number of 'tablets which Nabopolassar, king of the Sealand, carried off as plunder from the city of Uruk'. The text says the tablets were copied in the land of Elam and it is unlikely that their place of storage can have been other than a temple at Susa. While saying nothing directly about religious practice at Susa in the Seleucid period, the circumstances of the tablet's provenience suggest the possibility that temples in which cuneiform was still used existed side by side with newer shrines, like the one to Nanaya. This is an intriguing insight into the life of the city long after it had come under Achaemenid and finally Greek influence.

Masjid-i Solaiman

Some forty kilometres east of Shushtar as the crow flies are two sites of importance for the period under discussion. The earlier of these, in use during the Seleucid period and therefore treated first, is Masjid-i Solaiman ('mosque of Solomon'), a site located in what has long been one of the centres of Iran's oil industry. The major monument of Masjid-i Solaiman is a stone terrace (Fig. 10.5) of irregular shape measuring *c.* 54×91.4 m accessible by staircases on the north, south and east sides. Roughly in the middle of the terrace stood the so-called 'great temple'. Soundings through the floors of this late Parthian/early Sasanian temple recovered numerous figurines in Greek style of cavalry riders wearing the Macedonian *kausia*, a Central Asian type of woollen hat resembling the caps worn today by Afghans and Pakistanis from the northwestern part of Pakistan, originally introduced into Greece in the wake of Alexander's Central Asian conquests (Kingsley 1981). The recovery of this material led Ghirshman to postulate the existence of a Seleucid garrison at Masjid-i Solaiman (Ghirshman 1976: 79–80), stationed along an important route leading north towards Gabiane with its capital Gabai/Tabae, long identified with the area of modern Isfahan (Hoffmann 1880: 132, n. 1130; Weissbach 1910a; 1910b). A bronze plaque showing a female bust and a bronze head likened to an image of Athena in turn prompted Ghirshman to suggest that the original temple beneath the later Parthian structure was a Macedonian temple sacred to Athena Hippia (Ghirshman 1976: 89), possibly the one said by Strabo to have been destroyed by a Parthian king (XVI.1.18).

Fifteen metres to the northwest of the 'great temple' were found the remains of a multi-roomed, rectangular structure (8.03×17.10 m) interpreted by Ghirshman as a temple to Heracles. This identification was based on the recovery of the torso, legs and head of a statue of Heracles strangling the Nemean lion which probably stood *c.* 2.4 m in height when it was complete. Ghirshman suggested that the evidence of the worship of these Greek cults at Masjid-i Solaiman might go back to the reign of Antiochus I (280–261 BC), although no compelling justification was given for such a date and the limited numismatic evidence would not support it. All of the six pre-Roman, Greek coins recovered at Masjid-i Solaiman (a late fourth cent. BC silver drachm from Lampsacus; a silver drachm of Alexander I Balas [150–145 BC] from Seleucia-on-the-Tigris; a bronze obol of the same king from Susa; two bronze obols of Tigraios [c. 138/7–133/2 BC]; and a bronze obol, possibly from Susa, of Antiochus I) were heavily worn and were found together with later coins, suggesting that they had been in circulation for a long time and arrived at the site well after they had been minted (Augé *et al.* 1979: 16). Nevertheless, even if the architectural and iconographic arguments adduced by Ghirshman for the date of the earliest remains at Masjid-i Solaiman are fragile (Hannestad and Potts 1990: 115), the ceramics from the site suggest a date in the third and early second century BC (Haerinck 1983: 14).

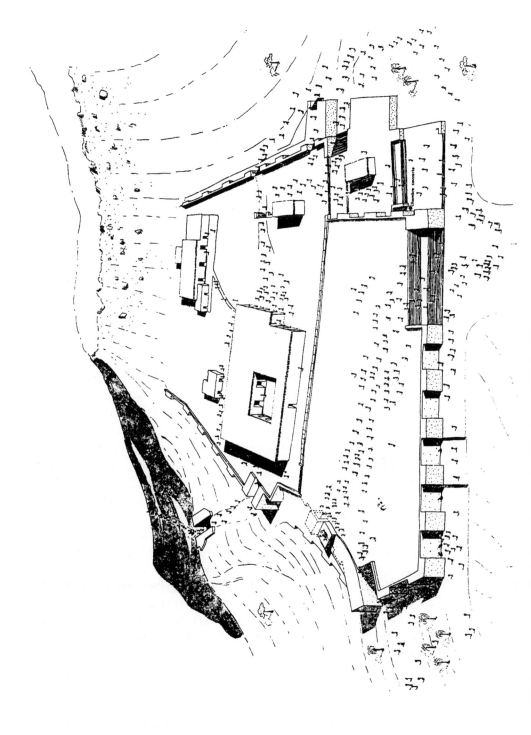

Figure 10.5 Artist's impression of Masjid-i Solaiman (after Ghirshman 1976: Fig. 42).

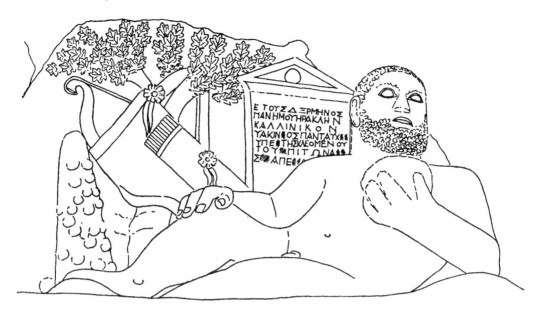

Figure 10.6 The Heracles relief and inscription at Behistun (after Huff 1984: Abb. 20).

As for the existence of a cult of Heracles at Masjid-i Solaiman, Ghirshman noted that if his identification of the Masjid-i Solaiman as the Heracles temple was correct, then it represented the first cult centre of the Greek god identified in Iran (Ghirshman 1976: 101). Other evidence of the veneration of Heracles in Iran includes the reclining Heracles relief at Behistun (Fig. 10.6), an image carved for Hyakinthos, son of Pantauchos, in honour of Kleomenis, the local Seleucid governor and dated in an adjacent Greek inscription to 148 BC (Bivar 1983: 33), i.e. the reign of Alexander I Balas (150–145 BC) (Luschey 1974: 122; 1990: 293; 1996; Vanden Berghe 1983: 118 and Pl. 10; Robert 1963: 76), and the inscription which states 'Here resides Heracles, nothing evil may enter' inside the cave of Qalah Karafto south of Hasanlu in Iranian Kurdistan (Bernard 1980). The significance of these occurrences in light of broader patterns of Greek-Iranian interaction have been largely ignored by ancient historians dealing with the period (e.g. Momigliano 1975: 137–50; Wolski 1977; 1989), but historians of religion have scarcely ceased discussing the problem of whether or not representations of a Greek Heracles in Iran reflect the worship of a genuinely Greek deity, or assimilation with the Iranian deity Verethragna (e.g. Bivar and Shaked 1964: 268; Scarcia 1979; von Gall 1986a: 212–13; Potts 1993: 352–3).

The Kossaeans

In Chapter 9, Kissia and the Kissians were discussed, and mention was made of later references to them post-dating the time of Alexander. According to Polybius (V.79), a Kissian contingent was present, along with Karmanians, Persians and Medes, among the 'subjects' who fought on Antiochus III's side at the battle of Raphia in 217 BC (Bar Kochva 1976: 50). Because this is the only post-Alexander reference to Kissians which does not go back to Herodotus, and because Polybius elsewhere (V.82) writes *Kissaious* or *Kassious*, Nöldeke (Nöldeke 1874: 178) dismissed Antiochus' Kissians as an error for *Kossaeans* (as at V.44). Nearly thirty years later, in 190 BC, Elymaeans were amongst the 'auxiliaries from subject or semi-independent nations or tribes' (Bar-Kochva 1976: 48 contends they were not, as Weissbach 1908: 2464 assumed, mercenaries) who fought by Antiochus' side at the battle of Magnesia (Livy 40.10.4). Let us examine these two ethnic groups, Kossaeans and Elymaeans.

If we begin with the Kossaeans, opinions have differed over the question of their relationship to the Kissians, discussed in Chapter 9. Some authorities consider them to be two distinct groups (e.g. Lehmann 1892; Cameron 1936: 92), while others see the names as two different variants of one and the same ethnicon, derived ultimately from Akkadian *Kaššu*, or 'Kassite' (nominative)/'Kassite' (adjective) (Delitzsch 1884; Billerbeck 1893: 36; Weissbach 1922b: 1501; for the use of the term, see Balkan 1954: 108), the earlier Kissioi reflecting a pronunciation *c.* 500 BC, the later Kossaioi a pronunciation of *c.* 300 BC, and the entire name complex to be located in the Pusht-i Kuh and Pish-i Kuh regions of Luristan (Herzfeld 1968: 190; see also Nöldeke 1874: 178; but note that Darius III's army at Gaugamela included 'those who dwelt in the mountains of the Cossaei' [Curtius, IV.12.10] and these are undoubtedly the Kossaeans). This, however, seems highly speculative. Equally speculative is the supposed connection between the Kassites, or their patron deity *dKaššu*, and the Kossaioi (Weissbach 1922b: 1501; Ziegler 1979; on the chronological range of *dKaššu*, see Balkan 1954: 108–9). A linguistically more acceptable derivation of the Greek toponym and ethnic would seem to be from the Hebrew and Aramaic rabbinic literature. In the Talmud Khuzistan is referred to in Hebrew as Be Huzae, in later Syriac sources as Beth Huzaje, and this has been taken by some Talmudic scholars as the source of Greek Kossaea (e.g. Obermeyer 1929: 204). Similarly the people known in the Talmud as Hoski/Hozki have been identified with the Kossaeans (Neubauer 1868: 378). Here we shall treat the Kossaeans as a unique group since their affiliation (or lack thereof) with the Kissians is of no relevance to an understanding of their role in the Seleucid and Parthian periods.

The Kossaeans were located in the mountains to the north of Susiana. According to Nearchus, the first Greek to provide firsthand knowledge of them, the territory of the Kossaeans neighboured that of the Medes, and the Persian king, in travelling from his winter capital of Susa to his summer capital at Ekbatana, had to cross the country of the Kossaeans (Strabo, *Geog.* XI.13.6). The same is said of Antigonus, who, according to Diodorus Siculus (XIX.19.2), had to laboriously fight his way through the land of the Kossaeans when going from Susiana to Ekbatana (see Nöldeke 1874: 179). Elsewhere Nearchus says that the Kossaeans were neighbours of the Uxians (*Anab.* VII.15.1). Strabo calls Kossaea an area 'inhabited by mountainous and predatory tribes' (*Geog.* XVI.1.17). According to Diodorus (V.44.7) the Kossaeans dwelt along with other tribes in the 'depressions and deep valleys' of Mount Zagrus (Zagros mountains). Other descriptions in ancient literature provide conflicting statements, e.g. when Arrian says that the Kossaeans lived in Persis (*Anab.* VII.23.1) or Strabo says that Kossaea extended as far north and east as the Caspian Gates (*Geog.* XVI.1.17), but these can probably be ignored.

Several ethnographic insights on the Kossaeans can be gleaned from the ancient authors. Polybius calls the Kossaeans one of the 'barbarous tribes' of the Zagros, 'with a high reputation for their warlike qualities' (V.44.7). Diodorus adds, 'These men, who have been independent from ancient times, live in caves, eating acorns and mushrooms, and also the smoked flesh of wild beasts' (XIX.19.3). The reference to acorns is particularly interesting for when Baron de Bode was travelling in the Bakhtiyari mountains in 1841 he met a foot-messenger sent by a Bakhtiyari nomad chief whose 'only provision for the journey was a bag filled with the moist flour or raw paste of the acorn . . . In the Bakhtiyárí mountains it forms the principal food of the wandering tribes. Their women gather the acorns as they drop ripe from the trees, and bruise them between two stones in order to extract the bitter juice, they then wash and dry the flour in the sun, and this is the whole process. They bake the cakes of it or eat the paste raw, and find it very palatable and nutritious' (de Bode 1843: 97–8).

Like the highland Uxians in Alexander's day, the Kossaeans wanted Antigonus to pay protection money for safe passage through their territory (Strabo actually says the Great King made such payments in order to pass from Ekbatana to Babylon [an error for Susa? Weissbach 1922b: 1500], *Geog.* XI.13.6). Refusing to do so, Antigonus and his men were harrassed by the Kossaeans, who, Diodorus tells us, 'kept rolling great rocks in quick succession upon the marching troops; and at the same time, sending arrows thick and fast' (XIX.19.4). Kossaean prowess in archery was renowned, and Strabo says that 'the Kossaeans, like the neighbouring mountaineers, are for the most part bowmen, and are always out on foraging expeditions; for they have a country that is small and barren, so that they must needs live at the expense of the other tribes. And they are of necessity a powerful people, for they are all fighters; at any rate, thirteen thousand Kossaeans joined the Elymaeans in battle, when the latter were warring against both the Babylonians and the Susians' (*Geog.* XVI.1.18; unfortunately, the political context of this episode is a mystery). They were also, he maintains, less 'interested in agriculture' than their neighbours, the Paraetaceni.

The Elymaeans

Let us turn now to the Kossaeans' neighbours, the Elymaeans. The phonetic similarity between Elymais and Elam is, of course obvious, and the identity of Elymais and Biblical Elam was posited centuries ago by Samuel Bochart (Nöldeke 1874: 189). Even if the identity of the Elamites and the Elymaeans has occasionally been called into question (e.g. Alizadeh 1985b), it is obvious that we are simply dealing with a Graecized form of the names Elam and Elamites, and the identity of Elymais/Elymaeans and Elam/Elamites is unassailable in light of the cuneiform evidence (Table 10.2). The Akkadian sources simply continue to speak of Elam and the Elamites, while the Greek and Latin texts use Elymais and Elymaeans.

Table 10.2. *Babylonian astronomical diaries, 145–77 BC, mentioning Elam*

Sachs-Hunger III	Date	Historical statements concerning Elymais
-144.obv.16'–18'	Aug/Sept 145 BC	'That month, I heard as follows: Ari'abu. [....] .... entered Babylon and the other rivers. The auxiliary troops of .... [....] .... the king of Elam with his numerous troops [....] from his land [....]'
-144.rev.20–22	Oct/Nov 145 BC	'this general [Ardaya] of Babylonia [....] from Babylon to fight with Kammashkiri [....] from the king?.... [....] Kammashkiri, king of Elam, marched around victoriously among the cities and rivers of Babylonia, they plundered this [...and] carried off their spoil. The people [....] their...., their animals [....] for fear of this Elamite to the house? [....] There was panic and fear in the land'.
-143.A.18'–21'	June/July 144 BC	'[...Th]at [month,] I heard as follows: the troops which to Susa .... of Susa [...] [...] many? [...] which had . . . to Elam, they made enter Susa [....] [...] the general of ...and the troops of Antiochus, son of Alexander, who retur[ned? ....] [...] departed. That month, redness occurred again and again in the east and west. That month, there was *simmu*-disease, scabies and scurf in the land'.
-140.C.obv.34–44	Nov/Dec 141 BC	'That month, I heard as follows: king Arsaces and his troops departed from Araqan'ia. I heard as follows: [on the] 6th, the Elamite and his troops departed towards Apamea which is on the river Silhu for fighting. That [month?], the people who dwell in Apamea went out to Bit-Karkudi; they burned Apamea. [....] An(tiochus) the general who is above the 4 generals, who was representing king Arsaces, went out from Sel[eucia which is on] the Tigris, towards the Elamite for fighting; from the river Kabari he departed, and the numerous troops....[...] went out for fighting. The people who were in Seleucia and the people who dwell in Babylon, [....] the belongings [....] to guard (them) before the . . . of the Elamite. I heard as follows: the troops who were in Bit-[....] set up [....] of the troops of the Elamite. That month, the people [....] their children, their possessions, and their wives [....] the nobles of the king who had entered Babylon and the few people they led to the sea [...].'

-140.C.rev.29′–35′	Dec/Jan 141/0 BC	[...] of the brickwork of the Marduk Gate they tore down and the brickwork [...] [...] on? the Euphrates from ...[...]′ 'That month, I heard as follows: on the 4th day, the citizens who were in Seleucia which is on the Tigris set up a curse on Antiochus, the general who is above the 4 generals, because? he made common cause with the Elamite; they had provided ?...for the general, and sent many troops with him towards the Elamite for fighting. They held back this Antiochus, but he escaped with a few troops, and the people of the land who were in Seleucia on the Tigris plundered his possessions which he had left in the land, and the troops of the king who were with him plundered the possessions which were in [...]. That month, the Elamite [went out . . .] towards Bit-Karkudî which is on the Tigris for fight[ing . . .]′
-140.D.obv.11′–13′	Jan/Feb 141(0) BC	'[....]...panic of the enemy occurred in the land. This Elamite enemy .... [...] .... [....] .... [....] [....] .... big? and small? inside this city .... [...] the [....] of Seleucia [....] [....] ..., son of Antiochus? the general? [....] .... [...]′
-137.A.rev.3′–7′	June/July 138 BC	'That month, the 28th day, ... [....] [....] general who was above the 4 generals entered Babylon. That month, a fall of cattle.... [....] [....] Uruk and the cities which are on the Kutha canal, the Suru canal, the Piqudu canal and the canals [....] [....] ....their...they took and brought (them) up to Elam'.
-137.B.rev.19′–21′	May/June 138 BC	'[....]...departed. I heard that on the 18th day the general [....] [....a mess]age? from king Arsaces to kill the general [....] [....] the province of Elam.... [...]′
-137.D.obv.8′–rev.3	Nov/Dec 138 BC	'That month, the 10th? day, [....] [...] pitched his camp [in....] on the Tigris. He returned and mustered his troops [....] [...] entered [...Seleucia which is on] the Tigris and the king's canal. That month, on an unknown day, the king's troops who guarded Babylonia came and .... [...] [....] .... dispersed their cohorts, took captives of them...they inflicted a defeat on them. They returned? [...] [....] panic of the Elamite enemy was strong in the land, and panic of the enemy fell on the people, . . . and reed marshes? they dispersed? [...]

Table 10.2. (cont.)

Sachs-Hunger III	Date	Historical statements concerning Elymais
		[....] of the lower Sealand, the cities and canals of the gulf [....] ..Iutra their names were ca[lled? ....] [....] and made them obey to his command; he imposed tribute on them, and Aspasine, son of [....] [....] this [Aspasi]ne searched for a sortie? against the Elamite enemy, and turned the cities [and? ca]na]ls? of the lower Sealand over to his own side, and made [them obey?] to his command [....] [....] in order to complete [....] of the lower Sea[land] who did not obey his command, ... [....] seized them in a revolt, took captives of them, plundered them [....] [....there was] panic in Elam, happiness and agreement in Babylonia[....]'
-132.B.rev.18–20	Sept/Oct 133 BC	'That month, I heard as follows: the forces of Aspasine, the enemy from the environs? of Mesene?, a friend of the Elamite enemy, came and fell on the harbour of ships in the Tigris and plundered this harbour of ships together with their possessions'.
-132.D₂.obv.8'–10'	Oct/Nov 133 BC	'That month, I heard [....] Susa they made, and killed many troops of the Elamite in fighting, and the . . . . [....] they ....
-132.D₂.rev.16'–23'	Dec/Jan 133/2 BC	'[... K]amnaskiri, the Elamite enemy, who had revolted against his father [....] lived in Babylonia, organized against their troops and left? [....] arratash, the river of Elam, they crossed, for one *beru* distance they pitched camp [....] departed [....] many [troops] for fighting [against] each other. In month VIII, the 7th, the troops [....] the troops [....] they brought about the defeat of the troops of the enemy?. Until sunset, the remainder [....] entered. Ur'a, the son of this Elamite enemy, [....] one bull and 5 (sheep) sacrifices opposite this messenger [....] .... and performed (it) for his life'.
-132.D₁.rev.7'–11'	Jan/Feb 133(2) BC	'[....] the general of Babylonia [went out] from Babylon to Seleucia [....] the Elamite enemy in guard with them .... [....] ....of the Babylonians.... [....] Seleucia to .... [....]'

Reference	Date	Text
-129.A₂.obv.19'	April/May 130 BC	'That [mo]nth, the 17th, a mess[enger] of the general…the harvest? of Elam […]
-124.B.obv.19'	Nov/Dec 125 BC	'[…] king Arsaces…of Susa departed to the area of Elam opposite Pittiti, the Elamite enemy, for? fighting'.
-124.B.rev.12'–14'	Dec/Jan 125/4 BC	'That month, the 2nd, …a message of Aspasine, king of Mesene?, which he had written to the general of Babylonia was brought near [….] was read [to the cit]izens who are in Babylon as follows: In this month, on the 15th?, king Arsaces and Pittit, the Elamite enemy, fought with each other. The king defeated the troops of Elam in battle. Pittit […] he seized..'
-124.B.rev.17'–19'	Dec/Jan 125/4 BC	'[…] a messenger of the king who carried a message entered Babylon. That day, the message of the king which was written to the governor of Babylon and the citizens who were in Babylon, was read in the House of observation, as follows: Fighting […] Pittit, the Elamite enemy, I made, and 15,000 battle troops among his troops I [overth]rew in battle; among my troops no … took place. Elam in its entirety I hit with weapons. Pittit […] … I seized'.
-90.rev.1–2	Dec/Jan 91/0 BC	'[…] departed? […] surroundings of Susa. A reduction of the equivalent happened in this city Susa. That day I heard […] (blank)'
-77.B.rev.13'–14'	Jan/Feb 78(7) BC	'[…] went [to] Elam and fought with Qabinashkiri, the king of Elam, and put […] in it, and the cities […] […]… the few troops which were with him, turned away from him and went up to the mountains. I heard that towards the mountains when […]'

The earliest source on Elymais is the account given by Nearchus as preserved by Strabo, according to which the Elymaeans were a plundering group in the neighbourhood of the Susians and Persians (*Geog.* XI.13.6). Elsewhere Strabo says, 'Neighbouring Susis is the part of Babylonia which was formerly called Sitacenê, but is now called Apolloniatis. Above both, on the north and towards the east, lie the countries of the Elymaei and the Paraetaceni, who are predatory peoples and rely on the ruggedness of their mountains' (*Geog.* XV.3.12). The proximity of Elymais to Susiana, Media, and the 'region of the Zagros' is repeated elsewhere by Strabo (*Geog.* XVI.1.17), who emphasizes that the land of the Elymaeans was both 'larger and more diversified' than that of their neighbours the Paraetaceni (the area of *Paraitakene* was first mentioned by Herodotus, *Hist.* I.101; see also Arrian, *Anab.* 3.19.2; for discussion, see Treidler 1965). 'Now all of it that is fertile', he writes, 'is inhabited by farmers, whereas the mountainous part of it is a nursery of soldiers' (*Geog.* XVI.1.18). Strabo names three provinces of 'Elymaea', viz. Gabiane (or Gabiene; see also Gabae, Weissbach 1910a), Massabatene (Weissbach 1930; Spiegel 1971: 117 identified this with Medieval Persian Mah-sabadan), and Korbiane (*Geog.* XVI.118; for which see Weissbach 1922a). Although Tarn suggested long ago that these were the *eparchies* or local administrative divisions of the region under Seleucid rule which continued to survive under the eventually independent Elymaean state (see below) (Tarn 1930: 132), Bengtson showed that the sources adduced by him were inconsistent and hardly susceptible to such a strict interpretation (Bengtson 1964/II: 30–8).

Over a century ago Hoffmann suggested that *Elymaea* denoted the Elamite 'realm', of which *Elymais* itself was, along with the abovementioned places, a province (Hoffmann 1880: 132). This recalls Vallat's distinction between Elam *sensu strictu* as the highlands of Fars, and Elam in its wider, geo-political sense as southwestern Iran. But whether Hoffmann was right is open to question, for immediately after stating that 'both Gabiane and Massabatice are provinces of Elymaea', Strabo goes on to say, 'and Corbiane is also a province of Elymais', which makes it sound as though he used the terms Elymaea and Elymais interchangeably. Gabiene appears in other ancient sources (e.g. Diodorus Siculus XIX.26.1 and 34.7; Polyaenus IV.6.13) in a variety of cognate forms, and as noted above has long been identified with the area of modern Isfahan (Andreas *apud* Hoffmann 1880: 132, n. 1130; Weissbach 1910b).

Elymaean archers, probably similar to the one depicted in the lifesize (1.88 m) rock relief (Fig. 10.7) at Gardaneh Gulmash, near Qir in Fars province (Huff 1984; Vanden Berghe 1986b), fought in the huge Seleucid army amassed by Antiochus III at Magnesia. Bar-Kochva has observed that the 'various national contingents mentioned in the great campaigns generally included mercenaries, allies, allied-mercenaries, and subjects-vassals, but the status of very few contingents can be established with certainty' (Bar-Kochva 1976: 48). Nevertheless, he classified the Elymaeans among the 'auxiliaries from subject or semi-independent nations or tribes'. Just how independent the semi-independent Elymaeans may have been is difficult to ascertain, but Nöldeke was certainly of the opinion that the foundation of an independent Elymaean kingdom was only possible after Antiochus III's defeat by Rome in 190 BC (Nöldeke 1874: 190).

Figure 10.7 The relief at Qir (after Huff 1984: Abb. 6).

The Seleucid defeat at Magnesia brought with it the imposition of severe penalties. Not only was Anatolia lost, Seleucid naval movement restricted, and the Seleucid elephant corps impounded, but reparations in the sum of 15,000 talents of silver were due. This was to be paid in a series of installments: 500 talents immediately; 2500 talents upon ratification of the treaty of Apamea by the Roman populace; and 12,000 talents thereafter in the form of an annual tribute of 1000 talents of silver per year for the next twelve years (Mørkholm 1966: 22–37). According to the Book of Maccabees (I. 3.31, 37; 6.1–3; II. 1.13–17) this desperate financial situation drove Antiochus to launch an attack in 187 BC on the temple of Bel in Elymais (Diodorus Siculus 28.3; 29.15; for the date, see Holleaux 1942: 254), an attack which cost the Seleucid emperor and most of his army their lives (according to a late cuneiform king list, Antiochus III died either on 3 July 187 BC [25 III 125 SE] or on the same day of the preceding month, see Sachs and Wiseman 1954: 207). Mørkholm believed, however, that there was more to this campaign than a mere quest for plunder, and instead saw it as a reassertion of Seleucid authority in the east following the humiliation of Antiochus by Rome (Mørkholm 1966: 29). But in general, most scholars have viewed Antiochus' adventurous attempt 'to lay his hands on the treasures of a temple of Bel in Elymais . . . [as an] eloquent testimon[y] to the financial difficulties of the king[s]' (Mørkholm 1966: 31). Moreover, this act of aggression against what had ostensibly been an ally (viz. the provision of archers at Magnesia) was seen by von Gutschmid as the defining moment in early Elymaean history, the moment when Elymais began to break away from the Seleucid kingdom and to establish its independence (von Gutschmid 1888: 39).

The location of the Bel temple in Elymais has long puzzled scholars. W.B. Henning postulated the presence of a sanctuary to Bel at Tang-i Sarvak, an important cluster of rock reliefs north of Behbehan, based on the presence of the personal name Bel-dusha on Monument A, which 'may indicate that he was a priest of Bel' (Henning 1977: 381). However, Henning scrupulously avoided identifying Tang-i Sarvak with the site of the Bel temple attacked by Antiochus III, no doubt because the reliefs and associated inscriptions date to the first centuries AD. Later, Bivar and Shaked suggested that 'the altar of Bel (?)' was mentioned in an inscription at Shimbar/Tang-i Butan, but as they dated this to the second century AD no association with the early Elymaean temple was posited (Bivar and Shaked 1964: 272). More recently, Vanden Berghe and Schippmann have suggested that the temple of Ahuramazda excavated by Ghirshman at Bard-e Nechandeh in the Bakhtiyari mountains is the best candidate for the Elymaean temple of Bel attacked by Antiochus III (Vanden Berghe and Schippmann 1985: 17). Such an explanation, of course, requires the acceptance of an assimilation between the Semitic divine name Bel and the Iranian deity Ahuramazda (Colpe 1983: 823). According to Herodotus (I.189), the Greek equivalent of Ahuramazda was Zeus (see also Teixidor 1990: 71; Duchesne-Guillemin 1983: 867), and it is clear that in Greek treatments of Babylonian religion, Bel was assimilated with Marduk (Kuhrt and Sherwin-White 1987). Doubting the Zoroastrianism of the Elymaeans, Hansman preferred to see the Elymaean Bel as 'a traditional Elamite god' but was unable to suggest which one (Hansman 1985: 245).

The death of Antiochus III did not, however, signal the end of Seleucid rule in the east, for coin issues show that the Seleucid mints at Susa and Ekbatana continued to operate until the Seleucids lost Susiana and Media to the Parthians. At Susa issues post-dating Antiochus III were struck by Seleucus IV (187–175 BC), Antiochus IV (175–164 BC), Demetrius I (162–150 BC), Alexander I Balas (150–145 BC), and Demetrius II (146–140 BC) (LeRider 1965a; Mørkholm 1965: 144–5, 148–50; Houghton 1983: 105–7). At Ekbatana in Media, on the other hand, issues minted by Seleucus IV, Antiochus IV, Antiochus V (164–162 BC), the satrap Timarchus (161 BC) who briefly claimed the title 'king', Demetrius I, and Alexander I Balas are known (Houghton 1983: 113–17).

No less audacious than Antiochus III's attack on the temple of Bel in Elymais was the attempt by his grandson, Antiochus IV, twenty-three years later, to invade Elymais once again in search of revenue. A number of ancient authors, including Polybius (XXXI.9), Appian (Syr. 66), Josephus (*Jewish Antiquities* XII.358–9), Porphyrius (FGH II no. 260, F 53 and 56), and St. Jerome (*Dan.* 718, 722) as well as I Maccabees 6.1–17 and II Maccabees 1.13–17 and 9.1–4, recount the tale of Antiochus IV's expedition to the temple of Artemis (Polybius, Josephus)/Aphrodite (Appian)/Diana (Porphyrius, St. Jerome)/Nanay(a) (II Maccabees), and although the similarity between the two expeditions is striking, Holleaux has shown that there can be no question of a confusion of names and a single event (Holleaux 1942; see also Mørkholm 1966: 170ff.; contra Bartlett 1973: 82; Green 1990: 512). Driven back by the hostility of the local Elymaeans, no battle was in fact fought, but Antiochus IV died, whether from divine retribution for his prior assault on the temple of Jerusalem, or simply from sickness, at Tabae in Paraitakene (probably Gabae, i.e. Isfahan, although Gera and Hurowitz 1997: 250, n. 71 suggest a location near Ekbatana), in November of 164 BC (Mørkholm 1966: 171; for the date, see Wacholder 1980; Hyldahl 1990: 196–7).

The deity involved is unclear. Holleaux, following G. Radet and F. Cumont, believed that the Iranian goddess Anahita could be represented in Greco-Roman sources as either Artemis or Aphrodite, noting further that a temple to Anahita in Elymais is mentioned by Aelian (AD 165/70–230/5) in his work *On the nature of animals* (XII.1.18) (Holleaux 1942: 268, n. 2; 271). Hoffmann, on the other hand, basing himself on II Maccabees, suggested that Nana or Nanay(a) was the oriental deity meant in references to the episode of Antiochus IV's death (Hoffmann 1880: 131–2; see also Tarn 1938: 463–6). Certainly Nanaya is by far the most frequently attested deity in the extant Greek inscriptions from Susa (Table 10.1).

As with the Elymaean temple of Bel, suggestions for the location of the temple of Elymaean Artemis/Aphrodite/Diana/Nanay(a) have varied. Tarn's belief that a shrine at Susa was meant (Tarn 1938: 463) had already been anticipated and rejected almost sixty years earlier by Hoffmann, who noted that if the attack had been on Susa, Polybius would surely have said so (Hoffmann 1880: 131). Vanden Berghe and Schippmann, on the other hand, point to the presence of a temple to Anahita and Mithra at Bard-e Nechandeh, although they note that Ghirshman dated the structure to the first–second centuries AD (Vanden Berghe and Schippmann 1985: 20). In searching for the temples plundered by Antiochus III and IV, however, one should not forget the obvious royal importance of Masjid-i Solaiman, clearly indicated by the recovery there of a relief portrait (Fig. 10.8) of an unidentified Elymaean king (von Gall 1980).

One passage in Strabo which has remained a mystery to scholars is his reference (*Geog.* XVI.1.18) to 13,000 Kossaeans joining 'the Elymaeans in battle, when the latter were warring against both the Babylonians and the Susians'. Nöldeke suggested that the campaign in question may have witnessed the beginning of an Elymaean drive for independence from Seleucid rule (Nöldeke 1874: 190). He argued that, as the account of Molon's assault on Diogenes, eparch of Susiana, had shown (Polybius V.48), Susa was an important node of Seleucid military force in the east, hence Strabo's reference to the 'Susians'. By the 'Babylonians', on the other hand, Strabo may have meant the Seleucid satrap of Babylonia and his forces. Certainly this is a possibility, but one which unfortunately cannot be verified by any other literary or epigraphic evidence. While Nöldeke believed that no Elymaean attempt to achieve independence of the Seleucid kingdom could have preceded Antiochus III's defeat at Magnesia, he did not say whether he felt that it occured prior to or after Antiochus IV's death in 164 BC. The likelihood would seem strong, however, that the push for Elymaean independence followed the demise of Antiochus IV (Sellwood 1983: 307), just as Wiesehöfer has suggested for developments in Persis (Wiesehöfer 1994: 124).

Elymais and the Parthian empire

The waning of Seleucid power in the east may have provided an opportunity for Elymaean consolidation (Sherwin-White and Kuhrt 1993: 225), but it was attended by the waxing of Parthian power on the Iranian plateau. From the Elymaean point of view, it is arguable which foreign power was the greater threat. Each made claims to Elymaean territory and most probably each was equally noxious to Elymaean nationalists.

At Susa the appearance of a new political order was heralded by the minting of coins in the name of Kamniskires I Nikephoros of Elymais (Hill 1922: clxxxvi). Attributing a coin minted at Susa to Demetrius II (146–140 BC) instead of Demetrius I (162–150 BC), Mørkholm suggested that Kamniskires I could not have begun minting before *c.* 145 BC (Mørkholm 1965: 151). LeRider and Houghton, on the other hand, believed that Kamniskires occupied Susa *c.* 147 BC, that the city was re-taken by Demetrius II who briefly issued coinage there *c.* 145 BC, and that it thereafter reverted to Elymaean rule (LeRider 1978: 35; Houghton 1983: 101).

How extensive Kamniskires' rule in Iran may have been we do not know, but Hansman has suggested, on the basis of symbols (e.g. the horse protome) shared by both Kamniskires' and Seleucid issues from Ekbatana, that his influence may have extended into Media (Hansman 1990: 2). A badly preserved Aramaic inscription from Bard-e Nechandeh, dated by Harmatta to *c.* 180–160 BC, has been restored as '*[kbnš] k [y]r mlk*' . . .', i.e. 'Kabnashkir the king' (Harmatta 1976: 289–300). If the dating of this text is correct, it may refer to Kamniskires I, and this would then imply control over the site.

Figure 10.8 Fragmentary bust of an Elymaean king from Masjid-i Solaiman (after von Gall 1980: Abb. 2).

Who was Kamniskires? To begin with the name, Henning noted that on some coins of a later, homonymous Kamniskires the legend, written in Aramaic, was *kbnškyr* (Henning 1977: 164; see also Alram 1986: 137–53; Schmitt 1991b: 212), which he considered remarkably similar to the Achaemenid Elamite title *kap-nu-iš-ki-ra* meaning 'treasurer' (Hinz and Koch 1987/I: 434; see also Kawase 1986). Henning suggested therefore that the Elamite title may have been applied originally to the satraps of Susiana whose chief duty was 'to protect the royal treasures stored at Susa' (Henning 1977: 165). Harmatta has gone so far as to suggest that Kamniskires I may have been the treasurer of the Elymaean temple of Bel which Antiochus III attempted to raid, and that he assumed the title 'king' in the wake of this disastrous expedition (Harmatta 1981: 209; see also Vanden Berghe and Schippmann 1985: 15). Surely this is rank speculation. Moreover, when Henning wrote his study of the Tang-i Sarvak inscriptions the Elamite onomasticon was largely unstudied. Today, as a result of Zadok's publications (1984b; 1991), it is much easier to isolate probable Elamite elements in Kamniskires which could be suggestive of alternative etymologies.

But did Kamniskires and the Elymaeans of his day speak Elamite, or a late version thereof? The only epigraphic evidence from Kamniskires' reign is found on his coins. Although examples of these have been found at Susa (LeRider 1965a: 360–361) and Bard-e Nechandeh (Augé *et al.* 1979: 51), these are modelled iconographically on Seleucid issues and have terse Greek legends, e.g. *ΒΑΣΙΛΕΩΣ ΚΑΜΝΙΣΚΙΡΟΥ ΝΙΚΗ-ΦΟΡΟΥ* ('king Kamniskires Nikephoros'). The use of Greek on a second century BC coin legend, however, tells us nothing about the language of the Elymaean population at the time, for Greek issues were widely copied by peoples of diverse linguistic background. To go further with the linguistic question, we are forced, therefore, to consider Elymaean inscriptions of later date. All later Elymaean texts, whether on coins or on rock faces, as at Tang-i Sarvak, use a form of the Middle Aramaic script which is closely related to that used in southern Mesopotamia in the second and third centuries AD (Klugkist 1986: 116). As Henning observed, however, whereas the later Elymaean tetradrachms and inscriptions at Tang-i Sarvak are written in pure Aramaic, the smaller coin denominations, e.g. those issued by Orodes (WRWD), use a number of Aramaic ideograms which 'proves that the language that underlay these legends is not Aramaic; it may have been an Iranian dialect or it may have been a surviving form of Elamite . . . Perhaps the lowlands of Khuzistan were peopled by speakers of Aramaic while in the highlands to the north an Iranian (or Elamite?) language was spoken; and the mints of the Kamnaskires dynasty, to accommodate both national groups, issued coins with legends in both languages for local circulation' (Henning 1977: 166). If Henning was correct in this suggestion, then the distinction between Aramaic-speakers in the lowlands and Elamite (or Iranian) speakers in the highlands of Elymais would represent one more example of the ethno-linguistic duality in Elam commented upon by scholars such as Amiet (1979a; 1979b; 1986c; 1992a) and Vallat (1980a).

According to LeRider, the tetradrachms of Kamniskires with an obverse monogram consisting of an *epsilon* (E) above an *alpha* (A) were probably struck immediately after the end of Demetrius II's control of Susa *c.* 145 BC. These are linked stylistically to several rare issues with the same E/A monogram but bearing the name *OKKONAΨOY*, i.e. Okkonapses, an otherwise unknown figure whom LeRider believes must have reigned immediately after Kamniskires (LeRider 1978: 34–5; not Hycnaspes as previously thought, and not *c.* 162 BC as once suggested, for which see Sellwood 1983: 307).

LeRider has identified half a dozen bronze issues with the E/A obverse monogram which bear the name of a king Tigraios and believes that the monogram designated the moneyer responsible for manufacturing all three series, i.e. those of Kamniskires, Okkonapses and Tigraios. Furthermore, LeRider suggests that Tigraios reigned at Susa either immediately after Okkonapses, or between Okkonapses and Phraates II, until 133/2 BC (LeRider 1965a: 381; 1978: 35; see also Unvala 1935: 158–60). Without citing specific examples, LeRider noted that various Elamite specialists considered Okkonapses the Greek transcription of an Elamite name (LeRider 1978: 36). M. Mayrhofer tentatively suggested that the Greek Okkonapses rendered an Elamite name such as *Ukka-napsa (Hinz and Koch 1987: 1213), but this is nothing more than a speculation (R. Schmitt, pers. comm.). In any case, one can say without doubt that the Elamite onomasticon contains numerous names beginning with the syllables *Ú-*, *Ú-ka*, or *Uk-ku-* which might have been transformed into a Greek form beginning *Okkon-* (Zadok 1984a: 81).

To return to Kamniskires, unexpectedly we have contemporary sources from Babylonia which attest to Kamniskires' activities there. The late Babylonian astronomical diaries, while recording astronomical observations, are a mine of incidental yet precious historical information, most of it closely dated, which was inserted by the scribes whose main interest was astrological and astronomical (Sachs and Hunger 1996). One such text (Table 10.2) from October/November 145 BC reports that Kammashkiri, king of Elam, i.e. Kamniskires I of Elymais, 'marched around victoriously among the cities and rivers of Babylonia', plundering, despoiling and causing 'panic and fear in the land'. A report from August/September, i.e. two months earlier, also mentions 'the king of Elam with his numerous troops' and must presumably refer to the same invasion. A counter-attack, dating to June/July 144 BC, under the command of an unnamed general in the service of Antiochus VI (145–142 BC), son of Alexander I Balas (150–146 BC), is recorded in another text. It is difficult to reconcile this new information with LeRider's suggestion that Demetrius II was striking coins at Susa *c.* 145 BC.

Whether or not the Elymaeans recaptured Susa after the counter-attack of 144 BC, they certainly regained enough strength to attack Babylonia again in 141 BC (Table 10.2), when 'the Elamite and his troops' advanced on Apamea. According to Pliny (*Nat. Hist.* VI.31.132) Apamea, which was located in Mesene (i.e. southernmost Babylonia), was named by Antiochus I after his mother and was 'surrounded by the Tigris'. The city has been located by most authorities near modern Kut al-Amara, perhaps synonymous with the Famiya or Fam of the as-Silh district which lay on the canal of the same name (see also the 'river' or more probably canal named Silhu on which Apamea was situated according to our astronomical text, known to Stephen of Byzantium as the Sellas) known in various Arabic geographical sources (Streck 1901: 306; LeStrange 1905: 28, 38; Tscherikower 1927: 93–4; Obermeyer 1929: 86–90; Oppenheimer 1983: 32ff.).

Although Parthian troops were sent out from Seleucia to meet the Elymaean contingent their success is not apparent for the text records the fear of the inhabitants of both Seleucia and Babylon of the Elymaean invaders. Moreover, a text written a short while later (Table 10.2) informs us that the citizens of Seleucia tried to put a curse on the military commander who had been sent to repel the Elymaean force, one Antiochus, 'the general who is above the four generals', on the grounds that 'he made common cause with the Elamite'. Having first provided the general with troops, and obviously dissatisfied with the result, they apprehended him only to have him escape. The Seleucians exacted their revenge by plundering those 'possessions which he had left in the land', but this did not alter the fact that the Elymaeans were advancing on Bit-Karkudî, somewhere on the Tigris (location unknown). 'Panic of the enemy' was rife in early 140 BC, suggesting that the Elamite threat was still very real.

The information just reviewed is of paramount importance for our understanding of Elymaean-Seleucid relations in the mid-second century BC and flatly contradicts earlier reconstructions of those relations based on evidence of questionable veracity. Thus, for example, according to a notice in Justin, Elymaean, Bactrian and Persian forces fought alongside the Seleucids against Mithridates I in the spring of 141 BC (XXXVI.1.4), but this was certainly not the case, for the Elymaeans were actively campaigning against both the Seleucids *and* the Parthians in Babylonia. Moreover, the new edition (Sachs and Hunger 1996) of the diaries of November 141 through January 140 BC makes it perfectly clear that, contrary to A.T. Olmstead's treatment of the material and all subsequent reconstructions (Olmstead 1937: 13; Vanden Berghe and Schippmann 1985: 22), the Elymaeans were not defeated by the Parthians near the Babylonia-Susiana frontier in late 141/early 140 BC.

Into this situation we must re-introduce Demetrius II (146–140 BC), who, in the last year of his first reign, made an attempt to re-take Babylonia. Although Wolski has equivocated on the degree of success attending this campaign, and even suggested that in the action against Apamea it was uncertain whether the defence was led by the Seleucid or the Parthian forces (Wolski 1993: 82), we now know that it was most definitely the Parthians who were in control, for the diary of November/December 141 BC says explicitly that the general in charge of countering the Elymaean offensive 'was representing king Arsaces' who, as stated in line 34 of the same text, had 'departed from Araqan'ia', i.e. Hyrcania, the country near the southeast corner of the Caspian Sea (Herzfeld 1968: 320; Kiyani 1982; Vogelsang 1988), where we know from Justin as well (XXXVI.1.6) that Mithridates I was then engaged (Wolski 1993: 82).

LeRider has suggested that Susa was re-taken from Alexander I Balas by *c.* 148/7 BC by the Elymaeans, and then conquered by Mithridates I in 140/139 BC (see also Augé *et al.* 1979: 53). Certainly it is difficult to believe that the Parthian king would have left for Hyrcania with the Elymaeans comfortably settled at Susa. Vanden Berghe has even suggested that the rock relief at Hung-i Nauruzi (Fig. 10.9), near Izeh-Malamir, depicts Mithridates I receiving homage from the conquered Elymaeans (Vanden Berghe 1963b: 167), but this interpretation has been questioned by a number of scholars (Mathiesen 1992: 120 with bibl.). Although Nöldeke suggested that the loss of Susa only dented

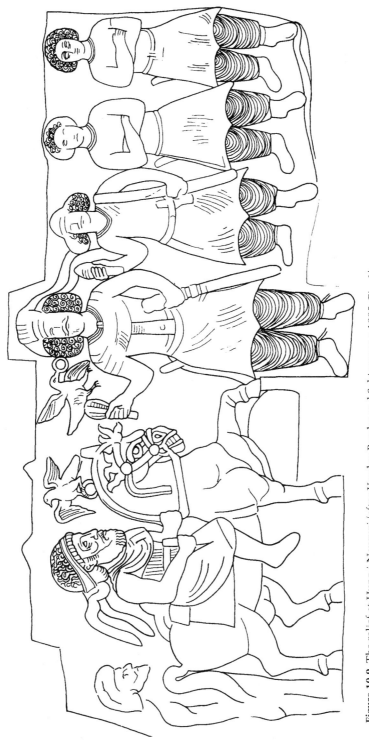

Figure 10.9 The relief at Hung-i Nauruzi (after Vanden Berghe and Schippmann 1985: Fig. 1).

Figure 10.10 A silver tetradrachm of Hyspaosines (after Waddington 1866: Pl. XI.2).

Elymaean independence, forcing upon the fledgling state the status of a tributary vassal vis-à-vis Parthia (Nöldeke 1874: 191), we can now see that 'the Elamite enemy' was certainly active in January/February of 140 BC and continued to be a nuisance as late as May/June 138 BC if one may infer that the order by the Parthian king 'to kill the general' refers to the Elamite commander.

The astronomical diaries also provide evidence which calls for a radically different understanding of the rise of the kingdom of Characene. It has long been believed that, upon the death of the Parthian king Phraates II in 128 or 127 BC, a former *eparch* of southern Babylonia under Antiochus IV by the name of Aspasine/Hyspaosines (Fig. 10.10) seized the opportunity to break away from Parthian domination and form a state of his own known as the kingdom of Characene (Nodelman 1960; Sellwood 1983: 310–14). We now know that Hyspaosines was active at least a decade earlier. Although the diary for November/December 138 BC is too fragmentary to tell what the involvement of the Parthians may have been, Hyspaosines seems clearly to have launched a raid into the borderland between Mesene and southwestern Khuzistan, the 'lower Sealand', 'against the Elamite enemy', bringing the cities and their inhabitants over to his side and causing 'panic in Elam, happiness and agreement in Babylonia'. But the diary from September/October 133 BC shows us that five years later Hyspaosines was regarded himself as an 'enemy', and 'a friend of the Elamite enemy'. What had happened in the interim is not hard to guess. Hyspaosines' move towards independence must have been viewed with concern by the Parthians and Hyspaosines was now classed as a rebel and co-conspirator with the Elymaeans.

As had happened so often in the Neo-Elamite period when rival claimants to the Elamite throne sought refuge in Assyria, we find that a year later an Elymaean named Kamniskiri (whether identical with Kamniskires I or II we cannot say) turned against his own father and 'lived in Babylonia', where he organized troops for an attack against his own people. Admittedly the diary for December/January 133/2 BC is difficult to follow, but it is clear that a battle took place between the two contending Elymaean sides. That 'Kamniskiri, the Elamite enemy' was not given official asylum in Babylonia, however, seems likely, for a diary entry from the following month reports the movement of the 'general of Babylonia' from Babylon to Seleucia, apparently escorting 'the Elamite enemy in guard with them'. Houghton believes that the Parthians held Susa until 130 BC when it fell to Antiochus VII, the brother of Demetrius II (Houghton 1983: 101). A year later, however, Antiochus VII was killed by a Parthian army under Phraates II and Susa once more fell under Parthian control (Davis and Kraay 1973: 217). That this state of affairs need not have impeded continued Elymaean independence further south near the borders of Babylonia and Susiana seems clear from the level of Elymaean military activity around this time.

Acknowledged in a text from Babylon of 127/6 BC as *sharru*, 'king' (Landsberger 1933: 299; Oelsner 1964: 271), Hyspaosines is called 'king of Mesene' in a diary from December/January 125/4 BC. But several scholars have misunderstood this particular text, believing it recorded yet another victorious campaign against Elymais by Hyspaosines (Pinches 1890; Nodelman 1960: 89). Nothing could be further from the truth, for in fact it is clear in the text that the Parthian king, here called simply 'Arsaces', fought with the Elamite Pittit and defeated a force of 15,000 Elamite troops. 'Elam in its entirety I hit with weapons', says the diary, and one can well imagine that settlements in southwesternmost Susiana mentioned in Greek and Latin sources, such as Aginis, Ampe and Aple (Andreas 1894a; 1894b; 1894c), must have borne the brunt of such an attack. Interestingly, Pittit, the general in command of the Elamite forces, bore a good Elamite name (Zadok 1984b: 35). This is yet another indication that the Elymaeans of the late period were linguistically 'late Elamites'.

According to an astronomical diary text Hyspaosines became ill and died in 124 BC (Sachs and Hunger 1996: 283, text -123.A.obv.18'). His realm, moreover, was short-lived, and by *c.* 120 BC the kingdom of Characene had been overrun by the Parthians, although they were not able to completely eradicate the quasi-independent state which continued to flourish to a greater or lesser extent for the next three hundred years (Nodelman 1960) and which, to judge from the circulation of Characene coinage at Susa (LeRider 1959), was constantly in contact with the ancient metropolis.

Elymais and Parthian Susa

Like his father, Mithridates I's son and successor Phraates II struck coins at Susa (Sellwood 1980: 45), a sure sign that he controlled the city during his reign (138–127 BC). Thereafter, we find a Parthian inter-regnal issue from *c.* 127 BC emanating from Susa, as well as coinage struck by Artabanus I (*c.* 127–124 BC), Mithridates II (*c.* 123–88 BC), Gotarzes I (*c.* 95–90 BC), Orodes I (*c.* 90–80 BC), an unknown king (*c.* 80–70 BC), Sinatruces (*c.* 75 BC), Darius (? *c.* 70 BC), Phraates III (*c.* 70–57 BC), Mithridates III (*c.* 57–54 BC), Orodes II (*c.* 57–38 BC), Phraates IV (*c.* 38–2 BC), Phraataces and his queen Musa (*c.* 2 BC – AD 4), Artabanus II (AD 10–38), Vardanes I (*c.* AD 40–5) and Gotarzes

II (c. AD 40–51) (Sellwood 1980: 55, 71, 76, 79–80, 83, 88, 92, 99–100, 104, 108–9, 116–18, 121, 125, 129–30, 145, 149, 165, 169, 174–5, 190, 201, 203, 210, 219). Thus, the Parthian mint at Susa was active from c. 138 BC (but see also the discussion of Tigraios above) to the mid-first century AD and is clear evidence that the Elymaeans, whatever else they may have done, did not control Susa during these two centuries.

The activity of the Parthian mint at Susa was mirrored by growth all across the site under the Arsacids. More than one author has spoken of the 'remarkable expansion' of Susa (e.g. Boucharlat 1985a: 76; de Miroschedji 1987: 51) and of the city's 'unprecedented prosperity' under Parthian rule (Amiet 1988c: 141). Ville Royale II, levels 3C, 3B, 3A, 2C and 2B, Ville Royale A, levels VIb, VI, and V, Ville Royale-Apadana, levels 4 and 3, Apadana East, levels 5d, 5c and 5a-b, and Shaur palace level 2b all show Parthian occupation extending from the late second century BC to the early third century AD (de Miroschedji 1987: Tab. 11). Large, well-built, private houses are attested, particularly in Ville Royale A, while richly furnished, barrel-vaulted brick tombs belonging to the so-called 'Parthian necropolis' in the Ville des Artisans (Ghirshman 1950a; Haerinck 1983: 16; Boucharlat 1985: 76), similar to those of Parthian Assur and ed-Dur in the United Arab Emirates, date to this period, as do individual pit graves and brick cist graves. Among other things, the Parthian-period graves of Susa have yielded a large number of interesting bone female figurines (Fig. 10.11) which find close parallels at contemporary sites in Mesopotamia, including Uruk, Seleucia-on-the-Tigris and Nuzi (Boucharlat and Haerinck 1994). The quantity of Parthian pottery recovered from Susa, both plain and glazed, is enormous (Haerinck 1983: 37–87).

Several decades after the Elymaean incursions into Babylonia, discussed above, we find renewed evidence of Elymaean assertiveness. From the year 82/1 or 79/8 BC (the Seleucid-era date on the coins can be read as either 231 or 234 SE) comes an issue in the names of a Kamniskires (II) and his wife Anzaze (Fig. 10.12), examples of which are known from Susa, Bard-e Nechandeh, Masjid-i Solaiman and various museum collections. Since Susa was under Parthian control at the time, LeRider believes these coins may have been minted at Seleucia-on-the-Hedyphon (LeRider 1965a: 190; Augé et al. 1979: 55ff.). Just a few years later the astronomical diaries inform us of a battle between a Parthian king and Kamniskires II. According to a diary dated to January/February 77 BC, '[Arsaces and the army] went to Elam and fought with Qabinashkiri, the king of Elam' (Table 10.2). The identification of the Parthian ruler in question with Orodes I is made possible via comparable notices in other astronomical diaries dating to 80, 78 and 76 BC, in which explicit reference is made to 'Arsaces, who is called Orodes, the king' and 'Ispubarza, his sister, the queen' (McEwan 1986: 93).

This text would seem to provide the context for a notice in Strabo, the date and context of which have long managed to elude scholars. Strabo (Geog. XVI.1.18) describes how a 'king of Parthia, though warned by what had happened to Antiochus [as discussed above], hearing that the temples in that country [Elymais] contained great wealth, and seeing that the inhabitants were disobedient subjects, made an invasion with a great force, and took both the temple of Athena and that of Artemis, the latter called Azara, and carried off treasures valued at ten thousand talents. And Seleuceia

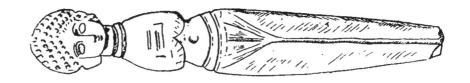

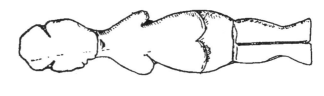

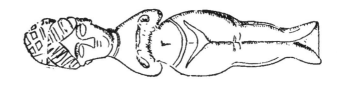

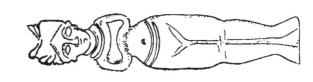

Figure 10.11 Parthian bone figurines from Susa (after de Mecquenem 1934: Fig. 65).

Figure 10.12 Elymaean coins of Kamniskires and Anzaze, upper, and a 'Kamniskires', lower (after Vaux
1856: Pl. opp. 139).

near the Hedyphon River, a large city, was also taken. In earlier times Seleucia was
called Soloce'. Some scholars have attributed this action to the Parthian king
Mithridates, linking it to his invasion of Susiana in 139 or 138 BC (e.g. Nodelman 1960:
87; Guépin 1965–6: 19; Hansman 1978: 154; Harmatta 1981: 207). But as Nöldeke noted
over a century ago, this is only a conjecture and the event may have occurred much
later (Nöldeke 1874: 192). If indeed LeRider was correct in locating the mint which produced the Kamniskires II and Anzaze issues at Seleucia-by-the-Hedyphon, then the
impertinence of the Elymaean ruler who dared to strike coinage in his own name, combined with the wealth which his striking of coins would imply, may well have provided
the impetus for the campaign described by Strabo and recorded in the Babylonian astronomical diary.

The reference to Soloce/Seleucia clearly points to the same settlement known to
Pliny as Seleucia-in-Elymais (*Nat. Hist.* VI.27.136) and because he calls the Hedyphon
(Hedypnus) a tributary of the Eluaios we are probably safe in attributing yet another ref-
erence to it, namely in the decree of Antioch-in-Persis (Tscherikower 1927: 98; Fraser

1996: 33, n. 70 for refs.). The site has been tentatively identified by Hansman with a large site shaped like an irregular parallelogram called Ja Nishin which is situated *c.* 80 km southeast of Ahwaz (Hansman 1978: 159). There are no grounds for believing, with Schippmann and Vanden Berghe, that Seleucia-by-the-Hedyphon was conquered by Kamniskires before he took Susa *c.* 145 BC (Vanden Berghe and Schippmann 1985: 25). As for the Hedyphon itself, this has long been identified with the Jarrahi river in eastern Khuzistan (e.g. Forbiger 1844: 581; LeRider 1965a: 261, 354; Hansman 1978: 156; Alizadeh 1985b: 180, n. 24; Rahimi-Laridjani 1988: 242; Christensen 1993: 107).

A second geographical issue raised by the passage just discussed is the location of Azara. Although Guépin argued that Azara was to be sought in a remote valley near the large cluster of rock reliefs at Tang-i Sarvak, these are probably to be dated (Mathiesen 1992: 35, 52, 57) to the late second and early third centuries AD (*c.* AD 150–225) and appear to have nothing to do with the sanctuary of Artemis mentioned by Strabo. Guépin completely overlooked the testimony of the Arab geographers such as al-Muqaddasi and Yaqut who attest to the existence of a city called Azar, one day out of Ram-Hormuz on the route to Ahwaz (Hoffmann 1880: 133; Sprenger 1864: 65). On the other hand, al-Muqaddasi also notes the existence of a town called 'Hazâr' or 'Âzâr Sâbûr' near Shiraz, which would place the sanctuary square in the heart of ancient Elam (LeStrange 1905: 280). Unfortunately, Strabo gives no indication of whether Azara was in lowland Khuzistan or highland Fars. A. Godard suggested many years ago that Azara be identified with the site of Bard-e Nechandeh between Ahwaz and Masjid-i Solaiman (Godard 1949: 159). Although the area between Ahwaz and Ram Hormuz was surveyed in 1948 by D. McCown, his materials (apart from a small selection of sites near Ahwaz), have not yet been published (Alizadeh 1985b: 176 and n. 6). Ghirshman identified the plundered temple with the site of Shami, 25 km northeast of Izeh-Malamir (Harmatta 1981: 207; Vanden Berghe and Schippmann 1985: 24). As noted in Chapter 4, it is tempting to suggest that Azara is the same place known in the third millennium as Zahara.

Strabo describes the population of Elymais as possessing 'a larger and more diversified country than the Paraetaceni. Now all of it that is fertile is inhabited by farmers, whereas the mountainous part of it is a nursery of soldiers, mostly bowmen; and since the latter part is extensive, it can furnish so large a military force that their king, since he possesses great power, refuses to be subject to the king of the Parthians like the other tribes; and their king was likewise disposed towards the Macedonians, who ruled Syria in later times' (*Geog.*, XVI.1.18). Unfortunately, we are again uncertain where to place such a notice chronologically, although Strabo's lifetime (*c.* 64 BC–AD +21) provides some parameters and we know that certain books of the *Geography* were composed in the reign of Tiberius and that the bulk of the material contained therein was collected between 20 and 7 BC (Lasserre 1979: 382). Given the brevity of Kamniskires I's hold over Susa and the newness of Parthian rule at that moment in time, it would seem unlikely that the reference pertains to the earliest phase of Elymaean independence. It would seem more plausible to associate this with a revival of Elymaean assertiveness in the first century BC such as that which occurred during the reign of Kamniskires II.

Two important epigraphic finds shed considerable light on Susa in the late first century BC and early first century AD. The first (SEG 7.12), dating to c. 37–32 BC, has been described as a 'verse chronicle' (Tarn 1932: 832) written by the Parthian king Phraates IV in honour of 'the faithful Zamaspes', an official who had been chosen by Tiridates, the general (*stratiarchos*) of Susa. The text is written in Greek and as such reflects the continued importance of this language at Susa long after the departure of the Seleucids. It shows us that the city at that time was probably under the rule of a military governor, if indeed this was Tiridates' role as *stratiarchos* (on the problem of his relationship with Phraates, see Tarn 1932). The text reads as follows (Potts 1989: 328–9, trans. A. Bülow-Jacobsen): 'Phraates heralds forever . . . the [immortal fame] of the noble Zamaspes . . . For the Lord by holy precepts . . . to the spirit of the all-mighty god Phraates . . . the staff-bearer of the king . . . and for the spirit of Tiridates . . . when he had been appointed general of Susa . . . chose for himself the faithful Zamaspes . . . he . . . the dried-out river Gondeisos . . . and [dug the stream] that had been blocked for a long time . . . he agreed with the city-dwellers . . . he led him before the crowds . . . and let him have his friend Heliodorus . . . first of all a man of action . . . for this reason now . . .'

Just as important as the political insights provided by the text are the economic/ecological data it provides. For Zamaspes was praised for his work on the 'dried-out river Gondeisos' which had been blocked 'for a long time', clearly bringing benefit to the city of Susa in so doing. It would seem that in recognition of his good works Zamaspes was later rewarded with appointment to higher office and a commemorative bronze statue. Thus, we find him identified as general and satrap of Susa in another text (SEG 7.13) dating to AD 1/2 which throws yet more light on the irrigation works of the Parthian administrator. The text reads as follows: 'See, oh stranger, the bronzen image of the general of Susa, Zamaspes, and learn of the public benefactions of that great man, who was great both by the providence of the immortals and by the spirit of the all-mighty god Phraates. [The king] having deemed him a patriotic and reputable companion chose him as a satrap who knew what was useful. Water of the Gondeisos, collected from high-up at the delicious sources, he made to flow and rendered richly flowing. In return for this the inhabitant guardians of the great hill-top Susa made him indestructible with a memory for future [generations], those people [i.e. the inhabitants] whose land, long since left dry, he saved and made fertile with the waves of Gondeisos. Year 313 [SE]. Ariston, son of Goras, wrote' (Potts 1989: 329, trans. A. Bülow-Jacobsen).

The Ab-i-Diz (Diz river) or one of its feeder tributaries (Wilhelm 1935: 80) is the prime candidate for identification with the Gondeisos (Potts 1989). Many years ago R. McC. Adams suggested that 'several impressive networks of canals which can be shown from aerial photographs to have antedated the still greater networks constructed early in the Sasanian period' might have been those of Zamaspes (Adams 1962: 8), while 'a dam or weir on the Dez which fed the area directly east of Susa' and which has been dated to the middle of the Parthian era (Wenke 1976: 117) is perhaps part of Zamaspes' irrigation project as well (Potts 1989: 331).

LeRider has suggested that, in the time of Phraates IV, Susa acquired the new name 'Phraata in Susa' as a sign of the town's significance in the period (LeRider 1965a: 409ff.;

see also Oppenheimer 1983: 431). Curiously, although Susa was a thoroughly Parthian settlement by then, Greek institutions continued to flourish and the Seleucid era was even used in preference to the Parthian era in the extant official records, although we should recall that these are largely written in Greek and the Parthian era may have been used to date no longer extant leather, parchment or papyrus documents. An interesting instance of the continued veneration of Greek deities at Parthian Susa is provided by an engraved paving stone (Cumont 1928: 89) which bears the fragmentary text of a first century AD (?) hymn in honour of Apollo by one Herodoros, son of Artemon, of Seleucia-by-the-Eulaios, i.e. Susa. The worship of a Greek deity at this late date is of interest but is hardly cause for surprise. After all, Plutarch (*Marcus Crassus*) recounts that when the head of the defeated Roman Marcus Crassus was brought to the Parthian king Orodes in 53 BC the latter was in the middle of watching a production of Euripides' *The Bacchae*. The Parthians, philhellenic to a degree, were inclined to worship Greek deities long after any vestige of Seleucid rule had been eradicated in the East.

The fact that Gotarzes II (*c.* AD 40–51) is the last Parthian king known to have minted coins at Susa (not Vardanes as previously thought, contra Oppenheimer 1983: 431), combined with the re-appearance of Elymaean issues after this date, has led scholars to assume a re-conquest of Susa around AD 45, even though Elymaean coins were not struck at the site until AD 70–5 (LeRider 1965a: 426ff.; Augé *et al.* 1979: 39). Indeed, as Augé has stressed, apart from a few inscriptions and several rock reliefs, the dates of which are difficult to determine, Elymaean coinage constitutes our primary source of knowledge about the succession of Elymaean kings during the second half of the first and all of the second centuries AD (Augé *et al.* 1979: 40; Harmatta 1982–1984: 174ff.).

The most important collections from this period are without doubt the foundation deposit from Bard-e Nechandeh and the hoard found in 1900 at Susa. Located to the north of Masjid-e Solaiman, Bard-e Nechandeh (Fig. 10.13) is the site of a second important terrace of irregular shape measuring maximally 67.5×45.3 m, topped by a small, so-called 'podium' and adjacent building (Ghirshman 1976: 13). Fragmentary bas-reliefs there once decorated the staircases leading up to the platform and illustrate, *inter alia*, men involved in a libation ceremony (e.g. Ghirshman 1976: Fig. 11; Mathiesen 1992: 151).

The succession of Elymaean kings in the first and second centuries AD (the so-called 'second period') has been studied for almost a century (for bibliography up to 1979, see Augé *et al.* 1979: 43–5), but the order and identity of more than one group has bedevilled attempts to come up with a secure sequence. As it would serve little purpose to review the various schemes proposed to date, we shall move straight to the most recent and refined sequence developed by R. Vardanian (Vardanian 1986; 1997), who in turn has built on the work of Augé and LeRider (Table 10.3). While far from providing a smooth and continuous sequence of rulers for the first and second centuries AD, Elymaean coinage does suggest certain developments in the history of the region. Vardanian believes that the alternation between Greek and Aramaic legends allows one to correlate the development of Elymaean coinage with that of the neighbouring kingdom of Characene. Furthermore, while LeRider has suggested that the

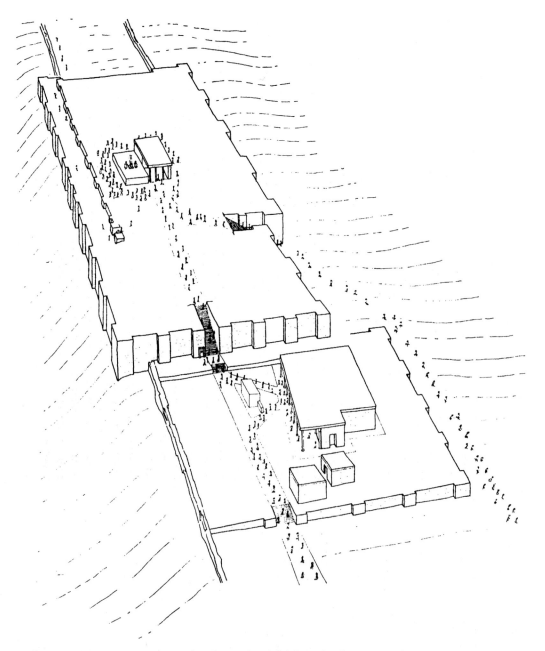

Figure 10.13 Artist's impression of Bard-e Nechandeh (after Ghirshman 1976: frontispiece).

Table 10.3. *Main features of Elymaean coinage*

Ruler	Approx. date	Description
Kamniskires Nikephoros	147–140 BC	tetradrachms: *obv.* diademed head of K., beardless, facing r.; *rev. Βασιλεως Καμνισχιρου Νιχηφ ορου* [king Kamniskires Nikephoros] nude Apollo seated on his omphalos, facing left and holding an arrow in his right hand drachms: *obv.* as above; *rev.* r. *Βασιλεως* [king], l. *Καμνισχιρου* [Kamniskires]; iconography as above
Kamniskires and Anzaze	82/81 or 79/78 BC	tetradrachms/drachms: *obv.* busts facing left of Anzaze and Kamniskires, bearded and diademed, anchor symbol; rev. Zeus seated on throne, torso nude, holding spear in left hand, supporting Nike proffering a wreath in right; legends *Βασιλεως* (above); *Καμνισχιρου* (right); *χαι Βασιλισσς* [left]; *Ανζαζης* (below);
Kamniskires	? to AD 58/9	tetradrachms/drachms: *obv.* diademed, bearded head, facing l., hair and diadem resembling a brimmed hat; star and crescent moon, anchor monogram; *rev.* pseudo-Greek legend, bearded masculine bust in the centre
Unknown king (Orodes I?)		tetradrachms: *obv.* bearded head facing l., wearing high, beaded tiara; crescent and star, anchor monogram behind head; Aramaic legend URUD MaLKA [Orodes king] in front of face; *rev.* pattern of vertical dashes, with or without an anchor in the centre
Kamniskires-Orodes	AD 110–120?	1st series, tetradrachms: *obv.* bearded head *en face*; hair rising up in diagonal waves, crescent and star, anchor, r.; Aramaic legend KUMaŠKIR/KaBNŠKIR URUD MaLKA BaRI URUD MaLKA [king Kamniskires-Orodes, son of king Orodes]; *rev.* pattern of dashes, normally vertical drachms: as above, but legend gives name only without filiation 2nd series: generally as above but hair arranged in horizontal waves
Orodes II		1st series, drachms: *obv.* bearded, diademed head en face; star and crescent, anchor r.; *rev.* Aramaic legend URUD MaLKA BaRI URUD [king Orodes, son of Orodes] around small, beardless head 2nd series, tetradrachms: *obv.* bearded head *en face*, tufted tiara; star and crescent, anchor r.; Aramaic legend URUD MaLKA left, *rev.* pattern of dashes; drachms: as above, but Aramaic legend as in 1st series, with filiation 3rd series, drachms: as 2nd series but tiara without tufts; legend gives filiation

Table 10.3. (cont.)

Ruler	Approx. date	Description
Phraates		1st series, drachms: *obv.* bearded head en face, tiara decorated with two crescents; star and crescent, anchor r.; *rev.* Greek legend Βασιλευς Πραατης or Φραατης; Artemis-Nanaya standing, facing right, holding bow in left hand, drawing arrow from a quiver on her back with right hand 2nd series, tetradrachms/drachms: *obv.* bearded head with high, spherical tiara, facing l., star and crescent on tiara; star and crescent, anchor r.; Aramaic legend PRAAT MaLKA [king Phraates, son of king Orodes]; *rev.* Artemis-Nanaya, as above, with Greek legend Βασιλευς Πραατης or Φραατης, or crescents or strokes in various patterns
Orodes III		tetradrachms: *obv.* bearded head with high tiara bearing anchor in profile, facing l.; star and crescent, anchor r.; Aramaic legend l., URUD MaLKA; *rev.* vertical dashes drachms: obv. as above; rev. Greek legend Υρωδης Βασιλευς, bust of Artemis-Nanaya in centre of field

vast majority of known Elymaean issues were minted at Seleucia-by-the-Hedyphon, Elymaean issues began to be minted at Susa by the 70s and Vardanian argues that a complete reunification of Susa and Elymais had been effected by the reign of Kamniskires-Orodes, roughly in the second decade of the second century AD (Vardanian 1986: 117).

Occasionally the numismatic evidence can be complemented by other types of data. Thus, a fragmentary inscription from Palmyra in Syria which mentions 'Susa' and 'Worod', i.e. Orodes, the name of at least three different Elymaean kings during the second century AD, raises the possibility that a Palmyrene merchant colony was established at the site in this period (Cantineau 1939: 278), a time when we know that Palmyrene merchants were active elsewhere in the region, e.g. in the kingdom of Characene and on Bahrain (Potts 1988). Contact between the Persian Gulf and Susiana was probably responsible for the limited diffusion of Elymaean coinage into eastern Arabia as well (Potts 1996: Fig. 9).

A square stone stele (Fig. 10.14) from Susa (Ghirshman 1950b; Mathiesen 1992/II: 168–9) depicting a seated nobleman wearing a crown and a standing figure in Parthian dress, both of whom grasp a ring, bears an inscription which reads, 'Artabanu, the king of kings, son of Walagashi [Vologases], the king of kings, built this "erection" which (is that) of Khwasak, the satrap of Susa' (Henning 1977: 384). The stele is dated 'year 462, month of Spandarmat, day of Mihr', i.e. 14 September AD 215 according to the Parthian era, and thus dates to the reign of Artabanus IV (c. AD 216–24), last of the Parthian kings. Henning believed the Susa stele may have been Khwasak's tomb stone and it is interesting to find him referred to as 'satrap of Susa'. Given the fact that the Parthian king Artabanus IV is only known to have struck coins at Ekbatana, not at Susa (Sellwood 1980: 290), his authority there may have been limited and Khwasak, the 'satrap of Susa', may have been an Elymaean with considerable political authority in Susiana at this time. Even so, it suggests that Parthian rule was not entirely absent from Susa at this late date, and some scholars believe it reflects the return of Susa to the Parthian political orbit after a century and a half of Elymaean control (Gyselen and Gasche 1994: 20). Lukonin noted that reliefs like Khwasak's 'were cut to the orders of these high personages, and reflected basically the same ideas as the rock carvings of the Sassanid Shahanshahs. Like them they proclaimed the ideas of legitimacy, like them they showed scenes of investiture; but with this difference that the governors derived their authority over the territories they ruled not from the gods but from the King of Kings of Iran' (Lukonin 1967: 156; von Gall 1990: 103). Within a few years, however, neither the Elymaeans nor the Parthians would be in control in Khuzistan. The rise of a new dynasty in Fars known as the Sasanians would put an end to all competition for hegemony in the region.

Elymaean rock reliefs

Apart from fragments of figural sculpture from sites such as Bard-e Nechandeh and Masjid-i Solaiman, the monumental art of Elymais consists of a series of rock reliefs in

Figure 10.14 The stele of Khwasak from Susa (after Ghirshman 1950b: Fig. 1).

the mountainous region east of lowland Khuzistan which perpetuate a far more ancient Elamite tradition (Vanden Berghe and Schippmann 1985: 99). In view of the difficulty of precisely defining the geographical limits of Elymais, a changing entity at all times vis-à-vis the boundaries of Parthian control, it is not always easy to classify a relief as Elymaean rather than Parthian (see Mathiesen 1992/I: 9), but there is generally broad agreement on the Elymaean attribution of the reliefs at a cluster of sites including Hung-i Nauruzi, Hung-i Yar-i 'Alivand, Hung-i Kamalvand, Tang-i Butan, Bard-i But, Kuh-i Taraz and Tang-i Sarvak (Figs. 10.15–17), the majority of which are located in the mountains north of Izeh and northeast of Shushtar (Vanden Berghe and Schippmann 1985).

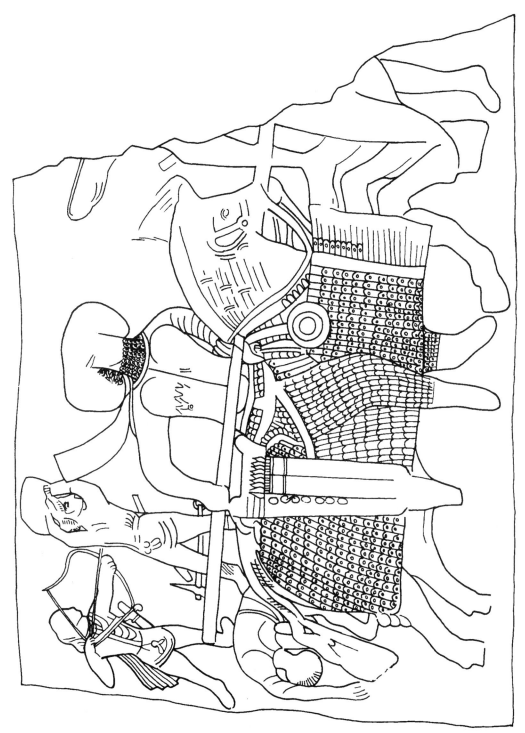

Figure 10.15 The Tang-i Sarvak III relief (after Vanden Berghe and Schippmann 1985. Fig. 12).

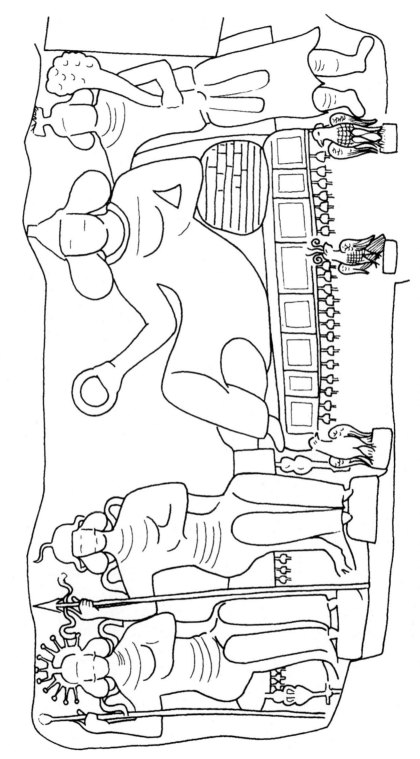

Figure 10.16 The Tang-i Sarvak II (northeast face, upper register) relief (after Vanden Berghe and Schippmann 1985: Fig. 9).

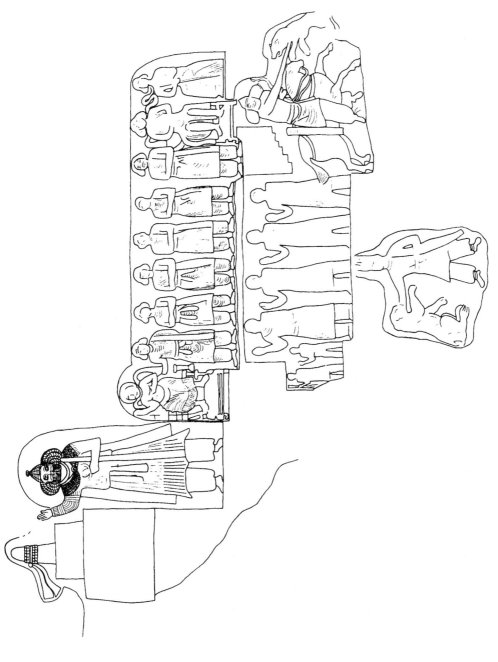

Figure 10.17 The Tang-i Sarvak II (north/northwest face) relief (after Vanden Berghe and Schippmann 1985: Fig. 11).

Having said that, the dating and interpretation of these reliefs have varied greatly over the years and only recently has a comprehensive analysis of their style, iconography and chronology been achieved which places them in the broader context of Parthian and Syro-Mesopotamian art of the last centuries BC and first centuries AD (Mathiesen 1992, superseding Vanden Berghe and Schippmann 1985). H.E. Mathiesen has assigned the corpus of Elymaean reliefs to four chronological groups (Table 10.4) which extend in time from *c.* 250 BC to AD 225. These include scenes of homage, worship, the hunt and equestrian combat (see Vanden Berghe and Schippmann 1985: 101–2). Although often badly weathered, the Elymaean reliefs still continue to display details of dress, weaponry and hairstyle which permit comparison with better preserved examples of Parthian, Hatran and Syrian (e.g. Dura Europus) art of the pre-Sasanian period. Stylistically, they are pervaded by a tendency towards frontality and static realism. In the absence of epigrams identifying specific figures, however, the identification of specific Elymaean princes or kings and deities is fraught with danger, and there is little agreement among specialists when it comes to these problematic issues.

Conclusion

Elymais, as we have seen, is nothing but the Graecized form of the more ancient name Elam, and as the sources make clear, the Elamites were, in their late manifestation, very much a part of the cultural and political landscape of southwestern Iran during the Seleucid and Parthian periods. Like their earlier forebears, they raided southern Mesopotamia on numerous occasions, and were subject to the oppression of foreign political powers, first the Seleucids and then the Parthians. Like the Elamites of earlier centuries, the Elymaeans were noted for their prowess in archery and had a reputation of being great warriors. There is more than a touch of the 'barbarian' in Greek and Latin ethnographic descriptions of the Elymaeans, even though agricultural pursuits are occasionally mentioned.

Of the non-political aspects of Elymaean history we are afforded few glimpses, but one notice preserved by Pliny is worth noting. Pliny commented (*Nat. Hist.* XII.38.78), 'so tired do mortals get of things that are their own, and so covetous are they of what belongs to other people', that the ancient inhabitants of Arabia used to 'send to the Elymaei for the wood of the bratum, a tree resembling a spreading cypress, with very white branches, and giving an agreeable scent when burnt. It is praised in the Histories of Claudius Caesar as having a marvellous property: he states that the Parthians sprinkle its leaves into their drinks, and that it has a scent very like cedar, and its smoke is an antidote against the effects of other woods. It grows beyond the Pasitigris on Mount Scanchrus in the territory of the city of Sostrata [i.e. Shushtar, see Weissbach 1927]'. This is a vignette of life in Elymais which adds a completely different dimension to our otherwise often intractable archaeological, epigraphic and literary sources.

Table 10.4. *Chronological distribution of Elymaean rock reliefs*

Period	Approx. date	Hung-i Nauruzi	Tang-i Sarvak	Tang-i Butan	Kuh-i Taraz	Hung-i Kamalwand	Hung-i Yar-i Alvand
Early	BC 250–0	relief, left side					
Middle	AD 0–150						
Late Ia	AD 150–190		CN, ANb, CE, BW, AWba_1 AWa, BS' left	Groups III–IV	relief		
Late Ib	AD 190–200		BS' right, BN, AWc	Group II		relief	relief
Late II	AD 200–25	relief, right side	ANa, ANW, AWbβ, D	Group I			

Note: According to Mathieson 1992.

Date	Lowlands	Highlands	Mesopotamia	'Elam'
323–316 BC	Susiana scene of fighting between successors of Alexander	fighting in Media	struggle amongst successors for control of Babylonia	
301–222 BC	Seleucus I gains control of Susiana, begins minting coins, founds and renames of cities in Khuzistan; Susa shows heavy occupation, much Hellenistic material; establishment of Seleucid military colony at Susa, transformation into a Greek *polis* with Greek institutions	Seleucus I in control of Fars, begins minting coins; independent *frataraka* dynasty in Persis after death of Seleucus I; foundation of Masjid-i Solaiman	Seleucus I gains control, Mesopotamia under Seleucid rule	
222–187 BC	Susiana joined to southern Babylonia administratively by the reign of Antiochus III; 'Kissians' fighting with Antiochus III represent Low-land contingent from Susiana	revolt in Media; Kossaeans and Elymaeans in Zagros; attack by Antiochus III on Bel temple in Elymais; Elymaean shrine at Bard-e Nechandeh	Seleucids in control, incursion by Ptolemy III?	Elymais and Elymaeans appear in Greek sources as region and ethnic group; political unity a reaction to Seleucid aggression? Elymaean deities
187–145 BC	activity of Susa's mint shows city remains Seleucid	Seleucid governor in Media, coins issued at Ecbatana; attack by Antiochus IV on Elymais		
145–130 BC	struggle for control of Susa between Elymaean	highlands under Elymaean control, early Elymaean rock	attacks by Elymaeans noted in Babylonian	Elymaean 'kingdom'

	king Kamniskires I and Parthians, Elymaean coin issues	reliefs	astronomical diaries; attempts by last Seleucids to re-assert authority, rise of Characene	shrinking of Elymais as political force
130–80 BC	Susa under Parthian control, Parthian coins issued there; massive occupation of site	Elymaeans in retreat? limited Parthian authority	Parthian control	
79 BC–AD 224	alternating rule of Elymaean and Parthian kings over Susa, alternative Elymaean 'capital' at Seleucia-on-the-Hedyphon? persistence of Greek institutions, Parthian investments in agriculture in Susiana	Elymaean/Parthian rivalry, series of important rock reliefs	Parthian control	shifting balance of power between Elymaean and Parthian Kings, signs of autonomy in areas of southwestern Iran

ELAM UNDER THE SASANIANS AND BEYOND

The Parthian empire was brought down by Ardashir, a native of Istakhr in Fars who successfully overthrew Artabanus IV, last of the Parthian kings, in AD 224, and thereby laid the foundations for what has become known as the Sasanian empire. There is no shortage of important archaeological sites in Fars and Khuzistan dating to the Sasanian period (AD 224–642), such as Susa, Gundeshapur and Ivan-e Kerkha. But where are the Elamites? By the Sasanian period it is difficult to discern elements of distinctive Elamite identity in southwestern Iran, although there are some indications that the Elamite language survived in places. After the Islamic conquest, however, we see the name 'Elam' used to identify the ecclesiastical province of the Nestorian church, a major branch of Christianity widespread in the Sasanian empire, located in Khuzistan. Sources dating to between the eighth and fourteenth centuries AD make frequent reference to the Nestorian ecclesiastical province of Elam which seems to have eventually succumbed to conquest by Tamerlane in about AD 1400. In this case the revival of the name Elam can be attributed to religious usage.

Introduction

As we have seen, the political status of Elymais in the late Parthian period is difficult to characterize on the basis of the very scarce data available to us today. However, thanks to the sources which touch upon the rise of the Sasanian dynasty in the first three decades of the third century, we are afforded another perspective on Elymais (Fig. 11.1) at the very end of the Parthian era. Early Arabic and Pahlavi sources differ in their identification of the eponymous Sasan, one alleging he was in charge of a temple of Anahita at Istakhr, near Persepolis (thus al-Tabari; Schippmann 1990: 11), another that he was a soldier (thus Ferdowsi), and a third that he was a shepherd of Achaemenid descent (thus the *Kar Namak-i Ardashir* or 'Book of Deeds of Ardashir', a Pahlavi 'novel' thought to have been written in the reign of the Sasanian king Hormizd I, c. AD 272/3) (Frye 1962: 207; 1983: 117). Whichever tradition one chooses to follow, the Ka'ba-i Zardosht (hereafter KZ) inscription at Naqshh-i Rustam near Persepolis stipulates descent from the eponymous Sasan through Papak (not necessarily Sasan's son; Frye 1983: 116; Felix 1985: 28) to Ardashir (Maricq 1958: 333). As for Ardashir himself (Fig. 11.2), there are various accounts of his career, the details of which are not always easy to reconcile (Christensen 1936; Frye 1971: 215; Widengren 1971; Piacentini 1984; 1985; Schippmann 1990), but it is clear that Darabgird in Fars was his centre of activity and that he became 'king' of Istakhr early in the third century, perhaps in AD 205/6 or 208 (for the date, see the discussion in Schippmann 1990: 13). This was an important step on the road to full-scale rebellion against the Parthian ruling house, culmi-

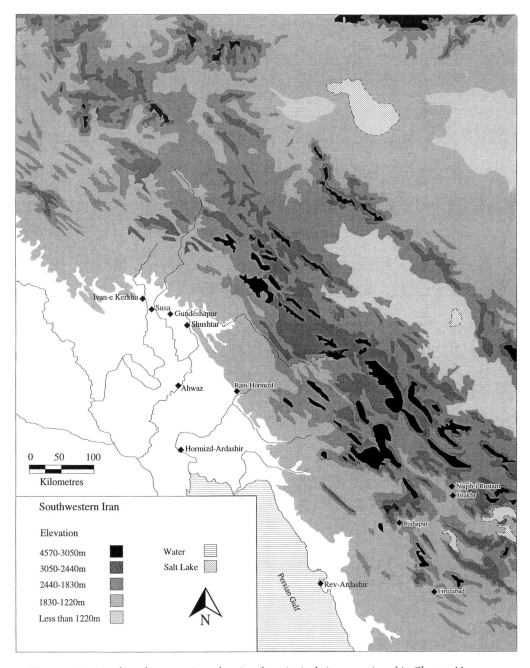

Figure 11.1 Map of southwestern Iran showing the principal sites mentioned in Chapter 11.

Figure 11.2 A Sasanian dirham of Ardashir I (after Sykes 1915/I: 422).

nating eventually in AD 224 with the victory of Ardashir over Artabanus (Fig. 11.3) and the birth of a new political power in Western Asia.

Elam in the early Sasanian period

Sometime shortly after AD 218 Ardashir (Fig. 11.4) battled and defeated an unnamed 'king of Ahwaz' who had been deputed by Artabanus to bring the Sasanian to him in chains, according to al-Tabari and Ibn al-Athir (Christensen 1936: 82; Widengren 1971: 737; Schippmann 1990: 15). Although Sellwood has suggested (Sellwood 1983: 310) that the 'king of Ahwaz' was one of the late Elymaean monarchs called 'Orodes' (Hill 1922: cxciv), this is attested neither in the ancient sources on Ardashir's reign (Felix 1985: 25–42) nor in the later Arabic accounts of his exploits. Widengren, who said simply, 'It is a difficult problem to say who is meant by "the king of al-Ahwaz",' noted that the only name one could possibly point to was that of Khwasak, the satrap of Susa under Artabanus V (Widengren 1971: 737–8) who was in office in AD 215 and whom we discussed in Chapter 10. Although we cannot be certain that the 'king of Ahwaz' was Khwasak, there seems little doubt that the 'kingdom of Ahwaz' was a semi-autonomous, late Parthian incarnation of Elymais, with or without the inclusion of Susiana, on the eve of its eventual capitulation to the new dynast (Widengren 1971: 738).

Having defeated the king of Ahwaz, Ardashir then invaded the territory of Khuzistan itself, marching through Arjan (near Behbehan) and several other districts near Ram-Hormuz before advancing to the region of Dauraq, near the ancient site of Seleucia-by-the-Hedyphon (Chapter 10). This he conquered and refounded as Hormizd-Ardashir (contested by Schwaigert 1989: 13, who considers it a foundation of Ardashir's grandson Hormizd I), which was later destroyed and refounded following the Muslim conquest as 'Ashkar Mukram, roughly halfway between Shushtar and al-Ahwaz (Fiey 1979: 130, n. 4). The (re-)foundation of Shushtar, Pliny's Sostra (Weissbach 1927), is also

Figure 11.3 The Firuzabad I relief showing Ardashir's triumph over Artabanus (after Vanden Berghe 1983: Fig. 8).

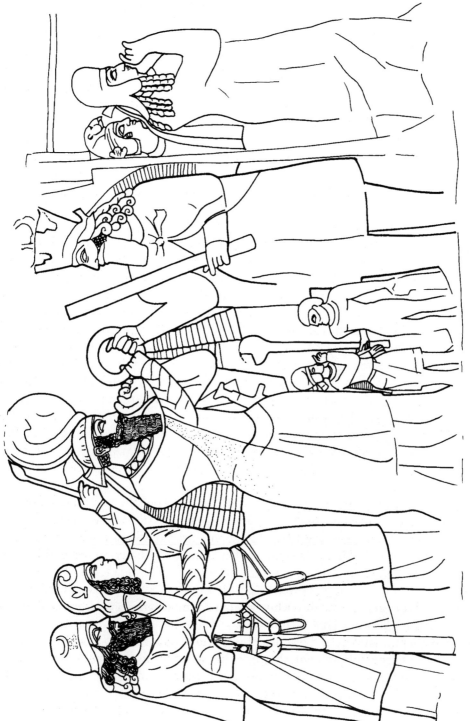

Figure 11.4 The Naqsh-i Rajab III relief showing the investiture of Ardashir (after Vanden Berghe 1983: Fig. 9).

attributed to Ardashir by the anonymous Persian work *Muǵmal at-tawarih* (Schwaigert 1989: 13). Laden with booty, Ardashir returned to Fars (Widengren 1971: 738). Shortly thereafter, he crossed the district again on his way to Mesene (southernmost Iraq).

The fact that Islamic historians writing on the reign of Ardashir used the term 'Ahwaz' in referring to the southwestern corner of Iran simply means that the names Elam and Elymais were no longer familiar to them, although the names certainly continued to figure in Christian and Jewish texts. But if we consider the sources on the career of Ardashir's son and successor, Shapur I, we find that we have both a more ancient and a more modern term in use. In the trilingual (Greek, Middle Persian and Parthian) KZ inscription of Shapur I, the king, after outlining his filiation, lists the countries which constituted his empire, beginning with Persis, Parthia and Susiana (Honigmann and Maricq 1953: 39; Maricq 1958: 304–5) as does, in all probability, the slightly later provincial list of Shapur's important priest Kartir (Gignoux 1971a: 86). In place of the classical Greek form Σουσιανη, KZ writes Οὐ[ζη]νήν (in the accusative), while the Parthian text uses the term *Hwzstn*, obviously the forerunner of modern Khuzistan. Οὐ[ζη]νήν, like the Greek ethnic Uxioi (Οὔξιοι), would seem to be derived from the Old Persian Huziya, the term used for the inhabitants of Huza (Szemerényi 1966: 194), as discussed in Chapter 9. The identity of all of these terms with the 'kingdom of Ahwaz' mentioned by Tabari and other late writers is also assured, since Arabic Ahwaz is nothing but the plural of New Persian Khûz, a cognate form of Old Persian Huziya which denoted the inhabitants of Khuzistan (Nöldeke 1874: 184).

The Elamite or Elymaean substratum of the inhabitants of this part of Iran is explicitly hinted at by two sources. According to the Babylonian Talmud (Megillah 18a), in answer to a question about when the Book of Esther was to be read, Raba (fl. reign of Shapur II, AD 309–79) said that the Jews of Susa read it every year on the 15 of Adar, the anniversary of the Purim uprising described in Esther 9.18. Furthermore, he said that it was read in the *native speech* of their country, which Obermeyer took to be Elymaean (Obermeyer 1929: 212; see also Oppenheimer 1983: 432) and which, in light of the evidence (e.g. Pittit's name) discussed in Chapter 10, must have been a late form of Elamite. Moreover, the tenth century writers al-Istakhri and Ibn Hawqal noted that, along with Persian and Arabic, the Khuz spoke another language which was neither Syriac nor Hebrew (Nöldeke 1874: 187; Fiey 1979: 224). Some form of Elamite seems implied by this statement. Nevertheless, it is striking that there is virtually no residual Elamite substratum in the New Persian dialects of southwestern Iran (de Blois 1996).

Like the Achaemenids and Elamites before them, the Sasanians, though indigenous to the highlands of Fars, moved into Khuzistan in an important way as soon as they had consolidated their power. This is not to say that they ignored Fars, as sites like Firuzabad, Bishapur, Istakhr and a series of important rock reliefs attest. But whether it was a matter of geographical centrality or political tradition, southwestern Iran once more assumed a level of geo-political importance which it had temporarily lost under the Parthians. At the same time, however, the military successes of the early Sasanian period had a profound impact on the topography, demography and religious make-up of Khuzistan in particular.

Figure 11.5 A Sasanian dirham of Shapur I (after Sykes 1915/I: 444).

Following in the footsteps of his father, Shapur I (AD 240–72) campaigned widely (Fig. 11.5), first as co-regent with Ardashir (e.g. in the campaign of AD 241 against Hatra in northern Mesopotamia), and later on his own (for the sources see Felix 1985: 43–89; Dodgeon and Lieu 1991; for the history, see e.g. Frye 1962: 212ff.; 1983: 124–7; Herrmann 1977: 96ff.; Kettenhofen 1982; Schippmann 1990: 19ff.). His victories over the Kushans in the east and the Romans in the west are the stuff of legend. He succeeded in defeating Gordian in AD 244, securing terms from Philip the Arab in the same year (Chaumont 1969: 44ff.; Kettenhofen 1982; 1995; Winter 1988: 100ff.), and capturing Valerian in AD 260, the latter an unprecedented achievement commemorated on rock reliefs at Darab, Bishapur and Naqsh-i Rustam (Pl. 11.1).

In Khuzistan, the direct consequences of Shapur's victories were enormous. To begin with, his capture of Antioch while in Syria in AD 256 on his second campaign, as recounted in the KZ inscription (Honigmann and Maricq 1953: 131ff.; Maricq 1958: 310) and in the *Chronicle of Seert*, a Nestorian Christian source of the eleventh century AD (Scher 1907: 220–3; Sachau 1916: 4; Peeters 1924: 295–7; Felix 1985: 57; Schwaigert 1989: 191, n. 4), resulted in the deportation of a large number of prisoners-of-war, indeed all who were not killed on the spot according to Zosimus (Chaumont 1988: 59). The *Chronicle of Seert* says explicitly that Shapur settled the prisoners in cities built by his father in Babylonia, Khuzistan and Persis, and in three new cities of his own construction, one in Mesene (Sad-Sabur), one in Persis (Sabur) and one on the Tigris (Buzurg-Sabur) (for these foundations, see the discussion in Peeters 1924: 298ff.). The *Chronicle of Seert* further specifies that Shapur 'rebuilt Gondisapor [Gundeshapur] which had fallen into ruins' and gave his prisoners land grants so that they might build homes and take up farming.

Apart from the sheer genetic and linguistic impact of this act, it is clear that the deportations introduced large numbers of skilled craftsmen and artisans. The Arab historian Masudi attributes the introduction to Persia of a number of industries to the

Plate 11.1 Detail of rock relief Naqsh-i Rustam VI showing Valerian kneeling before Shapur I.

talents of the deportees (Peeters 1924: 308), including sculptors and stone masons who, according to some scholars, were put to work on the reliefs and mosaics at Bishapur (Ghirshman 1956: 147; 1971: 177). Moreover, according to Tabari (Nöldeke 1879: 33, n. 2), captive Roman engineers built the *c.* 550 m long dam still visible (with thirty-five arches still extant) at Shushtar on the Karun river in Susiana as well as the 400 m long weir (with twenty-two arches) on the Diz river near Dizful, and possibly the 1 km wide weir at Ahwaz (Graadt van Roggen 1905: 174–90; Rahimi-Laridjani 1988: 238–9; Neely 1974; Christensen 1993: 109). Later Islamic and local folk tradition attributed the Shushtar constructions not just to Roman engineers but specifically to Valerian, calling them by such names as Pul-e Kaisar ('the emperor's bridge') or Band-e Kaisar ('the emperor's weir'), and even if there is little substance to such attributions they do make clear the perceived connection between irrigation works and Roman prisoners-of-war (Christensen 1993: 109). A sophisticated 'siphon bridge' across the Siah Mansur water course near Gundeshapur is also attributed to the Sasanian period (Adams and Hansen 1968: 59ff.). Considering the Sasanian interest in the professional qualifications of their prisoners, it is tempting to see the explosion in the construction of stone masonry irrigation works in Khuzistan as a direct result of these deportations. Just as the contribution of engineers to the French revolution has recently been highlighted (Alder 1997), so too it can be suggested that the implementation of Roman engineering had a catalytic effect on the Sasanian capacity for agricultural intensification, a necessity if the large population of Khuzistan in the third century was to be fed.

Further, we know from both the *Chronicle of Seert* and the twelfth century writer Mari Ibn Sulaiman (Westphal 1901) that among the deportees of AD 256 was Demetrianus, bishop of Antioch (Peeters 1924; Sachau 1916: 5). From a tactical point of view, the deportation of a community's religious leaders may have helped ensure more passive and orderly conduct on the part of the captives than would otherwise have been the case (Peeters 1924: 308). However that may be, the *Chronicle of Seert* says that from the time of this deportation onwards, Christianity flourished and spread widely throughout Iran (Selb 1981: 48–50, 161–5; Brock 1984: VI3–4; Schwaigert 1989: 20). Thus, despite the fact that Zoroastrianism was the 'state religion' of the ruling elites of the Sasanian court, the Nestorian church claimed a large share of the populace among its members and qualified, in many respects, to the claim of being a second 'state religion' (Labourt 1904). Indeed, Nöldeke believed that during the Sasanian period most of the population of Khuzistan was Christian (Nöldeke 1893: 44).

Shapur I's deportation of prisoners from Antioch in AD 256 was followed by a second one, explicitly noted in the *Chronicle of Seert*, in AD 261 (Peeters 1924: 310). Nor were these by any means unique in Sasanian history. Numerous other deportations impacted directly on Khuzistan. Arabic sources, including Yaqut and al-Tha'alibi, report that Shapur II (AD 309–79) deported prisoners from Amida (modern Diyarbakir near the Turkish-Iraqi border, see Dillemann 1962: 326), Bosra, Tuwana, Sinjar and other regions in northern Mesopotamia to Khuzistan. These new groups were meant to have been responsible for making brocade and other fine textiles at Shushtar, garments of silk at Susa, carpets and veils at Basinna and Mattut, and veils of inferior quality at Birud and Birdawn (Fiey 1979: 226). According to Tabari, Shapur II deported some prisoners from the Middle Euphrates (Peeters 1924: 305) to Eran-xwarrah-Shapur-Shahrestan, i.e. Ivan-e Kerkha, around AD 350. In AD 360 he sent around 9000 inhabitants of Finik, a town located near the eastern end of the Tur Abdin in what is today southeastern Turkey, to Susiana. A little later he deported a contingent of Christian Taghlib Arabs to Khuzistan, sending others to Kerman and Tawag, near Rev-Ardashir and modern Bushire on the Persian Gulf (Peeters 1924: 306). Between AD 502 and 506 Kawadh I deported part of the population of Theodosiopolis in Armenia, as well as groups from Amida and Maiperqat, to the borders of Persia and Khuzistan, founding the new city of Weh Amid-i Kavadh. Later deportations of Antiochans in AD 540 by Khusrau I, and of Palestinians by Khusrau II in AD 614, resulted principally in distributions of population around Seleucia-Ctesiphon in Babylonia (Peeters 1924: 307). In the absence of a clergyman, someone else might be assigned to assist the group of deportees. Thus, according to Tabari, Khusrau I chose a Christian and former inspector of public works from Khuzistan, one Baraz, to assist the Antiochans whom he settled at Rumia (Peeters 1924: 309).

Major settlements of the Sasanian period in Khuzistan

The influx of deportees, the consequent expansion of irrigation works in Khuzistan, and the foundation of new cities transformed southwestern Iran more profoundly than had ever been the case in the region's past. Let us now look at the major settlements of the region during the Sasanian period. As noted above, we know that Ardashir himself probably founded or re-founded several cities, including Hormizd-Ardashir and Shushtar (Fiey 1979: 130–40). Each became an important commercial centre as well as a Nestorian bishopric, well-attested in Nestorian and later Arabic sources, but neither has been excavated. Two cities associated with Shapur I, however, rank above all others in Sasanian Khuzistan: Gundeshapur and Eran-xwarrah-Shapur-sharestan, the former a royal residence and seat of the Christian metropolitan of the region, the latter the new administrative capital of the district.

Gundeshapur

The ruins of Gundeshapur (Fig. 11.6) are located south of the village of Shahabad in northern Khuzistan, *c.* 10 km south of Dizful. Investigated briefly in 1963 by Adams and Hansen, Gundeshapur is a vast site of 'sprawling, indistinct clusters of low mounds' with visible depressions intersecting at right angles (Adams and Hansen 1968: 53; see also Abbott 1968) which must represent the system of streets described by the Arab geographers, such as Hamza al-Isfahani and Yaqut, who state that the city was traversed in both its length and width by eight streets at right angles to each other (Chaumont 1988: 72, n. 84). The site is more than 3 km long and nearly 2 km wide in some places. Numerous scholars have recognized in the rectilinearity of Gundeshapur's grid-like street plan an example of Hippodamian urban design, almost certainly the work of Antiochan planners (Chaumont 1988: 73, n. 86; Fiey 1979: 228–9). It is possible that smaller sites with rectangular plans and cross-streets, such as Chogha Kal near Rasvand on the Izeh plain (Eqbal 1979: 116), reflect the same phenomenon.

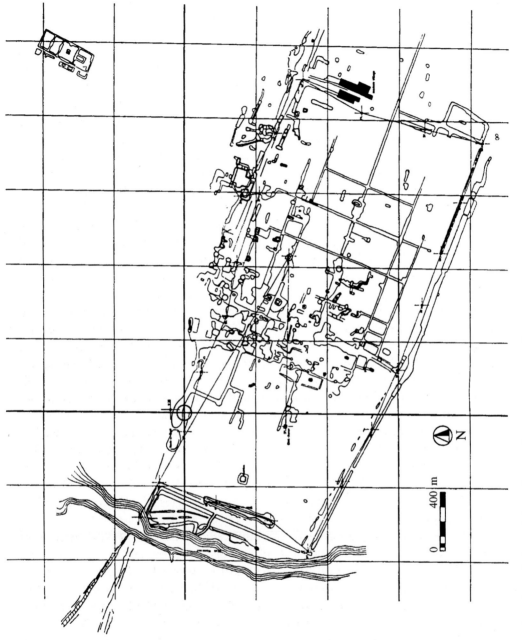

Figure 11.6 Plan of Gundeshapur (after Adams and Hansen 1968: Fig. 1).

As the *Chronicle of Seert* attests, the city is meant to have been re-founded by Shapur I, not created *ab novo*, and the distinction is important for the name, contrary to the many and varied suggestions put forward over the years, is almost certainly derived from that of a Parthian fortification, made up of *gund*, meaning military district or settlement, and *dêz*, meaning enclosure wall or fortress (Potts 1989: 332), which in turn gave its name to the river Gondeisos mentioned in the inscription of Zamaspes from Susa discussed in Chapter 10. The Parthian etymology of the name notwithstanding, Gundeshapur was given the Middle Persian epithet '(the) better (is the) Antioch of Shapur' (*why-'ndywk-šhpwhry*) following Shapur's capture of Antioch-on-the-Orontes. It is by this name that Gundeshapur is cited in the Pahlavi *Shahrastaniha i Eranshahr*, a listing of the provincial capitals of Iran compiled in the eighth century AD (Marquart 1931: 20). The Syriac name by which Gundeshapur appears throughout the Nestorian sources, in the Talmud and in Procopius, was Beth Lapat/Be Lapat/Belapaton, a name derived, according to a folk etymology preserved by Tabari, from that of its builder, Bel (see the discussion in Potts 1989: 324; Nöldeke 1879: 41–2, n. 2). According to the *Chronicle of Seert*, it was here that the captured Roman emperor Valerian became ill and died (Scher 1907: 220; Chaumont 1988: 63; Schwaigert 1989: 24 with references to the late accounts of Valerian's death preserved by Firmianus Lactantius, Eutropius, Aurelius Victor, Zosimas, Agathias Scholastikos and Zonaras).

Masudi says that Gundeshapur served as the Sasanian royal winter residence from its reconstruction during the reign of Shapur I (AD 240–72) (probably after the second capture of Antioch in AD 260 according to Schwaigert 1989: 24) through the reign of Hormizd II (AD 302–9), although Hamza al-Isfahani says that it continued to function in this capacity during the first thirty years of Shapur II's (AD 309–79) reign as well, prior to the foundation of the new Sasanian capital of Ctesiphon near Seleucia-on-the-Tigris (Nöldeke 1879: 42, n. 2). Gundeshapur's importance for the history of Manichaeism in the third century AD was also great, since the founder of the new religion, Mani, spent a great deal of time with Shapur and must therefore have lived at his winter residence on a regular basis (Hummel 1963: 2), just as we know that it was there that Mani met his death in AD 276 (Christensen 1936: 193; Fiey 1979: 234). Indeed the eighth/ninth century AD Syriac author Theodore bar Koni (Hespel 1983) says that Mani died at 'Beth Lapat, city of the Elamites' (Fiey 1979: 234).

In AD 270, two years before his death, Shapur is said to have married a daughter of the Roman emperor Aurelian. According to Bar Hebraeus, 'Aurelian gave his daughter to Sapor, and made peace with him. And Sapor built for himself in Persia a city which was like Constantinople. And its name was Gûndîshâbhôr, and he made his Roman wife to live therein. And there came with her distinguished Greek physicians, and they sowed the system of medicine of Hippocrates in the East' (Budge 1932: 56–7). This was the beginning of a unique medical academy which is attested as late as AD 869 (Hummel 1983: 54; Oppenheimer 1983: 88).

Equally if not more important was the city's role in the hierarchy of the Nestorian church (Table 11.1). At the synod of AD 410 convened by Mar Isaac at Seleucia-on-the-Tigris, a massive administrative re-organization of the Nestorian church was under-

Table 11.1. *Chronological and spatial distribution of early Christian and Nestorian (post AD 409) bishops in Khuzistan*

Date (AD)	Beth Lapat	Karka d'Ledan	Hormizd Ardashir	Shushtar	Susa	Ram Hormizd
[256–60]	[Demetrianus] [Ardaq[1]?]					
[330]					[Miles]	
341	Gadyaw[†2] M Sabina[†] Amaria[†3] Mqayma[†4]		John[†]			
?	Adona					
410	Yazdidad Agapit Mare Bar Shabtha Shila		John Batai	'Awdisho Simon Barduq	Z/Duqa Bar Shabtha	
420/424	Agapit M	Sawmai	'Abda[†] Batai	Gura Miles 'Abdisho	Duqa	
486	Papa? M	Paul b. Qaqai Salomon Emmanuel Samuel	Batai Shila	Pusai Yazdegerd	Papai	
497	Papa M Mar Marwai M					
524	Ya'qub M		Buzaq Paul			
534/7						
540					Khusrau	Simon
544	Paul M	Salmai	Shila	Elisee		
554	Joseph M	Surin	Shila	Elisee	Khusrau	
576	Dalai M	Moses	David	Daniel	Adhurhormizd	Mihr Shabur
585	Baraz M		David	Stephen		'Anan Isho
605		Pusai	Pusai	Ahishma	James	
630		Barsauma				
642/3	John M					
-646	Mar Emmeh M					
646	Sergius M					
650/9			Theodore	George		
-659	George of Kafra M					
680/1	John Bar Marta M	Isaac				
685–700	Narsai M					

Year					
751					
773–95	James M				
795	Ephrem M				
?	Sergius M				
799/804		Bar Sahde			Isho bar Nun
803	George b. al-Sayyah M				
828	George M				
835/7	Aba M	Michael			
837–48	Theodosius M				
840				Isho	
853			Abraham		
884	Paul M				
891	Shapur M				
893–900	Theodore M	Simon	Salomon	Isho'yaw	
900				Makarios	
960/1	George M				
986	Daylam M				
987	Hnanisho M				
987/97	Sawrisho M				
-1012			Emmanuel		
1012	Emmanuel M	Emmanuel			
-1064	Sawrisho Zanbur M				
1064	Steven (Abu 'Amr) M				
1075/90	Sawrisho M				
1111/32	Elias M				
	Yohannan M				
1176	Yuwanis M				
1222	'Awdisho M				
1256	Eliya M				
1257				Makkiha II	
1265				Yuhanna	
1283	Mar Ni'ma M				
1318	Joseph M				

Notes:

[1] reading of the name is uncertain.
[2] Gadimabh of the *Chronicle of Seert*.
[3] Marias of Sozomen.
[4] Mokinos of Sozomen.

M = metropolitan; B = bishop; † = martyred in that year.

taken and Gundeshapur became the capital of the ecclesiastical province of Beth Huzaye (Braun 1975 (1900): 28ff.; Chabot 1902: 253ff; Labourt 1904: 98). Several scholars (e.g. Westphal 1901: 63; Fiey 1979: 232) have suggested that, although never an official capital, Gundeshapur's importance as a royal residence accounts for the fact that it was chosen as the seat of the Nestorian metropolitan or archbishop who exercised jurisdiction over the bishops of Karka d'Ledan (Eran-xwarrah-Shapur-sharestan, Hormizd-Ardashir, Shushtar, Susa and Ram-Hormizd. Apart from the local importance of Gundeshapur in the Nestorian hierarchy of Khuzistan, the acts of the synod reveal a crucial demographic fact about the city. For in the last of twenty-one Canons or resolutions passed at the synod it is stated expressly that, after Seleucia itself (the ecclesiastical capital of the Nestorian church and comparable, in other words, to the status of the Vatican for the Roman Catholic church), the order and choice of the seats of the metropolitans (archbishops) of the church was based on the *size* of the cities in each region (Braun 1975 (1900): 28; Chabot 1902: 271). Hence, Gundeshapur was certainly the largest city of its day in Khuzistan and may well have been the second largest city in the Sasanian empire in AD 410 because of the fact that it is listed directly after Seleucia in the order of metropolitanates (Wiessner 1967: 289).

Interestingly, Canon XXI comments on the presence of two bishops in a single city in Beth Huzaye and the illegality of this state of affairs. It is generally thought that this was a by-product of the presence of two distinctly different Christian groups in Khuzistan at the time, the indigenous 'Aramaic' element, the origins of which may go back to the first century AD, and the 'Greek' element, composed of the deportees from Antioch and their descendants (Peeters 1924: 313; Fiey 1979: 236; Wiessner 1967: 293; Schwaigert 1989: 38). This cultural schism resulted in the use of two languages, Greek and Syriac, in the Christian liturgy of Khuzistan, and the perpetuation of these two languages is clearly signalled in the names of the rival bishops of Beth Huzaye, one group of which is Greek (e.g. Agapta, 'Αγαπητος) or Greco-Latin (e.g. Miles), while the other is non-Greek, principally Aramaic or Iranian (e.g. Yazdaidad) (Wiessner 1967: 293). One cannot help but be reminded of the much earlier Semitic (Akkadian)-Elamite (Anshanite) duality in Khuzistan and Elam generally of which Amiet and others have long been convinced. Although the reasons for the cultural and linguistic duality of Khuzistan in the Sasanian period were far different from those which may have applied in earlier times, the result was perhaps not that dissimilar in that a bi-cultural milieu, at least amongst the majority Christian community, seems to have prevailed.

Eran-xwarrah-Shapur-sharestan and its capital

While Gundeshapur enjoyed the status of a royal residence, the centre of local administration from the reign of Shapur II (AD 309–79) onwards lay elsewhere. Without going into detail on the subject of the administrative organization of the Sasanian empire (see e.g. Gignoux 1984 with earlier lit.; Zakeri 1995: 31–48), suffice it to say that there existed numerous administrative provinces, each with a provincial capital, and each composed of a variable number of administrative sub-districts. Reconstructing the administrative organization of Khuzistan on the basis of sealed clay bullae, Gyselen has identified three sub-districts within the province of Eran-xwarrah-Shapur: Shush i er-kar, Manestan i mar and . . . -shahrestan (Gyselen and Gasche 1994: 22; Gyselen 1989). Since the name of the provincial capital was usually composed of the name of the province plus the term *shahrestan*, Gyselen assumes that Eran-xwarrah-Shapur-sharestan was the capital of Khuzistan and that this was identical with the Eran-xwarrah-Shapur, 'which is called Karkha in Syriac', according to Tabari and Hamza al-Isfahani (Nöldeke 1879: 58; Marquart 1901: 145; Gyselen and Gasche 1994: 23). This is the Karka d'Ledan of the Nestorian sources, a city long identified with the site of Ivan-e Kerkha, *c.* 17 km northwest of Susa (e.g. Nöldeke 1879: 58, n. 1; Marquart 1901: 145; Chabot 1902: 674; Christensen 1936: 248).

Although it has sometimes been suggested that Susa was identical with Eran-xwarrah-Shapur-sharestan (see the discussion in Gyselen and Gasche 1994), the two are clearly distinguished in a number of souces. Thus, in the acts of the martyrdom of Yazdpanah of Beth Huzaye, Susa is described as 'a village close to Karka d'Ledan . . . in which many Magians [i.e. Zoroastrians] lived' (Hoffmann 1880: 87). In the work of Elias of Damascus, Karka d'Ledan is identified as a 'sister city' of Susa (Westphal 1901: 97). Similarly, Tabari says that Shapur II founded 'two cities in Ahwaz, namely Eran-xwarrah-Shapur, i.e. "Shapur and his land", called Karkh in Syriac, and Shush, a city which he built beside the fortress in which the sarcophagus with the corpse of the Prophet Daniel lies' (Nöldeke 1879: 58). Several pages later, in Tabari's story of an Indian doctor brought to Khuzistan by Shapur II, the physician is settled 'in Karkh near Susa' (Nöldeke 1879: 67). Finally, the *Chronicle of Seert* says explicitly of Shapur II that, 'In the tenth year of his reign, he imitated his predecessors and set himself to the con-struction of towns. He built one in Susiana [Al-Ahwaz], ringed it with fortifications, and called it . . . It is Karka d'Ledan. When he brought the Greeks into captivity, he established them there. Now [*c.* AD 1036, Schwaigert 1989: 145] it is in ruins. The inhabitants have been transported to Susa' (Scher 1907: 288).

The author of the *Acts of Pusai* gives a unique if not altogether unbiased perspective on Shapur II's philosophy in founding Karka d'Ledan. He says, 'Shapur [II] built the city of Karka d'Ledan, brought captives from various places and settled them there. He also had the idea of bringing about thirty families apiece from each of the ethnic groups living in the cities belonging to his realm, and settling them among the deported cap-tives, so that through intermarriage the latter should become tied down by the bonds of family and affection, thus making it less easy for them to slip away gradually in flight and return to the areas from which they had been deported. Such was Shapur's crafty plan, but God in his mercy turned it to good use, for thanks to intermarriage between the deported population and the native pagans, the latter were brought to knowledge of the faith' (Brock 1984: VI4). Fiey has suggested that Shapur II forsook Gundeshapur and made Karka d'Ledan his residence (Fiey 1974: 283).

In 1950 R. Ghirshman undertook a month of excavations at Ivan-e Kerkha, which he described as a rectangular settlement covering an area of roughly 390 ha (*c.* 3850 m [W]×3600 m [E]×950 m [N]×1000 m [S]; Gyselen and Gasche 1994: 30, n. 46). At that time he investigated a building considered to have been a palace as well as several other structures on which he published a brief account (Ghirshman 1952: 11). A royal workshop for silverworking at Karka d'Ledan is mentioned in the acts of the martyrdom of Pusai, the chief of the 'Greek' artisans there who was put to death on 18 April AD 341 as part of Shapur II's persecution of Christians (Fiey 1979: 125; Harper 1993: 151).

Shush i er-kar or Susa

Tabari explicitly attributed the foundation of Eran-xwarrah-Shapur to Shapur II (Nöldeke 1879: 58), a statement taken one step further by Ghirshman, who suggested that this event followed the destruction of Susa by the Sasanian monarch. Up to this point we have scarcely mentioned Susa. What can be said of its fate under the Sasanians?

Although Tha'alibi preserves a tradition according to which Shapur I spent the very end of his life at Susa consulting an Indian physician (Fiey 1979: 140; but Schwaigert 1989: 111 assigns this story to the reign of Shapur II), the history of Sasanian Susa is marked by its destruction c. AD 339 at the hands of Shapur II (Fig. 11.7). Ghirshman believed that the signs of destruction which he detected in level IV of his Ville Royale soundings were attributable to Shapur's noted persecution of Christians (Ghirshman 1952: 7), whom, it is said by Sozomenus, he suspected of harbouring pro-Roman sympathies (II.9; see Hartranft 1989: 264; Westphal 1901: 88; Brock 1984: VI4; Dodgeon and Lieu 1995: 90). But however real Shapur's persecution of Christians may have been, Fiey has noted that Susa was far from a Christian city, as indeed the career of Miles, bishop of Susa c. AD 330, clearly attests (Fiey 1979: 141). According to Sozomenus (II.14), Miles laboured for three years to convert the Susians, but 'failing in his efforts to convert the inhabitants to Christianity, he uttered imprecations against the city, and departed. Not long after, some of the principal citizens offended the king, and an army with three hundred elephants was sent against them; the city was utterly demolished and its land was ploughed and sown' (Hartranft 1989: 267). As Fiey has emphasized, to judge from Miles' lack of success in converting the population of Susa, the offending 'principal citizens' who, one presumes, conspired against Shapur were more likely to have been Zoroastrians than Christians (Fiey 1979: 141, n. 6a).

Turning to the archaeological evidence, while it is clear that the Sasanian level (IV) in the Ville Royale excavated by Ghirshman is much smaller in size and thickness than the earlier Parthian occupation (levels V-VI), it did contain some significant architecture including what has been described as an important building with frescoes depicting a hunting scene (Boucharlat 1987b: 358). The later level III 'intermediate', attributed by Ghirshman to the late fourth through sixth centuries AD, did not yield much material. More recent excavations by de Miroschedji have shown that in Ville Royale II there is a hiatus between the Parthian period and the beginning of the Islamic era, unless the two walls of level IIA are assigned a Sasanian date (de Miroschedji 1987: 52, Table 11), while in the Apadana East area, little remained of levels 5a (late Parthian/early Sasanian) and 4b-c (late Sasanian) (Boucharlat 1987a: 238, Table 28).

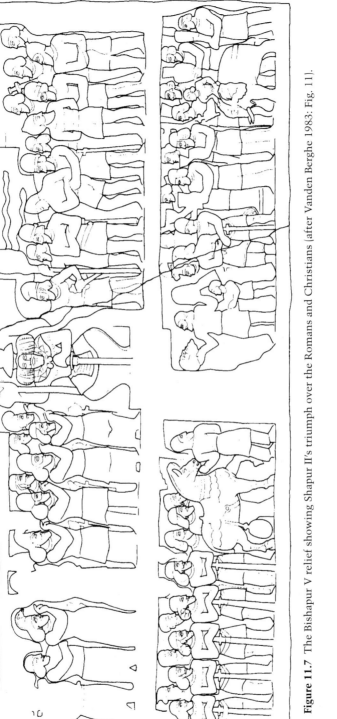

Figure 11.7 The Bishapur V relief showing Shapur II's triumph over the Romans and Christians (after Vanden Berghe 1983: Fig. 11).

Admittedly this is little material when one compares it to the earlier occupation levels of Susa, particularly those dating to the Parthian period, and one is tempted to interpret Susa's decline in light of the massive program of expansion pursued at Gundeshapur and Eran-xwarrah-Shapur-sharestan. Like Sozomenus, however, Ghirshman surely misrepresented the degree of destruction at Susa allegedly caused by Shapur II, for there are numerous other indications that the city continued to exist in the post-Shapur II period. For example, a long series of Nestorian bishops (Table. 11.1) are attested there from the year AD 410 through AD 605 (Chabot 1902: 683). Furthermore, if Gyselen is correct in her deductions based on sealed Sasanian bullae, Susa was re-christened Shush i er-kar, perhaps meaning 'Susa made Iranian', by which name it was known in administrative sources (Gyselen and Gasche 1994: 22). At least 33 Sasanian bullae, recovered by de Morgan, de Mecquenem and Ghirshman, are now in the Bibliothèque Nationale in Paris (Gignoux 1971b: 535). These contain the names of other cities with which Susa was in direct contact, including Rev-Ardashir on the Persian Gulf coast of Fars (near modern Bushire) and Vahman-Ardashir, a city situated along the Tigris (Gignoux 1971b: 540–1). As their names suggest, both were founded by Ardashir. In addition, the Susa bullae are important in giving us the titles of Sasanian officials connected with the site, including 'mlkly/hm'lkly, 'book-keeper, accountant', mǧw, 'magus, fire-priest', and mǧwpty, 'chief magus', the latter confirming the ongoing presence of Zoroastrians at Susa.

Evidence of two coin hoards dating to the reign of Khusrau II (AD 591–628) (Fig. 11.8) also suggests that Susa, while no longer a major city, was not marginalized. One of the hoards, discovered in 1930–1, contained coins originating in thirty different mints (Unvala 1934a), while the second, found in 1976 and consisting of no fewer than 1171 coins, consisted of coins from thirty-one mints (Gyselen 1977; Kervran 1985). Still, it is important to note that in contrast to the Seleucid and Parthian periods, no mint is attested at Susa during the Sasanian period (Boucharlat 1985: 78). Sellwood assigned the mint name AI or AIRAN to Eran-xwarrah-Shapur and, identifying this as an honorific title for Susa, suggested that Susa indeed had a Sasanian mint (Sellwood, Whitting and Williams 1985: 42). As we have seen, however, even if the identification of the abbreviated name AI with Eran-xwarrah-Shapur is correct, Susa does not thereby gain a mint, for the site in question is certainly Ivan-e Kerkha.

Aside from coinage, evidence of movable wealth at Susa in the Sasanian period is provided by the recovery of two Sasanian boat-shaped silver bowls thought to date to sometime 'after the middle of the Sasanian period' (Harper 1988: 336; Overlaet 1993: 228), as well as a high-footed silver bowl (Amiet 1967b; Overlaet 1993: 227). Similarly, a miniature rock crystal bowl in a gold, openwork mount, thought to have perhaps held cosmetics, is an item which bespeaks considerable wealth and social status (Harper 1978: 85; Overlaet 1993: 231). The bronze and iron noseband/halters and cheeked bits found by Ghirshman in level IV of the Ville Royale (Fig. 11.9) together with the incomplete skeleton of a horse (Ghirshman 1977; see also Herrmann 1989: Fig. 4) reflect equestrian equipment which is unlikely to have been in circulation amongst any but the elite of Sasanian society, particularly since similar tack is illustrated on royal mounts in rock reliefs and silver vessels (Harper 1978: 81). A white marble bust 'in

Plate 11.2 Stucco Christian plaque (Sb 9375, 13.6×8.5 cm) excavated by de Morgan at Susa. © Musée du Louvre, Antiquités Orientales

Figure 11.8 A Sasanian dirham of Khusrau II (after Sykes 1915/I: 516).

Roman Tetrarchic style' (Carter 1978: 171) of a bearded male, found in the Donjon and dated on stylistic grounds to the late third or early fourth century AD, should probably also be understood as an image reflecting the elite of Sasanian Susa (Martinez-Sève 1996).

Finally, the *Anonymous Syriac Chronicle* shows clearly that Susa was inhabited at the time of the Islamic conquest and was probably of some importance, for in the account of the Arab invasion of Khuzistan 'the fortress Shushan' is mentioned directly after Beth Lapat/Gundeshapur and Karka d'Ledan (Nöldeke 1893: 42), which, as we have seen, were the two most important cities in Sasanian Khuzistan.

Conclusion

The link between the ancient past of Khuzistan and its Sasanian incarnation was far more profound than one of simple geography. We have seen that as late as the tenth century AD, Arab writers confirm that a language other than Arabic, Persian, Hebrew or Aramaic was still being spoken in the region, and there are not many choices apart from a late form of Elamite. But beyond this, we also have the evidence of the later Nestorian sources. In contrast to earlier Nestorian sources which generally referred to the district as Beth Huzaye, an Aramaic term derived ultimately from the Old Persian Huza, later Syriac writers preferred to speak of 'Elam' (Fiey 1979: 223), and thus we find Theodore bar Koni referring to Beth Lapat as the 'city of the Elamites', and a synodal letter of AD 781/2 addressed to Ephrem, metropolitan of Beth Lapat, and to the 'bishops, priests and faithful of Elam' (Fiey 1979: 256). Similarly, another synodal letter of AD 790 sent by the catholicos Timothy notes that Ephrem held 'the seat and the throne of Elam', while his successor Sergius was called 'metropolitan of Elam' (Fiey

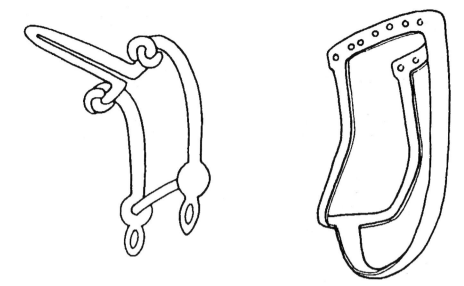

Figure 11.9 Cheeked bit and noseband from Susa (after Herrmann 1989: Fig. 4d [GS 2426] and 4c [GS 2425].

1979: 258). The Syriac codex 354 in the Bibliothèque Nationale in Paris, and the tables of Elias of Damascus, sources dating to *c.* AD 900, list the dioceses belonging to the ecclesiastical province of Elam as Susa or Karkha d'Ledan and Susa, Beth Huzaye or al-Ahwaz, Shushtrin/Tesr or Shushtar, and Mahraqan Qadaq (Fiey 1979: 264). In recounting the events surrounding two letters sent by the 'occidental fathers' to the catholicos Dadisho in AD 424, the fourteenth century AD writer 'Awdisho' of Nisibis (Gero 1981: 3; Vööbus 1965; Fiey 1977) names 'Agapit of Elam', the metropolitan of Beth Lapat, as the bearer of one if not both of the letters (Fiey 1970: 73, n. 38). As the last bishop from the area to attend a Nestorian synod was Joseph, present at the synod of Timothy II in AD 1318, Fiey has suggested that the ecclesiastical province of Elam finally succumbed to the onslaught of Tamerlane around AD 1400 (Fiey 1979: 267).

Date	Lowlands	Highlands	Mesopotamia	'Elam'
AD 205–26	Ardashir defeats Artabanus IV, last king of Parthian empire; foundation of new cities in Khuzistan	rise of Ardashir, 'king' of Istakhr, revolt and overthrow of Parthians	conquest by Ardashir, who was crowned 'king of kings' at Ctesiphon in Mesopotamia in AD 226	'kingdom of Ahwaz' possibly a relic of Elymaean semi-autonomy in late Parthian era?
AD 240–72	Shapur I deports prisoners from Antioch to Khuzistan, Roman engineers put to work on dams and bridges, re-building of Gundeshapur and Eran-xwarreh-Shapur-Sharestan, new capital of area; major influx of Christians; Susa eclipsed by new cities	settlement of Roman prisoners in Fars	under Sasanian control	
AD 309–79	deportations by Shapur II resulted in growth of textile industry in Khuzistan; Susa destroyed in AD 339 by Shapur II, refounded as Shush i er-kar			
AD 410–605	Nestorian bishops at Susa, Shushtar, Hormizd-Ardashir, Karka d'Ledan (Eran-xwarreh-Shapur-sharestan), archbishop at Gundeshapur			

AD 605–43	conquest of Khuzistan by Arabs in AD 638/9, revolt, reconquest in AD 642/3	Sasanian defeats at Jalula, Nihavend and Hamadan at hands of Arabs, AD 637–43	invasion of Mesopotamia, capture of Khusrau II's palace near Ctesiphon in AD 628 by Byzantine emperor Heraclius; destruction of Sasanian army in AD 637 at Qadisiyah by Arabs
AD 781–1318	Nestorian bishoprics survive Islamic conquest, referred to as being in 'Elam'	various Islamic dynasties	Abbasids in power in Khuzistan	Elam used to denote ecclesiastical province of Nestorian church

CONCLUSION

The history and archaeology of Elam are marked by the intermittent reconfiguration of the entity which we call by that name. Although continuities can be observed, there is as much if not more evidence of transformation and disjuncture. This chapter considers the archaeological and historical trajectory of Elam in the light of discussions in the field of history which have emphasized both long-term continuities and short-term cycles. It also looks at the problem of centre and periphery within Elam, between Elam and her neighbours, and in the study of Elam vis-à-vis Mesopotamia in modern scholarship. The topic of ethnogenesis, introduced at the beginning of this study, is again broached, while the question is asked, whether the foregoing study should be classified as history or archaeology? Finally, some suggestions are made which might impact on the enhancement of Elamite studies, and topics for further work are touched upon.

Beginning with the first references to Elam in the written record of the mid-third millennium BC, we have surveyed between three and four thousand years of Elamite history and archaeology. Along the way, a host of detailed issues have been explored. Many of the more salient points have been brought together in the summary tables provided in Chapters 3 through 11, and these should serve the reader as a ready reference to the main features of Elamite archaeology and history. At this point I would like to address a number of concepts which may prove useful in coming to grips with the mass of data dealt with above. These are aimed at re-orienting the reader from the details to generalities, and at putting some of the issues raised by a study of Elam into a larger perspective.

The courte durée

The first issue I would like to raise is one of structure. To what extent do the various incarnations of Elam attested in the archaeological and written record display evidence of underlying structures which could be said to underpin Elam in all its various manifestations? As we have seen throughout this book, it was not merely the boundaries of Elam which changed through time, but its very nature. We have, in fact, found evidence of many Elams. These include the changing representation of Elam in a variety of external sources. Both the earliest and the largest body of these comes from Mesopotamia, where a series of Elams with differing characteristics appeared over the course of two and a half thousand years.

From the mid-third millennium situation reflected in the *Sumerian King List* and the pre-Sargonic texts from Lagash to the parenthetical notes on Elam given in the late Babylonian astronomical diaries, Elam is alternately an enemy (Early Dynastic, late Ur III, Seleucid, Parthian periods), a subversive ally of other enemies (Neo-Assyrian era), a feared and respected neighbour (*sukkalmah* period), a source of raw materials (most periods), a mosaic of subject communities often dominated directly through provincial governors (Old Akkadian, Ur III periods), an independent force (Puzur-Inshushinak, Shimashkian kings), a land of great families tied to the royal house through dynastic inter-marriage (Middle Elamite period), and a religious community (early Islamic era).

A second corpus of 'external' sources are in fact local, but non-Elamite. Thus, we see Elam through the eyes of the Achaemenids, the Parthians and the Sasanians in periods when, in southwestern Iran, Elam was alternately a struggling political force (witness the early rebellions against Darius, the Uxii in the time of Alexander and his Seleucid successors, the Elymaean 'state' in the shadow of Parthia), a nursery of mountain warriors, feared for their prowess as bowmen (Achaemenid, Seleucid, Parthian eras), and an enduring linguistic and religious sub-culture, glimpses of which can be caught in Achaemenid royal and administrative texts and both Greek and Latin sources.

Finally, we have, of course, the testimony of the material and written record from Fars and Khuzistan itself, the vestiges of the Elams described by our external sources. These reflect regional ceramic and other artifactual variety, consistent with the image of a mosaic of constituents rather than a monolithic Elamite entity. Anshan, Marhashi, Shimashki, Zabshali, and the many other names which occasionally appear in the external sources no doubt identified sub-sets of that eastern entity which Mesopotamian scribes most often labelled simply 'Elam'. Differences abounded between the highland and lowland regions which made up Elam. Susiana came under much greater pressure from Mesopotamia throughout its history and as a result used Akkadian much more than Elamite, worshipping more Mesopotamian deities than was the case in the highlands as well. External sources show us alliances between various highland sub-regions and the lowlands in response to Mesopotamian aggression, and we get glimpses of alternate periods in which either the lowland or the highland element seems to dominate. Undoubtedly the entire Elamite area was heterogeneous, and Elamite was more a catch-all for highlanders and lowlanders east of Mesopotamia than an actual group, regardless of a certain degree of linguistic coherence (although non-Elamite names are amply attested in the highlands, suggesting the existence of many more linguistic groups than those to which we can put a name today).

Elam's repeated transformation through time is the defining theme running throughout its long history. Having begun as a Mesopotamian label used to identify certain eastern neighbours, Elam ended up as a designation for an ecclesiastical province of the Nestorian church, with numerous permutations in between. The use of the name Elam in the Nestorian sources was obviously anachronistic, derived from the Biblical tradition since, except in I and II Maccabees where the form *Elymais* occurs, the use of *Elam* by the Nestorian church has its roots in the Books of Genesis, Daniel and Jeremiah (Simons 1959: 27–8). But was the ecclesiastical province of Elam any less a reality than Elam of the *sukkalmah* period or Elymais of the Parthian period? Elam after the Islamic conquest was every bit as 'real' a concept in the minds of the Nestorian clergy as it was in the minds of Shamshi-Adad, Zimri-Lim, Hammurabi, Nebuchadnezzar I or Assurbanipal. That the tenth century AD and tenth century BC incarnations of Elam were far from identical is irrelevant. Elam was a reality and a construct which was characterized by its mutability and tendency to constantly reshape itself and be re-shaped by its observers. That process may have been halted as a result of Tamerlane's conquest of Iran, but it resumed as soon as the first Elamite texts were discovered at Persepolis. It continued throughout the unfolding of modern archaeological work on the subject, it continues in the writing of this book and it will continue long afterwards.

But this is not to say that the various forms of Elam which emerge from the historical and material record necessarily resembled each other either structurally or morphologically. To characterize the transformations (used here because it implies neither a positive progression nor a negative regression) of Elam using banal terms like 'continuity and change' trivializes the often profound changes which it underwent between the middle of the third millennium BC and the middle of the second millennium AD. Some readers may well disagree, but what I personally come away with after reviewing the evidence collected here is not a gradualist vision of adaptive change through time, but one of repeated reconfiguration at many levels.

It may be said of many archaeologists, whether processual or post-processual, as it has been said of historians, that they often tend to display a 'preoccupation . . . with quantitative social science, the *longue durée*, and immobile history', whereas microhistorians have been arguing for a return 'to interpreting utterances and beliefs, to describing brief dramatic events, and to envisioning a past characterized more by abrupt changes than by deep structural continuities' (Muir 1991: vii). Although I may have advocated the *histoire totale* of the *Annalistes* at the beginning of this book, I indicated that I was not advocating a belief in the *longue durée*, those alleged 'structures deeply rooted in time and space [which] are almost stationary' and 'move at near-imperceptible rates' (Hérubel 1994: 70). I reject the notion that 'history of events is . . . anathema, but, when informed by *la longue durée*, can be made useful and instructive' (Hérubel 1994: 105; Vovelle 1990: 126–53). Indeed the history of Elam as I read it is the very opposite of the *longue durée*.

To me, it seems characterized much more by what French economic historians have aptly termed *la courte durée* (Hérubel 1994: 8). It is the periodic realignment and transformation of Elam which strikes me most, not the extended historical cycle characterized by structural similarities. Elam emerges transformed after each brutal encounter (which may extend temporally over many years) with an 'other', whether Sumerian, Akkadian, Babylonian, Kassite, Assyrian, Macedonian, Seleucid, Parthian or Sasanian. In my opinion, only a superficial understanding of the archaeology and history of each formation of Elam could leave one with an impression of long-term continuity. And yet, while each Elam may have been structurally different from its predecessor(s), there are lineaments of continuity present such that we still speak of Elam throughout this long sweep of time. How can we do this while simultaneously denying the existence of deep structural continuity in Elam throughout history?

I believe that we must distinguish between a core or 'little tradition' of cultural and linguistic heritage, and the 'great tradition', which Yoffee has recently described in discussing Mesopotamia (Yoffee 1993). Elements of an Elamite 'great tradition' may exist as well. They seem particularly strong in the religious domain, where the repeated restoration of the Inshushinak temple at Susa affords a convenient example. But the manifestations of that 'great tradition' are by no means continuous and uninterrupted in the Elamite context and even if this is more a measure of the evidence than otherwise, I cannot help but think after studying the Elamite example that there seems to be much less of a 'great tradition' at work in Elam than in Mesopotamia. One ready explanation for this disparity seems to be afforded by the cultural, ethnic and to some extent linguistic and environmental diversity of Elam vis-à-vis ancient Mesopotamia, for as emphasized earlier, Elam was a name which subsumed a wide variety of disparate peoples in southwestern Iran who, although sometimes 'federated' politically, were not necessarily any more similar than the Kurds, Lurs, Bakhtiyari, Arabs and Qashqa'i of the last few centuries. We may see Elamite archers reappearing throughout the historical record, Elamite personal names still attested in the astronomical diaries of the second century BC, ethnic duality in the Susa II period and in Sasanian Khuzistan; and other signs of the core cultural-linguistic matrix intact over long periods of time, but these find their place in structurally altered contexts. This is why I reject the concept of the *longue durée* as an operational notion in assessing Elam, and prefer that of the *courte durée* interrupted by events and periods of destabilization followed by readjustments and reconstruction (for a very different but highly critical appraisal of the *longue durée*, see Östör 1993: 30–2).

Of centres, peripheries and mosaics

The second area I would like to explore is the domain of centres and peripheries. The fact that yet another book has been devoted to Elam might suggest that I for one do not consider that Elam was anything but central in antiquity, and yet many readers, whether scholars or laymen, would probably disagree. How do we deal with notions like centre and periphery in the particular case of Elam and its neighbours?

Few archaeologists or historians are ever satisfied with the quantity of evidence which forms the basis of the opinions which they freely hold and express in writing, but this rarely stops them from doing so. When it comes to Elam, no one would deny that the sources – epigraphic, archaeological and literary – are unsatisfactory in their pattern of distribution. Due to the particular history of modern archaeology in Iran, far more is known about Susa than about any other site which falls within the geographic limits of Elam, no matter what the period in question. By comparison the region and city of Anshan are but poorly known. We live and work today in a world which seems polarized on so many levels that 'centre and periphery' have become part of our daily vocabulary. Not surprisingly, therefore, centre and periphery have invaded archaeological and historical scholarship. But how is one to speak of centre and periphery, knowing that only a fraction of Tal-i Malyan has been excavated, that the settlements of Awan, Shimashki, Marhashi, etc. have yet to be identified, or that Seleucia-on-the-Hedyphon, Azara, Gundeshapur/Beth Lapat and numerous other important towns and cities of later antiquity are little more than names in historical sources? How fair is it to compare Susa and Uruk, to characterize the former as a 'small' centre, the latter as a 'world-class' urban metropolis, when the excavation technique and exposures realized at the two sites are so different? Knowing what was removed at Susa by excavators more adept at working in a mine shaft than an archaeological site, how can one reasonably compare the site with those cities to the west with which it interacted, such as Uruk or Ur? Still, no matter how many caveats one calls forth, comparisons will be made and must be made if we are to get any closer to an understanding of Elam in the wider Western Asiatic context. What then of the centre and periphery model, or the world systems view of ancient Western Asia? Where would Elam fit into schemes such as these? Was it a peer or a poor relation?

A miscellany of ethnically and linguistically diverse groups to the east of the alluvium, Elam nevertheless emerged as a coherent force in the second half of the third millennium BC with pretensions to influence on the political stage of Western Asia. Its fortunes varied considerably, as we have seen throughout this book. Periods of subjugation by the Old Akkadian and Ur III states were followed by flourishes of independence under the dynasties of Awan and Shimashki. Unprecedented influence and prestige were enjoyed under the *sukkalmahs*, while inter-marriage with the Kassite royal family in the later second millennium BC signalled the integration of Elam into a much wider web of inter-dynastic alliances during the Late Bronze Age. The rise of Assyria and a series of disastrous alliances with numerous Babylonian and several Assyrian leaders brought Elam's political fortunes to a low ebb, and the appearance of a new Iranian dynasty in Fars seemingly threatened to obliterate the ethnic and linguistic individuality of Elamites in southwestern Iran during the Achaemenid period. But the reign of the Achaemenids, the conquest of Alexander the Great, and the accession of the Seleucids all failed to bring about the complete absorption and assimilation of the Elamites, and just when the Parthians began to alter the balance of power in Western Asia once more, the Elamites re-emerged clearly in the historical record. There are indications that the Elamite language in fact survived into the tenth century AD, but Elam by this time had been transformed from a semi-autonomous polity in the shadow of Parthia into an ecclesiastical province of the Nestorian church, sometimes tolerated and sometimes persecuted viciously by the Sasanian government.

So where are the centres and where the peripheries in all of this? No one would deny that, in terms of sheer population density, there *were* centres in antiquity, just as there are today, and there *were* peripheries, if by that we mean geographically isolated or marginal areas, and areas with diminished political responsibility and prestige. These points do not seem to be in dispute. What is debatable, however, in the context of most centre-periphery studies today, is the implication that centres relied on the continual exploitation of peripheries over time, or that the identification of centres and peripheries is self-evident in the historical and archaeological record. Awan's appearance in the *Sumerian King List*, the desirability of marriages between the princesses of Ur and the princes of Anshan, the *sukkalmah's* influence over Assyria, Mari, Eshnunna or Babylon, Susa's role as an Achaemenid royal residence, or Beth Lapat's claim to being the second most important province in the Nestorian church are all counter-arguments to any assertion of marginality or peripheral status on Elam's part vis-à-vis any of the better known states or socio-religious formations of Western Asia. Whether or not tin flowed more freely into Mari as a result of its cordial relations with Elam, this alone can scarcely have been the justification for those relations in the first place, any more than the acquisition of raw materials from the Iranian Plateau can have been the justification for more than one king of the Third Dynasty of Ur giving his daughter in marriage to a prince of Anshan. Anshan may have been provincial and Susa may have been a quarter of the size of Uruk, but this did not stop the seemingly greater powers from entering into alliances, or expending resources in attempting to subjugate this 'periphery'. Our perception of what is peripheral and what is central must be very different from that of the ancients if we persist in viewing the Iranian Plateau as a periphery on the eastern margins of the greater Mesopotamian world. If that were the case, why would so much time and energy have been expended by the centre on this particular, eastern periphery? Clearly, we define peripheries according to criteria which are often far removed from those which must have obtained in the past. All too often, in trying to explain the *raison d'être* behind Mesopotamian-Iranian relations in antiquity we focus narrowly on natural resources, absent in the former area, abundant in the latter, ignoring the human aspects of such exercises in alliance-building. The prestige of being associated with a dynasty which could call up vast reserves of manpower, the honour of marrying into a group which could claim to have once subjugated Kish, the reflected glory of forging a link with a polity, the eastern borders of which were further than the horizon, these and other justifications may have been behind the push on the part of many a Mesopotamian dynast to build alliances with the Elamites, in the broadest sense of the term. And these are precisely the sorts of dynamics which we find hardest to isolate in the archaeological and epigraphic record.

But more to the point, we must stop looking at Western Asia in terms of diametrically opposed centres and peripheries, and begin to grapple with the far greater complexity posed by the overall matrix of relationships which characterized any moment in time. To understand the relationship between the Nestorian *catholicos* in Seleucia-Ctesiphon and the province of Beth Lapat, we must also appreciate the wider context in which that relationship functioned. We must look beyond the confines of the bilateral relationship itself. Similarly, we can see that in the early second millennium BC a complex network of relations was maintained between a dozen states, the permutations of which would be utterly lost to us were it not for the Mari letters. These and other examples point out the necessity of studying the entire matrix, the web of interrelationships, the mosaic of cultures in Western Asia, rather than focussing narrowly on the so-called centres and peripheries. The constituent parts of the mosaic each demand attention, each demand their own microhistories, and the synchronic structure and dynamics of the whole require study in order to appreciate particular developments and outcomes in specific contexts.

Ethnicity and ethnogenesis

The third area I would like the reader to think about is one which was introduced at the outset of this book, namely that of ethnogenesis and ethnicity. One of the most intriguing and intractable problems in archaeology revolves around the recognition of historically documented 'cultures' in assemblages of material remains. We are constantly enjoined not to equate 'pots' with 'people', and yet we live in a world in which ethnicity is a strong and pervasive factor, and nothing suggests that this was otherwise in Western Asia during the periods covered here. At the beginning of this book I noted that Elam's geographical parameters were difficult to define, for the simple reason that in the absence of written sources in Elamite, we have little way of knowing whether an area was or was not part of the Elamite body politic simply on the basis of its material culture (e.g. ceramics, burial types, metal weaponry, etc.). As noted earlier, the approach here has been a minimalist one, and doubtless other scholars would have incorporated more evidence from eastern Fars, Kerman, Luristan, Kurdistan and possibly even Baluchistan or Seistan, in their discussions of Elam.

But the problem of defining Elam archaeologically and historically is not limited to one of assigning ethnic labels to ceramic complexes. As shown in Chapters 3 and 4, when the name Elam appears in the historical record it is a label given by one literate, linguistic-cultural group to a heterogeneous group of not-so-near neighbours. Thus, if one is searching for the origins of the 'Elamites', the answer is, in one sense, to be found not in Elam but in Mesopotamia. On the other hand, identifying those groups covered by the name in terms of their material culture is almost impossible. Given the cultural and linguistic heterogeneity of western Iran in the late fourth and early third millennium BC, the term Elam must necessarily encompass culturally and linguistically heterogeneous groups living in an unspecified area to the east of the Mesopotamian alluvium.

The problem of 'becoming' Elamite is another matter. Examples abound both in antiquity and in the modern era of individuals changing nationality, language, and material culture within their own lifetime, and of similar changes being effected effortlessly on the part of a new generation by the children of parents born speaking a different language, on a different continent, with different material culture. In Seleucid Babylonia we can find parents with Akkadian names and whom one assumes were 'Babylonians' yet who freely gave Greek personal names to their children (e.g. Potts 1997: 293). In the twentieth century AD the upheavals of wars and subsequent exoduses of refugees from one country to another afford countless examples of nationality changing overnight, and there is nothing to suggest that, in the pre-passport age, given a bit of linguistic facility and desire, individuals were any less able to adopt new identities. This sort of assimilation and acculturation has often been invoked to help explain the disappearance of the Elamites within the Achaemenid melting pot, but the evidence of Elam and Elymais in the second century BC should warn us against the facile assumption that just because they may pass out of view for awhile, a people, whether the Elamites or any other, necessarily dissolves or disintegrates as soon as they cease to have a very prominent place in the written record. Archaeologists constantly confront 'new' material culture complexes, often characterized by distinctive pottery or stone tools, and ask themselves how representative these complexes may or may not be of ethnic groups. We know that material culture, biological identity, and language are all independent variables, and the example of Elam suggests that ethnicity and ethnogenesis are topics which are far from exhausted in the ancient Western Asiatic context.

History and archaeology

The fourth issue which ought to be raised in a book of this sort is the relationship between history and archaeology. Where does one begin and the other end? To what extent are they or are they not pursuing the same or similar goals? How does this study of Elam, at once historical and archaeological, contribute to the ongoing debate amongst archaeologists concerning historical civilizations and peoples without history? This book has provided no new formula for the successful integration of historical (epigraphic or literary) and archaeological evidence, and readers may well be asking whether the present work should be considered one of history or archaeology? It is not out of flippancy that I point out that the author of this book is an archaeologist and that the place of publication is in an archaeology series. These points alone might not satisfy all readers that the present work is a contribution to the archaeology of Elam. But as I hope I have made clear, we cannot hope for an *histoire totale* of Elam without constant recourse to all sorts of evidence – archaeological, epigraphic, literary, environmental, etc. – which must be used in a way which is neither rigidly materialist nor historicist.

Colleagues more accustomed to working at the prehistoric end of the temporal spectrum may wince or merely turn off when confronted with Strabo and Sozomenus, but that probably has more to do with the subject matter than the method of integrating historical and archaeological data. Prehistorians do not often concern themselves with Achaemenid, Seleucid, Parthian or Sasanian history, let alone the Nestorian church, and scholars embedded in these disciplines scarcely spend their days worrying about the natural resources available in the Zagros mountains, the firing temperature of bitumen compound, the historicity of the Awan-Shimashki kinglist, or the difficulties of establishing the order of succession in the Middle Elamite period. My own feeling has always been that if I am interested in a topic, then I am interested in it from beginning to end, from the origins of an entity until its final disappearance in the historical and archaeological record. I felt strongly about this long before I had ever heard the term *histoire totale*, or realized that my 'terrible craving for synthesis' belonged to a time-honoured intellectual tradition. In the case of Elam, as noted earlier, most treatments of the topic have concluded with the rise of the Achaemenid empire but, as I hope I have shown, there is no more justification for doing this than there would be for concluding at the end of the Middle Elamite or *sukkalmah* period. The story of Elam and the Elamites lasts much longer, and goes through several more important transformations, before it can be said to finally elude our grasp. The linguistic and cultural polarity of the Nestorian church in Beth Lapat is just as interesting as the Elamite-Semitic or Susian-Anshanite duality of Elam in its earlier days and it makes little sense to truncate Elamite history at the expense of the so-called 'late periods'.

None of these problems can be approached, however, by excluding the written evidence, or by acting as though we can reconstruct all that we would wish to know simply on the basis of the material record. Understanding Elam at whatever date is a difficult enough task without setting artificial limits on the data which may or may not be adduced to help illuminate it. The more archaeologists learn to feel familiar with epigraphic and literary sources, and the more historians and philologists learn to deal in more than a superficial manner with material evidence, the better will be the end result. To return to the question posed at the beginning of the section, is this a work of archaeology or a work of history? I have said on several occasions that this study aspires to the kind of *histoire totale* which some of the *Annalistes* have tried to write largely on the basis of written sources. It may well be rejected by historians as *histoire totale* because of the paucity of historical records used, and by archaeologists who believe that history is not archaeology. But if it is to be anything, then I would suggest that it is not *archéologie totale* for the simple reason that there are still far too many prehistorians who look with disdain on written sources and expect one to make all deductions from an analysis of material evidence. Elam is the object of the study, and to get closer to that object we must use all sources, of whatever type, recognizing their different virtues and limitations. My own disciplinary affiliation may be archaeology, but it is to be hoped that the end-product of this investigation is not narrowly archaeological in the sense in which that term is normally employed. If it is anything, then perhaps it is *antiquité totale*, a study of one aspect of antiquity in all its totality, using all types of evidence currently available. If dealing as intensively with numismatic, literary, archaeological, epigraphic, and environmental data makes one neither an historian nor an archaeologist, then perhaps it's time we reverted to calling ourselves 'antiquaries'. If so, then the pursuit of *antiquité totale* is what this book has been about.

Elam's progress

The fifth area which I would like readers to think about is where we go from here. How is the study of Elam to advance? Despite the fact that fieldwork in southwestern Iran by foreign expeditions has been virtually non-existent for the past two decades, it is a truism to say that much work remains to be done. At the time of the Iranian Revolution, more than one observer noted that the enforced pause in fieldwork would provide the time necessary to publish many of the excavations which had been conducted from the 1950s through the late 1970s. Unfortunately, this has only happened in several instances. More often than not, scholars involved in Iranian archaeology prior to the revolution have moved into other parts of Western Asia and become involved in new projects. Important work, therefore, remains to be done on many sites crucial to our understanding of Elamite and non-Elamite Iranian archaeology and history.

But there is a more insidious side to the interruption of fieldwork in Iran which is making itself felt more and more. Because it is no longer possible to involve students in fieldwork in Iran, the subject of Iranian archaeology is being taught less and less. I understand the logic of this argument, but in my opinion the logic is flawed. It is not a question of 'preparing for the day when we can all go back to Iran' by continuing to teach Iranian archaeology. Rather, we come back to the 'mosaic approach' to Western Asia adumbrated above. How are we to understand Mesopotamian or Arabian or Central Asian or Harappan archaeology if we neglect Iran? To cease teaching Iranian archaeology because the country is temporarily inaccessible for purposes of fieldwork is to commit a far graver academic sin. By this act scholars are excising an enormously important piece of the ancient Western Asiatic mosaic. This, in my opinion, is the most potent justification for teaching the archaeology of as many sub-regions of Western Asia as possible wherever the subject is represented in universities around the world. Accessibility is desirable but should never be confused with the intrinsic importance of the many different areas of Western Asia which we must strive to understand in order to make sense of developments there in the past.

On the other hand, one must ask, how common have courses in Elamite or Iranian archaeology ever been? The answer is surely, not very. Compared to the number of scholars working in the fields of Egyptology, Syro-Palestinian archaeology, or Mesopotamian studies, Iran has never claimed a large share of scholarship on a world-wide level. This is not to say that there is a shortage of first class material available for research and teaching. But it is surely true to say that we have lacked the same sorts of teaching materials in the field of Iranian and Elamite archaeology as those available in some of our neighbouring disciplines. And speaking from the perspective of one who teaches in an Anglophone university, the number of Anglophone students able to read modern European languages (principally French and German) seems to shrink annually in inverse proportion to the number of detailed studies produced by Austrian, Belgian, French, German, Italian, Spanish and other European colleagues. We suffer from the lack of an up-to-date, general text on Iranian archaeology in English with which to teach the subject. The present work is far narrower in scope, limited only to Elam, but will hopefully provide some sort of basis for invigorating the teaching of a subject which deserves to be given as much attention as any other archaeology in Western Asia, and which grows increasingly difficult to teach to Anglophone students for whom the specialist literature in European languages grows ever more inaccessible. If the subject isn't taught, it surely can't advance, and if basic texts are unavailable, the number of students likely to become interested in Elam or Iranian archaeology in general will decline to catastrophic levels.

Stories remaining to be written

Finally, I would like to conclude this study with a brief word about two subjects which have not been dealt with at all, but which hold out exciting prospects for scholars and students of a dozen different disciplines.

The first of these might be labelled 'Elamica in the mythical history of early Iran'. Although not the only source of this legendary history, the *Shah Nameh* or Book of Kings (completed in AD 1010) by the celebrated Persian poet Firdawsi (c. AD 935–1020) is the obvious place to start in any attempt to see whether anything of the remote Elamite past, whether mythical or historical, had filtered down into the tenth century traditions gathered by Daqiqi (d. c. AD 980) and later amalgamated and amplified by Firdawsi (Spiegel 1971: 508ff.). The early Pishdadiyan dynasty's first kings were identified with developments such as the discovery of fire and the introduction of domesticated animals (by Hoshang), or the introduction of writing and the creation of important urban centres, such as Merv, Babylon and Seleucia-on-the-Tigris (by Tahmurath). Zohak or Dahak, of Babylonian origin, was conceived as a human with a snake emanating from each of his shoulders. Can this latter image be connected with the Elamite imagery of a deity with snakes (Pl. 7.4, Fig. 7.5) or the serpent throne (Pls. 6.4–5, Figs. 6.8–9) of the *sukkalmah* era? These and many other points of possible congruence between Elamite and mythical Iranian tradition remain to be thoroughly investigated by scholars and students with the required background in the language, literature, iconography and history of both Elam and early Islamic Iran.

A second topic of potential interest to archaeologists, historians of science, scholars in cultural studies, and anthropologists concerned with early modern Europe is an investigation of the Elam re-invented in Paris by Maurice Pézard and Edmond Pottier in the Louvre Museum in 1913 (Pézard and Pottier 1926). Archaeologists have long been interested in the intellectual history of their discipline, but many of their studies have followed the course of scientific discovery without paying sufficient attention to its impact on the population at large and the reception of Near Eastern antiquity by Western audiences in the nineteenth and early twentieth centuries. Recent studies of the French expedition to Khorsabad (Fontan 1994) and the impact of Layard's discoveries at Nineveh on British taste and sensibilities (Russell 1997) have shown, however, that there is a fertile field here for exploration. The intellectual reception of Elam in the West as a result of the French discoveries at Susa has yet to be analyzed, although some early twentieth century literature does show that the 'scientific conquests' which did so much to honour France (Pézard and Pottier 1926: 5) did have an important impact in some circles (e.g. Cruveilhier 1921). Curiously, a recent survey of intellectual trends in French archaeology in the second half of the twentieth century makes absolutely no mention of the ongoing achievements of the French mission at Susa (Schnapp 1995), but there is no doubt in my mind that a study undertaken along the lines of McClellan's analysis of the origins and socio-political context of the Louvre in the eighteenth century (McClellan 1994), focussing particularly on the display, ideology and reception of Elamite antiquities in early twentieth century Paris, would be an interesting one. But that must be another book about yet another Elam, an Elam re-invented by the banks of the Seine.

REFERENCES

Abbott, N. (1968), 'Jundi Shahpur: a preliminary historical sketch', *Ars Orientalis* 7, 71–3.

Abraham, K. (1995), 'The Egibis in Elam', *Languages and Cultures in Contact: Programme and Abstracts of the 42e Rencontre Assyriologique Internationale*, Leuven: Katholieke Universiteit (unpaginated).

Ackroyd, P.R. (1990), 'The Biblical portrayal of Achaemenid rulers', *AH* 5, 1–16.

Adams, R.McC. (1962), 'Agriculture and urban life in early Southwestern Iran', *Science* 136, 109–22.

Adams, R.McC. and Hansen, D.P. (1968), 'Archaeological reconnaissance and soundings in Jundi Shahpur', *Ars Orientalis* 7, 53–73.

Adler, M.N. (1907), *The Itinerary of Benjamin of Tudela*, London.

Alberti, A. (1985), 'A reconstruction of the Abu Salabikh god-list', *SEL* 2, 3–23.

Alden, J.R. (1982a), 'Trade and politics in Proto-Elamite Iran', *Current Anthropology* 23, 613–40.

Alden, J.R. (1982b), 'Marketplace exchange as indirect distribution: an Iranian example', in Ericson, J.E. and Earle, T.K., eds., *Contexts for Prehistoric Exchange*, New York: Academic Press, 83–101.

Alder, K. (1997), *Engineering the Revolution: Arms and Enlightenment in France, 1763–1815*, Princeton: University Press.

Algaze, G. (1993), *The Uruk World System: the Dynamics of Expansion of Early Mesopotamian Civilization*, Chicago and London: University of Chicago Press.

Alizadeh, A. (1985a), 'A tomb of the Neo-Elamite period at Arjan, near Behbahan', *AMI* 18, 49–73.

(1985b), 'Elymaean occupation of Lower Khuzestan during the Seleucid and Parthian periods: a proposal', *IrAnt* 20, 175–95.

(1988), 'Socio-economic complexity in Southwestern Iran during the fifth and fourth millennia BC: the evidence from Tall-i Bakun A', *Iran* 26, 17–34.

(1992), *Prehistoric Settlement Patterns and Cultures in Susiana, Southwestern Iran: The Analysis of the F.G.L. Gremliza Survey Collection*, Ann Arbor: Museum of Anthropology Technical Report 24.

(1994), 'Social and economic complexity and administrative technology in a late prehistoric context', in Ferioli, P., Fiandra, E., Fissore, G.G., and Frangipane, M., eds., *Archives before Writing*, Rome: Centro Internazionale di Ricerche Archeologiche, Antropologiche e Storiche 1, 35–54.

Alram, M. (1986), *Nomina propria Iranica in nummis: Materialgrundlagen zu den iranischen Personennamen auf antiken Münzen*, Vienna: Österreichische Akademie der Wissenschaften.

Amiet, P. (1967a), 'Éléments émaillées du décor architectural néo-élamite', *Syria* 44, 27–46.

(1967b), 'Nouvelles acquisitions: Antiquités parthes et sassanides', *La Revue du Louvre* 17, 273–82.

(1972a), *Glyptique susienne*, Paris: MDP 43.

(1972b), 'Les ivoires achéménides de Suse', *Syria* 49, 167–91, 319–37.

(1973a), 'Glyptique élamite, à propos de nouveaux documents', *Arts Asiatiques* 26, 3–64.

(1973b), 'La glyptique de la fin de l'Elam', *Arts Asiatiques* 28, 3–45.

(1974a), 'Antiquités du désert de Lut: A propos d'objets de la Collection Foroughi', *RA* 68, 97–110.

(1974b), 'Quelques observations sur le palais de Darius à Suse', *Syria* 51, 65–73.

(1976), 'Disjecta membra aelamica: Le décor architectural en briques émaillées à Suse', *Arts Asiatiques* 32, 13–18.

(1979a), 'Archaeological discontinuity and ethnic duality in Elam', *Antiquity* 53, 195–204.

(1979b), 'Alternance et dualité. Essai d'interprétation de l'histoire élamite', *Akkadica* 15, 2–22.

(1979c), 'L'iconographie archaïque de l'Iran: Quelques documents nouveaux', *Syria* 56, 333–52.

(1980a), 'Antiquités de serpentine', *IrAnt* 15, 155–66.

(1980b), 'Roman Ghirshman (1895–1979)', *StIr* 9, 143–5.

(1980c), 'La glyptique du second millénaire en provenance des chantiers A et B de la Ville Royale de Suse', *IrAnt* 15, 133–47.

(1985a), 'Quelques témoins des contacts de Suse avec les pays du Levant au IIIe et IIe millénaire', in Durand, J.-M., and Kupper, J.-R., eds., *Miscellanea Babylonica: Mélanges offerts à Maurice Birot*, Paris: Editions Recherche sur les Civilisations, 9–15.

(1985b), 'A propos de l'usage et de l'iconographie des sceaux à Suse', *Paléorient* 11, 37–8.

(1986a), 'Antiquités trans-élamites', *RA* 80, 97–104.

(1986b), 'Au-delà d'Elam', *AMI* 19, 11–20.

(1986c), *L'âge des échanges inter-iraniens, 3500–1700 avant J.-C.*, Paris: Notes et Documents des Musées Nationaux 11.

(1986d), 'Kassites ou Elamites?', in Kelly-Buccellati, M., ed., *Insight through Images: Studies in Honor of Edith Porada*, Malibu: BiMes 21, 1–6.

(1986e), 'L'usage des sceaux à l'époque initiale de l'histoire de Suse', *FHE* 17–24.

(1986f), 'Susa and the Dilmun culture', in Al Khalifa, Shaikha H.A. and Rice, M., eds., *Bahrain through the Ages: The Archaeology*, London/New York/Sydney and Henley: Kegan Paul International, 262–8.

(1987a), 'Nouvelles acquisitions du département des Antiquités orientales', *La Revue du Louvre et des Musées de France*, 13–25.

(1987b), 'Temple sur terrasse ou forteresse?', *RA* 81, 99–104.

(1987c), 'Approche physique de la comptabilité à l'époque d'Uruk: les bulles-enveloppes de Suse', in Huot, J.-L., ed., *Préhistoire de la Mésopotamie*, Paris: Editions du CNRS, 331–44.

(1988a), 'Antiquités élamites et trans-élamites au musée du Louvre', *La Revue du Louvre et des Musées de France*, 361–9.

(1988b), 'Les modes d'utilisation des sceaux à Sue au IVe millénaire', *AMI* 21, 7–16.

(1988c), *Suse, 6000 ans d'histoire*, Paris: Monographies des musées de France.

(1989), 'Autour de Marlik', *AIO*, 311–22.

(1990a), 'Marlik et Tchoga Zanbil', *RA* 84, 44–7.

(1990b), 'Quelques épaves de la vaisselle royale perse de Suse', *MJP*, 213–24.

(1992a), 'Sur l'histoire Elamite', *IrAnt* 27, 75–94.

(1992b), 'Tiares élamites', *Studi Micenei ed Egeo-Anatolici* 30, 257–65.

(1992c), 'Bronzes élamites de la collection George Ortiz', *AMI* 25, 81–9.

(1994a), 'Un sceau trans-élamite à Suse', *RA* 88, 1–4.

(1994b), review of Algaze, G., *The Uruk World System*, *RA* 88, 92–3.

(1994c), 'Quelques sceaux élamites', *CDR*, 59–66.

(1994d), 'Un étage au palais de Darius à Suse?', in Dietrich, M. and Loretz, O., eds., *Beschreiben und Deuten in der Archäologie des Alten Orients: Festschrift für Ruth Mayer-Opificius*, Münster: Ugarit-Verlag, 1–5.

(1994e), 'Response', in Ferioli, P., Fiandra, E., Fissore, G.G., and Frangipane, M., eds., *Archives before Writing*, Rome: Centro Internazionale di Ricerche Archeologiche, Antropologiche e Storiche 1, 55–8.

(1994f), 'Sceaux et administration à Suse à l'époque d'Uruk', in Ferioli, P., Fiandra, E., Fissore,

G.G., and Frangipane, M., eds., *Archives before Writing*, Rome: Centro Internazionale di Ricerche Archeologiche, Antropologiche e Storiche 1, 87–94.

(1996), 'Observations sur les sceaux de Haft Tépé (Kabnak)', *RA* 90, 135–43.

André, B. and Salvini, M. (1989), 'Réflexions sur Puzur-Insusinak', *IrAnt* 24, 53–72.

Andreas, F.C. (1894a), 'Aginis', *RE* 1, 810–16.

(1894b), 'Ampe', *RE* 1, 1877–80.

(1894c), 'Aple', *RE* 1, 2810–12.

(1904), 'Über einige Fragen der ältesten persischen Geschichte', *Verhandlungen des XIII. internationalen Orientalisten-Kongresses, Hamburg September 1902*, Leiden: Brill, 93–7.

André-Salvini, B. (1992), 'Historical, Economic, and Legal Texts', in Harper, P.O., Aruz, J. and Tallon, F., eds., *The Royal City of Susa: Ancient Near Eastern Treasures in the Louvre*, New York: Metropolitan Museum of Art, 261–5.

Atkinson, J.E. (1994), *A commentary on Q. Curtius Rufus' Historiae Alexandri Magni Books 5 to 7.2*, Amsterdam: Acta Classica Supplement 1.

Aubin, J. (1977), 'La question de Sirgan au XIIIe siècle', *StIr* 6, 285–90.

Augé, C., Curiel, R. and LeRider, G. (1979), *Terrasses sacrées de Bard-è Néchandeh et Masjid-i Solaiman: Les trouvailles monétaires*, Paris: MDP 44.

Badian, E. (1975), 'Nearchus the Cretan', *Yale Classical Studies* 24, 147–70.

Balandier, G. (1972), *Political Anthropology*, Harmondsworth: Penguin.

Balkan, K. (1954), *Kassitenstudien 1. Die Sprache der Kassiten*, New Haven: AOS 37.

Bar-Kochva, B. (1976), *The Seleucid Army: Organization and Tactics in the Great Campaigns*, Cambridge: University Press.

Barth, F. (1969), 'Introduction', in Barth, F., ed., *Ethnic Groups and Boundaries: The Social Organization of Cultural Difference*, Boston: Little, Brown, 9–38.

Bartlett, J.R. (1973), *The First and Second Books of the Maccabees*, Cambridge: University Press.

Bayani, M.I. (1979), 'The Elamite periods on the Izeh Plain', in Wright, H.T., ed., *Archaeological Investigations in Northeastern Xuzestan, 1976*, Ann Arbor: University of Michigan Museum of Anthropology Technical Report No. 10, 99–105.

Beale, T.W. (1973), 'Early trade in highland Iran: a view from a source area', *World Archaeology* 5, 133–48.

Beaulieu, P.-A. (1989), *The Reign of Nabonidus, King of Babylon, 556–539 BC*, New Haven and London: Yale Near Eastern Researches 10.

Beckman, G. (1991), 'A stray tablet from Haft Tépé', *IrAnt* 26, 81–3.

Behm-Blancke, M.R. (1979), *Das Tierbild in der altmesopotamischen Rundplastik: Eine Untersuchung zum Stilwandel des frühsumerischen Rundbildes*, Mainz: Baghdader Forschungen 1.

Bellinger, A.R. (1950–1), 'An Alexander hoard from Byblos', *Berytus* 10, 37–49.

Bengtson, H. (1964[2]), *Die Strategie in der hellenistischen Zeit: Ein Beitrag zum antiken Staatsrecht*, 2 vols. Munich: Münchener Beiträge zur Papyrusforschung und antiken Rechtsgeschichte 32.

Berger, P.-R. (1973), *Die neubabylonischen Königsinschriften*, Kevelaer/Neukirchen-Vluyn: AOAT 4/1.

Bernard, P. (1980), 'Heraclès, les grottes de Karafto et le sanctuaire du mont Sambulos en Iran', *StIr* 9, 302–24.

Bernshtam, A. (1962), 'On the origin of the Kirgiz people', in Michael, H.N., ed., *Studies in Siberian Ethnogenesis*, Toronto: Arctic Institute of North America Anthopology of the North, Translations from Russian Sources/No. 2, 119–28.

Berthelot, A. (1935), 'La côte méridionale de l'Iran d'après les géographes grecs', in *Mélanges offerts à M. Octave Navarre par ses éléves et ses amis*, Toulouse: E. Privat, 11–24.

Berthoud, T., Bonnefous, S., Dechoux, M. and Françaix, J. (1980), 'Data analysis: towards a model of chemical modification of copper from ores to metal', in Craddock, P.T., ed., *Proceedings of the XIXth Symposium on Archaeometry*, London: British Museum Occasional Paper 20, 87–102.

Berve, H. (1926), *Das Alexanderreich auf prosopographischer Grundlage*, 2 vols. Munich: Beck.

Bewley, R.H. (1984), 'The Cambridge University archaeological expedition to Iran 1969, excavations in the Zagros mountains: Houmian, Mir Malas, and Barde Spid', *Iran* 22, 1–38.

Billerbeck, A. (1893), *Susa: Eine Studie zur alten Geschichte Westasiens*, Leipzig: Hinrichs.

Bintliff, J. (1991), ed., *The Annales School and Archaeology*, Leicester: University Press.

Bischof, G. and Pelinka, A. (1997), eds., *Austrian Historical Memory and National Identity*, New Brunswick/London: Contemporary Austrian Studies 5.

von Bissing, F.W. (1940), 'Ägyptische und ägyptisierende Alabastergefäße aus den Deutschen Ausgrabungen in Assur', *ZA* 46, 149–82.

Bittner, S. (1987[2]), *Tracht und Bewaffnung des persischen Heeres zur Zeit der Achaimeniden*, Munich: Klaus Friedrich Verlag.

Bivar, A.D.H. (1983), 'The political history of Iran under the Arsacids', *CHI* 3/1, 21–99.

Bivar, A.D.H. and Shaked, S. (1964), 'The inscriptions at Shimbar', *BSOAS* 27, 265–90.

Black, J. and Green, A. (1992), *Gods, Demons and Symbols of Ancient Mesopotamia*, London: British Museum Press.

Blackman, M.J. (1982), 'The manufacture and use of burned lime plaster at Proto-Elamite Anshan (Iran)', in Wertime, T. and S., eds., *Early Pyrotechnology: the Evolution of Fire using Industries*, Washington: Smithsonian Institution, 107–16.

Blois, F. de (1994, app. 1996), 'Elamite survivals in Western Iranian: a preliminary survey', *Studia Iranica, Mesopotamica & Anatolica* 1, 13–19.

Bobek, H. (1968), 'Vegetation', *CHI* 1: 280–93.

Bode, Baron C.A. de (1843), 'Extracts from a journal kept while travelling, in January, 1841, through the country of the Mamásení and Khógilú (Bakhtiyárí), situated between Kázerún and Behbehan', *JRGS* 13, 75–112.

Boese, J. (1971), *Altmesopotamische Weihplatten: Eine sumerische Denkmalsgattung des 3. Jahrtausends v. Chr.*, Berlin/New York: de Gruyter.

Bökönyi, S. (1977), *Animal Remains from the Kermanshah Valley, Iran*, Oxford: BAR Supplement Series 34.

Bollweg, J. (1988), 'Protoachämenidische Siegelbilder', *AMI* 21, 53–61.

Borger, R. (1956), *Die Inschriften Asarhaddons Königs von Assyrien*, Graz: AfO Beiheft 9.

Borger, R. (1982), Die Chronologie des Darius-Denkmals am Behistun-Felsen, *Nachrichten der Akademie der Wissenschaften in Göttingen, philosophische-historische Klasse* 3.

Bork, F. (1925), 'Elam', *Reallexikon der Vorgeschichte* 3, 69–83.

Börker, C. (1974), 'Griechische Amphorenstempel vom Tell Halaf bis zum persischen Golf', *BaM* 7, 31–49.

Born, H. and Seidl, U. (1995), *Schutzwaffen aus Assyrien und Urartu*, Mainz: Von Zabern.

Bosworth, A.B. (1980a), 'Alexander and the Iranians', *Journal of Hellenic Studies* 100, 1–21.

(1980b), *A Historical Commentary on Arrian's History of Alexander I*, Oxford: Clarendon Press.

(1987), 'Nearchus in Susiana', in Will, W. and Heinrichs, J., eds., *Zu Alexander d.Gr.: Festschrift G. Wirth zum 60. Geburtstag am 9.12.86*, Amsterdam: Hakkert, 541–66.

(1996), *Alexander and the East: the Tragedy of Triumph*, Oxford: Clarendon Press.

Bottema, S. (1978), 'The Late Glacial in the eastern Mediterranean and the Near East', in Brice, W.C., ed., *The Environmental History of the Near and Middle East since the Last Ice Age*, London/New York/San Francisco: Academic Press, 15–28.

Boucharlat, R. (1984), 'Monuments religieux de la Perse achéménide: Etat des questions', in Roux, G., ed., *Temples et Sanctuaires*, Lyon: TMO 7, 119–35.

(1985), 'Suse, marché agricole ou relais du grand commerce: Suse et la Susiane à l'époque des grands empires', *Paléorient* 11, 71–81.

(1987a), 'Les niveaux post-achéménides à Suse, secteur nord', *Cahiers de la DAFI* 15, 145–311.

(1987b), 'Suse à l'époque sasanide: Une capitale prestigieuse devenue ville de province', *Mesopotamia* 22, 357–66.

(1989), 'Cairns et pseudo-cairns du Fars: L'utilisation des tombes de surface au 1er millénaire de notre ère', *AIO*, 675–712.

(1990a), 'Suse et la Susiane à l'époque Achéménide: données archéologiques', *AH* 4, 149–75.

(1990b), 'La fin des palais Achéménides de Suse: Une mort naturelle', *MJP*, 225–33.

(1993), 'Pottery in Susa during the Seleucid, Parthian and early Sasanian periods', in Finkbeiner, U., ed., *Materialien zur Archäologie der Seleukiden- und Partherzeit im südlichen Babylonien und im Golfgebiet*, Tübingen: Wasmuth, 41–57.

(1997), 'Susa under Achaemenid rule', in Curtis, J., ed., *Mesopotamia and Iran in the Persian Period: Conquest and Imperialism, 539–331 BC*, London: British Museum, 54–67.

Boucharlat, R. and Haerinck, E. (1994), 'Das Ewig-weibliche: Figurines en os d'époque parthe de Suse', *IrAnt* 29, 185–99.

Boucharlat, R. and Labrousse, A. (1979), 'Le palais d'Artaxerxès II sur la rive droite du Chaour à Suse', *Cahiers de la DAFI* 10, 19–136.

Boucharlat, R. and Shahidi, H. (1987), 'Fragments architecturaux de type achéménide: Découvertes fortuites dans la ville de Shoush 1976–1979', *Cahiers de la DAFI* 15, 313–27.

Boyce, M. (1982), *A History of Zoroastrianism II. Under the Achaemenians*, Leiden/Cologne: HdO 8.i.2.

(1988), 'The religion of Cyrus the Great', *AH* 3, 5–31.

Braun, O. (1975; repr. of 1900 ed.), *Das Buch der Synhados oder Synodicon Orientale: Die Sammlung nestorianischer Konzilien, zusammengestellt im neunten Jahrhundert*, Amsterdam: Philo.

Braun-Holzinger, E. (1991), *Mesopotamische Weihgaben der frühdynastischen bis altbabylonischen Zeit*, Heidelberg: HSAO 3.

Brentjes, B. (1991), 'Humut-tabal ("nimm schnell hinweg") – ein Wunschname für eine Waffe?', *AMI* 24, 3–11.

(1993), 'Waffen der Steppenvölker 1. Dolch und Schwert im Steppenraum vom 2. Jahrtausend v. Chr. bis in die alttürkische Zeit', *AMI* 26, 5–45.

Briant, P. (1973), *Antigone le borgne: Les débuts de sa carrière et les problèmes de l'assemblée macédonienne*, Paris: Annales littéraires de l'Université de Besançon 152.

(1982), 'La campagne d'Alexandre contre les Ouxiens (début 330)', in *Rois, tributs et paysans*, Paris: Annales littéraires de l'Université de Besançon 269, 161–73.

(1984), 'La Perse avant l'empire (un état de la question)', *IrAnt* 19, 71–118.

(1990), 'The Seleucid kingdom, the Achaemenid empire and the history of the Near East in the first millennium BC', in Bilde, P., Engberg-Pedersen, T., Hannestad, L. and Zahle, J., eds., *Religion and Religious Practice in the Seleucid Kingdom*, Aarhus: Studies in Hellenistic Civilization 1, pp. 40–65.

(1991), 'De Sardes à Suse', *AH* 6, 67–82.

(1992a), *Darius, les Perses et l'empire*, Paris: Gallimard.

(1992b), 'Thémistocle sur la route royale', *DATA: Achaemenid History Newsletter*, 6.

(1993), 'Hérodote, Udjahorresnet et les palaces de Darius à Suse', *DATA: Achaemenid History Newsletter*, 2.

(1996), *Histoire de l'empire perse*, Paris: Fayard.

Brice, W.C. (1966), *South-West Asia*, London: A Systematic Regional Geography VIII.

(1978), 'The dessication of Anatolia', in Brice, W.C., ed., *The Environmental History of the Near and Middle East since the Last Ice Age*, London/New York/San Francisco: Academic Press, 141–7.

Bridges, S.J. (1981), *The Mesag Archive: a Study of Sargonic Society and Economy*, Ann Arbor: University Microfilms.

Brinkman, J.A. (1964), 'Merodach-Baladan II', in *Studies Presented to A. Leo Oppenheim, June 7, 1964*, Chicago: the Oriental Institute, 6–53.

(1965), 'Elamite military aid to Merodach-Baladan', *JNES* 24, 161–6.

(1968), *A Political History of Post-Kassite Babylonia, 1158–722 BC*, Rome: Analecta Orientalia 43.

(1973), 'Sennacherib's Babylonian problem: an interpretation', *JCS* 25, 89–95.

(1976), *Materials and Studies for Kassite History I: A Catalogue of Cuneiform Sources Pertaining to Specific Monarchs of the Kassite Dynasty*, Chicago: the Oriental Institute.

(1977), 'Mesopotamian chronology of the historical period', in Oppenheim, A.L., *Ancient Mesopotamia: Portrait of a dead civilization*, Chicago: University of Chicago Press, 335–48.

(1978), 'Notes on Arameans and Chaldeans in southern Babylonia in the early seventh century BC', *Or* 46, 304–25.

(1984), *Prelude to Empire: Babylonian Society and Politics, 747–626 BC*, Philadelphia: Occasional Publications of the Babylonian Fund 7.

(1986), 'The Elamite-Babylonian frontier in the Neo-Elamite Period, 750–625 BC', *FHE*, 199–207.

(1990), 'The Babylonian Chronicle revisited', in Abusch, T., Huehnergard, J. and Steinkeller, P., eds., *Lingering over Words: Studies in Ancient Near Eastern Literature in Honor of William L. Moran*, Atlanta: Scholars Press, 73–104.

(1991), 'Babylonia in the shadow of Assyria', *CAH* 3/2, 1–70.

(1993a), 'Meerland', *RlA* 8, 6–10.

(1993b), 'Babylonian influence in the Šēh Hamad texts dated under Nebuchadnezzar II', *SAAB* 7, 133–8.

(1995), 'Mušezib-Marduk', *RlA* 8, 455.

Brinkman, J.A. and Kennedy, D.A. (1983), 'Documentary evidence for the economic base of early Neo-Babylonian society: a survey of dated Babylonian economic texts, 721–626 BC', *JCS* 35, 1–90.

Brock, S. (1984), 'Christians in the Sasanid empire: a case of divided loyalties', in Brock, S., *Syriac Perspectives on Late Antiquity*, London: Variorum, pp. VI1–19.

Brookes, I.A. (1982), 'Geomorphological evidence for climatic change in Iran during the last 20,000 years', in Bintliff, J.L. and Van Zeist, W., eds., *Palaeoclimates, Palaeoenvironments and Human Communities in the Eastern Mediterranean Region in Later Prehistory*, Oxford: BAR International Series 133(i), 191–228.

(1989), *The Physical Geography, Geomorphology and Late Quaternary History of the Mahidasht Project Area, Qara Su Basin, Central West Iran*, Toronto: Royal Ontario Museum Mahidasht Project Vol. 1.

Budge, E.A.W. (1932), *The Chronography of Gregory Abû'l Faraj, the Son of Aaron, the Hebrew Physician, Commonly known as Bar Hebraeus, Being the First Part of his Political History of the World*, translated from the Syriac by Ernest A. Wallis Budge, London: Oxford University Press.

Butterlin, P. (1995), 'Problèmes de colonisation et de contacts à l'époque d'Uruk', *Sources Travaux Historiques* 36–7, 17–24.

Calmeyer, P. (1987), 'Greek historiography and Achaemenid reliefs', *AH* 2, 11–26.

(1988), 'Zur Genese altiranischer Motive X. Die elamisch-persische Tracht', *AMI* 21, 27–51.

(1989), 'Beobachtungen an der Silbervase aus Persepolis', *IrAnt* 24, 79–83.

(1992), 'Zur Genese altiranischer Motive XI. "Eingewebte Bildchen" von Städten', *AMI* 25, 95–124.

(1995a), 'Museum', *RlA* 8, 453–5.

(1995b), 'Middle Babylonian art and contemporary Iran', in Curtis, J., ed., *Later Mesopotamia and Iran: Tribes and Empires 1600–539 BC*, London: British Museum, 33–45.

Cameron, G.G. (1936), *History of Early Iran*, Chicago/London: University of Chicago.

(1957), 'An Elamite bronze plaque', in Schmidt, E.F., *Persepolis II: Contents of the Treasury and Other Discoveries*, Chicago: OIP 69, pp. 64–5.

Canal, D. (1978), 'La haute terrasse de l'Acropole de Suse', *Paléorient* 4, 169–76.

Cantineau, J. (1939), 'La Susiane dans une inscription palmyrénienne', in *Mélanges syriens offerts à Monsieur René Dussaud I*, Paris: Geuthner, 277–9.

Carter, E. (1980), 'Excavations in Ville Royale I at Susa: the third millennium BC occupation', *Cahiers de la DAFI* 11, 11–134.

(1981), 'Elamite ceramics', in Wright, H.T., *An Early Town on the Deh Luran Plain: Excavations at Tepe Farukhabad*, Ann Arbor: Memoirs of the Museum of Anthropology, University of Michigan, No. 13, 196–223.

(1985), 'Notes on archaeology and the social and economic history of Susiana', *Paléorient* 11, 43–8.

(1987), 'The Piedmont and the Pusht-i Kuh in the early third millennium BC', in Huot, J.-L., ed., *Préhistoire de la Mésopotamie*, Paris: Editions du CNRS, 73–83.

(1989), review of Seidl, U., *Die elamischen Felsreliefs von Kurangun und Naqš-e Rustam*, *ZA* 79, 145–8.

(1990), 'Elamite Exports', *MJP*, 89–100.

(1994a), 'The Middle Elamite building at Anshan (Tal-e Malyan)', *Iranian Journal of Archaeology and History* 7, 12–26.

(1994b), 'Bridging the gap between the Elamites and the Persians in southeastern Khuzistan', in Sancisi-Weerdenburg, H., Kuhrt, A., and Root, M.C., eds., *Achaemenid History VIII. Continuity and Change*, Leiden: Nederlands Instituut voor het Nabije Oosten, 65–95.

(1996), *Excavations at Anshan (Tal-e Malyan): the Middle Elamite period*, Philadelphia: University Museum Monograph 82 [= Malyan Excavation Reports 2].

Carter, E. and Stolper, M. (1984), *Elam: Surveys of Political History and Archaeology*, Berkeley/Los Angeles/London: University of California Publications, Near Eastern Studies 25.

Carter, M.L. (1978), 'White marble bust of a male', in Harper, P.O., *The Royal Hunter: Art of the Sasanian Empire*, New York: The Asia Society, 170–1.

Cassin, E. (1982), 'Le mort: Valeur et représentation en Mésopotamie ancienne', in Gnoli, G. and Vernant, J.-P., eds., *La mort, les morts dans les sociétés anciennes*, Cambridge and Paris: Cambridge University Press and Editions de la Maison des Sciences de l'Homme, 355–72.

Castellino, G.R. (1972), *Two Šulgi hymns (BC)*, Rome: Studi Semitici 42.

Chabot, J.B. (1902), *Synodicon orientale ou recueil de synodes nestoriens*, Paris: Notices et extraits des manuscrits de la Bibliothèque Nationale 37.

Chamaza, G.W. (1994), 'Der VIII. Feldzug Sargons II', *AMI* 27, 91–118.

Charpin, D. (1986), 'Les Elamites à Šubat-Enlil', *FH E*, 129–137.

(1987), 'A propos du site de Tell Harmal', *NABU*, 117.

(1990), 'Une alliance contre l'Elam et le rituel du *lipit napištim*', *MJP*, 109–18.

(1992), 'L'enterrement du roi d'Ur Šu-Sîn à Uruk', *NABU*, 106.

Charpin, D. and Durand, J.-M. (1991), 'La suzeraineté de l'empereur (sukkalmah) d'Elam sur la Mésopotamie et le "nationalisme" Amorrite', *MHEOP* 1, 59–66.

Chaumont, M.-L. (1969), *Recherches sur l'histoire d'Arménie de l'avènement des Sassanides à la conversion du royaume*, Paris: Geuthner.

(1988), *La christianisation de l'empire iranien: Des origines aux grandes persécutions du IVe siècle*, Louvain: *CSCO* 499 [= *Subsidia* 80].

Choksy, J.K. (1990), 'Gesture in ancient Iran and Central Asia I: the raised hand', *AcIr* 30 [= *Textes et Mémoires 16, Iranica Varia: Papers in honor of Professor Ehsan Yarshater*], 30–7.

Christensen, A. (1936), *L'Iran sous les Sassanides*, Copenhagen/Paris: Annales du Musée Guimet, Bibliothèque d'Études 48.

Christensen, P. (1993), *The Decline of Iranshahr: Irrigation and Environments in the History of the Middle East, 500 BC to AD 1500*, Copenhagen: Museum Tusculanum.

Civil, M. (1996), 'Sin-iddinam in Emar and SU.A = Šimaški', *NABU*, 41.

Clairmont, C. (1957), 'Greek pottery from the Near East II. Black vases', *Berytus* 11/2, 85–142.

Cogan, M. and Tadmor, H. (1981), 'Ashurbanipal's conquest of Babylon: the first official report – Prism K', *Or* 50, 229–40.

Cohen, G.M. (1978), *The Seleucid Colonies: Studies in Founding, Administration and Organization*, Wiesbaden: Historia Einzelschriften 30.

Colpe, C. (1983), 'Development of religious thought', *CHI* 3/2, 819–65.

Connan, J. and Deschesne, O. (1996), *Le bitume à Suse: Collection du Musée du Louvre*, Paris: Éditions de la Réunion des musées nationaux.

Córdoba, J.M. (1997), 'Die Schlacht am Ulaya-Fluß: Ein Beispiel assyrischer Kriegführung während der letzten Jahre des Reiches', in Waetzoldt, H. and Hauptmann, H., eds., *Assyrien im Wandel der Zeiten: XXXIXe Rencontre Assyriologique Internationale, Heidelberg 6.-10. Juli 1992*, Heidelberg: HSAO 6, 7–18.

Cressey, G.B. (1958), 'The Shatt al-Arab basin', *Middle East Journal* 12, 448–60.

Cruveilhier, P. (1921), *Les principaux résultats des nouvelles fouilles de Suse*, Paris: Geuthner.

Cumont, F. (1928), 'Inscriptions grecques de Suse publiées d'après les notes de Bernard Haussoullier', *MDP* 20, 77–98.

    (1930), 'Nouvelles inscriptions grecques de Suse', *CRAIBL*, 208–20.

    (1931), 'Inscriptions grecques de Suse', *CRAIBL*, 233–50.

    (1932a), 'Une lettre du roi Artaban III à la ville de Suse', *CRAIBL*, 238–60.

    (1932b), 'Nouvelles inscriptions grecques de Suse', *CRAIBL*, 271–86.

    (1933), 'Deux inscriptions de Suse', *CRAIBL*, 260–8.

Curtis, J. (1993), 'William Kennett Loftus and his excavations at Susa', *IrAnt* 28, 1–55.

Dalley, S. (1993), 'Nineveh after 612 BC', *AoF* 20: 134–47.

Dalley, S. and Postgate, J.N. (1984), *The Tablets from Fort Shalmaneser*, London: British School of Archaeology in Iraq [=Cuneiform Texts from Nimrud 3].

Damerow, P. and Englund, R.K. (1985), 'Die Zahlzeichensysteme der Archaischen Texte aus Uruk', in Green, M.W. and Nissen, H.J., *Zeichenliste der Archaischen Texte aus Uruk*, Berlin: Gebr. Mann [=Archaische Texte aus Uruk 2], 117–56.

    (1989), *The Proto-Elamite Texts from Tepe Yahya*, Cambridge: American School of Prehistoric Research Bulletin 39.

Dandamaev, M.A. (1976), *Persien unter den ersten Achämeniden (6.Jahrhundert v.Chr.)*, Wiesbaden: Ludwig Reichert.

    (1977), 'The dynasty of the Achaemenids in the early period', *AAASH* 25, 39–42.

    (1991), 'Elamite workers in Achaemenid Babylonia', *Bulletin of the Middle Eastern Culture Center in Japan* 5, 17–20.

    (1992), *Iranians in Achaemenid Babylonia*, Costa Mesa: Mazda Publishers.

    (1993a), 'Achaemenid Estates in Lahiru', *IrAnt* 27, 117–23.

    (1993b), 'Cyrus iii. Cyrus II the Great', *EnIr* 6, 516–21.

Dandamaev, M.A. and Lukonin, V.G. (1989), *The Culture and Social Institutions of Ancient Iran*, Cambridge: Cambridge University Press.

Davis, N. and Kraay, C.M. (1973), *The Hellenistic Kingdoms: Portrait Coins and History*, London: Thames and Hudson.

Delitzsch, F. (1884), *Die Sprache der Kossäer: Linguistisch-historische Funde und Fragen*, Leipzig.

Delougaz, P. (1952), *Pottery from the Diyala Region*, Chicago: OIP 63.

Dewan, M.L. and Famouri, J. (1968), 'Soils', *CHI* 1: 250–63.

Diakonoff, I.M. (1991), 'The cities of the Medes', in Cogan, M. and Eph'al, I., eds., *Ah,*

Assyria . . . Studies in Assyrian History and Ancient Near Eastern Historiography presented to Hayim Tadmor, Jerusalem: Scripta Hierosolymitana 33, 13–20.

Dietrich, M. (1970), *Die Aramäer Südbabyloniens in der Sargonidenzeit (700–648)*, Neukirchen-Vluyn: *AOAT* 7.

Dieulafoy, J. (1888), *A Suse: Journal des fouilles, 1884–1886*, Paris: Librairie Hachette.

Dieulafoy, M. (1893), *L'acropole de Suse d'après les fouilles exécutées en 1884, 1885, 1886 sous les auspices du Musée du Louvre*, Paris: Librairie Hachette.

Dillemann, L. (1962), *Haute Mésopotamie orientale et pays adjacents: Contribution à la géographie historique de la région du ve s. avant l'ère chrétienne au vie s. de cette ère*, Paris: *BAH* 72.

Dittmann, R. (1986), 'Susa in the Proto-Elamite period and annotations on the painted pottery of Proto-Elamite Khuzestan', in Finkbeiner, U. and Röllig, W., eds., *Ğamdat Naṣr: Period or Regional Style?*, Wiesbaden: TAVO Beiheft B 62, 171–98.

Dodgeon, M.H. and Lieu, S.N.C. (1991), *The Roman Eastern Frontier and the Persian Wars AD 226–363: a Documentary History*, London: Routledge.

(1995), 'Libanius and the Persian wars of Constantius II', in Cannuyer, C., Ries, J. and Van Tongerloo, A, eds., *War and Peace – Guerre et Paix*, Brussels/Louvain: Acta Orientalia Belgica, 83–109.

Dolce, R. (1978), *Gli intarsi mesopotamici dell'epoca protodinastica*, 2 vols., Rome: Serie Archeologica 23.

Dollfus, G. (1978), 'Djaffarabad, Djowi, Bendebal: Contribution à l'étude de la Susiane au Vᵉ millénaire et au début du IVᵉ millénaire', *Paléorient* 4, 141–67.

(1985), 'L'occupation de la Susiane au Vᵉ millénaire et au début du IVᵉ millénaire avant J.-C.', *Paléorient* 11, 11–20.

Dombart, T. (1929), 'Das Zikkuratrelief aus Kujundschik', *ZA* 38, 39–64.

Dossin, G. (1962), 'Bronze inscrits du Luristan de la Collection Foroughi', *IrAnt* 2, 149–64.

Duchene, J. (1986), 'La localisation de Huhnur', *FHE*, 65–74.

Duchesne-Guillemen, J. (1979), 'Kambyses 2', *KP* 3, 99–100.

(1983), 'Zoroastrian religion', *CHI* 3/2, 866–908.

Durand, J.-M. (1986), 'Fragments rejoints pour une histoire élamite', *FHE*, 111–128.

(1990), 'Commerce de l'étain à Mari', *NABU*, 69.

(1992), 'Rapports entre l'Élam et Ourouk', *NABU*, 62.

(1994), 'L'empereur d'Elam et ses vassaux', *CDR*, 15–22.

Dyson, R.H., Jr. (1987), 'The relative and absolute chronology of Hissar II and the Proto-Elamite horizon of northern Iran', in Aurenche, O., Evin, J. and Hours, F., eds., *Chronologies in the Near East*, Oxford: BAR International Series 379, 647–78.

Edel, E. and Mayrhofer, M. (1971), 'Notizen zu Fremdnamen in ägyptischen Quellen', *Or* 40, 1–10.

Edzard, D.O. (1957), *Die "zweite Zwischenzeit" Babyloniens*, Wiesbaden: Harrassowitz.

(1959–60), 'Neue Inschriften zur Geschichte von Ur III unter Šūsuen', *AfO* 19, 1–32.

(1967a), 'The Early Dynastic period', in Bottéro, J., Cassin, E. and Vercoutter, J., eds., *The Near East: the Early Civilizations*, New York: Delacorte Press, 52–90.

(1967b), 'The Third Dynasty of Ur – its empire and its successor states', in Bottéro, J., Cassin, E. and Vercoutter, J., eds., *The Near East: the Early Civilizations*, New York: Delacorte Press, 133–176.

Egmond, F. and Mason, P. (1997), *The Mammoth and the Mouse: Microhistory and Morphology*, Baltimore/London: Johns Hopkins University Press.

Eidem, J. (1985), 'News from the eastern front: the evidence from Tell Shemshara', *Iraq* 47, 83–107.

(1992), *The Shemshara Archives 2: the Administrative Texts*, Copenhagen: Det Kongelige Danske Videnskabernes Selskab, Historisk-filosofiske Skrifter 15.

Eilers, W. (1954), 'Der Name Demawend', *ArOr* 22, 267–374.

(1964), 'Kyros', *Beiträge zur Namenforschung* 15, 180–236.

(1974), 'The name of Cyrus', *AcIr* 3 [= *Commémoration Cyrus. Hommage Universel III*], 3–9.

(1982), 'Geographische Namengebung in und um Iran', *Bayerische Akademie der Wissenschaften, philosophische-historische Klasse Sitzungsberichte*. 5, 3–67.

Englund, R.K. (1994), *Archaic Administrative Texts from Uruk: the Early Campaigns*, Berlin: Ausgrabungen der Deutschen Forschungsgemeinschaft in Uruk-Warka 15 [=Archaische Texte aus Uruk 5].

(in press), 'Texts from the Late Uruk period', in Bauer, J., Englund, R.K. and Krebernik, M., eds., *Mesopotamien: Späturuk- und Frühdynastische Zeit*.

Englund, R.K. and Grégoire, J.-P. (1991), *The Proto-Cuneiform Texts from Jemdet Nasr I: Copies, Transliterations and Glossary*, Berlin: MSVO 1.

Englund, R.K. and Nissen, H.J. (1993), *Die lexikalischen Listen der archaischen Texte aus Uruk*, Berlin: Ausgrabungen der Deutschen Forschungsgemeinschaft in Uruk-Warka 13 [=Archaische Texte aus Uruk 3].

Eqbal, H. (1979), 'The Seleucid, Parthian, and Sasanian periods on the Izeh Plain', in Wright, H.T., ed., *Archaeological Investigations in Northeastern Xuzestan, 1976*, Ann Arbor: University of Michigan Museum of Anthropology Technical Report No. 10, 114–23.

Falconer, S.E. and Savage, S.H. (1995), 'Heartlands and hinterlands: alternative trajectories of early urbanization in Mesopotamia and the southern Levant', *American Antiquity* 60, 37–58.

Fales, F.M. (1973), *Censimenti e catasti di epoca Neo-Assira*, Rome: Studi economici e tecnologici 2.

Fales, F.M. and Postgate, J.N. (1992), *Imperial Administrative Records, pt. 1: Palace and Temple Administration*, Helsinki: State Archives of Assyria 7.

Falkenstein, A. (1950), 'Ibbisîn – Išbi'erra', *ZA* 49, 59–79.

Farber, W. (1975), 'Eine elamische Inschrift aus der 1. Hälfte des 2. Jahrtausends', *ZA* 64, 74–86.

Felix, W. (1985), *Antike literarische Quellen zur Außenpolitik des Sasanidenstaates I (224–309)*, Vienna: Sitzungsberichte der Österreichische Akademie der Wissenschaften, philosophische-historische Klasse 456 [=Veröffentlichungen der Iranischen Kommission 18].

Fiandra, E. (1982), 'Porte e chiusure di sicurezza nell'antico oriente', *Bollettino d'Arte* (6th ser.) 67, 1–18.

Fiey, J.M. (1970), *Jalons pour une histoire de l'église en Iraq*, Louvain: *CSCO* 310 [= *Subsidia* 36].

(1974), 'Les communautés syriaques en Iran des premiers siècles à 1552', *AcIr* 3 [=*Hommage universel* 3], 279–97.

(1977), *Nisibe, métropole syriaque orientale et ses suffragants des origines à nos jours*, Louvain: *CSCO* 388 [=*Subsidia* 54].

(1979), 'L'Elam, la première des métropoles ecclésiastiques syriennes orientales', in Fiey, J.M, *Communautés syriaques en Iran et Irak des origines à 1552*, London: Variorum, 123–53, 221–67.

Fincke, J. (1993), *Die Orts- und Gewässernamen der Nuzi-Texte*, Wiesbaden: RGTC 10.

Fisher, W.B. (1968), 'Physical Geography', *CHI* I, 3–110.

Flannery, K.V. (1969), 'Origins and ecological effects of early domestication in Iran and the Near East', in Ucko, P.J. and Dimbleby, G.W., eds., *The domestication and exploitation of plants and animals*, London: Duckworth, 73–100.

(1983), 'Early pig domestication in the Fertile Crescent: a retrospective look', in Young, T.C. Jr., Smith, P.E.L. and Mortensen, P., eds., *The Hilly Flanks and Beyond: Essays on the Prehistory of Southwestern Asia presented to Robert J. Braidwood, November 15, 1982*, Chicago: SAOC 36, 163–88.

Fontan, E. (1994), *De Khorsabad à Paris: La découverte des Assyriens*, Paris: Notes et documents des musées de France 26.

Forbiger, A. (1844), *Handbuch der alten Geographie aus den Quellen bearbeitet*, ii, Leipzig: Mayer and Wigand.

Foster, B.R. (1982), 'Archives and record-keeping in Sargonic Mesopotamia', *ZA* 72, 1–27.

(1985), 'The Sargonic victory stele from Telloh', *Iraq* 47, 15–30.

(1993), *Before the muses: An anthology of Akkadian literature*, 2 vols., Bethesda: CDL Press.

Frahm, E. (1997), *Einleitung in die Sanḥerib-Inschriften*, Horn: *AfO* Beiheft 26.

Frame, G. (1992), *Babylonia 689–627 BC: A Political History*, Leiden: Uitgaven van het Nederlands Historisch-Archaeologisch Instituut te Istanbul 69.

Frankfort, H. (1954; rev. 1970), *The Art and Architecture of the Ancient Near East*, Harmondsworth: Penguin.

(1955), *Stratified Cylinder Seals from the Diyala Region*, Chicago: OIP 72.

Fraser, J.B. (1826), *Travels and Adventures in the Persian Provinces on the Southern Banks of the Caspian Sea. With an Appendix, containing Short Notices on the Geology and Commerce of Persia.* London: Longman, Rees, Orme, Brown and Green.

Fraser, P.M. (1996), *Cities of Alexander the Great*, Oxford: Clarendon Press.

Frayne, D.R. (1991), 'Historical Texts in Haifa: Notes on R. Kutscher's "Brockmon Tablets"', *BiOr* 48, 378–409.

(1992), *The Early Dynastic List of Geographical Names*, New Haven: AOS 74.

(1993), *Sargonic and Gutian periods (2334–2113 BC)*, Toronto: The Royal Inscriptions of Mesopotamia, Early Periods, vol. 2.

Friberg, J. (1978), *The Third Millennium Roots of Babylonian Mathematics I. A Method for the Decipherment, through Mathematical and Metrological Analysis, of Proto-Sumerian and Proto-Elamite Semi-pictographic Inscriptions*, Gothenburg: Chalmers University of Technology and the University of Gothenburg.

(1979), *The Early Roots of Babylonian Mathematics II. Metrological Relations in a Group of Semi-pictographic Tablets of the Jemdet Nasr Type, probably from Uruk-Warka*, Gothenburg: Chalmers University of Technology and the University of Gothenburg.

(1994), 'Preliterate counting and accounting in the Middle East', *OLZ* 89, 477–502.

Frye, R.N. (1962), *The Heritage of Persia*, London: Widenfeld and Nicolson.

(1971), 'History and Sasanian inscriptions', in *La Persia nel medioevo*, Rome: Accademia Nazionale dei Lincei Quaderno 160, 215–24.

(1983), 'The political history of Iran under the Sasanians', *CHI* 3/1, 116–80.

(1984), 'Religion in Fars under the Achaemenids', *AcIr* 23 [=*Hommages et Opera Minora 9. Orientalia J. Duchesne-Guillemin Emerito Oblata*], 171–8.

Fuchs, A. (1994), *Die Inschriften Sargons II. aus Khorsabad*, Göttingen: Cuvillier Verlag.

Fullbrook, M. (1993), ed., *National Histories and European History*, London: UCL Press.

Ganji, M.H. (1968), 'Climate', *CHI* 1, 212–49.

(1978), 'Post-glacial climatic changes on the Iranian Plateau', in Brice, W.C., ed., *The Environmental History of the Near and Middle East since the Last Ice Age*, London/New York/San Francisco: Academic Press, pp. 149–63.

Garrison, M.B. (1991), 'Seals and the elite at Persepolis: some observations on early Achaemenid Persian art', *Ars Orientalis*, 1–29.

Garrison, M.B. and Root, M.C. (1996), 'Persepolis seal studies: an introduction with provisional concordances of seal numbers and associated documents on Fortification Tablets 1–2087', *AH* 9, 1–141.

Gassan, M., (1986) 'Une inscription cassite d'Iran', *FHE*, 187–9.

Gelb, I.J. and Kienast, B. (1990), *Die altakkadischen Königsinschriften des dritten Jahrtausends v.Chr.*, Stuttgart: Freiburger altorientalische Studien 6.

Gensheimer, T.R. (1984), 'The role of shell in Mesopotamia: evidence for trade exchange with Oman and the Indus Valley', *Paléorient* 10, 65–73.

George, A.R. (1996), 'The Akkadian word for "moustache"', *NABU*, 60.

Gera, D. and Hurowitz, W. (1997), 'Antiochus IV in life and death: evidence from the Babylonian astronomical diaries', *JAOS* 117, 240–52.

Gerardi, P. (1987), *Assurbanipal's Elamite Campaigns: a Political and Literary Study*, Ann Arbor: University Microfilms.

(1992), 'The Arab campaigns of Assurbanipal: scribal reconstruction of the past', *SAAB* 6/2, 67–103.

Gero, S. (1981), *Barsauma of Nisibis and Persian Christianity in the Fifth Century*, Louvain: *CSCO* 426 [= *Subsidia* 63].

Ghirshman, R. (1950a), 'The town which three hundred elephants rased to the ground: the newly excavated fourth level of Susa and the Partho-Seleucid necropolis', *Illustrated London News* (7 October), 571–3.

(1950b), 'Un bas-relief d'Artaban V avec inscription en Pehlevi Arsacide', *Monuments et mémoires publiés par l'Académie des Inscriptions et Belles-Lettres* 44, 97–107.

(1952), 'Cinq campagnes de fouilles à Suse (1946–1951)', *RA* 46, 1–18.

(1954), *Village perse-achéménide*, Paris: MDP 36.

(1956), *Bîchâpour II. Les mosaïques sassanides*, Paris: Musée du Louvre, Dépt. des Antiquités Orientales, Série Archéologique 7.

(1965), 'L'architecture élamite et ses traditions', *IrAnt* 5, 93–102.

(1966), *Tchoga Zanbil (Dur-Untash) I. La ziggurat*, Paris: MDP 39.

(1968), *Tchoga Zanbil (Dur-Untash) II. Temenos, temples, palais, tombes*, Paris: MDP 40.

(1971), *Bîchâpour I*, Paris: Musée du Louvre, Dépt. des Antiquités Orientales, Série Archéologique 6.

(1976), *Terrasses sacrées de Bard-è Néchandeh et Masjid-i Solaiman*, Paris: MDP 45.

(1977), 'Le harnais de tête en Iran', in Rosen-Ayalon, M., ed., *Studies in Memory of Gaston Wiet*, Jerusalem: Magnes, 1–5.

Gibson, McG. (1974), 'Violation of fallow and engineered disaster in Mesopotamian civilization', in Downing, T.E. and Gibson, McG., eds., *Irrigation's Impact on Society*, Tucson: Anthropological Papers of the University of Arizona 25, 7–19.

Gignoux, P. (1971a), 'La liste des provinces de l'Ērān dans les inscriptions de Šābuhr et de Kirdīr', *AAASH* 19, 83–94.

(1971b), 'Les collections de sceaux et de bulles sassanides de la Bibliothèque Nationale de Paris', in *La Persia nel medioevo*, Rome: Accademia Nazionale dei Lincei Quaderno 160, 535–42.

(1984), 'L'organisation administrative sasanide: Le cas du *marzbān*', *Jerusalem Studies in Arabic and Islam* 4, 1–29.

Gilbert, A.S. (1991), 'Equid remains from Godin Tepe, Western Iran: an interim summary and interpretation, with notes on the introduction of the horse into Southwest Asia', in Meadow, R.H. and Uerpmann, H.-P., eds., *Equids in the Ancient World*, vol. 2, Wiesbaden: Beihefte zum TAVO, Reihe A 19/2, 75–122.

Gillis, J.R. (1994), ed., *Commemorations: the Politics of National Identity*, Princeton: University Press,.

Glassner, J.-J. (1986), *La chute d'Akkadé, l'événement et sa mémoire*, Berlin: *BBVO* 5.

(1988), 'La chute d'Akkadé: addenda et corrigenda', *NABU*, 51.

(1991), 'Les textes de Haft Tépé, la Susiane et l'Elam au 2ème millénaire', *MHEOP* 1, 109–26.

(1994), 'Ruḫušak – mār aḫatim: la transmission du pouvoir en Elam', *JA* 282, 219–236.

(1996), 'Les dynasties d'Awan et de Šimaški', *NABU*, 34.

Gnoli, G. (1980), *Zoroaster's time and homeland*, Naples: Istituto Universitario Orientale, Seminario di Studi Asiatici Series Minor 7.

Godard, A. (1949), 'Badr Neshandi', *Athar-e Iran* 4, 153–162.

Gomi, T. (1984), 'On the critical economic situation at Ur early in the reign of Ibbisin', *JCS* 36, 211–42.

Graadt van Roggen, D.L. (1905), 'Notice sur les anciens travaux hydrauliques en Susiane', *MDP* 7, 166–208.

Grayson, A.K. (1975), *Assyrian and Babylonian Chronicles*, Locust Valley: Texts from Cuneiform Sources 5.

(1991), 'Assyria 668–635 BC: the reign of Ashurbanipal', *CAH* 3/2, 142–61.

Green, M.W. (1978), 'The Eridu lament', *JCS* 30, 127–67.

(1981), 'The construction and implementation of the cuneiform writing system', *Visible Language* 15, 345–72.

Green, P. (1990), *Alexander to Actium*, London: Thames and Hudson.

Grégoire, J.-P. (1970), *Archives administratives sumériennes*, Paris: Geuthner.

Grillot, F. (1986), 'Kiririša', FHE, 175–80.

Grillot, F. and Glassner, J.-J. (1990), 'L'inscription élamite de Siwepalarhuhpak', *NABU*, 65.

(1991), 'Problèmes de succession et cumuls de pouvoirs: une querelle de famille chez les premiers sukkalmah?', *IrAnt* 26, 85–99.

(1993), 'Chronologie susienne', *NABU*, 18.

Grillot, F. and Vallat, F. (1978), 'Le verbe élamite "pi(š)ši"', *Cahiers de la DAFI* 8, 81–84.

(1984), 'Dédicace de Šilhak-Inšušinak à Kiririša', *IrAnt* 19, 21–9.

Gropp, G. (1989), 'Ein elamischer Baderitus', *AIO*, 239–72.

Guépin, J.P. (1965–6), 'A contribution to the location of Ta Azara, the chief sanctuary of Elymais', *Persica* 2, 19–26.

Guichard, M. (1996), 'À la recherche de la pierre bleue', *NABU*, 36.

Gutschmid, A. von (1888), *Geschichte Irans und seiner Nachbarländer von Alexander dem Grossen bis zum Untergang der Arsaciden*, Tübingen: Laupp'schen Buchhandlung.

Gyselen, R. (1977), 'Trésor de monnaies sasanides trouvé à Suse', *Cahiers de la DAFI* 7, 61–74.

(1989), *La géographie administrative de l'empire sassanide: Les témoignages sigillographiques*, Bures-sur-Yvette: Res Orientales 1.

Gyselen, R. and Gasche, H. (1994), 'Suse et Ivān-e Kerkha, capitale provinciale d'Ērān-Xwarrah-Šāpūr', *StIr* 23, 19–35.

Hachmann, R. (1995), 'Die Völkerschaften auf den Bildwerken von Persepolis', in Finkbeiner, U., Dittmann, R. and Hauptmann, H., eds., *Beiträge zur Kulturgeschichte Vorderasiens: Festschrift für Rainer Michael Boehmer*, Mainz: von Zabern, 195–223.

Haerinck, E. (1983), *La céramique en Iran pendant la période parthe (ca. 250 av. J.C. à 225 après J.C.): typologie, chronologie et distribution*, Leuven: Peeters.

(1986), 'The Chronology of Luristan, Pusht-i Kuh in the late fourth and first half of the third millennium BC', in Huot, J.-L., ed., *Préhistoire de la Mésopotamie*, Paris: Editions du CNRS, 55–72.

(1997), 'Babylonia under Achaemenid rule', in Curtis, J., ed., *Mesopotamia and Iran in the Persian Period: Conquest and Imperialism, 539–331 BC*, London: British Museum, 26–34.

Haller, A. (1954), *Die Gräber und Grüfte von Assur*, Berlin: WVDOG 65.

Hallo, W.W. (1956), 'Zariqum', *JNES* 15, 220–5.

(1957), *Early Mesopotamian Royal Titles: a Philologic and Historical Analysis*, New Haven: AOS 43.

(1960), 'A Sumerian amphictyony', *JCS* 14, 88–114.

(1971), 'Gutium', *RlA* 3, 708–20.

(1976), 'Women of Sumer', in Schmandt-Besserat, D., ed., *The Legacy of Sumer*, Malibu: Bibliotheca Mesopotamica 4, 24–40.

(1980), 'Royal titles from the Mesopotamian periphery', *Anatolian Studies* 30, 189–95.

Hallock, R.T. (1969), *Persepolis Fortification Tablets*, Chicago: OIP 92.

Hamilton, J.R. (1987), 'Alexander's Iranian policy', in Will, W., ed., *Zu Alexander d.Gr.: Festschrift G.Wirth zum 60. Geburtstag am 9.12.86*, Amsterdam: Adolf M. Hakkert, 467–86.

Hannestad, L. and Potts, D.T. (1990), 'Temple architecture in the Seleucid kingdom', in Bilde, P., Engberg-Pedersen, T., Hannestad, L. and Zahle, J., eds., *Religion and Religious Practice in the Seleucid Kingdom*, Aarhus: Studies in Hellenistic Civilization 1, 91–124.

Hansman, J. (1978), 'Seleucia and the three Dauraks', *Iran* 16, 154–61.

(1985), 'The great gods of Elymais', *AcIr* 24 [*Hommages et Opera Minora*], 229–46.

(1990), 'Coins and mints of ancient Elymais', *Iran* 28, 1–11.

Harmatta, J. (1976), 'Inscriptions élyméennes', in Ghirshman, R., *Terrasses sacrées de Bard-è Néchandeh et Masjid-i Solaiman*, Paris: MDP 45, 287–303.

(1981), 'Parthia and Elymais in the 2nd century BC', *AAASH* 29, 189–217.

(1982–4), 'King Kabneškir son of King Kabneškir', *AAASH* 30, 167–80.

Harper, P.O. (1978), *The Royal Hunter: Art of the Sasanian Empire*, New York: Asia House Gallery.

(1988), 'Boat-shaped bowls of the Sasanian period', *IrAnt* 23, 331–45.

(1993), 'Evidence for the existence of state controls in the production of Sasanian silver vessels', in Boyd, S.A. and Mango, M.M., eds., *Ecclesiastical Silver Plate in Sixth-Century Byzantium*, Washington, D.C.: Dumbarton Oaks Research Library and Collection, 147–53.

Harper, P.O., Aruz, J. and Tallon, F. (1992), eds., *The Royal City of Susa: Ancient Near Eastern Treasures in the Louvre*, New York: Metropolitan Museum of Art.

Hartranft, C.D. (1989), 'Sozomenus: Church history from AD 323–425', in Schaff, P. and Wace, H., eds., *A Select Library of Nicene and Post-Nicene Fathers of the Christian Church II*, Grand Rapids: Eerdmans, 179–454.

Häser, J. (1988), *Steingefäße des 2. vorchristlichen Jahrtausends im Gebiet des Arabischen/Persischen Golfes: Typologie der Gefäße und Deckel aus Serpentinit, Chlorit, Steatit und verwandten Steinarten*, unpubl. MA thesis, Free University of Berlin.

Haussoullier, B. (1902), 'Inscriptions grecques de l'extrême-orient grec', in *Mélanges Perrot, recueil de mémoires concernant l'archéologie classique, la littérature et l'histoire anciennes dédié à Georges Perrot*, Paris: Fontemoing, 155–59.

Helbaek, H. (1969), 'Plant collecting, dry-farming, and irrigation agriculture in prehistoric Deh Luran', in Hole, F., Flannery, K.V., and Neely, J.A., *Prehistory and Human Ecology of the Deh Luran Plain*, Ann Arbor: Memoirs of the Museum of Anthropology of the University of Michigan 1, 383–426.

Heltzer, M. (1994), 'Mordekhai and Demaratos and the question of historicity', *AMI* 27, 119–21.

Henning, W.B. (1977), 'The monuments and inscriptions of Tang-i Sarvak', *AcIr* 15 [*Hommages et Opera Minora* 6. *W.B. Henning Selected Papers* 2], 359–86.

Henrickson, R.C. (1984), 'Šimaški and central western Iran: the archaeological evidence', *ZA* 74, 98–122.

Herbordt, S. (1992), *Neuassyrische Glyptik des 8.-7. Jh. v. Chr.*, Helsinki: State Archives of Assyria Studies 1.

Herrenschmidt, C. (1993a), 'La poste achéménide', *DATA: Achaemenid History Newsletter*, 4.

(1993b), 'aggarêion-aggaros', *DATA: Achaemenid History Newsletter*, 5.

Herrero, P. (1976), 'Tablettes administratives de Haft-Tépé', *Cahiers de la DAFI* 6, 93–116.

Herrero, P. and Glassner, J.J. (1990), 'Haft-Tépé: Choix de textes I', *IrAnt* 25, 1–45.

(1991), 'Haft-Tépé: Choix de textes II', *IrAnt* 26, 39–80.

Herrmann, G. (1977), *The Iranian revival*, Oxford: Elsevier-Phaidon.

(1989) 'Parthian and Sasanian saddlery: New light from the Roman west', *AIO*, 757–809.

Hérubel, J.-P.V.M. (1994), *Annales Historiography and Theory: a Selective and Annotated Bibliography*, Westport/London: Greenwood Press.

Herzfeld, E. (1908), 'Pasargadae: Untersuchungen zur persischen Archäologie', *Klio* 8, 1–68.

(1920), *Am Tor von Asien: Felsdenkmale aus Irans Heldenzeit*, Berlin: Reimer.

(1968), *The Persian Empire*, Wiesbaden: Steiner.

Hespel, R. (1983), *Théodore Bar Koni, Livre des scolies (recension d'Urmiah)*, Louvain: CSCO 448 [=*Scriptores Syri* 194].

Hesse, B. (1979), 'Rodent remains and sendentism in the Neolithic: Evidence from Tepe Ganj Dareh, western Iran', *Journal of Mammalogy* 60, 856–7.

(1982), 'Slaughter patterns and domestication: the beginnings of pastoralism in western Iran', *Man* NS 17, 403–417.

Hill, G.F. (1922), *Catalogue of the Greek Coins of Arabia, Mesopotamia and Persia*, London: British Museum.

Hinz, W. (1957–71), 'Gott C. Nach elamischen Texten', *RlA* 3, 546–7.

(1962), 'Die elamischen Inschriften des Hanne', in Henning, W.B. and Yarshater, E., eds., *A Locust's Leg: Studies in Honour of S.H. Taqizadeh*, London, 105–16.

(1967), 'Elams Vertrag mit Narâm-Sîn von Akkade', *ZA* 24, 66–96.

(1968), 'Die Entstehung der altpersischen Keilschrift', *AMI* 1, 95–8.

(1969), *Altiranische Funde und Forschungen*, Berlin: de Gruyter.

(1971a), 'Eine altelamische Tonkrug-aufschrift vom Rande der Lut', *AMI* 4, 21–4.

(1971b), 'Persia, *c.* 2400–1800 BC', *CAH* 1/2, 644–80.

(1972), *The Lost World of Elam*, London: Sidgwick and Jackson.

(1973), *Neue Wege im Altpersischen*, Wiesbaden: Göttinger Orientforschungen III/1.

(1972–5), 'Hallušu-Inšušinak', *RlA* 4, 61–2.

(1976–80), 'Inšušinak', *RlA* 5, 117–19.

Hinz, W. and Koch, H. (1987), *Elamisches Wörterbuch I–II*, Berlin: *AMI* Ergänzungsband 17.

Hirsch, S.W. (1985), *The Friendship of the Barbarians: Xenophon and the Persian Empire*, Hanover and London: University Press of New England.

Hobsbawm, E.J. (1990), *Nations and Nationalism since 1780: Programme, Myth, Reality*, Cambridge: University Press.

Hobsbawm, E.J. and Ranger, T. (1983), eds., *The Invention of Tradition*, Cambridge: University Press.

Hoffmann, G. (1880), *Auszüge aus syrischen Akten persischer Märtyrer*, Leipzig: Abhandlungen für die Kunde des Morgenlandes VII/3.

Hole, F. (1977), *Studies in the Archaeological History of the Deh Luran Plain: the Excavation of Chagha Sefid*, Ann Arbor: Memoirs of the Museum of Anthropology of the University of Michigan 9.

(1983), 'Symbols of religion and social organization at Susa', in Young, T.C. Jr., Smith, P.E.L. and Mortensen, P., eds., *The Hilly Flanks and Beyond: Essays on the Prehistory of Southwestern Asia presented to Robert J. Braidwood, November 15, 1982*, Chicago: SAOC 36, 315–31.

(1984) 'Analysis of structure and design in prehistoric ceramics', *World Archaeology* 15, 326–47.

(1985) 'The organization of Susiana society: periodization of site distributions', *Paléorient* 11, 21–4.

(1987), 'Archaeology of the village period', in Hole, F., ed., *The Archaeology of Western Iran: Settlement and Society from Prehistory to the Islamic conquest*, Washington DC and London: Smithsonian Institution Press, 29–78.

(1989), 'Patterns of burial in the fifth millennium', in Henrickson, E.F. and Thuesen, I., eds., *Upon this Foundation – the 'Ubaid Reconsidered*, Copenhagen: CNIP 10, 149–80.

(1990), 'Cemetery or mass grave? Reflections on Susa I', *MJP*, 1–13.

Hole, F., Flannery, K.V., and Neely, J.A. (1969), *Prehistory and Human Ecology of the Deh Luran Plain*, Ann Arbor: Memoirs of the Museum of Anthropology of the University of Michigan 1.

Holladay, W.L. (1989), *Jeremiah 2: a Commentary on the Book of the Prophet Jeremiah Chapters 26–52*, Minneapolis: Fortress Press.

Holleaux, M. (1942), 'La mort d'Antiochos IV Epiphanès', *Études d'épigraphie et d'histoire grecques III*, Paris: De Boccard, 255–79.

Honigmann, E., and Maricq, A. (1953), *Recherches sur les* Res Gestae Divi Saporis, Brussels: Memoires de l'Académie Royale de Belgique, Classe des Lettres et des Sciences Morales et Politiques 47/4.

Houghton, A. (1983), *Coins of the Seleucid Empire from the Collection of Arthur Houghton*, New York: Ancient Coins in North American Collections 4.

Hrouda, B. (1976), *Sarpol-i Zohab*, Berlin: Iranische Denkmäler 7/II/C.

(1994), 'Der elamische Streitwagen', *CDR*, 53–7.

Hubbard, R. (1990), 'Archaeobotany of Abdul Hosein', in Pullar, J., *Tepe Abdul Hosein: a Neolithic site in Western Iran, Excavations 1978*, Oxford: BAR International Series 563, 217–21.

Huff, D. (1984), 'Das Felsrelief von Qir (Fars)', *AMI* 17, 221–47.

(1994), 'Iranische Steinbruchtechniken', in Wartke, R.-B., ed., *Handwerk und Technologie im Alten Orient: Ein Beitrag zur Geschichte der Technik im Altertum*, Mainz: Von Zabern, 31–6.

Hummel, K. (1963), 'Die Anfänge der iranischen Hochschule Gundischapur in der Spätantike', *Tübinger Forschungen* 9, 1–4.

(1983), 'Die medizinische Akademie von Gundischapur', *Iranzamin* 2, 54–61.

Hüsing, G. (1908), 'Der Zagros und seine Völker: Eine archäologisch-ethnographische Skizze', *AO* 9/3–4, 3–66.

Hyldahl, N. (1990), 'The Maccabean Rebellion and the question of "Hellenization"', in Bilde, P., Engberg-Pedersen, T., Hannestad, L. and Zahle, J., eds., *Religion and Religious Practice in the Seleucid Kingdom*, Aarhus: Studies in Hellenistic Civilization 1, pp. 188–203.

Ingham, B. (1994), 'Ethno-linguistic links between southern Iraq and Khuzistan', in McLachlan, K., ed., *The Boundaries of Modern Iran*, London: UCL Press, 93–100.

Intelligence Department (1918), *Geology of Mesopotamia and its Borderlands*, London: H.M. Stationery Office, Admiralty Naval Staff I.D. 1177.

Jacobs, B. (1994), *Die Satrapienverwaltung im Perserreich zur Zeit Darius' III.*, Wiesbaden: Beihefte zum TAVO B 87.

Jacobs, L. (1980), *Darvazeh Tepe and the Iranian Highlands in the Second Millennium BC*, Ann Arbor: University Microfilms.

(1994), 'Darvaza Tepe', *EnIr* 7, 71–2.

Jacobsen, T. (1939), *The Sumerian King List*, Chicago: AS 11.

(1953), 'The myth of Inanna and Bilulu', *JNES* 12, 160–187.

(1970), 'The reign of Ibbī-Suen', in Moran, W.L., ed., *Toward the Image of Tammuz and Other Essays on Mesopotamian History and Culture*, Cambridge: Harvard University Press, 173–186.

(1982), *Salinity and irrigation agriculture in antiquity. Diyala basin archaeological projects: report on essential results, 1957–1958*. Malibu: *BiMes* 14.

James, T.G.H. (1991), 'Egypt: the Twenty-Fifth and Twenty-Sixth Dynasties', *CAH* III/2, 677–747.

Jean, C.-F. (1922), 'L'Élam sous la dynastie d'Ur: Les indemnités allouées aux "chargés de mission" des rois d'Ur', *RA* 19, 1–44.

Jenkins, G.K. (1978), 'Coins', in Stronach, D., Pasargadae, Oxford: Clarendon Press, 185–98.

Jéquier, G. (1905), 'Fouilles de Suse de 1899 à 1902', *MDP* 7, 9–41.

Jeyes, U. (1980), 'The act of extispicy in ancient Mesopotamia: an outline', *Assyriological Miscellanies* 1, 13–32.

Joannès, F. (1988), '*ig-gur^{ki} = Suse', *NABU*, 1.

(1990), 'Textes babyloniens de Suse d'époque achéménide', *MJP*, 173–80.

(1991), 'L'étain, de l'Elam à Mari', *MHEOP* 1, 68–76.

Johnson, G.A. (1973), *Local Exchange and Early State Development in Southwestern Iran*, Ann Arbor: Anthropological Papers of the Museum of Anthropology 51.

(1988/9), 'Late Uruk in greater Mesopotamia: Expansion or collapse?', *Origini* 14, 595–613.

Jones, T.B. and Snyder, J.W. (1961), *Sumerian Economic Texts from the Third Ur Dynasty*, Minneapolis: University of Minnesota Press.

Kantor, H.J. (1977), 'The Elamite cup from Chogha Mish', *Iran* 15, 11–14.

Kantor, H.J. and Delougaz, P. (1996), *Choga Mish, Vol. 1, The first five seasons, 1961–1971*, Chicago: OIP 101.

Kawase, T. (1986), 'Kapnuški in the Persepolis fortification texts', *FHE*, 263–75.

Kent, R.G. (1953), *Old Persian: Grammar, Texts, Lexicon*, New Haven: AOS 33.

Kervran, M. (1985), 'Transformations de la ville de Suse et de son économie de l'époque sasanide à l'époque abbaside', *Paléorient* 11, 91–100.

Kervran, M., Stronach, D., Vallat, F. and Yoyotte, J. (1972), 'Une statue de Darius découverte à Suse', *JA* 260, 235–66.

Kettenhofen, E. (1982), *Die römisch-persischen Kriege des 3.Jh. n. Chr. nach der Inschrift Šāhpuhrs I. an der Ka'be-ye Zartošt (ŠKZ)*, Wiesbaden: Beihefte zum TAVO B 55.

 (1995), *Tirdad und die Inschrift von Paikuli: Kritik der Quellen zur Geschichte Armeniens im späten 3. und frühen 4. Jh. n. Chr.*, Wiesbaden: Reichert.

Keylor, W.R. (1975), *Academy and Community: the Foundation of the French Historical Profession*, Cambridge: Harvard University Press.

King, L.W., and Campbell Thompson, R. (1907), *The sculptures and inscription of Darius the Great on the rock of Behistûn in Persia*, London: British Museum.

Kingsley, B.M. (1981), 'The cap that survived Alexander', *AJA* 85, 39–46.

Kinneir, J.M. (1813), *A Geographical Memoir of the Persian Empire*, London: John Murray.

Kirkby, M.J. (1977), 'Land and water resources of the Deh Luran and Khuzistan plains', in Hole, F. ed., *Studies in the Archaeological History of the Deh Luran Plain: the Excavation of Chagha Sefid*, Ann Arbor: Memoirs of the Museum of Anthropology 9, 251–88.

Kiyani, M.Y. (1982), *Parthian Sites in Hyrcania: the Gurgan Plain*, Berlin: *AMI* Ergänzungsband 9.

Kleiss, W. (1995), 'Qal'eh Tall-e Kabud, eine eisenzeitliche Befestigung südlich von Shiraz', in Finkbeiner, U., Dittmann, R. and Hauptmann, H., eds., *Beiträge zur Kulturgeschichte Vorderasiens: Festschrift für Rainer Michael Boehmer*, Mainz: Von Zabern, 289–93.

Klugkist, A. (1986), 'The origin of the Mandaic script', in Vanstiphout, H.L.J., Jongeling, K., Leemhuis, F. and Reinink, G.J., eds., *Scripta Signa Vocis: Studies about Scripts, Scriptures and Languages in the Near East, Presented to J.H. Hospers by his Pupils, Colleagues, and Friends*, Groningen: Forsten, 111–20.

Knapp, A.B. (1992), ed., *Archaeology, Annales and Ethnohistory*, Cambridge: University Press.

Koch, H. (1977), *Die religiösen Verhältnisse der Dareioszeit: Untersuchungen an Hand der elamischen Persepolistäfelchen*, Wiesbaden: Göttinger Orientforschung III.4.

 (1986), 'Die achämenidische Poststrasse von Persepolis nach Susa', *AMI* 19, 33–147.

 (1989), 'Tribut und Abgaben in Persis und Elymais', in Briant, P. and Herrenschmidt, C., eds., *Le tribut dans l'empire perse*, Paris: Travaux de l'Institut d'Études Iraniennes de l'Université de la Sorbonne Nouvelle 13, 121–28.

 (1990), *Verwaltung und Wirtschaft im persischen Kernland zur Zeit der Achämeniden*, Wiesbaden: Beihefte zum TAVO Reihe B 89.

 (1991), 'Zu Religion und Kulten im achämenidischen Kernland', in Kellens, J., ed., *La religion iranienne à l'époque achéménide*, Gent: *IrAnt* Supplement 5, 87–109.

 (1993), *Achämeniden-Studien*, Wiesbaden: Harrassowitz.

 (1996), review of Vallat, F., *Les noms géographiques des sources suso-élamites*, *BiOr* 53, 144–50.

 (1997), review of Malbran-Labat, *Les inscriptions royales de Suse*, *Or* 66, 109–10.

König, F.W. (1931), 'Geschichte Elams', *AO* 29/4, 1–38.

 (1938), 'Elam (Geschichte)', *RlA* 2, 324–38.

 (1957–1971), 'Geschwisterehe in Elam', *RlA*: 3, 224–31.

 (1965), *Die elamischen Königsinschriften*, Graz: *AfO* Beiheft 16.

Koschaker, P. (1931), 'Über einige griechische Rechtsurkunden aus den östlichen Randgebieten des Hellenismus', *Abhandlungen der Sächsischen Akademie* 42, 68–83.

(1933), 'Fratriarchat, Hausgemeinschaft und Mutterrecht in Keilschriftrechten', *ZA* 41, 1–89.

Kuhrt, A. (1995), *The Ancient Near East, c. 3000–330 BC*, vol. 1, London and New York: Routledge History of the Ancient World.

Kuhrt, A., and Sherwin-White, S. (1987), 'Xerxes, destruction of Babylonian temples', *AH* 2, 69–78.

Kutscher, R. (1979), 'A note on the early careers of Zariqum and Šamši-illat', *RA* 73, 81–2.

(1989), *The Brockmon Tablets at the University of Haifa: the Royal Inscriptions*, Haifa: Haifa University Press.

Labat, R. (1975), 'Elam, c. 1600–1200 BC', *CAH* II/2³, 482–506.

Labourt, J. (1904), *Le christianisme dans l'empire perse sous la dynastie sassanide 224–632*, Paris: Victor Lecoffre.

Lackenbacher, S. (1994), 'Les bénédictions dans les lettres de Suse', *NABU*, 54.

Læssøe, J. (1963), *People of Ancient Assyria: their Inscriptions and Correspondence*, London: Routledge and Kegan Paul.

Lamberg-Karlovsky, C.C. (1978), 'The Proto-Elamites on the Iranian Plateau', *Antiquity* 52, 114–20.

(1988), 'The "Intercultural Style" carved vessels', *IrAnt* 23, 45–95.

(1996a), *Beyond the Tigris and Euphrates: Bronze Age Civilizations*, Jerusalem: Beer-Sheva 9.

(1996b), 'The archaeological evidence for international commerce: Public and/or private enterprise in Mesopotamia?', in Hudson, M. and Levine, B.A., eds., *Privatization in the Ancient Near East and Classical World*, Cambridge: Peabody Museum Bulletin 5, 73–108.

Lambert, M. (1967), 'Shutruk-Nahunte et Shutur-Nahunte', *Syria* 44, 47–51.

(1971), 'Investiture de fonctionnaires en Elam', *JA* 259, 217–21.

(1972), 'Hutélutush-Inshushinak et le pays d'Anzan', *RA* 66, 61–76.

(1976), 'Tablette de Suse avec cachet du Golfe', *RA* 70, 71–2.

(1979), 'Le prince de Suse Ilishmani et l'Elam, de Naramsin à Ibisîn', *JA* 267, 11–40.

Lambert, W.G. (1979), 'Near Eastern seals in the Gulbenkian Museum of Oriental Art, University of Durham', *Iraq* 41, 1–46.

(1991), 'The Akkadianization of Susiana under the Sukkalmahs', *MHEOP* 1, 53–7.

(1992), 'Further notes on a seal of Ebarat', *RA* 86, 85–6.

(1994), 'The fall of the Cassite dynasty to the Elamites: an historical epic', *CDR*, 67–72.

Lamprc, G. (1900), 'Travaux de l'hiver, 1897–1898, tranchées nos. 7 et 7a', *MDP* 1, 100–10.

Landsberger, B. (1933), review of Unger, E., *Babylon die heilige Stadt nach der Beschreibung der Babylonier*, *ZA* 41, 255–299.

Langdon, S. (1905/6), 'Les inscriptions de Nebuchadnezzar trouvées à Suse', *ZA* 29, 142–147.

(1912), *Die neubabylonischen Königsinschriften*, Leipzig: VAB 4.

Langsdorff, A. and McCown, D.E. (1942), *Tall-i-Bakun A: Season of 1932*, Chicago: OIP 59.

Larsen, J.O. and Rhodes, P.J. (1996), 'Federal states', *Oxford Classical Dictionary*³, 591–2.

Lassere, F. (1979), 'Strabon', *KP* 5, 381–5.

Laufer, B. (1919), *Sino-Iranica: Chinese Contributions to the History of Civilization in Ancient Iran*, Chicago: Field Museum of Natural History Publication 201, Anthropological Series, Vol. 15:3.

Layard, A.H. (1842), 'Ancient sites among the Baktiyari mountains, with remarks on the rivers of Susiana, and the site of Susa, by Professor Long, V.P.', *JRGS* 12, 102–9.

(1846), 'A description of the province of Khúzistán', *JRGS* 16, 1–105.

(1882), *Nineveh and Babylon: a Narrative of a Second Expedition to Assyria during the Years 1849, 1850, and 1851*, London: John Murray.

LeBrun, A. (1978), 'Suse, chantier "Acropole 1"', *Paléorient* 4, 177–92.

(1985), 'Le niveau 18 de l'acropole de Suse. Mémoire d'argile, mémoire du temps', *Paléorient* 11, 31–6.

(1990), 'Les documents économiques du niveau 18 de l'Acrople de Suse et leurs modes de groupement', *MJP*, 61–6.

LeBrun, A., and Vallat, F. (1978), 'L'origine de l'écriture à Suse', *Cahiers de la DAFI* 8, 11–59.

Lecoq, P. (1997), *Les inscriptions de la Perse achéménide*, Paris: Gallimard.

Legrain, L. (1913), 'Tablettes de comptabilité, etc. de l'époque de la dynastie d'Agadê', *MDP* 14, 62–126.

Lehmann, C.F. (1892), 'Noch einmal Kassû: Κίσσιοι, nicht Κοσσαῖοι', *ZA* 7, 328–34.

Leriche, P. (1977), 'Problèmes de la guerre en Iran et en Asie Centrale dans l'empire perse et à l'époque hellénistique', in Deshayes, J., ed., *Le Plateau Iranien et l'Asie Centrale des origines à la conquête islamique*, Paris: Editions du CNRS, 297–312.

LeRider, G. (1959), 'Monnaies de Characène', *Syria* 36, 229–53.

(1965a), *Suse sous les Séleucides et les Parthes*, Paris: MDP 38.

(1965b), 'Un atelier monétaire séleucide dans la province de la Mer Érythrée?', *RN*, 36–43.

(1978), 'Deux nouveaux tétradrachmes frappés à Suse', *RN* 20, 33–7.

LeStrange, G. (1905), *The Lands of the Eastern Caliphate*, Cambridge: University Press.

Levine, L. (1972), *Two Neo-Assyrian Stelae from Iran*, Toronto: Royal Ontario Museum Art and Archaeology Occasional Paper 23.

(1973), 'Geographical studies in the Neo-Assyrian Zagros I', *Iran* 11, 1–27.

(1974), 'Geographical studies in the Neo-Assyrian Zagros II', *Iran* 12, 99–124.

(1982), 'Sennacherib's southern front: 704–689 BC', *JCS* 34, 28–58.

Levine, L. and Young, T.C., Jr. (1987), 'A summary of the ceramic assemblages of the central western Zagros from the middle Neolithic to the late third millennium BC', in Huot, J.-L., ed., *Préhistoire de la Mésopotamie*, Paris: Editions du CNRS, 15–53.

Lindemeyer, E. and Martin, L. (1993), *Uruk Kleinfunde III. Kleinfunde im Vorderasiatischen Museum zu Berlin: Steingefäße und Asphalt, Farbreste, Fritte, Glas, Holz, Knochen/Elfenbein, Muschel/Perlmutt/Schnecke*, Mainz: Ausgrabungen in Uruk-Warka Endberichte 9.

Littauer, M.A. and Crouwel, J.H. (1979), *Wheeled Vehicles and Ridden Animals in the Ancient Near East*, Leiden/Cologne: HdO 7/1.

(1989), 'Metal wheel tyres from the ancient Near East', *AIO*, 111–26.

Littauer, M.A., Crouwel, J.H. and Hauptmann, H. (1991), 'Ein spätbronzezeitliches Speichenrad vom Lidar Höyük in der Südost-Türkei', *Archäologischer Anzeiger*, 349–58.

Liverani, M. (1995), 'The Medes at Esarhaddon's court', *JCS* 47, 57–62.

(1993), ed., *Akkad, the First World Empire: Structure, Ideology, Traditions*, Padua: Sargon.

Loftus, W.K. (1856), 'On the excavations undertaken at the ruins of Susa in 1851–52', *Transactions of the Royal Society of Literature* 5, 422–53.

Luckenbill, D.D. (1924), *The Annals of Sennacherib*, Chicago: OIP 2.

Lukonin, V.G. (1967), *Persia II*, Geneva/Paris/Munich: Nagel.

Luschey, H. (1968), 'Studien zu dem Darius-Relief von Bisutun', *AMI* 1, 63–94.

(1974), 'Bisutun: Geschichte und Forschungsgeschichte', *Archäologischer Anzeiger* 89, 114–49.

(1990), 'Bisotun ii. Archeology', *EnIr* 4, 291–9.

(1996), 'Die seleukidische Heraklesfigur', in Kleiss, W. and Calmeyer, P., eds., *Bisutun: Ausgrabungen und Forschungen in den Jahren 1963–1967*, Berlin: Teheraner Forschungen 7, 59–60.

Lyon, B. (1987), 'Marc Bloch: historian', *French Historical Studies* 15, 195–207.

Mahboubian, H. (1995), *Treasures of the Mountains: the Art of the Medes*, London: self-publication.

Malbran-Labat, F. (1975), 'Nabû-bêl-šumâte, prince du Pays-de-la-Mer', *JA* 263, 7–37.

(1982), *L'armée et l'organisation militaire de l'Assyrie d'après les lettres des Sargonides trouvées à Ninive*, Paris: École Pratique des Hautes Études, Hautes Études Orientales 19.

(1994), *La version akkadienne de l'inscription trilingue de Darius à Behistun*, Rome: Documenta Asiana 1.

(1995), *Les inscriptions royales de Suse: Briques de l'époque paléo-élamite à l'Empire néo-élamite*, Paris: Éditions de la Réunion des musées nationaux.

Mallowan, M.E.L. (1970), 'Elamite problems', *Proceedings of the British Academy* 55, 255–92.

Mander, P. (1986), *Il pantheon di Abu-Salabikh: Contributo allo studio del pantheon sumerico arcaico*, Naples: Istituto Universitario Orientale, Dipartimento di Studi Asiatici Series Minor 26,.

Maricq, A. (1958), 'Classica et orientalia 5. Res gestae divi saporis', *Syria* 35, 295–360.

Marquart, J. (1901), *Ērānšahr nach der Geographie des Ps. Moses Xorenac'i*, Berlin: Abhandlungen der königlichen Gesellschaft der Wissenschaften zu Göttingen, philosophische-historische Klasse, NF Bd. iii/2.

(1931), *A Catalogue of the Provincial Capitals of Ērānshahr*, Rome: Analecta Orientalia 3.

Marschner, R.-F., Duffy, L.J. and Wright, H.T. (1978), 'Asphalts from ancient town sites in southwestern Iran', *Paléorient* 4, 97–112.

Marsden, E.W. (1969), *Greek and Roman Artillery: Historical Development*, Oxford: Clarendon Press.

Martinez-Sève, L. (1996), 'Une statuette romaine trouvée à Suse et la chronologie du Donjon', *Collectanea*, 171–80.

Mathiesen, H.E. (1992), *Sculpture in the Parthian Empire: a Study in Chronology*, 2 vols. Aarhus: Aarhus University Press.

Mathis, F. (1997), '1,000 years of Austria and Austrian identity: founding myths', in Bischof, G. and Pelinka, A., eds., *Austrian Historical Memory and National Identity*, New Brunswick/London: Contemporary Austrian Studies 5, 20–31.

Matthews, D.M. (1992), *The Kassite Glyptic of Nippur*, Freiburg and Göttingen: Universitätsverlag and Vandenhoeck and Ruprecht.

Mayer, W. (1995), *Politik und Kriegskunst der Assyrer*, Münster: Abhandlungen zur Literatur Alt-Syrien-Palästinas und Mesopotamiens 9.

Mayrhofer, M. (1973), *Onomastica Persepolitana: Das altiranische Namengut der Persepolis-Täfelchen*, Vienna: Österreichische Akademie der Wissenschaften, philosophische-historische Klasse Sitzungsberichte 286.

McClellan, A. (1994), *Inventing the Louvre: Art, Politics, and the Origins of the Modern Museum in Eighteenth-Century Paris*, Cambridge: University Press.

McEwan, G.J.P. (1986), 'A Parthian campaign against Elymais in 77 BC', *Iran* 24, 91–4.

Mecquenem, R. de (1911), 'Constructions élamites du tell de l'Acropole de Suse', *MDP* 12, 65–78. –

(1934), 'Fouilles de Suse, 1929–1933', *MDP* 25, 177–237.

(1943), 'Fouilles de Suse, 1933–1939', *MDP* 29, 3–161.

(1947), 'Contribution à l'étude du palais achéménide de Suse', *MDP* 30, 1–119.

(1949), 'Épigraphie proto-élamite', *MDP* 31, 5–150.

(1953), 'Têtes de cannes susiennes en métal', *RA* 47, 79–82.

(1980), 'Les fouilleurs de Suse', *IrAnt* 15, 1–48.

Meder, O. (1979), *Klimaökologie und Siedlungsgang auf dem Hochland von Iran in vor- und frühgeschichtlicher Zeit*, Marburg: Marburger Geographische Schriften 80.

Meyer, L. de (1966), 'Een Tilmoeniet te Suse', *Orientalia Gandensia* 3, 115–17.

(1986), 'Les archives d'Igibuni', *FHE*, 75–7.

Michalowski, P. (1978), 'Foreign tribute to Sumer during the Ur III period', *ZA* 68, 34–49.

(1989), *The Lamentation over the Destruction of Sumer and Ur*, Winona Lake: Eisenbrauns.

Milburn, W. (1813), *Oriental Commerce; Containing a Geographical Description of the*

Principal Places in the East Indies, China, and Japan, with their Produce, Manufactures, and Trade, including the Coasting or Country Trade from Port to Port; also the Rise and Progress of the Trade of the Various European Nations with the Eastern World, particularly that of the English East India Company, from the Discovery of the Passage round the Cape of Good Hope to the Present Period; with an Account of the Company's Establishments, Revenues, Debts, Assets, &c. at Home and Abroad, Vol. 1, London: Black, Parry and Co.

Millard, A.R. (1964), 'Another Babylonian Chronicle text', *Iraq* 26, 14–35.

Miller, N.F. (1981), 'The plant remains', in Wright, H.T., *An Early Town on the Deh Luran plain: Excavations at Tepe Farukhabad*, Ann Arbor: Memoirs of the Museum of Anthropology, University of Michigan, No. 13, 227–32.

(1984), 'The interpretation of some carbonized cereal remains as remnants of dung cake fuel', *Bulletin on Sumerian Agriculture* 1, 45–7.

(1985), 'Paleoethnobotanical evidence for deforestation in ancient Iran: a case study of urban Malyan', *Journal of Ethnobiology* 5, 1–19.

(1990a), 'Clearing land for farmland and fuel: archaeobotanical studies of the ancient Near East', in Miller, N.F., ed., *Economy and Settlement in the Near East: Analyses of Ancient Sites and Materials*, Philadelphia: MASCA Research Papers in Science and Archaeology Suppl. to Vol. 7, 71–8.

(1990b), 'Archaeobotanical perspectives on the rural-urban connection', in Miller, N.F., ed., *Economy and Settlement in the Near East: Analyses of Ancient Sites and Materials*, Philadelphia: MASCA Research Papers in Science and Archaeology Suppl. to Vol. 7, 79–83.

Miller, N.F. and Smart, T.L. (1984), 'Intentional burning of dung as fuel: A mechanism for the incorporation of charred seeds into the archeological record', *Journal of Ethnobiology* 4, 15–28.

Miroschedji, P. de (1973), 'Vases et objets en stéatite susiens du Musée du Louvre', *Cahiers de la DAFI* 3, 9–79.

(1978), 'Stratigraphie de la période néo-élamite à Suse', *Paléorient* 4, 213–27.

(1981a), 'Le dieu élamite au serpent et aux eaux jaillissantes', *IrAnt* 16, 1–25.

(1981b), 'Fouilles du chantier Ville Royale II à Suse (1975–1977). I. Niveaux élamites', *Cahiers de la DAFI* 12, 9–136.

(1981c), 'Observations dans les couches néo-élamites au nord-ouest du tell de la Ville Royale à Suse', *Cahiers de la DAFI* 12, 143–67.

(1982), 'Notes sur la glyptique de la fin de l'Elam', *RA* 76, 51–63.

(1985), 'La fin du royaume de l'Anšan et de Suse et la naissance de l'empire perse', *ZA* 75, 265–306.

(1986), 'La localisation de Madaktu et l'organisation politique de l'Elam à l'époque Neo-Elamite', *FHE*, 209–25.

(1987), 'Fouilles du chantier Ville Royale II à Suse (1975–1977) II. Niveaux d'époques achéménide, parthe et islamique', *Cahiers de la DAFI* 15, 11–143.

(1990), 'La fin de l'Elam: essai d'analyse et d'interprétation', *IrAnt* 25, 47–95.

Momigliano, A. (1975), *Alien Wisdom: the Limits of Hellenization*, Cambridge: University Press.

Montagne, C. and Grillot-Susini, F. (1996), 'Les inscriptions royales de Suse, Musée du Louvre (R.M.N., Paris, 1995), par Florence Malbran-Labat', *NABU*, 33.

Moorey, P.R.S. (1982), 'Archaeology and pre-Achaemenid metalworking in Iran: a fifteen year retrospective', *Iran* 20, 81–101.

Moortgat, A. (1969), *The Art of Ancient Mesopotamia*, London and New York: Phaidon.

Morgan, J. de (1900), 'Recherches archéologiques', *MDP* 1.

(1905), 'Recherches archéologiques', *MDP* 7.

Mørkholm, O. (1965), 'A Greek coin hoard from Susiana', *Acta Archaeologica* 36, 127–56.

(1966), *Antiochus IV of Syria*, Copenhagen: Classica et Mediaevalia Dissertationes 8.

Mousavi, A. (1990), 'Tépé Horreeye, le bit akitu de Tchogha Zanbil?', *MJP*, 143–5.

(1996), 'Early archaeological adventures and methodological problems in Iranian archaeology: the evidence from Susa', *IrAnt* 31, 1–16.

Muir, E. (1991), 'Introduction: observing trifles', in Muir, E. and Ruggiero, G., eds., *Microhistory and the Lost Peoples of Europe: Selections from Quaderni Storici*, Baltimore/London: Johns Hopkins, vii–xxviii.

Müller, B. (1994), ed., *Marc Bloch, Lucien Febvre et les* Annales d'Histoire Économique et Sociale, *Correspondance, Tome Premier 1928–1933*, Paris: Fayard.

Müller, G.G.W. (1994), *Studien zur Siedlungsgeographie und Bevölkerung des mittleren Osttigrisgebietes*, Heidelberg: HSAO 7.

Nash, M. (1989), *The Cauldron of Ethnicity in the Modern World*, Chicago/London: University of Chicago Press.

Nassouhi, E. (1924–5), 'Prisme d'Assurbânipal daté de sa trentième année, provenant du temple de Gula à Babylone', *Archiv für Keilschriftforschung* 2, 97–106.

Neely, J.A. (1974), 'Sassanian and early Islamic water-control and irrigation systems on the Deh Luran plain, Iran', in Downing, T.E. and Gibson, McG., eds., *Irrigation's Impact on Society*, Tucson: Anthropological Papers of the University of Arizona 25, pp. 21–42

Neely, J.A. and Wright, H.T. (1994), *Early Settlement and Irrigation on the Deh Luran Plain: Village and Early State Societies in Southwestern Iran*, Ann Arbor: University of Michigan Museum of Anthropology Technical Report 26.

Negahban, E.O. (1990), 'The Haft Tepe bronze plaque: an example of Middle Elamite art', *MJP*, 137–42.

(1991), *Excavations at Haft Tepe*, Iran, Philadelphia: University Museum Monograph 70.

(1994), 'The artist's workshop of Haft Tepe', *CDR*, 31–41.

Neubauer, A. (1868), *La géographie du Talmud*, Paris: Michel Lévy Frères.

Neumann, H. (1992), 'Bemerkungen zum Problem der Fremdarbeit in Mesopotamien (3. Jahrtausend v.u.Z.)', *AoF* 19, 266–75.

Newell, E.T. (1938), *The Coinage of the Eastern Seleucid Mints from Seleucus I to Antiochus III*, New York: Numismatic Studies 1.

Nicholas, I.M. (1990), *The Proto-Elamite Settlement at TUV*, Philadelphia: University Museum Monograph 69 [=Malyan Excavation Reports 1].

Nickerson, J. (1977), 'Malyan wall paintings', *Expedition* 19, 2–6.

Nickerson, J.L. (1991), 'Investigating intrasite variability at Tal-e Malyan (Anshan), Iran', *IrAnt* 26, 1–38.

Nicol, M. (1970), 'Excavations at Darvazeh Tepe: a preliminary report', *Bastan chenassi va honar-e Iran* 5, 19–22.

(1971), 'Darvazeh Tepe', *Iran* 9, 168–9.

Nissen, H.J. (1972), 'The city wall of Uruk', in Ucko, P.J., Tringham, R. and Dimbleby, G.W., eds., *Man, Settlement and Urbanism*, London: Duckworth, 794–8.

(1985a), 'Problems of the Uruk-period in Susiana, viewed from Uruk', *Paléorient* 11, 39–40.

(1985b), 'The emergence of writing in the ancient Near East', *Interdisciplinary Science Reviews* 10, 349–61.

(1986), 'The development of writing and glyptic art', in Finkbeiner, U. and Röllig, W., eds., *Ğamdat Naṣr: Period or Regional Style?*, Wiesbaden: TAVO Beiheft B 62, 316–31.

(1993), 'The Early Uruk period – a sketch', in Frangipane, M., Hauptmann, H., Liverani, M., Matthiae, P., and Mellink, M., eds., *Between the Rivers and Over the Mountains: Archaeologica anatolica et mesopotamica Alba Palmieri dedicata*, Rome: University of Rome 'La Sapienza', 123–31.

Nissen, H.J. Damerow, P., and Englund, R.K. (1990), *Frühe Schrift und Techniken der Writschaftsverwaltung im alten Vorderen Orient*, Bad Oldesloe: Franzbecker.

Nodelman, S.A. (1960), 'A preliminary history of Characene', *Berytus* 13, 83–122.

Nöldeke, T. (1874), 'Griechische Namen Susiana's', *Nachrichten von der Königl. Ges. der Wiss., und der G.A. Universität zu Göttingen* 8, 173–97.

(1879), *Geschichte der Perser und Araber zur Zeit der Sasaniden, aus der arabischen Chronik des Tabari*, Leiden: Brill.

(1893), 'Die von Guidi herausgegebene syrische Chronik', *Sitzungsberichte der Kaiserlichen Akademie der Wissenschaften, philosophische-historische Cl.* 128, 1–48.

Nunn, A. (1988), *Die Wandmalerei und der glasierte Wandschmuck im alten Orient*, Leiden/Cologne: HdO 7/1/2/6.

Nylander, C. (1970), *Ionians in Pasargadae: Studies in Old Persian architecture*, Uppsala: Acta Universitatis Upsaliensis 1.

(1974), 'Anatolians in Susa – and Persepolis (?)', *AcIr* 6 [= *Hommages et Opera Minora. Monumentum H.S. Nyberg III*], 317–23.

Oates, D. and Oates, J. (1994), 'Tell Brak: a stratigraphic summary, 1976–1993', *Iraq* 56, 167–76.

Oates, J. (1991), 'The fall of Assyria (635–609 BC)', *CAH* 3/2, 162–93.

(1993), 'Trade and power in the fifth and fourth millennia BC: new evidence from northern Mesopotamia', *World Archaeology* 24, 403–22.

Obermeyer, J. (1929), *Die Landschaft Babylonien im Zeitalter des Talmuds und des Gaonats: Geographie und Geschichte nach talmudischen, arabischen und anderen Quellen*, Frankfurt: Schriften der Gesellschaft zur Förderung der Wissenschaft des Judentums 30.

Oded, B. (1979), *Mass Deportations and Deportees in the Neo-Assyrian Empire*, Wiesbaden: Ludwig Reichert.

Oelsner, J. (1964), 'Ein Beitrag zur keilschriftlichen Königstitulaturen in hellenistischer Zeit', *ZA* 56, 262–74.

Olmstead, A.T. (1923), *History of Assyria*, Chicago and London: University of Chicago.

(1937), 'Cuneiform texts and Hellenistic chronology', *Classical Philology* 32, 1–14.

Oppenheimer, A. (1983), *Babylonia Judaica in the Talmudic Period*, Wiesbaden: Beihefte zum TAVO B 47.

Östör, Á. (1993), *Vessels of Time: an Essay on Temporal Change and Social Transformation*, Delhi: Oxford University Press.

Overlaet, B. (1997), 'A report on the 1952 and 1954/55 soundings at Tall-i Taimuran (Fars), Iran: a file-excavation at the Royal Museums of Art and History, Brussels', *IrAnt* 32, 1–51.

(1993), ed., *Hofkunst van de Sassanieden*, Brussels: Koninklijke Musea voor Kunst en Geschiedenis.

Pallis, S.A. (1954), 'Early exploration in Mesopotamia', *Det Kongelige Danske Videnskabernes Selskab, hist.-fil. Meddelelser* 33, 1–58.

Paper, H. (1954), 'Note préliminaire sur la date des trois tablettes élamites de Suse', in Ghirshman, R., *Village perse-achéménide*, Paris: MDP 36, 79–82.

Parpola, S. (1972), 'A letter from Šamaš-šumu-ukin to Esarhaddon', *Iraq* 34, 21–34.

(1980), 'The murderer of Sennacherib', in Alster, B., ed., *Death in Mesopotamia*, Copenhagen: Mesopotamia 8, 171–82.

Payne, S. (1991), 'Early Holocene equids from Tall-i-Mushki (Iran) and Can Hassan III (Turkey)', in Meadow, R.H. and Uerpmann, H.-P., eds., *Equids in the Ancient World*, vol. 2, Wiesbaden: Beihefte zum TAVO A 19/2, 132–77.

Peeters, P. (1924), 'S. Démétrianus, évêque d'Antioche?', *Analecta Bollandiana* 42, 288–314.

Perrot, J. (1971), 'Recherches archéologiques à Suse et en Susiane en 1969 et en 1970', *Syria* 48, 21–51.

(1981), 'L'architecture militaire et palatiale des Achéménides à Suse', in *150 Jahre Deutsches Archäologisches Institut 1829–1979*, Mainz: von Zabern, 79–94.

(1985), 'Suse à la période achéménide', *Paléorient* 11, 67–9.

Petit, T. (1990), *Satrapes et satrapies dans l'empire achéménide de Cyrus le Grand à Xerxès Ier*, Paris: Bibliothèque de la Faculté de Philosophie et Lettres de l'Université de Liège 254.

Pétrequin, G. (1990), 'Les vases k/guna(n)gi et la chronologie élamite', *NABU*, 16.

Pettinato, G. (1982), 'Il tesoro del nemico Elamita ovvero il bottino della guerra contro Anšan di Šulgi', *OrAnt* 20, 49–72.

Pézard, M. and Pottier, E. (1926), *Catalogue des Antiquités de la Susiane (Mission J. de Morgan)*, Paris: Musées Nationaux.

Piacentini, V.F. (1984), 'La presa di potere sassanide sul Golfo Persico tra leggenda e realtà', *Clio* 20, 173–210.

(1985), 'Ardashir i Papakan and the wars against the Arabs: working hypothesis on the Sasanian hold of the Gulf', *Proceedings of the Seminar for Arabian Studies* 15, 57–77.

Pickett, T.H. (1996), *Inventing Nations: Justifications of Authority in the Modern World*, Westport: Greenwood.

Piepkorn, A.C. (1933), *Historical Prism Inscriptions of Ashurbanipal I: Editions E, B_{1-5}, D, and K*, Chicago: University of Chicago Press.

Pigott, V.C. (1984), 'Ahan', *EnIr* 1, 624–33.

Pillet, M.L. (1914), *Le palais de Darius Ier à Suse*, Paris: Geuthner.

Pinches, T.G. (1890), 'A Babylonian tablet dated in the reign of Aspasine', *Babylonian and Oriental Record* 4, 131–5.

Pintore, F. (1978), *Il matrimonio interdinastico nel Vicino Oriente durante i secoli XV-XIII*, Rome: Orientis Antiqui Collectio 14.

Pittman, H. (1994), *The Glazed Steatite Glyptic Style: the Structure and Function of an Image System in the Administration of Protoliterate Mesopotamia*, Berlin: *BBVO* 16.

Pohanka, R. (1986), *Burgen und Heiligtümer in Laristan, Südiran: Ein Surveybericht*, Vienna: Österreichische Akademie der Wissenschaften, philosophische-historische Klasse Sitzungsberichte 466.

Pollock, S. (1989), 'Power politics in the Susa A period', in Henrickson, E.F. and Thuesen, I., eds., *Upon this Foundation – the 'Ubaid Reconsidered*, Copenhagen: CNIP 10, 281–92.

Pons, N. (1994), 'Tchoga Zanbil après Untas-Napirisa', *CDR*, 43–51.

Porada, E. (1965), *The Art of Ancient Iran*, New York: Crown.

(1970), *Tchoga Zanbil (Dur-Untash) Vol. IV. La Glyptique*, Paris: MDP 42.

(1971), 'Aspects of Elamite art and archaeology', *Expedition* 13/3–4, 28–34.

(1990), 'More seals of the time of the Sukkalmah', *RA* 84, 171–7.

Porter, B.N. (1993), *Images, Power, Politics: Figurative Aspects of Esarhaddon's Babylonian Policy*, Philadelphia: Memoirs of the American Philosophical Society 208.

Porter, Y., and Vesel, Œ. (1993), 'La joaillerie et la peinture: Approvisionnement en pierres et en pigments dans l'Iran médiéval', in Gyselen, R., ed., *Circulation des monnaies, des marchandises et des biens*, Bures-sur-Yvette: Res Orientales v, 141–57.

Postgate, J.N. (1993), 'The four "Neo-Assyrian" tablets from Seh Hamad', *SAAB* 7, 109–24.

Potter, D.S. (1996), 'hierodouloi', *Oxford Classical Dictionary*[3], 705.

Potts, D.T. (1986), 'The booty of Magan', *OrAnt* 25, 271–85.

(1988), 'Arabia and the kingdom of Characene', in Potts, D.T., ed., *Araby the Blest: Studies in Arabian Archaeology*, Copenhagen: CNIP 7, 137–67.

(1989), 'Gundešapur and the *Gondeisos*', *IrAnt* 24, 323–35.

(1990a), 'Notes on Some Horned Buildings in Iran, Mesopotamia and Iran', *RA* 84, 33–40.

(1990b), *The Arabian Gulf in Antiquity*, 2 vols. Oxford: Clarendon Press.

(1991), 'A note on rice cultivation in Mesopotamia and Susiana', *NABU*, 2.

(1993), 'Occidental and oriental elements in the religions of Babylonia and Iran during the third and second centuries BC', *Topoi* 3, 345–54.

(1996), 'The Parthian presence in the Arabian Gulf', in Reade, J.E., ed., *The Indian Ocean in Antiquity*, London/New York: Kegan Paul International, 269–85.

(1997), *Mesopotamian Civilization: the Material Foundations*, London: Athlone Publications in Egyptology and Near Eastern Archaeology.

Potts, D.T., Parpola, A., Parpola, S. and Tidmarsh, J. (1996), 'Guḫlu and Guggulu', *Wiener Zeitschrift für die Kunde des Morgenlandes* 86, 291–305.

Potts, T.F. (1989), 'Foreign stone vessels of the late third millennium BC from southern Mesopotamia: their origins and mechanisms of exchange', *Iraq* 51, 123–64.

Powell, M.A. (1981), 'Three problems in the history of cuneiform writing: origins, direction of script, literacy', *Visible Language* 15, 419–40.

   (1982), 'Merodach-Baladan at Dur-Jakin: a note on the defense of Babylonian cities', *JCS* 34, 59–61.

   (1985), 'Salt, seed and yields in sumerian agriculture: a critique of the theory of progressive salinization', *ZA* 75, 7–38.

Prášek, J.D. (1913), 'Kambyses', *AO* 14/2, 3–31.

Pritchard, J.B. (1969³), *Ancient Near Eastern Texts Relating to the Old Testament*, Princeton: Princeton University Press.

Pullar, J. (1990), *Tepe Abdul Hosein: a Neolithic Site in Western Iran, Excavations 1978*, Oxford: BAR International Series 563.

Quintana, E. (1996a), 'ELAM = halhatamti = high land', *NABU*, 50.

   (1996b), 'Le sukkalmah Kuknašur', *NABU*, 86.

   (1996c), 'Humban-numena I, un usurpateur à la royauté en Elam', *NABU*, 106.

   (1996d), '¿Trilogía de poder en Elam en el primer milenio?', *NABU*, 109.

   (1998), 'De nuevo sobre la dinastía elamita de Šimaški', *NABU*, 4.

Rahimi-Laridjani, F. (1988), *Die Entwicklung der Bewässerungslandwirtschaft im Iran bis in sasanidisch-frühislamische Zeit*, Wiesbaden: Beiträge zur Iranistik 13.

Reade, J.E. (1972), 'The Neo-Assyrian court and army: Evidence from the sculptures', *Iraq* 34, 87–112.

   (1976), 'Elam and Elamites in Assyrian sculpture', *AMI* 9, 97–105.

   (1978), 'Kassites and Assyrians in Iran', *Iran* 16, 137–43.

   (1983), *Assyrian Sculpture*, London: The British Museum.

   (1992a), 'An early Warka tablet', in Hrouda, B. *et al.*, ed., *Von Uruk nach Tuttul*, Munich, 177–9.

   (1992b), 'The Elamite tablets from Nineveh', *NABU*, 119.

   (1995), 'Iran in the Neo-Assyrian period', in Liverani, M., ed., *Neo-Assyrian Geography*, Rome: Quaderni di Geografia Storica 5, 31–42.

Redding, R.W. (1981), 'The faunal remains', in Wright, H.T., *An Early Town on the Deh Luran Plain: Excavations at Tepe Farukhabad*, Ann Arbor: Memoirs of the Museum of Anthropology, University of Michigan, No. 13, 233–61.

Reiner, E. (1969), *The Elamite Language*, Leiden/Cologne: HdO I/II/1/2/2, 54–118.

   (1973a), 'The location of Anšan', *RA* 67, 57–62.

   (1973b), 'Inscription from a Royal Elamite tomb', *AfO* 24, 87–102.

Roaf, M. (1973), 'The diffusion of the "salles à quatre saillants"', *Iraq* 35, 83–93.

Robert, L. (1936), 'Études d'épigraphie grecque XLIII. Sur les affranchissements de Suse', *Revue de Philologie* 10, 137–52.

   (1963), review of Fraser, P.M., Samothrace Vol. 2/1. *The Inscriptions on Stone, Gnomon* 35, 50–79.

Rochberg-Halton, F. (1991), 'The Babylonian astronomical diaries', *JAOS* 111, 323–32.

Roche, C. (1986), 'Les ziggurats de Tchogha Zanbil', *FHE*, 191–7.

Rogers, R.W. (1900), *A History of Babylonia and Assyria*, vol. 1, New York: Eaton and Mains and Cincinnati: Jennings and Pye.

Roosens, E.E. (1989), *Creating Ethnicity: The Process of Ethnogenesis*, Frontiers of Anthropology 5, Newbury Park/London/New Delhi: Sage Publications.

Root, M.C. (1979), *The King and Kingship in Achaemenid Art*, Leiden: AcIr 19 [= *Textes et Mémoires* 9].

Ross, R. (1996), 'Henri Pirenne and the legitimisation of Belgium', in Atkinson, J.A., Banks, I. and O'Sullivan, J., eds., *Nationalism and Archaeology*, Glasgow: Cruithne Press, 143–54.

Rostovtzeff, M. (1941), *The Social and Economic History of the Hellenistic World*, I-III, Oxford: Clarendon Press.

Rova, E. (1994), *Ricerche sui sigilli a cilindro vicino-orientali del periodo da Uruk/Jemdet Nasr*, Rome: Oriens Antiqui Collectio 20.

Rowton, M.B. (1967, app. 1969), 'Watercourses and water rights in the official correspondence from Larsa and Isin', *JCS* 21, 267–74.

Russell, J.M. (1997), *From Nineveh to New York: the Strange Story of the Assyrian Reliefs in the Metropolitan Museum and the Hidden Masterpiece at Canford School*, New Haven/London: Yale University Press.

Sachau, E. (1916), *Vom Christentum in der Persis*, Berlin: Sitzungsberichte der königlich Preussischen Akademie der Wissenschaften, philosophische-historische Klasse 39.

Sachs, A. and Hunger, H. (1988), *Astronomical Diaries and Related Texts from Babylonia I. Diaries from 652 BC to 262 BC*, Vienna: Österreichische Akademie der Wissenschaften, philosophische-historische Klasse, Denkschriften 195.

(1989), *Astronomical diaries and related texts from Babylonia II. Diaries from 261 BC to 165 BC*, Vienna: Österreichische Akademie der Wissenschaften, philosophische-historische Klasse, Denkschriften 210.

(1996), *Astronomical diaries and related texts from Babylonia III. Diaries from 164 BC to 61 BC*, Vienna: Österreichische Akademie der Wissenschaften, philosophische-historische Klasse, Denkschriften 247.

Sachs, A. and Wiseman, D.J. (1954), 'A Babylonian king list of the Hellenistic period', *Iraq* 16, 202–11.

Saggs, H.W.F. (1963), 'Assyrian warfare in the Sargonid period', *Iraq* 25, 145–54.

Sajjidi, M. and Wright, H.T. (1979), 'Test excavations in the Elamite layers at the Izeh East Face', in Wright, H.T., ed., *Archaeological Investigations in Northeastern Xuzestan, 1976*, Ann Arbor: University of Michigan Museum of Anthropology Technical Report No. 10, 106–13.

Salonen, E. (1965), *Die Waffen der alten Mesopotamier*, Helsinki: Studia Orientalia 33.

Sancisi-Weerdenburg, H. (1988), 'Was there ever a Median empire?', *AH* 3, 197–212.

Sarre, F. and Herzfeld, E. (1910), *Iranische Felsreliefs: Aufnahmen und Untersuchungen von Denkmälern aus alt- und mittelpersischer Zeit*, Berlin: Wasmuth.

Sasson, J.M. (1995), 'King Hammurabi of Babylon', *CANE*, 901–15.

Sawyer, Lt. Col. H.A. (1894), 'The Bakhtiyari mountains and Upper Elam', *Geographical Journal* 4, 481–505.

Scarcia, G. (1979), 'Ricognizione a Shimbar: Note sull'Eracle iranico', *OrAnt* 18, 255–75.

Schacht, R.M. (1975), 'A preliminary report on the excavations at Tepe Sharafabad, 1971', *Journal of Field Archaeology* 2, 307–29.

Scheil, V. (1900), *Textes élamites-sémitiques, première série*, Paris: MDP 2.

(1902), *Textes élamites-sémitiques, deuxième série*, Paris: MDP 4.

(1904), *Textes élamites-anzanites, deuxième série*, Paris: MDP 5.

(1905), *Textes élamites-sémitiques, troisième série*, Paris: MDP 6.

(1907), *Textes élamites-anzanites, troisième série*, Paris: MDP 9.

(1908), *Textes élamites-sémitiques, quatrième série*, Paris: MDP 10.

(1911), *Textes élamites-anzanites, quatrième série*, Paris: MDP 11.

(1917), 'Déchiffrement d'un document anzanite relatif aux présages' *RA* 14, 29–59.

(1927), 'Suse et l'empire néo-babylonien', *RA* 24, 47–8.

(1930), *Actes juridiques susiens*, Paris: MDP 22.

(1931), 'Dynasties élamites d'Awan et de Šimaš', *RA* 28: 1–8.

(1933), *Actes juridiques susiens; inscriptions des Achéménides*, Paris: MDP 24.

(1939), *Mélanges épigraphiques*, Paris: MDP 28.

Scher, A. (1907), *Histoire Nestorienne (Chronique de Séert), Pt. 1*, Paris: Patrologia Orientalis IV/3,.

Schippmann, K. (1990), *Grundzüge der Geschichte des sasanidischen Reiches*, Darmstadt: Wissenschaftliche Buchgesellschaft.

Schmandt-Besserat, D. (1981), 'From tokens to tablets: A re-evaluation of the so-called "numerical tablets"', *Visible Language* 15, 321–44.

(1986), 'Tokens at Susa', *OrAnt* 25, 93–125.

Schmidt, E.F. (1953), *Persepolis I*, Chicago: OIP 68.

(1957), *Persepolis II*, Chicago: OIP 69.

Scmidt, E.F., Van Loon, M.N. and Curvers, H.H. (1989), *The Holmes Expeditions to Luristan*, vols. I-II, Chicago: OIP 108.

Schmitt, H.H. (1964), *Untersuchungen zur Geschichte Antiochos' des Grossen und seiner Zeit*, Wiesbaden: Historia Enzelschriften 6.

Schmitt, R. (1973), 'Die Kosenamensuffixe -ina- und -uka-', in Mayrhofer, M., *Onomastica Persepolitana: Das altiranische Namengut der Persepolis-Täfelchen*, Vienna: Österreichische Akademie der Wissenschaften, philosophische-historische Klasse Sitzungsberichte 286, 287–98.

(1990a), 'Epigraphisch-exegetische Noten zu Dareios' Bisutun-Inschriften', *Öster. Akademie der Wissenschaften, philosophische-historische Klasse Sitzungsberichte* 561, 3–88.

(1990b), 'Bisotun iii. Darius's inscriptions', *EnIr* 4, 299–305.

(1991a), 'Name und Religion: Anthroponomastisches zur Frage der religiösen Verhältnisse des Achaimenidenreiches', in Kellens, J., ed., *La religion iranienne à l'époque achéménide*, Gent: *IrAnt* Supplement 5, 111–35.

(1991b), review of Harmatta, J., ed, *From Alexander the Great to Kül Tegin: Studies in Bactrian, Pahlavi, Sanskrit, Arabic, Aramaic, Armenian, Chinese, Türk, Greek and Latin Sources for the History of Pre-Islamic Central Asia*, Kratylos 36, 211–14.

(1991c), *The Bisitun Inscriptions of Darius the Great. Old Persian Text*, London: Corpus Inscriptionum Iranicarum I/1/1.

Schnapp, A. (1995), 'L'archéologie', in Bédarida, F., ed., *L'histoire et le métier d'historien en France 1945–1995*, Paris: Éditions de la Maison des sciences de l'homme, pp. 255–69.

Schroeder, O. (1925), Elam. A. Geschichte. *Reallexikon der Vorgeschichte* 3, 69–70.

Schwaigert, W. (1989), *Das Christentum in Ḫūzistān im Rahmen der frühen Kirchengeschichte Persiens bis zur Synode von Seleukia-Ktesiphon im Jahre 401*, diss. Marburg/Lahn.

Seibert, J. (1985), *Die Eroberung des Perserreiches durch Alexander d. Gr. auf kartographischer Grundlage*, Wiesbaden: Beihefte zum TAVO B 68.

Seibt, G.F. (1977), *Griechische Söldner im Achaimenidenreich*, Bonn: Habelts Dissertationsdrucke, Reihe Alte Geschichte 11.

Seidl, U. (1968), 'Die babylonischen Kudurru-Reliefs', *BaM* 4, 7–220.

(1986), *Die elamischen Felsreliefs von Kurangun und Naqš-e Rustam*, Berlin: Iranische Denkmäler 12/II/H.

(1990), 'Altelamische Siegel', *MJP*, 129–35.

(1997), 'Izeh', in Meyers, E.M., ed., *The Oxford Encyclopedia of Archaeology in the Near East*, vol. 3, New York and Oxford: Oxford University Press, 199–203.

Sekunda, N. (1988), 'Achaemenid military terminology', *AMI* 21, 69–77.

Selb, W. (1981), *Orientalisches Kirchenrecht, Band I, Die Geschichte des Kirchenrechts der Nestorianer (von den Anfängen bis zur Mongolenzeit)*, Vienna: Österreichische Akademie der Wissenschaften, philosophische-historische Klasse Sitzungsberichte 388.

Sellwood, D. (1980²), *An Introduction to the Coinage of Parthia*, London: Spink and Son.

(1983), 'Minor states in southern Iran', *CHI* 3/1, 299–321.

(1985), Whitting, P. and Williams, R., *An Introduction to Sasanian Coins*, London: Spink and Son.

Selz, G. (1989), 'lú-su-a vs. LU₂.SU.A', *NABU*, 94.

(1991), '"Elam" und "Sumer" – Skizze einer Nachbarschaft nach inschriftlichen Quellen der vorsargonischen Zeit', *MHEOP* 1, 27–43.

Shahbazi, A.S. (1993), 'Cyrus ii. Cyrus I', *EnIr* 6, 516.

Sherwin-White, S. and Kuhrt, A. (1993), *From Samarkhand to Sardis: a New Approach to the Seleucid Empire*, London: Duckworth.

Sigrist, M. (1986), 'Les courriers de Lagaš', *FHE*, 51–63.

(1988), *Isin Year Names*, Berrien Springs: Andrews University Institute of Archaeology Publications, Assyriological Series II.

(1990), *Larsa Year Names*, Berrien Springs: Andrews University Institute of Archaeology Publications, Assyriological Series II.

(1992), *Drehem*, Bethesda: CDL Press.

Sigrist, M. and Butz, K. (1986), 'Wirtschaftliche Beziehungen zwischen der Susiana und Südmesopotamien in der Ur-III-Zeit', *AMI* 19, 27–31.

Sigrist, M. and Gomi, T. (1991), *The Comprehensive Catalogue of Published Ur III Tablets*, Bethesda: CDL Press.

Simons, J. (1959), *The Geographical and Topographical Texts of the Old Testament*, Leiden: Brill.

Sollberger, E. and Kupper, J.-R. (1971), *Inscriptions royales sumériennes et akkadiennes*, Paris: Littératures du Proche-Orient 3.

Southall, A. (1956), *Alur Society*, Cambridge: Heffer and Sons.

Spiegel, F. (1971; repr. of 1873 ed.), *Erânische Altertumskunde*, 3 vols., Amsterdam: Oriental Press.

Sprenger, A. (1864), *Die Post- und Reiserouten des Orients*, Leipzig: Abhandlungen der Deutschen Morgenländischen Gesellschaft III/3.

Spycket, A. (1981), *La statuaire du Proche-Orient ancien*, Leiden/Cologne: HdO 7/I/2/B/2.

(1992), *Les figurines de Suse*, Paris: MDP 52.

Starr, I. (1985), 'Historical omens concerning Ashurbanipal's war against Elam', *AfO* 32, 60–7.

Steible, H. (1975), *Rimsîn, mein König: Drei kultische Texte aus Ur mit der Schlußdoxologie ᵈri-im-ᵈsîn lugal-mu*, Wiesbaden: FAOS 1.

(1982), *Die altsumerischen Bau- und Weihinschriften, I-II*, Wiesbaden: FAOS 5.

Steinkeller, P. (1981), 'Early history of the Hamrin basin in the light of textual evidence', Gibson, McG., ed., *Uch Tepe 1*, Copenhagen: Akademisk Forlag, 163–8.

(1982a), 'The Question of Marhaši: a contribution to the historical geography of Iran in the third millennium BC', *ZA* 72, 237–64.

(1982b), 'The Mesopotamian god Kakka', *JNES* 41, 289–94.

(1984), 'Sumerian Miscellanea', *Aula Orientalis* 2, 137–42.

(1987), 'The administrative and economic organization of the Ur III state: the core and the periphery', in Gibson, McG. and Biggs, R.D., eds., *The Organization of Power: Aspects of Bureaucracy in the Ancient Near East*, Chicago: SAOC 46, 19–41.

(1988a), 'On the identity of the toponyms LÚ.SU(.A)', *JAOS* 108, 197–202.

(1988b), 'The date of Gudea and his dynasty', *JCS* 40, 47–53.

(1989), 'Marhaši', *RlA* 7, 381–2.

(1990), 'More on LÚ.SU(.A)=Šimaški', *NABU*, 13.

(1993), 'Settlement patterns and material culture of the Akkadian period: continuity and discontinuity', in Liverani, M., ed., *Akkad, the First World Empire: Structure, Ideology, Traditions*, Padua: History of the Ancient Near East/Studies v, 91–129.

Steve, M.-J. (1967), *Tchoga Zanbil (Dur-Untash) III. Textes élamites et accadiens de Tchoga Zanbil*, Paris: MDP 41.

(1968), 'Fragmenta Elamica', *Or* 37, 290–307.

(1987), *Nouveaux mélanges épigraphiques, Inscriptions royales de Suse et de la Susiane*, Nice: MDP 53.

(1991), 'Elam: histoire continue ou discontinue?', *MHEOP* 1, 1–9.

(1992), *Syllabaire élamite: Histoire et paléographie*, vol. 1, Neuchâtel-Paris: Civilisations du Proche-Orient, Ser. II, Philologie.

(1994), 'Suse: La couche XII du Chantier "A" de la "Ville Royale" et la fin de l'époque des sukkalmah', *CDR*, 23–30.

Steve, M.-J., and Gasche, H. (1971), *L'Acropole de Suse*, Paris and Leiden: MDP 46.

(1990), 'Le tell de l'Apadana avant les Achéménides: Contribution à la topographie de Suse', *MJP*, 15–60.

(1996) 'L'accès à l'au-delà, à Suse', *Collectanea*, 329–48.

Steve, M.-J., Gasche, H., and de Meyer, L. (1980), 'La Susiane du deuxième millénaire: à propos d'une interprétation des fouilles de Suse', *IrAnt* 15, 49–154.

Steve, M.-J. and Vallat, F. (1989), 'La dynastie des Igihalkides: nouvelles interprétations', *AIO*, 223–38.

Stol, M. (1976), *Studies in Old Babylonian History*, Leiden: Uitgaven van het Nederlands Historisch-Archaeologisch Instituut te Istanbul 40.

Stolper, M.W. (1978), 'Inscribed fragments from Khuzistan', *Cahiers de la DAFI* 8, 89–91.

(1982), 'On the dynasty of Šimaški and the Early Sukkalmahs', *ZA* 72, 42–67.

(1984), *Texts from Tall-i Malyan, I. Elamite Administrative Texts (1972–1974)*, Philadelphia: Occasional Publications of the Babylonian Fund 6.

(1985), 'Proto-Elamite texts from Tall-i Malyan', *Kadmos* 24, 1–12.

(1986), 'A Neo-Babylonian text from the reign of Hallušu', *FHE*, 235–41.

(1987–90), 'Malamir. B. Philologisch', *RlA* 7, 276–80.

(1989), 'Awan', *EnIr* 3, 113–14.

(1992), 'The Murašu Texts from Susa', *RA* 86, 69–77.

Stolper, M.W. and Wright, H.T. (1990), 'Elamite brick fragments from Choga Pahn East and related fragments', *MJP*, 151–63.

Stordeur, D. and Anderson-Gerfaud, P. (1985), 'Les omoplates encochées néolithiques de Ganj Dareh (Iran): Étude morphologique et fonctionnelle', *Cahiers de l'Euphrate* 4, 289–313.

Streck, M. (1901), *Die alte Landschaft Babylonien nach den arabischen Geographen, II. Teil*, Leiden: Brill.

(1916), *Assurbanipal und die letzten assyrischen Könige bis zum Untergange Niniveh's*, 3 vols., Leipzig: Hinrichs.

Strommenger, E. (1994), 'Elamier, Perser und Babylonier', in Dietrich, M. and Loretz, O., eds., *Beschreiben und Deuten in der Archäologie des Alten Orients: Festschrift für Ruth Mayer-Opificius*, Münster: Ugarit-Verlag, 312–25.

Stronach, D. (1974), 'Achaemenid Village I at Susa and the Persian Migration to Fars', *Iraq* 36, 239–48.

(1978), *Pasargadae*, Oxford: Clarendon Press.

(1984), 'Notes on religion in Iran in the seventh and sixth centuries BC', *AcIr* 23 [= *Hommages et Opera Minora 9. Orientalia J. Duchesne-Guillemin Emerito Oblata*], 479–90.

(1985), 'The Apadana: a signature of the line of Darius I', in Huot, J.-L., Yon, M. and Calvet, Y., eds., *De l'Indus aux Balkans: Recueil à la mémoire de Jean Deshayes*, Paris: Editions Recherche sur les Civilisations, 433–45.

(1989a) 'The royal garden at Pasargadae: evolution and legacy', *AIO*, 475–502.

(1989b), 'Early Achaemenid coinage: perspectives from the homeland', *IrAnt* 24, 255–79.

(1990a), 'The garden as a political statement: some case studies from the Near East in the first millennium BC', *Bulletin of the Asia Institute* 4, 171–80.

(1990b), 'On the genesis of the Old Persian cuneiform script', *MJP*, 195–203.

(1994), 'Parterres and stone watercourses at Pasargadae: notes on the Achaemenid contribution to garden design', *Journal of Garden History* 14, 3–12.

(1997), 'Anshan and Parsa: early Achaemenid history, art and architecture on the Iranian Plateau', in Curtis, J., ed., *Mesopotamia and Iran in the Persian Period: Conquest and Imperialism, 539–331 BC*, London: British Museum, 35–53.

Sumner, W.M. (1974), 'Excavations at Tall-i Malyan, 1971–72', *Iran* 12, 155–80.

(1985), 'The Proto-Elamite city wall at Tal-i Malyan', *Iran* 23, 153–61.

(1986a), 'Proto-Elamite civilization in Fars', in Finkbeiner, U. and Röllig, W., eds., *Ğamdat Naṣr – period or regional style?*, Wiesbaden: TAVO Beiheft B 62, 199–211.

(1986b), 'Achaemenid settlement in the Persepolis plain', *AJA* 90, 3–31.

(1988a), 'Prelude to Proto-Elamite Anshan: the Lapui phase', *IrAnt* 23, 23–43.

(1988b), 'Maljan, Tall-e (Anšan)', *RlA* 7, 306–20.

(1989), 'Anshan in the Kaftari phase: patterns of settlement and land use', *AIO*, 135–61.

(1992), 'Ceramics VI. Uruk, Proto-Elamite, and Early Bronze Age in southern Persia', *EnIr* 5, 284–8.

(1994), 'Archaeological measures of cultural continuity and the arrival of the Persians in Fars', *AH* 8, 97–105.

Sykes, Lt.-Col. P.M. (1915), *A History of Persia*, 2 vols., London: Macmillan.

Szemerényi, O. (1966), 'Iranica II', *Die Sprache* 12, 191–226.

Tadmor, H. (1958), 'The campaigns of Sargon II of Assur: A chronological-historical study', *JCS* 12, 22–40, 77–100.

Tallon, F. (1987), *Métallurgie susienne. De la fondation de Suse au XVIIIe siècle av. J.-C.*, 2 vols., Paris: Editions de la Réunion des musées nationaux.

Tallon, F., Hurtel, L., and Drilhon, F. (1989), 'Un aspect de la métallurgie du cuivre à Suse: La petite statuaire du IIe millénaire avant J.-C.', *IrAnt* 24, 121–51.

Tarn, W.W. (1930), 'Seleucid-Parthian Studies', *Proceedings of the British Academy* 16, 105–35.

(1932), 'Tiridates II and the Young Phraates', in *Mélanges Gustave Glotz II*, Paris: Presses Universitaires de France, 831–7.

(1938), *The Greeks in Bactria and India*, Cambridge: University Press.

Tarn, W.W. and Vickers, M. (1996), 'Susa', *Oxford Classical Dictionary*[3], 1458.

Teich, M. and Porter, R. (1993), eds., *The National Question in Europe in Historical Context*, Cambridge: University Press.

Teixidor, J. (1990), 'Interpretations and misinterpretations of the East in Hellenistic times', in Bilde, P., Engberg-Pedersen, T., Hannestad, L. and Zahle, J., eds., *Religion and Religious Practice in the Seleucid Kingdom*, Aarhus: Studies in Hellenistic Civilization 1, 66–78.

Thompson, J.A. (1980), *The Book of Jeremiah*, Grand Rapids: Eerdmans.

Thordeman, B. (1939), *Armour from the Battle of Wisby 1361*, vol. 1. Stockholm: Kungl. Vitterhets Historie och Antikvitets Akademien.

Thureau-Dangin, F. (1907), *Die sumerischen und akkadischen Königsinschriften*, Leipzig: VAB 1/1,.

(1912), 'Notes assyriologiques', *RA* 9, 21–5.

Tinney, S. (1995), 'A new look at Naram-Sin and the "Great Rebellion"', *JCS* 47, 1–14.

Tomaschek, W. (1890), 'Topographische Erläuterungen der Küstenfahrt Nearchs vom Indus bis zum Euphrat', *Sitzungsberichte der Kaiserlichen Akademie der Wissenschaften in Wien, philosophische-historische Cl.* CXXI, 1–88.

Tourovets, A. (1996), 'La glyptique de Bani Surmah, Pusht-i Kuh-Luristan', *IrAnt* 31, 19–45.

(1997), 'Observations concernant l'existence d'une ancienne voie cérémonielle au nord-est du site de Tchoga Zanbil', *IrAnt* 32, 71–90.

Treidler, H. (1965), 'Paraitakene', *RE Suppl.* 10, 478–82.

Trichet, J. and Vallat, F. (1990), 'L'origine égyptienne de la statue de Darius', *MJP*, 205–8.

Trokay, M. (1991), 'Les origines du dieu élamite au serpent', *MHEOP* 1, 154–61.

Trümpelmann, L. (1976), 'Metrologische Untersuchungen am Kyrosgrab in Pasargadae', *The Memorial Volume of the VIth International Congress of Iranian Art and Archaeology, Oxford, September 11–16th 1972*, Tehran, 319–26.

(1981), 'Eine Kneipe in Susa', *IrAnt* 16, 35–44.

(1988), 'Zur Herkunft von Medern und Persern', *AMI* 21, 79–90.

Tscherikower, V. (1927), *Die hellenistischen Städtegründungen von Alexander dem Grossen bis auf die Römerzeit*, Leipzig: Philologus Supplementband 29/1.

Tuplin, C. (1996), *Achaemenid Studies*, Stuttgart: Historia Enzelschriften 99.

Uchitel, A. (1991), 'Foreign workers in the fortification archive', *MHEOP* 1, 127–35.

Uerpmann, H.-P. (1987), *The Ancient Distribution of Ungulate Mammals in the Middle East*, Wiesbaden: Beihefte zum TAVO Reihe A 27.

Unger, E. (1938), 'Elam und Elamiten in assyrischer Darstellung', *RlA* 2, 353–4.

Unvala, J.-M. (1934a), 'Monnaies sassanides trouvées dans un vase', *MDP* 25, 68–76.

(1934b), 'Tessères et médaillons frustes', *MDP* 25, 239–44.

(1935), 'Notes des numismatique (fouilles de Suse, 1934)', *RN* 38, 155–62.

Vallat, F. (1971), 'Deux nouvelles "chartes de fondation" d'un palais de Darius Ier à Suse', *Syria* 48, 53–9.

(1972), 'Deux inscriptions élamites de Darius 1er (DSf et DSz)', *StIr* 1, 3–13.

(1978), 'Une brique élamite de Hutelutush-Insushnak', *Cahiers de la DAFI* 8, 97–107.

(1980a), *Suse et l'Elam*, Paris: Recherche sur les grandes civilisations.

(1980b), 'Documents épigraphiques de la Ville Royale I (1972 et 1975)', *Cahiers de la DAFI* 11, 135–9.

(1981), 'L'inscription de la stèle d'Untash-Napirisha', *IrAnt* 16, 27–33.

(1983a), 'Le dieu Enzak: une divinité dilmunite venérée à Suse', in Potts, D.T., ed., *Dilmun: New Studies in the Archaeology and Early History of Bahrain*, Berlin: *BBVO* 2, 93–100.

(1983b), 'Un fragment de tablette achéménide et la turquoise', *Akkadica* 33, 63–8.

(1984a), 'Une inscription cunéiforme de Bouchir', *Dédalo* 23, 255–60.

(1984b), 'Kidin-Hutran et l'époque néo-élamite', *Akkadica* 37, 1–17.

(1985a), 'Hutelutuš-Inšušinak et la famille royale élamite', *RA* 79, 43–50.

(1985b), 'Éléments de géographie élamite (Résumée)', *Paléorient* 11, 49–54.

(1986a), 'The most ancient scripts of Iran: the current situation', *World Archaeology* 17, 335–47.

(1986b), 'Table accadienne de Darius Ier (DSaa)', *FHE*, 277–87.

(1987a), 'Elamite nulkippi', *NABU*, 88.

(1987b), '^{d}U = élamite *usan/iššan*', *NABU*, 89.

(1988a), 'Légendes élamites de fragments de statues d'Untaš-Napiriša et Tchogha Zanbil', *IrAnt* 23, 169–77.

(1988b), 'A propos de l'origine des tablettes élamites dites "de Ninive" conservées au British Museum', *NABU*, 39.

(1988c), '^{d}Umu à l'époque néo-élamite', *NABU*, 14.

(1989a), 'Le scribe Ibni-Adad et les premiers sukkalmah', *NABU*, 34.

(1989b), 'L'expression ADDA LUGAL an-ša-an ù MÙŠ.EREN^{ki} dans un texte d'Atta-hušu', *NABU*, 101.

(1989c), 'L'inscription du sceau-cylindre du sukkalmah Tan-Uli', *NABU*, 117.

(1990a), 'Reflexions sur l'époque des sukkalmah', *MJP*, 119–27.

(1990b), 'Les cornes élamites', *NABU*, 136.

(1990c), 'Une inscription élamite de Tépé Horreeye', *MJP*, 147–9.

(1991), 'La géographie de l'Elam d'après quelques textes mésopotamiens', *MHEOP* 1, 11–21.

(1992), 'Les prétendus fonctionnaires *unsak* des textes néo-élamites et achéménides', *DATA: Achaemenid History Newsletter* 1/4, 5.

(1993a), *Les noms géographiques des sources suso-élamites*, Wiesbaden: RGTC 11.

(1993b), 'Kuk-Našur et Ammiṣaduqa', *NABU*, 39.

(1994), 'Succession royale en Elam au IIème millénaire', *CDR*, 1–14.

(1995a), 'Susa and Susiana in second-millennium Iran', *CANE*, 1023–33.

(1995b), 'Šutruk-Nahunte, Šutur-Nahunte et l'imbroglio néo-élamite', *NABU*, 44.

(1996a), 'Šu-ilišu, Iddin-Dagan et Imazu, roi d'Anšan', *NABU*, 87.

(1996b), 'Le retour de Hutelutus-Insusnak à Suse', *NABU*, 88.

(1996c), 'Le royaume élamite de SAMATI', *NABU*, 31.

(1996d), 'Nouvelle analyse des inscriptions néo-élamites', *Collectanea*, 385–95.

(1996e), 'L'Élam à l'époque paléo-babylonienne et ses relations avec la Mésopotamie', in Durand, J.-M., ed., *Mari, Ébla et les Hourrites, dix ans de travaux, première partie*, Paris: Amurru 1, 297–319.

(1996f), 'ELAM: *haltamti/Elamtu*', *NABU*, 89.

(1997a), 'Nouveaux problèmes de succession en Elam', *IrAnt* 32, 53–70.

(1997b), 'La politesse élamite à l'époque des Igihalkides', *NABU*, 74.

(1997c), 'Les trois Kuk-Našur', *NABU*, 110.

(1997d), 'Inšušinak, Ea et Enzag', *NABU*, 111.

(1997e), 'La lettre élamite d'Arménie', *ZA* 87, 258–70.

Vanden Berghe, L. (1959), *Archéologie de l'Iran ancien*, Leiden: Brill.

(1963a), 'Les reliefs élamites de Malamir', *IrAnt* 3, 22–39.

(1963b), 'Le relief parthe de Hung-i Nauruzi', *IrAnt* 3, 155–68.

(1968), 'La nécropole de Bani Surmah, aurore d'une civilisation du Bronze', *Archéologia* 24, 52–63.

(1971), 'La nécropole de Bard-i Bal au Luristan', *Archéologia* 43, 14–23.

(Dec. 1973) 'Le Luristan à l'âge fu Fer: La nécropole de Kut-i Gulgul', *Archéologia* 65, 16–29.

(1983), *Reliefs rupestres de l'Iran ancien*, Brussels: Musées Royaux d'Art et d'Histoire.

(1986a), 'Données nouvelles concernant le relief rupestre élamite de Kurangun', *FHE*, 157–73.

(1986b), 'Le relief rupestre de Gardanah Galumushk (Qir)', *IrAnt* 21, 141–55.

(1987), 'Luristan, Pusht-i Kuh au Chalcolithique moyen (les nécropoles de Parchinah et de Hakalan)', in Huot, J.-L., ed., *Préhistoire de la Mésopotamie*, Paris: Editions du CNRS, 91–126.

Vanden Berghe, L. and Schippmann, K. (1985), *Les reliefs rupestres d'Elymaïde (Iran) de l'époque parthe*, Gent: IrAnt Supplement 3.

Van den Boorn, G.P.F., Houtkamp, J.M. and Verhart, L.B.M. (1989), 'Surface finds from KS-sites east of Haft Tepe (Khuzistan)', *IrAnt* 24, 13–43.

Van der Spek, R.J. (1993), 'The astronomical diaries as a source for Achaemenid and Seleucid history', *BiOr* 50, 91–101.

Van Dijk, J. (1970), 'Remarques sur l'histoire d'Elam et d'Ešnunna', *AfO* 23, 63–72.

(1978), 'Išbi'erra, Kindattu, l'homme d'Elam, et la chute de la ville d'Ur', *JCS* 30, 189–208.

(1986), 'Die dynastischen Heiraten zwischen Kassiten und Elamern: eine verhängnisvolle Politik', *Or* 55, 159–70.

Van Loon, M.N. (1988), 'Two Neo-Elamite cylinder seals with mounted huntsmen', *IrAnt* 23, 221–6.

Van Zeist, W. (1967), 'Late Quaternary vegetation history of western Iran', *Review of Palaeobotany and Palynology* 2, 301–11.

Vardanian, R. (1986), 'Elymaean coins: a chronological systematization of bronze emissions in the second century AD', *VDI* 176/1, 99–117 (in Russian with English summary).

(1997), 'A propos de la datation de Tang-i Sarvak II', *IrAnt* 32, 151–61.

Vaux, W.S.W. (1856), 'On some coins, chiefly Greek, which have been lately brought from the East', *Numismatic Chronicle* 18, 137–52.

Vértesalji, P.P. (1989), 'Were there supralocal cemeteries in southern Mesopotamia in late Chalcolithic times?', in Henrickson, E.F. and Thuesen, I., eds., *Upon this Foundation – the 'Ubaid Reconsidered*, Copenhagen: CNIP 10, 181–98.

Villard, P. (1995), 'Shamshi-Adad and sons: the rise and fall of an Upper Mesopotamian empire', *CANE*, 873–883.

Vogelsang, W. (1988), 'Some observations on Achaemenid Hyrcania: a combination of sources', *AH* 3, 121–35.

Voigt, M. and Dyson, R.H. (1992), 'The Chronology of Iran, ca. 8000–2000 BC', in Ehrich, R.W., ed., *Chronologies in Old World Archaeology*[3], Chicago/London: University of Chicago, 122–78.

Von Gall, H. (1980), 'Relieffragment eines elymäischen Königs aus Masǧed-e Soleiman', *IrAnt* 15, 241–50.

(1986a), 'Einleitung F. Zu Eigenart, Verwertbarkeit und Bestand der literarischen und archäologischen Primärquellen', in Haussig, W., ed., *Götter und Mythen der kaukasischen und iranischen Völker*, Stuttgart: Wörterbuch der Mythologie 4, 195–219.

(1986b), 'Nana(i)(a)', in Haussig, W., ed., *Götter und Mythen der kaukasischen und iranischen Völker*, Stuttgart: Wörterbuch der Mythologie 4, 409–11.

(1990), 'The figural capitals at Taq-e Bostan and the question of the so-called investiture in Parthian and Sasanian art', *Silk Road Art and Archaeology* 1, 99–122.

Von Voigtlander, E.N. (1978), *The Bisitun Inscription of Darius the Great: Babylonian Version*, London: Corpus Inscriptionum Iranicarum 1/II/1.

Von der Osten-Sakken, E. (1996), review of Pittman, H., *The Glazed Steatite Glyptic Style*, *BiOr* 91, 566–71.

Vööbus, A. (1965), *History of the School of Nisibis*, Louvain: *CSCO* 266 [= *Subsidia* 26].

Vovelle, M. (1990), *Ideologies and Mentalities*, Cambridge: Polity Press, 126–53.

Wacholder, B.Z. (1980), 'The date of the death of Antiochus IV Epiphanes and 1 Macc. 6:16–17', in Burstein, S.M. and Okin, L.A., eds., *Panhellenica: Essays in Ancient History and Historiography in Honor of Truesdell S. Brown*, Lawrence: Coronado, 129–32.

Waddington, W.H. (1866), 'Numismatique et chronologie des rois de la Characène', *RN* 11, 303–33.

Waele, E. de (1972), 'Shutruk-Nahunte II et les reliefs rupestres dits néo-élamites d'Iseh/Malamir', *Revue des Archéologues et Historiens d'Art de Louvain* 5, 17–32.

(1976), 'Remarques sur les inscriptions élamites de Šekaf-e Salman et Kul-e Farah près Izeh I. Leur corrélation avec les bas-reliefs', *Le Muséon* 89, 441–50.

(1981)'Travaux archéologiques à Šekaf-e Salman et Kul-e Farah près d'Izeh (Malamir)', *IrAnt* 16, 45–61.

(1989), 'Musicians and musical instruments on the rock reliefs in the Elamite sanctuary of Kul-e Farah (Izeh)', *Iran* 27, 29–38.

Walker, C.B.F. (1980), 'Elamite inscriptions in the British Museum', *Iran* 18, 75–81.

(1981), *Cuneiform Brick Inscriptions in the British Museum, the Ashmolean Museum, Oxford, the City of Birmingham Museums and Art Gallery, the City of Bristol Museums and Art Gallery*, London: British Museum Press.

Walser, G. (1980), *Persepolis: Die Königspfalz des Darius*, Tübingen: Wasmuth.

Wasilewska, E. (1991), 'To be or not to be a temple? Possible identification of a Banesh period temple at Tall-i Malyan, Iran', *MHEOP* 1, 143–52.

Weeks, L.R. (in press), 'Lead isotope analyses from Tell Abraq, United Arab Emirates: new data regarding the "tin problem" in Western Asia', *Antiquity*.

Wehrli, C. (1968), *Antigone et Démétrios*, Geneva: Droz.

Weidner, E.F. (1931–2), 'Die älteste Nachricht über das persische Königshaus: Kyros I. ein Zeitgenosse Assurbânaplis', *AfO* 7, 1–7.

(1939), 'Jojachin, König von Juda, in babylonischen Keilschrifttexten', *Mélanges syriens offerts à Monsieur René Dussaud II*, Paris: Geuthner, 923–935.

(1954–1956), 'Hochverrat gegen Asarhaddon', *AfO* 17, 5–9.

(1959), *Die Inschriften Tukulti-Ninurtas I. und seiner Nachfolger*, Graz: *AfO* Beiheft 12.

Weisberg, D.B. (1984), 'The length of the reign of Hallušu-Inšušinak', *JAOS* 104, 213–17.

Weiss, H. (1977), 'Periodization, population and early state formation in Khuzistan', in Levine, L.D. and Young, T.C., Jr., eds., *Mountains and Lowlands: Essays in the Archaeology of Greater Mesopotamia*, Malibu: BiMes 7, 347–69.

Weissbach, F.H. (1902), 'Susische Thontäfelchen', *Beiträge zur Assyriologie* 4, 168–74.

(1908), 'Elymais', *RE* 5, 2458–67.

(1909), 'Eulaios', *RE* 6, 1061–3.

(1910a), 'Γαβαι', *RE* 7, 411.

(1910b), 'Gabiene', *RE* 7, 420.

(1911), *Die Keilinschriften der Achämeniden*, Leipzig: VAB 3.

(1921), 'Κισσία', *RE* 11, 519–21.

(1922a), 'Κορβιανη', *RE* 11, 1382.

(1922b), 'Κοσσαῖοι', *RE* 11, 1499–1503.

(1927), 'Sostra', *RE²* 5, 1199.

(1930), 'Μασσαβατιχη', *RE²* 28, 2123.

Wenke, R.J. (1976), 'Imperial investments and agricultural developments in Parthian and Sasanian Khuzestan: 150 BC to AD 640', *Mesopotamia* 10–11, 31–221.

(1981), 'Elymeans, Parthians, and the evolution of empires in southwestern Iran', *JAOS* 101, 303–15.

Westenholz, A. (1970), 'berūtum, damtum, and Old Akkadian KI.GAL: burial of dead enemies in Ancient Mesopotamia, *AfO* 23, 27–31.

(1979), 'The Old Akkadian empire in contemporary opinion', in Larsen, M.T., ed., *Power and Propaganda: a Symposium on Ancient Empires*, Copenhagen: Mesopotamia 7, 107–24.

(1987), *Old Sumerian and Old Akkadian texts in Philadelphia*, Copenhagen: CNIP 3.

Westenholz, J.G. (1997), 'Nanaya: lady of mystery', in Finkel, I.L. and Geller, M.J., eds., *Sumerian Gods and their Representations*, Groningen: Cuneiform Monographs 7, 57–84.

Westphal, G. (1901), *Untersuchungen über die Quellen und die Glaubwürdigkeit der Patriarchenchroniken des Mari Ibn Sulaiman, ʿAmr Ibn Matai und Saliba Ibn Johannan I. Bis zum Beginn des nestorianischen Streites*, Kirchhain: Inaug.-Diss. submitted to the Philosophical Faculty of the University of Strasbourg.

Widengren, G. (1971), 'The establishment of the Sasanian dynasty in the light of new evidence', in *La Persia nel medioevo*, Rome: Accademia Nazionale dei Lincei Quaderno 160, 711–82.

Wiesehöfer, J. (1978), *Der Aufstand Gaumātas und die Anfänge Dareios' I.*, Bonn: Habelts Dissertationsdrucke, Reihe Alte Geschichte 13.

(1994), *Die 'dunklen Jahrhunderte' der Persis: Untersuchungen zu Geschichte und Kultur von Fāers in frühhellenistischer Zeit (330–140 v.Chr.)*, Munich: Zetemata 90.

Wiessner, G. (1967), 'Zu den Subskriptionslisten der ältesten christlichen Synoden in Iran', in *Festschrift für Wilhelm Eilers*, Wiesbaden: Harrassowitz, 288–98.

Wiggermann, F.A.M. (1992), *Mesopotamian Protective Spirits: the Ritual Texts*, Groningen: STYX and PP Publications.

(1996), 'Scenes from the shadow side', in Vogelzang, M.E. and Vanstiphout, H.L.J., eds., *Mesopotamian Poetic Language: Sumerian and Akkadian*, Groningen: Cuneiform Monographs 6 [=Proceedings of the Groningen Group for the Study of Mesopotamian Literature Vol. 2], 207–30.

Wilcke, C. (1987), 'Inschriften 1983–1984 (7.-8. Kampagne)', in Hrouda, B., *Isin-Išān Bahrīyāt III*, Munich: Bayr. Akademie der Wissenschaften, philosophische-historische Klasse, Abh. N.F. 94, 83–120.

Wilhelm, A. (1935), 'Drei griechische Epigramme aus Susa und aus Heliopolis-Baalbek', *Nachrichten von der Gesellschaft der Wissenschaften zu Göttingen, philosophische-historische Klasse, Fachgruppe 1*, NF I/4, 79–94.

Will, E. (1979), *Histoire politique du monde hellénistique (323–30 av. J.-C.)*, Vol. 1, Nancy: Annales de l'Est, Mémoire 30.

Willcox, G. (1990), 'Charcoal remains from Tepe Abdul Hosein', in Pullar, J., *Tepe Abdul Hosein: A Neolithic site in western Iran, excavations 1978*, Oxford: BAR International Series 563, 223–7.

(1992), 'Timber and trees: ancient exploitation in the Middle East: evidence from plant remains', *Bulletin on Sumerian Agriculture* 6, 1–31.

Windfuhr, G.L. (1974), 'Isoglosses: a sketch on Persians and Parthians, Kurds and Medes', *AcIr* 5 [=*Hommages et Opera Minora. Monumentum H.S. Nyberg II*], 457–72.

Winter, E. (1988), *Die sasanidisch-römischen Friedensverträge des 3. Jahrhunderts n. Chr. – ein Beitrag zum Verständnis der außenpolitischen Beziehungen zwischen den beiden Großmächten*, Frankfurt: Europäische Hochschulschriften Reihe III, Geschichte und ihre Hilfswissenschaften 350.

Winter, I. (1996), 'Artists' trial pieces from Susa?', *Collectanea*, 397–406.

Wiseman, D.J. (1956), *Chronicles of the Chaldaean kings (626–556 BC) in the British Museum*, London: British Museum.

(1984), *Nebuchadrezzar and Babylon*, Oxford: Oxford University Press.

(1991), 'Babylonia 605–539 BC', *CAH* 3/2, 229–51.

Wolski, J. (1977), 'L'Iran dans la politique des séleucides', *AAASH* 25, 149–56.

(1983), 'Les relations de Justin et de Plutarque sur les esclaves et la population dépendante dans l'empire parthe', *IrAnt* 18, 145–57.

(1989), 'L'hellénisme et l'Iran', in Mactoux, M.-M. and Geny, E., eds., *Mélanges Pierre Lévêque 2. Anthropologie et société*, Paris: Annales littéraires de l'Université de Besançon 377, 439–46.

(1993), *L'empire des Arsacides*, AcIr 32 [=*Textes et Mémoires* 18].

Wright, H.T. (1981), *An Early Town on the Deh Luran Plain: Excavations at Tepe Farukhabad*, Ann Arbor: Memoirs of the Museum of Anthropology, University of Michigan, No. 13.

Wright, H.T. and Johnson, G.A. (1985), 'Regional perspectives on southwest Iranian state development', *Paléorient* 11, 25–30.

Wu, Y. (1994), *A Political History of Eshnunna, Mari and Assyria during the Early Old Babylonian Period (from the end of Ur III to the death of Šamši-Adad)*, Changchun: Supplement to the Journal of Ancient Civilizations 1.

Wulff, H.E. (1966), *The Traditional Crafts of Persia: their Development, Technology and Influence on Eastern and Western civilizations*, Cambridge: M.I.T. Press.

Wunsch, C. (1993), *Die Urkunden des babylonischen Geschäftsmannes Iddin-Marduk: Zum Handel mit Naturalien im 6. Jahrhundert v. Chr.*, Groningen: Cuneiform Mongraphs 3a–b.

Yang, Z. (1989), *Sargonic inscriptions from Adab*, Changchun: Northeast Normal University.

Yoffee, N. (1993), 'The late great tradition in ancient Mesopotamia', in Cohen, M.E., Snell, D. and Weisberg, D, eds., *The Tablet and the Scroll: Near Eastern Studies in Honor of William W. Hallo*, Bethesda: CDL Press, 300–8.

Young, T.C., Jr. (1986), 'Godin Tepe VI/V and central western Iran at the end of the fourth millennium', in Finkbeiner, U. and Röllig, W., eds., *Ğamdat Naṣr: Period or Regional Style?*, Wiesbaden: TAVO Beiheft B 62, 212–28.

Young, T.C., Jr. and Levine, L.D. (1974), *Excavations of the Godin Project: Second Progress Report*, Toronto: Royal Ontario Museum Art and Archaeology Occasional Paper 26.

Yusifov, Y.B. (1974), 'The problem of the order of succession in Elam again', *AAASH* 22, 321–31.

Zaccagnini, C. (1979), *The Rural Landscape of the Land of Arrapḫe*, Rome: Quaderni di Geografia Storica 1.

Zadok, R. (1976a), 'On the connections between Iran and Babylonia in the sixth century BC', *Iran* 14, 61–78.

(1976b), review of W. Hinz, *Altiranisches Sprachgut der Nebenüberlieferungen*, BiOr 33, 213–19.

(1977), 'On five Biblical names', *Zeitschrift für die alttestamentliche Wissenschaft* 89, 266–8.

(1979a), 'On some non-Semitic names in cuneiform sources', *Beiträge zur Namenforschung* 14, 294–301.

(1979b), 'On some foreign population groups in first-millennium Babylonia', *Tel Aviv* 6, 164–81.

(1983b), 'A tentative structural analysis of Elamite hypocoristica', *Beiträge zur Namenforschung* 18, 93–120.

(1984a), 'On some non-Semitic names in the ancient Near East', *Beiträge zur Namenforschung* 19, 385–9.

(1984b), *The Elamite Onomasticon*, Naples: AION Suppl. 40.

(1985), *Geographical Names according to New- and Late-Babylonian Texts*, Wiesbaden: Beihefte zum TAVO B 7.

(1986a), 'Some non-Semitic names in Akkadian sources', *Beiträge zur Namenforschung* 21, 243–8.

(1986b), 'Notes on Esther', *Zeitschrift für die alttestamentliche Wissenschaft* 98, 105–10.

(1987), 'Peoples from the Iranian plateau in Babylonia during the second millennium BC', *Iran* 25, 1–26.

(1990), 'Some Elamite names in Mesopotamian sources', *NABU*, 39.

(1991), 'Elamite Onomastics', *SEL* 8, 225–37.

(1993), 'Hurrians as well as individuals bearing Hurrian and strange names in Sumerian sources', in Rainey, A.F., ed., *kinattūtu ša dārātī: Raphael Kutscher Memorial Volume*, Tel Aviv: Journal of the Institute of Archaeology of Tel Aviv University Occasional Publications No. 1, 219–45.

(1994), 'Elamites and other peoples from Iran and the Persian Gulf region in early Mesopotamian sources', *Iran* 32, 31–51.

(1995a), 'On the Late-Assyrian Texts from Dur-Katlimmu and the significance of the NA Documentation for ethno-linguistic classification', *NABU*, 2.

(1995b), 'A document concerning work in Elam: BM 49718', *NABU*, 4.

(1995c), 'The ethno-linguistic character of the Jezireh and adjacent regions in the 9th-7th centuries (Assyria proper vs. periphery)', in Liverani, M., ed., *Neo-Assyrian Geography*, Rome: Quaderni di Geografia Storica 5, 217–82.

Zakeri, M. (1995), *Sasanid Soldiers in Early Muslim Society: the Origins of 'Ayyaran and Futuwwa*, Wiesbaden: Harrassowitz.

Zawadzki, S. (1988), *The Fall of Assyria and Median-Babylonian Relations in Light of the Nabopolassar Chronicle*, Poznan: Seria Historia 149.

(1996a), 'The first Persian journey of Itti-Marduk-Balatu', *AMI* 27, 123–6.

(1996b), 'Bardiya, Darius and Babylonian usurpers in the light of the Bisitun inscription and Babylonian sources', *AMI* 27, 127–46.

Zeder, M. (1986), 'The equid remains from Tal-e Malyan, southern Iran', in Meadow, R.H. and Uerpmann, H.-P., eds., *Equids in the Ancient World*, vol. 1, Wiesbaden: Beihefte zum TAVO, Reihe A 19/1, 366–412.

(1991), *Feeding Cities: Specialized Animal Economy in the Ancient Near East*, Washington and London: Smithsonian Institution Press.

Ziegler, K. (1979), 'Kossaioi', *KP* 3, 316.

INDEX